The California
Family Law Paralegal

The California Family Law Paralegal

THIRD EDITION

Dianna L. Noyes

CAROLINA ACADEMIC PRESS
Durham, North Carolina

Library of Congress Cataloging-in-Publication Data

Noyes, Dianna L.
  The California family law paralegal / Dianna L. Noyes. -- Third edition.
      pages cm
  Includes bibliographical references and index.
  ISBN 978-1-61163-561-4 (alk. paper)
  1. Domestic relations--California. 2. Legal assistants--California--Handbooks, manu-
als, etc. I. Title.
  KFC115.N69 2014
  346.79401'5--dc23
                              2014017117

Carolina Academic Press
700 Kent Street
Durham, NC 27701
Telephone (919) 489-7486
Fax (919) 493-5668
www.cap-press.com

Printed in the United States of America

This book is dedicated to my parents
without whom my education and quest for knowledge
would not have been possible. The desire to teach
and share the knowledge and skills that I have developed
would still be filed away without them.

I also want to thank my fellow paralegals
for their help and encouragement as well as the many students
I have taught over the years who have served as my Petri dish.

There are many others, attorney, educators, friends, and mentors—
too numerous to mention—who have helped and encouraged me
throughout the years as a paralegal, educator, and author.

And last, but far from least, I am blessed to have wonderful friends and family
who have seen me through good and hard times.

Contents

Preface

Family law is probably the most diverse of all practice areas. It is also one of the most emotional, personal and volatile areas of law. Family law also requires a basic knowledge of other areas of law such as real estate, bankruptcy, personal injury, taxes, business and probate. This third edition, has been modified to incorporate changes in statute, case law, and the Judicial Council forms used in family law. The changes with regard to the Supreme Court's rejection of the definition of marriage, known as the Defense of Marriage Act (DOMA) which was formally adopted by California, will continue to change and evolve. As of the writing and revision of this 3rd Edition, the Family Code still defines marriage as between a man and a woman. The author has tried to incorporate as much information as possible regarding any changes in order to be able to update the text. That said, a family law paralegal should constantly check for updates and review resources in order to stay current with the statutes, cases, and in particular Judicial Council forms that are constantly being modified to fit the needs of the public as well as be consistent with statutory and court rule changes.

Most people think of divorce when they hear the term family law. The field of family law includes: dissolution of marriage, legal separation, annulment, paternity, adoption, domestic violence, pre and post-marital agreements and cohabitation agreements, domestic partnerships, and can cross into the areas of guardianships and conservatorships, which are typically overseen in probate courts in California. As of 2005 family law statutes also address the custody, support and the division of property in non-marital relationships. All of these areas will be covered, to some extent, in this textbook.

As a family law paralegal, one must draw on many skills, knowledge, and plain life experience. I decided to write this book to give California paralegals a true sense of their value and place in the family law firm. I also wanted a textbook that thoroughly prepares students for what they will encounter in the "real world" as a family law paralegal. Each client and firm is different, and family law paralegals need to be adept in balancing the many clients and facts of each case. Paralegals are an invaluable asset and provide quality and affordable legal services to the firm's clients.

California courts require the utilization of Judicial Council forms by practitioners and those litigants representing themselves in dissolutions of marriage, and other family law related matters. The California Judicial Council has certainly made these forms more "user-friendly." As a family law paralegal, one needs to learn the many nuances in the utilization of these forms, based on each clients unique needs. You will need to keep in mind that the Judicial Council forms were created for ease of use and to attempt to facilitate "fill-in-the-blank" and "check-the-box" situations. A paralegal working in a law firm will often find it necessary to supplement information and orders through the use of attachments.

This textbook assumes that the reader has little or no prior knowledge of the subject matter, as a student or a new paralegal in a law firm. It provides an introduction to the field of family law by utilizing a combination of theory, procedure and practical application. This book will provide the student with an overview of the family law codes and case law—past and present, as well as provide the basic terminology, procedure and process of a dissolution of marriage.

This book will become a handy reference for the paralegal in the family law firm. The text will discuss the utilization of a paralegal in the law firm, as well as the qualities and personalities which are well-suited to this area of practice. The student will be provided with a history of family law, trends and changes in the law, and basic information on how to complete forms, research, and obtain information from the client, his or her spouse and other sources. It is essential that the paralegal understand the forms, types of documents and information which must be disclosed during the course of the dissolution and other family law matters in order to effectively do their job and be an asset to the firm. It is also critical that the family law paralegal understands the other areas of law which may have an effect on the ultimate division and settlement of the marital property. Thus the areas of real estate, business, probate, bankruptcy, taxes, and personal injury will also be covered as they relate to family law.

The paralegal student will be provided a case study, basic guidelines, legal theory, and the tools to apply their knowledge and skills to each unique client. The text is organized in a manner which will take the student through a dissolution start-to-finish. Potential ethical hazards which seem to be inherent with family law are also included. The student will become familiar with many of the ethical considerations that are unique to family law so that they can avoid the unauthorized practice of law and particularly potential malpractice on the part of the attorney for whom the paralegal will work.

The California Family Law Paralegal also covers modification and enforcement of family law orders. Students will utilize Judicial Council forms and apply theory and practice in petitioning the court for orders of enforcement and/or modification, as well as learn the various enforcement mechanisms. Sample declarations and information are included for reference. The final chapter will discuss *other* family law issues which are often dealt with by paralegals in a family law practice: emancipation, adoption, pre and post-marital agreements, and cohabitation agreements. California's domestic partnership laws will be covered and precedent-setting case law applying these newest family law statutes will be discussed as well as much information is available at the time of publication as it relates to how the legislature ultimately redefines marriage.

Many students will find this text interesting from a personal perspective. Perhaps they have previously been through a divorce, or are considering one. Almost everyone knows someone who has been divorced, and perhaps they couldn't understand why certain rulings were made, why property was divided in a certain manner or why support was ordered at a specific amount. This course is also helpful to students who haven't yet married, as it gives them a different perspective on the subjects of cohabitation, having children, commingling property, and domestic partnerships. One of the most important things to remember in family law is that regardless of our experience on a personal level with family law issues, we must put aside our personal perspectives and relate professionally to the client, as this is a very personal issue with them. Also, students must remember that although they may have been involved in a personal family law matter, that matter was *their personal case* and may not reflect the other cases in which they may be involved within the law office environment.

It is my goal that each student will be able to apply the legal theory learned in this text to practical application at the completion of the course. The knowledge and hands-on experience will make the student more comfortable and confident as he or she transitions from student to practicing paralegal. At the conclusion, the student should have a portfolio that can be utilized for interviews and reference in the family law environment.

Dianna L. Noyes, M.S., RP®

The California
Family Law Paralegal

Chapter One

Introduction to Family Law

Introduction to Family Law in California

This text will contain practical, hands-on information specific to California for the student who is interested in the area of family law. At the completion of this course, you will gain the confidence necessary to assist an attorney in all phases of the dissolution process. You will also receive a general overview of other family law matters including: adoption, premarital and post-marital agreements, guardianship, conservatorship, emancipation, domestic violence and the domestic partnership laws. Coursework will also acquaint you with other areas of law that may affect family law clients and the ultimate conclusion of the dissolution of marriage.

Working in a family law practice is unique from most other areas of the law. Each client and his/her particular situation is different. There will be commonalities, but no two cases are ever exactly the same. The primary reason for this is we are human beings and therefore, we react differently, care differently about certain issues, and have different needs and wants from other people. You might find, for example, two families comprising the following: Husband and wife with an 11-year marriage, two children, two automobiles, a house, some small investments, both parties work, and various similar items of furniture, furnishings, tools and appliances. One would think that these dissolutions would be handled and resolved exactly the same. However, if you throw in additional information and issues such as: whether either or both parties have pension(s); the ability to work (full-time or part-time, or self-employed), or the inability to work; gambling, drug or alcohol issues; the age and needs of the children; whether either party has children from another marriage or relationship; debt ratio of each couple; separate property of either or both parties; how amicably the parties wish to dissolve their marriage; and numerous other factors. You now have two cases which are uniquely different.

As a paralegal in a family law office, you will also find that no two days are entirely alike. In a litigation practice, you might expect to be drafting motions, reviewing and summarizing depositions, or preparing for trial. In an estate planning/probate practice you can expect to draft wills and trusts, or handle probate and estate administrations on a daily basis — very similar activities on most days. This is not to say that any of those areas of practice are not interesting or challenging. They are just uniquely different from family law. Again, because you are dealing with the human element and psychological issues incorporated with a process that has many similarities to litigation, the information, problems and issues that you will encounter daily are unique. As we go through different situations during this course you will learn some of the nuances of why family law is different from other areas of law. You will also need to remain attentive to the fact that family law cases might be impacted by the inability of one or both of the parties to pay their debts resulting in a bankruptcy; if one of the parties has been injured (personally or on the job); if there is a change in employment and earnings; whether they own a business—the kind of entity, the value, and the product or service provided; the manner in which title to property is held by the parties; if they own property in another state; as well as numerous other factors. These will be discussed and you will be provided legal theory, statute and case law as they apply to those variables. Thus it is important to have a basic understanding of other areas of law as they relate to family law issues. You will learn to look for situations which might arise so that the attorney can be made aware of potential problems and issues that will need to be resolved. As a family law paralegal you will learn a great deal that is not available in a textbook.

As a paralegal in family law office, you will often be the first-line of contact for the client. Very often, it will be you with whom the client wants to speak when they call in with questions or to need information. You will quickly become the eyes and ears for the attorney.

This course will discuss potential malpractice and ethical considerations of which you will have to be aware. What happens when clients want to relay information or call asking you what to do about their situations? A family law paralegal, more than any other practice area, often walks a fine line under the California Rules of Professional Conduct and the Unauthorized Practice of Law (UPL) statutes. Every paralegal should be aware of Business & Professions Code § 6450 et seq. which set forth definitions of who can be called a paralegal. The Rules of Professional Conduct and UPL statutes will address what you can and cannot do under California Law. You will likely have already discussed some of these rules and issues in a previous class. You should also be familiar with the aforementioned Rules and should abide by them. The attorney is responsible for your work, and if you violate those Rules, the attorney is ultimately accountable, however it will significantly lead to the inability to find work as a paralegal and could lead to a personal civil and/or criminal case against you.

As a family law paralegal you will need to be able to be empathetic to clients' situations without becoming personally involved, or taking their reactions personally. This is an emotionally charged area of law. It is, in many cases, the only time the client will have ever had to seek legal advice. The client can be filled with anxiety, not only about the loss of the marriage and how it will affect the parties' lives from this time forward, but will be fearful of the entire legal process. The clients may know only what they have seen on court TV, read in the media or gained through helpful information from family and friends who want to share tales of what happened to them.

A family law paralegal must be a good listener. The paralegal must be able to separate the wheat from the chaff and not comment about the factual and non-factual information that is received. At the same time, the paralegal must be sensitive to clients, their situations and their needs. The paralegal should be tactful and diplomatic, maintain his/her cool and sense of humor. And, the paralegal must be able to recognize and tell the attorney when the client is pushing the envelope legally and emotionally or is requesting that the paralegal commit UPL.

I encourage you to keep the work you produce in this class in a condition that can be used as a portfolio should you decide to interview for a paralegal position with a family law firm. Once your instructor has reviewed your work, you may want to make the corrections so that your portfolio will be complete and accurate. Your instructor will provide you with more specifics on creating this portfolio at the beginning of the course. As you have read in the preface, family law is predominantly a "forms-driven" practice. The California Judicial Council has created the forms that you will utilize from the beginning to the end of the dissolution process and throughout this course. As you progress through the dissolution process, your instructor will provide you with additional information about the client and discuss the forms in greater detail. This text will provide you with background concerning the various forms, their history, the process and procedure for which each is used, and other information relative to their use. As you progress through the course, you will also be provided with samples of declarations, attachments and pleadings that are relevant, as well as learn to write them.

The Family Law Firm Environment

Depending upon the size of the law firm, you may be the first person with whom a new client speaks. Most family law firms are either sole practitioners or small, two- to five-attorney firms. Paralegals in a firm of this size can expect, once they have some experience, to be an integral part of most family law cases from the beginning to the end. With the exception of setting fees, appearing in court, and giving the client advice, the paralegal will be actively involved in most aspects of the case while working under the supervision of the attorney. Typical tasks include: calendaring, gathering information from the client, preparing disclosure and discovery documents, and the preparation of Judicial Council forms and pleadings. These may include informal discovery and exchange of information, depositions, subpoenas, interrogatories, and requests for production of documents from the opposing party, as well as from other persons and/or entities which may have relevant information. As you gain experience, you may draft special interrogatories, as well as obtain property valuations, prepare settlement conference statements, trial briefs, joinders, Qualified Domestic Relations Orders (QDROs), and Marital Settlement Agreements. You will work with opposing counsel (and his or her staff) to schedule depositions, settlement conferences and trial dates, or to obtain relevant information in a less formal manner. This list is not meant to be inclusive.

As a paralegal in this environment, your attorney will give you as much responsibility as your experience and skills allow. You will work closely with the attorney to develop the case plan and the attorney will come to rely on your experience and knowledge. The attorney may also rely on you to anticipate various procedures that need to be accomplished and to track dates that were calendared for preparing documents, answering discovery requests and other documents prior to the due dates.

You will, most often, be the front-line for the client. When clients call and need to speak with the attorney and the attorney is not available, they will ask for you. Early on in the relationship with clients, you will need to set some guidelines. It is hoped that the attorney has introduced you and informed the client that you are a paralegal and are part of the team who will be working on his or her case. The attorney should also let clients know that although you may be more readily available to speak with them when they call, that you are not an attorney and cannot give them legal advice. Most clients are very excited to know that a paralegal will be working with the attorney on their case. You will need to reiterate your role when you speak with the client so that they have a clear understanding of your role and that you may not be able to answer their questions. This is one of the first, and most common, ethical dilemmas that you will face in the family law office. There will be times when a client needs answers to questions that you will simply have to tell the client that you "will let the attorney know as soon as he/she has returned to the office or is finished speaking with another client." You can, of course, relay to the attorney what those questions and concerns might be. In fact, it is important that you keep detailed notes as to the content of your conversations with a client. I have found that, due to the emotional nature of the dissolution proceedings, clients will often forget to give you information, or may provide you with incorrect or only pieces of information. They may also, at a future time, state that you gave them certain information or that he/she told you something or gave you information that they did not. If you have documented the conversation and/or information to the file, you have a record as to the exact nature of the conversation and what was, or wasn't, said. It will reduce confusion and misunderstandings. The conversation may be relevant later, for example, if the call was about a potential domestic violence situation that might escalate in the future. Such information might be important to demonstrate previous occasions of similar behavior and actions, and you have documented the history.

Calendaring events is another area of potential malpractice and may cause problems. It will often be the paralegal's job to make sure that all documents, procedures and tasks requiring calendaring are calendared. As soon as you are hired, you should become familiar with the type(s) of calendars that are kept by both the firm and the attorney. It is also a good idea to ask for a calendar of your own or to set up reminders within your computer software for important dates for each case. In fact, missed statutes and deadlines are the most common malpractice claim.

The Initial Client Interview and Appointment

You may likely take the initial calls from clients regarding retaining the firm. The clients will usually have numerous questions and are often anxious to see the attorney and get the ball rolling, or they may have been served with documents and have a deadline for filing the responsive documents. In their emotional state, they might begin asking you many questions, none of which you will be able to answer, other than when the soonest appointment might be, when they can expect a return call from the attorney, or general information about the firm. Depending upon the firm's policy, it is wise to obtain the potential client's full name and the name of their spouse as soon as you have scheduled the appointment. This will allow you to provide the names to the attorney and to run a conflict of interest check to confirm that your firm has not represented this client and/or their spouse in a previous matter, that someone with the firm has not already scheduled an appointment, and/or has been retained by the caller's spouse. There would be an inherent conflict of interest if any of these situations occurred. You should ask about the firm's intake policy and how they want you to handle potential new clients.

The firm may want you to send a letter to new clients confirming the appointment and/or providing them with a questionnaire or lists of information that he/she should bring with them. If this is the firm's policy, they may wish for the letter to go to a different address, in the event he/she may still be living with the spouse. You should confirm the address to which the potential client wants the letter sent. Other firms, as well as potential clients, only want to meet to determine if the client does, in fact, want to retain the firm. And the firm may also want to consider if it is a good business decision to take on a new client. Smaller firms may only be able to handle a specific number of active clients at a time. They may consider the size and complexity of the case in determining whether to accept new clients. You should be familiar with the firm's policy prior to scheduling appointments for potential clients. Clients may state that they want to only have a specific part of the matter handled, the situation could be a post-judgment enforcement and/or modification, or strictly Domestic Violence Protection. You should know whether your firm handles these types of matters. If you don't know, ask.

At the first meeting, the attorney will primarily listen to the client, his/her situation, concerns and answer legal questions such as: "Am I entitled to Spousal Support"; "Will I have to pay Spousal Support"; "How much Child Support can I expect to receive"; "How much Child Support can I expect to pay"; "Can my spouse take the children and move away without my permission"; "My spouse threatened me, what can I do about it" and "How do I get my spouse to move out of the house if he/she is still living there, even after I told him/her I want a divorce." One of the other determinations that need to be made by the attorney is whether the client can file for a divorce according to California law. (We will discuss later in this chapter the qualifications and remedies if a client does not meet the California residence requirements for a dissolution of marriage.)

It is my opinion that while it is beneficial for the paralegal to have as much early contact with the client as possible, the paralegal should not conduct the initial client meeting without the attorney being present, unless it is an emergency. I also don't believe this can be the best use of a paralegal's time to be present during the first meeting, but this can be determined on a case-by-case basis. The attorney and the client are getting to know one another—sizing each other up, if you will. The client is listening to the attorney's answers and also using the time to determine if the attorney is really listening and will be their best advocate. The attorney will gauge the complexity of the case, deciding if this client is going to be able to afford his/her services, if the client is listening to his/her answers or simply hearing only what the client wants to hear, and ultimately deciding if this is a case that the attorney really wants to handle. Additionally, the attorney will be listening for clues that will help him/her decide whether or not to take the case.

As soon as the initial meeting is finished and the client has indicated he/she will retain the firm, I believe that now is the time to introduce the paralegal to the client. In my experience, it has worked well for the attorney to sit down with the new client and the paralegal and go over the information that was discussed in the initial meeting. You might also, at this time, discuss the information that the client brought with them, or advise the client about the information that he or she needs to bring to the office in order to get the dissolution process started. If you or the attorney have not already done so, provide the client the client questionnaire. You and the attorney can discuss with the client time frames for getting the initial documents filed with the court, how the spouse will be served and other procedural information which should be discussed and clarified, and about which the client should be aware. Clients have often been misinformed by "helpful" family and friends. These people have good intentions, but unless you are practicing in the family law area on a daily basis, it is difficult to understand the process and relay the information correctly. Thus, the client often has a misunderstanding about the entire dissolution process, their rights, what is going to happen, and when and why it is going to happen.

Prior to preparing any documents, the attorney and client should each sign a fee agreement, most commonly called a Retainer Agreement, which you may likely prepare. The Retainer Agreement sets forth the parameters and scope of work to be performed as well as the attorney's hourly rate, the paralegal's hourly rate, how out-of-pocket costs will be paid, and the lump-sum or retainer that the client will be required to pay to commence the representation. The firm will likely have a template of this agreement for you to use in preparing the retainer agreement.

Effective January 1, 2004, California allows attorneys to provide "un-bundled" legal representation to a client. Prior to 2004, if an attorney agreed to take on a dissolution of marriage, the attorney was required to represent the client from the start to the finish of the legal action, unless the client found other representation or the attorney was granted a withdrawal in the case because the client was being uncooperative or owed the attorney a substantial sum of money. This new rule allows attorneys to contract with a client to provide limited and specific services. Thus, the Retainer should specifically state the services or scope of work to be done. Once the work is complete, the attorney will simply withdraw from the case, which returns the client to the status of "representing" him or herself. You will want to check the Judicial Counsel forms as there have been some specific forms created for "un-bundled" services.

Ethics and the Paralegal

The paralegal should be diligent throughout the entire case and be aware of potential conflicts of interest, as well as other ethical considerations. Before meeting the client and/or being retained, a conflict check should be undertaken. The California Rules of Professional Conduct (CRPC) address potential conflicts of interest which are unique to family law. The paralegal should be well versed and understand these Rules. One of the most common potential conflicts would be the attorney representing both sides of a family law matter. CRPC 3-310 addresses these potential conflicts, as follows:

3-310(A): If an attorney has or had a relationship with another party in the litigation or is interested in the subject matter of the litigation, that attorney cannot accept or continue the representation without first obtaining the client's *informed written consent*.

3-310(B): No dual representation of both sides of a proceeding where their respective interests conflict is allowed without first obtaining *both* of their *informed written consent*.

3-310(C): An attorney must not undertake representation adverse to the interests of a former client (that is, must not represent someone who is suing a former client of the lawyer's) if, by virtue of the former representation that lawyer has obtained *confidential information* pertinent to the current subject matter of the representation, without first obtaining the former client's *informed written consent*.

3-310(F): This section defined *informed* as used above in the context of consent as a *disclosure and advice* to the client as to any actual or likely adverse effects to the client. Any client who is in the position of signing such an *informed written consent* must first be referred to some other attorney to advise him of the consequences of that act.

There are two common situations wherein the above rules *must* be reviewed and applied:

1) Husband and Wife schedule an appointment together with the attorney and tell the attorney that they "agree on everything." They further request that the attorney "just prepare the paperwork and the agreement" so that it is correct and official. The California Bar Association and the courts frown on dual representation. Clearly the above scenario would present a conflict of interest for the attorney. The attorney may consider taking the case, if: 1) the parties simply are requesting that the attorney assist in terminating the marital status **only**, no property, custody or support issues can be resolved; and 2) the parties execute an *informed written consent* setting forth the services the attorney is to perform, and stating that they understand that there is a potential conflict.

2) Attorney previously represented Husband and/or Wife in another legal matter. For instance, if the attorney prepared a will or a bankruptcy petition for Husband and Wife, or the attorney represented one of the parties in a personal injury, business, collection or some other matter for which the attorney might have *confidential* information about one or both of the parties that would make it difficult to advocate for either client.

There are many other less blatant examples of conflict of interest, the following are just a few:

1) If the attorney has a "social" relationship with either or both of the parties;

2) If the attorney has a "confidential" relationship with opposing counsel; or

3) If the attorney represented one of the party's immediate family members.

Notwithstanding the signing of an *informed written consent*, at such time as the attorney and/or client feels that the confidential information has been or may be disclosed or that the parties realize they cannot agree, the attorney representing them must completely withdraw from the case. Therefore, although it is not strictly prohibited for an attorney to provide dual representation, in most situations it is not advisable.

In the event that the parties have been made aware by the attorney of the potential conflicts, made an informed decision, sign the written consent and still request that the attorney represent them both, the attorney still, technically, may only represent one of the parties. The firm may have a specific policy of never handling cases where there are inherent conflicts.

If the attorney chooses to be retained in these situations, he or she will have to decide which party he/she will represent. The attorney will have to inform the other party that once the agreement and all other relevant documents are drafted, the party must take all documentation to another attorney for review. Additionally, the agreement should also contain a statement that the attorney drafting the document did not represent and/or advise the other party, nor did that party rely solely on any information provided by the attorney, and that the non-represented party was advised to seek independent legal advice, indicating whether they have done so, or waived the right. In fact, it is advisable to have the attorney who reviewed the documents sign a statement stating that he/she has reviewed the documents.

Other Malpractice Concerns

Errors in calendaring is one of the most common areas of malpractice. It is therefore, essential that the paralegal understand calendaring if he/she is responsible for that function in the office. If there is another individual assigned to calendaring, the paralegal should always double-check any calendared dates to make sure any and all dates are complete and accurate as it is likely to be the paralegal's responsibility to ensure the work is complete and ready for the attorney's review prior to the deadline.

Calendars may be topical, a central firm calendar (which may or may not be computerized), an attorney's personal calendar, and any other calendaring system the firm maintains. The paralegal will often maintain his or her own calendar as a back up for any of the aforementioned calendaring systems. Calendaring information should at a minimum include: the client or case name; the document received or filed, from or to whom and on what date; the hearing or appearance date; the date any responses are due. Subsequent entries should include any other relevant dates based on the type of document received. Once the documents are calendared, the paralegal should bring them to the attorney's attention. You will need to be diligent in providing copies of the documents received to the client, letting the client know what information the attorney needs in order to respond, giving the client a time-line for providing the information, preparing the responses in proper legal format, and finally providing drafts for the attorney to review and sign prior to sending the final documents and any exhibits (attachments) to the opposing party or their counsel.

The paralegal should always be careful about *giving legal advice* to the client (otherwise known as the Unauthorized Practice of Law or UPL). Although it may not be the client's intent, it is very easy to fall into a trap of answering clients' questions. For instance, if the client calls and says, "I believe that my [husband/wife] came into our home yesterday when I was at work and took all of the financial data in the roll top desk. What do I do? Can I change the locks?" You cannot give that client advice on whether they can change the locks or other legal remedies—even if you know the answer. You must wait to relay the information to the attorney. The attorney will either call the client and advise him/her, or the attorney may (in his/her discretion) ask you to call the client and relay specific information. The client will understandably be upset. It is disconcerting having someone, particularly an estranged spouse, come into the home when one isn't there. The client is already emotional and distraught and will want to have an answer right away. However, you **cannot** tell the client what to do. That is considered giving legal advice and is a violation of UPL Statutes. There are many more examples, which your instructor will discuss with you.

Confidentiality

The paralegal should never share information about clients and their cases with family or friends and should not discuss a client's case, even with the attorney, in an elevator or other public place where details about the client might be overheard by others. Additionally, one needs to be mindful that in some offices telephone conversations can also be overheard by others, and legal documents should never be left in areas where other clients or persons coming into the office might be able to see them. In many cases, a family law firm may seem more casual than a big firm that practices in the area of litigation. Regardless of the size of the firm—a solo practitioner or several attorneys—the confidentiality of each client needs to be of primary concern to every person affiliated with the law firm.

A paralegal must insure and protect his or her interests with respect to being protected in the law firm. It is undecided whether Errors and Omissions Insurance extends to the paralegal. Although Business & Professions Code states that a paralegal's work must be supervised by an attorney, the paralegal's liability may be at question and unprotected. Under the concept of *respondeat superior*, an employer is considered liable for any negligence of their employees as long as the employees are working within the course and scope of their employment at the time the negligent act occurred. This concept does not protect the employee, it does however, extend the negligence to other persons and/or the law firm. You should discuss this with the firm to be clear on whether or not you are listed on their malpractice coverage.

Ethical Wall

Family law paralegals do not seem to change jobs as frequently as litigation and other types of paralegals. However, because the family law "community" may be very small in some jurisdictions, it should be noted that a potential employer should be made aware of all cases on which the paralegal is working, particularly where the new employer might represent the opposing party.

In the event there may be a conflict of interest an ethical wall may have to be established. The National Federation of Paralegal Associations, Inc. (NFPA) has an outstanding publication titled "The Ethical Wall" which details the requirements of creating and maintaining the ethical wall. I would encourage you to obtain and read that publication if, in the future, you plan to seek employment with another family law attorney in your community. The same situation could occur when moving to another type of law firm. For example, perhaps the couple owned a business or other property together. The attorney/firm should be advised of your having assisted in the dissolution matter so that the firm can determine whether there is a conflict and an ethical wall needs to be created.

Family Code and Other Relevant California Codes

There are thousands of codes which have been enacted by the California legislature that relate to Family Law. The foundation of our legal system is from common law. Over time, many of the codes have been enacted by the legislature due to court rulings and opinions, others have been the result of the need for access to justice, as well as changes in social mores and public policy. The Family Code was created by the legislature in 1994 as a result of the judiciary recommending that California needed to have a collection of family law related statutes in one section rather than scattered throughout a variety of related codes. Prior to that date, dissolution of marriage laws were primarily found under the Family Law Act, Division 4 (General Provisions) Part 5 of the California Civil Code, Section 4000, Title 1, "Marriage." However, additional laws were found in at least five different California Codes. The legislature took on the task of reorganizing and updating the various codes into one body of work. The process of creating the Family Code began in 1989 and took over five years, as careful attention was paid to eliminating conflicts of pre-existing laws, duplication, and reorganization. The Family Code consists of 14 sections (or Divisions).

One of the most complex areas of the Family Code is covered by §§ 2500 et seq., which provide for the equal division of community property. While this code section codifies the rules with respect to the division of property, court decisions and further legislation addressing additional, unique situations regarding this subject have made it one of the most complex areas of law. Another very complex section is found within Family Code § 3020, et seq. which addresses child custody.

You will find that there are many other codes to which you will need to refer in certain situations. The following is not meant to be an exclusive list, but will give you an idea of the complexity of family law matters and the other laws with which a paralegal should be familiar.

Service of Documents — Code of Civil Procedure § 413.10

Venue — Code of Civil Procedure § 395(a)

Conservatorship — Probate Code §§ 1400 et seq.

Guardianship — Probate Code §§ 1400 et seq.

Spousal Abuse — Penal Code §§ 273.8 et seq.

Juvenile Court Law — Welfare & Institutions Code §§ 200 et seq.

Withholding Orders — California Code of Procedure §§ 706.030 et seq.

Discovery — Code of Civil Procedure §§ 2002 to 2076

The paralegal will find many secondary sources, which will be helpful in order to understand more fully the legislature's and/or the court's intentions in enacting laws and making rulings. There are numerous secondary resources which provide history, theory and sample documents to be utilized by the family law paralegal. Some of them are as follows:

- Hogoboom & King, *Family Law* (The Rutter Group);
- *California Practice Guide, Family Law* (Thomson-West Group);
- *Practice Under the Family Code* (Continuing Education of the Bar);
- Witkin, *Summary of California Law*;
- Witkin, *California Procedure*;
- Adams, *California Family Law Practice* (CFLR, Sausalito, California);
- *California Rules of Court*

There are numerous other publications and on-line services available and to which your firm may subscribe. It is also helpful to join your local bar association's family-law practice section (if they allow paralegal or associate membership) as they may be able to provide you with recent updates, continuing education, and timely information about local court rules, as well as proposed changes to the law, judicial council forms, and other family law related issues. If you are unable to become a member of the local bar, you should attend their luncheons and other Continuing Legal Education (CLE) offerings as frequently as possible. You might also want to join your local paralegal association, or consider joining the sections of the California State Bar that allow paralegals to join, such as the Solo and Small Firm Practice section. Membership in other associations such as the National Federation of Paralegal Associations, Inc. (NFPA) and the National Association of Legal Assistants (NALA) will also give you an opportunity to network with other paralegals, as well as find affordable CLE offerings.

Where do we start once the firm has been retained? One of the primary issues is whether the client has the ability to file the action in California.

Jurisdiction

In order for the court to hear a family law matter, the issue of jurisdiction must first be resolved. Specifically, does the California court, as well as the county court, have jurisdiction over the dissolution of marriage (the people, property, and/or children)? One of the first questions an attorney needs to ask when talking to a potential client is: "Where are you residing and for how long?"

In rem (Personal) Jurisdiction

The concept of person or "in rem" jurisdiction is whether the court has personal jurisdiction or the ability to exercise power over the parties. The California Constitution states that California may exercise personal jurisdiction and may make determinations over the personal rights of that individual, based on the following:

- physical presence in the state
- domicile in the state where action commenced
- consent to exercise personal jurisdiction
- "minimum contacts"

California Code of Civil Procedure § 410.10 defines personal jurisdiction and clarifies mere "physical presence" which would allow personal jurisdiction. Those conditions are as follows:

- presence in the state
- domicile in the state
- residence in the state
- citizen in the state
- doing business in the state
- causing an *effect* in the state
- consent of the person in question
- ownership of property within the state
- any other such relationship with the state which makes the exercise of personal jurisdiction reasonable

The California Courts interpret personal jurisdiction very broadly. If you would like to read more about personal jurisdiction and how it is determined in California, please read: *Burnham v. Superior Ct*, 495 U.S. 604, 110 S. Ct. 2105 (1990).

What happens if two different jurisdictions (States) declare that they have personal jurisdiction over the dissolution of marriage or, specifically the custody of the minor children? In most cases, the state which first acquired jurisdiction (who was the first to serve dissolution documents) will be the forum for resolution, regardless of which party filed first. There is also a question of domicile, which we will discuss shortly, and may be the exception to this rule. The paralegal should remember that in most cases, the first to **serve** controls the case, not the first person to **file**. From time to time you may be called upon to make sure that a party gets served immediately upon filing of the documents in order to preserve personal jurisdiction over the party. If a person is improperly served or there is no jurisdiction, it may be necessary to file a Motion to Quash Service of Summons, which will be covered in Chapter Two. Alternatively, the firm may find they will be representing the client to try to defend that Motion.

Residence and Domicile

Domicile is defined as the **permanent** place the party lives within a certain state. A person can have only one domicile, but can reside in more than one place. In order to file for a dissolution of marriage in California, at least one of the parties must be domiciled here. Thus, domicile establishes personal jurisdiction. The party who lives here must **intend** to make California his or her **permanent** residence.

The concept of domicile, as opposed to residence, can be proven by ownership of property, payment of state (personal) taxes, a driver's license, execution of a will, and voter registration. Oftentimes it takes evidence of several or all of these to resolve the issue of domicile, since a person may own real property in more than one state, may pay taxes in more than one state (because of a business), and may have a driver's license in more than one state, if the state(s) allow. However, a person can only, legally, execute a will and be registered to vote in one place — their **permanent** domicile. The **intent** to be domiciled in one location must be proved to establish jurisdiction that is in question, and that jurisdiction may be difficult to prove. For instance:

> A person may have more than one residence. They might have a house in Sacramento County, a house in Lake Tahoe, Nevada, and time shares in Maui and Florida, spending time equally in all places. Those would all be residences.

> Another example would be someone in the military who was stationed for a period of time overseas. Where is their domicile? In most cases, it is the point of entry of their military service, but further research would need to be done to confirm where the person has registered to vote or in some manner changed their domicile since enlisting.

The paralegal may need to assist the attorney in determining the proper jurisdiction for the dissolution of marriage. In the above-mentioned scenario, it would have to be determined which location was the domicile and which were merely residences. It has also been my experience that sometimes the client forgets to give the attorney all of the information about where people reside, and you might need to bring this issue to the attorney's attention so that he or she can make a determination as to whether or not there is a question of domicile.

The existence of domicile in California is important, because if California doesn't have jurisdiction, then the only matter which can be adjudicated, will be the marital status of the parties. A Judgment with any other orders such as custody, support and the division of property is considered void if the California court does not have jurisdiction. Additionally, it should be noted that the court's power over these issues is warranted only when personal jurisdiction has been established over the **responding** party.

Family Code § 2320 establishes the residence (domicile) requirements for a dissolution of marriage. The requirements are **six months** in the State of California and **three months** in the county immediately prior to the filing of the dissolution in that venue. This requirement applies only to dissolutions and not to legal separations or annulments. If a client does not meet the domicile requirements for a dissolution, the client may wish to file for a legal separation. After the Petitioner has met the requirements under FC § 2320 for a dissolution, the Petitioner can file an amended Petition to change from a legal separation to a dissolution. This procedure is found in Family Code § 2321, and will be discussed in more detail later in this chapter.

Subject Matter Jurisdiction

California Family Code §§ 2000 and 2010, state that the **Superior** court has exclusive subject matter jurisdiction to hear **all** issues arising from Family Code matters, including, but not limited to, the dissolution of marriage. For example, you will not file for child support in small claims court. All issues concerning the status of the marriage, child custody, visitation and support, spousal support, division of marital property and any other related matters must be heard in Superior court.

Venue

The venue is the county where the action will be filed. As stated above, to file for a dissolution, one of the parties must have resided in the County (venue) for three months immediately preceding the commencement of the action. *California Code of Civil Procedure § 395(a).* Venue may be challenged, if "inconvenient forum" can be proved, provided the inconvenienced party can show that the county is not the best location for the trial, or if it can be proved that the filing party did not meet the consecutive three-month residency requirement.

Family Code § 300 — Definition of a Marriage

Valid Marriage

Family Code § 300 sets forth the requirements for a valid marriage in the state of California. A valid marriage is established by consent and a contract between a man and a woman. A license must be issued and there must be a ceremony which solemnizes the marriage. The parties must be at least 18 years of age. If either is not, the parent(s) must consent or the minor must have been emancipated.

One of the criteria for a valid marriage is its "solemnization" which means that a ceremony was conducted. There is no specific reference to the kind of ceremony, "but the parties must declare, in the presence of the person solemnizing the marriage, and the necessary witnesses, that they take each other as husband and wife...." Any religious clergy, a judge, retired judge, magistrate, commissioner of civil marriages, or even a person authorized to perform a ceremony through registration with the county recorder may perform a marriage. (*Family Code § 420 et seq.*)

There continues to be debate, as well as, constitutional challenges made to Family Code § 308.5 which states: "Only marriage between a man and a woman is valid or recognized in California." Unlike common law marriages, there is no provision in the Family Code stating that if a same sex marriage is valid in another state it would be considered valid in California. As previously mentioned, this language was deemed unconstitutional in 2008 and again in 2013, but the statutes have not been modified as of the publication date of this text.

Confidential Marriage

A confidential marriage may be applied for by persons who have been living together prior to the marriage. A health certificate is not required. (Family Code § 300) The parties simply present themselves before the County Clerk where they reside, complete the application, affidavit, and pay the fees. The County Clerk will then perform (solemnize) the ceremony. The confidential marriage records are maintained in a secure location by the County Recorder, and the public is not allowed to inspect them. The clerk is allowed to search the records to determine the existence of a marriage, but may provide no other information, such as date and location of the marriage, except on court order.

Common Law Marriage and Cohabitation

California does not typically recognize common law marriages. It does not matter how long a man and woman have lived together, they are not *legally* married, and the division of their property and the issues regarding the custody and support of their children cannot be decided by the family court under the dissolution statutes. (Cohabitation agreements will be discussed in Chapter 11.) Child custody and support fall within the Family Code "Paternity" statutes; which will be addressed later in the text. However, since there is no requirement for a valid marriage to have children, this is a different issue and not specifically related to common law marriage and the statutes that determine a legal and valid marriage.

California may recognize a marriage that was "contracted outside this state that would be valid by the laws of the jurisdiction in which the marriage was contracted is valid in this state." (Family Code § 308.) Thus a common law marriage that is recognized in another state would be recognized in California as a valid marriage.

The primary exception to the common law and cohabitation statutes in California is a *palimony* case known as *Marvin v. Marvin*. (Marvin v. Marvin 18 Cal.3d 660, 1976) Prior to 1976, the courts felt that, based on public policy, it was wrong to consider cohabitation a valid marriage, because to do so would advocate sexual relations outside of marriage, which would ultimately erode the institution of marriage. The relevant facts of the case are as follows: Lee Marvin and Michelle Triola lived together for seven years, but never married. During that time, they accumulated over one million dollars in assets, held solely in the name of Lee Marvin (the Defendant). The parties also "held themselves out" as being married, thus Ms. Triola actually used the name of Michelle Marvin. When the parties separated, Ms. Marvin sued Mr. Marvin for support and for a share of the assets accumulated while they lived together. Ms. Marvin stated that she had expressly given up her musical career in order to provide domestic services to Mr. Marvin and in exchange, Mr. Marvin would support Michelle financially. They also agreed that they would combine any earnings and share in any accumulated wealth as would a married couple. (See Appendix 1A for the decision on this case.)

In 1976, the California Supreme Court broke with tradition and rejected Mr. Marvin's claim that the sexual aspect of the relationship was bound with the contractual aspect of the relationship and severed the two issues. The court recognized that this situation was different, because the parties had an express contract. Thus the laws governing contracts were applied in this situation (as they would in a valid marriage) and the "services" to be provided by Ms. Marvin were separated from the argument, although those services were "consideration."

Historically the courts have determined that most people who intend to co-habitate do not negotiate and formalize their relationship, resulting in a contractual agreement. Therefore, the issues of property and support are not considered express contracts and subject to the *Marvin* doctrine. Additionally, the courts have hesitated to use this "test" in most subsequent cases, as there is concern that it will appear that public policy advocates non-marital relationships.

The term *palimony* was actually coined by the media and not the court. It has, however, become a legal term-of-art associated with one party asking for alimony (spousal support) from another when there is not a valid marriage.

Dissolution, Legal Separation or Annulment

Once either or both parties have decided they no longer wish to be married and wish to terminate their relationship, they must decide the appropriate manner by which to dissolve the marriage. The first step might be to seek legal counsel to determine the proper procedure and determine each party's legal rights.

After initially meeting with the client, the attorney must make some initial assessments if he or she is going to take the case:

1) Determine if this is a valid marriage. Were the couple legally married and do they have a marriage certificate? Family Code § 300 establishes the criteria for a valid marriage in California;

2) Establish personal jurisdiction so that the matter can be filed in the California Superior Court in the appropriate county; and,

3) Determine the grounds, if applicable, for the appropriate manner of dissolving the marriage, as set forth below.

Dissolution of Marriage

If the client has resided in the state of California for a minimum of six months and if they have resided in the County for a minimum of three months in which the dissolution will be filed, a dissolution of marriage can be filed in that county.

Family Code § 2310: Grounds for Dissolution or Legal Separation states that: *Dissolution of the marriage or legal separation of the parties may be based on either of the following grounds, which shall be pleaded generally:*

(a) Irreconcilable differences, which have caused an irremedial breakdown of the marriage.

(b) Incurable insanity.

(*Ed. Note: this is "or" not both; only Irreconcilable difference is "no fault".*)

Prior to 1970, people obtaining a divorce in California were required to show that there was fault for the breakdown of the marriage. Some states still require that fault be determined. The grounds in these states, and in California prior to 1970, are: adultery, mental cruelty, and insanity. In 1970, when the Family Law Act became effective, the legislature codified this new "common ground" and made California a "no fault" state. This means that a party seeking a dissolution or legal separation simply states that there are **irreconcilable differences** which have caused an **irremedial breakdown** of the marriage. As long as one of the parties is prepared to testify and declare these grounds, as well as state that there is no possibility of the marriage being saved, the termination of marital status will be granted.

Should a party wish to state the grounds of incurable insanity, then insanity has to be proven. It is, therefore, usually simpler, quicker, and much less expensive, to request a judgment based on irreconcilable differences; or *no fault*.

In most cases at the completion of the process the marital status will be terminated and the parties will be restored to single status. A spouse may also request that the court restore the former (maiden) name as part of the dissolution proceeding.

Family Code § 2339 states that the "earliest the parties' marital status may be terminated is **six months after the court acquires jurisdiction** over the respondent." Thus, when a Petition for Dissolution is filed on behalf of the client, the six-month "waiting" period does not begin on the date the documents were **filed**, but on the date the respondent was **served**. The court, however, requires that a full day be added to any statutory waiting periods, therefore, the soonest the marital status can be terminated is **6 months, plus one day** from the **date of service** of the Summons and Petition.

Legal Separation

A Judgment for Dissolution of Marriage and a Judgment of Legal Separation are essentially the same process. The differences between the two are:

1) Residency (six months in the State and three months in the County) does not have to be established to file for a legal separation;

2) There is no six-month "waiting period; and,

3) A Legal Separation does not terminate the marital status of the parties.

The issues of child custody, support, division of property, injunctive relief, and any other relevant orders may be made as they would in a dissolution proceeding. However, at the conclusion of the matter, and upon entry of Judgment, the parties are still legally married. A Judgment of Legal Separation does not allow a spouse to return to the former name.

Both parties must consent to a legal separation. If a party objects to the Petition for Legal Separation, a Response requesting a dissolution must be filed. It should be noted that a default or non-appearance by respondent is considered consent.

There may be several reasons why a person would pursue a legal separation rather than a dissolution of marriage.

1) Residency requirements are not met;

2) Religious or moral reasons; or,

3) A legal separation affords both parties the opportunity to maintain benefits which would otherwise be terminated by a dissolution of marriage. Some of these benefits might be:

Continuation of health and dental benefits

Death benefits — either through employment or as a surviving spouse of decedent

Continuation of tax filing status

Nullity (Annulment)

The primary reason a party may choose to petition the court for an annulment is to contest the validity of the marriage. As stated, a party who petitions for a dissolution of marriage is asking the court to terminate a valid marriage. Although not frequently sought due to the ease of obtaining a dissolution under the "no fault" premise, it may be necessary to void a marriage or prove that it is voidable based on very specific circumstances. Should a client meet with the attorney and state, "I want my marriage annulled," you will likely assist the attorney in determining if the client meets the statutory requirements for an annulment. You will also assist in gathering documentation and preparing declarations to prove the marriage is invalid. It is extremely important that the Family Code Section which applies to each type of void or voidable marriage be reviewed carefully to confirm that the client has the ability to seek an annulment rather than a divorce. Those references are below:

Void and Voidable Marriages

Void:	Family Code § 2200	Incestuous Marriage
	Family Code § 2201	Bigamous; polygamous marriages
Voidable:	Family Code § 2210(a)	Petitioner's age at the time of marriage
	Family Code § 2210(b)	Prior existing marriage
	Family Code § 2210(c)	Unsound mind
	Family Code § 2210(d)	Fraud
	Family Code § 2210(e)	Force
	Family Code § 2210(f)	Physical incapacity

Void Marriages

There are only two grounds upon which a marriage may be determined as **void**, or as though it never had any force or effect. These are marriages that are considered incestuous or bigamous/polygamous. An incestuous marriage is described as a marriage which is between "parents and children," "brothers and sisters," (including half-brothers and sisters); "uncles and nieces," "aunts and nephews," and "ancestors and descendants of every degree." Family Code § 2200.

Bigamous and polygamous marriages are described as a marriage that occurred when a person subsequently marries another person **without having terminated the first marriage**. A bigamist has two spouses, and the polygamist has three or more spouses.

There are exceptions to this rule. See Family Code § 2201. Generally, in cases where a spouse has been missing for five years or more, or who are presumed to be or have been declared dead, then the remaining or surviving spouse may presume that he or she is free to marry. However, although rare, you should always review the applicable code sections with the attorney to address any questions or concerns which arise in these situations.

Voidable Marriages

A voidable marriage is one that appeared to be valid on its face but is later declared void, having no force or effect. The legal defect must have occurred at the time of the marriage and not later. If it occurs at a later date and time, the parties must obtain a divorce. A person who is not a party [to the marriage] is also able to file a Petition for Annulment, such as a parent on behalf of a child under the age of 18, or where a person does not have the mental capacity to consent to marriage; typically this would be someone who is a guardian or conservator of the adult person. In the event no one, even a third party, brings this matter to the court's attention, the marriage will continue as though it is valid. There may also be a statute of limitations which must be considered and be verified prior to bringing this type of action.

A new case law has established under what circumstances fraud may be used as a ground for annulment. In re the Marriage of Meagher & Meleki (2005) 131 Cal.App.4th 1, 31 Cal. Rptr.3d 663 held that a marriage may be nullified only if "the misrepresentation goes to the party's intentions with respect to the sexual or procreative aspect of marriage." Nor may either party "question the validity of the marriage upon the ground of reliance upon the express or implied representations of the other with respect to such matters as character, habits, chastity, business or social standing, financial worth or prospects, or matters of similar nature."

A marriage may be terminated under the following grounds:

- Age. The age of consent in California is 18   Family Code § 2210(a)
- Missing or presumed dead   Family Code § 2210(b)
- Unsound mind (ability to give legal consent)   Family Code § 2210(c)
- Fraud   Family Code § 2210(d)
- Force   Family Code § 2210(e)
- Physical incapacity   Family Code § 2210(f)

There is no six-month waiting period for an annulment, nor is there a residency requirement. An annulment can be achieved as quickly as the firm can compile the information, file and serve the documents, and obtain a hearing date. Upon entry of Judgment, the parties are restored to the status of unmarried persons. Again, because evidence and documentation must be obtained, this is not necessarily a speedy process.

Putative Spouse

A putative spouse is defined as a person who believes, in good faith, that their marriage was valid. If a marriage is void or voidable, the spouse, who was the innocent party, should not be punished for the wrongs of the "bad spouse." The putative spouse, must have believed, in good faith, that his/her marriage was valid and, as such he/she is entitled to receive the benefits of community and quasi-community property acquired during the marriage. (Family Code § 2500) This most commonly occurs in a bigamous or polygamous situation but can occur where any of the other elements for an annulment are met.

Family Code §§ 2251–2255 set forth the guidelines the court must use to determine whether a person may be considered a putative spouse, and if the person is entitled to spousal support, the community and quasi-community property acquired during the marriage, attorney fees, and any other relevant matters.

Summary Dissolution

There is also a very simple and inexpensive mechanism for obtaining a dissolution. This process can be easily completed without the assistance of attorneys. However, this type of dissolution is very narrow in scope and will not work for many couples.

A potential client may consult with the attorney to discuss a dissolution. The attorney may determine that the client meets the criteria below and since the matter is uncontested, the attorney may recommend that the client file a Petition for Summary Dissolution. This may be applicable in an instance where both husband and wife jointly meet with the attorney and ask the law firm to assist them in completing the documents necessary to obtain the Judgment. As a paralegal practicing in a family law firm, this area is perfectly suited for such knowledge and skills. It is recommended that you be familiar with the provisions set forth in Family Code §§ 2400 to 2406, and the accompanying brochure, so that, at the direction of the attorney, you can assist clients in expeditiously and inexpensively obtaining a summary dissolution, provided they qualify for the procedure.

In order to file for a **Summary Dissolution**, there are some specific criteria that need to be met.

Clients that meet the criteria should be encouraged to obtain a "booklet" from the court clerk (it costs about $20.00, depending upon the county). The booklet contains all of the forms and instructions needed to prepare and file the documents. No court hearing or appearance is required. The process, however, does **require** that the parties meet **all** the following criteria:

- At least one of the parties must be a resident of the State of California for at least six months and the county in which the action is commenced for at least three months before the action is filed;

- Irreconcilable differences have caused an "irremedial breakdown" of marriage, and the marriage should be dissolved;

- There are no natural children of the relationship;

- There are no adopted children under the age of 18;

- The wife is not pregnant;

- The parties have been married to each other for no more than five years before filing the petition for summary dissolution;

- Neither party owns any interest in any real property, except a *lease* of the residence in which they live, so long as the lease does not contain an option to purchase of the property. Furthermore, such a lease must terminate by its own terms within one year of filing the petition;

- There are no debts incurred during the marriage by either of the spouses greater than $6,000, with the exception of a car loan;

- The total fair market value of all assets acquired during the marriage does not exceed $40,000 (except automobiles), and neither party has separate property assets (except automobiles) that exceed $40,000 in value[1];

- The parties have signed an agreement dividing all their assets and debts and have also signed all other documents necessary to transfer title of assets to give effect to the terms of the agreement;

- Both parties must indicate to the court that they have read and understood the brochure contemplated in Family Code Section 2406, and that they are desirous of dissolving the marriage.

Although rare, should the parties change their minds about going forward with the Summary Dissolution, there are procedures for revoking a petition or setting aside (challenging) the judgment once it is entered. The brochure that accompanies the Summary Dissolution package should be reviewed and followed carefully.

Determination of Action

Now that you know the types of legal remedies for the new family law client, you will be more fully able to assist the attorney and the client in preparing the documents required. Does the client want a divorce or a legal separation? What is the client's goal? Is the client simply asking to separate assets and debts but have the marital status remain in tact? Did the client come to the office stating that he/she wanted a divorce, but the attorney has determined that they don't meet the residency requirements? Did the client state that he/she wanted their marriage annulled, but after careful review of the applicable Family Code sections, it has been determined that providing "proof" of a void or voidable marriage would be embarrassing to the client or difficult to prove, so a *no fault* dissolution would be the more appropriate procedure? If you are uncertain as to what the attorney has advised the client, you need to ask. Once you have this information, you can begin obtaining information (via the client information package or other method used by the firm) and completing the applicable Judicial Council forms, or begin obtaining the evidence and documentation required for a *provable* action.

For the purposes of this class, we will be focusing on a Dissolution of Marriage. There will be instances as we progress where we will discuss aspects of other remedies as they relate to the codes, rules and forms, but our primary course of action will be to reach a Judgment for a Dissolution of Marriage.

---

1. Note that FC§ 2400 states that the Judicial Council may adjust these amounts according to the California Consumer Price Index in odd-numbered years. These amounts should be verified prior to confirming the client's ability to qualify for the Summary Dissolution based on the current CPI.

Client Files

Your instructor may provide you with an example of a client file and any applicable guidelines and details for preparing your client file to be used as a portfolio for your class "law firm." If you intend to use this client file as a portfolio, it is highly suggested, that you correct any work that has been graded by your instructor.

The following is a general outline of what is involved in opening and keeping a client file:

> Each firm will have its own procedure for creating and opening a file. Additionally, each attorney may want his/her staff to organize documents in a particular manner. When you begin your job as a paralegal, the creation of client files will be one of the first things you will want to learn. Of primary importance, regardless of the initial steps, is that once the file is open, any person within the firm should be able to obtain basic client information, ascertain what information is in the file, and have easy access that information. Most firms will place labels on the file/folder indicating the party's name, address, telephone, other contact information and whether they are the Petitioner or the Respondent. Additionally, it is helpful if the other party's contact information is also on the outside of the folder, including the name of his/her attorney and his/her contact information, if the party is represented. Having this information easily accessible on the outside of folder saves time when anyone within the firm needs to contact the party or the attorney.

> In most cases a client file will be divided into at least two parts: Correspondence and Pleadings. Likewise, this information should be inserted into any electronic database(s) the firm maintains. This could include: software for conflicts checks, calendaring, billing, and specific legal specialty form packages, to name a few.

> Correspondence can consist of any of the following: Contract/retainer agreement; client information (form); letters; correspondence to and from opposing counsel, experts, counselors and mediators; memoranda between firm attorneys and other staff memorializing actions taken and/or conversations with the client; and any other information which is relevant to the case.

> Pleadings may include, but are not limited to the following: Petition; Response; Motions or Request for Hearing pleadings, declarations and exhibits; Orders; Judgments; copies of documents filed by the opposing side; and, disclosure and/or discovery documents. Pleadings can further be broken down into categories. Again, this depends upon how the attorney prefers the documents be organized. For instance, the attorney may want a separate section or category which contains financial information, depositions or other discovery, or valuation of property.

> For the purposes of this course you are going to keep it simple, unless your instructor tells you differently. Unless otherwise noted, references to the dissolution process will also mean legal separation and annulments.

Case Study

Your instructor will provide you with the name of the client who has retained your firm to be utilized through this course. You will also be provided with the name of the client's spouse, their children, the ages of their children and where they live and work. You will also need to know how long they have resided in the State of California and the county in which the dissolution will be filed. A sample *Client Information form* is provided as Appendix 2A. This form is not meant to be exclusive. It does, however, contain the minimum amount of information you will need from clients to process an *uncontested* dissolution. Each firm will have its own version of this intake information/questionnaire, and the form may request much more information than the basic one provided herein. It is highly suggested that the form be completed in its entirety as soon as the client has retained the firm. It is my experience that if the information is not provided initially, you will find yourself constantly having to find alternative ways to acquire this information.

Your instructor will review this form with you and will assist you in completing the information based on the "sample client" provided. Your instructor will also provide you with supplemental information as you progress through the dissolution process.

Oftentimes, you will need to assist the client in completing the information. Many clients are too overwhelmed and/or emotional at the time of the initial meeting to focus on what information they need to provide. Some clients will find the need for personal information invasive, but they need to understand that California requires that all assets and debts, community and separate, be disclosed. A paralegal with good interviewing skills, can glean much information just by talking with the person. You can ask simple questions. Familiarity with the format of the form is essential, as often the client will provide you with random information as it comes to mind and not in the order presented in the form. The client may also provide you with information that is not required on the form but may be relevant in the future. While it is still fresh in your mind, the information should be noted in a memorandum at the conclusion of your meeting. You may also need to provide the client with a list of additional information that the client will need to provide. Copies of earnings statements (for both parties, if available), tax returns, insurance policies, retirement and investment statements, deeds and vehicle registrations should be provided as soon as possible. If the client does not have this information available, as the paralegal, you will need to determine how to find that information. This process will be discussed later in Chapter Five, Disclosure and Discovery.

As a paralegal, this can be some of your most rewarding work—working with clients, assuring them and making them as comfortable as possible with the process. You are building confidence and trust between yourself, the firm and the client. The client should feel at the end of the interview that any information provided will be kept in strict confidence. The client should also have a better sense of what to expect from the firm throughout the dissolution process.

Litigation Process

What do you do now that you have the basic information?

All cases must have a legal document which is used to commence the action. In family law, that document is called the Petition. The Petition is similar to the Complaint which is filed in civil matters and which sets forth the allegation. Since California is a "no fault" state, it is not necessary to have allegations as to why the marriage should be terminated. You will simply indicate that there are irreconcilable differences, which have led to an *irremedial breakdown* of the marriage. If the action is based on incurable insanity or is a Petition for Annulment, then allegations must be included and subsequently proven.

Family law is a forms driven practice in California. As such, most of the pleadings that are prepared must be done on the Judicial Council forms. These forms are **mandatory**. It is always helpful to look at the bottom left corner of each Judicial Council form to see whether it says that it is approved, adopted or mandatory. If it is approved, that means that the court will allow you to use either the form or submit a written pleading. If the form says adopted or mandatory, then it means that you **must** use that form. There should also be a "rule" number on the bottom right corner of the form which indicates the rule number(s) and/or code section(s) which references the form and its use(s). There may be exceptions to these rules and if you have a question you should consult the California Rules of Court and your local county rules to determine whether there are any exceptions. You should also look at the date on the form (bottom left corner) to determine if it is the most current form. For instance, if you submit a Petition for Dissolution on a form dated 1/1/01, the court will most likely return the documents to you unfiled. The most recent, updated (as of the publication of this text) Petition should contain the date 1/1/2005, or a subsequent date. The court may also change judicial council forms mid-year. Therefore, some forms may contain a 7/1 revision date or some other alternative revision date.

In California, the person who initiates the action is called the Petitioner, or the person who would be the Plaintiff in civil matters. The Respondent is the Defendant and the person expected to answer the Petition with a Response. Once the person is the Petitioner, they will **always** be the Petitioner, even if later in the matter, or after the judgment is entered, the responding party, who is always known as the Respondent files for additional orders with the court. The party who files a Motion or a Request for Order with the court is the *moving party* and can be the Petitioner or the Respondent. In this respect family law is similar to civil actions, however, the terminology is just different. Once the initial documents are filed with the court and served, some of the processes and procedures are different from what takes place in the civil process. Those differences will be discussed as we progress through the dissolution process.

In order to commence a dissolution of marriage, legal separation or an annulment, the other document that **must** be filed with the Petition is the Summons. In addition, there may be other documents which can accompany the Summons and Petition upon the initial filing. However, those documents are based on other legal requirements and/or the needs of the client. For instance, the Declaration Under Uniform Child Custody Jurisdiction Act, **must** be filed whenever there are minor children. Additional forms and their functions will be discussed in future chapters as you explore their need and relevance with your instructor.

The "litigation process" of a dissolution has many similarities to a civil case; it also has several differences. As stated previously, the Petitioner (the person initiating the action) is the same as the Plaintiff. The Respondent (the person answering) is the same as the Defendant. You will note that when you begin looking at the Judicial Council forms that the captions contain these titles (in most cases) rather than Plaintiff and Defendant. You will also note that most of the forms already state that they are Superior Court cases.

The initial action must be commenced with a Summons and Petition. Those documents must be filed with the court. You should always provide the court with the original documents and at least two copies. The court will assign a case number, will keep the originals for its file, and will return the filed copies to your office. Local rules will also determine whether the court issues any other orders or documents relative to the case. For instance, if there are minor children and you have also submitted a Declaration Under Uniform Child Jurisdiction Act, then the court may issue orders with regard to mediation. You should become familiar with the local family law rules in the counties where your firm primarily practices. It is helpful if you can relay to the client what kinds of things or procedures the Court will require from them.

As an example: Placer County will issue an Order for Orientation/Mediation with the issuance of the Summons and the filing of the Petition. The Order will contain a date on which the parties need to appear at the Family Law Mediation office to discuss how divorce affects families and to determine if the parties agree to custody, parenting and visitation. If you don't prepare the client for receiving this document, they may call and tell you: "I don't need to go to this because my spouse and I have agreed to share custody and this is an uncontested divorce." While that may be true, the court requires that the parties attend at least the orientation. If, at the orientation, they sign an agreement resolving any custody, parenting and/or visitation issues, they are not referred to mediation. If this is an uncontested dissolution, that agreement, when provided to your office, becomes the foundation of the Judgment or any agreement that will be eventually executed by the parties. If the parties cannot reach an agreement, they will be required to attend mediation, which will be conducted by a person approved by the court and assigned to the case to meet with the parties and assist them in reaching an agreement. Oftentimes, this process keeps the parties from filing motions and having hearings. The issues of mediation and motions will be discussed in later chapters. However, you can see how Placer County's local rules may impact the process and why this information should be relayed to the client prior to the filing of any documents with the court.

As previously indicated, the Petitioners do not need to list any specific allegations in a Dissolution of Marriage. They just simply state they no longer want to be married and that there is no chance of reconciliation. Irreconcilable differences is simply cited as the reason.

Another difference in family law is that you are required to serve "reciprocal" documents. This means that when you serve the Respondent with the Summons and Petition, you must also provide the Respondent with a blank Response form. If a Declaration Under Uniform Child Custody Jurisdiction and Enforcement Act (UCCJEA) has been filed and is also served with the initial documents, you must also serve a "blank" UCCJEA form on the Respondent. With few exceptions, this rule exists throughout the family law process. You will note as you become familiar with the various family law forms that they provide instructions and/or indicate the procedures which must be followed, the reciprocal forms that must be served, and the time-lines required for service and filing. As a paralegal, you should pay close attention to these details, as the attorney may rely on you to be familiar with these procedures.

Additionally, the time-lines that are required in California civil cases are different in family law. Whereas the Summons and Complaint must be served within 60 days of filing in most California Superior Court cases, family law does not have the same requirement. With the exception of discovery deadlines (interrogatories, production of documents, depositions) and motions, the accelerated "trial" deadlines do not normally apply. The Family Code, the Civil Code of Procedure and local rules should be consulted to determine if there are any rules and statutes which require documents to be filed and served within specific time frames. You should also note that frequently the Judicial Council forms will contain the required time-lines and/or references to the code sections to which you will need to refer.

Preliminary Declaration of Disclosure

A clarification to the Family Code regarding the service of the Preliminary Declaration of Disclosure, should be noted as it now must be served either concurrently with the initial documents or within 60 days of filing them. This will also be an event that must be calendared if it will occur after the date of filing, which will also serve as a potential malpractice hazard. This subject will be discussed in more detail in subsequent chapters.

Additionally, there is now a specific form and procedure to request orders regarding non-compliance with disclosure requirements, which will be addressed in chapter five.

Less Litigious Ways to Resolve Dissolutions

Although this text will primarily discuss the dissolution process you should be aware that the cases do not have to be litigious. The parties may agree at the beginning of the process that they wish to avoid the adversarial battleground, anger, conflict and other emotions that can surface during the "conventional" dissolution process.

There are two methods of non-litigation for resolving marital issues: Mediation and Collaborative Practice.

Mediation

As the name infers, the parties may agree to hire an attorney to mediate any separation issues they are unable to resolve themselves. This type of mediation may include property, support, and custody. There is usually just one attorney, who will not represent either person, but will serve as an objective third party to help the parties reach an amicable resolution of the issues.

The parties usually execute some form of agreement, stating that they wish to mediate their dissolution and specifying the terms and conditions under which they will work with the mediator. In the event the parties are unable to reach an agreement, the parties will have to seek the services of their own individual counsel and proceed through the convention method of ending the marriage (litigation).

Court-ordered mediation is required under Family Code §§ 1850–1852 for all custody and visitation issues. This will be discussed further in Chapter Four.

Collaborative Negotiation or Practice

The Collaborative Practice is considered a "kinder, gentler approach" to the dissolution process. It begin in San Mateo and Santa Clara Counties in 1994. Minnesota is the first state to have initiated this process in family practice. Many California Counties now have their own Collaborative groups.

Effective January 1, 2007, the California Legislature enacted the Collaborative Family Law Act. (Family Code § 2013.) The Act authorizes parties to dissolution, legal separation, or nullity proceedings to utilize a collaborative law process by written agreement. The statute provides that, "if a written agreement is entered into by the parties, they may utilize a collaborative law process to resolve **any** matter governed by the Family Code over which the court is granted jurisdiction pursuant to Family Code § 2000. FC§ 2013 defines collaborative law process to mean: "the process in which the parties and any professionals engaged by the parties to assist them agree in writing to use their best efforts and to make a good faith attempt to resolve disputes related to family law matters as referenced in Family Code § 2013(a) on an agreed basis without resorting to adversary judicial intervention."

The benefits of resolving matters through collaboration are reduction in attorney fees and costs; less (if not entire avoidance of) emotional impact; constructive resolution to co-parenting issues; and the ultimate agreement will be tailored to the parties needs.

These goals are achieved through informal exchange of information and discussions between the parties and their attorneys. The process also enlists the assistance of a "divorce coach," financial consultants, as well as "child" specialists. Each "expert," along with the parties and their attorneys, become a team that is committed to helping the parties respect each other and ultimately to have more control over the dissolution process.

Procedurally, the parties will each chose an attorney from the list of Collaborative practitioners in their jurisdiction. Each party will sign an agreement with the attorney as to the guidelines that will govern the process. Part of the agreement will be a commitment to be honest, to cooperate, to compromise, and to act professionally in all aspects of the process in order to maximize the settlement options, minimize economic impact, as well as the emotional and social consequences of the parties and their children. Once the parties have met with their respective attorneys to identify the issues, a meeting will be scheduled between the parties and their attorneys to begin the negotiation process and to determine what additional "experts" will need to be involved.

Informal Discovery

The parties may agree individually, or through their attorneys to provide all documentation regarding their income, assets, debts and property in a more informal manner, rather than through Interrogatories, Depositions, Requests for Production, etc. The parties must comply with Disclosure as set forth in Family Code §§ 2100–2113. (These will be discussed further in Chapter Seven.)

This method allows the parties to reduce animosity, as well as attorney's fees, by not having to draft discovery documents, pay witness or subpoena fees for records and the like. It is certainly much easier and less time-consuming for the paralegal if both parties are willing to provide all of the documentation that relates to the individual party's property. It save the parties time and avoids animosity if they don't have to "pry" each bit of information out of their respective spouses.

Key Terms

- Jurisdiction
- Service of Process
- Minimum Contacts
- Family Code
- Irreconcilable Differences
- Irremedial Breakdown
- California Rules of Professional Conduct
- Conflict of Interest
- Domicile
- Residence
- Putative Spouse
- No Fault State
- Common Law Marriage
- Summary Dissolution
- Summons
- Petition
- Dissolution
- Legal Separation
- Annulment
- Uniform Child Custody Jurisdiction and Enforcement Act
- Collaborative Law Practice

Chapter Two

Commencing the Dissolution Process

Family law is a "forms driven practice." As such, a course utilizing this text will consist of reading assignments, lecture, and completion of the Judicial Council forms that are required to complete a dissolution of marriage in California.

Each chapter will contain "sample" forms based on the client matter or "case study" you will develop for this course. The instructor will review and discuss the Judicial Council forms and their purpose. The instructor will also provide you with information as to variations on these forms based on different types of matters, clients and scenarios that you might encounter in the typical family law firm. Some of these forms have multiple uses. For instance, the Petition (form) will be used whether the matter is for a dissolution, legal separation or an annulment. The student will learn which "boxes to check" for the appropriate matters and the issues to be resolved. The client information package should be completed and handy as you proceed with the preparation of these forms. The required forms are also included in each related chapter as you progress through the text.

Summons

In simple terms, the purpose of the Summons is to provide judicial notice to a party that there is a legal matter pending before the court. (*Code of Civil Procedures §§ 412.10–412.20*) Also, pursuant to the Due Process Clause of the Constitution of the United States, a person must be given notice of the action and an opportunity to be heard. The Summons must be properly served upon the litigant, who in family law is the Respondent. If there is improper service, any Judgment subsequent to that service may be set aside and considered void.

A family law Summons (form FL-110) must be used in *all* dissolutions, legal separations, or annulments. The family law Summons is also unique, in that it contains "Automatic Temporary Restraining Orders" on the reverse side of the Summons. These Orders initially became effective in 1991 and include all subsequent changes since that time.

The Automatic Temporary Restraining Orders ("ATROs") apply to the Petitioner upon the signing of the Petition, and to the Respondent, once he or she is served. The Orders contain language that requires each party to maintain the status quo of the marriage, until the court can make orders to the contrary or the parties have signed an agreement. **It is important to note that these restraining orders** *do not* **provide any protection with respect to domestic violence or other** *personal* **protections.** There is one exception however, and that is with respect to the custody of minor children. Family Code §§ 2040 and 3134.5 were amended effective 1/1/13. The court has the ability to freeze the assets and/or restrict the passport of a party who allegedly takes **unlawful** custody of a child. Otherwise, any orders with respect to protection from abuse or harassment must be addressed in a separate set of documents and under different rules and criteria (which will be discussed under Domestic Violence Protection Orders). Once the Petitioner signs the Petition, these Orders also apply to him or her. The Orders are self-explanatory. However, it is important that you know that the client has read and understands them. Oftentimes, it is best if the attorney or paralegal review them with the client. This will eliminate potential misunderstanding later in the proceedings as to what the person can or cannot do particularly with respect to the parties' children and property. It has also been my experience that some clients have difficulty reading due to poor eye sight, limited education, or stress. By going over the Orders with the client you will be assured that he/she has been made aware of the significance of the ATROs.

Petition

The Petition is the document which sets forth the potential issues that require resolution so that a dissolution of marriage, legal separation, or annulment can be achieved on behalf of the client. This document should contain as much information as is relative to the action. In most cases, the Petition does not need to contain specific dollar values and/or detailed descriptions of the party's various assets or debts. That information will be required later during the disclosure period. You will want to review the client information carefully to confirm that you have all the basic information required to complete the Petition. If you do not have the necessary information, you will need to contact the client and stress the importance of obtaining the information so that the initial pleading is complete and accurate. Should you submit any incomplete information to the court, the clerk is likely to return it to your office unfiled, which may delay the matter. In the event you provide inaccurate information, the Petition might have to be amended and then served again on the Respondent. This could delay the resolution of the matter and give the Respondent additional time to respond.

It is also important to gather as much information as possible from the client, even information about finances and property that the client does not think are relevant or the "business" of the other party, these is especially critical in light of the clarification and requirements of FC§ 2104 where service of the Preliminary Declarations of Disclosure must be served within 60 days of filing the Petition. For example, the client has received a lump sum settlement for a worker's compensation claim, but he/she doesn't want his/her spouse to know about it. The issue of whether this is separate or community property will be discussed later. While this information may not need to be included in the Petition, the attorney needs to know about it and its existence must be disclosed, although the attorney will need to prove, at a later time, whether the asset would be considered separate or community property and at what point any value will be disclosed.

Specifically, FC§ 2104 was amended to clarify the time frame for serving the Preliminary Declaration of Disclosure in dissolutions, legal separations, and annulments. The statute now requires that preliminary declarations of disclosure be served on the Respondent either concurrently with the Petition or within sixty (60) days of **filing** the Petition. The same is true for the Respondent and the filing of the Response. The disclosure must include all tax returns filed by the party within the past two (2) years. This change now requires the firm to step up the gathering of this information from the client as the rules are not as lax as in previous years. Note that the parties can agree or stipulate to another date, but this agreement must be in writing.

The parties to a marital action in California are required to disclose information regarding all of their assets and debts, whether community or separate. It will not help the client if the attorney is "blind-sided" by information as he or she is preparing for trial, if that information was not previously disclosed as required. It is difficult for the attorney to be an advocate for the client if he/she doesn't have **all** of the information, even information which may show the client in a negative light, such as a history of drug and alcohol abuse or a previously abusive relationship. An attorney is required to keep such information confidential, and the client needs to be aware of the attorney-client privilege and assured that the privilege will be maintained. Issues such as habitual drug or alcohol abuse and domestic violence may now impact orders relating to support and property so it is important that an attorney be aware of the need for advocacy and the protection of his/her client's rights in light of recent case law. For example, *In re Marriage of Freitas* (2012) CalApp Lexis 1039 (FC§ 4325) allows for the termination of temporary spousal support to a spouse convicted of domestic violence; and FC§ 3011 requires that the court take into account a parent's habitual or continual abuse of controlled substances and/or alcohol if the person is seeking custody of or visitation with a minor child. These situations will be discussed in greater detail within their respective topics later in the text.

Legal Separation

Does the client want a legal separation? Does the client understand that the marital status will **not** be terminated upon the entry of Judgment of a Legal Separation? If so, then you will prepare the Petition and check the appropriate boxes for a Legal Separation. The "grounds" are the same as for a Dissolution.

Does the client want a Dissolution but does not meet the residency requirements for the state and/or county? Please make sure that the residency requirements are met. If they are not and you have prepared a Petition for Dissolution, which has been filed and served, there is a risk of either having the Respondent file a Motion to Quash or a Motion to Change Venue (both of which will be discussed in detail in the next chapter). Either of these motions may affect the client's ability to proceed with the Dissolution matter in a timely fashion.

Last, the Respondent must agree to a Judgment for Legal Separation. If the Respondent does not agree and wishes to be divorced (provided the residency requirements are met) then he/she can file a Response requesting a Dissolution. The marriage will then be dissolved and the marital status terminated, regardless of the Petitioner's wishes. The attorney will need to advise the client that this is a possible implication prior to completing and signing the Petition.

Annulment

A Petition for Annulment is initiated by completing the form and checking the appropriate boxes. You will note that page two of the Petition requires that the box relative to a void or voidable marriage be checked as to the Family Code section that will be alleged for the annulment. As previously discussed, the boxes on the Petition give the applicable Family Code section. These references and allegations should be confirmed, as they will provide the requirements for the **proof** that the client will need to provide. These code sections will also cover any statutes of limitations that apply to the client's particular situation.

Family Code § 2211 provides the periods of limitations that are available to the petitioner. For example, if the client states they were underage at the time of the marriage, pursuant to FC§ 2210(a), the underage person has four (4) years from the time they turn eighteen (18) to bring the action. However, if a parent or guardian wishes to bring the action, it must be done **before** the underage married person becomes an adult (18). A petitioner requesting an annulment due to fraud, must bring the action within four (4) years of **discovering** the fraud.

Since there is no waiting period for an annulment, in most cases, the attorney is going to want to schedule a hearing for the client, so that the annulment can be obtained in the minimum amount of time. You will achieve this by filing a Request for Order, any applicable Judicial Council forms, along with declarations and applicable exhibits. Should the client be asking for support or attorney's fees relative to the annulment (Putative Spouse) you will also need to prepare the appropriate Income and Expense Declarations, as well as the Preliminary Declaration of Disclosure. Please refer to Chapter Four for more specific information on preparing and filing the documents, setting the hearing, and serving a Request for Order.

If the client wishes to have the marriage annulled based on fraud, you must first establish that he/she became aware of the fraud within the four year limit. Once the time frame is established and can be documented, you will then need to obtain a declaration from the client concerning the circumstances of the fraud, as well as, obtain any supporting documentation that will substantiate the claim. You may also need to obtain declarations from other persons or witnesses to the fraud, which will be included in the Request for Order and provided to the court.

Dissolution of Marriage — Completing the Forms

Let's get started! As you begin to use the Judicial Council forms, always look to see that you have the most current form. The "revised" date at the bottom left corner of the form will give you the last date of that form. You can also search the Judicial Council website for the form, as the most recent version of the form will be available there. Although there is usually a grace period (60 days) if you submit an outdated form, the court clerk will return all of the documents received after that date to you, unfiled. Many firms also subscribe to a "forms" service such as Legal Solutions, Martin Dean, HotDocs, or SmartLaser.

Summons

The significance of the document called the Summons (FL-110) has been previously discussed. Therefore, a specific Family Law Summons has been created and it is mandatory that this document is utilized when initiating a Dissolution, Legal Separation or Annulment.

First let's look at the form. The form indicates what kind of document it is and also gives you the Judicial Counsel form reference at both the top and the bottom of the form. The Summons is two pages, and as with most Judicial Council forms, it is meant to be printed two-sided, heel-to-toe. This means that when you have the form in the file folder and want to look at the back side, you will simply turn up the form from the bottom and the bottom of the back side should actually be the top. This is done so that you don't have to remove the page from the file or turn the folder around in order to read it. Some firms refer to this as "tumbling."

Second, this is a **NOTICE** to **Respondent** and you will need to insert the Respondent's name. The **Petitioner**'s name will be placed immediately after the space left open for his or her name.

You will see that there is a square on the upper right corner of the form, which says for court use only. This is where the court will endorse the document indicating it has been filed (or in some cases it is endorsed). There is then a space for the case number. The clerk will issue the case number when the initial documents are filed, so this space will also be left blank.

The next section contains instructions to the Respondent about filing the Response (also written in Spanish in the opposite box). You should read this section so that you know about the process and what is expected from the Respondent.

The following section, "**NOTICE**," spells out the Automatic Standard Restraining Orders (ATROs). As previously indicated, you should make sure that the client is familiar with this notice and the restraining orders on the back (page two) as they apply to both parties. The Orders on the back are self-explanatory; however, if you have any questions, please ask your instructor for further clarification. Also refer to FC§§ 2040 and 3134.5 with regard to updates, changes, and clarification in the court's ability to freeze assets in the event of illegal custody activity.

The bottom section will also need to be completed by you.

1. The name and address of the court is:

[Insert the name and address of the court as provided by your instructor.]

The example in the book contains the information for Sacramento County to use as a reference for how the text should appear.

2. The name, address and telephone number of petitioners' attorney, or petitioner without an attorney is:

[Insert the name, State Bar Number, address and telephone number of the attorney as provided by your instructor.]

Please note: The attorney's California State Bar Number must be included, or the clerk may return the documents unfiled.

The remainder of the form should be left blank. The clerk will stamp the date and his/her name where indicated on the form. The clerk will keep the original, which will contain a seal at the bottom left corner of the form. You should make at least three copies: the original for the court clerk (court's file); one copy to retain in your file; and two copies to submit to the court. Once you have filed copies back from the court, the unfiled "holding copy" can be removed from the file and shredded.

Petition

The first section of the form is the Caption. Please see the sample on the Petition provided herein, and using the information provided by your instructor as to the attorney, state bar number, firm, firm's address and telephone number, and the client's name, complete the caption.

The second section contains the court information. You will note that it states: **Superior Court of California, County of** *[blank—you will insert name of the county]*. As previously stated, this indicates that the Superior Court has subject matter jurisdiction. You will simply fill in the name of the county (venue) where the client will be filing the matter, based on their county of residence.

The third section indicates who the parties are in this matter. The Petitioner will be the client, and you will place his/her name after the colon. Do the same for the Respondent. Most courts prefer each person's **full** name. At the very minimum you should provide a first name, middle initial, and last name. The reason for this is that if you have two court files open with the name of "John Smith" as the Petitioner, it could be confusing. Although most court files are kept by case number, rather than name, the court is not infallible. Therefore, the more detailed and specific the information that you can provide the clerk, the easier it will be to avoid confusion.

The final section is where you will indicate what kind of matter this will be: Dissolution, Legal Separation, or Nullity. You will check the appropriate box. You will also note there is a place to check denoting an Amended Petition.

You may amend the Petition for a couple of reasons. One, which we have already discussed: is that the client did not meet the residency requirements but wanted to get the matter started, let's say for financial reasons. Financial reasons might include the need to establish child support or spousal support if the parties have not been living together for several months, or if it is necessary to establish a specific date when any property (assets and/or debts) acquired by a party would be considered their separate property. If you filed a Petition for Legal Separation and the client has now resided in California and/or the county for the requisite time, you can now amend for a dissolution.

Another reason that a Petition may have to be amended would be if the original Petition contained incorrect or incomplete information. Examples might be the date of birth of one of the children is incorrect, separate property was not listed which should have been, or asset and debt information was incomplete or inaccurate. As we previously discussed, getting **all** of the information from the client prior to completing these forms, having the client sign them, filing them with the court, and then serving them on the Respondent are **very** important.

Your firm does not want to be in the position of having to amend the Petition because it is not correct. Should the Petition have to be amended, re-filed with the court, and then re-served on the Respondent, the Respondent would then be allowed another thirty days from the date the amended Petition was served to respond.

Please follow the instructor's instructions as they apply to the client information you have obtained or been provided when completing items 1 through 9 on the Petition. You should also use the example provided in the text. Take special notice of item 10, which is a statement about the responsibility of each parent to the maintenance of support of the minor children. The support of the children is an issue that is *always* before the court. While the other portions of the Petition allow the Petitioner to state which issues are before the court and put the Respondent on notice as to the specific relief being sought, this statement automatically puts the Respondent on notice as long as there are minor children involved.

You should also carefully read each component of the form and ask your instructor to explain any of the items on the Petition that you don't understand. You will also note that in several instances you can attach other Judicial Council forms to the Petition. Most family law practitioners will want the paralegal to complete the form in its entirety. These additional form attachments have been created and are often utilized by *pro se* clients (those representing themselves). You are encouraged to review the numerous forms referenced on the Petition, as well as other forms as we progress through the course.

As you complete the property information, keep in mind that you may not have been provided with every item or detail concerning the party's separate and community property. Most firms will put general language in these sections which are "catch all" phrases for items that may not have been included. Your instructor will provide you with sample language to use in items 4 and 5. In general a phrase such as: "Any and all property, unknown to the Petitioner at this time, subject to proof," can be included. Keep in mind that if you do not list property and do not include such a phrase, should the Respondent default (not respond), the court can only issue orders for division of property that is based on the information on the Petition. If you do not provide the court with this information initially, it is possible that the court will reject the Default Judgment at a later date, because the court did not have sufficient evidence on which to base its decision. You should not rely on the preparation and service of the Preliminary Declaration of Disclosure as those documents are **not** filed with the court—they are served on the opposing party and not part of the court record at this point.

At the bottom of page two of the Petition is a **Notice**. This language is a reminder that certain rights may be affected by a dissolution or legal separation. Although the parties are restrained from altering or changing a spouse's rights to certain property (refer to the Restraining Orders on the Summons) it does notify them, that once the Judgment is entered, the parties will want to review these documents and change them accordingly.

Upon completion of the Summons and Petition (or any other documents that you have prepared), the attorney should review all the documents for accuracy. At that point the attorney will sign the Petition, and it is then ready for the client's signature.

Declaration Under Uniform Child Custody Jurisdiction and Enforcement Act

This specific form must be completed any time the parties have minor children *of this marriage*. Children from other relationships of either party, unless the child has been adopted by one of the parties, are not listed because those children are not subject to any orders made herein. If you check the box that says there are "no minor children" of this marriage listed on the Petition, the form is not necessary.

The Uniform Child Custody Jurisdiction and Enforcement Act provisions can be found at Family Code § 3400 et seq. The court requires that, in family law matters, the parties must establish who has jurisdiction over the minor child(ren). Specifically, the court needs to know if one or both of the parties have had care and control over the child(ren) for the past five years. Additionally, the court wants to know if the child(ren) have been subject to any other jurisdiction, which jurisdiction, the nature and status of the proceeding and if any other person, not a party to the current matter, has physical custody of the child(ren). The court also requires that it be notified should any of the information or circumstances of the custody change.

Family Code §§ 3400–3465 contain the Uniform Child Custody Jurisdiction and Enforcement Act (UCCJEA). In the case of *Brossoit v. Brossoit* (1995) 31 CA4th 361, the court held that: "Generally speaking, the UCCJEA … is designed to avoid competition between jurisdictions and conflicts between courts and different states in the resolution of child custody disputes. This is designed to keep the parties from bouncing their children all over the county or all over the state in an attempt to obtain a favorable ruling, and to promote cooperation between courts of the various states with the ultimate goal that the child custody decree be rendered in the state best equipped to deal with the particular case." This is often referred to as "forum shopping." The court further stated: "the UCCJEA is seen in the UCCJEA's intention to bring provisions more in line with the Federal Parental Kidnapping Prevention Act (FPKPA)…, and to clarify and strengthen the basic jurisdictional standards employed by the courts." The Federal Parental Kidnapping Prevention Act (FPKPA) is found at 28 U.S.C. § 1738A, et seq., and is similar in nature to the California UCCJEA laws. UCCJEA rules do not govern Native American children, who are, in most cases, subject to tribal law only.

Conversely, the UCCJEA statutes provide for resolution of the custodial jurisdiction over the children, including children who are not present in the state, as well as juvenile court and dependency issues. These laws have nothing to do with the personal jurisdiction over parents. All states, as well as the District of Columbia and the Virgin Islands, have adopted some form of the UCCJEA establishing "uniform" standards as the title infers. The concept behind the UCCJEA statutes was to determine the state where the child has the most significant **contacts**. The California court, when making determinations as to the jurisdiction over the children, will, however, consider itself as having control, regardless of another state's **implied** jurisdiction.

California passed the Indian Welfare Act in 2007, which became effective January 1, 2008. In the event any child subject to the proceeding is a Native American, this Act should be reviewed and the attorney will need to determine if the child(ren) is subject to any tribal laws or the Act. There are a specific set of forms that must be prepared and submitted, as set forth in the Act, in that event. These statutes are beyond the scope of this text and are only mentioned so that the paralegal is aware that the laws and forms created by the Act, which are found under a separate subsection within the Judicial Council forms, should be reviewed carefully.

Once the matter is filed, the court has jurisdiction to resolve any custody and visitation matters relative to the children of the marriage, and no other court will have jurisdiction over the minor children. This section and other related federal codes will be discussed further in Chapter Four.

The Judicial Council has created a informational form, FL-314-INFO called Child Custody Order Information. While this form is primarily created for pro se parties, it does contain information the client may find helpful regarding their rights to have the court hear the matter, enforcement, and mediation information. As of this writing the form is not required by those parties represented by counsel, but that is subject to change. Some Courts (counties) may, at some point, require that a client sign a declaration stating that he/she has read the form.

Other Applicable Initial Remedies

It is possible that the attorney will determine, after speaking with the client, that he or she needs to obtain immediate orders. Examples could be domestic violence issues, custody, visitation, child support, spousal support, the payment of community debts, (property) restraining orders, and orders removing a party from the property.

For example, at the initial meeting, the client provides the following information:

He has three minor children, ages: 5, 8 and 12. His wife is a native of Greenland and travels there frequently to visit her family. Since the parties separated, Wife has repeatedly told Husband that she intends to take the children "home" and that if she does, he will never see her or the children again. Additionally, she has told Husband that once she returns to Greenland, she will file for a divorce there and they have different laws. She has told him that he can expect to pay a lot more child support once the children are in Greenland because the laws there state that if he cheated on her, he will have to pay more. Husband does indicate that he had an affair prior to separation.

The attorney may decide to file immediately for restraining orders requesting that Wife be restrained from leaving the county or the country, even for a visit with her family, without written permission of Husband. Temporary child custody, visitation and support may need to be immediately established so that Wife cannot flee the country making it difficult for Husband to assert his legal rights to custody and visitation as a parent. Once custody, visitation and child support are established pursuant to the California guidelines, Greenland will not likely be able to assert jurisdiction over the children and this marriage.

The attorney has directed you to prepare a Request for Order to be filed at the same time as the Summons and Petition are filed so that "we will get Wife served right away."

This is just one example. There are thousands of such scenarios, which will impact other documents the attorney may ask you to prepare relative to the dissolution.

Another consideration may be that the Court determines that the child needs counsel appointed to speak on his or her behalf. In that event, the attorney who is appointed must complete and submit a Declaration of Counsel for a Child Regarding Qualifications (FL-322). The Court will also issue an Order Appointing Counsel for Child (FL-323). In the event the law firm may be appointed by the Court to act in such capacity, it may fall to the paralegal to prepare the form prior to or subsequent to the hearing at which the appointment is made.

Application for Waiver of Court Fees and Costs; Order

In the event that your office is representing an indigent client or has taken a pro bono case, the court allows a waiver of the filing fees. See Government Code § 68511.3 and the local rules regarding an application and an order for waiver of court fees and costs. The forms you will be primarily using for this process are: Application for Waiver of Court Fees & Costs, (form 982(a)(17)) and Order on Application for Waiver of Court Fees & Costs (form 982(a)(18)). Read the instructions carefully.

Filing the Documents

Now that you have completed the Summons, Petition, and UCCJEA, if applicable (which it is in our case), and any other documents, the attorney will need to review them for accuracy. Do not be discouraged by your first attempt at completing all of these documents. You will become more proficient as you gain experience working with the attorney on different cases and documents.

Once the documents have been reviewed and approved by the attorney, the client will need to review and sign them. The attorney will decide if he or she will meet with the client to accomplish this, or if you will be the one to meet with the client. Once you become more experienced, the attorney will likely have you regularly meet with clients at this step.

After the client has signed the documents, make copies for the client to take home with him or her. Remind the client about the Restraining Orders (ATROs) on the Summons. In my experience, unless the local court rules indicate otherwise, you should have the client sign in blue ink. This will make it easier for you, anyone in your office, and the court clerk to differentiate between the original and copies of any pleadings.

The original and (at least) two copies should be sent to the court, along with the filing fee. The court clerk will assign a case number to the file, will stamp that number on all documents received. The clerk will keep the original of each document and will return the copies to your office. If you have requested a hearing date for a matter, that date will also be given and the matter will be assigned to a judge. Your firm will determine if documents are going to be filed by mail, a courier service or if someone in your office has responsibility for filing documents. In the event you file documents by mail, **always**, enclose a self-addressed, stamped envelope so that the documents will be returned to you.

Now that the documents have been filed what do you do?

As soon as you have received them, you should send a copy to the client and advise the client of anything further that is needed. For instance:

- Is an orientation required when there are minor children? If so, please advise as to when or where the orientation will take place, or who must be called to schedule such an appointment. Also remind the client to fill out any paperwork they receive from the mediator prior to the appointment or to call the office if there are questions about completing the paperwork.

- Must the client attend mediation to attempt to resolve custody and visitation issues?

- Has a hearing date been set? If so, advise the client of the date, time, location, and whether the attorney needs to see the client prior to the hearing or if the attorney will meet them [give the client a time frame, i.e., 30 minutes] prior to the hearing. Make sure the client knows where the courthouse is located and to allow for unexpected things like construction or rush hour traffic. Clients are very nervous about these types of matters, and they might not think about having to allow extra time for traffic if they never "go that direction" early in the morning. In some cases, you may want to suggest that they make a trial run so they know how to get to the courthouse.

Now you are ready to serve the documents on the Respondent. The documents that *require service* are: the Summons, the Petition and a blank Response. In cases where there are minor children, completed (and filed) and blank UCCJEA forms must be served also. Don't forget to consult your local rules to determine if any other documents are required, such as mediation provider information/notices or notices regarding attendance at mediation when there are minor children. Some documents, per local rule, must be **personally** served.

Remember also, if you haven't served the Preliminary Declaration of Disclosure with the initial documents, they must be prepared, reviewed, signed and served as soon as possible, but no later than 60 days from the date filed.

Service of Process

The methods of service can be found in the Code of Civil Procedure at sections §§ 415.10 et seq. It is recommended that students or paralegals, who are working in a law firm setting where they will be involved in serving documents, review and be familiar with this portion of the Code of Civil Procedure.

Unlike civil cases (particularly those governed by the Trial Delay Act), the court does not require that the Summons and Petition (Complaint) be served on the Respondent within a particular time frame. Note that while there is no requirement, the changes to FC§ 2104, which now require service of the Preliminary Declaration of Disclosure within 60 days of filing, may muddy the waters as to which statute will take priority. Historically, the legislature and courts have been hesitant to force service upon a Respondent as it might appear that the legislature was encouraging dissolutions and legal separations. It was felt that if there was any possibility of reconciliation, the legislature would seem to be advocating to the contrary by pushing a party to move the matter along.

In most cases, a court will not contact a Petitioner for a minimum of three years (and sometimes longer) if a Proof of Service has not been filed, verifying that the Respondent was served. The court may contact the Petitioner and request confirmation that they wish the case to remain open. If the Petitioner responds affirmatively, the case will remain open. If the Petitioner does not respond the court may dismiss the matter on their own motion. The Petitioner may also file a Request for Dismissal with the court asking that the matter be closed.

Personal Service

Code of Civil Procedure § 415.10. A summons may be served by personal delivery of a copy of the summons and of the complaint [Petition in family law] to the person to be served. Service of a summons in this manner is deemed complete at the time of such delivery.

Personal service is always the **preferred** method of service, especially with regard to the initial family law documents or the Summons and Petition in this matter. The attorney will not want to run the risk of having service questioned if the Respondent is not personally served with the documents.

The documents may be personally served by any person who is over the age of eighteen (18). The attorney may choose to have a process server deliver the documents to the Respondent. Alternatively, the client may want to have a friend or family member deliver the documents to the Respondent. Your office should work with the client to determine which is the best and most expedient method of serving the documents. Personal service is effectuated by the person serving the documents personally handing the documents to the Respondent.

In the event that the person is not reasonably available to be personally handed the documents, the documents may be served by substitute service, as follows:

Code of Civil Procedure § 415.20.

(a) In lieu of personal delivery of a copy of the summons and complaint to the person to be served as specified in Section 416.10, 416.20, 416.30, 416.40, or 416.50, a summons may be served by leaving a copy of the summons and complaint during usual office hours in his or her office or, if no physical address is known, at his or her usual mailing address, other than a United States Postal Service post office box, with the person who is apparently in charge thereof, and by thereafter mailing a copy of the summons and complaint by first-class mail, postage prepaid to the person to be served at the place where a copy of the summons and complaint were left. When service is effected by leaving a copy of the summons and complaint at a mailing address, it shall be left with a person at least 18 years of age, who shall be informed of the contents thereof. Service of a summons in this manner is deemed complete on the 10th day after the mailing.

(b) If a copy of the summons and complaint cannot with reasonable diligence be personally delivered to the person to be served, as specified in Section 416.60, 416.70, 416.80, or 416.90, a summons may be served by leaving a copy of the summons and complaint at the person's dwelling house, usual place of abode, usual place of business, or usual mailing address other than a United States Postal Service post office box, in the presence of a competent member of the household or a person apparently in charge of his or her office, place of business, or usual mailing address other than a

United States Postal Service post office box, at least 18 years of age, who shall be informed of the contents thereof, and by thereafter mailing a copy of the summons and of the complaint by first-class mail, postage prepaid to the person to be served at the place where a copy of the summons and complaint were left. Service of a summons in this manner is deemed complete on the 10th day after the mailing.

If it appears that the Respondent is going to be difficult to serve, it is best to leave this process to a Process Server who is registered with the State of California. This person or company, will be familiar with the rules governing the service of the documents.

Service by Mail

It is also possible to serve the Respondent by mail. There are specific guidelines for serving individuals if they reside in California, as well as if they reside in another state.

If the Respondent resides in California, pursuant to Code of Civil Procedure § 415.30, the documents must be served by Notice and Acknowledgment of Receipt [form FL-117].

This code section states in part:

(a) A summons may be served by mail as provided in this section. A copy of the summons and of the complaint shall be mailed (by first-class mail or airmail, postage prepaid) to the person to be served, together with two copies of the notice and acknowledgment provided for in subdivision

(b) and a return envelope, postage prepaid, addressed to the sender. The documents **cannot** be served by certified mail if mailed to an address within California.

This section (and the form) state that "Failure to complete this form and return it to the sender within 20 days may subject you (or the party on whose behalf you are being served) to liability for the payment of any expenses incurred in serving a summons upon you in any other manner permitted by law."

CCP § 415.30 provides that the summons is deemed served on the date of execution of an acknowledgment of receipt of summons.

If the client and the attorney agree that service by mail is the best method for serving the Respondent, in most cases, the paralegal will be mailing these documents to the Respondent. You will need to complete form FL-117—"Notice And Acknowledgment of Receipt," making two originals, both of which you will sign. (The form is included in the text and your instructor will determine if you will utilize this form.) This form has several boxes for you to check which indicate what documents were enclosed/served on the Respondent. As stated in CCP§ 415.30, you will also need to provide the Respondent with a self-addressed, stamped, return envelope so that he or she may sign the form and return it to your office.

Service outside of California may be accomplished by Certified Mail. The Receipt that is signed by the recipient serves as the acknowledgment of the date of service. When serving the Respondent by mail, the paralegal will also then complete the Proof of Service of Summons, as instructed below.

Some offices will also want you to prepare a cover letter to the Respondent which contains the instructions on completing the Notice and Acknowledgment of Receipt. This letter serves to identify the law firm as representing the Petitioner; remind the Respondent that they must sign and return the form within 20 days; and indicates that a return envelope has been provided. Your firm should have a standard (form) letter or template for you to use in this situation.

There is a down-side to serving the documents by mail, and that is causing delay of service, which may be important to the client. If the Respondent does not sign the form, and after the 20-day period has run, you will then have to arrange for the documents to be personally served, which may cause delay. If you have set the matter for hearing, you may need to re-set the hearing date to allow for time for service of the documents.

Once the form has been signed and returned to the office, it will be submitted to the court, with the Proof of Service of Summons that has been executed by the paralegal (or person mailing the Notice & Acknowledgment of Receipt), for filing. As always, you will want to submit the originals and two copies to be returned for your file.

Service by Publication

Service by Publication is the **least** preferred method of service for these documents. The law firm will have to make a special request of the court to be allowed to publish the Summons. This can only happen after every other means of locating and delivering the documents to the Respondent have been exhausted. See CCP§ 415.50 below for the specific instructions on service by publication.

The rules governing service by publication can be found at *Code of Civil Procedure § 415.50.*

(a) A summons may be served by publication if upon affidavit it appears to the satisfaction of the court in which the action is pending that the party to be served cannot with reasonable diligence be served in another manner specified in this article and that either: (1) A cause of action exists against the party upon whom service is to be made or he or she is a necessary or proper party to the action. (2) The party to be served has or claims an interest in real or personal property in this state that is subject to the jurisdiction of the court or the relief demanded in the action consists wholly or in part in excluding the party from any interest in the property.

(b) The court shall order the summons to be published in a named newspaper, published in this state, that is most likely to give actual notice to the party to be served. If the party to be served resides or is located out of this state, the court may also order the summons to be published in a named newspaper outside this state that is most likely to give actual notice to that party. The order shall direct that a copy of the summons, the complaint, and the order for publication be forthwith mailed to the party if his or her address is ascertained before expiration of the time prescribed for publication of the summons ... (e) As a condition of establishing that the party to be served cannot with reasonable diligence be served in another manner specified in this article, the court may not require that a search be conducted of public databases where access by a registered process server to residential addresses is prohibited by law or by published policy of the agency providing the database, including, but not limited to, voter registration rolls and records of the Department of Motor Vehicles.

(Note: it has become extremely difficult to obtain certain types of personal information because of privacy laws. Your firm may need to hire the services of a company that is permitted to obtain this type of information.)

Proof of Service

This is a very important document, and it should never leave the client's file until it is to be filed with the court. Once the Proof of Service (and the Notice and Acknowledgment of Receipt, if the Respondent has been served by mail) have been filed with the court, the filed copies should be retained in the file. It has been my experience that these documents, if misplaced by the clerk, will be essential in proving that the Respondent was properly served and that the Respondent's Default may be taken if a Response was not timely filed. The date of service will be needed as you prepare additional pleadings, so you will want to make sure the information is easily accessible.

In the event that the Respondent is served and retains counsel, the attorney may receive a letter or telephone call requesting an extension in which to file and serve the Response. If the attorney agrees to the extension, a confirming letter should be prepared either by your office, or by Respondent's attorney which states the date the Response will be received. This date should be calendared.

Overviews of Domestic Violence Issues

Domestic Violence Prevention Act (DVPA) can be found at Family Code §§ 6200 et seq. These codes provide the framework and definitions for domestic violence. The California Penal Code also contains related statutes because Domestic Violence is criminal in nature.

A Protective Order can be obtained either as part of the dissolution process, prior to, or after the dissolution is final. The DVPA is different than standard restraining orders. There are different standards for the DVPA and a different set of forms. The differences between Standard Restraining Orders (ATROs) found on the Summons and DVPA Orders will be discussed in greater detail in Chapter Four, under Request for Order.

At this point you are given an overview of custody, visitation and property definitions so that you will understand the differences as they relate to completing the Petition for Dissolution. These topics will be discussed in more detail in Chapters Four and Seven, respectively.

Child Custody and Visitation

It is appropriate at this time to take a preliminary look at child custody and visitation. These topics will be discussed in greater detail in Chapter Four. However, it will be necessary for the attorney and client to determine the type of custody and/or visitation the client will be requesting on the Petition. Child Custody and Visitation terms are defined as follows:

Legal Custody—The rights and responsibility for the health, education and welfare of the minor child(ren) of the parties. The parties may have joint legal custody for which they will be equally responsible for all decisions, rights and responsibility for the health, education and welfare of the child(ren).

Physical Custody—Usually determined by the parent with whom the child(ren) reside and/or spend significant periods of time. The parties can share physical custody so that each parent spends significant periods of time with the minor child(ren). Or one party may request and be awarded primary physical custody. This means that the custodial parent will be responsible for the daily activities of the child(ren), such as getting them to school and extra curricular activities, bathing, homework, and providing food, clothing and shelter. If one party has primary physical custody, they are referred to as the "**custodial**" parent.

Visitation—A parent who does not equally share physical custody with the other parent, will have visitation with the minor(s). This person is defined as the "**non-custodial**" parent. There is nothing in the Family Code which specifies a visitation plan as to the non-custodial parent. Family Code § 3020 states that there must be "**frequent and continuing contact**" with both parents.

The Family Code and subsequent case law establish that the needs and the best interests of the child(ren) be met. Thus, the possibilities are endless. Chapter Four will also discuss new statutes that restrict custody and visitation for those with a history of abuse or who have been convicted as a sexual predator. The laws have also changed with respect to incorporating permanent restraining orders in a settlement agreement.

Community, Quasi-Community and Separate Property Definitions (An Overview)

Community Property

Community property is defined as: All property, real or personal, wherever situated, acquired by a person during marriage while domiciled in California.

Quasi-Community Property

Quasi-Community property is property that would have been community property had it been acquired by the parties while they were married and domiciled in California.

Separate Property

Separate property is owned by one of the parties prior to marriage, property acquired by a married person by gift, bequest, or inheritance, or property acquired after the date of separation.

Chapter Seven will discuss in greater detail the definitions of types of property and how property is divided. For the purposes of completing the Petition, the client will need to inform you of any separate property assertions. Also keep in mind that property, such as a condo in Kauai, is also subject to California community property laws. In Chapter 7, you will also read about the various case law and statutes which govern the division of all types of marital property, which, as previously indicated, is the largest and most complex area of the Family Code.

Maintenance of Status Quo of Property

At this point, the attorney will need to determine, based on the way title is held to marital property, whether the client's interests in any of the property needs to be established and/or protected.

> For instance, how is title held on the family home? Is it held in only one party's name, is it in joint tenancy or some other form of ownership? Is there a possibility that the client's spouse could cash in the couple's retirement, insurance or some other form of investments?

In these instances, it may be necessary to bring that property as a third party to the action. In the case of real property, the attorney may file a **Lis Pendens** with the county recorder. This document, which can only be removed by the person recording it, clouds the title to the property. Should the person whose name is listed as the owner try to sell the property, the attorney will be notified of any such action. Lis Pendens is Latin for pending litigation. This action protects the client if he or she is the person whose name is not on the title, but who has an interest in the property.

A **Joinder** can be filed by an attorney on a pension plan or other marital asset. The Joinder essentially puts a hold on the distribution of the property and notifies the "holder" of the asset that this property is pending litigation. Chapter Seven will discuss this issue in greater detail.

Additionally, a grandparent can request a Joinder with respect to the minor child(ren). This will be discussed in greater detail in Chapter Four.

The Joinder allows a "third party" to assert their rights as an "interested party" in the matter. In the event these assertions need to be made to protect marital property, it is relevant at this point.

In subsequent chapters we will progress through the Dissolution process and the various forms and documents you will need to prepare. The format will be such that the general discussion about the various areas of law as they relate to family law in general, the Dissolution issues and the documents will be discussed first. At the end of each informational section, you will be provided with instruction and information (and as supplemented by your instructor as needed) to complete the forms applicable to that chapter. It will be necessary for you to read the entire chapter before you begin to fill out the documents, as there will be information presented that will be necessary for you to complete the assignments.

Forms Associated with Topic

Summons (FL-110)

Petition (FL-100)

Declaration Under Uniform Child Custody Jurisdiction and Enforcement Act (FL-105)

(See examples of some forms on the following pages)

Key Terms

- Summons
- Petition
- Uniform Child Custody Jurisdiction and Enforcement Act
- Application and Order for Waiver of Court Fees & Costs
- Automatic Temporary Restraining Orders
- Preliminary Declaration of Disclosure
- Dissolution
- Legal Separation
- Nullity (Annulment)
- Void Marriage
- Voidable Marriage
- Community Property
- Quasi-Community Property
- Separate Property
- Service of Process
- Notice & Acknowledgment of Receipt
- Domestic Violence
- Non-Custodial Parent
- Custodial Parent
- Joinder
- Lis Pendens

Summons (Family Law) FL-110

FL-110

SUMMONS (Family Law)	CITACIÓN (Derecho familiar)

NOTICE TO RESPONDENT *(Name):* ROCKY SHORES
AVISO AL DEMANDADO (Nombre):

> **You are being sued.** *Lo están demandando.*

Petitioner's name is: SANDIE SHORES
Nombre del demandante:

> To keep other people from seeing what you entered on your form, please press the Clear This Form button at the end of the form when finished.

CASE NUMBER *(NÚMERO DE CASO):*

You have **30 calendar days** after this *Summons* and *Petition* are served on you to file a *Response* (form FL-120 or FL-123) at the court and have a copy served on the petitioner. A letter or phone call will not protect you.

If you do not file your *Response* on time, the court may make orders affecting your marriage or domestic partnership, your property, and custody of your children. You may be ordered to pay support and attorney fees and costs. If you cannot pay the filing fee, ask the clerk for a fee waiver form.

If you want legal advice, contact a lawyer immediately. You can get information about finding lawyers at the California Courts Online Self-Help Center *(www.courtinfo.ca.gov/selfhelp)*, at the California Legal Services Web site *(www.lawhelpcalifornia.org)*, or by contacting your local county bar association.

Tiene **30 días corridos** después de haber recibido la entrega legal de esta Citación y Petición para presentar una Respuesta *(formulario FL-120 ó FL-123)* ante la corte y efectuar la entrega legal de una copia al demandante. Una carta o llamada telefónica no basta para protegerlo.

Si no presenta su Respuesta a tiempo, la corte puede dar órdenes que afecten su matrimonio o pareja de hecho, sus bienes y la custodia de sus hijos. La corte también le puede ordenar que pague manutención, y honorarios y costos legales. Si no puede pagar la cuota de presentación, pida al secretario un formulario de exención de cuotas.

Si desea obtener asesoramiento legal, póngase en contacto de inmediato con un abogado. Puede obtener información para encontrar a un abogado en el Centro de Ayuda de las Cortes de California (www.sucorte.ca.gov), en el sitio Web de los Servicios Legales de California (www.lawhelpcalifornia.org) o poniéndose en contacto con el colegio de abogados de su condado.

NOTICE: The restraining orders on page 2 are effective against both spouses or domestic partners until the petition is dismissed, a judgment is entered, or the court makes further orders. These orders are enforceable anywhere in California by any law enforcement officer who has received or seen a copy of them.

AVISO: Las órdenes de restricción que figuran en la página 2 valen para ambos cónyuges o pareja de hecho hasta que se despida la petición, se emita un fallo o la corte dé otras órdenes. Cualquier autoridad de la ley que haya recibido o visto una copia de estas órdenes puede hacerlas acatar en cualquier lugar de California.

NOTE: If a judgment or support order is entered, the court may order you to pay all or part of the fees and costs that the court waived for yourself or for the other party. If this happens, the party ordered to pay fees shall be given notice and an opportunity to request a hearing to set aside the order to pay waived court fees.

AVISO: Si se emite un fallo u orden de manutención, la corte puede ordenar que usted pague parte de, o todas las cuotas y costos de la corte previamente exentas a petición de usted o de la otra parte. Si esto ocurre, la parte ordenada a pagar estas cuotas debe recibir aviso y la oportunidad de solicitar una audiencia para anular la orden de pagar las cuotas exentas.

1. The name and address of the court are *(El nombre y dirección de la corte son):*
   SACRAMENTO SUPERIOR COURT, 3341 POWER INN ROAD, SACRAMENTO, CA 95826

2. The name, address, and telephone number of the petitioner's attorney, or the petitioner without an attorney, are:
   (El nombre, dirección y número de teléfono del abogado del demandante, o del demandante si no tiene abogado, son):
   JOAN CARE-ACTOR, 75000 WHY ME LANE, SACRAMENTO, CA 95826; 916-555-1234

Date *(Fecha):* _____ Clerk, by *(Secretario, por)* _____, Deputy *(Asistente)*

[SEAL]

NOTICE TO THE PERSON SERVED: You are served
AVISO A LA PERSONA QUE RECIBIÓ LA ENTREGA: Esta entrega se realiza

a. ☐ as an individual. *(a usted como individuo.)*
b. ☐ on behalf of respondent who is a *(en nombre de un demandado que es):*
   (1) ☐ minor *(menor de edad)*
   (2) ☐ ward or conservatee *(dependiente de la corte o pupilo)*
   (3) ☐ other *(specify) (otro – especifique):*
   (Read the reverse for important information.) *(Lea importante información al dorso.)*

Page 1 of 2

Form Adopted for Mandatory Use
Judicial Council of California
FL-110 [Rev. July 1, 2009]

SUMMONS
(Family Law)

Family Code §§ 232, 233, 2040,7700;
Code of Civil Procedure, §§ 412.20, 416.60–416.90
Government Code, § 68637
www.courtinfo.ca.gov

Summons (Family Law) FL-110

WARNING—IMPORTANT INFORMATION

WARNING: California law provides that, for purposes of division of property upon dissolution of a marriage or domestic partnership or upon legal separation, property acquired by the parties during marriage or domestic partnership in joint form is presumed to be community property. If either party to this action should die before the jointly held community property is divided, the language in the deed that characterizes how title is held (i.e., joint tenancy, tenants in common, or community property) will be controlling, and not the community property presumption. You should consult your attorney if you want the community property presumption to be written into the recorded title to the property.

STANDARD FAMILY LAW RESTRAINING ORDERS

Starting immediately, you and your spouse or domestic partner are restrained from

1. Removing the minor child or children of the parties, if any, from the state without the prior written consent of the other party or an order of the court;

2. Cashing, borrowing against, canceling, transferring, disposing of, or changing the beneficiaries of any insurance or other coverage, including life, health, automobile, and disability, held for the benefit of the parties and their minor child or children;

3. Transferring, encumbering, hypothecating, concealing, or in any way disposing of any property, real or personal, whether community, quasi-community, or separate, without the written consent of the other party or an order of the court, except in the usual course of business or for the necessities of life; and

4. Creating a nonprobate transfer or modifying a nonprobate transfer in a manner that affects the disposition of property subject to the transfer, without the written consent of the other party or an order of the court. Before revocation of a nonprobate transfer can take effect or a right of survivorship to property can be eliminated, notice of the change must be filed and served on the other party.

You must notify each other of any proposed extraordinary expenditures at least five business days prior to incurring these extraordinary expenditures and account to the court for all extraordinary expenditures made after these restraining orders are effective. However, you may use community property, quasi-community property, or your own separate property to pay an attorney to help you or to pay court costs.

ADVERTENCIA – INFORMACIÓN IMPORTANTE

ADVERTENCIA: De acuerdo a la ley de California, las propiedades adquiridas por las partes durante su matrimonio o pareja de hecho en forma conjunta se consideran propiedad comunitaria para los fines de la división de bienes que ocurre cuando se produce una disolución o separación legal del matrimonio o pareja de hecho. Si cualquiera de las partes de este caso llega a fallecer antes de que se divida la propiedad comunitaria de tenencia conjunta, el destino de la misma quedará determinado por las cláusulas de la escritura correspondiente que describen su tenencia (por ej., tenencia conjunta, tenencia en común o propiedad comunitaria) y no por la presunción de propiedad comunitaria. Si quiere que la presunción comunitaria quede registrada en la escritura de la propiedad, debería consultar con un abogado.

ÓRDENES DE RESTRICCIÓN NORMALES DE DERECHO FAMILIAR

En forma inmediata, usted y su cónyuge o pareja de hecho tienen prohibido:

1. *Llevarse del estado de California a los hijos menores de las partes, si los hubiera, sin el consentimiento previo por escrito de la otra parte o una orden de la corte;*

2. *Cobrar, pedir prestado, cancelar, transferir, deshacerse o cambiar el nombre de los beneficiarios de cualquier seguro u otro tipo de cobertura, tal como de vida, salud, vehículo y discapacidad, que tenga como beneficiario(s) a las partes y su(s) hijo(s) menor(es);*

3. *Transferir, gravar, hipotecar, ocultar o deshacerse de cualquier manera de cualquier propiedad, inmueble o personal, ya sea comunitaria, cuasicomunitaria o separada, sin el consentimiento escrito de la otra parte o una orden de la corte, con excepción las operaciones realizadas en el curso normal de actividades o para satisfacer las necesidades de la vida; y*

4. *Crear o modificar una transferencia no testamentaria de manera que afecte al destino de una propiedad sujeta a transferencia, sin el consentimiento por escrito de la otra parte o una orden de la corte. Antes de que se pueda eliminar la revocación de una transferencia no testamentaria, se debe presentar ante la corte un aviso del cambio y hacer una entrega legal de dicho aviso a la otra parte.*

Cada parte tiene que notificar a la otra sobre cualquier gasto extraordinario propuesto, por lo menos cinco días laborales antes de realizarlo, y rendir cuenta a la corte de todos los gastos extraordinarios realizados después de que estas órdenes de restricción hayan entrado en vigencia. No obstante, puede usar propiedad comunitaria, cuasicomunitaria o suya separada para pagar a un abogado o para ayudarle a pagar los costos de la corte.

For your protection and privacy, please press the Clear This Form button after you have printed the form.

Save This Form   **Print This Form**   **Clear This Form**

Petition—Marriage (Family Law) FL-100

FL-100

ATTORNEY OR PARTY WITHOUT ATTORNEY (Name, State Bar number, and address):	
JOAN CARE-ACTOR, SBN ******* LAW OFFICES OF JOAN CARE-ACTOR 75000 WHY ME LANE SACRAMENTO, CA 95826 TELEPHONE NO.: 916-555-1234 FAX NO. (Optional): 916-555-1233 E-MAIL ADDRESS (Optional): joan@care-actorlaw.com ATTORNEY FOR (Name): SANDIE SHORES, Petitioner	To keep other people from seeing what you entered on your form, please press the Clear This Form button at the end of the form when finished.

SUPERIOR COURT OF CALIFORNIA, COUNTY OF SACRAMENTO
STREET ADDRESS: 3341 Power Inn Road
MAILING ADDRESS: 3341 Power Inn Road
CITY AND ZIP CODE: Sacramento, CA 95826
BRANCH NAME: Family Law

MARRIAGE OF
PETITIONER: SANDIE SHORES

RESPONDENT: ROCKY SHORES

PETITION FOR	CASE NUMBER:
☑ **Dissolution of Marriage** ☐ **Legal Separation** ☐ **Nullity of Marriage** ☐ **AMENDED**	

1. RESIDENCE (Dissolution only) ☑ Petitioner ☐ Respondent has been a resident of this state for at least six months and of this county for at least three months immediately preceding the filing of this *Petition for Dissolution of Marriage.*

2. STATISTICAL FACTS
   a. Date of marriage: June 20, 2003
   b. Date of separation: August 30, 2014
   c. Time from date of marriage to date of separation (specify):
      Years: 11   Months: 2

3. DECLARATION REGARDING MINOR CHILDREN (include children of this relationship born prior to or during the marriage or adopted during the marriage):
   a. ☐ There are no minor children.
   b. ☑ The minor children are:

Child's name	Birthdate	Age	Sex
EDDY WADE SHORES	5/1/05	9	MALE
SHELLY PEBBLES SHORES	10/15/09	4	FEMALE

   ☐ Continued on Attachment 3b.
   c. If there are minor children of the Petitioner and Respondent, a completed *Declaration Under Uniform Child Custody Jurisdiction and Enforcement Act (UCCJEA)* (form FL-105) must be attached.
   d. ☐ A completed voluntary declaration of paternity regarding minor children born to the Petitioner and Respondent prior to the marriage is attached.

4. SEPARATE PROPERTY
   Petitioner requests that the assets and debts listed ☐ in *Property Declaration* (form FL-160) ☐ in Attachment 4
   ☑ below be confirmed as separate property.

Item	Confirm to
Garnet necklace and earrings	Petitioner
2001 Honda motorcyle	Respondent
All property acquired prior to marriage, during marriage by gift bequest, inheritance, or after the date of separation	Respective Party

NOTICE: You may redact (black out) social security numbers from any written material filed with the court in this case other than a form used to collect child or spousal support.

Page 1 of 2

Petition—Marriage (Family Law) FL-100

MARRIAGE OF (last name, first name of parties): SHORES, SANDIE & ROCKY	CASE NUMBER:

5. DECLARATION REGARDING COMMUNITY AND QUASI-COMMUNITY ASSETS AND DEBTS AS CURRENTLY KNOWN
    a. ☐ There are no such assets or debts subject to disposition by the court in this proceeding.
    b. ☑ All such assets and debts are listed ☐ in *Property Declaration* (form FL-160) ☐ in Attachment 5b.
          ☑ below *(specify):*
             Home located at 11155 Turtle Dove Ct. Folsom, CA w/debt; property located on Wilderness
             Rd, Mokuleme Hill, CA; 2005 Dodge Caravan, 2010 Dodge P-U w/debt; Retirement, Banks

6. **Petitioner requests**
    a. ☑ dissolution of the marriage based on   d. ☐ nullity of voidable marriage based on
        (1) ☑ irreconcilable differences. (Fam. Code, § 2310(a).)   (1) ☐ petitioner's age at time of marriage.
        (2) ☐ incurable insanity. (Fam. Code, § 2310(b).)   (Fam. Code, § 2210(a).)
    b. ☐ legal separation of the parties based on   (2) ☐ prior existing marriage.
        (1) ☐ irreconcilable differences. (Fam. Code, § 2310(a).)   (Fam. Code, § 2210(b).)
        (2) ☐ incurable insanity. (Fam. Code, § 2310(b).)   (3) ☐ unsound mind. (Fam. Code, § 2210(c).)
    c. ☐ nullity of void marriage based on   (4) ☐ fraud. (Fam. Code, § 2210(d).)
        (1) ☐ incestuous marriage. (Fam. Code, § 2200.)   (5) ☐ force. (Fam. Code, § 2210(e).)
        (2) ☐ bigamous marriage. (Fam. Code, § 2201.)   (6) ☐ physical incapacity. (Fam. Code, § 2210(f).)

7. **Petitioner requests** that the court grant the above relief and make injunctive (including restraining) and other orders as follows:

	Petitioner	Respondent	Joint	Other
a. Legal custody of children to	☐	☐	☑	☐
b. Physical custody of children to	☑	☐	☐	☐
c. Child visitation be granted to	☐	☑		☐

        As requested in form: ☐ FL-311 ☐ FL-312 ☐ FL-341(C) ☐ FL-341(D) ☐ FL-341(E) ☐ Attachment 7c.
    d. ☐ Determination of parentage of any children born to the Petitioner and Respondent prior to the marriage.

	Petitioner	Respondent
e. Attorney fees and costs payable by	☐	☑
f. Spousal support payable to (earnings assignment will be issued)	☑	☐

    g. ☑ Terminate the court's jurisdiction (ability) to award spousal support to Respondent.
    h. ☑ Property rights be determined.
    i. ☑ Petitioner's former name be restored to *(specify):* SANDIE BEACH
    j. ☐ Other *(specify):*

        ☐ Continued on Attachment 7j.

8. **Child support**–If there are minor children born to or adopted by the Petitioner and Respondent before or during this marriage, the court will make orders for the support of the children upon request and submission of financial forms by the requesting party. An earnings assignment may be issued without further notice. Any party required to pay support must pay interest on overdue amounts at the "legal" rate, which is currently 10 percent.

9. **I HAVE READ THE RESTRAINING ORDERS ON THE BACK OF THE SUMMONS, AND I UNDERSTAND THAT THEY APPLY TO ME WHEN THIS PETITION IS FILED.**

I declare under penalty of perjury under the laws of the State of California that the foregoing is true and correct.

Date:

SANDIE SHORES   ▶
    (TYPE OR PRINT NAME)   (SIGNATURE OF PETITIONER)

Date:

JOAN CARE-ACTOR   ▶
    (TYPE OR PRINT NAME)   (SIGNATURE OF ATTORNEY FOR PETITIONER)

NOTICE: Dissolution or legal separation may automatically cancel the rights of a spouse under the other spouse's will, trust, retirement plan, power of attorney, pay on death bank account, survivorship rights to any property owned in joint tenancy, and any other similar thing. It does not automatically cancel the right of a spouse as beneficiary of the other spouse's life insurance policy. You should review these matters, as well as any credit cards, other credit accounts, insurance polices, retirement plans, and credit reports to determine whether they should be changed or whether you should take any other actions. However, some changes may require the agreement of your spouse or a court order (see Family Code sections 231–235).

For your protection and privacy, please press the Clear This Form button after you have printed the form.

| Save This Form | Print This Form | Clear This Form |

UCCJEA FL-105/GC-120

FL-105/GC-120

ATTORNEY OR PARTY WITHOUT ATTORNEY (Name, State Bar number, and address):	
JOAN CARE-ACTOR, SBN ******** LAW OFFICES OF JOAN CARE-ACTOR 75000 WHY ME LANE SACRAMENTO, CA 95826 TELEPHONE NO.: 916-555-1234 FAX NO. (Optional): 916-555-1233 E-MAIL ADDRESS (Optional): ATTORNEY FOR (Name): SANDIE SHORES	To keep other people from seeing what you entered on your form, please press the Clear This Form button at the end of the form when finished.

SUPERIOR COURT OF CALIFORNIA, COUNTY OF   SACRAMENTO

STREET ADDRESS: 3341 Power Inn Road
MAILING ADDRESS: 3341 Power Inn Road
CITY AND ZIP CODE: Sacramento, CA 95826
BRANCH NAME: Family Law Division

PETITIONER: SANDIE SHORES

RESPONDENT: ROCKY SHORES

DECLARATION UNDER UNIFORM CHILD CUSTODY JURISDICTION AND ENFORCEMENT ACT (UCCJEA)	CASE NUMBER:

1. **I am a party** to this proceeding to determine custody of a child.
2. ☐ My present address is not disclosed. It is confidential under Family Code section 3429. I have listed the address of the children presently residing with me as confidential.
3. *(Number):* TWO   minor children are subject to this proceeding as follows:
   (Insert the information requested below. The residence information must be given for the last FIVE years.)

a. Child's name EDDY WADE SHORES	Place of birth POCATELLO, ID	Date of birth 5/1/05	Sex M
Period of residence	Address	Person child lived with (name and present address)	Relationship
3/2004 to present	11155 Turtle Dove Court, Folsom ☐ Confidential	Rocky Shores & Sandie Shores 11155 Turtle Dove Ct., Folsom, CA	Parents
to			
to			
to			
to			

b. Child's name SHELLY PEBBLES SHORES ☑ Residence information is the same as given above for child a. (If NOT the same, provide the information below.)	Place of birth CARMICHAEL, CA	Date of birth 10/15/09	Sex F
Period of residence	Address	Person child lived with (name and present address)	Relationship
to present	☐ Confidential		
to			
to			
to			

c. ☐ Additional children are listed on Attachment 3c. *(Provide all requested information for additional children.)*

Page 1 of 2

Form Approved for Optional Use
Judicial Council of California
FL-105/GC-120 [Rev. January 1, 2007]

**DECLARATION UNDER UNIFORM CHILD CUSTODY
JURISDICTION AND ENFORCEMENT ACT (UCCJEA)**

Family Code, § 3400 et seq.
Probate Code, §§ 1510(f), 1512
www.courtinfo.ca.gov

American LegalNet, Inc.
www.FormsWorkflow.com

UCCJEA FL-105/GC-120

FL-105/GC-120

SHORT TITLE:	CASE NUMBER:
IN RE MARRIAGE OF SHORES	

4. Have you participated as a party or a witness or in some other capacity in another litigation or custody proceeding, in California or elsewhere, concerning custody of a child subject to this proceeding?
   ☑ No ☐ Yes   *(If yes, provide the following information):*
   a. Name of each child:

   b. I was a: ☐ party ☐ witness ☐ other *(specify):*

   c. Court *(specify name, state, location):*

   d. Court order or judgment *(date):*

5. Do you have information about a custody proceeding pending in a California court or any other court concerning a child in this case, other than that stated in item 4?
   ☑ No ☐ Yes   *(If yes, provide the following information):*

   a. Name of each child:
   b. Nature of proceeding: ☐ dissolution or divorce ☐ guardianship ☐ adoption ☐ other *(specify):*
   c. Court *(specify name, state, location):*
   d. Status of proceeding:

6. ☐ One or more domestic violence restraining /protective orders are now in effect. (Attach a copy of the orders if you have one.)
   The orders are from the following court or courts *(specify county and state):*
   a. ☐ Criminal: County/state: _____   c. ☐ Juvenile: County/state: _____
        Case No. *(if known):* _____   Case No. *(if known):* _____
   b. ☐ Family: County/state: _____   d. ☐ Other: County/state: _____
        Case No. *(if known):* _____   Case No. *(if known):* _____

7. Do you know of any person who is not a party to this proceeding who has physical custody or claims to have custody of or visitation rights with any child in this case?
   ☑ No ☐ Yes *(If yes, provide the following information):*

a. Name and address of person	b. Name and address of person	c. Name and address of person
☐ Has physical custody ☐ Claims custody rights ☐ Claims visitation rights	☐ Has physical custody ☐ Claims custody rights ☐ Claims visitation rights	☐ Has physical custody ☐ Claims custody rights ☐ Claims visitation rights
Name of each child	Name of each child	Name of each child

I declare under penalty of perjury under the laws of the State of California that the foregoing is true and correct.
Date:

SANDIE SHORES
_____   ▶   _____
(TYPE OR PRINT NAME)   (SIGNATURE OF DECLARANT)

8. ☐ Number of pages attached after this page: _____

> **NOTICE TO DECLARANT:** You have a continuing duty to inform this court if you obtain any information about a custody proceeding in a California court or any other court concerning a child subject to this proceeding.

FL-105/GC-120 [Rev. January 1, 2007]   **DECLARATION UNDER UNIFORM CHILD CUSTODY JURISDICTION AND ENFORCEMENT ACT (UCCJEA)**   Page 2 of 2

Print This Form	For your protection and privacy, please press the Clear This Form button after you have printed the form.	Clear This Form

Summons—Marriage (Family Law) FL-110

FL-110

SUMMONS (Family Law)	CITACIÓN (Derecho familiar)

NOTICE TO RESPONDENT *(Name):*

AVISO AL DEMANDADO (Nombre):

> **You are being sued.** *Lo están demandando.*

To keep other people from seeing what you entered on your form, please press the Clear This Form button at the end of the form when finished.

Petitioner's name is:

Nombre del demandante:

CASE NUMBER *(NÚMERO DE CASO):*

You have **30 calendar days** after this *Summons* and *Petition* are served on you to file a *Response* (form FL-120 or FL-123) at the court and have a copy served on the petitioner. A letter or phone call will not protect you.

If you do not file your *Response* on time, the court may make orders affecting your marriage or domestic partnership, your property, and custody of your children. You may be ordered to pay support and attorney fees and costs. If you cannot pay the filing fee, ask the clerk for a fee waiver form.

If you want legal advice, contact a lawyer immediately. You can get information about finding lawyers at the California Courts Online Self-Help Center *(www.courtinfo.ca.gov/selfhelp)*, at the California Legal Services Web site *(www.lawhelpcalifornia.org)*, or by contacting your local county bar association.

*Tiene **30 días corridos** después de haber recibido la entrega legal de esta Citación y Petición para presentar una Respuesta (formulario FL-120 ó FL-123) ante la corte y efectuar la entrega legal de una copia al demandante. Una carta o llamada telefónica no basta para protegerlo.*

Si no presenta su Respuesta a tiempo, la corte puede dar órdenes que afecten su matrimonio o pareja de hecho, sus bienes y la custodia de sus hijos. La corte también le puede ordenar que pague manutención, y honorarios y costos legales. Si no puede pagar la cuota de presentación, pida al secretario un formulario de exención de cuotas.

Si desea obtener asesoramiento legal, póngase en contacto de inmediato con un abogado. Puede obtener información para encontrar a un abogado en el Centro de Ayuda de las Cortes de California (www.sucorte.ca.gov), en el sitio Web de los Servicios Legales de California (www.lawhelpcalifornia.org) o poniéndose en contacto con el colegio de abogados de su condado.

NOTICE: The restraining orders on page 2 are effective against both spouses or domestic partners until the petition is dismissed, a judgment is entered, or the court makes further orders. These orders are enforceable anywhere in California by any law enforcement officer who has received or seen a copy of them.

AVISO: Las órdenes de restricción que figuran en la página 2 valen para ambos cónyuges o pareja de hecho hasta que se despida la petición, se emita un fallo o la corte dé otras órdenes. Cualquier autoridad de la ley que haya recibido o visto una copia de estas órdenes puede hacerlas acatar en cualquier lugar de California.

NOTE: If a judgment or support order is entered, the court may order you to pay all or part of the fees and costs that the court waived for yourself or for the other party. If this happens, the party ordered to pay fees shall be given notice and an opportunity to request a hearing to set aside the order to pay waived court fees.

AVISO: Si se emite un fallo u orden de manutención, la corte puede ordenar que usted pague parte de, o todas las cuotas y costos de la corte previamente exentas a petición de usted o de la otra parte. Si esto ocurre, la parte ordenada a pagar estas cuotas debe recibir aviso y la oportunidad de solicitar una audiencia para anular la orden de pagar las cuotas exentas.

1. The name and address of the court are *(El nombre y dirección de la corte son):*

2. The name, address, and telephone number of the petitioner's attorney, or the petitioner without an attorney, are:
   (El nombre, dirección y número de teléfono del abogado del demandante, o del demandante si no tiene abogado, son):

Date *(Fecha):* _____ Clerk, by *(Secretario, por)* _____, Deputy *(Asistente)*

[SEAL]

NOTICE TO THE PERSON SERVED: You are served

AVISO A LA PERSONA QUE RECIBIÓ LA ENTREGA: Esta entrega se realiza

a. ☐ as an individual. *(a usted como individuo.)*

b. ☐ on behalf of respondent who is a *(en nombre de un demandado que es):*

   (1) ☐ minor *(menor de edad)*

   (2) ☐ ward or conservatee *(dependiente de la corte o pupilo)*

   (3) ☐ other *(specify) (otro – especifique):*

(Read the reverse for important information.) *(Lea importante información al dorso.)*

Page 1 of 2

Form Adopted for Mandatory Use
Judicial Council of California
FL-110 [Rev. July 1, 2009]

SUMMONS
(Family Law)

Family Code §§ 232, 233, 2040,7700;
Code of Civil Procedure, §§ 412.20, 416.60–416.90
Government Code, § 68637
www.courtinfo.ca.gov

Summons—Marriage (Family Law) FL-110

WARNING—IMPORTANT INFORMATION

WARNING: California law provides that, for purposes of division of property upon dissolution of a marriage or domestic partnership or upon legal separation, property acquired by the parties during marriage or domestic partnership in joint form is presumed to be community property. If either party to this action should die before the jointly held community property is divided, the language in the deed that characterizes how title is held (i.e., joint tenancy, tenants in common, or community property) will be controlling, and not the community property presumption. You should consult your attorney if you want the community property presumption to be written into the recorded title to the property.

STANDARD FAMILY LAW RESTRAINING ORDERS

Starting immediately, you and your spouse or domestic partner are restrained from

1. Removing the minor child or children of the parties, if any, from the state without the prior written consent of the other party or an order of the court;

2. Cashing, borrowing against, canceling, transferring, disposing of, or changing the beneficiaries of any insurance or other coverage, including life, health, automobile, and disability, held for the benefit of the parties and their minor child or children;

3. Transferring, encumbering, hypothecating, concealing, or in any way disposing of any property, real or personal, whether community, quasi-community, or separate, without the written consent of the other party or an order of the court, except in the usual course of business or for the necessities of life; and

4. Creating a nonprobate transfer or modifying a nonprobate transfer in a manner that affects the disposition of property subject to the transfer, without the written consent of the other party or an order of the court. Before revocation of a nonprobate transfer can take effect or a right of survivorship to property can be eliminated, notice of the change must be filed and served on the other party.

You must notify each other of any proposed extraordinary expenditures at least five business days prior to incurring these extraordinary expenditures and account to the court for all extraordinary expenditures made after these restraining orders are effective. However, you may use community property, quasi-community property, or your own separate property to pay an attorney to help you or to pay court costs.

ADVERTENCIA – INFORMACIÓN IMPORTANTE

ADVERTENCIA: De acuerdo a la ley de California, las propiedades adquiridas por las partes durante su matrimonio o pareja de hecho en forma conjunta se consideran propiedad comunitaria para los fines de la división de bienes que ocurre cuando se produce una disolución o separación legal del matrimonio o pareja de hecho. Si cualquiera de las partes de este caso llega a fallecer antes de que se divida la propiedad comunitaria de tenencia conjunta, el destino de la misma quedará determinado por las cláusulas de la escritura correspondiente que describen su tenencia (por ej., tenencia conjunta, tenencia en común o propiedad comunitaria) y no por la presunción de propiedad comunitaria. Si quiere que la presunción comunitaria quede registrada en la escritura de la propiedad, debería consultar con un abogado.

ÓRDENES DE RESTRICCIÓN NORMALES DE DERECHO FAMILIAR

En forma inmediata, usted y su cónyuge o pareja de hecho tienen prohibido:

1. *Llevarse del estado de California a los hijos menores de las partes, si los hubiera, sin el consentimiento previo por escrito de la otra parte o una orden de la corte;*

2. *Cobrar, pedir prestado, cancelar, transferir, deshacerse o cambiar el nombre de los beneficiarios de cualquier seguro u otro tipo de cobertura, tal como de vida, salud, vehículo y discapacidad, que tenga como beneficiario(s) a las partes y su(s) hijo(s) menor(es);*

3. *Transferir, gravar, hipotecar, ocultar o deshacerse de cualquier manera de cualquier propiedad, inmueble o personal, ya sea comunitaria, cuasicomunitaria o separada, sin el consentimiento escrito de la otra parte o una orden de la corte, con excepción las operaciones realizadas en el curso normal de actividades o para satisfacer las necesidades de la vida; y*

4. *Crear o modificar una transferencia no testamentaria de manera que afecte el destino de una propiedad sujeta a transferencia, sin el consentimiento por escrito de la otra parte o una orden de la corte. Antes de que se pueda eliminar la revocación de una transferencia no testamentaria, se debe presentar ante la corte un aviso del cambio y hacer una entrega legal de dicho aviso a la otra parte.*

Cada parte tiene que notificar a la otra sobre cualquier gasto extraordinario propuesto, por lo menos cinco días laborales antes de realizarlo, y rendir cuenta a la corte de todos los gastos extraordinarios realizados después de que estas órdenes de restricción hayan entrado en vigencia. No obstante, puede usar propiedad comunitaria, cuasicomunitaria o suya separada para pagar a un abogado o para ayudarle a pagar los costos de la corte.

SUMMONS
(Family Law)

For your protection and privacy, please press the Clear This Form button after you have printed the form.

| Save This Form | Print This Form | Clear This Form |

Petition—Marriage (Family Law) FL-100

ATTORNEY OR PARTY WITHOUT ATTORNEY *(Name, State Bar number, and address):*	**To keep other people from seeing what you entered on your form, please press the Clear This Form button at the end of the form when finished.**
TELEPHONE NO.: FAX NO. *(Optional):*	
E-MAIL ADDRESS *(Optional):*	
ATTORNEY FOR *(Name):*	

SUPERIOR COURT OF CALIFORNIA, COUNTY OF

STREET ADDRESS:

MAILING ADDRESS:

CITY AND ZIP CODE:

BRANCH NAME:

MARRIAGE OF

PETITIONER:

RESPONDENT:

PETITION FOR	CASE NUMBER:
☐ **Dissolution of Marriage** ☐ **Legal Separation** ☐ **Nullity of Marriage** ☐ **AMENDED**	

1. RESIDENCE (Dissolution only) ☐ Petitioner ☐ Respondent   has been a resident of this state for at least six months and of this county for at least three months immediately preceding the filing of this *Petition for Dissolution of Marriage.*

2. STATISTICAL FACTS
   a. Date of marriage:
   b. Date of separation:
   c. Time from date of marriage to date of separation *(specify):*
      Years: Months:

3. DECLARATION REGARDING MINOR CHILDREN *(include children of this relationship born prior to or during the marriage or adopted during the marriage):*
   a. ☐ There are no minor children.
   b. ☐ The minor children are:

Child's name	Birthdate	Age	Sex

   ☐ Continued on Attachment 3b.
   c. If there are minor children of the Petitioner and Respondent, a completed *Declaration Under Uniform Child Custody Jurisdiction and Enforcement Act (UCCJEA)* (form FL-105) must be attached.
   d. ☐ A completed voluntary declaration of paternity regarding minor children born to the Petitioner and Respondent prior to the marriage is attached.

4. SEPARATE PROPERTY
   Petitioner requests that the assets and debts listed ☐ in *Property Declaration* (form FL-160) ☐ in Attachment 4 ☐ below   be confirmed as separate property.

Item	Confirm to

NOTICE: You may redact (black out) social security numbers from any written material filed with the court in this case other than a form used to collect child or spousal support.

Page 1 of 2

Form Adopted for Mandatory Use
Judicial Council of California
FL-100 [Rev. January 1, 2005]

PETITION—MARRIAGE
(Family Law)

Family Code, §§ 2330, 3409;
www.courtinfo.ca.gov

Petition—Marriage (Family Law) FL-100

MARRIAGE OF *(last name, first name of parties):*	CASE NUMBER:

5. DECLARATION REGARDING COMMUNITY AND QUASI-COMMUNITY ASSETS AND DEBTS AS CURRENTLY KNOWN
   a. ☐ There are no such assets or debts subject to disposition by the court in this proceeding.
   b. ☐ All such assets and debts are listed ☐ in *Property Declaration* (form FL-160) ☐ in Attachment 5b.
      ☐ below *(specify):*

6. **Petitioner requests**
   a. ☐ dissolution of the marriage based on
      (1) ☐ irreconcilable differences. (Fam. Code, § 2310(a).)
      (2) ☐ incurable insanity. (Fam. Code, § 2310(b).)
   b. ☐ legal separation of the parties based on
      (1) ☐ irreconcilable differences. (Fam. Code, § 2310(a).)
      (2) ☐ incurable insanity. (Fam. Code, § 2310(b).)
   c. ☐ nullity of void marriage based on
      (1) ☐ incestuous marriage. (Fam. Code, § 2200.)
      (2) ☐ bigamous marriage. (Fam. Code, § 2201.)
   d. ☐ nullity of voidable marriage based on
      (1) ☐ petitioner's age at time of marriage.
          (Fam. Code, § 2210(a).)
      (2) ☐ prior existing marriage.
          (Fam. Code, § 2210(b).)
      (3) ☐ unsound mind. (Fam. Code, § 2210(c).)
      (4) ☐ fraud. (Fam. Code, § 2210(d).)
      (5) ☐ force. (Fam. Code, § 2210(e).)
      (6) ☐ physical incapacity. (Fam. Code, § 2210(f).)

7. **Petitioner requests** that the court grant the above relief and make injunctive (including restraining) and other orders as follows:

	Petitioner	Respondent	Joint	Other
a. Legal custody of children to	☐	☐	☐	☐
b. Physical custody of children to	☐	☐	☐	☐
c. Child visitation be granted to	☐	☐	☐	☐

   As requested in form: ☐ FL-311 ☐ FL-312 ☐ FL-341(C) ☐ FL-341(D) ☐ FL-341(E) ☐ Attachment 7c.
   d. ☐ Determination of parentage of any children born to the Petitioner and Respondent prior to the marriage.
   e. Attorney fees and costs payable by .... ☐ ☐
   f. Spousal support payable to (earnings assignment will be issued) .... ☐ ☐
   g. ☐ Terminate the court's jurisdiction (ability) to award spousal support to Respondent.
   h. ☐ Property rights be determined.
   i. ☐ Petitioner's former name be restored to *(specify):*
   j. ☐ Other *(specify):*

      ☐ Continued on Attachment 7j.

8. **Child support**–If there are minor children born to or adopted by the Petitioner and Respondent before or during this marriage, the court will make orders for the support of the children upon request and submission of financial forms by the requesting party. An earnings assignment may be issued without further notice. Any party required to pay support must pay interest on overdue amounts at the "legal" rate, which is currently 10 percent.

9. I HAVE READ THE RESTRAINING ORDERS ON THE BACK OF THE SUMMONS, AND I UNDERSTAND THAT THEY APPLY TO ME WHEN THIS PETITION IS FILED.

I declare under penalty of perjury under the laws of the State of California that the foregoing is true and correct.

Date:

▶

_____   _____
(TYPE OR PRINT NAME)   (SIGNATURE OF PETITIONER)

Date:

▶

_____   _____
(TYPE OR PRINT NAME)   (SIGNATURE OF ATTORNEY FOR PETITIONER)

NOTICE: Dissolution or legal separation may automatically cancel the rights of a spouse under the other spouse's will, trust, retirement plan, power of attorney, pay on death bank account, survivorship rights to any property owned in joint tenancy, and any other similar thing. It does not automatically cancel the right of a spouse as beneficiary of the other spouse's life insurance policy. You should review these matters, as well as any credit cards, other credit accounts, insurance polices, retirement plans, and credit reports to determine whether they should be changed or whether you should take any other actions. However, some changes may require the agreement of your spouse or a court order (see Family Code sections 231–235).

For your protection and privacy, please press the Clear This Form button after you have printed the form.

Save This Form   Print This Form   Clear This Form

UCCJEA FL-105/GC-120

ATTORNEY OR PARTY WITHOUT ATTORNEY *(Name, State Bar number, and address):*	
TELEPHONE NO.: FAX NO. *(Optional):* E-MAIL ADDRESS *(Optional):* ATTORNEY FOR *(Name):*	To keep other people from seeing what you entered on your form, please press the Clear This Form button at the end of the form when finished.

SUPERIOR COURT OF CALIFORNIA, COUNTY OF

STREET ADDRESS:

MAILING ADDRESS:

CITY AND ZIP CODE:

BRANCH NAME:

PETITIONER: *(This section applies only to family law cases.)*

RESPONDENT:

OTHER PARTY:

(This section apples only to guardianship cases.)

GUARDIANSHIP OF *(Name):*   Minor

CASE NUMBER:

DECLARATION UNDER UNIFORM CHILD CUSTODY JURISDICTION AND ENFORCEMENT ACT (UCCJEA)

1. **I am a party** to this proceeding to determine custody of a child.

2. ☐   My present address and the present address of each child residing with me is confidential under Family Code section 3429 as I have indicated in item 3.

3. There are *(specify number):*   minor children who are subject to this proceeding, as follows:
   (Insert the information requested below. The residence information must be given for the last FIVE years.)

a. Child's name		Place of birth	Date of birth	Sex
Period of residence	Address	Person child lived with *(name and complete current address)*		Relationship
to present	☐ Confidential	☐ Confidential		
	Child's residence *(City, State)*	Person child lived with *(name and complete current address)*		
to				
	Child's residence *(City, State)*	Person child lived with *(name and complete current address)*		
to				
	Child's residence *(City, State)*	Person child lived with *(name and complete current address)*		
to				

b. Child's name		Place of birth	Date of birth	Sex
☐ Residence information is the same as given above for child a. *(If NOT the same, provide the information below.)*				
Period of residence	Address	Person child lived with *(name and complete current address)*		Relationship
to present	☐ Confidential	☐ Confidential		
	Child's residence *(City, State)*	Person child lived with *(name and complete current address)*		
to				
	Child's residence *(City, State)*	Person child lived with *(name and complete current address)*		
to				
	Child's residence *(City, State)*	Person child lived with *(name and complete current address)*		
to				

c. ☐   Additional residence information for a child listed in item a or b is continued on attachment 3c.

d. ☐   Additional children are listed on form *FL-105(A)/GC-120(A)*. *(Provide all requested information for additional children.)*

Page 1 of 2

Form Adopted for Mandatory Use
Judicial Council of California
FL-105/GC-120 [Rev. January 1, 2009]

DECLARATION UNDER UNIFORM CHILD CUSTODY JURISDICTION AND ENFORCEMENT ACT (UCCJEA)

Family Code, § 3400 et seq.;
Probate Code, §§ 1510(f), 1512
www.courtinfo.ca.gov

UCCJEA FL-105/GC-120

FL-105/GC-120

SHORT TITLE:	CASE NUMBER:

4. Do you have information about, or have you participated as a party or as a witness or in some other capacity in, another court case or custody or visitation proceeding, in California or elsewhere, concerning a child subject to this proceeding?
  ☐ Yes ☐ No *(If yes, attach a copy of the orders (if you have one) and provide the following information):*

Proceeding	Case number	Court *(name, state, location)*	Court order or judgment *(date)*	Name of each child	Your connection to the case	Case status
a. ☐ Family						
b. ☐ Guardianship						
c. ☐ Other						

Proceeding	Case Number	Court *(name, state, location)*
d. ☐ Juvenile Delinquency/ Juvenile Dependency		
e. ☐ Adoption		

5. ☐ One or more domestic violence restraining/protective orders are now in effect. *(Attach a copy of the orders if you have one and provide the following information):*

Court	County	State	Case number *(if known)*	Orders expire *(date)*
a. ☐ Criminal				
b. ☐ Family				
c. ☐ Juvenile Delinquency/ Juvenile Dependency				
d. ☐ Other				

6. Do you know of any person who is not a party to this proceeding who has physical custody or claims to have custody of or visitation rights with any child in this case? ☐ Yes ☐ No *(If yes, provide the following information):*

a. Name and address of person	b. Name and address of person	c. Name and address of person
☐ Has physical custody ☐ Claims custody rights ☐ Claims visitation rights	☐ Has physical custody ☐ Claims custody rights ☐ Claims visitation rights	☐ Has physical custody ☐ Claims custody rights ☐ Claims visitation rights
Name of each child	Name of each child	Name of each child

I declare under penalty of perjury under the laws of the State of California that the foregoing is true and correct.

Date:

▶

_____
(TYPE OR PRINT NAME)

_____
(SIGNATURE OF DECLARANT)

7. ☐ Number of pages attached: _____

NOTICE TO DECLARANT: You have a continuing duty to inform this court if you obtain any information about a custody proceeding in a California court or any other court concerning a child subject to this proceeding.

FL-105/GC-120 [Rev. January 1, 2009] **DECLARATION UNDER UNIFORM CHILD CUSTODY JURISDICTION AND ENFORCEMENT ACT (UCCJEA)** Page 2 of 2

For your protection and privacy, please press the Clear This Form button after you have printed the form. **Save This Form** **Print This Form** **Clear This Form**

Chapter Three

Dissolution: Second Steps

Once the Summons and Petition (and UCCJEA and other documents by local rule) have been served on the Respondent, the six-month waiting period begins. The firm will have to be ready for the next steps depending upon what additional documents have been served on the Respondent, the issues raised in the Petition and supporting documents, and whether the Respondent wishes to participate in the dissolution process.

Once served, the Respondent has three options:

1) To challenge the court's jurisdiction;

2) To file and serve a Response (accept the court's jurisdiction); or

3) Default (do nothing).

Challenging the Court's Jurisdiction

Family Code § 2012 provides for the appearance of the Respondent to contest the court's jurisdiction during the pendency of a motion without inadvertently submitting to the court's jurisdiction. This is called a *special* appearance.

Special Appearance

A special appearance may be made by filing a Motion with the court. The grounds normally available to the Respondent are: Motion to Quash Service of the Summons; Motion to Quash the Proceeding; Motion to Change Venue; or a Motion to Strike.

A Motion to Quash Service of the Summons alleges that the California Court does not have personal jurisdiction or that there was improper service of process (CCP§ 418.10(a)(1)). The Respondent may also simultaneously file a Motion to Quash the Proceeding or a Motion to Strike. If the motion is denied, the Respondent may petition for a writ of mandate. Until the writ proceedings are complete, the Respondent still will not have made an appearance. If the writ is denied, the Respondent will be ordered to file a Response. However, if successful, the Court will deny the Petitioner the capacity to seek relief against the Respondent in California.

A Motion to Quash the Proceeding (CRC § 1230) challenges the Petitioner's capacity to file a lawsuit, usually stating that the residency requirements have not been met or that there is another action already pending between the parties in another jurisdiction. A Motion to Quash the Proceeding is the same as a demurrer in civil proceedings. The Respondent may move on one or more of the following four grounds: 1) lack of legal capacity to sue; 2) prior judgment or action pending in another jurisdiction; 3) residence requirements not satisfied; 4) nullity action barred by statute of limitations.

A Motion to Change Venue (CRC § 1235) challenges the Petitioner's capacity to file the dissolution of marriage in a specific county. In the event the Petitioner has not met the statutory requirements as a resident of the County (lived there for at least 3 months) and as long as the Respondent has not filed a Response, the venue may be changed to the proper County. CCP § 397 provides the rules and grounds for changing venue.

A Motion to Strike (CRC § 1229(a)) allows the Respondent to request that the court remove certain items contained in the Petition which are not required by CRC 1281, or which do not apply to this action, such as allegations of misconduct and claims for relief not related to the marital status and/or rights and obligations arising out of the marriage.

The Respondent must file his or her Motion within the thirty (30) day period in which they have to file a Response. The documents which should be filed are: Notice of Motion; (written) Declaration of the Respondent (and evidence, if any) supporting the facts; and a Memorandum with Points and Authorities. (Your instructor will provide you with more detail. An example of a Declaration and Points and Authorities for a Motion to Quash Proceeding is provided in Appendix 3A and 3B.)

Once filed, the Respondent must then have the Petitioner served with the documents. CCP§ 1005(a)(13)-(b) currently provides that a Motion must be served at least 16 **court** days by personal service and 21 **court** days, if by mail (known as the *five day mail rule*). **Note: service of process dates with regard to any motion should always be confirmed. Also, always check the dates to see if they are calendar days or court days.** The Code of Civil Procedure also sets forth the dates for Responsive Declarations and Reply Declarations. You will also need to check for any local rule requirements that must be followed.

Filing a Motion

In most cases, the hearing on a Motion will be set for a period far enough in advance for matters other than a special appearance, to allow for the time to serve the documents. If your office is representing the Petitioner, you will want to confirm, upon receipt of the documents, that timely service was complete. You will also want to calendar the following dates: 1) date of the hearing; 2) date when the Responsive Declaration will be due; 3) the date the Petitioner's Reply Declaration is due. **You should always confirm these dates on the forms and with the Code of Civil Procedure and any local rules that are subject to change.**

If your office represents the Respondent, you will calendar the following dates: 1) date of the hearing; 2) date when the documents were served on the Respondent (and by what method); 3) date when the Responsive Declaration is due; and 4) date the Reply Declaration due.

It has been my experience that some family law attorneys *do not* closely follow the required time-lines for the serving and exchange of documents. In the event your office or client has not been served in the proper manner, within the prescribed legal time limit, or the responsive declaration is not filed and served within the prescribed time, the attorney can request that the Motion be denied, or that the date be reset to allow for sufficient time to respond to the moving party's rebuttal and/or allegations. It is within the court's discretion to do so. The attorney will consider whether it is more detrimental to delay the hearing of the matter or to have less time to respond and/or prepare for the hearing. Alternatively, the attorney may have conferred with opposing counsel and agreed to a different time-line. These changes should be noted on the calendar and in the client file.

A person requesting a Motion is asking that the court hear a matter of **law**, as opposed to an issue of **fact**. An issue of fact, e.g., whether a party should receive spousal or child support, or other types of relief, should be obtained through a Request for Order (form FL-300) rather than a Notice of Motion. Many offices have used Judicial Council forms and methods interchangeably, but they are technically different.

A Notice of Motion, as previously stated, should be used for obtaining orders regarding legal standing or for interpretation of the law. During a special appearance, the Respondent is asking the court whether the Petitioner has legal standing to file the petition, serve the petition, file the petition in that venue, and/or file a petition requesting certain types of relief that may not be appropriate.

The Declarations that will be attached to the Notice of Motion will also provide the court with the legal background as to why the court should rule in the moving party's favor. These are considered the Points and Authorities. The Points and Authorities, which you should have discussed in an entry level course, apply the law to the facts in the case and present argument of why the Court should apply the "rule of law" based on statute and/or case law. Any evidence that can verify the party's position should also be attached. For instance, a Motion to Quash Summons will contain legal argument and case law as to why California does not have jurisdiction. It should cite applicable case law, as well as the California Rules of Court that apply to jurisdiction. Contained within the Notice of Motion (see Appendix 3C) at the end of the chapter are examples of declarations for the various motions discussed herein. As a paralegal in the law office environment you will need to research the appropriate "Authorities" to apply the legal remedies to these declarations. (Several sample "Authorities" can be found at Appendix 3D.)

It should also be noted that a Notice of Motion does not require an appearance by the person against whom relief is being sought—in this case, the Petitioner. In fact, the Notice of Motion (as opposed to the Request for Order) does not have a statement that "you are ordered to appear." Additionally, because the person is not being ordered to appear, the attorney may sign the Notice. And, in most cases the court presumes that the Motion will be served by mail rather than personally. Although, due to the "five (5) day rule" for mailing, and in the interest of time, it may be necessary to personally serve the other party or his/her attorney. A final difference between a Notice of Motion and a Request for Order is that no witnesses may appear at the Motion hearing. The Request for Order allows the moving party to subpoena witnesses and experts to appear. Only the parties and their attorneys (if represented) may appear at a Motion hearing.

You will want to see if there are any local rules which require that the attorney use one method over the other. For instance, if you are calling witnesses, you will only be allowed to do so for what is referred to as a "long cause" hearing.

Remember that the Petitioner is always the Petitioner and the Respondent is always the Respondent. In the instance where the Respondent has filed a Notice of Motion to the Court, although he or she is "petitioning" the Court for relief, that person is still the Respondent. They are simply called the "moving party" whenever they file a Motion or Request for Order with the court. This remains true even after a Judgment has been entered.

You will also want to check each county's local rules to determine if the court offers tentative rulings for family law. Although tentative rulings may be required for civil cases, in some counties tentative rulings are not available for family law matters.

Once the opposing party (or his/her attorney) has been served with the Notice of Motion, they must file a Responsive Declaration with the court, as well as personally serve same, at least nine (9) **court** days prior to the hearing. (**Remember also the five (5) day mailing rule.**) In the event the client wishes to file a Reply Declaration, it must be filed and personally served five (5) **court** days prior to the hearing. There is presently no fee for filing a Responsive Declaration to a Motion and/or Request for Order. Always check CCP§ 1003 to confirm the current rules governing motions and hearings.

Another issue to keep in mind is that if the Petitioner filed a Request for Order which may be scheduled to be heard before the Motion (requesting a special appearance only) can be heard, the Respondent must make an appearance at that Request for Order hearing in order to oppose any requests for relief by the Petitioner. It is therefore, a good idea to have the Respondent's Motion filed on or before the hearing date, so that the Court can be informed of the pending hearing and take that information under submission. For instance, the Court may delay making orders for spousal support if the Court is aware that there is a question of jurisdiction over the entire matter. The Court may delay some or all of the relief requested in Petitioner's Request for Order until Respondent's Motion is heard and the issue of jurisdiction has been resolved. This hearing may also be a good time to serve the other party with the Motion, if this has not already been done, provided the date is within the time-frame allowed for personal service.

At the hearing, the Judge may 1) grant the Respondent's Motion—in which case the Summons is Quashed and the case closed "on the court's own motion"; or 2) the Judge may deny the Respondent's (moving party) Motion, order the Respondent to respond, granting him or her up to 30 days to file a Response to the Petition and most likely to file a Responsive Declaration to the underlying Request for Order.

Response

The Respondent has thirty days from the date he or she is served the Summons and Petition to Respond to the action (or as indicated above, to file a motion, if appropriate). Upon the filing of the Response, the Respondent has accepted the Court's jurisdiction and waives any right to object to the court having personal jurisdiction. Thus, the Respondent has made a *general appearance*.

The Respondent must complete the Response (remember that a blank one was served with the Summons and Petition) and serve a copy on the Petitioner, with a Proof of Service by Mail (form FL-335). The Response may be served by mail and pursuant to CCP § 1410 cannot be served by the Respondent. The Response is served by an individual over the age of 18 years, who is a resident of the United States, and who is not a party to the action. This person may be the paralegal who works for the Respondent's attorney, if an attorney has been retained.

A special note regarding service of documents: When the Summons and Petition are served, or any other initial documents such as a complaint, they **must** be served personally (see Chapter 2 regarding service). However, once the Respondent/Defendant is served, most other documents can be served by mail, unless the law states otherwise.

The Response will be filed with the court along with the Proof of Service (for the Response) and the appropriate filing fee. If there are minor children, the Respondent will also need to file a Declaration Under the Uniform Child Custody Jurisdiction Enforcement Act, confirming with the court that the children are in the custody of the natural parent(s), that no other person has been given custody or guardianship, and that there is not a concurrent case in another jurisdiction. The Preliminary Declaration of Disclosure should also be served if the Petitioner has already served theirs.

In the event the Respondent is unable to pay the filing fee, he/she should submit the Application for Order and Waiver of Court Fees and Costs.

As in most other actions, once the Response has been served and filed, the parties may begin the discovery process. This will include either the informal exchange of information or formal discovery such as Interrogatories, Requests for Admissions and Depositions. These will be discussed in Chapter Five.

In the case of Disclosure declarations (which will be discussed more thoroughly in Chapter Seven), all preliminary Disclosure documents must be exchanged and served within sixty (60) days following the date the Respondent was served. It is therefore important that you begin gathering this information as soon as possible. Although the preliminary disclosure only requires a listing of the assets and debts along with Income & Expense Declarations, you will want to have the client provide as much information as early in the process as possible.

Default

The Respondent's third option is to not do anything. In other words, the Respondent may simply ignore the matter entirely. In that event, the Petitioner may take the Respondent's Default thirty-one (31) days after the date the Respondent was served. You will recall that the Summons informed the Respondent that they had thirty (30) days to respond once he/she had been served. The Court requires that the Petitioner wait until the full 30-day period has expired before filing a Default. Therefore, if you are working on this family law case, you should calendar the "default date" as 30 days after service, but you should note that the Default can only be filed with the court on the next business day after the 30-day period has expired.

> Example: If the Respondent was served on June 1, he or she has until July 1 to serve and file their Response. Thus, you cannot take (file) the Default of the Respondent until July 2. However, let's assume that July 2 is a Saturday, which then makes Monday, July 4, a holiday. You cannot file the Default with the court until Tuesday, July 5, which is the next "business" day.

The Default is significant because in the eyes of the court once the default has been entered that "party" no longer exists. The Petitioner then can ask the court to make any fair and equitable orders it deems appropriate and based on the Petition that was filed with the court. Going back to the discussion of preparing the Petition, it becomes extremely important that the client has accurately reflected all of the issues and relief requested with respect to custody, support and the division of property, as that information is what the court will utilize to issue the final Judgment.

For instance, if the Petitioner stated that they wished to share joint legal and physical custody with the other parent that is the only order that the court can make. This is true even though the Petitioner may have now decided that he/she wants to be granted sole legal and physical custody. In the event, the Petitioner wants to change, correct or add any relief sought, he/she will have to file an amended Petition and have it served *again* on the Respondent. This will allow the Respondent another thirty (30) day window in which to file a Response—essentially, starting the process over. Although sometimes necessary, it is usually not in the client's best interests to amend the Petition.

Whenever the Petition requests any financial relief or property division, the necessary Judicial Council forms will have to be completed by the Petitioner and served on the Respondent. If the Petition requests support, an Income & Expense Declaration must be prepared and served. When property issues are listed on the Petition, the Petitioner must have a Property Declaration served on the Respondent. The forms submitted to the court along with the Judgment will require the Petitioner to state, under penalty of perjury, that these forms were completed and served as applicable, along with the Preliminary Disclosure documents.

Also, the court will only award, even through default, what is just and equitable. Thus, the court will not enter a Judgment wherein the Petitioner receives the house, pensions, automobile and other assets, while giving the Respondent all of the debts and ordering him or her to pay child and spousal support to the Petitioner. California is a community property state and, regardless of the circumstances, the Court must order that **all** assets and liabilities, as well as the support of any minor children, be shared equally, and based on current statutes.

The default of any member of the military on active duty cannot be taken. This means that if the client's spouse is deployed, as set forth in the Soldiers & Sailors Act of 1940 and as revised in Section 511 et seq. of the Servicemembers Civil Relief Act (50 U.S.C. Appen. § 501 et seq.), the attorney will have to determine how to make sure that the service member files a Response. The Respondent's rights must be protected, particularly his/her military pensions and other benefits which must be joined as part of the proceedings.

You will note on the Request to Enter Default (form FL-165) there is a place for the client or the attorney to declare under penalty of perjury that the Respondent is "not a member of the military service."

Consolidation of Cases

In the event that both parties file a Petition for Dissolution, the controlling party will be the person who **served** the Summons and Petition first. The person serving first will become the Petitioner and the person being served will become the Respondent, regardless of who filed the documents first.

Since each party in the case will have a different case number, the court has developed a form to be submitted to the court telling the court which party is to be considered the Petitioner and which party is the Respondent and which case number will be the lead or controlling case. (See Notice of Consolidation, Judicial Council form FL-920). This form helps the court avoid confusion in the future as to which party is which and assists the law firm staff as well. Additionally, the parties can usually stipulate that the "Petition" filed by the Respondent will be considered a Response, so that another Response does not have to be filed. It also eliminates the Respondent having to pay another fee, since each paid one at the time of filing the Petition.

This makes it important to get the Summons and Petition, which you have prepared and filed on behalf of the client, served on the Respondent as soon as possible. Unless the client (the Petitioner) requests you to delay the service of these documents, it is a good idea to get them served. Although there is no legal advantage, although there may be emotional, personal, or psychological reasons, to being the first one to "strike," it simply eliminates the need to go through the consolidation process.

Child Support History, Issues and Calculations

The Obligation to Support

Below are the primary Family Code Sections which relate to Child Support:

Family Code §§ 3500–3830 (Part 1) Definitions and General Provisions

Family Code §§ 3900–4203 (Part 2) Child Support

Family Code §§ 3900 et seq. sets forth the general obligation of **both** parents to support their minor child(ren). A valid marriage does not need to exist for this obligation to support. The law with respect to minor children, does not refer to the "legitimacy" of the child's birth. This code section is most often interpreted strictly as it relates to "*minor*" children, it can, however, extend to children who are older than 19, who have special needs, or where there are special and other circumstances.

> Family Code § 3901 defines a minor child as follows: any "unmarried child who is under the age of 18 years, a full time high school student, who is not self-supporting, until the child completes the 12th grade or attains the age of 19 years, whichever occurs first."

Child support is broadly defined as monetary contributions made by one parent to the other parent. The parent paying support is, in most cases, referred to as the "*non-custodial*" parent, who is paying support to the "*custodial*" parent. The person paying support may also be referred to as the "*obligor*," while the person receiving support would be called the "*obligee*."

The Family Code does not allow a parent to ignore the obligation to support the minor child, even though the other parent has adequate income and means to support the child. Family Code § 4000 provides "If a parent has the duty to provide for the support of the child and willfully fails to so provide, the other parent, or the child's guardian ad litem, may bring an action against the parent to enforce the duty." Thus, both parents have a reciprocal responsibility of support which **cannot** be relinquished, except by a **complete** termination of the "statutory duty" to support and/or parental rights (such as adoption) through the court system.

Family Code § 4001 states: "In a proceeding where there is at issue the support of a minor child, or a child for whom support is authorized under section 3901 or 3910, the court may order either or both parents to pay an amount necessary for the support of the child." The definition of a child, however, may be broadened at the court's discretion. As set forth in Family Code § 3910: "The father and mother have an equal responsibility to maintain, to the extent of their ability, a child of whatever age, who is incapacitated from earning a living and without sufficient means." This means that although a child has passed the age of "minority" **both** parents have an obligation to support a child who cannot support him or herself. However, this statute is interpreted very strictly. Support does not extend to an adult child who is capable of working and does not. This interpretation **does** extend to an adult child, who is still living at home with a parent, who has a specific mental or physical disability which renders him/her unable to support his/herself, or for whom government assistance may not be available. Likewise, a parent is not responsible, unless the parties have agreed otherwise, to pay for college of a child who is considered an adult, although the child may still be residing at home, or for the child's living expenses while enrolled in college. The parties may agree, in writing, to provide for the child(ren) while they are enrolled in college. However, these sums are **not** usually considered support.

The law also provides that, if a parent fails to provide the child with the "*necessities of life*" and a third party provides the child with these "*necessities of life*" the third party may recover reasonable value from the parent, plus interest. Necessities of life is defined as: food, clothing and shelter (and preferably health care). It is based upon those items for which Welfare would pay.

The law also requires that children continue to be covered on health insurance if the child is in school or being supported past the age of majority or in college, so this may need to be addressed. Typically, this may not be included in any initial orders but may be addressed in a future modification when the child is closer to the age of majority.

When a "third party" provides a child(ren) with the "necessities of life," Family Code § 3950 provides: "If a parent neglects to provide articles necessary for the parent's child who is under the charge of the parent, according to the circumstances of a parent, a third person may in good faith supply the necessities and recover their reasonable value from the parent." The duty to support does not extend to "abandonment" by a parent or parents. However, abandonment may be subjective and can only be determined by review of the circumstances or specific facts of each individual case.

The law also extends to a child who is in foster care, juvenile hall or other court-ordered care. In such cases, the parents are equally responsible for the costs related to the care of the child. The County will assess the costs of such care to the parents.

If the parent with whom the child(ren) resides, or alternatively if the child(ren) has been placed in the guardianship of a grandparent(s), and that person has applied for Welfare or other public assistance, that agency is able to request reimbursement from the non-supporting parent(s). Grandparents may also seek reimbursement for the support of the child(ren) from a parent, or both parents, when a parent is not contributing to the necessities of life for the child(ren).

Careful attention should be paid to Family Code § 3951 which states that: "(a) A parent is not bound to compensate the other parent, or a relative, for the voluntary support of the parent's child, or without an agreement for compensation, (b) compensate a stranger for the support of a child who has abandoned the parent without just cause ..." Thus it is important for persons who are providing care for a child, to do so under court order, or they may be unable to seek reimbursement from a non-supporting parent. A person providing care for a child may also seek legal remedies for reimbursement through the civil court, but only after being appointed as a Guardian Ad Litem.

History of Child Support

Historically, each court made its own decision regarding the amount of child support. The court would examine the needs of the child(ren); each party's earning capacity; and any other factors the court deemed relevant and which had a bearing on the child's standard of living. The court could consider the standards during marriage, as well as post separation.

The California legislature, in an attempt to close the gap between the support ordered by the courts and the amount paid by Welfare, enacted the *Agnos Child Support Standards Act of 1984* (previously Civil Code §§ 4720 et seq.). The *Agnos Act* established two levels of guidelines for determining support: 1) Minimum **mandatory** statewide standards with allowable mandatory add-ons and 2) Discretionary add-ons.

Mandatory add-ons include:

Hardship deductions

Child care costs

Reasonable uninsured health care costs for the child(ren)

Discretionary add-ons include:

Costs related to educational and/or special needs of the child(ren)

Travel expenses for visitation

The Federal Government established *The Family Support Act of 1988* 42 U.S.C. §667(a) (b) 2. The "Act" required the states to establish uniform guidelines, within the state, if they wanted to continue to receive federal welfare monies.

The California Legislature enacted California Rule of Court 1274, effective March 1, 1991. This "Rule" established uniform statewide guidelines and eliminated the Courts' previous discretion in child support orders. This "Rule" is considered to be a continuation of the concepts of *The Agnos Act* and was in compliance with The Family Support Act of 1988. Technically, Rule 1274 repealed and replaced *The Agnos Act*. In July 1992, permanent, mandatory child support guidelines were established for use throughout California.

Upon the revisions of the California Codes and the establishing of the separate *Family Code* in July 1994, the guidelines were further refined. Family Code § 4053 sets forth the *Mandatory Adherence Principles*.

The minimum standards, or "*guideline*" support as it has come to be known, and upon which *The Agnos Act* and subsequent legislation and code was based, affect child support in two ways. First, the minimum standards were what Welfare (Aid for Dependent Children) would pay a custodial parent for the care, food, shelter and clothing, of the minor child(ren). Second, a person receiving welfare or AFDC must release their right to receive child support from the non-custodial parent. The legislature said that if the government (state, county or other agency) is making the child support payment on behalf of the non-custodial parent, the government is entitled to reimbursement. The government is essentially fulfilling the role as caretaker and has a right to recover the sums that would have been the responsibility of the non-custodial parent. Therefore, **at least** the amount of reimbursement is the minimum amount that can be ordered.

By establishing this guideline (minimum standard) all courts within the State of California utilized the AFDC standard as the minimum amount to be awarded for the necessities of life. Thus, most courts are in compliance with "*The Act*" and are consistent for most of the State.

The court, however, still has discretion to consider other factors, called "add-ons" in ordering child support. This holds true except where AFDC is already established, then the court must order reimbursement at that sum. The discretionary factors referenced previously will be discussed in greater detail later in this chapter.

California courts must have jurisdiction over the issue of child support. The Superior Court system has subject matter jurisdiction whether or not there is a valid marriage. The jurisdiction extends to: dissolutions, legal separations, annulments, paternity, and proceedings for custody and support wherein the parties are married, but not seeking a resolution to other marital issues. It also holds jurisdiction over all future modifications, enforcement or orders, and/or other orders relative to the children (whether minors or adults) where the court has retained jurisdiction.

The California courts must also have personal jurisdiction over at least one of the parties. Since the personal rights of the obligor and obligee are affected, the affected person must either be a resident of California, have appeared in California, or have otherwise agreed to California having personal jurisdiction. If the obligor is a resident of California, Family Code § 3550 states that "*every* obligor resident of this state is required to adhere to the duty of support as defined in sections 3900, 3901, 3910, 4300, and 4400, regardless of the residence of obligee."

Current Child Support Calculations

With the enactment of the Family Code in January 1994, Civil Code § 4721 became Family Code §§ 4050, et seq. Article 2 of the Family Code is titled "Statewide Uniform Guidelines." This Article incorporates the legislative intent and goals for compliance with Federal Rules or "*The Act*." Family Code § 4053 very specifically sets forth the established guideline for the courts to use when calculating child support. Per Family Code § 4053, the mandatory adherence to principles, are as follows:

In implementing the statewide uniform guideline, the courts shall adhere to the following principles:

(a) A parent's first and principal obligation is to support his or her minor children according to the parent's circumstances and station in life.

(b) Both parents are mutually responsible for the support of their children.

(c) The guideline takes into account each parent's actual income and level of responsibility for the children.

(d) Each parent should pay for the support of the children according to his or her ability.

(e) The guideline seeks to place the interests of children as the state's top priority.

(f) Children should share in the standard of living of both parents. Child support may therefore appropriately improve the standard of living of the custodial household to improve the lives of the children.

(g) Child support orders in cases in which both parents have high levels of responsibility for the children should reflect the increased costs of raising the children in two homes and should minimize significant disparities in the children's living standards in two homes.

(h) The financial needs of the children should be met through private financial resources as much as possible.

(i) It is presumed that a parent having primary physical responsibility for the children contributes a significant portion of available resources for the support of the children.

(j) The guideline seeks to encourage fair and efficient settlements of conflicts between parents and seeks to minimize the need for litigation.

(k) The guideline is intended to be presumptively correct in all cases, and only under special circumstances should child support orders fall below the child support mandated by the guideline formula.

(l) Child support orders must ensure that children actually receive fair, timely, and sufficient support reflecting the state's high standard of living and high costs of raising children compared to other states.

Family Code § 4054 requires the Judicial Council to monitor the effectiveness and make periodic recommendations to the legislature regarding the above principles.

The legislature also created an algebraic formula to determine the minimum standard of child support. The formula below (which is for calculating support for one child) can be found at Family Code § 4055, and is as follows:

$$CS = K [HN-(H\%)(TN)]$$

The symbols in the above formula are below:

CS: Child Support

K: amount of both parents' income to be allocated for child support

HN: high earner's net monthly disposable income

H%: higher earner's approximate time of physical responsibility for the children

TN: the parties' total monthly net income

In the event there is more than one child for whom child support must be calculated, the formula result (CS) will be calculated by using a multiplier. Thus, if there are two children the multiplier is 1.6 (Example: $CS \times 1.6 =$ total support payable by the higher earner for two children). Multipliers for three to six children are as follows:

Three children:	2.0
Four children:	2.3
Five children:	2.5
Six children:	2.65

Multipliers for seven to ten children can be found in Family Code § 4055(b)(4).

These mathematical calculations are further complicated by variables in the parties' incomes. As defined in Family Code § 4055(b)(3), the "K factor" is the amount of **both parents' income to be allocated to child support**. The "K factor" must reflect the parents **net disposable** income which is further defined at FC§ 4058 and FC§ 4059. Generally, Courts use the IRS definitions of gross and net income in making these determinations. The IRS guidelines state that *gross income* is "income from all sources." *Net disposable income* is the gross income less allowable deductions, such as, state and federal taxes, union dues, mandatory retirement. The party may also be entitled to statutory **mandatory add-ons**, such as health insurance and work-related child care expenses (*Family Code § 4062*). Necessary job-related expenses may also be deductible.

Other variables may include the following: if either party is self-employed; if either party is receiving public assistance or other benefits such as TANF, GA, SSI, SSD, SDI, Unemployment, or Workers' Compensation; if either party is receiving spousal support, or pension/retirement funds; and/or if either party has a hardship deduction. (Note: TANF is Temporary Aid for Needy Families which replaced AFDC.) A **hardship deduction** is defined (*Family Code §§ 4070 and 4071*) as:

1) Extraordinary health expenses for which the parent is financially responsible, and uninsured catastrophic losses.

2) The minimum basic living expenses of either parent's natural or adopted children for whom the parent has an obligation to support from other marriages or relationships who reside with the parent.

The court requires the party requesting a hardship deduction to specify the period of time for the requested deduction, as well as written verification of the amount of the deduction and how it was calculated. For instance, if it is for a catastrophic loss, one must show bills or receipts; if it is for a child, the age of the child, or alternatively when the child will reach the age of majority. The court must document the reason that the party was allowed the hardship deduction.

The court has discretion to consider **discretionary add-ons** such as travel expenses for visitation and/or costs related to education or special needs of the child(ren). In most cases the discretionary add-ons will be allocated equally to both parents, unless the court finds good cause to do otherwise.

The "K factor" also requires that the amount of time spent with the children by the *high earner* (HN) be determined. This is referred to as *time share*. The time share must then be multiplied by the fraction set forth in FC§ 4055(b)(3). If the *high earner* has less than a 50% time share, the calculation is done one way. If the *high earner* has more than a 50% share, the calculation is done another way. (Time share will be discussed in greater detail in Chapter 4.)

Family Code § 4055(b)(7) sets forth the per child allocation in the event there is more than one child. For the sake of discussion let us say that there are three children and that guideline child support is $2,995 per month. The court allocates the largest portion of support to the youngest child, rather than allocating it equally. The rationale for this is that as the oldest child reaches majority and is no longer subject to child support, the parties will know the specific amount of reduction in child support, and that the younger children or youngest child, will receive the guideline amount of support, without the necessity of going back to court. (See Appendix 3E.)

There is often the question of the effect of a "new spouse" on the calculation of child support. Family Code § 4057.5 addresses this issue, as follows:

(a)(1) The income of the obligor parent's subsequent spouse or nonmarital partner shall not be considered when determining or modifying child support, except in an extraordinary case where excluding that income would lead to extreme and severe hardship to any child subject to the child support award, in which case the court shall also consider whether including that income would led to an extreme and severe hardship to any child supported by the obligor or by the obligor's subsequent spouse or nonmarital partner.

Extraordinary is defined as, "a parent who voluntarily or intentionally quits or reduces their income and thus relies on the [new] subsequent spouse or nonmarital partner's income."

In fact, you will note that when the *new spouse* income is included in the support calculation software, that the child support amount may actually be reduced. In most cases, this is a result of the change in tax filing status and tax bracket of the combined income of the obligor and the new spouse. (See Appendix 3F.)

One of the most effective ways to see how the various factors affect child support is to utilize the software programs: XSpouse™, SupporTax™, or Dissomaster™. As you can probably tell, based on the information above, calculating child support can be onerous and easily subject to error when done manually using the statutory formula in FC§ 4055 et seq. The various computer programs are customized spreadsheets which allow the user to estimate the amount of guideline child support. The various courts may dictate which of these programs are used. Should the parties find themselves in court to resolve the issue of child support, having this information prior to the hearing will give them some idea of the approximate amount of support that will be paid or received. Additionally, in an attempt to resolve the support issues without the necessity of going to court, these programs also allow attorneys to negotiate prior to the hearing.

Several Dissomaster™ printouts utilizing the case scenario you are using in the class are included for your reference. You will be able to compare the amount of guideline support based on the information which has been entered into the program even if you do not have access to either Dissomaster™ or XSpouse™. (Appendix 3G.) These "scenarios" also deal with support where there is a spousal support order and where there is none.

The Legislature directed the court to approve child support orders if the orders complied with and contained the following language (Family Code § 4065):

(1) They are fully informed of their rights concerning child support.

(2) The order is being agreed to without coercion or duress.

(3) The agreement is in the best interest of the children involved.

(4) The needs of the children will be adequately met by the stipulated amount.

(5) The right to support has not been assigned to the county pursuant to Section 11147 of the Welfare and Institutions Code and no public assistance application is pending.

The above language **must** appear, in its entirety, in any stipulated and/or agreed orders made, as well as the Judgment (at the conclusions of the matter) with regard to child support. You will note as you begin completing forms that deal with child support orders, that this language is also included on the Judicial Council forms. If you prepare any Stipulations and/or Orders in pleading format, be sure to include the above language in its entirety.

Standard of Living

One might assume that since California has "guideline" child support standards, that would be all the support a parent will have to pay. However, the court has broad discretion to determine the parent's, and thus the child's, standard of living when making an award **above** the minimum guidelines. The guideline is simply that—a guideline and the minimum standard for the child's food, shelter and clothing. Case law has clearly established that a parent must provide more than just the necessities of life, if the parent can afford more, and that children are entitled to the same standard of living as that of their parent and/or parents. The courts have a policy of making sure that a child enjoys any "good fortune" of their parent(s). By the same token, a parent who is deliberately reducing income or refuses to work though able to do so, will find the court unlikely to order a lower amount of support. For instance, if a licensed physician has chosen to work at a fast food restaurant in order to reduce support based on the "**ability to pay**" (or actual earnings) he or she will be ordered by the court to pay child support based on his/her "**ability to earn**."

Other Statutes Affecting Child Support

In addition to the guideline child support, the court has the ability to make other orders per California statutes.

Health Insurance

As defined by Family Code § 3750, health insurance includes all of the following:

(a) Vision care and dental coverage whether the vision care or dental coverage is part of an existing health insurance coverage or is issued as a separate policy or plan.

(b) Provision for the delivery of health care services by a fee for service, health maintenance organization, preferred provider organization, or any other type of health care delivery system under which medical services could be provided to a dependent child of an absent parent.

Family Code § 3751 mandates health insurance coverage for a supported child, as follows:

(a)(1) Support orders issued or modified pursuant to this chapter shall include a provision requiring the child support obligor to keep the agency designated under Title IV-D of the Social Security Act (42 U.S.C. Sec. 651, et seq.) informed of whether the obligor has health insurance coverage at a reasonable cost and, if so, the health insurance policy information.

(2) The court shall require that health insurance coverage for a supported child shall be maintained by either or both parents if that insurance is available at no cost or at a reasonable cost to the parent. Health insurance coverage shall be rebuttably presumed to be reasonable in cost if the cost to the responsible parent providing medical support does not exceed 5 percent of his or her gross income. (See additional language for clarification of income.)

(b) If the court determines that health insurance coverage is not available at no or reasonable cost, the court's order for support shall contain a provision that specifies that health insurance coverage shall be obtained if it becomes available at no or reasonable costs. Upon health insurance coverage at no or reasonable cost becoming available to a parent, the parent shall apply for that coverage.

Sections 3760 to 3772 of the Family Code provide that health insurance can be maintained and/or secured without the cooperation of the employee parent. All child support orders must contain provisions for health care coverage based on the above code sections. A *Notice of Rights and Responsibilities—Health Care Costs and Reimbursement Procedures and Information Sheet on Changing a Child Support Order* (form FL-192) **must** be attached to all Agreements, Stipulations, Judgments and most Orders processed through the court. In the event that the employee parent decides to reduce expenses and remove the children from his or her health insurance coverage, or the employee parent refuses to enroll, secure, or pay for the coverage, the court provides for a procedure to obtain a *Health Insurance Coverage Assignment Order*. Upon receipt of the "Order," within ten (10) days of receipt, the employer must enroll the child(ren) in the plan in which the employee parent is enrolled, or if not enrolled, any plan available. The premium will then be deducted from the obligor's pay check. If the employer fails to comply with the Order, Family Code § 3768 provides the mechanism for enforcement.

Deferred Sale of Family Home

The court has the discretion to provide child support "in kind" rather than "in cash." The mechanism most often used in this instance is referred to as the *Deferred Sale of Home Order*, which is often called the *"Duke Order."*

In re Marriage of Duke (1980) 101 CA3d 152, 161 CR. 444. The Court established specific circumstances compelling additional awards of child support and establishing specific circumstances as follows: "Where adverse economic, emotional and social impacts on minor children and the custodial parent which would result from an immediate loss of a long-established family home are not out-weighed by economic detriment to the non-custodial party, the court shall, upon request, reserve jurisdiction and defer sale on appropriate conditions." The *Duke* court failed to specify any standards, on which future cases may rely, other than those considered in the instant case. However, the *Duke* court did **require** that future courts reserve jurisdiction, when requested by the custodial parent.

Two cases prior to *Duke* did establish and define the delayed sale as an alternative to child support, when it was more feasible than selling and/or awarding the house to one parent. They were: *In re Marriage of Bozeman* (1973) 31 CA3d 372, 107 CR. 232 and *In re Marriage of Herrmann* (1978) 84 CA3d. 361, 148 CR 550.

The *Duke Orders* were incorporated in the Civil Code at Section 4800.7 in 1985 and were then converted to Family Code §§ 3800 to 3810. This statute established the Deferred Sale of the Family Home Order and required the Court, upon the request of a party, to determine whether it is economically feasible to delay the sale of the family home as an additional component of child support. The definition of "Deferred Sale of Home Order" found in Family Code § 3800(b) is as follows:

(b) "Deferred Sale of Home Order" means an order that temporarily delays the sale and awards the temporary exclusive use and possession of the family home to the custodial parent of a minor child or child for whom support is authorized under Sections 3900 and 3901 or under Section 3910 whether or not the custodial parent has sole or joint custody in order to minimize the adverse impact of dissolution of marriage or legal separation of the parties on the welfare of the child.

The *Duke Order* was based on the following conditions and facts: The party's most significant asset was the family residence. At the time of this case, it was common for people to stay in a home for 15 to 20 years and thus acquire significant equity in the property. Upon separation, if the custodial parent is the one staying in the home, they are most often the "supported spouse" or what is referred to in *Duke* as the "*in spouse.*" The court has found that it may be difficult for the *in spouse* to find comparable housing at a reasonable cost—either a rental or to purchase; particularly, if the current mortgage payment is low. Historically, the courts, counselors and the child(ren) have preferred to maintain the status quo where the children are concerned. By remaining in the family home, the children will remain in their familiar neighborhood, attend the same schools and have the same friends. Children who are experiencing their parents' dissolution of marriage are already having difficulty and to "transport then to an entirely new environment" is considered by many to **not** be in their best interests.

In cases where the "*out spouse*" is able to cash out the *in spouse*, or when there are enough community assets for one party to take an asset of equal value (to be discussed further in Chapter Seven) then this is a non-issue. However, if the *in spouse* can continue paying the mortgage, insurance, property taxes, and maintain the property, the court may determine that it is in the best interests of the parties as well as the children to delay the sale of the home as long as the children are minors and remain in the home. While this may be a great situation for the *in spouse*, the *out spouse* may find it a less than desirable situation. A *Duke Order* means that the parties have unfinished business which must be resolved when the children reach majority. The *out spouse*'s ability to purchase other property of equal value or at a reasonable cost, as well as tax considerations, may be affected. In the event the *in spouse* fails to make the mortgage, insurance or property tax payments, or fails to maintain the property causing it to deteriorate, or otherwise affect the equity in the home, the *out spouse*'s credit and/or future fair market value of the property may be affected. Often the *in spouse* will be unable to refinance the property in his or her own name, leaving the name of the *out spouse* on the mortgage. Should the *in spouse* fail to make the payments, the mortgage company may come to the *out spouse* for payment. Thus the *out spouse*, who had agreed to a waiver of child support in lieu of the future interest in the family home, may be responsible for the mortgage payments in order to protect his/her credit and to keep the property from going into foreclosure. If the property should go into foreclosure, both parties can lose the equity they had in the property.

The Court must carefully weigh current and future factors which could affect the property, including but not limited to each party's ability to pay. Therefore, the court has great discretion over making *Duke Orders*. In the event the situation changes, the court also has the ability to rescind the Order. In that case, the *out spouse* will usually file for a post-judgment modification hearing (see Chapter 10) asking the court to require that the property be sold, the proceeds split, and that child support be commenced.

The Court also has the ability to order, or the parties may agree, that an insurance policy or annuity be maintained or established by the supporting parent. The maintenance of said policy or annuity will assure that in the event the supporting parent dies before the children reach the age of majority, the child's needs will be met through said policy. Although the parties may agree to the concept of having the policy or annuity, they may often disagree as to the appropriate person to be the beneficiary of the policy/

annuity. In most cases, if the minor children are named as the beneficiary(ies), upon the death of the parent, a guardian ad litem will have to be established for the children and the account set up as a custodial account through the court system. This can add a degree of difficulty through the court system as well as in the ability to obtain needed funds for the children. However, if the parties can agree that the surviving parent, or a third party (for example, aunt, uncle, grandparent, or god-parent) can be named as beneficiary of the policy or annuity, then that person will have more control of the maintenance of the funds and the ability to use them for the needs of the children.

Child Care

As previously indicated, work-related child care costs may be included as a "mandatory add-on." Likewise, work-related child care is considered to be payable equally by both parents. A child support order will often include language stating that each parent "shall pay one-half" of all work-related child care. It is up to the discretion of the court and/or the agreement of the parties, whether the child care should be payable as child support.

For instance, if the non-custodial parent is ordered to pay **all** work-related day care, the court may reduce the amount of child support the parent is paying to the custodial spouse. Or, alternatively, the court may increase the amount of support as it may be deductible from that person's taxes or may being deducted as a pre-tax employee benefit. These options should be discussed between the parties, and their attorneys and tax preparer(s).

Suffice it to say, every Order should address the issue of how work-related child care expenses are to be paid.

Family Support

Family Support is a concept which was created for tax purposes. Family Support includes a combination of Spousal Support and Child Support. While Spousal Support is included in a person's taxes, Child Support is not. The courts devised the family support concept to generate additional "income" for support. This is a very complex, tax driven, means of calculating support. It should be left to attorneys and tax professionals, as it can create problems and issues, that if not handled properly, can ultimately cost the person paying family support more money in taxes. Orders for family support should carefully detail how the support is to be allocated. (Spousal and child support amounts otherwise there could be negative and costly tax consequences incurred.)

Stepparent Obligation of Support

There is no direct responsibility for a stepparent to provide support to a child. In fact, the Family Code provides a right of reimbursement to the stepparent, against the natural parent, in the event community property is used to satisfy a child support obligation that was ordered prior to the marriage. A continuing child support order from a previous marriage is treated as a pre-marital debt. If the parent who is paying the support remarries, then that party's portion of the community property acquired with the new spouse may be subject to collection for existing (or non-payment of) child support. In that instance it may "appear" as though the stepparent is liable for support of the stepchild.

If a stepparent has legally adopted a child, the parental rights of the natural parent have been terminated (this will be discussed in more detail in Chapter Eleven, "Adoption"), only then does the stepparent have an obligation to support the child should the parties dissolve their marriage. This is because the stepparent is deemed the parent of the child and has accepted the obligation to support as part of the adoption this is always specifically stated in the adoption decree.

The information provided in this chapter is just an overview of the way the courts calculate child support. There are many more variables which will affect guideline child support. If you work in a family law firm, you will become more proficient in learning the tax implications, as well as how the guidelines can vary from county to county.

The California Department of Child Support Services (CDCSS) provides a child support calculator available on-line at: www.childsup.ca.gov/Resources. This site also provides great information about child support and an individual may also apply to the California CDCSS to assist in collecting support through this website. While these calculations may be different than what the Court will ultimately order it will assist a *pro se* individual, as well as the student, with general information and approximate guideline support based on the information entered.

Tax Exemptions and Considerations

The Internal Revenue Code states that federal child tax credit may be claimed **only** by the parent who is entitled to take a dependency exemption for the child for the same tax year. *IRC§ 24*. Specifically, the parent with *physical custody* for the "greater portion of the tax year" is entitled to claim the child as a dependent (exemption). *IRC § 152(c)(1)*. However, the parties may agree, in writing, that the *non-custodial* parent may make the exemption. The *custodial* parent will need to sign a declaration stating that he or she will not claim the child as a dependent. *IRC§ 152(c)(2)*. This declaration (IRS form 8332) will have to be completed for each year that it applies.

California law conforms with the IRS and federal law in this respect. However, when the parents share *joint physical custody* a parent must be specified as to which parent will claim the dependent and/or who will sign the declaration releasing the dependency exemption. This will avoid issues both with the IRS and between the parties.

It is also important to consider who will most likely benefit from the exemption. A party who makes very little income may not benefit, while the higher earner may have the greater benefit, thus creating more *disposable* income to pay child support. Conversely, an extremely high earner may not benefit, as federal law has eliminated dependency exemptions for some taxpayers in high income brackets. *IRC§ 151(c)(3)*. The attorney and a tax consultant should work together to determine the tax benefits or ramifications of the dependency exemption(s). In some instances, if there are two children and the parties have similar incomes, they may agree to each claim a child as a dependency exemption.

A child may also be receiving Social Security due to the death of a parent. That "income" must also be considered.

Forms Associated with Topic

Notice and Acknowledgment of Receipt (FL-117)

Proof of Service by Mail (FL-335)

Motions (special appearance) w/ Supporting Declaration, Declaration, and Points & Authorities (FL-301) and (FL-310)

Response with Proof of Service (FL-120 and FL-335)

(See examples of some forms on the following pages)

Key Terms

- Consolidation of Cases
- General Appearance
- Special Appearance
- Default
- Points and Authorities
- Notice of Motion
- Request for Order
- Child Support
- Family Support
- Agnos Act
- Mandatory Adherence to Principles
- Mandatory Add-Ons
- Discretionary Add-Ons
- *Duke Order*
- Deferred Sale of Family Home Order
- Minor Child
- Rule 1274
- Guideline Child Support
- Gross v. Net Income
- Wage Assignment
- Necessities of Life
- Custodial Parent
- Non-Custodial Parent

Notice and Acknowledgment of Receipt

FL-117

ATTORNEY OR PARTY WITHOUT ATTORNEY (Name, State Bar number, and address):　SBN **********	FOR COURT USE ONLY
JOAN CARE-ACTOR LAW OFFICES OF JOAN CARE-ACTOR 75000 WHY ME LANE, SACRAMENTO, CA 95826 　TELEPHONE NO.: 916-555-1234　　FAX NO. (Optional): 916-555-1233 E-MAIL ADDRESS (Optional): joan@care-actorlaw.com 　ATTORNEY FOR (Name): SANDIE SHORES, Petitioner	To keep other people from seeing what you entered on your form, please press the Clear This Form button at the end of the form when finished.

SUPERIOR COURT OF CALIFORNIA, COUNTY OF SACRAMENTO
STREET ADDRESS: 3341 POWER INN ROAD
MAILING ADDRESS: 3341 POWER INN ROAD
CITY AND ZIP CODE: SACRAMENTO, CA 95826
BRANCH NAME: FAMILY LAW DIVISION

PETITIONER: SANDIE SHORES
RESPONDENT: ROCKY SHORES
OTHER PARENT/PARTY:

NOTICE AND ACKNOWLEDGMENT OF RECEIPT	CASE NUMBER: 14FLXXXXXXX

To (name of individual being served): ROCKY SHORES

NOTICE

The documents identified below are being served on you by mail with this acknowledgment form. You must personally sign, or a person authorized by you must sign, this form to acknowledge receipt of the documents.

If the documents described below include a summons and you fail to complete and return this acknowledgment form to the sender within 20 days of the date of mailing, you will be liable for the reasonable expenses incurred after that date in serving you or attempting to serve you with these documents by any other methods permitted by law. If you return this form to the sender, service of a summons is deemed complete on the date you sign the acknowledgment of receipt below. This is **not** an answer to the action. If you do not agree with what is being requested, you must submit a completed *Response* form to the court within 30 calendar days.

Date of mailing: XX/XX/2014

SUSIE Q. DILIGENT, PARALEGAL
　　　(TYPE OR PRINT NAME)　　　　　　　　　　　▶
　　　　　　　　　(SIGNATURE OF SENDER—MUST NOT BE A PARTY IN THIS CASE
　　　　　　　　　AND MUST BE 18 YEARS OR OLDER)

ACKNOWLEDGMENT OF RECEIPT
(To be completed by sender before mailing)

I agree I received the following:

a. [✔] Family Law: *Petition-Marriage* (form FL-100), *Summons* (form FL-110), and blank *Response-Marriage* (form FL-120)

b. [ ] Family Law—Domestic Partnership: *Petition—Domestic Partnership/Marriage* (form FL-103), *Summons* (form FL-110), and blank *Response—Domestic Partnership/Marriage* (form FL-123)

c. [ ] Uniform Parentage: *Petition to Establish Parental Relationship* (form FL-200), *Summons* (form FL-210), and blank *Response to Petition to Establish Parental Relationship* (form FL-220)

d. [ ] Custody and Support: *Petition for Custody and Support of Minor Children* (form FL-260), *Summons* (form FL-210), and blank *Response to Petition for Custody and Support of Minor Children* (form FL-270)

e. [✔]
(1) [ ] Completed and blank *Declaration Under Uniform Child Custody Jurisdiction and Enforcement Act (UCCJEA)* (form FL-105)
(2) [✔] Completed and blank *Declaration of Disclosure* (form FL-140)
(3) [ ] Completed and blank *Schedule of Assets and Debts* (form FL-142)
(4) [✔] Completed and blank *Income and Expense Declaration* (form FL-150)
(5) [ ] Completed and blank *Financial Statement (Simplified)* (form FL-155)
(6) [ ] *Request for Order* (form FL-300) and blank *Responsive Declaration to Request for Order* (form FL-320)
(7) [ ] Other (specify):

(To be completed by recipient)
Date this acknowledgment is signed: _____

ROCKY SHORES
　　(TYPE OR PRINT NAME)　　　　　　　　　▶
　　　　　　　　　(SIGNATURE OF PERSON ACKNOWLEDGING RECEIPT)

Page 1 of 1

Form Approved for Optional Use Judicial Council of California FL-117 [Rev. July 1, 2013]	**NOTICE AND ACKNOWLEDGMENT OF RECEIPT** (Family Law)	Code of Civil Procedure, §§ 415.30, 417.10 www.courts.ca.gov

For your protection and privacy, please press the Clear This Form button after you have printed the form.

Save This Form　　Print This Form　　Clear This Form

Proof of Service of Summons

FL-115

ATTORNEY OR PARTY WITHOUT ATTORNEY (Name, State Bar number, and address): JOAN CARE-ACTOR, SBN ******* Care-Actor Law Firm 75000 Why Me Lane, Sacramento, CA 95826 TELEPHONE NO.: 916-555-1234 FAX NO. (Optional): 916-555-1233 E-MAIL ADDRESS (Optional): joan@care-actorlaw.com ATTORNEY FOR (Name): SANDIE SHORES, Petitoner	FOR COURT USE ONLY To keep other people from seeing what you entered on your form, please press the Clear This Form button at the end of the form when finished.

SUPERIOR COURT OF CALIFORNIA, COUNTY OF SACRAMENTO
STREET ADDRESS: 3341 Power Inn Road
MAILING ADDRESS: 3341 Power Inn Road
CITY AND ZIP CODE: Sacramento, CA 95826
BRANCH NAME: Family Law Division

PETITIONER: SANDIE SHORES

RESPONDENT: ROCKY SHORES

PROOF OF SERVICE OF SUMMONS	CASE NUMBER: 14FLXXXXXXX

1. At the time of service I was at least 18 years of age and not a party to this action. **I served the respondent with copies of:**
   a. [✔] Family Law—Marriage: *Petition—Marriage* (form FL-100), *Summons* (form FL-110), and blank *Response—Marriage* (form FL-120)

   –or–

   b. [ ] Family Law—Domestic Partnership: *Petition—Domestic Partnership* (form FL-103), *Summons* (form FL-110), and blank *Response—Domestic Partnership* (form FL-123)

   –or–

   c. [ ] Uniform Parentage: *Petition to Establish Parental Relationship* (form FL-200), *Summons* (form FL-210), and blank *Response to Petition to Establish Parental Relationship* (form FL-220)

   –or–

   d. [ ] Custody and Support: *Petition for Custody and Support of Minor Children* (form FL-260), *Summons* (form FL-210), and blank *Response to Petition for Custody and Support of Minor Children* (form FL-270)

   and

   e. [✔] (1) [✔] Completed and blank *Declaration Under Uniform Child Custody Jurisdiction and Enforcement Act* (form FL-105)

   (2) [✔] Completed and blank *Declaration of Disclosure* (form FL-140)

   (3) [✔] Completed and blank *Schedule of Assets and Debts* (form FL-142)

   (4) [✔] Completed and blank *Income and Expense Declaration* (form FL-150)

   (5) [ ] Completed and blank *Financial Statement (Simplified)* (form FL-155)

   (6) [ ] Completed and blank *Property Declaration* (form FL-160)

   (7) [ ] *Request for Order* (form FL-300), and blank *Responsive Declaration to Request for Order* (form FL-320)

   (8) [ ] Other (specify):

2. Address where respondent was served:
   10000 Q STREET, SACRAMENTO, CA 95816

3. I served the respondent by the following means (check proper box):
   a. [✔] **Personal service.** I personally delivered the copies to the respondent (Code Civ. Proc., § 415.10) on (date): XX/XX/2014   at (time): 11:49 AM
   b. [ ] **Substituted service.** I left the copies with or in the presence of (name):
   who is (specify title or relationship to respondent):

   (1) [ ] **(Business)** a person at least 18 years of age who was apparently in charge at the office or usual place of business of the respondent. I informed him or her of the general nature of the papers.
   (2) [ ] **(Home)** a competent member of the household (at least 18 years of age) at the home of the respondent. I informed him or her of the general nature of the papers.

Page 1 of 2

PROOF OF SERVICE OF SUMMONS
(Family Law—Uniform Parentage—Custody and Support)

Code of Civil Procedure, § 417.10
www.courts.ca.gov

Proof of Service of Summons

PETITIONER: SANDIE SHORES	CASE NUMBER:
RESPONDENT: ROCKY SHORES	14FLXXXXXXX

3. b. *(cont.)* on *(date):*   at *(time):*

I thereafter mailed additional copies (by first class, postage prepaid) to the respondent at the place where the copies were left (Code Civ. Proc., § 415.20b) on *(date):*

A **declaration of diligence** is attached, stating the actions taken to first attempt personal service.

c. ☐ **Mail and acknowledgment service.** I mailed the copies to the respondent, addressed as shown in item 2, by first-class mail, postage prepaid, on *(date):*   from *(city):*

(1) ☐ with two copies of the *Notice and Acknowledgment of Receipt* (form FL-117) and a postage-paid return envelope addressed to me. **(Attach completed *Notice and Acknowledgment of Receipt* (form FL-117).)** (Code Civ. Proc., § 415.30.)

(2) ☐ to an address outside California (by registered or certified mail with return receipt requested). **(Attach signed return receipt or other evidence of actual delivery to the respondent.)** (Code Civ. Proc., § 415.40.)

d. ☐ **Other** *(specify code section):*

☐ Continued on Attachment 3d.

4. The "NOTICE TO THE PERSON SERVED" on the *Summons* was completed as follows (Code Civ. Proc., §§ 412.30, 415.10, 474):

a. ☑ As an individual **or**

b. ☐ On behalf of respondent who is a

(1) ☐ minor. (Code Civ. Proc., § 416.60.)

(2) ☐ ward or conservatee. (Code Civ. Proc., § 416.70.)

(3) ☐ other *(specify):*

5. **Person who served papers**

Name: JOHNNY PROCESS SERVER

Address: 800 GETTEM LANE, SACRAMENTO, CA 95814

Telephone number: 916-XXX-XXXX

This person is

a. ☐ exempt from registration under Business and Professions Code section 22350(b).

b. ☑ not a registered California process server.

c. ☐ a registered California process server: ☐ an employee or ☐ an independent contractor

(1) Registration no.:

(2) County:

d. **The fee** for service was *(specify):* $ 35.00

6. ☑ **I declare** under penalty of perjury under the laws of the State of California that the foregoing is true and correct.

—or—

7. ☐ **I am a California sheriff, marshal, or constable,** and I certify that the foregoing is true and correct.

Date: XX/XX/2014

JOHNNY PROCESS SERVER   ▶
_____   _____
(NAME OF PERSON WHO SERVED PAPERS)   (SIGNATURE OF PERSON WHO SERVED PAPERS)

FL-115 [Rev. July 1, 2012]   **PROOF OF SERVICE OF SUMMONS**   Page 2 of 2
                            (Family Law—Uniform Parentage—Custody and Support)

For your protection and privacy, please press the Clear This Form button after you have printed the form. | Save This Form | Print This Form | Clear This Form |

Notice of Motion

		FL-301

ATTORNEY OR PARTY WITHOUT ATTORNEY *(Name, State Bar number, and address):*

SAM E. SPACE, SBN **********
LAW OFFICES OF SPADE, PICKS & SHOVEL
99999 DEFENSE COURT
SACRAMENTO, CA 95826
TELEPHONE NO.: 916-555-9999   FAX NO. *(Optional):* 916-555-9998
E-MAIL ADDRESS *(Optional):* Sam@spadelawcorp.com
ATTORNEY FOR *(Name):* ROCKY SHORES, Respondent

To keep other people from seeing what you entered on your form, please press the Clear This Form button at the end of the form when finished.

SUPERIOR COURT OF CALIFORNIA, COUNTY OF SACRAMENTO
STREET ADDRESS: 3341 POWER INN ROAD
MAILING ADDRESS: 3341 POWER INN ROAD
CITY AND ZIP CODE: SACRAMENTO, CA 95826
BRANCH NAME: FAMILY LAW DIVISION

PETITIONER/PLAINTIFF: SANDY SHORES
RESPONDENT/DEFENDANT: ROCKY SHORES

NOTICE OF MOTION
- ☐ Child Custody
- ☐ Child Support
- ☐ Attorney Fees and Costs

MODIFICATION
- ☐ Child Custody
- ☐ Visitation
- ☐ Spousal Support

- ☐ Injunctive Order
- ☑ Other *(specify):*
  MOTION TO QUASH

CASE NUMBER:
14FLXXXXXX

1. TO *(name):* SANDIE SHORES & HER ATTORNEY OF RECORD

2. A hearing on this motion for the relief requested in the attached application will be held as follows:

   a. Date: Time: ☐ Dept.:   ☐ Rm.:

   b. Address of court ☑ same as noted above ☐ other *(specify):*

3. Supporting attachments:
   a. Completed *Application for Order and Supporting Declaration* (form FL-310) and a **blank** *Responsive Declaration* (form FL-320)
   b. ☐ Completed *Income and Expense Declaration* (form FL-150) and a **blank** *Income and Expense Declaration*
   c. ☐ Completed *Financial Statement (Simplified)* (form FL-155) and a **blank** *Financial Statement (Simplified)*
   d. ☐ Completed *Property Declaration* (form FL-160) and a **blank** *Property Declaration*
   e. ☑ Points and authorities
   f. ☑ Other *(specify):*
      SUPPORTING DELCARATION

Date:
SAM E. SPADE
_____   ▶   _____
(TYPE OR PRINT NAME)   (SIGNATURE)

ORDER

4. ☐ Time for ☐ service ☐ hearing   is shortened. Service must be on or before *(date):*

5. Any responsive declaration must be served on or before *(date):*

6. If child custody or visitation is an issue in this proceeding, *Family Code* section 3170 requires mediation before or concurrently with the hearing listed above. The parties are ordered to attend orientation and mandatory custody services as follows:

Date:
_____
JUDICIAL OFFICER

NOTICE: If you have children from this relationship, the court is required to order payment of child support based on the incomes of both parents. The amount of child support can be large. It normally continues until the child is 18. You should supply the court with information about your finances. Otherwise, the child support order will be based on the information supplied by the other parent.

You do not have to pay any fee to file declarations in response to this *Notice of Motion* (including a completed Income and Expense Declaration (form FL-150) or Financial Statement *(Simplified)* (form FL-155) that will show your finances). In the absence of an order shortening time, the original of the responsive declaration must be filed with the court and a copy served on the other party at least nine court days before the hearing date. Add five calendar days if you serve by mail within California. (See Code of Civil Procedure 1005 for other situations.) To determine court and calendar days, go to *www.courtinfo.ca.gov/selfhelp/courtcalendars/.*

Form Adopted for Mandatory Use
Judicial Council of California
FL-301 [Rev. January 1, 2007]

NOTICE OF MOTION

Page 1 of 2
Government Code, § 26826
www.courtinfo.ca.gov

American LegalNet, Inc.
www.FormsWorkflow.com

Notice of Motion

FL-301

PETITIONER/PLAINTIFF: SANDY SHORES	CASE NUMBER:
RESPONDENT/DEFENDANT: ROCKY SHORES	14FLXXXXXX

7. PROOF OF SERVICE BY MAIL

  a. I am at least age 18, **not a party to this action,** and am a resident or employed in the county where the mailing took place. My residence or business address is:

    WALTER SMITH-WESSON, LAW OFFICES OF SAM E. SPADE, 99999 DEFENSE COURT, SACRAMENTO, CA 95826

  b. I served copies of the following documents by enclosing them in a sealed envelope with postage fully prepaid, depositing them in the United States mail as follows:

    (1) Papers served:

      (a) *Notice of Motion* and a completed *Application for Order and Supporting Declaration* (form FL-310) **and** a blank *Responsive Declaration* (form FL-320)

      (b) ☐ Completed *Income and Expense Declaration* (form FL-150) **and** a blank *Income and Expense Declaration*

      (c) ☐ Completed *Financial Statement (Simplified)* (form FL-155) **and** a blank *Financial Statement (Simplified)*

      (d) ☐ Completed *Property Declaration* (form FL-160) **and** a blank *Property Declaration*

      (e) ☑ Points and authorities

      (f) Other *(specify):*

      RESPONDENT'S WRITTEN DECLARATION IN SUPPORT OF MOTION

    (2) Manner of service: MAIL

      (a) Date of deposit: XX/XX/2014

      (b) Place of deposit *(city and state):* SACRAMENTO, CA 95826

      (c) Addressed as follows:

      JOAN CARE-ACTOR

      LAW OFFICES OF JOAN CARE-ACTOR

      75000 WHY ME LANE

      SACRAMENTO, CA 95826

  c. I declare under penalty of perjury under the laws of the State of California that the foregoing is true and correct.

Date: XX/XX/2014

WALTER SMITH-WESSON

    (TYPE OR PRINT NAME)   ▶   (SIGNATURE OF DECLARANT)

Requests for Accommodations

Assistive listening systems, computer-assisted real-time captioning, or sign language interpreter services are available if you ask at least five days before the proceeding. Contact the clerk's office or go to *www.courtinfo.ca.gov/forms* for *Request for Accommodations by Persons With Disabilities and Response* (Form MC-410). (Civil Code, § 54.8.)

Print This Form	For your protection and privacy, please press the Clear This Form button after you have printed the form.	Clear This Form

Response — Marriage

<table>
<tr>
<td colspan="2">

ATTORNEY OR PARTY WITHOUT ATTORNEY *(Name, State Bar number, and address):*
SAM E. SPADE, SBN *********
LAW OFFICES OF SPADE, PICKS & HOVEL
99999 DEFENSE COURT
SACRAMENTO, CA 95826
TELEPHONE NO.: 916-555-9999   FAX NO. *(Optional):* 916-555-9998
E-MAIL ADDRESS *(Optional):* sam@spadelawcorp.com
ATTORNEY FOR *(Name):* ROCKY SHORES, Respondent

</td>
<td>

FL-120

To keep other people from seeing what you entered on your form, please press the Clear This Form button at the end of the form when finished.

</td>
</tr>
</table>

SUPERIOR COURT OF CALIFORNIA, COUNTY OF SACRAMENTO
STREET ADDRESS: 3341 POWER INN ROAD
MAILING ADDRESS: 3341 POWER INN ROAD
CITY AND ZIP CODE: SACRAMENTO, CA 95826
BRANCH NAME: FAMILY LAW DIVISION

MARRIAGE OF

PETITIONER: SHORES, SANDIE

RESPONDENT: SHORES, ROCKY

RESPONSE ☑ **and REQUEST FOR**	CASE NUMBER:
☑ **Dissolution of Marriage**	14FLXXXXXX
☐ **Legal Separation**	
☐ **Nullity of Marriage** ☐ AMENDED	

1. RESIDENCE (Dissolution only) ☐ Petitioner ☑ Respondent has been a resident of this state for at least six months and of this county for at least three months immediately preceding the filing of the *Petition for Dissolution of Marriage.*

2. STATISTICAL FACTS
   a. Date of marriage: June 20, 2003
   b. Date of separation: August 30, 2014
   c. Time from date of marriage to date of separation *(specify):*
   Years: 11   Months: 2

3. DECLARATION REGARDING MINOR CHILDREN *(include children of this relationship born prior to or during the marriage or adopted during the marriage):*
   a. ☐ There are no minor children.
   b. ☑ The minor children are:

Child's name	Birthdate	Age	Sex
EDDY WADE SHORES	5/1/05	9	MALE
SHELLY PEBBLE SHORES	10/15/09	4	FEMALE

   ☐ Continued on Attachment 3b.
   c. If there are minor children of the Petitioner and Respondent, a completed *Declaration Under Uniform Child Custody Jurisdiction and Enforcement Act (UCCJEA)* (form FL-105) must be attached.
   d. ☐ A completed voluntary declaration of paternity regarding minor children born to the Petitioner and Respondent prior to the marriage is attached.

4. SEPARATE PROPERTY
   Respondent requests that the assets and debts listed ☐ in *Property Declaration* (form FL-160) ☐ in Attachment 4
   ☑ below be confirmed as separate property.

Item	Confirm to
2001 Honda Motorcyle	Respondent
Real Property located on Wilderness Rd. Mokuleme Hill, CA	Respondent
All other property acquired prior to marriage, during marriage by gift, bequest, inheritance or after the date of separation	Respective Party

NOTICE: You may redact (black out) social security numbers from any written material filed with the court in this case other than a form used to collect child or spousal support.

Form Adopted for Mandatory Use
Judicial Council of California
FL-120 [Rev. January 1, 2005]

RESPONSE—MARRIAGE
(Family Law)

Page 1 of 2
Family Code, § 2020
www.courtinfo.ca.gov

Response — Marriage

MARRIAGE OF *(last name, first name of parties):*	CASE NUMBER:
SHORES, SANDIE SHORES, ROCKY	14FLXXXXXX

5. **DECLARATION REGARDING COMMUNITY AND QUASI-COMMUNITY ASSETS AND DEBTS AS CURRENTLY KNOWN**
    a. ☐   There are no such assets or debts subject to disposition by the court in this proceeding.
    b. ☑   All such assets and debts are listed ☐ in *Property Declaration* (form FL-160) ☐ in Attachment 5b.
          ☐   below *(specify):*

             Family home located at 11155 Turtle Dove Ct, Folsom w/debt; 2005 Dodge Caravan, 2010
             Dodge P/U w/debt; Husband's Retirement, Bank, Savings and Stock Accounts. Misc.
             household furniture, furnishings & appliances

6. ☐   **Respondent contends** that the parties were never legally married.
7. ☐   **Respondent denies** the grounds set forth in item 6 of the petition.
8. **Respondent requests**
    a. ☑   dissolution of the marriage based on   d. ☐   nullity of voidable marriage based on
        (1) ☑   irreconcilable differences. (Fam. Code, § 2310(a).)   (1) ☐   respondent's age at time of marriage.
        (2) ☐   incurable insanity. (Fam. Code, § 2310(b).)   (Fam. Code, § 2210(a).)
    b. ☐   legal separation of the parties based on   (2) ☐   prior existing marriage.
        (1) ☐   irreconcilable differences. (Fam. Code, § 2310(a).)   (Fam. Code, § 2210(b).)
        (2) ☐   incurable insanity. (Fam. Code, § 2310(b).)   (3) ☐   unsound mind. (Fam. Code, § 2210(c).)
    c. ☐   nullity of void marriage based on   (4) ☐   fraud. (Fam. Code, § 2210(d).)
        (1) ☐   incestuous marriage. (Fam. Code, § 2200.)   (5) ☐   force. (Fam. Code, § 2210(e).)
        (2) ☐   bigamous marriage. (Fam. Code, § 2201.)   (6) ☐   physical incapacity. (Fam. Code, § 2210(f).)

9. **Respondent requests** that the court grant the above relief and make injunctive (including restraining) and other orders as follows:

	Petitioner	Respondent	Joint	Other
a. Legal custody of children to	☐	☐	☑	☐
b. Physical custody of children to	☐	☐	☑	☐
c. Child visitation be granted to	☐	☐	☐	☐

        As requested in form: ☐ FL-311 ☐ FL-312 ☐ FL-341(C) ☐ FL-341(D) ☐ FL-341(E) ☐ Attachment 9c.
    d. ☐   Determination of parentage of any children born to the Petitioner and Respondent prior to the marriage.

	Petitioner	Respondent	
e. Attorney fees and costs payable by	☑	☑	

    f. ☐   Spousal support payable to (wage assignment will be issued)   ☐   ☐
    g. ☑   Terminate the court's jurisdiction (ability) to award spousal support to Petitioner.
    h. ☑   Property rights be determined.
    i. ☐   Respondent's former name be restored to *(specify):*
    j. ☐   Other *(specify):*

           ☐   Continued on Attachment 9j.

10. **Child support**– If there are minor children born to or adopted by the Petitioner and Respondent before or during this marriage, the court will make orders for the support of the children upon request and submission of financial forms by the requesting party. An earnings assignment may be issued without further notice. Any party required to pay support must pay interest on overdue amounts at the "legal" rate, which is currently 10 percent.

I declare under penalty of perjury under the laws of the State of California that the foregoing is true and correct.

Date:

__ROCKY SHORES_____   ▶   _____
          (TYPE OR PRINT NAME)   (SIGNATURE OF RESPONDENT)
Date:

_____   ▶   _____
          (TYPE OR PRINT NAME)   (SIGNATURE OF ATTORNEY FOR RESPONDENT)

The original response must be filed in the court with proof of service of a copy on Petitioner.

FL-120 [Rev. January 1, 2005]   **RESPONSE—MARRIAGE**   Page 2 of 2
                             (Family Law)

For your protection and privacy, please press the Clear This Form button after you have printed the form.		Save This Form	Print This Form	Clear This Form

UCCJEA

FL-105/GC-120

ATTORNEY OR PARTY WITHOUT ATTORNEY (Name, State Bar number, and address): SAM E. SPADE, SBN ******* LAW OFFICES OF SPADE, PICKS, & HOVEL 99999 DEFENSE COURT SACRAMENTO, CA 95826 TELEPHONE NO.: 916-555-9999 FAX NO. (Optional): 916-555-9998 E-MAIL ADDRESS (Optional): same@spadelawcorp.com ATTORNEY FOR (Name): ROKY SHORES	To keep other people from seeing what you entered on your form, please press the Clear This Form button at the end of the form when finished.

SUPERIOR COURT OF CALIFORNIA, COUNTY OF SACRAMENTO
STREET ADDRESS: 3341 POWER INN ROAD
MAILING ADDRESS: 3341 POWER INN ROAD
CITY AND ZIP CODE: SACRAMENTO, CA 95826
BRANCH NAME: FAMILY LAW DIVISION

(This section applies only to family law cases.) PETITIONER: SANDIE SHORES RESPONDENT: ROCKY SHORES OTHER PARTY:	

(This section applies only to guardianship cases.) GUARDIANSHIP OF (Name): Minor	CASE NUMBER: 14FLXXXXXX

DECLARATION UNDER UNIFORM CHILD CUSTODY JURISDICTION AND ENFORCEMENT ACT (UCCJEA)	

1. **I am a party** to this proceeding to determine custody of a child.

2. ☐ My present address and the present address of each child residing with me is confidential under Family Code section 3429 as I have indicated in item 3.

3. There are *(specify number):* 2 minor children who are subject to this proceeding, as follows:
   (Insert the information requested below. The residence information must be given for the last FIVE years.)

a. Child's name EDDY WADE SHORES		Place of birth POCATELLO, ID	Date of birth 5/1/05	Sex MALE
Period of residence 2006 to present	Address 11155 Turtle Dove Ct Folsom, CA ☐ Confidential		Person child lived with *(name and complete current address)* Rocky & Sandie Shores, 11155 Turtle Dove ☐ Confidential Folsom, CA	Relationship Parents
	Child's residence *(City, State)*		Person child lived with *(name and complete current address)*	
to				
	Child's residence *(City, State)*		Person child lived with *(name and complete current address)*	
to				
	Child's residence *(City, State)*		Person child lived with *(name and complete current address)*	
to				

b. Child's name SHELLY PEBBLES SHORES ☑ Residence information is the same as given above for child a. *(If NOT the same, provide the information below.)*		Place of birth CARMICHAEL, CA	Date of birth 10/15/09	Sex FEMALE
Period of residence to present	Address ☐ Confidential		Person child lived with *(name and complete current address)* ☐ Confidential	Relationship
	Child's residence *(City, State)*		Person child lived with *(name and complete current address)*	
to				
	Child's residence *(City, State)*		Person child lived with *(name and complete current address)*	
to				
	Child's residence *(City, State)*		Person child lived with *(name and complete current address)*	
to				

c. ☐ Additional residence information for a child listed in item a or b is continued on attachment 3c.

d. ☐ Additional children are listed on form *FL-105(A)/GC-120(A)*. *(Provide all requested information for additional children.)*

Page 1 of 2

Form Adopted for Mandatory Use Judicial Council of California FL-105/GC-120 [Rev. January 1, 2009]	**DECLARATION UNDER UNIFORM CHILD CUSTODY JURISDICTION AND ENFORCEMENT ACT (UCCJEA)**	Family Code, § 3400 et seq.; Probate Code, §§ 1510(f), 1512 www.courtinfo.ca.gov

UCCJEA

	FL-105/GC-120
SHORT TITLE: In Re Marriage of Shores	CASE NUMBER: 14FLXXXXXX

4. Do you have information about, or have you participated as a party or as a witness or in some other capacity in, another court case or custody or visitation proceeding, in California or elsewhere, concerning a child subject to this proceeding?

☐ Yes ☑ No *(If yes, attach a copy of the orders (if you have one) and provide the following information):*

Proceeding	Case number	Court *(name, state, location)*	Court order or judgment *(date)*	Name of each child	Your connection to the case	Case status
a. ☐ Family						
b. ☐ Guardianship						
c. ☐ Other						

Proceeding	Case Number	Court *(name, state, location)*
d. ☐ Juvenile Delinquency/ Juvenile Dependency		
e. ☐ Adoption		

5. ☐ One or more domestic violence restraining/protective orders are now in effect. *(Attach a copy of the orders if you have one and provide the following information):*

Court	County	State	Case number *(if known)*	Orders expire *(date)*
a. ☐ Criminal				
b. ☐ Family				
c. ☐ Juvenile Delinquency/ Juvenile Dependency				
d. ☐ Other				

6. Do you know of any person who is not a party to this proceeding who has physical custody or claims to have custody of or visitation rights with any child in this case? ☐ Yes ☑ No *(If yes, provide the following information):*

a. Name and address of person	b. Name and address of person	c. Name and address of person
☐ Has physical custody ☐ Claims custody rights ☐ Claims visitation rights	☐ Has physical custody ☐ Claims custody rights ☐ Claims visitation rights	☐ Has physical custody ☐ Claims custody rights ☐ Claims visitation rights
Name of each child	Name of each child	Name of each child

I declare under penalty of perjury under the laws of the State of California that the foregoing is true and correct.

Date:

ROCKY SHORES   ▶

_____
(TYPE OR PRINT NAME)

_____
(SIGNATURE OF DECLARANT)

7. ☐ Number of pages attached:_____

NOTICE TO DECLARANT: You have a continuing duty to inform this court if you obtain any information about a custody proceeding in a California court or any other court concerning a child subject to this proceeding.

FL-105/GC-120 [Rev. January 1, 2009]

DECLARATION UNDER UNIFORM CHILD CUSTODY JURISDICTION AND ENFORCEMENT ACT (UCCJEA)

Page 2 of 2

For your protection and privacy, please press the Clear This Form button after you have printed the form.

Save This Form   Print This Form   Clear This Form

Proof of Service by Mail

FL-335

ATTORNEY OR PARTY WITHOUT ATTORNEY *(Name, State Bar number, and address):*	FOR COURT USE ONLY
CLASS E. ATTORNEY, SBN ****** CLASS & ASSOCIATES 150000 FOREVERMORE CIRCLE SACRAMENTO, CA 95826 TELEPHONE NO.: 916-555-9876 FAX NO. *(Optional):* 916-555-9877 E-MAIL ADDRESS *(Optional):* class@classandassociates.com ATTORNEY FOR *(Name):* ROCKY SHORES, Respondent	To keep other people from seeing what you entered on your form, please press the Clear This Form button at the end of the form when finished.

SUPERIOR COURT OF CALIFORNIA, COUNTY OF SACRAMENTO
STREET ADDRESS: 3341 POWER INN ROAD
MAILING ADDRESS: 3341 POWER INN ROAD
CITY AND ZIP CODE: SACRAMENTO, CA 95826
BRANCH NAME: FAMILY LAW

PETITIONER/PLAINTIFF: SANDIE SHORES	CASE NUMBER: 14FLXXXXXXX
RESPONDENT/DEFENDANT: ROCKY SHORES	*(If applicable, provide):*
OTHER PARENT/PARTY:	HEARING DATE:
PROOF OF SERVICE BY MAIL	HEARING TIME: DEPT.:

NOTICE: To serve temporary restraining orders you must use personal service (see form FL-330).

1. I am at least 18 years of age, not a party to this action, and I am a resident of or employed in the county where the mailing took place.

2. My residence or business address is:
    LAW OFFICES OF CLASS & ASSOCIATES
    5000 FOREVERMORE CIRCLE, SACRAMENTO, CA 95826

3. I served a copy of the following documents *(specify):*
    RESPONSE , DECLARATION UNDER UNIFORM CHILD CUSTODY JURISTICTION ACT

    by enclosing them in an envelope AND
    a. ☐ **depositing** the sealed envelope with the United States Postal Service with the postage fully prepaid.
    b. ☑ **placing** the envelope for collection and mailing on the date and at the place shown in item 4 following our ordinary business practices. I am readily familiar with this business's practice for collecting and processing correspondence for mailing. On the same day that correspondence is placed for collection and mailing, it is deposited in the ordinary course of business with the United States Postal Service in a sealed envelope with postage fully prepaid.

4. The envelope was addressed and mailed as follows:
    a. Name of person served: JOAN CARE-ACTOR, CARE-ACTOR LAW OFFICE
    b. Address: 75000 WHY ME LANE, SACRAMENTO, CA 95826

    c. Date mailed: XX/XX/2014
    d. Place of mailing *(city and state):* SACRAMENTO, CA

5. ☐ I served a request to modify a child custody, visitation, or child support judgment or permanent order which included an address verification declaration. *(Declaration Regarding Address Verification—Postjudgment Request to Modify a Child Custody, Visitation, or Child Support Order* (form FL-334) may be used for this purpose.)

6. I declare under penalty of perjury under the laws of the State of California that the foregoing is true and correct.

Date:

SALLIE P. PARALEGAL
(TYPE OR PRINT NAME)   ▶   (SIGNATURE OF PERSON COMPLETING THIS FORM)

Page 1 of 1

Form Approved for Optional Use
Judicial Council of California
FL-335 [Rev. January 1, 2012]

PROOF OF SERVICE BY MAIL

Code of Civil Procedure, §§ 1013, 1013a
www.courts.ca.gov

For your protection and privacy, please press the Clear This Form button after you have printed the form.

Save This Form   Print This Form   Clear This Form

Notice and Acknowledgment of Receipt

FL-117

ATTORNEY OR PARTY WITHOUT ATTORNEY *(Name, State Bar number, and address)*:	FOR COURT USE ONLY
TELEPHONE NO.: FAX NO. *(Optional)*: E-MAIL ADDRESS *(Optional)*: ATTORNEY FOR *(Name)*:	To keep other people from seeing what you entered on your form, please press the Clear This Form button at the end of the form when finished.

SUPERIOR COURT OF CALIFORNIA, COUNTY OF
STREET ADDRESS:
MAILING ADDRESS:
CITY AND ZIP CODE:
BRANCH NAME:

PETITIONER:

RESPONDENT:

OTHER PARENT/PARTY:

NOTICE AND ACKNOWLEDGMENT OF RECEIPT	CASE NUMBER:

To *(name of individual being served)*: _____

NOTICE

The documents identified below are being served on you by mail with this acknowledgment form. You must personally sign, or a person authorized by you must sign, this form to acknowledge receipt of the documents.

If the documents described below include a summons and you fail to complete and return this acknowledgment form to the sender within 20 days of the date of mailing, you will be liable for the reasonable expenses incurred after that date in serving you or attempting to serve you with these documents by any other methods permitted by law. If you return this form to the sender, service of a summons is deemed complete on the date you sign the acknowledgment of receipt below. This is **not** an answer to the action. If you do not agree with what is being requested, you must submit a completed *Response* form to the court within 30 calendar days.

Date of mailing: _____

▶

_____   _____
(TYPE OR PRINT NAME)   (SIGNATURE OF SENDER—MUST NOT BE A PARTY IN THIS CASE
                                              AND MUST BE 18 YEARS OR OLDER)

ACKNOWLEDGMENT OF RECEIPT
(To be completed by sender before mailing)

I agree I received the following:

a. ☐ Family Law: *Petition-Marriage* (form FL-100), *Summons* (form FL-110), and blank *Response-Marriage* (form FL-120)

b. ☐ Family Law—Domestic Partnership: *Petition—Domestic Partnership/Marriage* (form FL-103), *Summons* (form FL-110), and blank *Response—Domestic Partnership/Marriage* (form FL-123)

c. ☐ Uniform Parentage: *Petition to Establish Parental Relationship* (form FL-200), *Summons* (form FL-210), and blank *Response to Petition to Establish Parental Relationship* (form FL-220)

d. ☐ Custody and Support: *Petition for Custody and Support of Minor Children* (form FL-260), *Summons* (form FL-210), and blank *Response to Petition for Custody and Support of Minor Children* (form FL-270)

e. ☐

(1) ☐ Completed and blank *Declaration Under Uniform Child Custody Jurisdiction and Enforcement Act (UCCJEA)* (form FL-105)

(2) ☐ Completed and blank *Declaration of Disclosure* (form FL-140)

(3) ☐ Completed and blank *Schedule of Assets and Debts* (form FL-142)

(4) ☐ Completed and blank *Income and Expense Declaration* (form FL-150)

(5) ☐ Completed and blank *Financial Statement (Simplified)* (form FL-155)

(6) ☐ *Request for Order* (form FL-300) and blank *Responsive Declaration to Request for Order* (form FL-320)

(7) ☐ Other *(specify)*:

(To be completed by recipient)
Date this acknowledgment is signed: _____

▶

_____   _____
(TYPE OR PRINT NAME)   (SIGNATURE OF PERSON ACKNOWLEDGING RECEIPT)

Page 1 of 1

Form Approved for Optional Use
Judicial Council of California
FL-117 [Rev. July 1, 2013]

NOTICE AND ACKNOWLEDGMENT OF RECEIPT
(Family Law)

Code of Civil Procedure, §§ 415.30, 417.10
www.courts.ca.gov

For your protection and privacy, please press the Clear This Form button after you have printed the form.   Save This Form   Print This Form   Clear This Form

Proof of Service of Summons

ATTORNEY OR PARTY WITHOUT ATTORNEY *(Name, State Bar number, and address)*:	FOR COURT USE ONLY
TELEPHONE NO.: FAX NO. *(Optional)*: E-MAIL ADDRESS *(Optional)*: ATTORNEY FOR *(Name)*:	To keep other people from seeing what you entered on your form, please press the Clear This Form button at the end of the form when finished.

SUPERIOR COURT OF CALIFORNIA, COUNTY OF
STREET ADDRESS:
MAILING ADDRESS:
CITY AND ZIP CODE:
BRANCH NAME:

PETITIONER:
RESPONDENT:

PROOF OF SERVICE OF SUMMONS	CASE NUMBER:

1. At the time of service I was at least 18 years of age and not a party to this action. **I served the respondent with copies of:**

   a. ☐ Family Law—Marriage: *Petition—Marriage* (form FL-100), *Summons* (form FL-110), and blank *Response—Marriage* (form FL-120)

   –or–

   b. ☐ Family Law—Domestic Partnership: *Petition—Domestic Partnership* (form FL-103), *Summons* (form FL-110), and blank *Response—Domestic Partnership* (form FL-123)

   –or–

   c. ☐ Uniform Parentage: *Petition to Establish Parental Relationship* (form FL-200), *Summons* (form FL-210), and blank *Response to Petition to Establish Parental Relationship* (form FL-220)

   –or–

   d. ☐ Custody and Support: *Petition for Custody and Support of Minor Children* (form FL-260), *Summons* (form FL-210), and blank *Response to Petition for Custody and Support of Minor Children* (form FL-270)

   and

   e. ☐ (1) ☐ Completed and blank *Declaration Under Uniform Child Custody Jurisdiction and Enforcement Act* (form FL-105)

       (2) ☐ Completed and blank *Declaration of Disclosure* (form FL-140)

       (3) ☐ Completed and blank *Schedule of Assets and Debts* (form FL-142)

       (4) ☐ Completed and blank *Income and Expense Declaration* (form FL-150)

       (5) ☐ Completed and blank *Financial Statement (Simplified)* (form FL-155)

       (6) ☐ Completed and blank *Property Declaration* (form FL-160)

       (7) ☐ *Request for Order* (form FL-300), and blank *Responsive Declaration to Request for Order* (form FL-320)

       (8) ☐ Other *(specify):*

2. Address where respondent was served:

3. I served the respondent by the following means *(check proper box):*

   a. ☐ **Personal service.** I personally delivered the copies to the respondent (Code Civ. Proc., § 415.10) on *(date):*   at *(time):*

   b. ☐ **Substituted service.** I left the copies with or in the presence of *(name):*
   who is *(specify title or relationship to respondent):*

       (1) ☐ **(Business)** a person at least 18 years of age who was apparently in charge at the office or usual place of business of the respondent. I informed him or her of the general nature of the papers.

       (2) ☐ **(Home)** a competent member of the household (at least 18 years of age) at the home of the respondent. I informed him or her of the general nature of the papers.

Page 1 of 2

PROOF OF SERVICE OF SUMMONS
(Family Law—Uniform Parentage—Custody and Support)

Proof of Service of Summons

PETITIONER:	CASE NUMBER:
RESPONDENT:	

3. b. *(cont.)* on *(date):*   at *(time):*

☐ I thereafter mailed additional copies (by first class, postage prepaid) to the respondent at the place where the copies were left (Code Civ. Proc., § 415.20b) on *(date):*

☐ A declaration of diligence is attached, stating the actions taken to first attempt personal service.

   c. ☐   **Mail and acknowledgment service.** I mailed the copies to the respondent, addressed as shown in item 2, by first-class mail, postage prepaid, on *(date):*   from *(city):*

   (1) ☐   with two copies of the *Notice and Acknowledgment of Receipt* (form FL-117) and a postage-paid return envelope addressed to me. **(Attach completed *Notice and Acknowledgment of Receipt* (form FL-117).)** (Code Civ. Proc., § 415.30.)

   (2) ☐   to an address outside California (by registered or certified mail with return receipt requested). **(Attach signed return receipt or other evidence of actual delivery to the respondent.)** (Code Civ. Proc., § 415.40.)

   d. ☐   **Other** *(specify code section):*

         ☐   Continued on Attachment 3d.

4. The "NOTICE TO THE PERSON SERVED" on the *Summons* was completed as follows (Code Civ. Proc., §§ 412.30, 415.10, 474):

   a. ☐   As an individual   **or**

   b. ☐   On behalf of respondent who is a

      (1) ☐   minor. (Code Civ. Proc., § 416.60.)

      (2) ☐   ward or conservatee. (Code Civ. Proc., § 416.70.)

      (3) ☐   other *(specify):*

5. **Person who served papers**

   Name:

   Address:

   Telephone number:

   This person is

   a. ☐   exempt from registration under Business and Professions Code section 22350(b).

   b. ☐   not a registered California process server.

   c. ☐   a registered California process server: ☐   an employee or   ☐   an independent contractor

      (1) Registration no.:

      (2) County:

   d. **The fee** for service was *(specify):* $

6. ☐   **I declare** under penalty of perjury under the laws of the State of California that the foregoing is true and correct.

                    –or–

7. ☐   I am a **California sheriff, marshal, or constable,** and I certify that the foregoing is true and correct.

Date:

▶

_____   _____
(NAME OF PERSON WHO SERVED PAPERS)   (SIGNATURE OF PERSON WHO SERVED PAPERS)

For your protection and privacy, please press the Clear This Form button after you have printed the form.	Save This Form	Print This Form	Clear This Form

Notice of Motion

FL-301

ATTORNEY OR PARTY WITHOUT ATTORNEY *(Name, State Bar number, and address)*:	To keep other people from seeing what you entered on your form, please press the Clear This Form button at the end of the form when finished.

TELEPHONE NO.:   FAX NO. *(Optional)*:

E-MAIL ADDRESS *(Optional)*:

ATTORNEY FOR *(Name)*:

SUPERIOR COURT OF CALIFORNIA, COUNTY OF

STREET ADDRESS:

MAILING ADDRESS:

CITY AND ZIP CODE:

BRANCH NAME:

PETITIONER/PLAINTIFF:

RESPONDENT/DEFENDANT:

NOTICE OF MOTION ☐ **MODIFICATION** ☐	CASE NUMBER:
☐ **Child Custody** ☐ **Visitation** ☐ **Injunctive Order**	
☐ **Child Support** ☐ **Spousal Support** ☐ **Other** *(specify)*:	
☐ **Attorney Fees and Costs**	

1. TO *(name)*:

2. A hearing on this motion for the relief requested in the attached application will be held as follows:

 a. Date: Time: ☐ Dept.:   ☐ Rm.:

 b. Address of court ☐ same as noted above ☐ other *(specify)*:

3. Supporting attachments:

 a. Completed *Application for Order and Supporting Declaration* (form FL-310) and a **blank** *Responsive Declaration* (form FL-320)

 b. ☐ Completed *Income and Expense Declaration* (form FL-150) and a **blank** *Income and Expense Declaration*

 c. ☐ Completed *Financial Statement (Simplified)* (form FL-155) and a **blank** *Financial Statement (Simplified)*

 d. ☐ Completed *Property Declaration* (form FL-160) and a **blank** *Property Declaration*

 e. ☐ Points and authorities

 f. ☐ Other *(specify)*:

Date:

     (TYPE OR PRINT NAME)   ▶   (SIGNATURE)

ORDER

4. ☐ Time for ☐ service ☐ hearing is shortened. Service must be on or before *(date)*:

5. Any responsive declaration must be served on or before *(date)*:

6. If child custody or visitation is an issue in this proceeding, *Family Code* section 3170 requires mediation before or concurrently with the hearing listed above. The parties are ordered to attend orientation and mandatory custody services as follows:

Date:

                  JUDICIAL OFFICER

NOTICE: If you have children from this relationship, the court is required to order payment of child support based on the incomes of both parents. The amount of child support can be large. It normally continues until the child is 18. You should supply the court with information about your finances. Otherwise, the child support order will be based on the information supplied by the other parent.

You do not have to pay any fee to file declarations in response to this *Notice of Motion* (including a completed Income and Expense Declaration (form FL-150) or Financial Statement *(Simplified)* (form FL-155) that will show your finances). In the absence of an order shortening time, the original of the responsive declaration must be filed with the court and a copy served on the other party at least nine court days before the hearing date. Add five calendar days if you serve by mail within California. (See Code of Civil Procedure 1005 for other situations.) To determine court and calendar days, go to *www.courtinfo.ca.gov/selfhelp/courtcalendars/*.

Form Adopted for Mandatory Use
Judicial Council of California
FL-301 [Rev. January 1, 2007]   **NOTICE OF MOTION**   Page 1 of 2
Government Code, § 26826
www.courtinfo.ca.gov

American LegalNet, Inc.
www.FormsWorkflow.com

Notice of Motion

PETITIONER/PLAINTIFF:	CASE NUMBER:
RESPONDENT/DEFENDANT:	

7. PROOF OF SERVICE BY MAIL

   a. I am at least age 18, **not a party to this action,** and am a resident or employed in the county where the mailing took place. My residence or business address is:

   b. I served copies of the following documents by enclosing them in a sealed envelope with postage fully prepaid, depositing them in the United States mail as follows:

     (1) Papers served:

       (a) *Notice of Motion* and a completed *Application for Order and Supporting Declaration* (form FL-310) **and** a blank *Responsive Declaration* (form FL-320)

       (b) ☐ Completed *Income and Expense Declaration* (form FL-150) **and** a blank *Income and Expense Declaration*

       (c) ☐ Completed *Financial Statement (Simplified)* (form FL-155) **and** a blank *Financial Statement (Simplified)*

       (d) ☐ Completed *Property Declaration* (form FL-160) **and** a blank *Property Declaration*

       (e) ☐ Points and authorities

       (f) Other *(specify):*

     (2) Manner of service:

       (a) Date of deposit:

       (b) Place of deposit *(city and state):*

       (c) Addressed as follows:

   c. I declare under penalty of perjury under the laws of the State of California that the foregoing is true and correct.

Date:

▶

_____
(TYPE OR PRINT NAME)

_____
(SIGNATURE OF DECLARANT)

Requests for Accommodations
Assistive listening systems, computer-assisted real-time captioning, or sign language interpreter services are available if you ask at least five days before the proceeding. Contact the clerk's office or go to *www.courtinfo.ca.gov/forms* for *Request for Accommodations by Persons With Disabilities and Response* (Form MC-410). (Civil Code, § 54.8.)

Print This Form	For your protection and privacy, please press the Clear This Form button after you have printed the form.	Clear This Form

Proof of Service by Mail

FL-335

ATTORNEY OR PARTY WITHOUT ATTORNEY *(Name, State Bar number, and address)*:	FOR COURT USE ONLY
TELEPHONE NO.: FAX NO. *(Optional)*: E-MAIL ADDRESS *(Optional)*: ATTORNEY FOR *(Name)*:	To keep other people from seeing what you entered on your form, please press the Clear This Form button at the end of the form when finished.

SUPERIOR COURT OF CALIFORNIA, COUNTY OF
STREET ADDRESS:
MAILING ADDRESS:
CITY AND ZIP CODE:
BRANCH NAME:

PETITIONER/PLAINTIFF:	CASE NUMBER:
RESPONDENT/DEFENDANT:	*(If applicable, provide)*:
OTHER PARENT/PARTY:	HEARING DATE:
PROOF OF SERVICE BY MAIL	HEARING TIME: DEPT.:

NOTICE: To serve temporary restraining orders you must use personal service (see form FL-330).

1. I am at least 18 years of age, not a party to this action, and I am a resident of or employed in the county where the mailing took place.

2. My residence or business address is:

3. I served a copy of the following documents *(specify)*:

   by enclosing them in an envelope AND
   a. ☐ **depositing** the sealed envelope with the United States Postal Service with the postage fully prepaid.
   b. ☐ **placing** the envelope for collection and mailing on the date and at the place shown in item 4 following our ordinary business practices. I am readily familiar with this business's practice for collecting and processing correspondence for mailing. On the same day that correspondence is placed for collection and mailing, it is deposited in the ordinary course of business with the United States Postal Service in a sealed envelope with postage fully prepaid.

4. The envelope was addressed and mailed as follows:
   a. Name of person served:
   b. Address:

   c. Date mailed:
   d. Place of mailing *(city and state)*:

5. ☐ I served a request to modify a child custody, visitation, or child support judgment or permanent order which included an address verification declaration. *(Declaration Regarding Address Verification—Postjudgment Request to Modify a Child Custody, Visitation, or Child Support Order (form FL-334) may be used for this purpose.)*

6. I declare under penalty of perjury under the laws of the State of California that the foregoing is true and correct.

Date:

_____ _____
(TYPE OR PRINT NAME) (SIGNATURE OF PERSON COMPLETING THIS FORM)

Page 1 of 1

Form Approved for Optional Use Judicial Council of California FL-335 [Rev. January 1, 2012]	**PROOF OF SERVICE BY MAIL**	Code of Civil Procedure, §§ 1013, 1013a www.courts.ca.gov

For your protection and privacy, please press the Clear This Form button after you have printed the form. Save This Form Print This Form Clear This Form

Response — Marriage

FL-120

ATTORNEY OR PARTY WITHOUT ATTORNEY *(Name, State Bar number, and address):*	
	To keep other people from seeing what you entered on your form, please press the Clear This Form button at the end of the form when finished.

TELEPHONE NO.:   FAX NO. *(Optional)*:
E-MAIL ADDRESS *(Optional)*:
ATTORNEY FOR *(Name)*:

SUPERIOR COURT OF CALIFORNIA, COUNTY OF
    STREET ADDRESS:
    MAILING ADDRESS:
    CITY AND ZIP CODE:
    BRANCH NAME:

MARRIAGE OF
    PETITIONER:
    RESPONDENT:

RESPONSE ☐ **and REQUEST FOR**
  ☐ **Dissolution of Marriage**
  ☐ **Legal Separation**
  ☐ **Nullity of Marriage**   ☐ AMENDED

CASE NUMBER:

1. RESIDENCE (Dissolution only) ☐ Petitioner ☐ Respondent has been a resident of this state for at least six months and of this county for at least three months immediately preceding the filing of the *Petition for Dissolution of Marriage.*

2. STATISTICAL FACTS
  a. Date of marriage: c. Time from date of marriage to date of separation *(specify)*:
  b. Date of separation: Years: Months:

3. DECLARATION REGARDING MINOR CHILDREN *(include children of this relationship born prior to or during the marriage or adopted during the marriage)*:
  a. ☐ There are no minor children.
  b. ☐ The minor children are:

Child's name	Birthdate	Age	Sex

  ☐ Continued on Attachment 3b.
  c. If there are minor children of the Petitioner and Respondent, a completed *Declaration Under Uniform Child Custody Jurisdiction and Enforcement Act (UCCJEA)* (form FL-105) must be attached.
  d. ☐ A completed voluntary declaration of paternity regarding minor children born to the Petitioner and Respondent prior to the marriage is attached.

4. SEPARATE PROPERTY
  Respondent requests that the assets and debts listed ☐ in *Property Declaration* (form FL-160) ☐ in Attachment 4 ☐ below be confirmed as separate property.

Item	Confirm to

NOTICE: You may redact (black out) social security numbers from any written material filed with the court in this case other than a form used to collect child or spousal support.

Form Adopted for Mandatory Use
Judicial Council of California
FL-120 [Rev. January 1, 2005]

RESPONSE—MARRIAGE
(Family Law)

Family Code, § 2020
www.courtinfo.ca.gov.

Response — Marriage

MARRIAGE OF (last name, first name of parties):	CASE NUMBER:

5. DECLARATION REGARDING COMMUNITY AND QUASI-COMMUNITY ASSETS AND DEBTS AS CURRENTLY KNOWN

    a. ☐ There are no such assets or debts subject to disposition by the court in this proceeding.

    b. ☐ All such assets and debts are listed ☐ in *Property Declaration* (form FL-160) ☐ in Attachment 5b.

        ☐ below *(specify)*:

6. ☐ **Respondent contends** that the parties were never legally married.

7. ☐ **Respondent denies** the grounds set forth in item 6 of the petition.

8. Respondent requests

  a. ☐ dissolution of the marriage based on   d. ☐ nullity of voidable marriage based on
     (1) ☐ irreconcilable differences. (Fam. Code, § 2310(a).)   (1) ☐ respondent's age at time of marriage.
     (2) ☐ incurable insanity. (Fam. Code, § 2310(b).)   (Fam. Code, § 2210(a).)
  b. ☐ legal separation of the parties based on   (2) ☐ prior existing marriage.
     (1) ☐ irreconcilable differences. (Fam. Code, § 2310(a).)   (Fam. Code, § 2210(b).)
     (2) ☐ incurable insanity. (Fam. Code, § 2310(b).)   (3) ☐ unsound mind. (Fam. Code, § 2210(c).)
  c. ☐ nullity of void marriage based on   (4) ☐ fraud. (Fam. Code, § 2210(d).)
     (1) ☐ incestuous marriage. (Fam. Code, § 2200.)   (5) ☐ force. (Fam. Code, § 2210(e).)
     (2) ☐ bigamous marriage. (Fam. Code, § 2201.)   (6) ☐ physical incapacity. (Fam. Code, § 2210(f).)

9. Respondent requests that the court grant the above relief and make injunctive (including restraining) and other orders as follows:

	Petitioner	Respondent	Joint	Other
a. Legal custody of children to	☐	☐	☐	☐
b. Physical custody of children to	☐	☐	☐	☐
c. Child visitation be granted to	☐	☐		☐

    As requested in form: ☐ FL-311 ☐ FL-312 ☐ FL-341(C) ☐ FL-341(D) ☐ FL-341(E) ☐ Attachment 9c.

  d. ☐ Determination of parentage of any children born to the Petitioner and Respondent prior to the marriage.

	Petitioner	Respondent		
e. Attorney fees and costs payable by	☐	☐		
f. Spousal support payable to (wage assignment will be issued)	☐	☐		

  g. ☐ Terminate the court's jurisdiction (ability) to award spousal support to Petitioner.

  h. ☐ Property rights be determined.

  i. ☐ Respondent's former name be restored to *(specify)*:

  j. ☐ Other *(specify)*:

        ☐ Continued on Attachment 9j.

10. Child support– If there are minor children born to or adopted by the Petitioner and Respondent before or during this marriage, the court will make orders for the support of the children upon request and submission of financial forms by the requesting party. An earnings assignment may be issued without further notice. Any party required to pay support must pay interest on overdue amounts at the "legal" rate, which is currently 10 percent.

I declare under penalty of perjury under the laws of the State of California that the foregoing is true and correct.

Date:

▶

_____   _____
(TYPE OR PRINT NAME)   (SIGNATURE OF RESPONDENT)

Date:

▶

_____   _____
(TYPE OR PRINT NAME)   (SIGNATURE OF ATTORNEY FOR RESPONDENT)

The original response must be filed in the court with proof of service of a copy on Petitioner.

For your protection and privacy, please press the Clear This Form button after you have printed the form.

Save This Form   Print This Form   Clear This Form

Chapter Four

Obtaining Court Orders

Regardless of the status of the Dissolution proceeding, it is often necessary to obtain certain orders on behalf of the client. The requests for orders may include, but are not limited to: Child custody (confirmation of temporary or permanent legal and physical custody and/or requiring the parties to attend mediation); Child visitation; Child Support (including work-related child care and health insurance); Spousal Support (including ordering a spouse to seek or obtain a job); Enforcement of Standard Restraining Orders (stopping a party from selling, transferring or encumbering community property); Orders regarding which party has control of certain property; Attorney Fees; Requiring a party to comply with previously made Orders; and any other Orders the "Court deems just and equitable."

As indicated in Chapter Three an attorney (or a party if appearing pro se) may file a Request for Order to obtain any of the above requests for relief and subsequent orders. A Request for Order is considered a request for relief that is factual rather than legal. Therefore, in most cases a Request for Order should be filed rather than a Notice of Motion.

In the case of Domestic Violence Orders, there is a special set of forms. These forms are found in Appendix 4A of this book. The forms are very "user friendly" as they are primarily designed with pro se clients in mind. However, there may be times, when you will be required to complete these forms. Therefore, we will discuss them briefly, and later in the chapter you will be provided with the basic information as these forms relate to the dissolution process.

It is possible to obtain "Temporary Restraining Orders" as part of the Request for Order process. However, these Orders are different from Domestic Violence Orders, and will be discussed below.

Request for Order

A Request for Order may be filed at any time. The Petitioner may file a Request for Order with the Summons and Petition. He or she may file one after the Respondent is served, even if the Respondent hasn't filed a Response. The Respondent may file a Notice of Motion if they are making a special appearance as soon as they have been served with the Summons and Petition.

The Petitioner may want to wait to file a Request for a hearing until after the Respondent is served to see if the parties can reach an amicable solution to some or all of the issues. Immediately filing for a hearing, may seem "defensive," while, waiting may appear to be more *friendly* and demonstrate a willingness to negotiate the terms of the settlement. It will be up to the attorney and the client to determine the best of course of action.

The Request for Order can be filed several weeks or several months after the Respondent has been served or alternatively as issues arise. Possible reasons either party may seek relief are: support, getting the other party removed from the family home, requesting mediation and/or a resolution to custody and support issues and/or to require a party to pay or reimburse the other for payments on community debts. As indicated in Chapter One, each marriage is unique. Thus the issues to be resolved, although they may be the same categorically due to the specific circumstances surrounding the families, will be different. Emotional issues also enter the mix, which will further complicate matters.

As you will note as you review the Request for Order "face sheet" and the supplemental forms, there are a number of issues which can be resolved, as well as an "other" box for issues which do not fit within any of the other categories. These are standardized forms and can be customized by including additional information in the form of attachments and exhibits. The forms can also be used with the various attachment pages which were created by the Judicial Council, as seen in Appendix 4B.

The Request for Order can also be used for resolving issues in any of the following types of matters: Dissolution, Legal Separation, Annulment, Paternity, Child Custody and Support Petition, and Post Judgment Modification and Enforcement.

You will need to sit down with the attorney and determine exactly what the needs of the client are, what is the time frame for those needs, and which forms will need to be completed and attached. You will need to work with the client to obtain information which will verify or substantiate the client's position or claim. Some of the questions that need to be asked of the client to determine whether a hearing is necessary are as follows:

1) Does the client need support (child and/or spousal)?

2) Have the parties agreed on custody and visitation if they have minor children, and if they have not, have they been through a court-mandated mediation process?

3) Are the parties still residing in the same home and does one of them need to move out?

4) Is there a disagreement about who will take or retain certain property and/or pay certain bills?

5) Has one (or both) of the parties liquidated assets, or are any of the "community" assets only in one party's name?

6) Is the client unemployed or the person who earns less in the marriage and have they paid attorneys fees?

7) Are their issues of child care, ability to earn or return to work, support arrearages?

8) Is a determination of parentage needed?

9) Does health care need to be provided for the children?

10) Has the opposing party threatened to take the children away from the other and/ or leave the state or country with them?

11) Are there issues regarding previous orders which require enforcement and/or modification?

If the parties have been unable to reach an agreement outside of the courtroom, all of the above, and more, can be resolved through a hearing. In most cases a hearing will be set for a minimum of 35 days after the filing of the documents to allow time for the documents to be served on the opposing side. (Check with the court clerk for approximate dates.) As previously indicated either party may file a Request for Order.

Part of your job as a paralegal, especially as you gain experience, is to review all of the information and glean the most important items and facts from the information that the client has provided to you and then prepare the required Declarations. Remember that this is a very emotional time for the client. The client will want to lament and cast blame. You must keep the client focused on what information is going to be the most important for the court to review. Most judges have only 10–15 minutes prior to a hearing to review the file as well as the documents you have prepared. If you attach a 15-page declaration to the request, the Judge is unlikely to have an opportunity to read it. Alternatively, it is going to be reviewed by the law clerk who is going to prepare a summary for the Judge. It is, therefore, in the client's best interest to keep the information clear, concise, and to the point. (If you don't, the law clerk is going have to summarize the request and declarations for the Judge.)

The Request for Hearing from is very user-friendly and will provide you with the names and numbers of any forms that will be needed to be completed and attached. As you begin your family law course, you should look at the form carefully before you begin the process of collecting information and completing the form.

The attorney (or your Instructor within the framework of the coursework) can guide you in determining if the client needs any of the following forms submitted with the Request for Order.

- Custody and Visitation — FL311; FL341
- Child Support — Income & Expense Declarations — FL150
- Spousal Support — FL157
- Attorney Fees — FL158
- Additional forms and declarations as needed; e.g. MC-013

Keep in mind that under Family Code §§ 1850–1852 mediation is required for custody, visitation, and related issues. The attorney will want to make sure that the client has either attended or requested mediation in order to be in compliance with this statute. It is recommended that you review this section of the Family Code to understand that reason that the legislature mandates the "Statewide Coordination of Family Mediation."

You will also need to prepare an Income & Expense Declaration whenever you are requesting the opposing party to pay for anything (support, bills, reimbursements, attorneys fees, or arrears). There are few exceptions to this rule.

Standard or Temporary Restraining Orders — Domestic Violence

Standard or Temporary Restraining Orders

Automatic (Standard) or Temporary Restraining Orders (ATROs) can be obtained via a Request for Order ("Request"). It is often necessary to reiterate and/or clarify specifically the ATROs that are contained in the Summons. It is quite common for both of the clients to ignore the language on the Summons, often because of the emotional nature of these proceedings. In the event the Standard Restraining Orders are ignored and/or violated or there are issues that need to be resolved, which are not considered Domestic Violence, a Request for Order is the proper mechanism for resolution.

In some instances, however, it will be necessary to obtain **immediate** relief for the client.

> For example, if the husband is the client and he informs the attorney that his wife said that she is taking the children to New York to live with her parents, and that she has purchased airline tickets for herself and the children to leave in two weeks, it may be necessary to bring the Court's attention to this situation immediately.

In such an event, you would likely file the Request as soon as it can be prepared and request that an expedited or *Ex Parte* hearing occur. This procedure will be discussed a little later in the chapter. In other words, will this follow the normal course in which the client will fill out the necessary paperwork and get it back to you so that you can prepare it for filing with court or do you need to sit down with the client (and/or the attorney) immediately and get the documents prepared and filed requesting an "Order Shortening time" or a court appearance within the next 24 hours and then request an Ex Parte hearing.

In the event that the client requires Restraining Orders, the attorney will need to be certain what kind he/she is requesting. If the Orders are Domestic Violence Prevention Act (restraining) Orders you will need to review the following section. However, if a parent is going to take the child(ren) on vacation without permission; if the client is asking that his/her spouse be removed from the family home because he or she just doesn't want to move out; or if the spouse has cleaned out the joint checking and savings accounts or trying to sell real or personal property without the other person's consent, then you must utilize the Request for Order mechanism. In the event it is an extreme emergency you can request an Ex Parte hearing, at which time the court will issue "temporary" orders restraining the party from that activity or those activities, pending the regular hearing. Also, at the hearing, the restraining orders can be ordered continued, denied, or dropped because the underlying issues have been resolved. More information regarding Temporary Restraining Orders (TROs) can be found near the end of this Chapter.

State, Federal and International "Kidnapping"

If a parent is threatening to take the children out of state or to another country with the intent of keeping the children and denying the other parent their parental rights, there may be Federal Statute violations which will require immediate action. In addition to the California Penal Code, there may be a different set of codes and rules to be applied. The following state and federal statutes may apply in these *"kidnapping"* cases:

California Penal Code § 227 states (in part): Every person having a right of custody of the child who maliciously takes, detains, conceals, or entices away that child within or without the state, without good cause, and with the intent to deprive the custody right of another person…, shall be punished … This same section provides the punishment for violation of this section.

California Penal Code § 2278.5 states: Every person who has a right to physical custody of or visitation with a child pursuant to an order, judgment, or decree of any court which grants another person, guardian or public agency the right to physical custody or visitation with that child, and who within or without the state detains, conceals, takes, or entices away that child with the intent to deprive the other person of that right to custody or visitation shall be punished by imprisonment in the state prison for 16 months, or two or three years, a fine of not more than Ten Thousand Dollars ($10,000.00), or both, or by imprisonment in a county jail for a period of not more than one year, a fine of not more than One Thousand Dollars ($1,000.00) or both.

28 U.S.C. § 534, *The Missing Children Act*, allows the FBI to track missing persons, and can be provided to local law enforcement agencies, in the event there is a kidnapping. The FBI may, under this statute, provide assistance to local law enforcement in locating the missing children.

18 U.S.C. § 1073, *The Federal Fugitive Act*. This statute allows the federal government to intercede, extradite, and/or prosecute any individual who crosses the state lines to avoid child abduction prosecution in another state. This statute also provides the penalties for violation of The Federal Fugitive Act.

There is also an International Treaty, known as the *Hague Convention*. This treaty, which was signed in 1965, ensures the cooperation of the countries that have signed the treaty in returning children who have been kidnapped from the custodial parent. The following countries signed the Treaty: Australia, Austria, Canada, China, France, Norway, Portugal, Spain, Sweden, Switzerland, United Kingdom, United States. It is rare that you will be involved in this type of case. However, if the occasion should arise, you would need to carefully read the **entire** text of the Treaty before initiating any type of action. It is also likely that your firm will need to hire an expert in this area of law.

Family Code § 3030 was amended in 2006 changing the circumstances under which a child may be placed in a home where a registered sex offender or child abuser resides. The court previously had to first make a determination that there was "no significant risk to the child." This amendment closed an unintentional loophole in the pre-existing law. The statute now specifically prohibits custody or visitation with a known sexual predator, denies unsupervised visitation, and/or visitation in a location where a registered sex offender or child abuser resides. This applies to not only the parent of the child(ren) in question, but any other person or family member in the home. In the event the court permits visitation to occur in this type of environment, the court must state its reasons in writing or on the record.

Indian Child Welfare Act

As indicated in Chapter Two, these laws became effective January 1, 2008. In the event a child subject to dissolution or paternity is considered a Native American, this statute and the subsequent Judicial Council forms that were created should be reviewed and utilized as needed.

Domestic Violence Protection Act (Restraining Orders)

Domestic Violence Protection Act (DVPA) Orders have very specific requirements and time-lines. They are also differentiated from Standard or Temporary Restraining Orders because, in most cases, once ordered are quasi-criminal in nature. In fact, some of the statutes concerning these Orders and their history are found in the Penal Codes.

The Judicial Council has created a special set of forms and rules with regard to obtaining DVPA Orders that are easy to follow. For the purposes of this text, unless your instructor chooses otherwise, you will not spend a great deal of time discussing those rules and forms at this time.

For the purposes of this text you will need to be aware of the following:

1) Domestic Violence Protection Act (DVPA) is found in Family Code §§ 6200 et seq.

2) There does **not** have to be a marriage to obtain domestic violence restraining orders.

3) Domestic violence restraining orders can be obtained against any person who is residing or has resided in the same home (a spouse or former spouse, significant other, male or female roommate, or in a parent-child relationship if the parties involved are adults) or who was a previous co-habitant as defined under FC§ 6209; or against a party in which there are mutual children, if the Orders requested also include the children.

4) There are no fees for filing a Domestic Violence Petition.

5) Domestic Violence Orders may be (and should as appropriate) be included in any related family law stipulations, agreements and/or judgments subsequently filed.

6) Will the DVPA Orders need to be renewed? If so, the renewal date must be calendared.

If the client, or potential client, has previously obtained domestic violence restraining orders, you will want to make sure that your office obtains a copy of those orders for the file and that the attorney is aware of them. The DVPA Orders might impact whether it will be appropriate for the parties to be present at the same time for mediation and even for hearings. You may need to alert mediators, the court, and any other relevant individuals of special circumstances about which they will need to be aware when dealing with these individuals who have DVPA Orders against them.

Effective January 1, 2007, Family Code §§ 6345, 6361 give the Court the discretion of issuing restraining orders for up to five years after the date of the hearing for personal conduct, stay-away and residence exclusions. Previously, the orders could only be effective for three years from the date of the hearing. Additionally, Family Code § 3100(c) was modified to require that if criminal protective orders are issued under Penal Code § 136.2, any custody or visitation order **must** reference and acknowledge the existence and the enforcement of the Order.

Another amendment effective January 1, 2007, which closed a loophole in preexisting law is Family Code § 6389, requires the **immediate** relinquishing of firearms by a person subject to a protective order. The receipt must be filed with the court within 48 hours of being served with the Order. Previously a person subject to a protective order had 24 hours from the time they were served with the Order to relinquish firearms and they had 72 hours in which to file a receipt with the court.

Family Codes §§ 4320 and 4324.5 were amended in 2012 by the legislature (effective 1/1/13) to "preclude an award of spousal support during dissolution proceedings to a spouse who has been convicted of a violent sexual felony perpetrated against the other spouse if the dissolution is 'filed before five years following the conviction and any time served in custody, on probation, or on parole.' In that instance, the legislature also provides special rules for the payment of attorney fees from the community property, altering the date of separation, and the award of the injured spouse's retirement and pension benefits." (2013 *Practice Under the California Family Code — Case and Legislation Highlights*, California Education of the Bar, page xx)

All DVPA Orders should be served on the police and/or sheriff's department having jurisdiction. It will be necessary to serve the documents on any law enforcement entities which include multiple locations from which the person is restrained, such as: place of employment, children's school, child care provider, and even the grandparents' home. It is important that the Orders be entered into the computer system of the appropriate department(s) in case they are called to enforce them. The client should also have a copy of the Order in their possession in the event law enforcement is called, and the Orders have not been logged in the system.

For instance, if the client Sue has restraining orders against Fred who is the father of her children, and these parents need to go to mediation to discuss the custody and visitation of their children, the mediator will need to be aware of the restraining orders against Fred. In most cases, if there are restraining orders of this nature, the restrained party (or there may be mutual restraining orders) will most likely not be able to be near the other party, whether it is at home, place of employment, children's school, or any other designated places. It is often necessary, in this case, for the parents to meet with a mediator at separate times, and/or agree, in writing, that they can both attend mediation at the same time. You can see that it is important to have a copy of the DVPA Orders in you file so that you can make any needed special arrangements ahead of time. And, in this instance, the mediator will also want to have a copy of those DVPA Orders, as they may impact the custody and/or visitation arrangements, and should be noted in the mediator's report, findings and recommendation as well.

Two significant changes were made in 2007 with respect to domestic violence orders, they are as follows:

- Family Code § 6250.3 (addition) clarified the statute with respect to who can issue a protective order. The statute requires that emergency protective orders are valid only if issued after a specific request by a law enforcement officer and on the basis of statutory findings. Pre-existing law required the presiding judge to designate a judge or commissioner to issue protective orders. (FC § 6241). However, in some jurisdictions standing emergency protective orders were acted upon by law enforcement, rather than requiring that new orders be obtained. The additional section provides that law enforcement personnel must make a separate request of a judicial officer, with the specific facts of each case, when requesting a EPO.

- Family Code § 6389 was amended to require an immediate relinquishing of firearms by persons subject to a protective order. Previously a person subject to a protective order had 24 hours from the time they are served with the order to relinquish firearms. The person also had 72 hours to file the a receipt with the court. The person must now file the receipt within 48 hours of service of the order.

There are many organizations as well as some courts throughout the state which offer "self-help" clinics to assist persons who need to complete the Judicial Council forms, obtain a hearing, serve the Respondent, and obtain Protective Orders from a Judge.

Ex Parte Hearings and Issues

As previously indicated, Ex Parte hearings are for resolving emergency-type issues or restraining either or both parties from a specific action; *Ex Parte* means that the responding party is not given the usual notice time.

CCP§ 1005(a)(13)-(b) requires that all Motions (including Requests for Hearing) be served 16 **court** days, by personal service, plus five calendar days for mailing. Therefore, most courts set hearings for 35–40 days after the date they are filed. There are instances when issues need to be resolved sooner than that, such as immediate support, removing a disruptive parent from the home, or keeping a parent from taking the children from the home.

Check the Court's local rules for any special requirements they have regarding giving Ex Parte notice. For instance, some courts require a minimum of six hours notice, others require 24 hours notice to the opposing party or his/her attorney. Other Courts require that you notify the court of your intent to have an Ex Parte hearing so they can give you a date and time, as they restrict the number of Ex Parte hearing applications each day. Some counties will set Ex Parte hearings for several weeks out. Some judges will require that an Ex Parte hearing only be heard either on the afternoon or morning calendar and may require that the matter be heard only after all other regularly scheduled matters are heard. Thus, the attorney and client may have to wait an hour or more to be heard. You will also need to know if the Court requires a particular form or format Declaration of Notice of Ex Parte Hearing.

It is always a good idea to know the proper method, time frames for notifying the opposing party, and if the attorney needs to plan on being at the courthouse for a long period. This means you will have to clear all other appointments from his or her calendar or any other special requirements the court may have. Most Courts also require a "special" hearing fee in addition to the regular hearing fee. You will want to know the amount of each of those fees.

You can check the local court website for the most accurate filing fee information in most counties or www.calcourt.org. The "calcourt" website also provides a directory so that you can determine the correct county (jurisdiction) for filing documents if you have any question. If there is a question, you should call the clerk and confirm the cost.

In the event that you must prepare for an Ex Parte hearing, in addition to obtaining the local rules, you will need to do the following:

1) Prepare the Request for Order, applicable forms, with accompanying written declaration of the client; any necessary exhibits or attachments; and Income & Expense Declarations.

2) Discuss with the attorney who will give the notice. (The attorney or the paralegal may give notice as per the attorney's instructions.) Prepare the Declaration of Ex Parte Notice for signature by the person giving the notice. Some Counties have a form that they prefer that you use, so check the local rules. In the event that the Court does not have a preprinted form, a sample Declaration is found at Appendix 4C.

3) Give notice per local rules. Advise the attorney of any special requirements. Discuss how they will be handled or who will take care of them.

4) Complete the Declaration with the date, time and who was given notice, as well as date, time and court information of the hearing. Make sure the attorney has the original and two copies of the Declaration.

5) Make sure the attorney has an updated calendar with dates that are available to return for the next *regular* hearing date in this matter. The attorney should have the originals of all the documents listed under #1 above, as well as the Declaration referenced in #2 above, and any required filing fees (special and regular) ready for the hearing.

6) Notify the client of the date, time and location of the hearing, and provide the client with any special instructions from the attorney or the court.

Child Custody and Visitation

The Court's primary focus in a Dissolution of Marriage, Legal Separation, and Paternity is on the children. The Court is required by law to determine what is in the **best interest** of the children. In Chapter Two you learned of the different types of custody: Legal custody which can be Joint or Sole Legal Custody; and Physical Custody which can be Joint or Sole Physical Custody, as well as visitation rights of "other" interested persons. In the case of Joint Physical Custody the court often refers to this as Parenting. Sole Physical Custody gives the primary care of the child(ren) to one parent and the other parent (the "*non-custodial*" parent) will have visitation with the children. Another often used term of art is "*time-share*" which is used most often for calculating child support as you learned in Chapter Three.

Family Code §§ 3020–3031 establish California *public policy* as well as the court's authority to resolve custody disputes between parents. The California Legislature has made it very clear as to the definition of the **best interest of the child**, as well as the policy that children, except in abusive situations, should have **frequent and continuing contact with both parents**. The Court encourages that, whenever possible, both parents share the **rights and responsibilities** of rearing their child.

As indicated in Chapter Two, a Declaration Under the Uniform Child Custody Jurisdiction Act must be completed and filed with a Petition for Dissolution, Legal Separation, Annulment, or Paternity, whenever there are minor children.

Mediation

There are two primary types of Mediation: 1) Court-ordered, as discussed above and 2) Private (voluntary) mediation.

Court-Ordered Mediation

In the event that the parties disagree, which is often the case, about the custody of the children, prior to, or in conjunction with the hearing, the parties will be required to attend court-mandated mediation. This form of mediation was mandated under Family Code §§ 1850–1852. Many California counties, although not all, refer to their county-funded programs as Family Court Services (FCS). Additionally, each county will have their own local rules regarding when and how the parties attend mediation, as well as whether the mediator is allowed to make a recommendation to the court, absent the agreement of the parties, or as a supplement to an agreement. The statewide mandate states that in order to avoid unnecessary "litigation" with regard to custody and visitation issues, the parties are required to attend mediation in the hope that they will be able to reach an agreement regarding the parenting of their children. (*Family Code § 3160 et seq.*)

Some courts will automatically refer the parties to an orientation upon the filing of the Summons and Petition. In that instance, remember to serve the Respondent his or her copy of that Notice when the initial documents are being served. You are also going to want to make sure the client receives a copy of the Notice and is aware of the date and time the client is to attend. Thus, getting the Respondent served sooner, rather than later, may be important.

Other courts may request that the party complete a Petition (or Request) for Mediation only when there is a disagreement as to the custody and visitation needs of the child. The Petition may contain information such as, each party's personal information (home address, telephone number, etc.), as well as the names, ages, and schools of the children, the issues to be resolved, any previous mediation attended, and all applicable (and known) case numbers. Upon receipt of the Petition, the parties will be referred to mediation and they will receive a notice of the date and time to attend. The court will assign a mediator to meet with the parties. If one of the parties is not in the county, this person may attend by telephone. In most counties, the mediator will want to talk with children who are over the age of five. If there are children under the age of five, they should not be brought to the appointment. Should either party wish to provide any written documentation to the mediator, that party will need to serve copies of all of those documents on the other party prior to mediation. Types of documentation may include: medical records, doctor or school reports and grades, declarations from neighbors, family or church members who are familiar with the family and, in particular, the children who have an insight as to the best interests of the children. The parties will usually have only one meeting with the mediator. At the conclusion of the meeting, the mediator will write a report detailing any agreements made by the parties and/or any recommendations that the mediator has where there is no agreement, or only a partial agreement.

In most cases, if there is a date or time conflict, the court will allow the appointment to be rescheduled, but it has to be by agreement of **both** parties. The only exception to both parties attending mediation appointments at the same time is if there is a restraining order against one or both of them. As indicated earlier in this chapter, you will need to make the mediation department aware of any restraining orders as early as possible, so they can make reasonable accommodation.

The mediator will most likely prepare a report which will set forth any agreements made by the parties and/or will make recommendations as to any unresolved issues.

In general, the mediator's report is given great weight by the judicial system. It is not mandatory that the court adopt or that the parties accept the recommendation of the mediator but the judge will give the mediator's recommendation weighty consideration. A great deal of discretion with respect to making recommendations for alcohol and/or drug testing, anger management, counseling and psychological evaluations for the parties and the children are given to the mediator. The mediator's report is not public record but is part of the court's file and can be obtained by others within the judicial system. A mediator can also be called as a witness should the parties go to trial over the issue of custody. The local rules should be reviewed to determine the mediator's role, whether the mediator's recommendation/report is considered and in what manner, whether the mediator may appear at trial, and the scope of the mediator's testimony.

Family Code §3161 states that the purpose of mediation is: "to reduce acrimony which may exist between the parties" and "to develop an agreement assuring the child close and continuing contact with both parents that is in the best interest of the child."

Upon completion of the mediation process, if the parties have reached an agreement, that agreement will be memorialized in writing, pursuant to the local court rules, and some form of Stipulation and/or Agreement will be prepared (often by the paralegal) so that each party can sign the document. That document will then be submitted to the Court for the Judge's approval and signature. That document becomes an official "Order" of the Court. It is important to have an Order, as it becomes an enforceable court document. There are times, however, when other issues need to be resolved, and it may be best to wait and incorporate several or all issues into one document. The attorney will advise what, if anything, should be prepared at this stage.

In the event the parties have not been able to reach an agreement, the parties may request that the matter be set for a hearing, and they will take the issue before the Judge. The hearing also will often include any of the other unresolved issues, as it is best to have as many issues resolved at one time as possible, thus avoiding frequent trips to the courthouse.

Please note that court-ordered mediation through Family Court Services can only resolve issues with regard to custody and visitation. They will not discuss issues relative to child support, spousal support, or the division of property. If the parties have other issues they wish to resolve without litigation, they can consider other forms of mediation.

Carefully review all local court rules to determine what is allowed as part of the court-ordered mediation, as the foregoing is strictly an overview of the process and is not to be relied upon as the process may change or the county in which you work may have different rules.

Collaborative/Voluntary (Private) Mediation

The parties may prefer to choose a mutually agreed upon mediator rather than go through the referral system of their local court. Most courts have an attorney referral to mediators who have been credentialed by the court as an approved mediator. It is always preferable to have the parties sign an Agreement which sets forth the guidelines for the mediator and the mediation process. Once again, you should check the local rules to determine any special requirements, forms or conditions which must be met so that the client can utilize this type of mediation.

One advantage to private mediation over court-ordered mediation is that, in most cases, the mediator will have the parties return for supplemental appointments until such time as they have reached an agreement or an impasse. The parties will have to pay for private mediation, which for many individuals, is not affordable. However, the advantage is, it may save the parties money, in the long term, because they have reached an amicable resolution, that will likely save them attorneys fees, both now and in the future, because they haven't had to litigate. Additionally, the report created by the mediator is completely private. Only the formal agreement between the parties will become part of the court record, unless the parties request that it be sealed.

The parties can also request that the mediator discuss issues other than custody and visitation with the parties. Those issues should be included in the agreement for voluntary mediation. In the event the parties wish to have more than custody issues mediated, they should make sure that the mediator they choose has the education and experience in those types of matters and is willing to participate as a mediator with respect to all issues.

For more information about how the Collaborative Mediation Practice works go to the "Collaborative Practice California" website: www.cpcal.org.

The Best Interests of the Child

The Court will not make any orders with respect to child custody which are based on any of the following factors: race, sexual conduct or preference, religious practices, physical handicap or ability, or disparity of incomes. The Court's primary focus is on the best interests of the child and will only consider: the child's need for stability and continuity, emotional bonds, and which party is most likely to assure that there is frequent and continuing contact with the other parent. The Court will **not** enter an Agreement as an Order unless each party has 1) agreed, either in person or through their attorney of record, in Court or by Stipulation; or 2) one party failed to appear at the noticed hearing on the issues to be resolved in the Agreement; or 3) the Court deems the Agreement is not in the best interests of the child.

Although there is no *presumption* that Joint Legal Custody is in the best interests of the child, in most cases, the Court will give as much latitude as possible to establishing that both parents will be able to cooperate with one another with regard to the health, education and welfare of the children (their best interests). Where the parties have **mutually** agreed to Joint Legal Custody, there is *then* a presumption that it is in the best interests of the children.

Family Code § 3083, provides the Court with the following orders for Joint Legal Custody:

> In making an order for joint legal custody, the court shall specify the circumstances under which the consent of both parents is required to be obtained in order to exercise legal control of the child and the consequences of the failure to obtain mutual consent. In all other circumstances, either parent acting alone may exercise legal control of the child. An order of joint legal custody shall not be construed to permit an action that is inconsistent with the physical custody order unless the action is expressly authorized by the court.

As indicated above, the Court requires the parties to cooperate when making the "legal" decisions regarding the children. However, if the Court has, for instance, ordered sole physical custody to one parent, because of an abusive parent, they will **not** order Joint Legal Custody, which would be "inconsistent with the Physical Custody Order."

The Court's rely heavily on the following two cases with respect to making custody decisions: *In re Marriage of Carney* (1979) 24 C3d 725, 157 CR 383 and *Burchard v. Garay* (1986) 42 C3d 531, 229 CR 800. The *Carney* case is often quoted as it provides an excellent overview of what the court must consider when awarding custody to one parent over the other. A portion of that decision is quoted below:

> [c]ontemporary psychology confirms what wise families have perhaps always known—that the essence of parenting is not to be found in the harried rounds of daily carpooling endemic of modern suburban life, or even in the doggedly dutiful actions of "togetherness" committed every weekend by well-meaning fathers and mothers across America. Rather, its essence lies in the ethical, emotional, and intellectual guidance the parent gives to the child throughout his formative years, and often beyond. The sources of this guidance is the adults' own experience of life; its motive power is parental love and concern for the child's well-being; and its teachings deal with such fundamental matters as the child's feelings about himself, his relationship with others, his system of values, his standards of conduct, and his goals and priorities in life.
>
> We do not mean, of course, that the health or physical condition of the parents may not be taken into account in determining whose custody would best serve the child's interest. In relation to the issues at stake, however, this factor is ordinarily of minor importance. Whenever raised—whether in awarding custody originally or in changing it later—it is essential that the court weigh the matter with an informed and open mind.... Weighing these and all other relevant factors together, the court should then carefully determine whether the parent's condition will in fact have a substantial and lasting adverse effect on the best interests of the child ... [I]t has at last been understood that a boy need not prove his masculinity on the playing fields of Eton, nor must a man compete with his son in athletics in order to be a good father: their relationship is no less "normal" if it is built on shared experiences in such fields of interest as science, music, arts and crafts, history or travel, or in pursuing such classic hobbies as stamp or coin collecting. In short, an afternoon that a father or son spend together at a museum or the zoo is surely no less enriching than an equivalent amount of time spent catching either balls or fish.

The Court, in making custody orders, will also use such terminology as *minimum contacts* and *status quo*. In most cases, as you prepare the Request for Order, at this stage in the Dissolution process, the orders for both Legal and Physical Custody will be considered *temporary*. In other words, at the point in time when a final Judgment is entered (either by Agreement, Stipulation or after Trial) the custody orders will be considered permanent, or at least for a period of time. With that in mind, however, it is important to note that once the Court makes the "temporary" orders, it will hesitate to make sweeping changes once "permanent" orders are made, unless it can be proven that the temporary orders were inconsistent with the best interests of the child or significant change or event has occurred, and should not be become "permanent" and incorporated in the Judgment. The Court is unlikely to revise the temporary Orders in that instance as it will be necessary for the parties to attend mediation, if they have not previously done so and possibly to file another Request for Order. Additionally at some point, as the child's needs change, a parent wishes to move with the children, or any other number of factors which will be discussed in Chapter Ten, under Modification and Enforcement, the custody orders may be modified.

For the purposes of this chapter, we will focus on the *temporary* custody orders being requested at the hearing by the client during the interim. At this point, the Courts will consider the status quo to be very important. The child is facing a situation where their sense of security and stability is in a state of flux. The entire world as the child knows it is about to change. The parent who is able to quickly establish a loving and stable environment for the child may be in the best position to later request that the court continue the *status quo*.

Status quo may also refer to the type of contact and relationship the parent and child had during the marriage. It may be reflected in how the person requesting custody positions him/herself. For instance, if Mother is a stay-at-home mom and Father travels frequently for work, there is going to be a definite pattern to this type of "family lifestyle." It would not be the status quo for Father to be awarded primary physical custody. However, if both parents work and the parties have shared all of the child-rearing (school, homework, extracurricular activities, evening rituals such as bathing, homework, and bedtime reading) then it would be more consistent with the status quo to order joint physical custody. (**Note:** These are generalized statements for discussion purposes only and should not be construed as the only way to approach a client's request for certain types of custody orders. The attorney or instructor should offer you several different types of custody scenarios for discussion.)

Thus the *minimum contacts* standards come into play with regard to visitation (one parent has primary physical custody while the other has *visitation*). While Family Code § 3100 mandates that "the court *shall* grant reasonable visitation rights to a parent unless it is shown that the visitation will be detrimental to the best interest of the child," there is nothing in the Family Code that establishes conclusively what is "reasonable visitation." Thus the term "frequent and continuing contact" is construed to mean what is *reasonably practical*. The Courts have interpreted *reasonable* to mean the maximum possible visitation time available to the non-custodial parent, as long as it is in the best interests of the child, and which does not interfere with the custodial parent's time with the child.

Two 2003 cases addressed the issue of what was "frequent and continuing contact" and what is in the "best interests of the child" as set forth in Family Code §§ 3020 and 3040. *In re Marriage of Campos* (2003) 108 CA4th 1294. The Court ruled that the "rule" cannot be used when the party seeking custody (and the children) have been a victim (or victims) of Domestic Violence within the past five years by the non-custodial parent, and there is *not* a rebuttable presumption that it is in the best interest of the child under that circumstance. That presumption may be rebutted only by a preponderance of evidence subject to *Family Code § 3044(a)* which outlines the factors to be considered; such as whether the perpetrator has successfully completed program(s), as well as being in compliance with any other Court orders.

Additionally, the Court's ruling of *In re Marriage of Abargil* (2003) 106 CA4th 1294, 131 CR2d 429, states that the parent's rights must be preserved if the custodial parent moves (or wishes to move) to a foreign country. The Court found that in order to "protect the child's relationship with the non-custodial parent," the custodial parent may be ordered to (1) post a substantial bond to ensure compliance with the Court's orders; (2) be prohibited from applying for modification of the judgment in any but a California court; and (3) be required to register the California judgment with the foreign authorities before leaving the state.

Note: These issues will be discussed later under modification and enforcement of judgments in Chapter Ten. However, they need to be kept in mind when drafting custody orders to eliminate potential problems and issues in the future or when anticipating what the court may determine is frequent and continuing contact in that case/situation.

Many people think of joint physical custody as a 50/50 timeshare, which of course, would seem ideal. The reality, however, is that a 50/50 split is often difficult for the parents and children to maintain based on school and other activities in which the child may be involved, not to mention a parent's work-related schedules, such as overtime and/or travel. A 50/50 time share may actually **not** be the status quo or it is possible that such an arrangement does not maintain a stable and secure environment for the children.

A standard visitation schedule was established by a family law judge (Judge Freeman). He felt this schedule was the minimum amount of time (20%) that a child should spend with the non-custodial parent. It became known as the *Freeman Order* and is as follows:

1. Alternating weekends from Friday at 6:00 p.m. to Sunday at 6:00 p.m.;

2. One midweek dinner (or may be overnight) visit;

3. Equal division of holidays (see below);

4. Two uninterrupted weeks during the summertime for each parent; and

5. Equal division of school vacations (Christmas, Spring and/or other breaks).

The parties, of course, have great flexibility in establishing a schedule which is consistent with their lifestyles, school and activities of the children and any other relevant factors. You will note when using the child support software to calculate time share (one of the pull-down menus) that the Freeman Order is actually closer to 26% time share for the non-custodial parent.

Appendix 4D includes a typical schedule for alternating holidays, school vacations and breaks, which can be adopted by the parties. Judicial Council form FL-341(c) can also be used to "check the boxes."

In the event that the parties are at great odds regarding custody and visitation, it may be necessary for the Court to appoint an attorney or advocate to protect the rights of the child(ren). This may be particularly true when there are allegations of child abuse or violent behavior.

Child Abuse Considerations

The law in this area is evolving and changing. It is difficult, given the number of possible scenarios, for the legislature to develop a strict guideline for establishing with whom an abused child should live. Issues of child abuse are heard within the Juvenile Dependency Court system, which is entirely separate from Family Law. Welfare and Institutions Code § 300 sets forth the circumstances under which a child may become a "ward" of the court. It also provides for the protection of the child and the parent. These types of cases may involve grandparents, stepparents, relatives and other extended family members, as well as marital and non-marital partners. California Penal Code § 11166(a) states the situations under which one must report suspected child abuse, and the fines for failure to report can be found at PC§ 11172(e).

As indicated earlier Family Code § 3030 was amended in 2006 (effective 2007) to limit the circumstances under which a child may be placed and/or have visitation in a home where a suspected or known child abuser resides.

As a paralegal you should be aware of these code sections and your responsibility of reporting any suspected activity to the attorney for whom you work. In the event your firm practices in the area of Juvenile Dependency, you will want to become more familiar with the Judicial Council forms, the local court rules, the statutes and case law that govern that area of practice.

Other Issues and/or Orders Relating to Custody

The Court may, on its **own motion** (or as recommended by a mediator) make orders for any of the following:

Mental Health Evaluation

Counseling for Parents and/or Children (Abuse, Alcohol, Drug, Parenting)

Appointment of an Attorney for the Child

Investigation

Supervised Visitation when there are concerns of Abuse or Neglect

Restraining Orders

Additionally, if either party raises allegations related to the above, they may request that the court make orders, regarding those issues.

As you can see there are many considerations to be made with respect to child custody when preparing the Request for Order and/or the Petition. The attorney should have carefully examined all of these options, along with the statutory and case law foundations on which legal and physical custody are based. Although the client may absolutely abhor his/her spouse at this point in time, the attorney cannot let those feelings contradict what is in the best interest of the child. It is often a fine line between being an advocate for the client and doing what is best for the child.

You will want to carefully detail with the attorney and/or the client exactly what type of legal and physical custody is being requested in the Request for Order and obtain the factual bases for that request. You may also need to research the statutes and case law in order to provide the court with the foundation for the client's position and basis for his or her custody requests.

Child Support

Chapter Three discussed the history of Child Support and how it evolved to what is referred to currently as "guideline" child support. Oftentimes, parties will need to resolve the issue of custody or parenting time in order to calculate "time share" which is an important piece of information to have when calculating child support. These two issues are relational as well as volatile. You are dealing with usually the two most important things to a parent: the emotional attachment to the children and the parent's financial situation.

It is hoped that your firm will utilize either Dissomaster™, SupporTax™, or Xspouse™ software programs to calculate guideline child support. These programs will assist with calculating time share percentages as well. They also help to take the "personal" out of the calculation, since they are standard for **everyone**. Primarily the two greatest influences are: earnings and time share. As previously indicated, the Judge will use one of these programs, therefore, it is best if your office is using the same information in discussions with the client as the Court will use in calculating support.

The attorney will usually have talked with the client about the amount of **projected** support that the non-custodial parent will pay. By using the Dissomaster™ or Xspouse™ the attorney can anticipate different schemes, identify the various mandatory deductions, as well as project discretionary add-ons. The attorney will need pay stubs from both parties, and/or joint tax returns in order to accurately enter the income of each party. If the earnings information is not available, or is based on a party's self-employment income, the attorney will, with the assistance of the client and a tax preparer, determine the earnings. Worst case, the attorney may have to make an educated guess as to the earnings, using the child support software. Additional considerations would be if a party is attempting to hide income or has taken a job at less than their earning capacity. In that case, the findings will need to be based on the party's potential earning capacity.

The question of time share is also a factor if one or both of the parties wish to change the current custody arrangements, or they do not agree with the proposal of the other parent or the mediator's report. (See above section.) It is often necessary to prepare several "what-if" or anticipated time share schemes for the non-custodial parent in preparation for the hearing and the Judge's ruling or to present to the other party when attempting to reach an amicable resolution.

For the purposes of calculating child support, there is no calculation for a 50/50 time share. The reason is for tax purposes: only one party can be considered the custodian, which enables that person to claim the child on his or her taxes. Therefore, when using the child support software, the program will default to a 49/51 percent time share. The parties, however, can agree to waive the right to claim the child on their taxes, even if they are considered the custodial parent. (This will be discussed further in Chapter Nine, under Marital Settlement Agreement.)

The Court uses the Income & Expense Declaration (form FL-150) to assist in making Child Support Orders. It is important that each party provide as much information as is available so that the Court may have an accurate picture of the parent's incomes, allowable deductions, and any discretionary deductions. Each parent's pay stubs for the past two months **must** be attached to the Income & Expense Declaration ("I&E"). The form also asks for the average earnings for the past twelve (12) months, because in most cases, the Court uses the monthly *average earnings* to calculate support. If pay stubs are not available, tax returns or other verification of earnings should be attached.

Please note that you may redact Social Security Numbers on copies of any earnings related information that will be filed with the court.

The Court may also determine that child support may be less than the guideline. For example, as discussed in Chapter Three, a *Duke Order* may be in effect, and therefore the Court might reduce the amount of support to reflect those financial considerations. Alternatively, the non-custodial parent may be ordered (or agree) to pay the entire mortgage of the custodial parent who lives in the home. In that event, the Court would consider that financial obligation when factoring support. Therefore, it may as a technicality, be less then that what would be considered guideline child support.

The attorney may alternatively decide to file form FL-316, *Ex Parte Application and Order to Seal Financial Forms* requesting that the Court place the financial documents specified in the form in a confidential portion of the file, to which the public does not have access.

It is always preferred that you obtain copies of the actual pay-stubs as they usually provide the information on deductions such as FICA, SDI, Social Security/Medicare, State Taxes, Mandatory Retirement, Health Care Deductions, and Union Dues, all of which are allowable, mandatory deductions. The attorney will have an opportunity to review the deductions and argue that they are **not** allowable and must be added back in as income.

In the event that the earnings are based on fluctuating hours, bonuses, or commissions, all of which are considered income, the child support programs have a feature that will allow you to enter all of the income information. You can then go to the "Income" menu, and it will show the Income page (page 2 of the I&E) on which you will find the *total average gross monthly income,* as well as the standard tax deductions based on those earnings. If this information is for the client, you can then print out that page and utilize it in preparing the I&E or for imputing other parent's net income.

Gross income includes:

Taxable Income: Salary or Wages, Over-time, Commissions, Bonuses, Self-employment income, Pension or Retirement, Spousal Support (received), Military benefits (BAQ and BAF), Rental Income, Dividends and Interest, Trust Income

Non-taxable income: Social Security Disability, Workers Compensation, Unemployment, Public Assistance such as CalWORKS or Aid to Children (TANF), Supplemental Security Income (SSI) and General Assistance (GA/GR).

You will note that the Income & Expense Declaration does have an Expense component (page 3) which must be completed. However, for the purposes of child support, the Court has discretion as to whether it will consider this information or in what context. The Expense information will be used by the Court to make orders, if requested, as to the payment of community debts. The Expense information is also used to show standard of living, which is used most often in Spousal Support determinations. (See Chapter Five.) It can, however, provide the Court with insight as to the party's lifestyle which may be evidence of a *higher earner* who is trying to hide or reduce earnings in order to pay less child support. It also helps to confirm the filing status and allowable deductions.

For instance:

If the custodial parent is residing in the family home with the children and has a mortgage payment of $5,000 per month (not including property taxes, insurance and maintenance), yet only earns $2,500 and the non-custodial parent has indicated he/she only earn $3,000 per month, the Court will note this discrepancy (income vs. expenses) and assume that one or both of the parties are not providing accurate earnings information or that they are receiving money from an outside source (girlfriend, boyfriend, second job, etc.) which isn't reported on the I&E. The Court may also consider the high costs of two households and whether a decision needs to be made about the family residence.

If the parties cannot agree on the amount of "guideline" support, they will have to take the matter before a Judge for a final determination.

The Court can make this determination at any time that is appropriate. For example, the Court may make Orders for support under any of the following circumstances:

1) Support may have to be established early on in the process by requesting an Request for Order.

2) The Court can approve a Stipulation or Agreement between the parties which has been signed and is submitted as an Order.

3) After the hearing, or later in the process after a settlement conference or trial; as a request to modify support based on a change in circumstances of the parties; upon entry of a Judgment.

4) After the Dissolution, Legal Separation or Paternity Judgment has been entered, which would be considered a post-Judgment Modification.

It should also be noted, that if the client has applied for public assistance the Department of Child Support Services should be notified that this matter will be pending before the court. The department will need to be served with any documents related to a Request for Order or Motion at which child support will be determined. The Court will also require the departmental signatures on any new or modified orders.

Spousal Support

For the purposes of the Request for Order, we will be discussing "*temporary*" spousal support. Permanent Spousal Support orders will be discussed in Chapter Seven.

Temporary spousal support orders are designed to maintain the status quo of the marriage, and are usually ordered, unless otherwise agreed to by the parties, pending further litigation or resolution as to more permanent orders. Family Code § 3600 provides the statutory authority for the court to make temporary spousal support orders. It states that the Court can order "any amount" necessary for the support of the husband or wife. This section further indicates that the Court may also consider the *need* of the supported party, while weighing *the ability to pay* by the supporting party.

Oftentimes, the need vs. of ability to pay argument is the basis for requesting a determination of temporary spousal support. A supporting party may attempt to "deliberately and willfully suppress" or hide their income. The Court will apply the same laws with respect to spousal support as they do with child support in this instance. The Court has the discretion to consider and order support based on ability to earn or the standard of living which can be deduced by the evidence provided.

For example:

A person owning a home valued at a million dollars, vacation property, a Mercedes-Benz, a Hummer, a motorhome, membership at a prestigious golf club, etc. is probably not going to be working at a fast food restaurant.

One of the primary reasons for requiring a temporary order of spousal support is so that the spouse who requires support will **not** seek public assistance. The Legislature has enacted statutes putting in place mechanisms to avoid the state (public) having to support a person, when the Family Code (FC§ 4300) and public policy state there is an obligation to support while living together. This obligation continues during separation and included the use of separate property for said support, if so ordered.

As stated previously, the Income & Expense Declaration becomes critical with respect to evaluating the standard of living and needs of the spouse requesting spousal support in order to maintain the status quo. It should be noted that all supporting documentation should be provided as back-up to the I&E declarations. Such documentation may include copies of: all real property ownership documents (deeds, mortgage statements, property taxes, insurance, maintenance records); automobile ownership (registration, payment coupons, DMV fees, and insurance); credit card statements (showing purchases for furniture, furnishings, clothing, vacations/travel, meals, etc.); gym membership; personal grooming; children's school and activities; and any other evidence of the party's lifestyle and their related expenses.

Another consideration is the party's ability to work. The Court needs to determine whether the party has currently been working and the earnings, if any, or, if there is an ability to obtain work during the period. Some of the items the Court will consider are:

> Did they work prior to the marriage? What kind of job did they have or what kind of skills and/or education to they have? Are they a stay-at-home parent? Do they work part-time while the children are at school in order to be at home when the children are there? Have they ever worked outside the home? Do the costs of child care outweigh the earnings that the supported party would make?

> What are the community assets and obligations? How much is the mortgage, food, clothing, automobiles, and other expenses. Did the parties have a lifestyle during marriage where they took expensive vacations, ate out frequently, have the children enrolled in private schools and/or activities.

The California Court of Appeals ruled in 2006, *Marriage of Shaughnessy*, 139 CA4th 1225, 43 CR3d 642, that the Court may consider monetary gifts to a supported spouse from a third party when setting spousal support.

While there is no formal guideline as there is for child support, for the purposes of *temporary* spousal support, the same software that is used to calculate child support may be used for spousal support. The resulting calculation is based solely on earnings, however, and does not consider the standard of living. In most cases, however, the court will use the figure on the Dissomaster™ or Xspouse™ in order to at least provide the supported party some form of minimum "income" thus maintaining what they feel is the *status quo* until an order for permanent support can be made.

According to a recent ruling, it was confirmed that the court may retroactively modify—or order—spousal support if jurisdiction has been reserved. <u>Marriage of Freitas</u> (2012) 209 CA4th 1059, 147 CR3d 453.

It is always in the client's best interests, if they are the *lower earner*, to request spousal support when preparing for a hearing. The Court has the discretion to order the spousal support or may simply retain jurisdiction over the issue "until trial or further order of the Court." Either way, you have protected the client's interests in this issue.

Attorney's Fees

A request for attorney fees can be made at any point in the Dissolution process or as the result of modification or enforcement. The Court has discretion to order the higher earner to pay a portion or all of the other party's attorney fees and costs, or to simply retain jurisdiction over the issue. The statutes are somewhat vague when addressing the issue of attorney fees. *Family Code § 2030.* However, Family Code § 7605 was amended in 2013 to require the Court to determine, specifically, in parentage cases, whether there is a disparity between the parties in the ability to obtain counsel and whether one of the parties has the ability to pay for representation for both parties. It is likely that this statute will be applied in future cases in all areas of family law, not just under the *Uniform Parentage Act* (FC§§ 7600-7730). The Court typically has great latitude in determining need vs. ability to pay, coupled with the current financial situation of the parties. The Court also has the discretion to order the liquidation of assets, including separate property, for attorney fees.

Of primary importance to the Court is that each of the parties is able to protect and preserve their rights and interests, so they essentially have "equal litigating power." *In re Marriage of Green* (1992) 6 CA4th 584, 7 CR 872. Equal litigating power is particularly important where there are many complex issues to be resolved. It is also important if the party requesting the fees is not working, is the custodial parent, and/or does not have any funds available. In that event, the court is required to consider whether the fees paid would have to come from what should be used for the health and welfare (food, housing, clothing) of the children.

The concept of *ability to pay* must also be determined. Does the party have liquid assets available? If the person has liquid assets but they are separate property (such as an inheritance or savings account they had prior to marriage) the Court has the discretion to award fees paid from separate property. These types of orders may be subject to reimbursement by the other party upon conclusion of the matter. Again, that is at the Court's discretion.

The Court historically has held that it is "an abuse of discretion by the court not to award fees at a hearing for temporary orders." *In re Marriage of Hatch* (1985) 169 CA3d 1213. The court further stated that a spouse should not have to pay attorney fees out of support, and that the Court may order the Respondent to "go to other property" in order to pay attorney fees.

Attorney fees are requested through a noticed Motion or Request for Order, which is the mechanism you are using to obtain other relief on behalf of the client. Attorney's fees should always be requested when you are asking for any kind of financial relief for the client, and especially, where the other party is purposely delaying or being uncooperative in order to prolong litigation, or where you are requesting that the other party be compelled to comply with an order.

The client may also request that costs be reimbursed, subject to proof. They may request reimbursement for court filing fees, appraiser, accountant, actuary and other expert fees and costs which may be required during the litigation process.

The request for fees of any type must be accompanied by a declaration by the client and copies of any bills for which they are requesting reimbursement, as well as a declaration from the attorney stating the amount the client has paid, the amount owed, or the anticipated amount of fees. An I&E would also be required if it had not previously been provided. The court may, on its own motion, or within a Request for Order/Motion made by either party, order that attorney fees be paid if/when one of the parties has submitted an application for waiver of Court Fees and Costs.

Property Orders

There are numerous property issues that may need to be resolved at this point. Most of these, however, will be temporary in nature.

1) A party may need to have the other party removed from the family home. This is referred to as a "kick-out" order.

2) A party may need to enforce the standard restraining orders such as: restraining the party from listing the family home for sale without the consent of the other party; cashing in their retirement; deleting the spouse and/or the children from the health insurance plan of the employee spouse; requiring a party to pay or jointly pay any community debts.

3) Any other orders which would require a party from either ceasing or requiring a party to comply with any orders relating to the parties' community or quasi-community property, and in some cases a party's separate property, such as making a specific payment on an automobile, line of credit, credit card, etc.

Temporary Restraining Orders (TROs)

Orders which do not have to do with Domestic Violence issues (where DVPA forms must be used) fall into the general category of Temporary Restraining Orders (TROs). TROs can be similar to the property orders referenced above. They may be injunctive in nature, such as requesting that a grandparent or other person be able to have contact or not have contact with a child; a parent wanting to take a child on vacation to another state, when the parent has not notified and/or received written consent from the other parent pursuant to a current Order; or, the TRO may be requesting that a child be transferred or enrolled, or **not** be transferred or enrolled, in a school or with a child care provider, because the other parent hasn't consented.

TROs are usually limited in time frame and nature. The Judge has discretion to make Orders that he or she feels are necessary. If the TRO is granted at an Ex Parte hearing, it is only in effect until the hearing or until the party complies with the Order. At the regularly scheduled hearing, the Judge may deny the request or state that the issue has been resolved. In the event the Judge grants or extends the TRO at the regularly scheduled hearing, it will remain in effect until further order of the court (at a future hearing or trial) or for a maximum period of three years unless otherwise specified by the Judge. TROs which are granted for a three-year period must be renewed prior to the expiration of that period, if necessary, otherwise the TRO will expire. Note that the addition of FC § 6250.3 (as discussed above) allows the court to extend this Order to five years if it is considered a protective order. The TRO may be renewed upon application to the court 3 months prior to the expiration date. FC§ 6345(c) states that "failure to state the expiration date on the face of the form creates an order with a duration of three years from the date of issuance." Care must be taken by the attorney that the Judge specifically enters the expiration date preferred or requested on the *face* of the form to avoid any confusion and ambiguity as to the expiration date.

Other Issues Requiring Resolution

The "Other" section is simply a catchall for any other matters related to the Dissolution or Legal Separation (or Paternity) which do not fit in any of the other categories and for which a Request for Order must be filed.

This section is often used for post-Judgment enforcement requests. Examples would be: establishing support arrears; requesting that a party assign, transfer or sell property which was to be distributed pursuant to the Dissolution Judgment or comply with other orders made. It however, can contain pre-Judgment issues such as asking that another party or entity be joined in the matter, as well as other compliance issues.

Other Related Documents

There are numerous types of additional documents which may be prepared, filed and/or served with a Request for Order. Depending upon the type of relief requested, it may be beneficial, although not required, to prepare Points and Authorities ("P&A"). In fact, some Judges prefer to have Points and Authorities, particularly if there is a complex issue being heard. The Points and Authorities, as a separate but a related document, call special attention to the issue(s) and legal remedies as well as case law on which the Judge must rely. The Judge will then have the opportunity to review your firm's P.A. and research the issues prior to the hearing. As noted under Notice of Motion, P&As usually relate to issues of law. However, in a Request for Order, you may have both issues of fact and of law to be resolved by the court. Attorney's fees, for example, may be considered an issue of law and may thus warrant the preparation of P&As. It is always a good idea to research the local rules to determine when/if P&As should be filed, and/or keep a log of each Judge's preferences as you learn them.

When there are complex property issues, it may be a good idea to file a Property Declaration (FL-160) with the Court. When requesting that attorney fees be paid from the responding party's separate property, it will be beneficial to show the Court the community property assets and debts as well as the responding party's available separate assets.

There are occasions when it will be necessary to prepare Supplemental Declarations. In the event you receive information, such as a Family Court Services report, that is important to the case just prior to the hearing and you want to be able to present it to the court, you can only do so if you have provided notice to the other party. In that instance, it is wise to prepare a Supplemental Declaration of the attorney and/or the client presenting the information or attachments as appropriate. This document will then be served on the opposing party, or their attorney of record, and filed with the court, pursuant to the Notice requirements of CCP§ 1003. Alternatively, if you have received the Responsive Declaration and it contains erroneous information, statements that are false or that requires further clarification, it would be important to file a Reply Declaration, signed by the client. Again, the Declaration must be served on the other party and filed with the court in order for it to be considered by the Judge.

Preparation of the Request for Order

You will want to compile all of the information, which pertains to the client's case and the issues as referenced above. The issues raised in the Request for Order should be included in the applicable Judicial Council forms or written declarations where needed in proper sequence. The client's written declaration and any exhibits will then be attached. I have followed that same order in discussing each of the issues in this section. For instance, if there are issues of child custody and/or visitation that will be the first form and issue addressed in the document. Child support will be next, and so on.

If written declarations are used, you will also want to check with the appropriate person in the office to see if there are any standard templates or formats that the office prefers to use. Many offices will, over the course of time, develop templates for you to use in certain situations. Due to the complexity of issues and the uniqueness of each family law case, it may be difficult to use such a template, but a very least you will be able to review previously prepared Declarations so that you can have a feel for the manner and style by which the attorney likes them written. Each attorney in the firm may have their own stylistic preferences for format and language. However, whenever possible don't reinvent the wheel and don't be afraid to ask, in advance, as it will save you a lot of time in the long run.

For your reference, a very simple Declaration is included at Appendix 4E. This sample will give you an idea of the general format and the basic detail which should be provided, as well as information which may be included. I cannot stress enough, that if you have **never** drafted a family law declaration before, you should ask someone at the firm to provide you with samples. Always remember to keep the declaration clear, concise and to the point.

Prepare a first draft of the Declaration for the attorney's review and then have the client review it for accuracy. Once all of the Judicial Council forms are complete and the Declaration is ready, the attorney should review **all** of the documents. The client should then be called to come in and review and sign the documents. The documents are then ready for filing and a hearing date can be obtained.

In addition to submitting the *original* documents, which the Court will keep, you will want to make at least two additional copies. (I prefer to make three: one to retain in the file until I have received filed copies back from the court and two copies to be filed.) By having two complete filed copies you will always have one copy to retain in your file from which you can make a copy for the client. You will also have one that you will use for serving the opposing party. I have also found that if you place the "original" filed copy in the client's file it is less likely that pages will be misplaced or not copied resulting in missing or illegible pages. Oftentimes, the court's stamp is unreadable. As you begin making copies of copies, as time goes on, some of the information becomes illegible.

Along with the original and copies of the Request for Order and related documents, you will need to provide the court with possible dates for the hearings. Some courts will require or allow you to call the clerk and find out the dates available on the Court's calendar. You should find out what the local customs (sometimes it's a rule and sometimes what is customary) are in this regard and follow that procedure. You will also need to submit the filing fee with the Request for Order. Most counties now have their filing fees posted on their website. It is always a good idea to periodically check the court's fees to see if they have changed (or some courts may tell you when the next change will occur).

Upon receiving the filed documents from the Court, you will want to do the following: 1) calendar the hearing date; 2) send a copy to the client with a cover letter advising them of the date, time and location of the hearing and that the client's appearance is **mandatory**, and any other information the attorney wishes you to provide; 3) send the documents out for service on the opposing party or his/her attorney of record; 4) calendar the date the opposing party's response is due — which is nine (9) court days prior to the hearing; and 5) calendar the Reply Declaration, which is two (2) days prior to the hearing. You should also check local rules or the Court Clerk to determine if the documents must be filed prior to a certain time of the day.

Service of Motions and Request for Order Documents

In most cases a Request for Order **must** be personally served. It must be served at least 16 court days prior to the hearing. In the event the Request for Hearing is served by mail or fax, the 5-day mail or 2-day fax rules, as applicable, must be carefully followed. *CCP§ 1005(a)(13)-(b)*. [**Author's note:** *always* **check this code section to determine if these dates have been changed.**] A circumstance when you might serve by fax or mail would be if the opposing party's attorney has been informed or is expecting service. The attorney may suggest or agree to be served by a method other than personal service. In that event, as the paralegal, once the documents are served by fax or mail, you will want to make sure that you have the completed the proof of service, attached a copy of the fax transmission confirmation, and have the papers filed with the court as soon as possible after service of the documents.

Remember to send the "reciprocal" documents to the opposing party along with the filed documents. Whenever any kind of financial issue is raised in a Request for Order (or Motion), an Income & Expense Declaration must be completed and served by the moving party. Thus, a blank Income & Expense Declaration must also be served. See below for examples of "reciprocal" documents:

Filed Document	Reciprocal Document
Request for Order w/ Attachments	Blank Responsive Declaration
Income & Expense Declaration	Blank Income & Expense Declaration

As soon as the documents have been served, you will want to make sure that the Proof of Service is filed with the court. Many Courts will question whether the opposing party was properly served and whether the Court has the ability to hear the matter if they do not have a copy of the filed Proof of Service. In some cases, the Proof of Service will not have made it to the Court file after processing. Therefore it is imperative that the filed copy be in the client's file that goes with the attorney to Court.

Upon receipt of the Responsive Declaration and the accompanying I&E, you will want to send copies to the client. Often, the attorney will want to have the client come in and review the Responsive Declaration in case a Supplemental Declaration or a Rebuttal will need to be filed. The attorney will advise you on this, or as you become experienced, you can ask the attorney if that is the course he or she wants to take.

Department of Child Support Services

In all situations where a parent is receiving public assistance through the county where they reside, the California Department of Child Support Services (CDCSS) must be served a copy of the hearing documents. In some cases, the local court will require that the matter be set for a specific time on the Court's calendar. (Check your local rules or with the Court Clerk.) In the event the CDCSS is not served with the documents and the parent is receiving public assistance, the court will, on its own order, continue the matter until such time as the DCSS can have a representative present at the hearing.

Forms Associated with Topic

Request for Order (FL-300)

Spousal or Partner Support Declaration Attachment (FL-157)

Request for Attorneys Fees & Costs (FL-158)

Written declarations and exhibits (pleading)

Income & Expense Declarations (FL-150)

(See examples of some forms on the following pages)

Key Terms

- Domestic Violence Protection Act
- Request for Order
- Harassment
- Standard Restraining Orders
- Temporary Restraining Orders
- Legal Custody
- Physical Custody
- Mediation
- Collaborative Practice
- Ex Parte Declarations and Hearings
- Responsive Declaration
- Gross Income
- Net Income
- Income & Expense Declarations
- Standard of Living
- Temporary Spousal Support

Request for Order

	FL-300
ATTORNEY OR PARTY WITHOUT ATTORNEY (Name, State Bar number, and address): ⌐JOAN CARE-ACTOR, SBN ******** LAW OFFICES OF JOAN CARE-ACTOR 75000 WHY ME LANE SACRAMENTO, CA 95826 　TELEPHONE NO.: 916-555-1234　　FAX NO. (Optional): 916-555-1233 　E-MAIL ADDRESS (Optional): joan@ care-actorlaw.com 　ATTORNEY FOR (Name): SANDIE SHORES, Petitioner	FOR COURT USE ONLY To keep other people from seeing what you entered on your form, please press the Clear This Form button at the end of the form when finished.

SUPERIOR COURT OF CALIFORNIA, COUNTY OF SACRAMENTO
STREET ADDRESS: 3341 POWER INN ROAD
MAILING ADDRESS: 3341 POWER INN RAOD
CITY AND ZIP CODE: SACRAMENTO, CA 95826
BRANCH NAME: FAMILY LAW DIVISION

PETITIONER/PLAINTIFF: SANDIE SHORES
RESPONDENT/DEFENDANT: ROCKY SHORES
OTHER PARENT/PARTY:

REQUEST FOR ORDER ☑ Child Custody ☑ Child Support ☑ Attorney Fees and Costs	☐ **MODIFICATION** ☑ **Visitation** ☑ **Spousal Support**	☐ **Temporary Emergency Court Order** ☑ **Other** *(specify):*	CASE NUMBER:

1. TO (name): ROCKY SHORES

2. A hearing on this *Request for Order* will be held as follows: **If child custody or visitation is an issue in this proceeding, Family Code section 3170 requires mediation before or at the same time as the hearing *(see item 7.)***

a. Date:	Time:	☐ Dept.:	☐ Room.:

　b. Address of court　☑ same as noted above　☐ other *(specify):*

3. Attachments to be served with this *Request for Order:*
   a. A **blank** *Responsive Declaration* (form FL-320)
   b. ☑ Completed *Income and Expense Declaration* (form FL-150) and a **blank** *Income and Expense Declaration*

   c. ☐ Completed *Financial Statement (Simplified)* (form FL-155) and a **blank** *Financial Statement (Simplified)*
   d. ☐ Points and authorities
   e. ☐ Other *(specify):*

Date:
JOAN CARE-ACTOR　　　　　　　　　　　　　　　▶
　　　(TYPE OR PRINT NAME)　　　　　　　　　　　　　　　　　　(SIGNATURE)

☑ COURT ORDER

4. ☑ YOU ARE ORDERED TO APPEAR IN COURT AT THE DATE AND TIME LISTED IN ITEM 2 TO GIVE ANY LEGAL REASON WHY THE ORDERS REQUESTED SHOULD NOT BE GRANTED.

5. ☐ Time for ☐ service ☐ hearing is shortened. Service must be on or before *(date):*
6. Any responsive declaration must be served on or before *(date):*
7. The parties are ordered to attend mandatory custody services as follows:

8. ☐ You are ordered to comply with the *Temporary Emergency Court Orders* (form FL-305) attached.
9. ☐ Other *(specify):*

Date: _____
　　　　　　　　　　　　　　　　　　　　JUDICIAL OFFICER

To the person who received this *Request for Order:* If you wish to respond to this *Request for Order,* you must file a *Responsive Declaration to Request for Order* (form FL-320) and serve a copy on the other parties at least nine court days before the hearing date unless the court has ordered a shorter period of time. You do not have to pay a filing fee to file the *Responsive Declaration to Request for Order* (form FL-320) or any other declaration including an *Income and Expense Declaration (form FL-150)* or *Financial Statement (Simplified)* (form FL-155).

Page 1 of 4

Request for Order

FL-300

PETITIONER/PLAINTIFF: SANDIE SHORES	CASE NUMBER:
RESPONDENT/DEFENDANT: ROCKY SHORES	
OTHER PARENT/PARTY:	

REQUEST FOR ORDER AND SUPPORTING DECLARATION

[✔] **Petitioner** [ ] **Respondent** [ ] **Other Parent/Party** requests the following orders:

1. [✔] **CHILD CUSTODY** [ ] **To be ordered pending the hearing**

a. Child's name and age	b. Legal custody to (name of person who makes decisions about health, education, etc.)	c. Physical custody to (name of person with whom child will live)
EDDY SHORES - 9	JOINT	SANDIE SHORES
SHELLY SHORES - 4	JOINT	SANDIE SHORES

    d. [✔] As requested in form [✔] *Child Custody and Visitation Application Attachment* (form FL-311)
           [ ] *Request for Child Abduction Prevention Orders* (form FL-312)
           [ ] *Children's Holiday Schedule Attachment* (form FL-341(C))
           [ ] *Additional Provisions—Physical Custody Attachment* (form FL-341(D))
           [✔] *Joint Legal Custody Attachment* (form FL-341(E))
           [ ] *Other (Attachment 1d)*

    e. [ ] Modify existing order
        (1) filed on *(date):*
        (2) ordering *(specify):*

2. [✔] **CHILD VISITATION** *(PARENTING TIME)* [ ] **To be ordered pending the hearing**

    a. As requested in: (1) [✔] Attachment 2a (2) [✔] *Child Custody and Visitation Application Attachment* (form FL-311)
                (3) [ ] Other *(specify):*
    b. [ ] Modify existing order
        (1) filed on *(date):*
        (2) ordering *(specify):*

    c. [ ] One or more domestic violence restraining/protective orders are now in effect. *(Attach a copy of the orders if you have one.)* The orders are from the following court or courts *(specify county and state):*
        (1) [ ] Criminal: County/state: (3) [ ] Juvenile: County/state:
              Case No. *(if known):*   Case No. *(if known):*
        (2) [ ] Family: County/state: (4) [ ] Other: County/state:
              Case No. *(if known):*   Case No. *(if known):*

3. [✔] **CHILD SUPPORT** *(An earnings assignment order may be issued.)*

    a. Child's name and age   b. [✔] I request support based on the   c. Monthly amount requested (if not by guideline)
                      child support guidelines $

EDDY SHORES - 9
SHELLY SHORES - 4

    d. [ ] Modify existing order
        (1) filed on *(date):*
        (2) ordering *(specify):*

Notice: The court is required to order child support based on the income of both parents. It normally continues until the child is 18. You must supply the court with information about your finances by filing an *Income and Expense Declaration* (form FL-150) or a *Financial Statement (Simplified)* (form FL-155). Otherwise, the child support order will be based on information about your income that the court receives from other sources, including the other parent.

Request for Order

FL-300

PETITIONER/PLAINTIFF: SANDIE SHORES	CASE NUMBER:
RESPONDENT/DEFENDANT: ROCKY SHORES	
OTHER PARENT/PARTY:	

4. ☑ SPOUSAL OR PARTNER SUPPORT *(An earnings assignment order may be issued.)*

    a. ☑ Amount requested *(monthly)*: $ 2,000   c. ☐ Modify existing order

    b. ☐ Terminate existing order   (1) filed on *(date)*:

       (1) filed on *(date)*:   (2) ordering *(specify)*:

       (2) ordering *(specify)*:

    d. ☑ The *Spousal or Partner Support Declaration Attachment* (form FL-157) is attached *(for modification of spousal or partner support after judgment only)*

    e. An *Income and Expense Declaration* (form FL-150) must be attached

5. ☑ ATTORNEY FEES AND COSTS are requested on *Request for Attorney Fees and Costs Order Attachment* (form FL-319) or a declaration that addresses the factors covered in that form. An *Income and Expense Declaration* (form FL-150) must be attached. A *Supporting Declaration for Attorney Fees and Costs Order Attachment* (form FL-158) or a declaration that addresses the factors covered in that form must also be attached.

6. ☑ PROPERTY RESTRAINT   ☐ **To be ordered pending the hearing**

    a. The ☑ petitioner ☑ respondent ☐ claimant is restrained from transferring, encumbering, hypothecating, concealing, or in any way disposing of any property, real or personal, whether community, quasi-community, or separate, except in the usual course of business or for the necessities of life.

        ☑ The applicant will be notified at least five business days before any proposed extraordinary expenditures, and an accounting of such will be made to the court.

    b. ☑ Both parties are restrained and enjoined from cashing, borrowing against, canceling, transferring, disposing of, or changing the beneficiaries of any insurance or other coverage, including life, health, automobile, and disability, held for the benefit of the parties or their minor children.

    c. ☑ Neither party may incur any debts or liabilities for which the other may be held responsible, other than in the ordinary course of business or for the necessities of life.

7. ☑ PROPERTY CONTROL   ☐ **To be ordered pending the hearing**

    a. ☑ The petitioner ☐ respondent is given the exclusive temporary use, possession, and control of the following property that we own or are buying *(specify)*:

        11155 Turtle Dove Court, Folsom, CA 95630

    b. ☐ The petitioner ☑ respondent is ordered to make the following payments on liens and encumbrances coming due while the order is in effect:

Debt	Amount of payment	Pay to
Mortgage	600	XYZ MORTGAGE & LOAN

8. ☐ OTHER RELIEF *(specify)*:

NOTE: To obtain domestic violence restraining orders, you must use the forms *Request for Order (Domestic Violence Prevention)* (form DV-100), *Temporary Restraining Order (Domestic Violence)* (form DV-110), and *Notice of Court Hearing (Domestic Violence)* (form DV-109).

Request for Order

	CASE NUMBER:
PETITIONER/PLAINTIFF: SANDIE SHORES	
RESPONDENT/DEFENDANT: ROCKY SHORES	
OTHER PARENT/PARTY:	

9. ☐ **I request** that time for service of the *Request for Order* and accompanying papers be shortened so that these documents may be served no less than *(specify number):* _____ days before the time set for the hearing. I need to have this order shortening time because of the facts specified in item 10 or the attached declaration.

10. ☑ FACTS IN SUPPORT of orders requested and change of circumstances for any modification are *(specify)*:
      ☑ Contained in the attached declaration. (*You may use* Attached Declaration *(form MC-031) for this purpose. The attached declaration must not exceed 10 pages in length unless permission to file a longer declaration has been obtained from the court.*)

    ** SEE WRITTEN SAMPLE DECLATATION - APPENDIX 4E

I declare under penalty of perjury under the laws of the State of California that the foregoing is true and correct.

Date:

▶

_____
(TYPE OR PRINT NAME)

_____
(SIGNATURE OF APPLICANT)

Requests for Accommodations
Assistive listening systems, computer-assisted real-time captioning, or sign language interpreter services are available if you ask at least five days before the proceeding. Contact the clerk's office or go to *www.courts.ca.gov/forms* for *Request for Accommodations by Persons With Disabilities and Response* (form MC-410). (Civil Code, § 54.8.)

For your protection and privacy, please press the Clear This Form button after you have printed the form.

Save This Form   Print This Form   Clear This Form

Child Custody and Visitation Application

To keep other people from seeing what you entered on your form, please press the Clear This Form button at the end of the form when finished.

FL-311

PETITIONER/PLAINTIFF: SANDIE SHORES	CASE NUMBER:
RESPONDENT/DEFENDANT: ROCKY SHORES	

CHILD CUSTODY AND VISITATION APPLICATION ATTACHMENT

TO [✔] Petition, Response, Application for Order or Responsive Declaration   [ ] Other *(specify)*:

[ ] To be ordered now and effective until the hearing

1. [✔] **Custody.** Custody of the minor children of the parties is requested as follows:

Child's Name	Date of Birth	Legal Custody to *(person who makes decisions about health, education, etc.)*	Physical Custody to *(person with whom the child lives)*
EDDY SHORES	5/1/05	JOINT	SANDIE SHORES
SHELLY SHORES	10/15/09	JOINT	SANDIE SHORES

2. [✔] **Visitation.**

a. [✔] Reasonable right of visitation to the party without physical custody **(not appropriate in cases involving domestic violence)**

b. [ ] See the attached _____-page document dated *(specify date):*

c. [ ] The parties will go to mediation at *(specify location):*

d. [ ] No visitation

e. [✔] Visitation for the [ ] petitioner [✔] respondent will be as follows:

    (1) [✔] **Weekends starting** *(date):* 4/1/14

      (The first weekend of the month is the first weekend with a Saturday.)

      [✔] 1st [ ] 2nd [✔] 3rd [ ] 4th [✔] 5th   weekend of the month

      from FRIDAY   at 5   [ ] a.m. [✔] p.m.
      (day of week)   *(time)*

      to SUNDAY   at 6   [ ] a.m. [✔] p.m.
      (day of week)   *(time)*

      (a) [ ] The parents will alternate the fifth weekends, with the [ ] petitioner [ ] respondent having the initial fifth weekend, which starts *(date):*

      (b) [ ] The petitioner will have fifth weekends in [ ] odd [ ] even   months.

    (2) [ ] **Alternate weekends starting** *(date):*

      The [ ] petitioner [ ] respondent will have the children with him or her during the period

      from _____ at _____ [ ] a.m. [ ] p.m.
      (day of week)   *(time)*

      to _____ at _____ [ ] a.m. [ ] p.m.
      (day of week)   *(time)*

    (3) [✔] **Weekdays starting** *(date):* 4/1/14

      The [ ] petitioner [✔] respondent will have the children with him or her during the period

      from WEDNESDAY at 5 [ ] a.m. [✔] p.m.
      (day of week)   *(time)*

      to WEDNESDAY at 8 [ ] a.m. [✔] p.m.
      (day of week)   *(time)*

    (4) [ ] **Other** *(specify days and times as well as any additional restrictions):*

         [ ] See Attachment 2e(4).

Page 1 of 2

Form Approved for Optional Use
Judicial Council of California
FL-311 [Rev. July 1, 2005]

CHILD CUSTODY AND VISITATION APPLICATION ATTACHMENT

Family Code, § 3200 et seq
www.courtinfo.ca.gov

Child Custody and Visitation Application

PETITIONER: SANDIE SHORES

RESPONDENT: ROCKY SHORES

CASE NUMBER:

3. ☐ **Supervised visitation.**
I request that *(name):*   have supervised visitation with the minor children according to the
schedule set out on page 1 and that the visits be supervised by *(name):*
who is a ☐ professional ☐ nonprofessional supervisor. The supervisor's phone number is *(specify):*

I request that the costs of supervision be paid as follows: petitioner: percent; respondent: percent.

**If item 3 is checked, you must attach a declaration that shows why unsupervised visitation would be bad for your
children. The judge is required to consider supervised visitation if one parent is alleging domestic violence and is
protected by a restraining order.**

4. ☐ **Transportation for visitation and place of exchange.**
   a. ☐ Transportation **to** the visits will be provided by *(name):*
   b. ☐ Transportation **from** the visits will be provided by *(name):*
   c. ☐ Drop-off of the children will be at *(address):*
   d. ☐ Pick-up of the children will be at *(address):*
   e. ☐ The children will be driven only by a licensed and insured driver. The car or truck must have legal child restraint
       devices.
   f. ☐ During the exchanges, the parent driving the children will wait in the car and the other parent will wait in his or her
       home while the children go between the car and the home.
   g. ☐ Other *(specify):*

5. ☑ **Travel with children.** The ☐ petitioner ☑ respondent ☐ other *(name):*
   must have written permission from the other parent or a court order to take the children out of
   a. ☑ the state of California.
   b. ☐ the following counties *(specify):*
   c. ☐ other places *(specify):*

6. ☐ **Child abduction prevention.** There is a risk that one of the parents will take the children out of California without the other
   parent's permission. I request the orders set out on attached form FL-312.

7. ☑ **Children's holiday schedule.** I request the holiday and visitation schedule set out on the attached ☑ form FL-341(C)
   ☐ other *(specify):*

8. ☐ **Additional custody provisions.** I request the additional orders regarding custody set out on the attached
   ☐ form FL-341(D) ☐ other *(specify):*

9. ☐ **Joint legal custody provisions.** I request joint legal custody and want the additional orders set out on the attached
   ☐ form FL-341(E) ☐ other *(specify):*

10. ☐ **Other.** I request the following additional orders *(specify):*

For your protection and privacy, please press the Clear This Form
button after you have printed the form.   **Save This Form**   │ **Print This Form** │ │ **Clear This Form** │

Spousal or Partner Support Declaration

	FL-157
PETITIONER/PLAINTIFF: SANDIE SHORES RESPONDENT/DEFENDANT: ROCKY SHORES OTHER PARTY:	CASE NUMBER:

SPOUSAL OR PARTNER SUPPORT DECLARATION ATTACHMENT

[ ] Declaration for Default or Uncontested Judgment (form FL-170)   [ ] Supporting Declaration for Attorney's Fees and
[✔] Other (specify):   Costs Attachment (form FL-158)
    REQUEST FOR ORDER

1. **Spousal or domestic partner support.** I request that the court (check all that apply):
   a. [✔] Enter a judgment for spousal or domestic partner support for [✔] Petitioner [ ] Respondent.
   b. [ ] Modify the judgment for spousal or domestic partner support for [ ] Petitioner [ ] Respondent.
   c. [ ] Deny the request to modify the judgment for spousal or domestic partner support.
   d. [ ] Terminate jurisdiction to award spousal or domestic partner support to [ ] Petitioner [ ] Respondent.

2. [✔] **Attorney fees and costs.** I request that the court (check one):
   a. [✔] Order my attorney fees and costs to be paid by [✔] my spouse or domestic partner [ ] a joined party (specify):

   b. [ ] Deny the request for attorney fees and costs.

3. The facts in support of my request are:

   a. **Family Code section 4320(a)(1)**

   (1) The supported party has the following training, job skills, and work history:
   I AM CURRENTLY A STAY-AT-HOME MOM. I VOLUNTEER A FEW HOURS A WEEK AT OUR
   DAUGHTER'S DAY CARE TO OFF-SET THE COSTS SO THAT SHE CAN HAVE SOME PLAY AND
   SOCIALIZATION TIME. I HAVEN'T WORKED OUTSIDE THE HOME SINCE 2005 WHEN OUR OLDEST
   CHILD WAS BORN AND DO NOT HAVE ANY MARKETABLE SKILLS AT THIS TIME

   (2) The current job market for the job skills of the supported party described in item 3a(1) is:
   NONE.

   (3) The supported party would need the following time and expense to acquire the education or training to develop the job
   skills described in item 3a(1):
   I WOULD HAVE TO GO BACK TO SCHOOL AND FINISH MY DEGREE IN BUSINESS - WHICH I DID
   NOT FINISH BECAUSE OF THE BIRTH OF OUR FIRST CHILD. RESPONDENT AND I AGREED THAT
   I WOULD NOT WORK FORMALLY OUTSIDE THE HOME WHILE OUR CHILDREN WERE ENROLLED
   IN SCHOOL. I REQUEST THAT THE COURT MAINTAIN THAT STANDARD OF LIVING UNTIL OUR
   YOUNGEST CHILD IS IN SCHOOL AT LEAST 6 HOURS A DAY. AT WHICH TIME I WOULD GO BACK
   TO SCHOOL AND FINISH MY DEGREE SO THAT I COULD ENTER THE JOB MARKET.

   (4) To develop other, more marketable job skills or employment, the supported party would need the following retraining
   or education:
   SAME AS #3 ABOVE. I WOULD NEED THE APPROPRIATE SKILLS AND TRAINING CLOSER TO THE
   TIME I WILL RE-ENTER THE JOB MARKET. IT WAS MY GOAL TO ATTAIN AT LEAST AN A.A.
   DEGREE IN BUSINESS SO THAT I CAN WORK IN AN OFFICE. I WAS PREVIOUSLY AN
   ADMINISTRATIVE ASSISTANT IN AN INSURANCE FIRM.

Form Approved for Optional Use
Judicial Council of California
FL-157 [New January 1, 2012]
**SPOUSAL OR PARTNERSHIP SUPPORT
DECLARATION ATTACHMENT**
Family Code, §§ 270, 2030,2032, 4320,
5344, 7640
www.courts.ca.gov

Spousal or Partner Support Declaration

FL-157

PETITIONER/PLAINTIFF: SANDIE SHORES	CASE NUMBER:
RESPONDENT/DEFENDANT: ROCKY SHORES	
OTHER PARTY:	

3. Facts in support of request.

b. **Family Code section 4320(a)(2)**

Provide any facts that indicate the supported party's earning ability is, or is not, lower than it might be if he or she had not had periods of unemployment because of the time needed to attend to domestic duties *(explain)*:

I HAVE BEEN UNEMPLOYED SINCE 2005 AND MUCH HAS CHANGED IN THE BUSINESS WORLD SINCE THAT TIME. I HAVE LIMITED KNOWLEDGE OF USE OF COMPUTERS AND THE SOFTWARE USED IN THE BUSINESS ENVIRONMENT. MY HUSBAND AND I AGREED THAT I WOULD STAY AT HOME AND RAISE OUR CHILDREN RATHER THAN WORK. IT IS THE STATUS QUO IN OUR FAMILY AND I BELIEVE BEST FOR OUR CHILDREN IF THAT IS MAINTAINED.

c. **Family Code section 4320(b)**

Provide any facts that indicate that the supported party contributed to the education, training, career position, or license of the supporting party.

NONE

d. **Family Code section 4320(c)**

(1) The supporting party ☐ does ☐ does not   have the ability to pay spousal or domestic partner support.

(2) The supporting party's current gross income from employment or self-employment is *(specify):* $6,000

(3) The supporting party's current income from investments, retirement, other sources is *(specify):*

(4) The supporting party's current assets and their values and balances are *(specify):*

UNKNOWN AT THIS TIME.

(5) The supporting party's standard of living is *(describe, for example, type and frequency of vacations, value of home and other real estate, value of investments, type of vehicles owned, credit card use or nonuse):*

THE STANDARD OF LIVING IS PROVIDED WITHIN THE INCOME AND EXPENSE DECLARATION AND ALSO WILL BE SUBJECT TO PROOF WHEN RESPONDENT PROVIDES HIS INCOME & EXPENSE DECLARATIONS.
RESPONDENT HAS BEEN THE SOLE PROVIDER FOR THE FAMILY AND WE HAVE LIVED WITHIN THOSE MEANS DURING THE COURSE OF OUR MARRIAGE. TO FELT IT WAS BEST THAT RESPONDENT BE THE BREAD-WINNER AND THAT I (PETITIONER) BE THE PRIMARY CARE-GIVER FOR THE CHILDREN.

**SPOUSAL OR PARTNERSHIP SUPPORT
DECLARATION ATTACHMENT**

Spousal or Partner Support Declaration

	FL-157
PETITIONER/PLAINTIFF: SANDIE SHORES RESPONDENT/DEFENDANT: ROCKY SHORES OTHER PARTY:	CASE NUMBER:

3. Facts in support of request.

   e. **Family Code section 4320(d)**

     The supported party ☑ does ☐ does not need support to maintain the standard of living we enjoyed during the marriage or domestic partnership.

   f. **Family Code Section 4320(e)**

     (1) The supported party's assets and obligations, including separate property, are *(list values and balances)*:

        THIS INFORMATION IS PROVIDED IN THE INCOME & EXPENSE DECLARATION FILE/SERVED WITH THIS REQUEST FOR ORDER.

     (2) The supporting party's assets and obligations, including separate property, are *(list values and balances)*:

        UNKNOWN AT THIS TIME; SUPPORTING PARTY (RESPONDENT) HAS FAILED TO COOPERATE WITH PETITIONER WHICH IS WHY THIS REQUEST FOR ORDER IS BEING FILED.

Spousal or Partner Support Declaration

FL-157

PETITIONER/PLAINTIFF: SANDIE SHORES	CASE NUMBER:
RESPONDENT/DEFENDANT: ROCKY SHORES	
OTHER PARTY:	

3. Facts in support of request.

    g. **Family Code section 4320(f)**

        Length of marriage or domestic partnership *(specify)*:
        WE HAVE BEEN MARRIED FOR ELEVEN YEARS AND ONE MONTH.

    h. **Family Code section 4320(g)**

        Provide any facts indicating whether or not the supported party is able to work without unduly interfering with the interests of the children in his or her care *(describe)*: SEE PREVIOUS DECLARATIONS

    i. **Family Code section 4320(h)**

        (1) Petitioner's age is *(specify):* 35   Respondent's age is *(specify):* 38

        (2) Petitioner's current health condition is *(describe):*
            GOOD

        (3) Respondent's current health condition is *(describe):*
            BELIEVED TO BE GOOD

    j. **Additional factors (Family Code sections 4320(i)–(n))**

        The court will also consider the following factors before making a judgment for spousal or domestic partner support:

        (1) Any documented evidence of domestic violence between the parties as defined in Family Code section 6211.

        (2) The immediate and specific tax consequences for each party;

        (3) The balance of the hardships on each party;

        (4) The criminal conviction of an abusive spouse in reducing or eliminating support in accordance with Family Code section 4325;

        (5) The goal that the supported party will be self-supporting within a reasonable period of time; and

        (6) Any other factors the court determines are just and equitable.

        Describe below any additional information that will assist the court in considering the above factors:

        AS PREVIOUSLY STATED, PETITIONER HAS NOT WORKED SINCE 2005 AND THEREFORE LACKS THE SKILLS AND TRAINING TO ENTER THE WORK-FORCE IN HER PREVIOUS CAPACITY AS AN ADMINISTRATIVE ASSISTANT.

        ADDITIONALLY, THE PARTIES AGREED THAT UNTIL THE YOUNGEST CHILD WAS IN SCHOOL FOR A MINIMUM OF 6 HOURS PER DAY (MIDDLE SCHOOL) SHE WOULD NOT WORK. HER "JOB" WAS TO BE TO CARE FOR THE CHILDREN, INCLUDING HELPING THEM WITH HOMEWORK, MAKING SURE THAT THEY WERE ABLE TO PARTICIPATE IN AND ATTEND ACTIVITIES AND EXTRA-CURRICULAR ACTIVITIES SUCH AS SOCCER, BASEBALL, SCOUTS, MUSIC LESSONS, PLAY DATES, ETC.

**SPOUSAL OR PARTNERSHIP SUPPORT
DECLARATION ATTACHMENT**

For your protection and privacy, please press the Clear This Form
button after you have printed the form.

Save This Form   **Print This Form**   **Clear This Form**

Supporting Declaration for Attorney's Fees and Costs

FL-158

PETITIONER/PLAINTIFF: SANDIE SHORES	CASE NUMBER:
RESPONDENT/DEFENDANT: ROCKY SHORES	
OTHER PARTY:	

SUPPORTING DECLARATION FOR ATTORNEY'S FEES AND COSTS ATTACHMENT

To: ☑ *Request for Attorney's Fees and Costs Attachment* (form FL-319)

☐ *Responsive Declaration* (form FL-320)

1. I am
   a. ☑ the petitioner/plaintiff.
   b. ☐ the respondent/defendant.
   c. ☐ the other party.

2. I request that the court ☑ grant ☐ grant in part ☐ deny the request for attorney's fees and costs.

3. I am providing the following information ☑ in support of ☐ in opposition to the request for attorney's fees and costs.
   a. The ☐ petitioner/plaintiff ☑ respondent/defendant ☐ other party has the ability to pay
   (1) ☐ my attorney's fees and costs.
   (2) ☐ his or her own attorney's fees and costs.
   (3) ☑ both my and his or her own attorney's fees and costs.
   (4) ☐ other (specify):

   b. The attorney's fees and costs can be paid from the following sources:
   RESPONDENT MAKES A GOOD SALARY AND HAS LEFT THE CHILDREN AND I WITH THE MORTGAGE, HOUSEHOLD UTILITIES, BILLS, CREDIT CARD DEBT, ETC. WHILE I WORK ONLY PART-TIME AS A NURSE'S AID. I HAD TO BORROW THE MONEY FROM MY PARENTS TO PAY THE RETAINER.

   c. The court should consider the following facts in deciding whether to grant, grant in part, or deny the request for attorney's fees and costs (describe):
   ☑ See Attachment 3c.
   THE CHILDREN SHOULD NOT SUFFER BECAUSE OF RESPONDENT'S LACK OF CONCERN FOR THEIR WELL-BEING, CARE, AND NECESSITIES OF LIFE. IF I HAVE TO PAY ATTORNEY'S FEES I WOULD HAVE TO TAKE MONEY FROM WHAT SHOULD BE SPENT ON SHELTER, CLOTHING, FOOD AND THE NECESSITIES OF LIFE.

   d. If appropriate, describe the reasons why a non-spouse party or domestic partner is involved in the case and whether he or she should or should not pay attorney's fees and costs:
   ☐ See Attachment 3d.

Form Approved for Optional Use
Judicial Council of California
FL-158 [New January 1, 2012]

**SUPPORTING DECLARATION FOR ATTORNEY'S FEES
AND COSTS ATTACHMENT
(Family Law)**

Family Code, §§ 270, 2030, 2032, 3121, 3557, 4320, 7605; Cal. Rules of Court, rules 5.425, 5.93
www.courts.ca.gov

Supporting Declaration for Attorney's Fees and Costs

FL-158

PETITIONER/PLAINTIFF: SANDIE SHORES RESPONDENT/DEFENDANT: ROCKY SHORES OTHER PARTY:	CASE NUMBER:

4. Has an order already been made for payment of child support in this case?
   a. ☑ No.
   b. ☐ Yes. If so, describe the order:
      (1) The ☐ petitioner/plaintiff ☐ respondent/defendant ☐ other party must pay: $
      per month for child support.
      (a) This order has been in effect since *(date):*
      (b) The payments ☐ have been made ☐ have not been made ☐ have been made in part
      since the date of the order.
      (2) ☐ Additional information *(specify):*

5. Has an order already been made for payment of spousal, partner, or family support in this case?
   a. ☑ No.
   b. ☐ Yes. If so, describe the order:
      (1) The ☐ petitioner/plaintiff ☐ respondent/defendant ☐ other party must pay: $
      per month for ☐ spousal support ☐ partner support ☐ family support.
      (a) This order has been in effect since *(date):*
      (b) The payments ☐ have been made ☐ have not been made ☐ have been made in part
      since the date of the order.
      (2) ☐ Additional information *(specify):*

6. If you are or were married to, or in a domestic partnership with, the person you are seeking fees from, the court must consider the factors in Family Code section 4320 in determining whether it is just and reasonable under the relative circumstances to award attorney's fees and costs. Complete and attach *Spousal or Partner Support Declaration Attachment* (form FL-157) or a comparable declaration to provide the court with information about the factors described in section 4320.

7. You must complete, file, and serve a current *Income and Expense Declaration* (form FL-150). It is considered current if you have completed form FL-150 within the past three months and no facts have changed since the time of completion.

8. Number of pages attached to this *Supporting Declaration:* _____

I declare under penalty of perjury under the laws of the State of California that the information contained on all pages of this form and any attachments is true and correct.

Date:

SANDIE SHORES
_____   ▶ _____
(TYPE OR PRINT NAME)   (SIGNATURE)

For your protection and privacy, please press the Clear This Form button after you have printed the form.   Save This Form   Print This Form   Clear This Form

Income and Expense Declaration

FL-150

ATTORNEY OR PARTY WITHOUT ATTORNEY *(Name, State Bar number, and address):*	
JOAN CARE-ACTOR, SBN ******** CARE-ACTOR LAW FIRM 75000 WHY ME LANE SACRAMENTO, CA 95826 TELEPHONE NO.: 916-555-1234 E-MAIL ADDRESS *(Optional):* joan@care-actorlaw.com ATTORNEY FOR *(Name):* SANDIE SHORES, Petitioner	To keep other people from seeing what you entered on your form, please press the Clear This Form button at the end of the form when finished.

SUPERIOR COURT OF CALIFORNIA, COUNTY OF SACRAMENTO
STREET ADDRESS: 3341 POWER INN ROAD
MAILING ADDRESS: 3341 POWER INN ROAD
CITY AND ZIP CODE: SACRAMENTO, CA 95826
BRANCH NAME: FAMILY LAW DIVISION

PETITIONER/PLAINTIFF: SANDIE SHORES
RESPONDENT/DEFENDANT: ROCKY SHORES
OTHER PARENT/CLAIMANT:

INCOME AND EXPENSE DECLARATION	CASE NUMBER: 14FLXXXXXX

1. **Employment** *(Give information on your current job or, if you're unemployed, your most recent job.)*

    Attach copies of your pay stubs for last two months (black out social security numbers).

    a. Employer: GRETA'S SENIOR CARE FACILITY
    b. Employer's address: #6 SENILITY LANE, RANCHO CORDOVA, CA
    c. Employer's phone number: 916-555-5550
    d. Occupation: NURSE'S AID
    e. Date job started: 9/2013
    f. If unemployed, date job ended:
    g. I work about 20 hours per week.
    h. I get paid $ 2,000 gross (before taxes) ☑ per month ☐ per week ☐ per hour.

    (If you have more than one job, attach an 8½-by-11-inch sheet of paper and list the same information as above for your other jobs. Write "Question 1—Other Jobs" at the top.)

2. **Age and education**

    a. My age is *(specify):* 35
    b. I have completed high school or the equivalent: ☑ Yes ☐ No   If no, highest grade completed *(specify):*
    c. Number of years of college completed *(specify):* 1.5   ☐ Degree(s) obtained *(specify):*
    d. Number of years of graduate school completed *(specify):*   ☐ Degree(s) obtained *(specify):*
    e. I have: ☐ professional/occupational license(s) *(specify):*
       ☐ vocational training *(specify):*

3. **Tax information**

    a. ☑ I last filed taxes for tax year *(specify year):* 2013
    b. My tax filing status is ☐ single ☐ head of household ☑ married, filing separately
       ☐ married, filing jointly with *(specify name):*
    c. I file state tax returns in ☑ California ☐ other *(specify state):*
    d. I claim the following number of exemptions (including myself) on my taxes *(specify):* 3

4. **Other party's income.** I estimate the gross monthly income (before taxes) of the other party in this case at *(specify):* $
    This estimate is based on *(explain):* PREVIOUS TAX RETURNS

(If you need more space to answer any questions on this form, attach an 8½-by-11-inch sheet of paper and write the question number before your answer.) Number of pages attached: _____

I declare under penalty of perjury under the laws of the State of California that the information contained on all pages of this form and any attachments is true and correct.

Date:
SANDIE SHORES   ▶
_____   _____
(TYPE OR PRINT NAME)   (SIGNATURE OF DECLARANT)

Income and Expense Declaration

PETITIONER/PLAINTIFF: SANDIE SHORES	CASE NUMBER:
RESPONDENT/DEFENDANT: ROCKY SHORES	14FLXXXXXX
OTHER PARENT/CLAIMANT:	

Attach copies of your pay stubs for the last two months and proof of any other income. Take a copy of your latest federal tax return to the court hearing. *(Black out your social security number on the pay stub and tax return.)*

5. **Income** *(For average monthly, add up all the income you received in each category in the last 12 months and divide the total by 12.)*

		Last month	Average monthly
a.	Salary or wages (gross, before taxes)...	$2,000	2,000
b.	Overtime (gross, before taxes)...	$_____	_____
c.	Commissions or bonuses...	$_____	_____
d.	Public assistance (for example: TANF, SSI, GA/GR) ☐ currently receiving	$_____	_____
e.	Spousal support ☐ from this marriage ☐ from a different marriage..................	$_____	_____
f.	Partner support ☐ from this domestic partnership ☐ from a different domestic partnership	$_____	_____
g.	Pension/retirement fund payments..	$_____	_____
h.	Social security retirement (not SSI)	$_____	_____
i.	Disability: ☐ Social security (not SSI) ☐ State disability (SDI) ☐ Private insurance .	$_____	_____
j.	Unemployment compensation..	$_____	_____
k.	Workers' compensation...	$_____	_____
l.	Other (military BAQ, royalty payments, etc.) *(specify):*	$_____	_____

6. **Investment income** *(Attach a schedule showing gross receipts less cash expenses for each piece of property.)*

a.	Dividends/interest...	$_____	_____
b.	Rental property income	$_____	_____
c.	Trust income...	$_____	_____
d.	Other *(specify):*	$_____	_____

7. **Income from self-employment, after business expenses for all businesses**..................... $2,000   2,000

    I am the ☐ owner/sole proprietor ☐ business partner ☐ other *(specify):*

    Number of years in this business *(specify):*

    Name of business *(specify):*

    Type of business *(specify):*

    Attach a profit and loss statement for the last two years or a Schedule C from your last federal tax return. Black out your social security number. If you have more than one business, provide the information above for each of your businesses.

8. ☐ **Additional income.** I received one-time money (lottery winnings, inheritance, etc.) in the last 12 months *(specify source and amount):*

9. ☐ **Change in income.** My financial situation has changed significantly over the last 12 months because *(specify):*

10. **Deductions**   Last month

a.	Required union dues...	$_____
b.	Required retirement payments (not social security, FICA, 401(k), or IRA).............	$_____
c.	Medical, hospital, dental, and other health insurance premiums *(total monthly amount)*.......	$_____
d.	Child support that I pay for children from other relationships..........................	$_____
e.	Spousal support that I pay by court order from a different marriage.....................	$_____
f.	Partner support that I pay by court order from a different domestic partnership	$_____
g.	Necessary job-related expenses not reimbursed by my employer *(attach explanation labeled "Question 10g")*	$_____

11. **Assets**   Total

a.	Cash and checking accounts, savings, credit union, money market, and other deposit accounts	$100
b.	Stocks, bonds, and other assets I could easily sell	$2,000
c.	All other property, ☑ real and ☑ personal *(estimate fair market value minus the debts you owe)*	$unkn

FL-150 [Rev. January 1, 2007]   **INCOME AND EXPENSE DECLARATION**   Page 2 of 4

Income and Expense Declaration

FL-150

PETITIONER/PLAINTIFF: SANDIE SHORES	CASE NUMBER:
RESPONDENT/DEFENDANT: ROCKY SHORES	14FLXXXXXX
OTHER PARENT/CLAIMANT:	

12. The following people live with me:

Name	Age	How the person is related to me? *(ex: son)*	That person's gross monthly income	Pays some of the household expenses?
a. SANDIE SHORES	35	SELF	2,000	✔ Yes ☐ No
b. TOMAS CRUZ LINES	13	SON	NONE	☐ Yes ✔ No
c. EDDY WADE SHORES	8	SON	NONE	☐ Yes ✔ No
d. SHELLY SHORES	5	DAUGHTER	NONE	☐ Yes ✔ No
e.				☐ Yes ☐ No

13. Average monthly expenses   ☐ Estimated expenses ✔ Actual expenses ☐ Proposed needs

a. Home:

   (1) ☐ Rent or ✔ mortgage... $ 850

   If mortgage:

    (a) average principal: $ 150
    (b) average interest: $ 700

   (2) Real property taxes .... $ 100

   (3) Homeowner's or renter's insurance (if not included above) .... $ 100

   (4) Maintenance and repair .... $ 50

b. Health-care costs not paid by insurance.. $ 100

c. Child care .... $ ____

d. Groceries and household supplies....... $ 600

e. Eating out......................... $ 100

f. Utilities (gas, electric, water, trash) ...... $ 150

g. Telephone, cell phone, and e-mail ......$ 100

h. Laundry and cleaning .... $ 10

i. Clothes .... $ 200

j. Education .... $ ____

k. Entertainment, gifts, and vacation........ $ 100

l. Auto expenses and transportation (insurance, gas, repairs, bus, etc.) .... $ 350

m. Insurance (life, accident, etc.; do not include auto, home, or health insurance)... $ ____

n. Savings and investments.............. $ ____

o. Charitable contributions.............. $ ____

p. Monthly payments listed in item 14 *(itemize below in 14 and insert total here)*.. $ 220

q. Other *(specify)*: personal grooming ... $ 100

r. **TOTAL EXPENSES** (a–q) *(do not add in the amounts in a(1)(a) and (b))* $ 2930

s. Amount of expenses paid by others $ NONE

14. Installment payments and debts not listed above

Paid to	For	Amount	Balance	Date of last payment
Discover Card	Misc	$ 20	$ 2,000	current
VISA	Misc	$ 80	$ 8,000	current
MasterCard	Misc	$ 100	$ 10,000	current
Home Depot	Repairs/Supplies/Misc	$ 20	$ 2,000	current
		$	$	
		$	$	

15. Attorney fees *(This is required if either party is requesting attorney fees.)*:

  a. To date, I have paid my attorney this amount for fees and costs *(specify)*: $ 6,000
  b. The source of this money was *(specify)*: Borrowed from parents
  c. I still owe the following fees and costs to my attorney *(specify total owed)*: $
  d. My attorney's hourly rate is *(specify)*: $ 300

I confirm this fee arrangement.

Date:

JOAN CARE-ACTOR
   (TYPE OR PRINT NAME OF ATTORNEY)   ▶   (SIGNATURE OF ATTORNEY)

Income and Expense Declaration

PETITIONER/PLAINTIFF: SANDIE SHORES	CASE NUMBER:
RESPONDENT/DEFENDANT: ROCKY SHORES	14FLXXXXXX
OTHER PARENT/CLAIMANT:	

CHILD SUPPORT INFORMATION
(NOTE: Fill out this page only if your case involves child support.)

16. **Number of children**
    a. I have *(specify number):* 3   children under the age of 18 with the other parent in this case.
    b. The children spend   95   percent of their time with me and   5   percent of their time with the other parent.
    (If you're not sure about percentage or it has not been agreed on, please describe your parenting schedule here.)

17. **Children's health-care expenses**
    a. ☐ I do   ☑ I do not   have health insurance available to me for the children through my job.
    b. Name of insurance company:
    c. Address of insurance company:

    d. The monthly cost for the **children's** health insurance is or would be *(specify):* $
       (Do not include the amount your employer pays.)

18. **Additional expenses for the children in this case**   Amount per month
    a. Child care so I can work or get job training . . . . $ 800
    b. Children's health care not covered by insurance . . . . $
    c. Travel expenses for visitation . . . . $
    d. Children's educational or other special needs *(specify below):* . . . . $

19. **Special hardships.** I ask the court to consider the following special financial circumstances
    (attach documentation of any item listed here, including court orders):   Amount per month   For how many months?
    a. Extraordinary health expenses not included in 18b . . . . $
    b. Major losses not covered by insurance (examples: fire, theft, other
       insured loss) . . . . $
    c. (1) Expenses for my minor children who are from other relationships and
       are living with me . . . . $ 500   63
       (2) Names and ages of those children *(specify):*

       TOMAS CRUZ LINES - 13

       (3) Child support I receive for those children . . . . $ NONE

    The expenses listed in a, b, and c create an extreme financial hardship because *(explain):*
    I HAVE SOLE LEGAL AND PHYSICAL CUSTODY OF MY 13 YEAR OLD SON; HIS FATHER HAS
    NOT APID ANY SUPPORT IN OVER 10 YEARS.

20. **Other information I want the court to know concerning support in my case** *(specify):*

For your protection and privacy, please press the Clear This Form
button after you have printed the form.   Save This Form   Print This Form   Clear This Form

Request for Order

<table>
<tr>
<td colspan="2">

ATTORNEY OR PARTY WITHOUT ATTORNEY *(Name, State Bar number, and address)*:

TELEPHONE NO.:   FAX NO. *(Optional)*:
E-MAIL ADDRESS *(Optional)*:
ATTORNEY FOR *(Name)*:
</td>
<td>

FL-300

FOR COURT USE ONLY

To keep other people from seeing what you entered on your form, please press the Clear This Form button at the end of the form when finished.
</td>
</tr>
</table>

SUPERIOR COURT OF CALIFORNIA, COUNTY OF
STREET ADDRESS:
MAILING ADDRESS:
CITY AND ZIP CODE:
BRANCH NAME:

PETITIONER/PLAINTIFF:
RESPONDENT/DEFENDANT:
OTHER PARENT/PARTY:

REQUEST FOR ORDER ☐ **MODIFICATION** ☐ **Temporary Emergency**	CASE NUMBER:

REQUEST FOR ORDER
☐ **Child Custody**   ☐ **MODIFICATION**   ☐ **Temporary Emergency**
☐ **Child Support**   ☐ **Visitation**   **Court Order**
☐ **Attorney Fees and Costs** ☐ **Spousal Support**   ☐ **Other** *(specify):*

1. TO *(name):*

2. A hearing on this *Request for Order* will be held as follows: **If child custody or visitation is an issue in this proceeding, Family Code section 3170 requires mediation before or at the same time as the hearing *(see item 7.)***

   a. Date: Time: ☐ Dept.:   ☐ Room.:

   b. Address of court   ☐ same as noted above   ☐ other *(specify):*

3. Attachments to be served with this *Request for Order:*
   a. A **blank** *Responsive Declaration* (form FL-320)
   b. ☐ Completed *Income and Expense Declaration* (form FL-150) and a **blank** *Income and Expense Declaration*
   c. ☐ Completed *Financial Statement (Simplified)* (form FL-155) and a **blank** *Financial Statement (Simplified)*
   d. ☐ Points and authorities
   e. ☐ Other *(specify):*

Date:

▶

_____   _____
(TYPE OR PRINT NAME)   (SIGNATURE)

☐ COURT ORDER

4. ☐ YOU ARE ORDERED TO APPEAR IN COURT AT THE DATE AND TIME LISTED IN ITEM 2 TO GIVE ANY LEGAL REASON WHY THE ORDERS REQUESTED SHOULD NOT BE GRANTED.

5. ☐ Time for ☐ service ☐ hearing is shortened. Service must be on or before *(date):*

6. Any responsive declaration must be served on or before *(date):*

7. The parties are ordered to attend mandatory custody services as follows:

8. ☐ You are ordered to comply with the *Temporary Emergency Court Orders* (form FL-305) attached.

9. ☐ Other *(specify):*

Date:
               _____
                             JUDICIAL OFFICER

To the person who received this *Request for Order:* If you wish to respond to this *Request for Order*, you must file a *Responsive Declaration to Request for Order* (form FL-320) and serve a copy on the other parties at least nine court days before the hearing date unless the court has ordered a shorter period of time. You do not have to pay a filing fee to file the *Responsive Declaration to Request for Order* (form FL-320) or any other declaration including an *Income and Expense Declaration* (form FL-150) or *Financial Statement (Simplified)* (form FL-155).

Page 1 of 4

Form Adopted for Mandatory Use
Judicial Council of California
FL-300 [Rev. July 1, 2012]

REQUEST FOR ORDER

Family Code, §§ 2045, 2107, 6224,
6226, 6320–6326, 6380–6383
Government Code, § 26826
www.courts.ca.gov

Request for Order

FL-300

PETITIONER/PLAINTIFF:	CASE NUMBER:
RESPONDENT/DEFENDANT:	
OTHER PARENT/PARTY:	

REQUEST FOR ORDER AND SUPPORTING DECLARATION

☐ **Petitioner** ☐ **Respondent** ☐ **Other Parent/Party** requests the following orders:

1. ☐ CHILD CUSTODY ☐ **To be ordered pending the hearing**
   a. Child's name and age
   b. Legal custody to (name of person who makes decisions about health, education, etc.)
   c. Physical custody to (name of person with whom child will live)

   d. ☐ As requested in form
   ☐ Child Custody and Visitation Application Attachment (form FL-311)
   ☐ Request for Child Abduction Prevention Orders (form FL-312)
   ☐ Children's Holiday Schedule Attachment (form FL-341(C))
   ☐ Additional Provisions—Physical Custody Attachment (form FL-341(D))
   ☐ Joint Legal Custody Attachment (form FL-341(E))
   ☐ Other (Attachment 1d)

   e. ☐ Modify existing order
   (1) filed on (date):
   (2) ordering (specify):

2. ☐ CHILD VISITATION (PARENTING TIME) ☐ **To be ordered pending the hearing**
   a. As requested in: (1) ☐ Attachment 2a (2) ☐ Child Custody and Visitation Application Attachment (form FL-311)
   (3) ☐ Other (specify):
   b. ☐ Modify existing order
   (1) filed on (date):
   (2) ordering (specify):

   c. ☐ One or more domestic violence restraining/protective orders are now in effect. (Attach a copy of the orders if you have one.) The orders are from the following court or courts (specify county and state):
   (1) ☐ Criminal: County/state:
   Case No. (if known):
   (2) ☐ Family: County/state:
   Case No. (if known):
   (3) ☐ Juvenile: County/state:
   Case No. (if known):
   (4) ☐ Other: County/state:
   Case No. (if known):

3. ☐ CHILD SUPPORT (An earnings assignment order may be issued.)
   a. Child's name and age
   b. ☐ I request support based on the child support guidelines
   c. Monthly amount requested (if not by guideline) $

   d. ☐ Modify existing order
   (1) filed on (date):
   (2) ordering (specify):

Notice: The court is required to order child support based on the income of both parents. It normally continues until the child is 18. You must supply the court with information about your finances by filing an *Income and Expense Declaration* (form FL-150) or a *Financial Statement (Simplified)* (form FL-155). Otherwise, the child support order will be based on information about your income that the court receives from other sources, including the other parent.

Request for Order

FL-300

PETITIONER/PLAINTIFF: RESPONDENT/DEFENDANT: OTHER PARENT/PARTY:	CASE NUMBER:

4. ☐ SPOUSAL OR PARTNER SUPPORT *(An earnings assignment order may be issued.)*

    a. ☐ Amount requested *(monthly):* $ c. ☐ Modify existing order

    b. ☐ Terminate existing order   (1) filed on *(date):*

        (1) filed on *(date):*   (2) ordering *(specify):*

        (2) ordering *(specify):*

    d. ☐ The *Spousal or Partner Support Declaration Attachment* (form FL-157) is attached *(for modification of spousal or partner support after judgment only)*

    e. An *Income and Expense Declaration* (form FL-150) must be attached

5. ☐ ATTORNEY FEES AND COSTS are requested on *Request for Attorney Fees and Costs Order Attachment* (form FL-319) or a declaration that addresses the factors covered in that form. An *Income and Expense Declaration* (form FL-150) must be attached. A *Supporting Declaration for Attorney Fees and Costs Order Attachment* (form FL-158) or a declaration that addresses the factors covered in that form must also be attached.

6. ☐ PROPERTY RESTRAINT   ☐ **To be ordered pending the hearing**

    a. The ☐ petitioner ☐ respondent ☐ claimant   is restrained from transferring, encumbering, hypothecating, concealing, or in any way disposing of any property, real or personal, whether community, quasi-community, or separate, except in the usual course of business or for the necessities of life.

      ☐ The applicant will be notified at least five business days before any proposed extraordinary expenditures, and an accounting of such will be made to the court.

    b. ☐ Both parties are restrained and enjoined from cashing, borrowing against, canceling, transferring, disposing of, or changing the beneficiaries of any insurance or other coverage, including life, health, automobile, and disability, held for the benefit of the parties or their minor children.

    c. ☐ Neither party may incur any debts or liabilities for which the other may be held responsible, other than in the ordinary course of business or for the necessities of life.

7. ☐ PROPERTY CONTROL   ☐ **To be ordered pending the hearing**

    a. ☐ The petitioner ☐ respondent is given the exclusive temporary use, possession, and control of the following property that we own or are buying *(specify):*

    b. ☐ The petitioner ☐ respondent is ordered to make the following payments on liens and encumbrances coming due while the order is in effect:

Debt	Amount of payment	Pay to

8. ☐ OTHER RELIEF *(specify):*

NOTE: To obtain domestic violence restraining orders, you must use the forms *Request for Order (Domestic Violence Prevention)* (form DV-100), *Temporary Restraining Order (Domestic Violence)* (form DV-110), and *Notice of Court Hearing (Domestic Violence)* (form DV-109).

Request for Order

FL-300

PETITIONER/PLAINTIFF:	CASE NUMBER:
RESPONDENT/DEFENDANT:	
OTHER PARENT/PARTY:	

9. ☐ **I request** that time for service of the *Request for Order* and accompanying papers be shortened so that these documents may be served no less than *(specify number):*   days before the time set for the hearing. I need to have this order shortening time because of the facts specified in item 10 or the attached declaration.

10. ☐ FACTS IN SUPPORT of orders requested and change of circumstances for any modification are *(specify):*
    ☐ Contained in the attached declaration. (*You may use* Attached Declaration *(form MC-031) for this purpose. The attached declaration must not exceed 10 pages in length unless permission to file a longer declaration has been obtained from the court.)*

I declare under penalty of perjury under the laws of the State of California that the foregoing is true and correct.

Date:

▶

_____   _____
(TYPE OR PRINT NAME)   (SIGNATURE OF APPLICANT)

Requests for Accommodations
Assistive listening systems, computer-assisted real-time captioning, or sign language interpreter services are available if you ask at least five days before the proceeding. Contact the clerk's office or go to *www.courts.ca.gov/forms* for *Request for Accommodations by Persons With Disabilities and Response* (form MC-410). (Civil Code, § 54.8.)

For your protection and privacy, please press the Clear This Form button after you have printed the form.   **Save This Form** | **Print This Form** | **Clear This Form**

Child Custody and Visitation Application

> To keep other people from seeing what you entered on your form, please press the Clear This Form button at the end of the form when finished.

FL-311

PETITIONER/PLAINTIFF:	CASE NUMBER:
RESPONDENT/DEFENDANT:	

CHILD CUSTODY AND VISITATION APPLICATION ATTACHMENT

TO ☐ Petition, Response, Application for Order or Responsive Declaration ☐ Other *(specify):*

☐ To be ordered now and effective until the hearing

1. ☐ **Custody.** Custody of the minor children of the parties is requested as follows:

Child's Name	Date of Birth	Legal Custody to *(person who makes decisions about health, education, etc.)*	Physical Custody to *(person with whom the child lives)*

2. ☐ **Visitation.**

     a. ☐ Reasonable right of visitation to the party without physical custody **(not appropriate in cases involving domestic violence)**

     b. ☐ See the attached _____-page document dated *(specify date):*

     c. ☐ The parties will go to mediation at *(specify location):*

     d. ☐ No visitation

     e. ☐ Visitation for the ☐ petitioner ☐ respondent will be as follows:

         (1) ☐ **Weekends starting** *(date):*

            (The first weekend of the month is the first weekend with a Saturday.)

            ☐ 1st ☐ 2nd ☐ 3rd ☐ 4th ☐ 5th   weekend of the month

            from _____ at _____ ☐ a.m. ☐ p.m.
                 (day of week)   *(time)*

            to _____ at _____ ☐ a.m. ☐ p.m.
                (day of week)   *(time)*

            (a) ☐ The parents will alternate the fifth weekends, with the ☐ petitioner ☐ respondent having the initial fifth weekend, which starts *(date):*

            (b) ☐ The petitioner will have fifth weekends in ☐ odd ☐ even   months.

         (2) ☐ **Alternate weekends starting** *(date):*

            The ☐ petitioner ☐ respondent will have the children with him or her during the period

            from _____ at _____ ☐ a.m. ☐ p.m.
                (day of week)   *(time)*

            to _____ at _____ ☐ a.m. ☐ p.m.
                (day of week)   *(time)*

         (3) ☐ **Weekdays starting** *(date):*

            The ☐ petitioner ☐ respondent will have the children with him or her during the period

            from _____ at _____ ☐ a.m. ☐ p.m.
                (day of week)   *(time)*

            to _____ at _____ ☐ a.m. ☐ p.m.
                (day of week)   *(time)*

         (4) ☐ **Other** *(specify days and times as well as any additional restrictions):*

                                               ☐ See Attachment 2e(4).

Form Approved for Optional Use
Judicial Council of California
FL-311 [Rev. July 1, 2005]

CHILD CUSTODY AND VISITATION APPLICATION ATTACHMENT

Family Code, § 6200 et seq.
www.courtinfo.ca.gov

Child Custody and Visitation Application

PETITIONER:	CASE NUMBER:
RESPONDENT:	

3. ☐ **Supervised visitation.**
I request that *(name):* have supervised visitation with the minor children according to the schedule set out on page 1 and that the visits be supervised by *(name):*
who is a ☐ professional ☐ nonprofessional supervisor. The supervisor's phone number is *(specify):*

I request that the costs of supervision be paid as follows: petitioner: percent; respondent: percent.

If item 3 is checked, you must attach a declaration that shows why unsupervised visitation would be bad for your children. The judge is required to consider supervised visitation if one parent is alleging domestic violence and is protected by a restraining order.

4. ☐ **Transportation for visitation and place of exchange.**
   a. ☐ Transportation **to** the visits will be provided by *(name):*
   b. ☐ Transportation **from** the visits will be provided by *(name):*
   c. ☐ Drop-off of the children will be at *(address):*
   d. ☐ Pick-up of the children will be at *(address):*
   e. ☐ The children will be driven only by a licensed and insured driver. The car or truck must have legal child restraint devices.
   f. ☐ During the exchanges, the parent driving the children will wait in the car and the other parent will wait in his or her home while the children go between the car and the home.
   g. ☐ Other *(specify):*

5. ☐ **Travel with children.** The ☐ petitioner ☐ respondent ☐ other *(name):*
must have written permission from the other parent or a court order to take the children out of
   a. ☐ the state of California.
   b. ☐ the following counties *(specify):*
   c. ☐ other places *(specify):*

6. ☐ **Child abduction prevention.** There is a risk that one of the parents will take the children out of California without the other parent's permission. I request the orders set out on attached form FL-312.

7. ☐ **Children's holiday schedule.** I request the holiday and visitation schedule set out on the attached ☐ form FL-341(C)
   ☐ other *(specify):*

8. ☐ **Additional custody provisions.** I request the additional orders regarding custody set out on the attached
   ☐ form FL-341(D) ☐ other *(specify):*

9. ☐ **Joint legal custody provisions.** I request joint legal custody and want the additional orders set out on the attached
   ☐ form FL-341(E) ☐ other *(specify):*

10. ☐ **Other.** I request the following additional orders *(specify):*

For your protection and privacy, please press the Clear This Form button after you have printed the form.

Save This Form   Print This Form   Clear This Form

Spousal or Partner Support Declaration

FL-157

PETITIONER/PLAINTIFF:	CASE NUMBER:
RESPONDENT/DEFENDANT:	
OTHER PARTY:	

SPOUSAL OR PARTNER SUPPORT DECLARATION ATTACHMENT

[ ] **Declaration for Default or Uncontested Judgment (form FL-170)**   [ ] **Supporting Declaration for Attorney's Fees and Costs Attachment (form FL-158)**

[ ] **Other** *(specify):*

1. **Spousal or domestic partner support.** I request that the court *(check all that apply):*

    a. [ ]   Enter a judgment for spousal or domestic partner support for [ ] Petitioner [ ] Respondent.

    b. [ ]   Modify the judgment for spousal or domestic partner support for [ ] Petitioner [ ] Respondent.

    c. [ ]   Deny the request to modify the judgment for spousal or domestic partner support.

    d. [ ]   Terminate jurisdiction to award spousal or domestic partner support to [ ] Petitioner [ ] Respondent.

2. [ ]   **Attorney fees and costs.** I request that the court *(check one):*

    a. [ ]   Order my attorney fees and costs to be paid by [ ] my spouse or domestic partner [ ] a joined party *(specify):*

    b. [ ]   Deny the request for attorney fees and costs.

3. The facts in support of my request are:

    a. **Family Code section 4320(a)(1)**

       (1) The supported party has the following training, job skills, and work history:

       (2) The current job market for the job skills of the supported party described in item 3a(1) is:

       (3) The supported party would need the following time and expense to acquire the education or training to develop the job skills described in item 3a(1):

       (4) To develop other, more marketable job skills or employment, the supported party would need the following retraining or education:

Form Approved for Optional Use
Judicial Council of California
FL-157 [New January 1, 2012]

**SPOUSAL OR PARTNERSHIP SUPPORT
DECLARATION ATTACHMENT**

Family Code, §§ 270, 2030,2032, 4320,
6344, 7640
www.courts.ca.gov

Spousal or Partner Support Declaration

	FL-157
PETITIONER/PLAINTIFF: RESPONDENT/DEFENDANT: OTHER PARTY:	CASE NUMBER:

3. Facts in support of request.

   b. **Family Code section 4320(a)(2)**

     Provide any facts that indicate the supported party's earning ability is, or is not, lower than it might be if he or she had not had periods of unemployment because of the time needed to attend to domestic duties *(explain)*:

   c. **Family Code section 4320(b)**

     Provide any facts that indicate that the supported party contributed to the education, training, career position, or license of the supporting party.

   d. **Family Code section 4320(c)**

     (1) The supporting party ☐ does ☐ does not have the ability to pay spousal or domestic partner support.

     (2) The supporting party's current gross income from employment or self-employment is *(specify)*:

     (3) The supporting party's current income from investments, retirement, other sources is *(specify)*:

     (4) The supporting party's current assets and their values and balances are *(specify)*:

     (5) The supporting party's standard of living is *(describe, for example, type and frequency of vacations, value of home and other real estate, value of investments, type of vehicles owned, credit card use or nonuse)*:

Spousal or Partner Support Declaration

	FL-157
PETITIONER/PLAINTIFF: RESPONDENT/DEFENDANT: OTHER PARTY:	CASE NUMBER:

3. Facts in support of request.

   e. **Family Code section 4320(d)**

      The supported party ☐ does ☐ does not need support to maintain the standard of living we enjoyed during the marriage or domestic partnership.

   f. **Family Code Section 4320(e)**

     (1) The supported party's assets and obligations, including separate property, are *(list values and balances):*

     (2) The supporting party's assets and obligations, including separate property, are *(list values and balances):*

Spousal or Partner Support Declaration

FL-157

PETITIONER/PLAINTIFF: RESPONDENT/DEFENDANT: OTHER PARTY:	CASE NUMBER:

3. Facts in support of request.

   g. **Family Code section 4320(f)**
     Length of marriage or domestic partnership *(specify):*

   h. **Family Code section 4320(g)**
     Provide any facts indicating whether or not the supported party is able to work without unduly interfering with the interests of the children in his or her care *(describe):*

   i. **Family Code section 4320(h)**

     (1) Petitioner's age is *(specify):*   Respondent's age is *(specify):*

     (2) Petitioner's current health condition is *(describe):*

     (3) Respondent's current health condition is *(describe):*

   j. **Additional factors (Family Code sections 4320(i)–(n))**
     The court will also consider the following factors before making a judgment for spousal or domestic partner support:
     (1) Any documented evidence of domestic violence between the parties as defined in Family Code section 6211.
     (2) The immediate and specific tax consequences for each party;
     (3) The balance of the hardships on each party;
     (4) The criminal conviction of an abusive spouse in reducing or eliminating support in accordance with Family Code section 4325;
     (5) The goal that the supported party will be self-supporting within a reasonable period of time; and
     (6) Any other factors the court determines are just and equitable.

     Describe below any additional information that will assist the court in considering the above factors:

For your protection and privacy, please press the Clear This Form button after you have printed the form.   Save This Form   Print This Form   Clear This Form

Supporting Declaration for Attorney's Fees and Costs

FL-158

PETITIONER/PLAINTIFF:	CASE NUMBER:
RESPONDENT/DEFENDANT:	
OTHER PARTY:	

SUPPORTING DECLARATION FOR ATTORNEY'S FEES AND COSTS ATTACHMENT

To: ☐ *Request for Attorney's Fees and Costs Attachment* (form FL-319)

☐ *Responsive Declaration* (form FL-320)

1. I am
   a. ☐ the petitioner/plaintiff.
   b. ☐ the respondent/defendant.
   c. ☐ the other party.

2. I request that the court ☐ grant ☐ grant in part ☐ deny   the request for attorney's fees and costs.

3. I am providing the following information ☐ in support of ☐ in opposition to   the request for attorney's fees and costs.
   a. The ☐ petitioner/plaintiff ☐ respondent/defendant ☐ other party   has the ability to pay
      (1) ☐ my attorney's fees and costs.
      (2) ☐ his or her own attorney's fees and costs.
      (3) ☐ both my and his or her own attorney's fees and costs.
      (4) ☐ other *(specify):*

   b. The attorney's fees and costs can be paid from the following sources:

   c. The court should consider the following facts in deciding whether to grant, grant in part, or deny the request for attorney's fees and costs *(describe):*
      ☐ See Attachment 3c.

   d. If appropriate, describe the reasons why a non-spouse party or domestic partner is involved in the case and whether he or she should or should not pay attorney's fees and costs:
      ☐ See Attachment 3d.

Form Approved for Optional Use
Judicial Council of California
FL-158 [New January 1, 2012]

**SUPPORTING DECLARATION FOR ATTORNEY'S FEES
AND COSTS ATTACHMENT
(Family Law)**

Family Code, §§ 270,
2030, 2032, 3121, 3557,
4320, 7605; Cal. Rules of
Court, rules 5.425, 5.93
www.courts.ca.gov

Supporting Declaration for Attorney's Fees and Costs

FL-158

PETITIONER/PLAINTIFF: RESPONDENT/DEFENDANT: OTHER PARTY:	CASE NUMBER:

4. Has an order already been made for payment of child support in this case?

     a. ☐   No.

     b. ☐   Yes. If so, describe the order:

         (1) The ☐ petitioner/plaintiff ☐ respondent/defendant ☐ other party   must pay: $
         per month for child support.

         (a) This order has been in effect since (date):

         (b) The payments ☐ have been made ☐ have not been made ☐ have been made in part
         since the date of the order.

         (2) ☐   Additional information (specify):

5. Has an order already been made for payment of spousal, partner, or family support in this case?

     a. ☐   No.

     b. ☐   Yes. If so, describe the order:

         (1) The ☐ petitioner/plaintiff ☐ respondent/defendant ☐ other party   must pay: $
         per month for ☐ spousal support ☐ partner support ☐ family support.

         (a) This order has been in effect since (date):

         (b) The payments ☐ have been made ☐ have not been made ☐ have been made in part
         since the date of the order.

         (2) ☐   Additional information (specify):

6. If you are or were married to, or in a domestic partnership with, the person you are seeking fees from, the court must consider the factors in Family Code section 4320 in determining whether it is just and reasonable under the relative circumstances to award attorney's fees and costs. Complete and attach *Spousal or Partner Support Declaration Attachment* (form FL-157) or a comparable declaration to provide the court with information about the factors described in section 4320.

7. You must complete, file, and serve a current *Income and Expense Declaration* (form FL-150). It is considered current if you have completed form FL-150 within the past three months and no facts have changed since the time of completion.

8. Number of pages attached to this *Supporting Declaration:* _____

I declare under penalty of perjury under the laws of the State of California that the information contained on all pages of this form and any attachments is true and correct.

Date:

_____
(TYPE OR PRINT NAME)

▶ _____
(SIGNATURE)

For your protection and privacy, please press the Clear This Form button after you have printed the form.

Save This Form	Print This Form	Clear This Form

Income and Expense Declaration

FL-150

ATTORNEY OR PARTY WITHOUT ATTORNEY *(Name, State Bar number, and address):* TELEPHONE NO.: E-MAIL ADDRESS *(Optional):* ATTORNEY FOR *(Name):*	To keep other people from seeing what you entered on your form, please press the Clear This Form button at the end of the form when finished.

SUPERIOR COURT OF CALIFORNIA, COUNTY OF

STREET ADDRESS:

MAILING ADDRESS:

CITY AND ZIP CODE:

BRANCH NAME:

PETITIONER/PLAINTIFF:

RESPONDENT/DEFENDANT:

OTHER PARENT/CLAIMANT:

INCOME AND EXPENSE DECLARATION	CASE NUMBER:

1. **Employment** *(Give information on your current job or, if you're unemployed, your most recent job.)*

<table>
<tr><td rowspan="8">Attach copies of your pay stubs for last two months (black out social security numbers).</td><td>a.</td><td>Employer:</td></tr>
<tr><td>b.</td><td>Employer's address:</td></tr>
<tr><td>c.</td><td>Employer's phone number:</td></tr>
<tr><td>d.</td><td>Occupation:</td></tr>
<tr><td>e.</td><td>Date job started:</td></tr>
<tr><td>f.</td><td>If unemployed, date job ended:</td></tr>
<tr><td>g.</td><td>I work about   hours per week.</td></tr>
<tr><td>h.</td><td>I get paid $ gross (before taxes) ☐ per month ☐ per week ☐ per hour.</td></tr>
</table>

(If you have more than one job, attach an 8½-by-11-inch sheet of paper and list the same information as above for your other jobs. Write "Question 1—Other Jobs" at the top.)

2. **Age and education**

   a. My age is *(specify):*

   b. I have completed high school or the equivalent: ☐ Yes ☐ No   If no, highest grade completed *(specify):*

   c. Number of years of college completed *(specify):*   Degree(s) obtained *(specify):*

   d. Number of years of graduate school completed *(specify):*   Degree(s) obtained *(specify):*

   e. I have: ☐ professional/occupational license(s) *(specify):*

        ☐ vocational training *(specify):*

3. **Tax information**

   a. ☐ I last filed taxes for tax year *(specify year):*

   b. My tax filing status is ☐ single ☐ head of household ☐ married, filing separately

        ☐ married, filing jointly with *(specify name):*

   c. I file state tax returns in ☐ California ☐ other *(specify state):*

   d. I claim the following number of exemptions (including myself) on my taxes *(specify):*

4. **Other party's income.** I estimate the gross monthly income (before taxes) of the other party in this case at *(specify):* $

   This estimate is based on *(explain):*

(If you need more space to answer any questions on this form, attach an 8½-by-11-inch sheet of paper and write the question number before your answer.) Number of pages attached: _____

I declare under penalty of perjury under the laws of the State of California that the information contained on all pages of this form and any attachments is true and correct.

Date:

▶

_____   _____
(TYPE OR PRINT NAME)   (SIGNATURE OF DECLARANT)

Form Adopted for Mandatory Use
Judicial Council of California
FL-150 [Rev. January 1, 2007]   **INCOME AND EXPENSE DECLARATION**   Family Code, §§ 2030–2032,
2100–2113, 3552, 3620–3634,
4050–4076, 4300–4339
www.courtinfo.ca.gov

Income and Expense Declaration

PETITIONER/PLAINTIFF:	CASE NUMBER:
RESPONDENT/DEFENDANT:	
OTHER PARENT/CLAIMANT:	

Attach copies of your pay stubs for the last two months and proof of any other income. Take a copy of your latest federal tax return to the court hearing. *(Black out your social security number on the pay stub and tax return.)*

5. **Income** *(For average monthly, add up all the income you received in each category in the last 12 months and divide the total by 12.)*

		Last month	Average monthly
a.	Salary or wages (gross, before taxes). . . . . $		
b.	Overtime (gross, before taxes) . . . . $		
c.	Commissions or bonuses. . . . . $		
d.	Public assistance (for example: TANF, SSI, GA/GR) ☐ currently receiving . . . . $		
e.	Spousal support ☐ from this marriage ☐ from a different marriage . . . . $		
f.	Partner support ☐ from this domestic partnership ☐ from a different domestic partnership $		
g.	Pension/retirement fund payments. . . . . $		
h.	Social security retirement (not SSI) . . . . $		
i.	Disability: ☐ Social security (not SSI) ☐ State disability (SDI) ☐ Private insurance . $		
j.	Unemployment compensation . . . . $		
k.	Workers' compensation . . . . $		
l.	Other (military BAQ, royalty payments, etc.) (specify): . . . . $		

6. **Investment income** *(Attach a schedule showing gross receipts less cash expenses for each piece of property.)*

a.	Dividends/interest. . . . . $		
b.	Rental property income . . . . $		
c.	Trust income. . . . . $		
d.	Other (specify): . . . . $		

7. **Income from self-employment, after business expenses for all businesses.** . . . . $____

I am the ☐ owner/sole proprietor ☐ business partner ☐ other *(specify):*
Number of years in this business *(specify):*
Name of business *(specify):*
Type of business *(specify):*

Attach a profit and loss statement for the last two years or a Schedule C from your last federal tax return. Black out your social security number. If you have more than one business, provide the information above for each of your businesses.

8. ☐ **Additional income.** I received one-time money (lottery winnings, inheritance, etc.) in the last 12 months *(specify source and amount):*

9. ☐ **Change in income.** My financial situation has changed significantly over the last 12 months because *(specify):*

10. **Deductions**   Last month

a.	Required union dues . . . . $
b.	Required retirement payments (not social security, FICA, 401(k), or IRA). . . . . $
c.	Medical, hospital, dental, and other health insurance premiums (total monthly amount). . . . . $
d.	Child support that I pay for children from other relationships. . . . . $
e.	Spousal support that I pay by court order from a different marriage. . . . . $
f.	Partner support that I pay by court order from a different domestic partnership . . . . $
g.	Necessary job-related expenses not reimbursed by my employer (attach explanation labeled "Question 10g") . . . . . $

11. **Assets**   Total

a.	Cash and checking accounts, savings, credit union, money market, and other deposit accounts . . . . $
b.	Stocks, bonds, and other assets I could easily sell . . . . $
c.	All other property, ☐ real and ☐ personal (estimate fair market value minus the debts you owe) . . . . $

Income and Expense Declaration

PETITIONER/PLAINTIFF:	CASE NUMBER:
RESPONDENT/DEFENDANT:	
OTHER PARENT/CLAIMANT:	

12. The following people live with me:

Name	Age	How the person is related to me? *(ex: son)*	That person's gross monthly income	Pays some of the household expenses?
a.				☐ Yes ☐ No
b.				☐ Yes ☐ No
c.				☐ Yes ☐ No
d.				☐ Yes ☐ No
e.				☐ Yes ☐ No

13. Average monthly expenses   ☐ Estimated expenses   ☐ Actual expenses   ☐ Proposed needs

a. Home:

   (1) ☐ Rent or ☐ mortgage. . . $ _____

   If mortgage:

     (a) average principal: $ _____

     (b) average interest: $ _____

   (2) Real property taxes . . . . $ _____

   (3) Homeowner's or renter's insurance (if not included above) . . . . $ _____

   (4) Maintenance and repair . . . . $ _____

b. Health-care costs not paid by insurance. . . $ _____

c. Child care . . . . $ _____

d. Groceries and household supplies. . . . . . $ _____

e. Eating out. . . . . $ _____

f. Utilities (gas, electric, water, trash) . . . . . $ _____

g. Telephone, cell phone, and e-mail . . . . . . $ _____

h. Laundry and cleaning . . . . $ _____

i. Clothes . . . . $ _____

j. Education . . . . $ _____

k. Entertainment, gifts, and vacation. . . . . . . $ _____

l. Auto expenses and transportation (insurance, gas, repairs, bus, etc.) . . . . . . $ _____

m. Insurance (life, accident, etc.; do not include auto, home, or health insurance). . . $ _____

n. Savings and investments. . . . . $ _____

o. Charitable contributions. . . . . $ _____

p. Monthly payments listed in item 14 (itemize below in 14 and insert total here). . $ _____

q. Other *(specify):* . . . . $ _____

r. **TOTAL EXPENSES** (a–q) *(do not add in the amounts in a(1)(a) and (b))* $ _____

s. **Amount of expenses paid by others** $ _____

14. Installment payments and debts not listed above

Paid to	For	Amount	Balance	Date of last payment
		$	$	
		$	$	
		$	$	
		$	$	
		$	$	
		$	$	

15. Attorney fees *(This is required if either party is requesting attorney fees.):*

  a. To date, I have paid my attorney this amount for fees and costs *(specify):* $

  b. The source of this money was *(specify):*

  c. I still owe the following fees and costs to my attorney *(specify total owed):* $

  d. My attorney's hourly rate is *(specify):* $

I confirm this fee arrangement.

Date:

▶

_____   _____
(TYPE OR PRINT NAME OF ATTORNEY)   (SIGNATURE OF ATTORNEY)

Income and Expense Declaration

FL-150

PETITIONER/PLAINTIFF:	CASE NUMBER:
RESPONDENT/DEFENDANT:	
OTHER PARENT/CLAIMANT:	

CHILD SUPPORT INFORMATION
(NOTE: Fill out this page only if your case involves child support.)

16. **Number of children**
 a. I have *(specify number):*   children under the age of 18 with the other parent in this case.
 b. The children spend   percent of their time with me and   percent of their time with the other parent.
 (If you're not sure about percentage or it has not been agreed on, please describe your parenting schedule here.)

17. **Children's health-care expenses**
 a. ☐ I do   ☐ I do not   have health insurance available to me for the children through my job.
 b. Name of insurance company:
 c. Address of insurance company:

 d. The monthly cost for the **children's** health insurance is or would be *(specify):* $
 (Do not include the amount your employer pays.)

18. **Additional expenses for the children in this case**   Amount per month
 a. Child care so I can work or get job training . . . . $ _____
 b. Children's health care not covered by insurance . . . . $ _____
 c. Travel expenses for visitation . . . . $ _____
 d. Children's educational or other special needs *(specify below):* . . . . $ _____

19. **Special hardships.** I ask the court to consider the following special financial circumstances
 (attach documentation of any item listed here, including court orders):   Amount per month   For how many months?
 a. Extraordinary health expenses not included in 18b. . . . . $ _____ _____
 b. Major losses not covered by insurance (examples: fire, theft, other
    insured loss) . . . . $ _____ _____
 c. (1) Expenses for my minor children who are from other relationships and
       are living with me . . . . $ _____ _____
    (2) Names and ages of those children *(specify):*

    (3) Child support I receive for those children. . . . . $ _____

 The expenses listed in a, b, and c create an extreme financial hardship because *(explain):*

20. **Other information I want the court to know concerning support in my case** *(specify):*

For your protection and privacy, please press the Clear This Form button after you have printed the form.	Save This Form	Print This Form	Clear This Form

Chapter Five

Hearings, Discovery and Disclosure

Hearings and Continuances

Chapter Four discussed the process for preparing the Request for Order. Now that the documents have been filed and served, you need to prepare for the hearing.

First, you should find out if the attorney will need any additional information to take to the hearing. Also, is a meeting with the client a day or two prior to the hearing necessary? In some instances, the attorney will want to take the applicable Order forms to the hearing. In that case, the forms should be prepared in advance and reviewed by the attorney. Once approved, additional copies should be made so that the attorney can file the documents and still have copies to place in the file.

Continuance

It is often necessary to continue a hearing for a variety of reasons. Two of the most common reasons for a hearing to be continued are: 1) The Respondent has just retained an attorney who has not had time to prepare for the hearing or has a calendar conflict; or 2) the parties are in the process of reaching an agreement, but it has not been finalized or formalized.

You will need to check your local rules to determine if the Court allows a hearing to be continued and under what circumstances, as well as what their requirements are for granting the continuance. Most counties require a minimum number of hours or days notice to the Court to request the continuance. If that minimum time is not met, then the attorney will have to appear at the hearing and request that the matter be continued. In the event you are requesting a continuance telephonically with the clerk, the clerk will usually need a specific date for the continuance. The clerk will also ask that the request and confirmation of the new date be followed up in writing and that the opposing party, or attorney of record, also receive a copy of the letter. Some courts only allow the moving party to request the continuance, while others will require that both parties confirm that they are agreeable to having the matter continued, while other counties will require that the parties sign a Stipulation for Continuance, which is then submitted to the Court for the Judge's approval and signature. Another method is for the attorney to go to the Department Clerk when he or she is appearing on another matter and obtain the permission to continue at that time.

It is very important that you learn the local Court rules about the requirements for a continuance. Most Courts will not allow you to simply leave a message. Some Courts also have a time deadline for notifying them that the parties have agreed to continue the matter. If you do leave a message and no one appears at the hearing, the Court will likely drop the matter from the calendar. As a result you have to file the documents again, pay another filing fee, get another hearing date, and have the documents served notifying the opposing party of the new date and time. Thus, it will cause a delay in obtaining orders, as well as additional expense for the client. Such errors could be grounds for malpractice.

If your attorney is practicing in multiple counties, it is helpful to keep the local rules handy, or make yourself a "cheat sheet" which contains the requirements as the rules will vary between counties, even those in close proximity.

Minute Orders, Findings & Orders, Transcripts, Stipulations and Formal Orders

Minute Orders, Findings & Orders and Transcripts

In some cases you will be preparing the Order after the hearing based on what is called a "Minute Order." The Minute Order, which is used in many counties, is a checklist of issues that were addressed in the hearing. In other counties, you will need to request a copy of the Court transcript to confirm any orders that were made on the record. Check your local rules or with the attorney so that you can be prepared to obtain the necessary Court records as soon as possible after the hearing.

It should be stressed that, without leave of Court, any issues **not** raised in the Request for Order or Motion, technically cannot be raised at the hearing. If you are able to acquire the Minute Order, it will reflect the Orders the Court has made during the hearing. The Minute Order format will usually follow the same format (or order of items) Request for Order (form) and subsequent attachments. In other words, Child Custody is the first item, followed by Visitation, Child Support (and related health care and day care issues), Spousal Support, Attorney Fees, and property issues. There is also a place at the end of the form for "any other orders." Each Court will have its own specific form and will determine whether it is the clerk's function to complete the Minute Order or if the Judge will ask an attorney to complete the form as an "officer of the court."

In the event you need to obtain a transcript of the proceedings, those proceedings will also follow the same format as the issues raised as set forth above.

CCP§632 requires the Court to issue a statement of decision at the request of either party after a custody trial. However, most courts will apply this statute to hearings as well.

Court Form Stipulation & Order

Some Court's utilize a Stipulation & Order form that can be obtained from the Court Clerk. If the parties reach an agreement at the hearing and wish to put such orders on the record, they may request that the Stipulation be entered at that time. Each issue addressed will be indicated on the form which is usually several pages long and each party, and their attorney of record, signs the Stipulation before the Judge. The Judge will also sign the Stipulation and the clerk will "enter" the Orders. This document does not eliminate the Minute Order; the court (Judge or clerk and even sometimes the attorney) will, in fact, complete both forms.

In the event that the attorney returns to the office with such a Stipulation and Order you will need to ask who has received a copy of the Stipulation & Order. It is likely that you will have to send a copy to the client unless the attorney made a copy for him or her while at the courthouse. In some cases opposing counsel or opposing party, if unrepresented, may not have received a copy. In that event, you will have to serve a copy of the Stipulation & Order on the opposing party/attorney and file the Proof of Service of same with the Court.

Findings & Order After Hearing

At this stage of the proceeding, a formal order can be a Stipulation & Order or a Findings & Order After Hearing. (Stipulations and Orders, other than those mentioned in the preceding section, will be discussed in more detail in Chapter Six.) The Minute Order is not a formal, *enforceable* Order. The Stipulation & Order and Findings & Order After Hearing, once filed with the Court are *enforceable* orders.

A Findings & Order After Hearing is prepared after a hearing and using the Minute Order. It is therefore crucial that once the attorney has returned to the office with the file and the Minute Order that you review the information and any notes with the attorney. It is always a good idea to review everything while it is fresh in the attorney's mind. The Minute Order, in most cases, contains very little space and is mostly a "fill-in-the-blank" type form. Therefore, the attorney will often have made quick, cryptic notes on a legal pad, which may need to be incorporated in the formal order. Just as you have found in the classroom, you take notes, often in a quick and sometimes illegible or shorthand fashion. If you don't go back and review those notes soon after you have taken them, you may forget what they mean. The same is true of the attorney. You need to get clarification of the terms of the Order or agreement while they are still fresh in his/her mind.

You will note that in the counties that utilize the Minute Order, the form will also contain the Rules of Court governing the time frame for which the Findings & Order, or other documents, must be prepared, sent to the opposing party or attorney for review, as well as the filing of same with the Court. You will want to calendar these dates to assure that you are in compliance, as well as to make sure that you receive the documents back (assuming you are the one preparing the Orders) and when they will need to be filed with the court. In the event you don't receive the proposed Order back from the opposing party or counsel within the required time limits, you must contact them about the noncompliance and give them a *date specific* (within a reasonable time) by which to return the signed Order, or you will request that the Judge enter the Orders without their signature. You must to attach a copy of the letter to any request to the Judge to enter the Order without a signature. (You should also consult any local rules regarding a noncompliance with signing Orders.)

Of particular importance is the date the Request for Order was filed with the Court. This is the date the Court will most likely use for the commencement of any support orders. For instance, if a Request for Order is filed on March 5, but the hearing does not occur until April 30th, any support or other orders will most likely become effective on March 5, unless the attorney has requested or the Judge ordered otherwise. You will note, that in all likelihood, the date of any such orders on the Minute Order will reflect that date, unless the parties have agreed otherwise, or the court deems it necessary to have another commencement date. In most instances, child support cannot be retroactive further back than the date of filing the Request for Order. Spousal support can be retroactive, but the request must be made in the Request, and may be at the Judge's discretion as to whether support should be retroactive prior to the filing date. If the client has requested or agreed to a continuance, the client will need to be informed that any support orders will most likely commence on the date of filing the Request for Hearing, and not the date of the hearing. Thus, if they are the obligor, any ordered support will be considered already in arrears on the hearing date.

The *Findings & Order After Hearing* (form FL-340) is considered a "face sheet" much like the Request for Order. In most cases, it will be prepared by the attorney for the *moving party*. If the moving party files *pro se* then the Judge will likely order the attorney for the represented party to prepare the documents, as the attorney will have a better understanding of the requirements. The Findings & Order will contain attachment pages based on the issues that were raised and which were resolved at the hearing. They should be added in the order consistent with the order on the F&O face sheet.

The attachment pages can be any of the following:

Joint Legal Custody Attachment (FL-341(E))

Child Custody & Visitation Order Attachment (FL-341)

Supervised Visitation Order (FL-341(A))

Child Abduction Prevention Order Attachment (FL-341(B))

Children's Holiday Schedule Attachment (FL-341(C))

Additional Provisions—Physical Custody Attachment (FL-341(D))

Child Support Order Attachment (FL-342)

Non-Guideline Child Support Findings Attachment (FL-342(A))

Spousal Support, Partner, or Family Support Order Attachment (FL-343)

Property Order Attachment (FL-344)

Attorney Fees Order Attachment (FL-346)

Temporary [Restraining] Order Attachment (FL-305)

Additional pages and/or attachments may be incorporated into the Orders, such as a copy of the adopted mediator's recommendation and Dissomaster™, SupporTax™ or XSpouse™ printouts which the court has approved, or other attachments as appropriate. **Note:** if the court has generated a Dissomaster™, SupporTax™ or XSpouse™ support calculation, you must attach the Court's **official** finding and not one prepared by the attorney's office. If the Court has produced a Minute Order, the support printout is usually attached to the Minute Order at the hearing.

All pages of the Findings & Order After Hearing should be numbered with the total number of pages being written on the bottom right of each form used. Several of these forms contain more than one page, others are a single page. This will insure that all forms, attachments or exhibits are in the proper sequence and are contained in the orders. The attachment forms should be in sequential order as set forth on the Application for Order and Supporting Declaration and the Minute Order (or Stipulation if applicable).

You will also want to make sure that the client receives a copy of the Minute Order and any attachments immediately after the hearing. This will be the interim Order to which the client must comply until the formal Order is signed by the Judge and filed. In the event a Stipulation & Order was entered at the hearing, you will need to make sure they receive a copy of the Order as indicated above. You may also need to serve a copy of the Order on the opposing party or their attorney, with a Proof of Service.

Once the Findings & Order has been prepared and reviewed by the attorney it will need to be sent to the opposing party or the attorney of record for review and signature. As referenced above, they will have a limited time frame in which to review the documents and contact your office if they are requesting any changes to the Order. If the Orders are correct, they must sign the Order and return it within the time limitation. Should there be a disagreement about the Order, you may request a copy of the Court's Transcript. Once the signed Order has been returned to your office, it will need to be confirmed that no changes were made to the document without the attorney's approval, and then it will be copied and submitted to the Court for the Judge's signature and filing.

The paralegal will also need to assist the attorney in the preparation of any collateral documents, such as Wage Assignments or other enforcement documents. It is always advisable that as soon as an Order has been made, or has been modified, particularly with respect to support, that an *Income Withholding for Support* (FL-195) be prepared and filed with the Court. The actual preparation of this document will be discussed further in Chapter 9. At this stage, you should be aware that this document should be submitted either immediately after the hearing (if a Stipulation & Order was made at the hearing) or along with the Findings & Order After Hearing.

Whenever there are minor children, regardless of whether child support has been ordered or modified, you are required to submit a *Child Support Case Registry* form (FL-191). This form **must** be completed and submitted with any Order involving minor children. Even if there is no change in the support order itself, this document will need to be submitted indicating that there is no change. Although the form indicates that you have 10 days after an Order is made to submit the form, it has been my experience, that if a law office is submitting any type of Order relating to children, the clerk will not process the Order without this form. Please note that the first two pages are to be completed, while pages 3 and 4 are instructional and do not normally have to be submitted to the court with the first two pages, unless local rules specify otherwise.

Upon receipt of the filed Findings & Order After Hearing, a copy should be sent to the client. You are also required to serve a copy on the opposing party and then file the Proof of Service by Mail (FL-335) with the court showing that the document was served as required. In the event you submitted an Order/Notice to Withhold Child Support, or any other collateral documents to the Court that require service, you will need to serve those documents as soon as possible on the appropriate person. (This form and process will be discussed further in Chapter Nine.)

Proceeding with the Case

Once the attorney has determined the manner in which this case will proceed, you will begin gathering additional information as necessary. In the event the Respondent has failed to file a Response within the 31 days and no extension has been requested, the matter will proceed by Default. The attorney will then be better able to determine exactly how much information is needed from the client and/or what other information will be needed to be obtained by other means. Regardless of the amount of information needed to complete the dissolution process on behalf of the client, the attorney is required to comply with FC§2104 (effective 1/1/14) and proceed with completing and serving the Preliminary Declaration of Disclosure that contains information on the assets, debts, taxes, income and expenses of the parties involved in this matter. Below is the statutory language.

2104. (a) Except by court order for good cause, as provided in Section 2107, in the time period set forth in subdivision (f), each party shall serve on the other party a preliminary declaration of disclosure, executed under penalty of perjury on a form prescribed by the Judicial Council. The commission of perjury on the preliminary declaration of disclosure may be grounds for setting aside the judgment, or any part or parts thereof, pursuant to Chapter 10 (commencing with Section 2120), in addition to any and all other remedies, civil or criminal, that otherwise are available under law for the commission of perjury. The preliminary declaration of disclosure shall include all tax returns filed by the declarant within the two years prior to the date that the party served the declaration.

(b) The preliminary declaration of disclosure shall not be filed with the court, except on court order. However, the parties shall file proof of service of the preliminary declaration of disclosure with the court.

(c) The preliminary declaration of disclosure shall set forth with sufficient particularity, that a person of reasonable and ordinary intelligence can ascertain, all of the following:

(1) The identity of all assets in which the declarant has or may have an interest and all liabilities for which the declarant is or may be liable, regardless of the characterization of the asset or liability as community, quasi-community, or separate.

(2) The declarant's percentage of ownership in each asset and percentage of obligation for each liability where property is not solely owned by one or both of the parties. The preliminary declaration may also set forth the declarant's characterization of each asset or liability.

(d) A declarant may amend his or her preliminary declaration of disclosure without leave of the court. Proof of service of any amendment shall be filed with the court.

(e) Along with the preliminary declaration of disclosure, each party shall provide the other party with a completed income and expense declaration unless an income and expense declaration has already been provided and is current and valid.

(f) The petitioner shall serve the other party with the preliminary declaration of disclosure either concurrently with the petition for dissolution, or within 60 days of filing the petition. The respondent shall serve the other party with the preliminary declaration of disclosure either concurrently with the response to the petition, or within 60 days of filing the response. The time periods specified in this subdivision may be extended by written agreement of the parties or by court order.

As previously stated, although it can't be emphasized enough, it is very important for the attorney to have knowledge of all community and separate property assets and debts in order to provide the best representation and achieve the best possible result for the client.

Even though the disclosure rules have been clarified, codified, and must be followed, that does not mean that the information will be received timely or completely. Many clients balk at having to disclose this *personal* information or the amount of time and energy that is required to collect it and will thus procrastinate as much as possible. It will usually be up to the paralegal to stay on top of getting this information from the client in a timely manner and particularly to allow time for the paralegal to prepare the documents for service and for the attorney to review all the information before it is sent to the opposing party or his/her counsel.

Family Code § 2107 addresses the process and procedure for action to be taken if a party fails to serve the Preliminary Declaration of Disclosure within the prescribed, or otherwise agreed to time. The Judicial Council has created a form — FL-316 — Request for Orders Regarding Noncompliance with Disclosure Requirements that can be used in this event. This form would be attached to a Request for Hearing and sent to the court for a hearing to be set on the matter. Since a Judge can impose money sanctions against the non-complying party along with attorney's fees and court costs, it does not look very good for the attorney in the eyes of the court and/his or her client if the requirements are not met. Additionally, the court may set aside a judgment or previously made orders, disallow the non-complying party from presenting evidence regarding the property during trial, as well as any other orders the court deems appropriate.

2107. (a) If one party fails to serve on the other party a preliminary declaration of disclosure under Section 2104 or a final declaration of disclosure under Section 2105, or fails to provide the information required in the respective declarations with sufficient particularity, and if the other party has served the respective declaration of disclosure on the noncomplying party, the complying party may, within a reasonable time, request preparation of the appropriate declaration of disclosure or further particularity.

(b) If the noncomplying party fails to comply with a request under subdivision (a), the complying party may do one or more of the following:

(1) File a motion to compel a further response.

(2) File a motion for an order preventing the noncomplying party from presenting evidence on issues that should have been covered in the declaration of disclosure.

(3) File a motion showing good cause for the court to grant the complying party's voluntary waiver of receipt of the noncomplying party's preliminary declaration of disclosure pursuant to Section 2104 or final declaration of disclosure pursuant to Section 2105. The voluntary waiver does not affect the rights enumerated in subdivision (d).

(c) If a party fails to comply with any provision of this chapter, the court shall, in addition to any other remedy provided by law, impose money sanctions against the noncomplying party. Sanctions shall be in an amount sufficient to deter repetition of the conduct or comparable conduct, and shall include reasonable attorney's fees, costs incurred, or both, unless the court finds that the noncomplying party acted with substantial justification or that other circumstances make the imposition of the sanction unjust.

(d) Except as otherwise provided in this subdivision, if a court enters a judgment when the parties have failed to comply with all disclosure requirements of this chapter, the court shall set aside the judgment. The failure to comply with the disclosure requirements does not constitute harmless error. If the court granted the complying party's voluntary waiver of receipt of the noncomplying party's preliminary declaration of disclosure pursuant to paragraph (3) of subdivision (b), the court shall set aside the judgment only at the request of the complying party, unless the motion to set aside the judgment is based on one of the following:

(1) Actual fraud if the defrauded party was kept in ignorance or in some other manner was fraudulently prevented from fully participating in the proceeding.

(2) Perjury, as defined in Section 118 of the Penal Code, in the preliminary or final declaration of disclosure, in the waiver of the final declaration of disclosure, or in the current income and expense statement.

(e) Upon the motion to set aside judgment, the court may order the parties to provide the preliminary and final declarations of disclosure that were exchanged between them. Absent a court order to the contrary, the disclosure declarations shall not be filed with the court and shall be returned to the parties.

Discovery

As in all types of litigation, it is often necessary to obtain information that the client does not have and that affects his or her case. The methods used in family law are the same as those used in civil litigation and are governed by Code of Civil Procedure §§ 2016–2036. These CCP sections contain provisions for both formal and informal discovery. Informal discovery may consist of a release or an authorization and/or an agreement to exchange or disclose information. Formal discovery consists of taking depositions (of persons and/or business records), interrogatories, subpoena, admissions, and exchange of expert witness information.

The Continuing Education of the Bar reference book *Practice Under the California Family Code* (Sections 13.9–13.17) contains a excellent information on "Developing a Plan" for family law cases. I recommend reviewing this section and developing your own checklist for proceeding with disclosure and discovery in any contested Family Law matters. Or, check with your firm to determine if a checklist has previously been developed or requires updating.

For instance, if the client has copies of documents that identify all of the marital assets and debts at his/her disposal such as deeds, loan/mortgage documents, vehicle registrations, bank accounts, investments, IRAs or other retirement accounts, credit card statements, insurance policies, payroll or taxable earnings information, etc., you should be able to complete the Schedule of Assets and Debts and Income & Expense Declarations with the information provided. The client's spouse, if he/she has filed a Response, will also (it is hoped) be complying with the disclosure rules so that you can verify his or her information against what the client has provided.

However, if the client does not have access to that information and/or the matter is going to trial, that information, or more detailed information, may be obtained by other means. The attorney may request that you prepare Form or Special Interrogatories, Requests for Production, Subpoena or Production of Business Records, and/or Notice of Deposition. He or she may also determine it is necessary to retain experts to prepare valuations of property (such as real estate, investments or retirement) and those experts may have their depositions taken or they may be called as witnesses at trial. It may be necessary to wait to prepare the final declarations of disclosure until all of the above information has been received. Keep this in mind when setting the matter for trial. All of these issues will be discussed in greater detail under future chapters relating to division of property and trial procedures.

It is always important to have the client complete as much of the initial Client Information package as possible and provide you with as much supporting documentation as early in the process as possible. This will help the attorney in determining a discovery plan. The attorney will need to know what information to which the client will have access, what information will be obtained by other means, and the least expensive means, while providing the maximum amount of information. It will also help in working with the client to determine what he or she might be able to do in order to facilitate getting the information at the most reasonable cost. For instance, can the client make telephone calls to certain people and arrange for appraisals or request copies of bank statements, loan documents, etc., rather than have the law office do it. This would fall under "informal discovery." Always keep in mind, however, that you need to know how the client functions. If the client is a procrastinator, it may be best if the paralegal is appointed to start tracking down information and documentation, with the proper authorizations signed by the client, so that the information will be received in a timely manner. Copies of any information received will be sent to the client so he/she can verify information. You may want to cross check or verify the information to make sure that you have received complete information. Of course, the attorneys for both parties can also agree to exchange information and documents informally also.

It is my experience that information you receive from one source may lead you to other sources of information as they relate to the dissolution and community property. Examples would be—bank statements which show that funds have been transferred from another account, but the client did not provide you with that account information or there are large deposits or withdrawals for which the client has not provided detail. That information could lead the attorney to question additional accounts or sources of income that was not previously provided.

Discovery Methods

As previously stated, discovery in family law utilizes the same methods as a civil case.

Interrogatories: Interrogatories are typically a set of written questions to be answered under an oath by the other party, and which are sent to the opposing party. The party has thirty (30) days, plus five for mailing, in which to respond to the Interrogatories. (*CCP§ 2030, et. seq.*) Interrogatories, when answered, are considered admissions and become evidence in the case. This evidence can be used against the person if the matter goes to trial. The Interrogatories can take two forms: Form Interrogatories and Special Interrogatories. The (family law) Form Interrogatories (FL-145) contain a list of questions that are consistent with the information most requested in family law matters. (See Appendix 5A for the specific categories.) The Answers to Form Interrogatories must be verified and answered under penalty of perjury and sent with all requested supporting documentation to the propounding (asking) party as required by CCP§ 2030 et. seq. In most cases, the attorney is going to request that a Schedule of Assets & Debts and Income & Expense Declarations be served with the Form Interrogatories. This process is meant to insure that the information which must be disclosed is, in fact, disclosed as required by law. The answering party has the ability to object, but in most cases, the court will, on motion of the propounding party, order the answering party to comply with the standard information requested in the Form Interrogatories. You should always retain the original sets of Interrogatories (form and special) along with the original proof of service, you send copies to the answering party.

In the event that there is additional information needed which cannot be derived through the answers to the standard Form Interrogatory questions, the attorney may have you prepare a set of Special Interrogatories. Some attorneys will automatically send the Special Interrogatories with the Form Interrogatories. Others will wait until the answers to the Form Interrogatories have been returned to determine if additional information is needed that was not provided either in the answers or to which further detail or documents are needed. Oftentimes the time element may also be a factor. An approaching deposition or trial date may require you to get all discovery requests out as soon as possible. With regard to Special Interrogatories, always ask if there is a template or previous set that you can review or use, as the introduction contains required instructions and definitions, as well as the admonition that the answers must be given under an oath (penalty of perjury). The answering party must sign and date the verification.

When preparing Special Interrogatories, you must carefully follow CCP§ 2030 et. seq. with regard to the number of questions that can be propounded.

Neither the Interrogatories nor the Answers to Interrogatories are filed with the Court, unless they will be used as evidence at trial. The answers are normally sent to the propounding party with all supporting documentation within the time frame required in CCP§ 2030. The client should then be asked to come to the office to review the answers and supporting documentation to confirm that the Answer appears to be complete and accurate. The attorney may, at trial, show that the answering party provided contradictory evidence or may use the Answer to impeach a witness and/or discredit evidence. In the event that the Interrogatories will be used at trial, the originals will then be filed with the court, along with copies of the answering party's answers and documents.

As with the Special Interrogatories, an attorney will often wait until he/she receives, or is due to receive, the answers to any and all Interrogatories, and then set a date to take the spouse's deposition. If the attorney has the basic information requested prior to the Deposition, he/she can then tailor questions to specific topics or details for which more information is needed. This tactic will save time and money, as depositions can be expensive. For instance, if the client's spouse has a business and the Interrogatories propounded have been answered and documentation provided (such as tax returns, invoices, contracts), the attorney may not have to spend time during the Deposition asking for all of those items or information. The attorney can then focus on asking for clarification of information, or for more detail which may not have been disclosed. (See Depositions below.)

Demand for Production

A demand for Production of documents can be directed only to a party and can be sent no sooner than ten (10) days after the service of the Summons and Petition. The Respondent may serve a Demand for Production at any time. Demands for production are governed by CCP§ 2031 et. seq. which should be read and reviewed carefully prior to preparing and serving a Demand for Production.

As stated above, an attorney may prefer to receive the Answers to Interrogatories (form and/or special) prior to sending the Demand for Production. This will allow the attorney to customize the specific information that is required and/or may eliminate receiving repetitive or duplicate information. For example, if the Form Interrogatories have requested tax returns for the past three years, you don't really *need* to request these documents again on a Demand for Production unless you are asking for tax returns for the past *five* years or requesting actual supporting documentation that may not have been included in the tax return itself.

The Demand states that the request is for **production, inspection, and copying of documents that are in the answering party's possession, custody or control**. Thus, if the party does not have the information, it may not be provided. An example would be if you asked for current pension statements. Perhaps the party has not received their most recent pension statement and cannot readily obtain the statement. They may simply answer: "I do not have the information."

A responding party may raise a question of privilege and can file a motion for protective order pursuant to CCP§ 2031 et. seq. Please note, this code section should be reviewed if your office is planning to file the motion. A declaration must be attached to a motion indicating to the court that a "good faith" effort to resolve all of the issues presented in the motion has been made.

The documents may be produced in their entirety, or they may be provided at a specific time and place to be inspected and/or copied. This process is governed by CCP§ 2031(a)(1). CCP§ 2031(a)(2)–(3) addresses the inspection of *tangible things, land and other property*, and related requirements.

Subpoena

Subpoenas can take two forms: personal appearance and business records. There are three mandatory Judicial Council forms which must be used when requiring an appearance and/or business records. They are: Deposition Subpoena for Personal Appearance and Production of Documents and Things, form: SUBP-020; Deposition Subpoena for Personal Appearance, form: SUBP-015; and Deposition Subpoena for Production of Business Records, form: SUBP-010.

A Deposition Subpoena for Personal Appearance is used to compel the attendance of a deponent, party or non-party (or the party's representative). This document is most commonly used in the context of family law to require a person to give oral testimony, whether for a deposition or at trial. It may also be used to require the person to produce original records. In the event that the Subpoena is being used to obtain business or employment records in the possession of a business or entity, the Subpoena must be accompanied by a Notice to Consumer, as required by CCP§§ 1985.3, 1985.6, 2020: form SUBP-025. The statutes, rules and forms with regard to the production of documents change occasionally **please review them carefully**.

Also carefully review the forms to determine if there are any appearance fees that may be required. The appearance fees may have to be paid along with the Subpoena. Also, carefully read the instructions and the appropriate section of the Code of Civil Procedure which address the time frames required for notice. Some of the documents require only a *"reasonable time"* for production of documents, while others require specific time frames for a personal appearance.

You might want to consider using a "subpoena service" if your firm does not already utilize one. Check with your local paralegal association to see if they have a vendor list for such services. These services will prepare all of the documents, advance the fees, serve the subpoena and then bill the firm for cost of the subpoena service. They know all of the "ins and outs" of service, consumer notices, etc. and will save you a lot of headaches, if you are new to the process.

The original proof of service of each of these documents should be retained in the client's file in the event it is needed as an attachment to a Motion to Compel or produced for trial. These documents are served on the party or person and are not filed with the court until such time as they are required.

Deposition

A Notice of Taking Deposition is prepared in pleading format and is typically used only for requiring the appearance of a party in a family law matter. In the event, the attorney wishes to depose a non-party, one of the methods discussed above would be more appropriate.

The Petitioner may not serve a Notice of Taking Deposition until at least twenty (20) days after the service of the Summons and Petition, the appearance of the Respondent, or by special permission of the court. A Deposition Notice requires a minimum of ten (10) days notice (plus five days if mailed). Depositions requirements can be found at CCP§ 2025.

The Notice must contain the following information: person to be deposed, date, time, and location of the deposition. If the person to be deposed is not a party, the notice should also contain that person's address and telephone number. The person may also be required to bring documents to the deposition. If this is the case, please review the Code of Civil Procedure statutes that govern production of documents, as this will affect the notice and service requirements.

Request for Admissions—Are often combined with Special Interrogatories in family law matters as set forth above. However, there is a specific family law Request for Admission form (FL-100) which may be utilized if the attorney prefers. This Judicial Council form is **not** mandatory and therefore a pleading may also be prepared. (See CCP§ 2033 for further information and requirements of Requests for Admissions.)

Extensions

It is very common in the family law practice for a responding party to require an extension of time to provide answers to the propounding party. This is particularly true if you are working for a busy sole practitioner. Several possibilities might occur that would require an extension, such as the client has been unable to secure information requested because it has to come from a third party such as a pension plan; the attorney has been out of town or in court, and unable to meet with the client, review the information, and/or sign any declarations; or the paralegal has been busy working on other matters and unable to prepare the final documents.

In the event any of these things occur which may exceed the deadline for serving the documents, your office must ask for an extension of time. Most attorneys will grant an extension as a professional courtesy (the same thing happens in their offices from time to time) unless there are other dates pending such as trial, which will have an effect on any date extensions. If an extension is necessary, at the direction of the attorney, you should contact opposing counsel's office and request an extension and provide an exact date on which you will have the documents delivered to their office. This is referred to as a *date certain.* You must then confirm the extension granted, indicating the original date due and the newly agreed-upon date when the documents will be provided. The same is true if your office is granting the extension. You will want to make sure that the opposing counsel's office provides a confirmation letter. If they do not, you will need to write the letter confirming the agreement and the *date certain.* It is always good practice to send a copy of the letter by facsimile immediately and follow up by sending the original by mail.

It is very important that this step is done, as it will significantly affect any Motions to Compel that may need to be filed. For instance, if your office has not provided the documents to be produced by the required date and has not requested an extension (and confirmed it in writing), then the opposing counsel may file a Motion to Compel. Alternatively, if you have granted an extension with a *date certain* and the opposing party has not sent the propounded discovery by that new date, your attorney may need to file a Motion to Compel, to which you will want to attach a copy of the confirming letter showing the court that you have made a reasonable effort to obtain the discovery. In both instances, a second letter should also be sent indicating that the party or the attorney of record has missed the discovery due date and that requests a reasonable time (3–5 days) for presenting the discovery or a Motion to Compel will be filed. This letter should be attached to the Motion as an exhibit.

Demand for Exchange of Expert Trial Witness Information

A Demand for Exchange of Expert Trial Witness Information is done in pleading format. It may also contain a demand that any reports, documents or other writings prepared by the Expert who will be called to testify at trial be produced to the opposing party. CCP§ 2034 governs the exchange of Expert Witness information and documents. CCP§ 2034.010–2034.730 states that the parties must participate in "mutual and simultaneous" exchange of information. These sections contain the specific information required in the exchange and should be reviewed to assure that your office is in compliance with the process setting forth the information that is required to be exchanged.

The above is a guideline based on the Code of Civil Procedure to which each section relates. **Always** follow the instructions of the attorney and his/her "Discovery Plan." For instance, some attorneys will send out all of the above types of discovery demands, except expert trial witness exchange information, immediately upon filing the Response. Other attorneys will wait to see how the exchange of information flows between the parties as the case progresses. The Discovery Plan is a matter of the attorney's personal or the firm's prerogative and should be followed by the paralegal.

Forms Associated with Topic

Preliminary Declaration of Disclosure (FL-140)

Responsive Declaration (FL-320)

Proof of Service by Mail (FL-335)

Findings & Order After Hearing (FL-340)

Attachments to Findings & Order:

Child Custody and Visitation Attachment (FL-341)

Children's Holiday Schedule Attachment (FL-341(C))

Child Support Information and Order Attachment (FL-342)

Spousal, Partner or Family Support Order Attachments (FL-343)

Attorney Fees and Costs Attachment (FL-346)

Property Order Attachment (FL-344)

Request for Orders Regarding Noncompliance with Disclosure Requirements (FL-316)

(See examples of some forms on the following pages)

Key Terms

- Minute Order
- Findings & Order After Hearing
- Continuance
- Interrogatories
- Request for Admissions
- Demand for Production
- Deposition
- Subpoena
- Demand for Exchange of Expert Trial Witness Information
- Notice to Consumer
- Date Certain

Responsive Declaration to Request for Order

FL-320

ATTORNEY OR PARTY WITHOUT ATTORNEY *(Name, State Bar number, and address):*	FOR COURT USE ONLY
SAM E SPADE, SBN ********** LAW OFFICES OF SPADE, PICKS & HOVEL 99999 DEFENSE COURT SACRAMENTO, CA 95826 TELEPHONE NO. 916-555-9999 FAX NO. *(Optional):* 916-555-9998 E-MAIL ADDRESS *(Optional):* sam@ spadelawcorp.com ATTORNEY FOR *(Name):* ROCKY SHORES, Respondent	To keep other people from seeing what you entered on your form, please press the Clear This Form button at the end of the form when finished.

SUPERIOR COURT OF CALIFORNIA, COUNTY OF SACRAMENTO
STREET ADDRESS: 3341 POWER INN ROAD
MAILING ADDRESS: 3341 POWER INN ROAD
CITY AND ZIP CODE: SACRAMENTO, CA 95826
BRANCH NAME: FAMILY LAW DIVISION

PETITIONER/PLAINTIFF: SANDIE SHORES

RESPONDENT/DEFENDANT: ROCKY SHORES

OTHER PARTY:

RESPONSIVE DECLARATION TO REQUEST FOR ORDER	CASE NUMBER: 14FLXXXXXXX
HEARING DATE: XX/XX/2014	TIME: 9 AM	DEPARTMENT OR ROOM: ***

1. ☑ CHILD CUSTODY
   a. ☐ I consent to the order requested.
   b. ☑ I do not consent to the order requested, but I consent to the following order:
   Joint legal and physical custody

2. ☑ CHILD VISITATION (PARENTING TIME)
   a. ☐ I consent to the order requested.
   b. ☑ I do not consent to the order requested, but I consent to the following order:
   Joint legal and physical custody - frequent and continuing contact

3. ☑ CHILD SUPPORT
   a. ☐ I consent to the order requested.
   b. ☑ I consent to guideline support.
   c. ☐ I do not consent to the order requested, but I consent to the following order:
   (1) ☐ Guideline
   (2) ☐ Other *(specify):*

4. ☑ SPOUSAL OR PARTNER SUPPORT
   a. ☐ I consent to the order requested.
   b. ☑ I do not consent to the order requested.
   c. ☐ I consent to the following order:

Form Adopted for Mandatory Use
Judicial Council of California
FL-320 [Rev. July 1, 2012]

RESPONSIVE DECLARATION TO REQUEST FOR ORDER

Responsive Declaration to Request for Order

PETITIONER/PLAINTIFF: SANDIE SHORES	CASE NUMBER:
RESPONDENT/DEFENDANT: ROCKY SHORES	14FLXXXXXXX
OTHER PARTY:	

5. ☑ ATTORNEY'S FEES AND COSTS
    a. ☐ I consent to the order requested.
    b. ☑ I do not consent to the order requested.
    c. ☐ I consent to the following order:

6. ☑ PROPERTY RESTRAINT
    a. ☐ I consent to the order requested.
    b. ☑ I do not consent to the order requested.
    c. ☐ I consent to the following order:

7. ☑ PROPERTY CONTROL
    a. ☐ I consent to the order requested.
    b. ☑ I do not consent to the order requested.
    c. ☐ I consent to the following order:

8. ☐ OTHER RELIEF
    a. ☐ I consent to the order requested.
    b. ☐ I do not consent to the order requested.
    c. ☐ I consent to the following order:

9. ☑ SUPPORTING INFORMATION
    ☑ Contained in the attached declaration. (You may use *Attached Declaration* (form MC-031) for this purpose).
    Since the time of our separation Petitioner has been very angry and antagonistic. She has refused to allow any contact with the children. She has refused to discuss anything to do with resolving our marital issues. I agree to attend court-ordered mediation regarding the custody and visitation of our children. Based on the results of that mediation, I would then agree to guideline child support based on the time-share agreed.

NOTE: To respond to domestic violence restraining orders requested in the *Request for Order (Domestic Violence Prevention)* (form DV-100), you must use the *Answer to Temporary Restraining Order (Domestic Violence Prevention)* (form DV-120).

I declare under penalty of perjury under the laws of the State of California that the foregoing and all attachments are true and correct.

Date:

ROCKY SHORES   ▶
  (TYPE OR PRINT NAME)   (SIGNATURE OF DECLARANT)

For your protection and privacy, please press the Clear This Form button after you have printed the form.	Save This Form	Print This Form	Clear This Form

Proof of Service by Mail

FL-335

ATTORNEY OR PARTY WITHOUT ATTORNEY *(Name, State Bar number, and address):*	FOR COURT USE ONLY
CLASS E. ATTORNEY, SBN ******* CLASS & ASSOCIATES 150000 FOREVERMORE CIRCLE SACRAMENTO, CA 95826 TELEPHONE NO.: 916-555-9876 FAX NO. *(Optional):* 916-555-9877 E-MAIL ADDRESS *(Optional):* class@classandassociates.com ATTORNEY FOR *(Name):* ROCKY SHORES, Respondent	To keep other people from seeing what you entered on your form, please press the Clear This Form button at the end of the form when finished.

SUPERIOR COURT OF CALIFORNIA, COUNTY OF SACRAMENTO
STREET ADDRESS: 3341 POWER INN ROAD
MAILING ADDRESS: 3341 POWER INN ROAD
CITY AND ZIP CODE: SACRAMENTO, CA 95826
BRANCH NAME: FAMILY LAW

PETITIONER/PLAINTIFF: SANDIE SHORES RESPONDENT/DEFENDANT: ROCKY SHORES OTHER PARENT/PARTY:	CASE NUMBER: 14FLXXXXXXX

PROOF OF SERVICE BY MAIL	*(If applicable, provide):* HEARING DATE: XX/XX/2014 HEARING TIME: 9 AM DEPT.: ***

NOTICE: To serve temporary restraining orders you must use personal service (see form FL-330).

1. I am at least 18 years of age, not a party to this action, and I am a resident of or employed in the county where the mailing took place.

2. My residence or business address is:

   LAW OFFICES OF CLASS & ASSOCIATES
   5000 FOREVERMORE CIRCLE, SACRAMENTO, CA 95826

3. I served a copy of the following documents *(specify):*
   RESPONSIVE DECLARATION TO REQUEST FOR ORDER

   by enclosing them in an envelope AND
   a. ☐ **depositing** the sealed envelope with the United States Postal Service with the postage fully prepaid.
   b. ☑ **placing** the envelope for collection and mailing on the date and at the place shown in item 4 following our ordinary business practices. I am readily familiar with this business's practice for collecting and processing correspondence for mailing. On the same day that correspondence is placed for collection and mailing, it is deposited in the ordinary course of business with the United States Postal Service in a sealed envelope with postage fully prepaid.

4. The envelope was addressed and mailed as follows:
   a. Name of person served: JOAN CARE-ACTOR, CARE-ACTOR LAW OFFICE
   b. Address: 75000 WHY ME LANE, SACRAMENTO, CA 95826

   c. Date mailed: XX/XX/2014
   d. Place of mailing *(city and state):* SACRAMENTO, CA

5. ☐ I served a request to modify a child custody, visitation, or child support judgment or permanent order which included an address verification declaration. *(Declaration Regarding Address Verification—Postjudgment Request to Modify a Child Custody, Visitation, or Child Support Order* (form FL-334) may be used for this purpose.)

6. I declare under penalty of perjury under the laws of the State of California that the foregoing is true and correct.

Date:

SALLIE P. PARALEGAL
(TYPE OR PRINT NAME)   ▶   (SIGNATURE OF PERSON COMPLETING THIS FORM)

Page 1 of 1

Form Approved for Optional Use Judicial Council of California FL-335 [Rev. January 1, 2012]	**PROOF OF SERVICE BY MAIL**	Code of Civil Procedure, §§ 1013, 1013a www.courts.ca.gov

For your protection and privacy, please press the Clear This Form button after you have printed the form.   Save This Form   Print This Form   Clear This Form

Findings and Order after Hearing

FL-340

ATTORNEY OR PARTY WITHOUT ATTORNEY *(Name, State Bar number, and address):* JOAN CARE-ACTOR, SBN XXXXXX CARE-ACTOR LAW OFFICES 75000 WHY ME LANE SACRAMENTO, CA 95826 TELEPHONE NO.: 916-555-1234 FAX NO. *(Optional):* 916-555-1233 E-MAIL ADDRESS *(Optional):* joan@care-actorlaw.com ATTORNEY FOR *(Name):* SANDIE SHORES, PETITIONER	FOR COURT USE ONLY To keep other people from seeing what you entered on your form, please press the Clear This Form button at the end of the form when finished.

SUPERIOR COURT OF CALIFORNIA, COUNTY OF SACRAMENTO
STREET ADDRESS: 3341 POWER INN ROAD
MAILING ADDRESS: 3341 POWER INN ROAD
CITY AND ZIP CODE: SACRAMENTO, CA 95826
BRANCH NAME: FAMILY LAW

PETITIONER/PLAINTIFF: SANDIE SHORES

RESPONDENT/DEFENDANT: ROCKY SHORES

OTHER PARTY:

FINDINGS AND ORDER AFTER HEARING	CASE NUMBER: 14FLXXXXXX

1. This proceeding was heard
   on *(date):*   xx/xx/2014   at *(time):*   9 A,M   in Dept.:   ***   Room:
   by Judge *(name):*   Samuel Clemons Twain   ☐ Temporary Judge
   On the order to show cause, notice of motion or request for order filed *(date):* xx/xx/14 by *(name):*   SANDIE SHORES

   a. ☑ Petitioner/plaintiff present   ☑ Attorney present *(name):* JOAN CARE-ACTOR
   b. ☑ Respondent/defendant present   ☑ Attorney present *(name):* CLASS E ATTORNEY
   c. ☐ Other party present   ☐ Attorney present *(name):*

THE COURT ORDERS

2. Custody and visitation/parenting time: As attached ☑ on form FL-341   ☐ Other   ☐ Not applicable
3. Child support: As attached ☑ on form FL-342   ☐ Other   ☐ Not applicable
4. Spousal or family support: As attached ☑ on form FL-343   ☐ Other   ☐ Not applicable
5. Property orders: As attached ☑ on form FL-344   ☐ Other   ☐ Not applicable
6. Attorney's fees: As attached ☑ on form FL-346   ☐ Other   ☐ Not applicable
7. Other orders: ☐ As attached   ☐ Not applicable
8. All other issues are reserved until further order of court.
9. ☐ This matter is continued for further hearing on *(date):*   at *(time):*   in Dept.:
   on the following issues:

Date: ▶ _____
                                              JUDICIAL OFFICER

Approved as conforming to court order.

▶ _____

SIGNATURE OF ATTORNEY FOR ☐ PETITIONER / PLAINTIFF ☑ RESPONDENT/DEFENDANT ☐ OTHER PARTY

Page 1 of 1

Form Adopted for Mandatory Use
Judicial Council of California
FL-340 [Rev. January 1, 2012]

FINDINGS AND ORDER AFTER HEARING
(Family Law—Custody and Support—Uniform Parentage)

www.courts.ca.gov

For your protection and privacy, please press the Clear This Form button after you have printed the form.   Save This Form   Print This Form   Clear This Form

Child Custody and Visitation Order Attachment

	FL-341
PETITIONER/PLAINTIFF: SANDIE SHORES	CASE NUMBER:
RESPONDENT/DEFENDANT: ROCKY SHORES	14FLXXXXXX

CHILD CUSTODY AND VISITATION (PARENTING TIME) ORDER ATTACHMENT

TO [✔] *Findings and Order After Hearing* (form FL-340)   [ ] *Judgment* (form FL-180)

[ ] *Stipulation and Order for Custody and/or Visitation of Children* (form FL-355)

[ ] *Other (specify):*

1. **Jurisdiction.** This court has jurisdiction to make child custody orders in this case under the Uniform Child Custody Jurisdiction and Enforcement Act (part 3 of the California Family Code, commencing with section 3400).

2. **Notice and opportunity to be heard.** The responding party was given notice and an opportunity to be heard, as provided by the laws of the State of California.

3. **Country of habitual residence.** The country of habitual residence of the child or children in this case is
   [✔] the United States [ ] other *(specify):*

4. **Penalties for violating this order.** If you violate this order, you may be subject to civil or criminal penalties, or both.

5. [✔] **Custody.** Custody of the minor children of the parties is awarded as follows:

Child's name	Date of birth	Legal custody to (person who makes decisions about health, education, etc.)	Physical custody to (person with whom the child lives)
EDDY WADES SHORES	5/1/05	JOINT	SANDIE SHORES, MOTHER
SHELLY P. SHORES	10/15/09	JOINT	SANDIE SHORES, MOTHER

6. [ ] **Child abduction prevention.** There is a risk that one of the parents will take the children out of California without the other parent's permission. (*Child Abduction Prevention Orders Attachment* (form FL-341(B)) must be attached and must be obeyed.)

7. [✔] **Visitation (parenting time)**

   a. [ ] Reasonable right of visitation to the party without physical custody **(not appropriate in cases involving domestic violence)**

   b. [ ] See the attached _____-page document.

   c. [ ] The parties will go to mediation at *(specify location):*

   d. [ ] No visitation

   e. [✔] Visitation (parenting time) for the [ ] petitioner [✔] respondent [ ] other *(name):*
   will be as follows:

   (1) [✔] **Weekends starting** *(date):* XX/XX/2014
   (The first weekend of the month is the first weekend with a Saturday.)

   [✔] 1st [ ] 2nd [✔] 3rd [ ] 4th [✔] 5th   weekend of the month

   from FRIDAY   at 6   [ ] a.m. [✔] p.m.
   (day of week)   *(time)*

   to SUNDAY   at 6   [ ] a.m. [✔] p.m.
   (day of week)   *(time)*

   (a) [ ] The parents will alternate the fifth weekends, with the [ ] petitioner [ ] respondent
   [ ] other *(name):*   having the initial fifth weekend, which starts *(date):*

   (b) [ ] The petitioner will have fifth weekends in [ ] odd [ ] even months.

THIS IS A COURT ORDER.

Page 1 of 3

CHILD CUSTODY AND VISITATION (PARENTING TIME) ORDER ATTACHMENT

Family Code, §§ 3020, 3022, 3025, 3040–3043, 3048, 3100, 6340, 7604
www.courts.ca.gov

Child Custody and Visitation Order Attachment

PETITIONER/PLAINTIFF: SANDIE SHORES	CASE NUMBER:
RESPONDENT/DEFENDANT: ROCKY SHORES	14FLXXXXXX

7. e. (2) ☐ **Alternate weekends starting** *(date):*

The ☐ petitioner ☐ respondent ☐ other *(name):* will have the children

with him or her during the period

from _____ at _____ ☐ a.m. ☐ p.m.

    (day of week)   *(time)*

to _____ at _____ ☐ a.m. ☐ p.m.

    (day of week)   *(time)*

(3) ☐ **Weekdays starting** *(date):*

The ☐ petitioner ☐ respondent ☐ other *(name):* will have the children

with him or her during the period

from _____ at _____ ☐ a.m. ☐ p.m.

    (day of week)   *(time)*

to _____ at _____ ☐ a.m. ☐ p.m.

    (day of week)   *(time)*

(4) ☐ **Other** *(specify days and times as well as any additional restrictions):*

☐ See Attachment 7e(4).

8. ☐ **The court acknowledges** that criminal protective orders in case number *(specify):*
in *(specify court):* relating to the parties in this case are in effect
under Penal Code section 136.2, are current, and have priority of enforcement.

9. ☐ **Supervised visitation.** Until ☐ further order of the court ☐ other *(specify):*
the ☐ petitioner ☐ respondent ☐ other *(name):* will have supervised visitation with
the minor children according to the schedule

set forth on page 1. **(You must attach *Supervised Visitation Order* (form FL-341(A).)**

10. ☐ **Transportation for visitation**

a. The children must be driven only by a licensed and insured driver. The car or truck must have legal child restraint devices.

b. ☐ Transportation **to** the visits will be provided by the ☐ petitioner ☐ respondent
☐ other *(specify):*

c. ☐ Transportation **from** the visits will be provided by the ☐ petitioner ☐ respondent
☐ other *(specify):*

d. ☐ The exchange point at the beginning of the visit will be at *(address):*

e. ☐ The exchange point at the end of the visit will be at *(address):*

f. ☐ During the exchanges, the parent driving the children will wait in the car and the other parent will wait in his or her home while the children go between the car and the home.

g. ☐ Other *(specify):*

11. ☑ **Travel with children.** The ☐ petitioner ☑ respondent ☐ other *(name):*
must have written permission from the other parent or a court order to take the children out of

a. ☑ the state of California.

b. ☐ the following counties *(specify):*

c. ☐ other places *(specify):*

THIS IS A COURT ORDER.

Child Custody and Visitation Order Attachment

PETITIONER/PLAINTIFF: SANDIE SHORES	CASE NUMBER:
RESPONDENT/DEFENDANT: ROCKY SHORES	14FLXXXXXX

12. ☑ **Holiday schedule.** The children will spend holiday time as listed ☐ below ☑ in the attached schedule. *(Children's Holiday Schedule Attachment* (form FL-341(C)) may be used for this purpose.)

13. ☐ **Additional custody provisions.** The parents will follow the additional custody provisions listed ☐ below ☐ in the attached schedule. *(Additional Provisions—Physical Custody Attachment* (form FL-341(D)) may be used for this purpose.)

14. ☑ **Joint legal custody.** The parents will share joint legal custody as listed ☐ below ☑ in the attached schedule. *(Joint Legal Custody Attachment* (form FL-341(E)) may be used for this purpose.)

15. ☐ **Other** *(specify)*:

THIS IS A COURT ORDER.

FL-341 [Rev. July 1, 2012]	**CHILD CUSTODY AND VISITATION (PARENTING TIME)** **ORDER ATTACHMENT**	Page 3 of 3

For your protection and privacy, please press the Clear This Form button after you have printed the form. | Print This Form | Save This Form | Clear This Form |

Children's Holiday Schedule Attachment

> To keep other people from seeing what you entered on your form, please press the Clear This Form button at the end of the form when finished.

FL-341(C)

PETITIONER: SANDIE SHORES	CASE NUMBER:
RESPONDENT: ROCKY SHORES	14FLXXXXX

CHILDREN'S HOLIDAY SCHEDULE ATTACHMENT

TO ☐ Petition or Application for Order ☑ Findings and Order After Hearing or Judgment
☐ Stipulation and Order for Custody and/or Visitation of Children

1. **Holiday parenting.** The following table shows the holiday parenting schedules. Write "Pet" or "Resp" to specify each parent's years—odd, even, or both ("every year")—and under "Time" specify the starting and ending days and times.

Holiday	Time (from when to when) (Unless otherwise noted, all single-day holidays start at ___ a.m. and end at ___ p.m.)	Every Year Petitioner/ Respondent	Even Years Petitioner/ Respondent	Odd Years Petitioner/ Respondent
January 1 (New Year's Day)				
Martin Luther King's Birthday (weekend)			Petitioner	Respondent
Lincoln's Birthday				
President's Day (weekend)			Respondent	Petitioner
Spring Break, first half			Petitioner	Respondent
Spring Break, second half				
Mother's Day		Petitioner		
Memorial Day (weekend)			Respondent	Petitioner
Father's Day		Respondent		
July 4th			Petitioner	Respondent
Labor Day (weekend)			Respondent	Petitioner
Columbus Day (weekend)				
Halloween			Petitioner	Respondent
Veteran's Day (weekend)			Respondent	Petitioner
Thanksgiving Day			Petitioner	Respondent
Thanksgiving weekend				
Winter Break, first half			Respondent	Petitioner
Winter Break, second half			Petitioner	Respondent
New Year's Eve				
Child's birthday			Respondent	Petitioner
Mother's birthday		Petitioner		
Father's birthday		Respondent		
Breaks for year-round schools				
Summer Break, first half			Petitioner	Respondent
Summer Break, second half			Respondent	Petitioner
Other (specify):				

☑ Any three-day weekend not specified above will be spent with the parent who would normally have that weekend.

☐ Other (specify):

2. **Vacations.** The ☐ petitioner ☑ respondent may take a vacation of up to (specify number): 14 ☑ days ☐ weeks with the children the following number of times per year (specify): 2 . They must notify the other parent in writing of their vacation plans a minimum of (specify number): 30 days in advance and provide the other parent with a basic itinerary that includes dates of leaving and returning, destinations, flight information, and telephone numbers for emergency purposes. ☑ The other parent has (specify number): 5 days to respond if there is a problem with the schedule.

a. ☐ This vacation may be outside California.

b. ☑ Any vacation outside ☑ California ☐ the United States requires prior written consent of the other parent or a court order.

c. ☐ Other (specify):

Page 1 of 1

Form Approved for Optional Use
Judicial Council of California
FL-341(C) [Rev. January 1, 2005]

CHILDREN'S HOLIDAY SCHEDULE ATTACHMENT

Family Code, §§ 3003, 3083
www.courtinfo.ca.gov

> For your protection and privacy, please press the Clear This Form button after you have printed the form.

Save This Form | **Print This Form** | **Clear This Form**

Child Support Information and Order Attachment

	FL-342
PETITIONER/PLAINTIFF: SANDIE SHORES RESPONDENT/DEFENDANT: ROCKY SHORES OTHER PARENT:	CASE NUMBER: 14FLXXXXXX

CHILD SUPPORT INFORMATION AND ORDER ATTACHMENT

TO [✔] **Findings and Order After Hearing (form FL-340)** [ ] **Judgment (form FL-180)**
[ ] **Restraining Order After Hearing (CLETS-OAH)(form DV-130)**
[ ] **Other** *(specify):*

THE COURT USED THE FOLLOWING INFORMATION IN DETERMINING THE AMOUNT OF CHILD SUPPORT:

1. [✔] A printout of a computer calculation and findings is attached and incorporated in this order for all required items not filled out below.

2. [ ] **Income**

	Gross monthly income	Net monthly income	Receiving TANF/CalWORKS
a. Each parent's monthly income is as follows:			
Petitioner/plaintiff:	$	$	[ ]
Respondent/defendant:	$	$	[ ]
Other parent:	$	$	[ ]

b. Imputation of income. The court finds that the [ ] petitioner/plaintiff [ ] respondent/defendant
[ ] other parent has the capacity to earn:
$ _____ per _____ and has based the support order upon this imputed income.

3. [✔] **Children of this relationship**

a. Number of children who are the subjects of the support order *(specify):* TWO
b. Approximate percentage of time spent with petitioner/plaintiff: 75 %
respondent/defendant: 25 %
other parent: %

4. [ ] **Hardships**

Hardships for the following have been allowed in calculating child support:

	Petitioner/ plaintiff	Respondent/ defendant	Other parent	Approximate ending time for the hardship
a. [ ] Other minor children:	$	$	$	
b. [ ] Extraordinary medical expenses:	$	$	$	
c. [ ] Catastrophic losses:	$	$	$	

THE COURT ORDERS

5. [ ] **Low-income adjustment**

a. [ ] The low-income adjustment applies.
b. [ ] The low-income adjustment does not apply because *(specify reasons):*

6. [✔] **Child support**

a. **Base child support**

[ ] Petitioner/plaintiff [✔] Respondent/defendant [ ] Other parent must pay child support beginning *(date):* _____ and continuing until further order of the court, or until the child marries, dies, is emancipated, reaches age 19, or reaches age 18 and is not a full-time high school student, whichever occurs first, as follows:

Child's name	Date of birth	Monthly amount	Payable to *(name):*
EDDY WADE SHORES	5/.1/05	800	SANDIE SHORES
SHELLY SHORES	10/15/09	950	SANDIE SHORES

Payable [✔] on the 1st of the month [ ] one-half on the 1st and one-half on the 15th of the month
[ ] other *(specify):*

THIS IS A COURT ORDER.

Form Adopted for Mandatory Use
Judicial Council of California
FL-342 [Rev. July 1, 2012]
CHILD SUPPORT INFORMATION AND ORDER ATTACHMENT
Family Code, §§ 4055–4069
www.courts.ca.gov

Child Support Information and Order Attachment

FL-342

PETITIONER/PLAINTIFF: SANDIE SHORES RESPONDENT/DEFENDANT: ROCKY SHORES OTHER PARENT:	CASE NUMBER: 14FLXXXXXX

THE COURT FURTHER ORDERS

6. b. ☐ **Mandatory additional child support**

    (1) ☐ Child-care costs related to employment or reasonably necessary job training

        (a) ☐ Petitioner/plaintiff must pay: % of total   or   ☐ $ per month   child-care costs.

        (b) ☐ Respondent/defendant must pay: % of total   or   ☐ $ per month   child-care costs.

        (c) ☐ Other parent must pay: % of total   or   ☐ $ per month   child-care costs.

        (d) ☐ Costs to be paid as follows *(specify)*:

  c. **Mandatory additional child support**

    (2) ☐ Reasonable uninsured health-care costs for the children

        (a) ☐ Petitioner/plaintiff must pay: % of total   or   ☐ $ per month.

        (b) ☐ Respondent/defendant must pay: % of total   or   ☐ $ per month.

        (c) ☐ Other parent must pay: % of total   or   ☐ $ per month.

        (d) ☐ Costs to be paid as follows *(specify)*:

  d. ☐ **Additional child support**

    (1) ☐ Costs related to the educational or other special needs of the children

        (a) ☐ Petitioner/plaintiff must pay: % of total   or   ☐ $ per month.

        (b) ☐ Respondent/defendant must pay: % of total   or   ☐ $ per month.

        (c) ☐ Other parent must pay: % of total   or   ☐ $ per month.

        (d) ☐ Costs to be paid as follows *(specify)*:

    (2) ☐ Travel expenses for visitation

        (a) ☐ Petitioner/plaintiff must pay: % of total   or   ☐ $ per month.

        (b) ☐ Respondent/defendant must pay: % of total   or   ☐ $ per month.

        (c) ☐ Other parent must pay: % of total   or   ☐ $ per month.

        (d) ☐ Costs to be paid as follows *(specify)*:

  e. ☐ **Non-Guideline Order**
      This order does not meet the child support guideline set forth in Family Code section 4055. *Non-Guideline Child Support Findings Attachment* (form FL-342(A)) is attached.

Total child support per month: $ 1750.00

7. **Health-care expenses**

  a. Health insurance coverage for the minor children of the parties must be maintained by the
    ☐ petitioner/plaintiff   ☑ respondent/defendant   ☐ other parent   if available at no or reasonable cost through their respective places of employment or self-employment. Both parties are ordered to cooperate in the presentation, collection, and reimbursement of any health-care claims. The parent ordered to provide health insurance must seek continuation of coverage for the child after the child attains the age when the child is no longer considered eligible for coverage as a dependent under the insurance contract, if the child is incapable of self-sustaining employment because of a physically or mentally disabling injury, illness, or condition and is chiefly dependent upon the parent providing health insurance for support and maintenance.

  b. ☐ Health insurance is not available to the   ☐ petitioner/plaintiff   ☐ respondent/defendant   ☐ other parent at a reasonable cost at this time.

  c. ☐ The party providing coverage must assign the right of reimbursement to the other party.

8. **Earnings assignment**
An earnings assignment order is issued. **Note:** The payor of child support is responsible for the payment of support directly to the recipient until support payments are deducted from the payor's wages and for payment of any support not paid by the assignment.

9. In the event that there is a contract between a party receiving support and a private child support collector, the party ordered to pay support must pay the fee charged by the private child support collector. This fee must not exceed 33 1/3 percent of the total amount of past due support nor may it exceed 50 percent of any fee charged by the private child support collector. The money judgment created by this provision is in favor of the private child support collector and the party receiving support, jointly.

10. ☐ **Employment search order (Family Code, § 4505)**
    ☐ Petitioner/plaintiff   ☐ Respondent/defendant   ☐ Other parent   is ordered to seek employment with the following terms and conditions:

THIS IS A COURT ORDER.

Child Support Information and Order Attachment

FL-342

PETITIONER/PLAINTIFF: SANDIE SHORES RESPONDENT/DEFENDANT: ROCKY SHORES OTHER PARENT:	CASE NUMBER: 14FLXXXXXX

11. **Other orders** *(specify):*

12. **Notices**

    a. *Notice of Rights and Responsibilities (Health-Care Costs and Reimbursement Procedures) and Information Sheet on Changing a Child Support Order* (form FL-192) must be attached and is incorporated into this order.

    b. If this form is attached to *Restraining Order After Hearing* (form DV-130), the support orders issued on this form (form FL-342) remain in effect after the restraining orders issued on form DV-130 end.

13. **Child Support Case Registry Form**

    Both parties must complete and file with the court a *Child Support Case Registry Form* (form FL-191) within 10 days of the date of this order. Thereafter, the parties must notify the court of any change in the information submitted within 10 days of the change by filing an updated form.

> **NOTICE:** Any party required to pay child support must pay interest on overdue amounts at the legal rate, which is currently 10 percent per year.

THIS IS A COURT ORDER.

For your protection and privacy, please press the Clear This Form button after you have printed the form. | Print This Form | Save This Form | Clear This Form |

Spousal, Partner, or Family Support Order Attachment

FL-343

PETITIONER/PLAINTIFF: SANDIE SHORES	CASE NUMBER:
RESPONDENT/DEFENDANT: ROCKY SHORES	14FLXXXXXXX
OTHER PARENT:	

SPOUSAL, PARTNER, OR FAMILY SUPPORT ORDER ATTACHMENT

TO [✔] *Findings and Order After Hearing* (form FL-340) [ ] *Judgment* (form FL-180)
[ ] *Restraining Order After Hearing (CLETS-OAH)* (form DV-130) [ ] *Other (specify):*
[ ] *Stipulation of Parties*

THE COURT FINDS

1. **Net income.** The parties' monthly income and deductions are as follows *(complete a, b, or both)*:

		Total gross monthly income	Total monthly deductions	Total hardship deductions	Net monthly disposable income
a. Petitioner:	[ ] receiving TANF/CalWORKS	$	$	$	$
b. Respondent:	[ ] receiving TANF/CalWORKS	$	$	$	$

2. [✔] A printout of a computer calculation of the parties' financial circumstances is attached for all required items not filled out above *(for temporary support only)*.

3. **Judgment for spousal or partner support**
   a. [ ] Modifies a judgment or order entered on *(date):*
   b. [✔] The parties were married for *(specify numbers):* 11 years 2 months.
   c. [ ] The parties were registered as domestic partners or the equivalent for *(specify numbers):* _____ years ____ months.
   d. [ ] The parties are both self-supporting, as shown on the *Declaration for Default or Uncontested Dissolution or Legal Separation* (form FL-170).
   e. [✔] The marital standard of living was *(describe):*
   > Petitioner has been primarily and stay-at-home mom; most recently getting an unskilled job for minimum wage only during the time that the children are in school. Respondent has been the primary support for the family. The court will maintain the status quo until the parties have an opportunity to reach a property settlement at which time the court will reevaluate any long term, permanent spousal support orders.
   [ ] See Attachment 3d.

THE COURT ORDERS

4. [ ] The issue of spousal or partner support for the [ ] petitioner [ ] respondent is reserved for a later determination.

5. [✔] The court terminates jurisdiction over the issue of spousal or partner support for the [ ] petitioner [✔] respondent.

6. a. The [ ] petitioner [✔] respondent must pay to the [ ] petitioner [ ] respondent
   as [✔] temporary [✔] spousal support [ ] family support [ ] partner support
   $ 1,000 per month, beginning *(date):* xx/xx/2014 , payable through *(specify end date):* review

   [ ] payable on the *(specify):* day of each month.
   [ ] Other *(specify):*

   b. [✔] Support must be paid by check, money order, or cash. The support payor's obligation to pay support will terminate on the death of either party, remarriage, or registration of a new domestic partnership of the support payee.

   c. [ ] An earnings assignment for the foregoing support will issue. (**Note:** The payor of spousal, family, or partner support is responsible for the payment of support directly to the recipient until support payments are deducted from the payor's earnings, and for any support not paid by the assignment.)

   d. [ ] Service of the earnings assignment is stayed provided the payor is not more than *(specify number):* days late in the payment of spousal, family, or partner support.

THIS IS A COURT ORDER.

Form Approved for Optional Use
Judicial Council of California
FL-343 [Rev. July 1, 2012]

SPOUSAL, PARTNER, OR FAMILY SUPPORT ORDER ATTACHMENT
(Family Law)

Family Code, §§ 150, 299, 3651, 3653, 3654, 4320, 4330, 4337
www.courts.ca.gov

Spousal, Partner, or Family Support Order Attachment

PETITIONER/PLAINTIFF: SANDIE SHORES RESPONDENT/DEFENDANT: ROCKY SHORES OTHER PARENT:	CASE NUMBER: 14FLXXXXXXX

7. [✔] The [✔] petitioner [ ] respondent should make reasonable efforts to assist in providing for his or her support needs.

8. [✔] The parties must promptly inform each other of any change of employment, including the employer's name, address, and telephone number.

9. [ ] This order is for family support. Both parties must complete and file with the court a *Child Support Case Registry Form* (form FL-191) within 10 days of the date of this order. The parents must notify the court of any change of information submitted within 10 days of the change by filing an updated form. A *Notice of Rights and Responsibilities (Health-Care Costs and Reimbursement Procedures) and Information Sheet on Changing a Child Support Order* (form FL-192) is attached.

10. [ ] Notice: If this form is attached to *Restraining Order After Hearing (CLETS-OAH) (Order of Protection)* (form DV-130), the orders issued on this form (FL-343) do not expire upon termination of the restraining orders issued on form DV-130.

11. [✔] Other orders (*specify*):

The parties will return to the court within one year of entry of this order for a review of the Petitioner's need for permanent, long term support; unless the parties reach an agreement prior to that time.

NOTICE: Any party required to pay support must pay interest on overdue amounts at the "legal" rate, which is currently 10 percent.

THIS IS A COURT ORDER.

For your protection and privacy, please press the Clear This Form button after you have printed the form.	Print This Form	Save This Form	Clear This Form

Attorney's Fees and Costs Order Attachment

FL-346

PETITIONER/PLAINTIFF: SANDIE SHORES RESPONDENT/DEFENDANT: ROCKY SHORES OTHER PARTY:	CASE NUMBER: 14FLXXXXXXX

ATTORNEY'S FEES AND COSTS ORDER ATTACHMENT

Attached to:

☑ **Findings and Orders After Hearing** (form FL-340)

☐ **Judgment (Uniform Parentage—Custody and Support)** (form FL-250)

☐ **Judgment** (form FL-180)

☐ Other *(specify):*

THE COURT FINDS

1. ☑ An award of attorney's fees and costs is appropriate because there is a demonstrated disparity between the parties in access to funds to retain or maintain counsel and in the ability to pay for legal representation.

    a. ☑ The party requested to pay attorney's fees and costs has or is reasonably likely to have the ability to pay for legal representation for both parties.

    b. ☑ The requested attorney's fees and costs are reasonable and necessary.

2. ☐ An award of attorney's fees and costs is not appropriate because *(check all that apply):*

    a. ☐ there is not a demonstrated disparity between the parties in access to funds to retain or maintain counsel or in the ability to pay for legal representation.

    b. ☐ the party requested to pay attorney's fees and costs does not have or is not reasonably likely to have the ability to pay for legal representation for both parties.

    c. ☐ the requested attorney's fees and costs are not reasonable or necessary.

3. ☐ Other *(specify):*

THE COURT ORDERS

4. a. The ☐ petitioner/plaintiff ☑ respondent/defendant ☐ other party to pay attorney's fees and costs in this legal proceeding

    b. in the amount of:

        (1) ☑ Fees: $ 6,000

        (2) ☑ Costs: $ 400

        (3) ☑ Interest is not included and is not waived.

    c. Payable to ☑ petitioner/plaintiff ☐ respondent/defendant ☐ other party

    d. ☐ From the payment sources of *(if specified):*

Form Approved for Optional Use
Judicial Council of California
FL-346 [New January 1, 2012] **ATTORNEY'S FEES AND COSTS ORDER ATTACHMENT**
(Family Law) Family Code, §§ 270, 2030, 3121, 3557,
7605; Cal. Rules of Court, rules 5.425, 5.93
www.courts.ca.gov

Attorney's Fees and Costs Order Attachment

FL-346

PETITIONER/PLAINTIFF: SANDIE SHORES	CASE NUMBER:
RESPONDENT/DEFENDANT: ROCKY SHORES	14FLXXXXXXX
OTHER PARTY:	

4. e.   With a payment schedule of *(specify):*

    (1) ☐ Due in full, on or before *(date):*

    (2) ☐ Due in installments, with monthly payments of *(specify):* $, on the *(specify):*   day of each month,
              beginning *(date):*   until paid in full.

    (3) ☐ If any payment is not timely made and more than   days overdue, the entire unpaid balance will
              immediately become due with interest at the legal rate, which is currently 10 percent per year, from the date of
              default to the date payment is finally made.

    (4) ☐ No interest will accrue as long as payments are timely made.

    (5) ☐ Other *(specify):*

5. ☐ This amount includes *(check all that apply):*

    a. ☐ a fee in the amount of *(specify)* $ to hire an attorney in a timely manner before the proceedings in the
          matter go forward.

    b. ☐ attorney's fees and costs incurred to date in the amount of *(specify):* $

    c. ☐ estimated attorney's fees and costs in the amount of *(specify):* $

    d. ☐ attorney's fees and costs for limited scope representation in the amount of *(specify):* $

    e. ☐ any amounts previously ordered that have not yet been paid *(specify):* $

    f. ☐ Other *(specify):*

6. ☐ Other orders *(specify):*

NOTICE: Any party required to pay attorney's fees and costs must pay interest on overdue amounts at the legal rate, which is currently 10 percent per year.

Save This Form   Print This Form   Clear This Form

Property Order Attachment to Findings and Order after Hearing

> To keep other people from seeing what you entered on your form, please press the Clear This Form button at the end of the form when finished.

	FL-344
PETITIONER : SANDIE SHORES	CASE NUMBER:
RESPONDENT: ROCKY SHORES	14FLXXXXXX

**PROPERTY ORDER ATTACHMENT
TO FINDINGS AND ORDER AFTER HEARING**

THE COURT ORDERS

1. ☑ **Property restraining orders**

   a. The ☐ petitioner ☑ respondent ☐ claimant   is restrained from transferring, encumbering, hypothecating, concealing, or in any way disposing of any property, real or personal, whether community, quasi-community, or separate, except in the usual course of business or for the necessities of life.

   b. The ☐ petitioner ☑ respondent   must notify the other party of any proposed extraordinary expenses at least five business days before incurring such expenses, and make an accounting of such to the court.

   c. The ☐ petitioner ☑ respondent   is restrained from cashing, borrowing against, cancelling, transferring, disposing of, or changing the beneficiaries of any insurance or other coverage, including life, health, automobile, and disability, held for the benefit of the parties or their minor child or children.

   d. The ☐ petitioner ☑ respondent   must not incur any debts or liabilities for which the other may be held responsible, other than in the ordinary course of business or for the necessities of life.

2. ☑ **Possession of property.** The exclusive use, possession, and control of the following property that the parties own or are buying is given as specified:

   Property
   11155 TURTLE DOVE COURT, FOLSOM

   Given to
   SANDIE SHORES, PETITIONER

   ☐ See Attachment 2.

3. ☑ **Payment of debts.** Payments on the following debts that come due while this order is in effect must be paid as follows:

Total debt	Amount of payments	Pay to	Paid by
$ 250,000	$ 950	XYZ MORTGAGE CO.	ROCKY SHORES
$	$		
$	$		
$	$		

   ☐ See Attachment 3.

4. ☑ These are temporary orders only. The court will make final orders at the time of judgment.

5. ☐ Other *(specify):*

Form Adopted for Mandatory Use
Judicial Council of California
FL-344 [Rev. January 1, 2007]

**PROPERTY ORDER ATTACHMENT
TO FINDINGS AND ORDER AFTER HEARING**
(Family Law)

Family Code, §§ 2045, 6324
www.courtinfo.ca.gov

> For your protection and privacy, please press the Clear This Form button after you have printed the form.

Save This Form   **Print This Form**   **Clear This Form**

Responsive Declaration to Request for Order

<table>
<tr>
<td colspan="2"></td>
<td align="right">FL-320</td>
</tr>
<tr>
<td colspan="2">ATTORNEY OR PARTY WITHOUT ATTORNEY (Name, State Bar number, and address):</td>
<td align="center">FOR COURT USE ONLY</td>
</tr>
<tr>
<td colspan="2">
TELEPHONE NO.:   FAX NO. (Optional):
E-MAIL ADDRESS (Optional):
ATTORNEY FOR (Name):
</td>
<td>To keep other people from seeing what you entered on your form, please press the Clear This Form button at the end of the form when finished.</td>
</tr>
<tr>
<td colspan="2">
SUPERIOR COURT OF CALIFORNIA, COUNTY OF
STREET ADDRESS:
MAILING ADDRESS:
CITY AND ZIP CODE:
BRANCH NAME:
</td>
<td></td>
</tr>
<tr>
<td colspan="2">
PETITIONER/PLAINTIFF:

RESPONDENT/DEFENDANT:

OTHER PARTY:
</td>
<td></td>
</tr>
<tr>
<td colspan="2">RESPONSIVE DECLARATION TO REQUEST FOR ORDER</td>
<td>CASE NUMBER:</td>
</tr>
<tr>
<td colspan="2">HEARING DATE: TIME: DEPARTMENT OR ROOM:</td>
<td></td>
</tr>
</table>

1. ☐ CHILD CUSTODY
   - a. ☐ I consent to the order requested.
   - b. ☐ I do not consent to the order requested, but I consent to the following order:

2. ☐ CHILD VISITATION (PARENTING TIME)
   - a. ☐ I consent to the order requested.
   - b. ☐ I do not consent to the order requested, but I consent to the following order:

3. ☐ CHILD SUPPORT
   - a. ☐ I consent to the order requested.
   - b. ☐ I consent to guideline support.
   - c. ☐ I do not consent to the order requested, but I consent to the following order:
     - (1) ☐ Guideline
     - (2) ☐ Other (specify):

4. ☐ SPOUSAL OR PARTNER SUPPORT
   - a. ☐ I consent to the order requested.
   - b. ☐ I do not consent to the order requested.
   - c. ☐ I consent to the following order:

Form Adopted for Mandatory Use
Judicial Council of California
FL-320 [Rev. July 1, 2012]

RESPONSIVE DECLARATION TO REQUEST FOR ORDER

www.courts.ca.gov

Responsive Declaration to Request for Order

PETITIONER/PLAINTIFF:	CASE NUMBER:
RESPONDENT/DEFENDANT:	
OTHER PARTY:	

5. ☐ ATTORNEY'S FEES AND COSTS
    a. ☐ I consent to the order requested.
    b. ☐ I do not consent to the order requested.
    c. ☐ I consent to the following order:

6. ☐ PROPERTY RESTRAINT
    a. ☐ I consent to the order requested.
    b. ☐ I do not consent to the order requested.
    c. ☐ I consent to the following order:

7. ☐ PROPERTY CONTROL
    a. ☐ I consent to the order requested.
    b. ☐ I do not consent to the order requested.
    c. ☐ I consent to the following order:

8. ☐ OTHER RELIEF
    a. ☐ I consent to the order requested.
    b. ☐ I do not consent to the order requested.
    c. ☐ I consent to the following order:

9. ☐ SUPPORTING INFORMATION
    ☐ Contained in the attached declaration. (You may use *Attached Declaration* (form MC–031) for this purpose).

NOTE: To respond to domestic violence restraining orders requested in the *Request for Order (Domestic Violence Prevention)* (form DV-100), you must use the *Answer to Temporary Restraining Order (Domestic Violence Prevention)* (form DV-120).

I declare under penalty of perjury under the laws of the State of California that the foregoing and all attachments are true and correct.

Date:

▶

_____
(TYPE OR PRINT NAME)

_____
(SIGNATURE OF DECLARANT)

FL-320 [Rev. July 1, 2012]   **RESPONSIVE DECLARATION TO REQUEST FOR ORDER**   Page 2 of 2

For your protection and privacy, please press the Clear This Form button after you have printed the form.

Save This Form | Print This Form | Clear This Form

Findings and Order after Hearing

	FL-340
ATTORNEY OR PARTY WITHOUT ATTORNEY (Name, State Bar number, and address):	FOR COURT USE ONLY
TELEPHONE NO.: FAX NO. (Optional):	To keep other people from seeing what you entered on your form, please press the **Clear This Form** button at the end of the form when finished.
E-MAIL ADDRESS (Optional):	
ATTORNEY FOR (Name):	

SUPERIOR COURT OF CALIFORNIA, COUNTY OF
STREET ADDRESS:
MAILING ADDRESS:
CITY AND ZIP CODE:
BRANCH NAME:

PETITIONER/PLAINTIFF:

RESPONDENT/DEFENDANT:

OTHER PARTY:

FINDINGS AND ORDER AFTER HEARING	CASE NUMBER:

1. This proceeding was heard
   on (date):   at (time):   in Dept.:   Room:
   by Judge (name):   ☐ Temporary Judge
   On the order to show cause, notice of motion or request for order filed (date):   by (name):

   a. ☐ Petitioner/plaintiff present   ☐ Attorney present (name):
   b. ☐ Respondent/defendant present   ☐ Attorney present (name):
   c. ☐ Other party present   ☐ Attorney present (name):

THE COURT ORDERS

2. Custody and visitation/parenting time: As attached ☐ on form FL-341 ☐ Other ☐ Not applicable

3. Child support: As attached ☐ on form FL-342 ☐ Other ☐ Not applicable

4. Spousal or family support: As attached ☐ on form FL-343 ☐ Other ☐ Not applicable

5. Property orders: As attached ☐ on form FL-344 ☐ Other ☐ Not applicable

6. Attorney's fees: As attached ☐ on form FL-346 ☐ Other ☐ Not applicable

7. Other orders: ☐ As attached   ☐ Not applicable

8. All other issues are reserved until further order of court.

9. ☐ This matter is continued for further hearing on (date):   at (time):   in Dept.:
   on the following issues:

Date: _____   ▶ _____
                                                    JUDICIAL OFFICER

Approved as conforming to court order.

▶ _____

SIGNATURE OF ATTORNEY FOR ☐ PETITIONER / PLAINTIFF ☐ RESPONDENT/DEFENDANT ☐ OTHER PARTY

Page 1 of 1

Form Adopted for Mandatory Use Judicial Council of California FL-340 [Rev. January 1, 2012]	**FINDINGS AND ORDER AFTER HEARING** (Family Law—Custody and Support—Uniform Parentage)	www.courts.ca.gov

For your protection and privacy, please press the Clear This Form button after you have printed the form.   Save This Form | Print This Form | Clear This Form

Child Custody and Visitation

FL-341

PETITIONER/PLAINTIFF:	CASE NUMBER:
RESPONDENT/DEFENDANT:	

CHILD CUSTODY AND VISITATION (PARENTING TIME) ORDER ATTACHMENT

TO ☐ *Findings and Order After Hearing (form FL-340)*   ☐ *Judgment (form FL-180)*

☐ *Stipulation and Order for Custody and/or Visitation of Children (form FL-355)*

☐ **Other** *(specify):*

1. **Jurisdiction.** This court has jurisdiction to make child custody orders in this case under the Uniform Child Custody Jurisdiction and Enforcement Act (part 3 of the California Family Code, commencing with section 3400).

2. **Notice and opportunity to be heard.** The responding party was given notice and an opportunity to be heard, as provided by the laws of the State of California.

3. **Country of habitual residence.** The country of habitual residence of the child or children in this case is ☐ the United States ☐ other *(specify):*

4. **Penalties for violating this order.** If you violate this order, you may be subject to civil or criminal penalties, or both.

5. ☐ **Custody.** Custody of the minor children of the parties is awarded as follows:

Child's name	Date of birth	Legal custody to *(person who makes decisions about health, education, etc.)*	Physical custody to *(person with whom the child lives)*

6. ☐ **Child abduction prevention.** There is a risk that one of the parents will take the children out of California without the other parent's permission. (*Child Abduction Prevention Orders Attachment* (form FL-341(B)) must be attached and must be obeyed.)

7. ☐ **Visitation (parenting time)**

   a. ☐ Reasonable right of visitation to the party without physical custody **(not appropriate in cases involving domestic violence)**

   b. ☐ See the attached _____-page document.

   c. ☐ The parties will go to mediation at *(specify location):*

   d. ☐ No visitation

   e. ☐ Visitation (parenting time) for the ☐ petitioner ☐ respondent ☐ other *(name):* will be as follows:

   (1) ☐ **Weekends starting** *(date):*
   (The first weekend of the month is the first weekend with a Saturday.)

   ☐ 1st ☐ 2nd ☐ 3rd ☐ 4th ☐ 5th   weekend of the month

   from _____ at _____   ☐ a.m. ☐ p.m.
        (day of week)   *(time)*

   to _____ at _____   ☐ a.m. ☐ p.m.
      (day of week)   *(time)*

   (a) ☐ The parents will alternate the fifth weekends, with the ☐ petitioner ☐ respondent ☐ other *(name):* having the initial fifth weekend, which starts *(date):*

   (b) ☐ The petitioner will have fifth weekends in ☐ odd ☐ even months.

THIS IS A COURT ORDER.

Form Approved for Optional Use
Judicial Council of California
FL-341 [Rev. July 1, 2012]

**CHILD CUSTODY AND VISITATION (PARENTING TIME)
ORDER ATTACHMENT**

Page 1 of 3

Family Code, §§ 3020, 3022, 3025,
3040–3043, 3048, 3100, 6340, 7604
www.courts.ca.gov

Child Custody and Visitation

PETITIONER/PLAINTIFF:	CASE NUMBER:
RESPONDENT/DEFENDANT:	

7. e. (2) ☐ **Alternate weekends starting** (date):

The ☐ petitioner ☐ respondent ☐ other (name):   will have the children with him or her during the period

from _____ at _____ ☐ a.m. ☐ p.m.
   (day of week)   (time)

to _____ at _____ ☐ a.m. ☐ p.m.
   (day of week)   (time)

(3) ☐ **Weekdays starting** (date):

The ☐ petitioner ☐ respondent ☐ other (name):   will have the children with him or her during the period

from _____ at _____ ☐ a.m. ☐ p.m.
   (day of week)   (time)

to _____ at _____ ☐ a.m. ☐ p.m.
   (day of week)   (time)

(4) ☐ **Other** (specify days and times as well as any additional restrictions):

☐ See Attachment 7e(4).

8. ☐ **The court acknowledges** that criminal protective orders in case number (specify):
in (specify court):   relating to the parties in this case are in effect under Penal Code section 136.2, are current, and have priority of enforcement.

9. ☐ **Supervised visitation.** Until ☐ further order of the court ☐ other (specify):
the ☐ petitioner ☐ respondent ☐ other (name):   will have supervised visitation with the minor children according to the schedule

set forth on page 1. **(You must attach** *Supervised Visitation Order* **(form FL-341(A).)**

10. ☐ **Transportation for visitation**

  a. The children must be driven only by a licensed and insured driver. The car or truck must have legal child restraint devices.

  b. ☐ Transportation **to** the visits will be provided by the ☐ petitioner ☐ respondent ☐ other (specify):

  c. ☐ Transportation **from** the visits will be provided by the ☐ petitioner ☐ respondent ☐ other (specify):

  d. ☐ The exchange point at the beginning of the visit will be at (address):

  e. ☐ The exchange point at the end of the visit will be at (address):

  f. ☐ During the exchanges, the parent driving the children will wait in the car and the other parent will wait in his or her home while the children go between the car and the home.

  g. ☐ Other (specify):

11. ☐ **Travel with children.** The ☐ petitioner ☐ respondent ☐ other (name):
must have written permission from the other parent or a court order to take the children out of

  a. ☐ the state of California.

  b. ☐ the following counties (specify):

  c. ☐ other places (specify):

THIS IS A COURT ORDER.

Child Custody and Visitation

PETITIONER/PLAINTIFF:	CASE NUMBER:
RESPONDENT/DEFENDANT:	

12. ☐ **Holiday schedule.** The children will spend holiday time as listed ☐ below ☐ in the attached schedule.
    (Children's Holiday Schedule Attachment (form FL-341(C)) may be used for this purpose.)

13. ☐ **Additional custody provisions.** The parents will follow the additional custody provisions listed ☐ below ☐ in the attached schedule. *(Additional Provisions—Physical Custody Attachment* (form FL-341(D)) may be used for this purpose.)

14. ☐ **Joint legal custody.** The parents will share joint legal custody as listed ☐ below ☐ in the attached schedule.
    (Joint Legal Custody Attachment (form FL-341(E)) may be used for this purpose.)

15. ☐ **Other** *(specify):*

THIS IS A COURT ORDER.

For your protection and privacy, please press the Clear This Form button after you have printed the form. | Print This Form | Save This Form | Clear This Form |

Children's Holiday Schedule Attachment

To keep other people from seeing what you entered on your form, please press the Clear This Form button at the end of the form when finished.	FL-341(C)

PETITIONER:	CASE NUMBER:
RESPONDENT:	

CHILDREN'S HOLIDAY SCHEDULE ATTACHMENT

TO ☐ Petition or Application for Order   ☐ Findings and Order After Hearing or Judgment
☐ Stipulation and Order for Custody and/or Visitation of Children

1. **Holiday parenting.** The following table shows the holiday parenting schedules. Write "Pet" or "Resp" to specify each parent's years—odd, even, or both ("every year")—and under "Time" specify the starting and ending days and times.

Holiday	Time (from when to when) (Unless otherwise noted, all single-day holidays start at ___ a.m. and end at ___ p.m.)	Every Year Petitioner/ Respondent	Even Years Petitioner/ Respondent	Odd Years Petitioner/ Respondent
January 1 (New Year's Day)				
Martin Luther King's Birthday (weekend)				
Lincoln's Birthday				
President's Day (weekend)				
Spring Break, first half				
Spring Break, second half				
Mother's Day				
Memorial Day (weekend)				
Father's Day				
July 4th				
Labor Day (weekend)				
Columbus Day (weekend)				
Halloween				
Veteran's Day (weekend)				
Thanksgiving Day				
Thanksgiving weekend				
Winter Break, first half				
Winter Break, second half				
New Year's Eve				
Child's birthday				
Mother's birthday				
Father's birthday				
Breaks for year-round schools				
Summer Break, first half				
Summer Break, second half				
Other (specify):				

☐ Any three-day weekend not specified above will be spent with the parent who would normally have that weekend.
☐ Other (specify):

2. **Vacations.** The ☐ petitioner ☐ respondent may take a vacation of up to (specify number): ☐ days ☐ weeks with the children the following number of times per year (specify): ___. They must notify the other parent in writing of their vacation plans a minimum of (specify number): ___ days in advance and provide the other parent with a basic itinerary that includes dates of leaving and returning, destinations, flight information, and telephone numbers for emergency purposes.
   ☐ The other parent has (specify number): ___ days to respond if there is a problem with the schedule.
   a. ☐ This vacation may be outside California.
   b. ☐ Any vacation outside ☐ California ☐ the United States requires prior written consent of the other parent or a court order.
   c. ☐ Other (specify):

Form Approved for Optional Use
Judicial Council of California
FL-341(C) [Rev. January 1, 2005]

CHILDREN'S HOLIDAY SCHEDULE ATTACHMENT

Family Code, §§ 3003, 3083
www.courtinfo.ca.gov

For your protection and privacy, please press the Clear This Form button after you have printed the form.		Save This Form	Print This Form	Clear This Form

Child Support Information and Order Attachment

FL-342

PETITIONER/PLAINTIFF:	CASE NUMBER:
RESPONDENT/DEFENDANT:	
OTHER PARENT:	

CHILD SUPPORT INFORMATION AND ORDER ATTACHMENT

TO ☐ **Findings and Order After Hearing (form FL-340)** ☐ **Judgment (form FL-180)**
☐ **Restraining Order After Hearing (CLETS-OAH)(form DV-130)**
☐ **Other** *(specify):*

THE COURT USED THE FOLLOWING INFORMATION IN DETERMINING THE AMOUNT OF CHILD SUPPORT:

1. ☐ A printout of a computer calculation and findings is attached and incorporated in this order for all required items not filled out below.

2. ☐ **Income**

a. Each parent's monthly income is as follows:

	Gross monthly income	Net monthly income	Receiving TANF/CalWORKS
Petitioner/plaintiff: $	$		☐
Respondent/defendant: $	$		☐
Other parent: $	$		☐

b. Imputation of income. The court finds that the ☐ petitioner/plaintiff ☐ respondent/defendant
☐ other parent has the capacity to earn:

$ _____ per _____ and has based the support order upon this imputed income.

3. ☐ **Children of this relationship**

a. Number of children who are the subjects of the support order *(specify):*

b. Approximate percentage of time spent with petitioner/plaintiff: _____ %
respondent/defendant: _____ %
other parent: _____ %

4. ☐ **Hardships**

Hardships for the following have been allowed in calculating child support:

		Petitioner/ plaintiff	Respondent/ defendant	Other parent	Approximate ending time for the hardship
a. ☐	Other minor children:	$	$	$	
b. ☐	Extraordinary medical expenses:	$	$	$	
c. ☐	Catastrophic losses:	$	$	$	

THE COURT ORDERS

5. ☐ **Low-income adjustment**

a. ☐ The low-income adjustment applies.

b. ☐ The low-income adjustment does not apply because *(specify reasons):*

6. ☐ **Child support**

a. **Base child support**

☐ Petitioner/plaintiff ☐ Respondent/defendant ☐ Other parent must pay child support beginning *(date):* _____ and continuing until further order of the court, or until the child marries, dies, is emancipated, reaches age 19, or reaches age 18 and is not a full-time high school student, whichever occurs first, as follows:

Child's name	Date of birth	Monthly amount	Payable to *(name):*

Payable ☐ on the 1st of the month ☐ one-half on the 1st and one-half on the 15th of the month
☐ other *(specify):*

THIS IS A COURT ORDER.

Form Adopted for Mandatory Use
Judicial Council of California
FL-342 [Rev. July 1, 2012]
CHILD SUPPORT INFORMATION AND ORDER ATTACHMENT
Family Code, §§ 4055–4069
www.courts.ca.gov

Child Support Information and Order Attachment

PETITIONER/PLAINTIFF: RESPONDENT/DEFENDANT: OTHER PARENT:	CASE NUMBER:

THE COURT FURTHER ORDERS

6. b. ☐ **Mandatory additional child support**

    (1) ☐ Child-care costs related to employment or reasonably necessary job training

        (a) ☐ Petitioner/plaintiff must pay: % of total or ☐ $ per month child-care costs.

        (b) ☐ Respondent/defendant must pay: % of total or ☐ $ per month child-care costs.

        (c) ☐ Other parent must pay: % of total or ☐ $ per month child-care costs.

        (d) ☐ Costs to be paid as follows *(specify)*:

  c. **Mandatory additional child support**

    (2) ☐ Reasonable uninsured health-care costs for the children

        (a) ☐ Petitioner/plaintiff must pay: % of total or ☐ $ per month.

        (b) ☐ Respondent/defendant must pay: % of total or ☐ $ per month.

        (c) ☐ Other parent must pay: % of total or ☐ $ per month.

        (d) ☐ Costs to be paid as follows *(specify)*:

  d. ☐ **Additional child support**

    (1) ☐ Costs related to the educational or other special needs of the children

        (a) ☐ Petitioner/plaintiff must pay: % of total or ☐ $ per month.

        (b) ☐ Respondent/defendant must pay: % of total or ☐ $ per month.

        (c) ☐ Other parent must pay: % of total or ☐ $ per month.

        (d) ☐ Costs to be paid as follows *(specify)*:

    (2) ☐ Travel expenses for visitation

        (a) ☐ Petitioner/plaintiff must pay: % of total or ☐ $ per month.

        (b) ☐ Respondent/defendant must pay: % of total or ☐ $ per month.

        (c) ☐ Other parent must pay: % of total or ☐ $ per month.

        (d) ☐ Costs to be paid as follows *(specify)*:

  e. ☐ **Non-Guideline Order**

    This order does not meet the child support guideline set forth in Family Code section 4055. *Non-Guideline Child Support Findings Attachment* (form FL-342(A)) is attached.

Total child support per month: $

7. **Health-care expenses**

  a. Health insurance coverage for the minor children of the parties must be maintained by the

    ☐ petitioner/plaintiff ☐ respondent/defendant ☐ other parent if available at no or reasonable cost through their respective places of employment or self-employment. Both parties are ordered to cooperate in the presentation, collection, and reimbursement of any health-care claims. The parent ordered to provide health insurance must seek continuation of coverage for the child after the child attains the age when the child is no longer considered eligible for coverage as a dependent under the insurance contract, if the child is incapable of self-sustaining employment because of a physically or mentally disabling injury, illness, or condition and is chiefly dependent upon the parent providing health insurance for support and maintenance.

  b. ☐ Health insurance is not available to the ☐ petitioner/plaintiff ☐ respondent/defendant ☐ other parent at a reasonable cost at this time.

  c. ☐ The party providing coverage must assign the right of reimbursement to the other party.

8. **Earnings assignment**

  An earnings assignment order is issued. **Note:** The payor of child support is responsible for the payment of support directly to the recipient until support payments are deducted from the payor's wages and for payment of any support not paid by the assignment.

9. In the event that there is a contract between a party receiving support and a private child support collector, the party ordered to pay support must pay the fee charged by the private child support collector. This fee must not exceed 33 1/3 percent of the total amount of past due support nor may it exceed 50 percent of any fee charged by the private child support collector. The money judgment created by this provision is in favor of the private child support collector and the party receiving support, jointly.

10. ☐ **Employment search order (Family Code, § 4505)**

    ☐ Petitioner/plaintiff ☐ Respondent/defendant ☐ Other parent is ordered to seek employment with the following terms and conditions:

THIS IS A COURT ORDER.

Child Support Information and Order Attachment

	FL-342
PETITIONER/PLAINTIFF: RESPONDENT/DEFENDANT: OTHER PARENT:	CASE NUMBER:

11. **Other orders** *(specify):*

12. **Notices**

    a. *Notice of Rights and Responsibilities (Health-Care Costs and Reimbursement Procedures) and Information Sheet on Changing a Child Support Order* (form FL-192) must be attached and is incorporated into this order.

    b. If this form is attached to *Restraining Order After Hearing* (form DV-130), the support orders issued on this form (form FL-342) remain in effect after the restraining orders issued on form DV-130 end.

13. **Child Support Case Registry Form**

Both parties must complete and file with the court a *Child Support Case Registry Form* (form FL-191) within 10 days of the date of this order. Thereafter, the parties must notify the court of any change in the information submitted within 10 days of the change by filing an updated form.

> **NOTICE: Any party required to pay child support must pay interest on overdue amounts at the legal rate, which is currently 10 percent per year.**

THIS IS A COURT ORDER.

For your protection and privacy, please press the Clear This Form button after you have printed the form.

| Print This Form | Save This Form | Clear This Form |

Spousal, Partner, or Family Support Order Attachment

FL-343

		CASE NUMBER:
PETITIONER/PLAINTIFF:		
RESPONDENT/DEFENDANT:		
OTHER PARENT:		

SPOUSAL, PARTNER, OR FAMILY SUPPORT ORDER ATTACHMENT

TO ☐ **Findings and Order After Hearing** (form FL-340) ☐ **Judgment** (form FL-180)

☐ **Restraining Order After Hearing (CLETS-OAH)** (form DV-130) ☐ **Other** (specify):

☐ **Stipulation of Parties**

THE COURT FINDS

1. **Net income.** The parties' monthly income and deductions are as follows (complete a, b, or both):

	Total gross monthly income	Total monthly deductions	Total hardship deductions	Net monthly disposable income
a. Petitioner: ☐ receiving TANF/CalWORKS	$	$	$	$
b. Respondent: ☐ receiving TANF/CalWORKS	$	$	$	$

2. ☐ A printout of a computer calculation of the parties' financial circumstances is attached for all required items not filled out above (for temporary support only).

3. **Judgment for spousal or partner support**

   a. ☐ Modifies a judgment or order entered on (date):

   b. ☐ The parties were married for (specify numbers): _____ years _____ months.

   c. ☐ The parties were registered as domestic partners or the equivalent for (specify numbers): _____ years _____ months.

   d. ☐ The parties are both self-supporting, as shown on the Declaration for Default or Uncontested Dissolution or Legal Separation (form FL-170).

   e. ☐ The marital standard of living was (describe):

   ☐ See Attachment 3d.

THE COURT ORDERS

4. ☐ The issue of spousal or partner support for the ☐ petitioner ☐ respondent is reserved for a later determination.

5. ☐ The court terminates jurisdiction over the issue of spousal or partner support for the ☐ petitioner ☐ respondent.

6. a. The ☐ petitioner ☐ respondent must pay to the ☐ petitioner ☐ respondent
   as ☐ temporary ☐ spousal support ☐ family support ☐ partner support
   $ _____ per month, beginning (date): _____ , payable through (specify end date): _____

   ☐ payable on the (specify): _____ day of each month.

   ☐ Other (specify):

   b. ☐ Support must be paid by check, money order, or cash. The support payor's obligation to pay support will terminate on the death of either party, remarriage, or registration of a new domestic partnership of the support payee.

   c. ☐ An earnings assignment for the foregoing support will issue. (**Note:** The payor of spousal, family, or partner support is responsible for the payment of support directly to the recipient until support payments are deducted from the payor's earnings, and for any support not paid by the assignment.)

   d. ☐ Service of the earnings assignment is stayed provided the payor is not more than (specify number): _____ days late in the payment of spousal, family, or partner support.

THIS IS A COURT ORDER.

Page 1 of 2

Form Approved for Optional Use
Judicial Council of California
FL-343 [Rev. July 1, 2012]

SPOUSAL, PARTNER, OR FAMILY SUPPORT ORDER ATTACHMENT
(Family Law)

Family Code, §§ 150, 299, 3651, 3653, 3654, 4320, 4330, 4337
www.courts.ca.gov

Spousal, Partner, or Family Support Order Attachment

PETITIONER/PLAINTIFF:	CASE NUMBER:
RESPONDENT/DEFENDANT:	
OTHER PARENT:	

7. ☐ The ☐ petitioner ☐ respondent should make reasonable efforts to assist in providing for his or her support needs.

8. ☐ The parties must promptly inform each other of any change of employment, including the employer's name, address, and telephone number.

9. ☐ This order is for family support. Both parties must complete and file with the court a *Child Support Case Registry Form* (form FL-191) within 10 days of the date of this order. The parents must notify the court of any change of information submitted within 10 days of the change by filing an updated form. A *Notice of Rights and Responsibilities (Health-Care Costs and Reimbursement Procedures) and Information Sheet on Changing a Child Support Order* (form FL-192) is attached.

10. ☐ Notice: If this form is attached to *Restraining Order After Hearing (CLETS-OAH) (Order of Protection)* (form DV-130), the orders issued on this form (FL-343) do not expire upon termination of the restraining orders issued on form DV-130.

11. ☐ Other orders (*specify*):

NOTICE: Any party required to pay support must pay interest on overdue amounts at the "legal" rate, which is currently 10 percent.

THIS IS A COURT ORDER.

FL-343 [Rev. July 1, 2012]	**SPOUSAL, PARTNER, OR FAMILY SUPPORT ORDER ATTACHMENT** **(Family Law)**	Page 2 of 2

For your protection and privacy, please press the Clear This Form button after you have printed the form.

Print This Form   Save This Form   Clear This Form

Attorney's Fees and Costs Order Attachment

FL-346

PETITIONER/PLAINTIFF: RESPONDENT/DEFENDANT: OTHER PARTY:	CASE NUMBER:

ATTORNEY'S FEES AND COSTS ORDER ATTACHMENT

Attached to:

☐ *Findings and Orders After Hearing* (form FL-340)

☐ *Judgment (Uniform Parentage—Custody and Support)* (form FL-250)

☐ *Judgment* (form FL-180)

☐ Other *(specify):*

THE COURT FINDS

1. ☐ An award of attorney's fees and costs is appropriate because there is a demonstrated disparity between the parties in access to funds to retain or maintain counsel and in the ability to pay for legal representation.

     a. ☐ The party requested to pay attorney's fees and costs has or is reasonably likely to have the ability to pay for legal representation for both parties.

     b. ☐ The requested attorney's fees and costs are reasonable and necessary.

2. ☐ An award of attorney's fees and costs is not appropriate because *(check all that apply):*

     a. ☐ there is not a demonstrated disparity between the parties in access to funds to retain or maintain counsel or in the ability to pay for legal representation.

     b. ☐ the party requested to pay attorney's fees and costs does not have or is not reasonably likely to have the ability to pay for legal representation for both parties.

     c. ☐ the requested attorney's fees and costs are not reasonable or necessary.

3. ☐ Other *(specify):*

THE COURT ORDERS

4. a. The ☐ petitioner/plaintiff ☐ respondent/defendant ☐ other party to pay attorney's fees and costs in this legal proceeding

     b. in the amount of:

         (1) ☐ Fees: $

         (2) ☐ Costs: $

         (3) ☐ Interest is not included and is not waived.

     c. Payable to ☐ petitioner/plaintiff ☐ respondent/defendant ☐ other party

     d. ☐ From the payment sources of *(if specified):*

Form Approved for Optional Use
Judicial Council of California
FL-346 [New January 1, 2012]

ATTORNEY'S FEES AND COSTS ORDER ATTACHMENT
(Family Law)

Page 1 of 2

Family Code, §§ 270, 2030, 3121, 3557,
7605; Cal. Rules of Court, rules 5.425, 5.93
www.courts.ca.gov

Attorney's Fees and Costs Order Attachment

	CASE NUMBER:
PETITIONER/PLAINTIFF:	
RESPONDENT/DEFENDANT:	
OTHER PARTY:	

4. e. With a payment schedule of *(specify)*:

     (1) ☐ Due in full, on or before *(date)*:

     (2) ☐ Due in installments, with monthly payments of *(specify)*: $, on the *(specify)*:   day of each month, beginning *(date)*:   until paid in full.

     (3) ☐ If any payment is not timely made and more than   days overdue, the entire unpaid balance will immediately become due with interest at the legal rate, which is currently 10 percent per year, from the date of default to the date payment is finally made.

     (4) ☐ No interest will accrue as long as payments are timely made.

     (5) ☐ Other *(specify)*:

5. ☐ This amount includes *(check all that apply)*:

     a. ☐ a fee in the amount of *(specify)* $ to hire an attorney in a timely manner before the proceedings in the matter go forward.

     b. ☐ attorney's fees and costs incurred to date in the amount of *(specify)*: $

     c. ☐ estimated attorney's fees and costs in the amount of *(specify)*: $

     d. ☐ attorney's fees and costs for limited scope representation in the amount of *(specify)*: $

     e. ☐ any amounts previously ordered that have not yet been paid *(specify)*: $

     f. ☐ Other *(specify)*:

6. ☐ Other orders *(specify)*:

NOTICE: Any party required to pay attorney's fees and costs must pay interest on overdue amounts at the legal rate, which is currently 10 percent per year.

For your protection and privacy, please press the Clear This Form button after you have printed the form.

| Save This Form | Print This Form | Clear This Form |

Property Order Attachment to Findings and Order after Hearing

To keep other people from seeing what you entered on your form, please press the Clear This Form button at the end of the form when finished.

FL-344

PETITIONER :	CASE NUMBER:
RESPONDENT:	

**PROPERTY ORDER ATTACHMENT
TO FINDINGS AND ORDER AFTER HEARING**

THE COURT ORDERS

1. ☐ **Property restraining orders**

   a. The ☐ petitioner ☐ respondent ☐ claimant is restrained from transferring, encumbering, hypothecating, concealing, or in any way disposing of any property, real or personal, whether community, quasi-community, or separate, except in the usual course of business or for the necessities of life.

   b. The ☐ petitioner ☐ respondent must notify the other party of any proposed extraordinary expenses at least five business days before incurring such expenses, and make an accounting of such to the court.

   c. The ☐ petitioner ☐ respondent is restrained from cashing, borrowing against, cancelling, transferring, disposing of, or changing the beneficiaries of any insurance or other coverage, including life, health, automobile, and disability, held for the benefit of the parties or their minor child or children.

   d. The ☐ petitioner ☐ respondent must not incur any debts or liabilities for which the other may be held responsible, other than in the ordinary course of business or for the necessities of life.

2. ☐ **Possession of property.** The exclusive use, possession, and control of the following property that the parties own or are buying is given as specified:

Property	Given to

   ☐ See Attachment 2.

3. ☐ **Payment of debts.** Payments on the following debts that come due while this order is in effect must be paid as follows:

Total debt	Amount of payments	Pay to	Paid by
$	$		
$	$		
$	$		
$	$		

   ☐ See Attachment 3.

4. ☐ These are temporary orders only. The court will make final orders at the time of judgment.

5. ☐ Other (specify):

Form Adopted for Mandatory Use
Judicial Council of California
FL-344 [Rev. January 1, 2007]

**PROPERTY ORDER ATTACHMENT
TO FINDINGS AND ORDER AFTER HEARING
(Family Law)**

Page 1 of 1
Family Code, §§ 2045, 6324
www.courtinfo.ca.gov

For your protection and privacy, please press the Clear This Form button after you have printed the form.

Save This Form | Print This Form | Clear This Form

Declaration of Disclosure

FL-140

ATTORNEY OR PARTY WITHOUT ATTORNEY *(Name, State Bar number, and address):*	
JOAN CARE-ACTOR, SBN XXXXXXX CARE-ACTOR LAW FIRM 75000 WHY ME LANE SACRAMENTO, CA 95826 TELEPHONE NO.: 916-555-1234 FAX NO. : 916-555-1233 E-MAIL ADDRESS: joan@care-actorlaw.com ATTORNEY FOR *(Name)*: SANDIE SHORES	

SUPERIOR COURT OF CALIFORNIA, COUNTY OF SACRAMENTO
STREET ADDRESS: 3341 POWER INN ROAD
MAILING ADDRESS: 3341 POWER INN ROAD
CITY AND ZIP CODE: SACRAMENTO, CA 95826
BRANCH NAME: FAMILY LAW DIVISION

PETITIONER: SANDIE SHORES
RESPONDENT: ROCKY SHORES
OTHER PARENT/PARTY:

DECLARATION OF DISCLOSURE	CASE NUMBER:
✓ Petitioner's ☐ Preliminary ☐ Respondent's ☐ Final	14FLXXXXXXX

DO NOT FILE DECLARATIONS OF DISCLOSURE OR FINANCIAL ATTACHMENTS WITH THE COURT

In a dissolution, legal separation, or nullity action, both a preliminary and a final declaration of disclosure must be served on the other party with certain exceptions. Neither disclosure is filed with the court. Instead, a declaration stating that service of disclosure documents was completed or waived must be filed with the court (see form FL-141).

- *In summary dissolution cases, each spouse or domestic partner must exchange preliminary disclosures as described in* Summary Dissolution Information *(form FL-810). Final disclosures are not required (see Family Code section 2109).*

- *In a default judgment case that is not a stipulated judgment or a judgment based on a marital settlement agreement, only the petitioner is required to complete and serve a preliminary declaration of disclosure. A final disclosure is not required of either party (see Family Code section 2110).*

- *Service of preliminary declarations of disclosure may not be waived by an agreement between the parties.*

- *Parties who agree to waive final declarations of disclosure must file their written agreement with the court (see form FL-144).*

The petitioner must serve a preliminary declaration of disclosure at the same time as the Petition or within 60 days of filing the Petition. The respondent must serve a preliminary declaration of disclosure at the same time as the Response or within 60 days of filing the Response. The time periods may be extended by written agreement of the parties or by court order (see Family Code section 2104(f)).

Attached are the following:

1. ☒ A completed *Schedule of Assets and Debts* (form FL-142) or ☐ A *Property Declaration* (form FL-160) for *(specify):*
   ☐ Community and Quasi-Community Property   ☐ Separate Property.

2. ☒ A completed *Income and Expense Declaration* (form FL-150).

3. ☒ All tax returns filed by the party in the two years before the date that the party served the disclosure documents.

4. ☒ A statement of all material facts and information regarding valuation of all assets that are community property or in which the community has an interest *(not a form)*.
   PETITIONER HAS NOT COMPLETED A VALUATION OF ALL COMMUNITY ASSETS

5. ☒ A statement of all material facts and information regarding obligations for which the community is liable *(not a form)*.
   PETITIONER HAS NOT COMPLETED DISCOVERY OF THE EXTENT OF OBLIGATIONS

6. ☒ An accurate and complete written disclosure of any investment opportunity, business opportunity, or other income-producing opportunity presented since the date of separation that results from any investment, significant business, or other income-producing opportunity from the date of marriage to the date of separation *(not a form)*.
   Petitioner has had no investment, business or income-producing opportunity since date of separation.

I declare under penalty of perjury under the laws of the State of California that the foregoing is true and correct.

Date:

SANDIE SHORES
_____
(TYPE OR PRINT NAME)   _____
                                                        SIGNATURE

Page 1 of 1

Form Adopted for Mandatory Use Judicial Council of California FL-140 [Rev. July 1, 2013]	**DECLARATION OF DISCLOSURE** **(Family Law)**	Family Code, §§ 2102, 2104, 2105, 2106, 2112 www.courts.ca.gov

For your protection and privacy, please press the Clear This Form button after you have printed the form. | Print this form | Save this form | | Clear this form |

Requests for Orders Regarding Noncompliance
with Disclosure Requirements

To keep other people from seeing what you entered on your form, please press the Clear This Form button at the end of the form when finished.

FL-316

PETITIONER:	CASE NUMBER:
RESPONDENT:	

REQUEST FOR ORDERS REGARDING NONCOMPLIANCE
WITH DISCLOSURE REQUIREMENTS

Attachment to *Request for Order* **(form FL-300)**

1. ☐ Petitioner ☐ Respondent   has complied with mandatory disclosure requirements (you must attach a copy of your filed *Declaration Regarding Service of Declaration of Disclosure and Income and Expense Declaration* (form FL-141)), and requests an order that

☐ petitioner ☐ respondent

a. ☐ provide a

(1) ☐ preliminary declaration of disclosure under Family Code section 2104 as directed by court order.

(2) ☐ final declaration of disclosure under Family Code section 2105 as directed by court order.

b. ☐ provide a further response to his or her ☐ preliminary ☐ final declaration of disclosure under Family Code section 2107(b)(1).

c. ☐ has failed to comply with disclosure requirements and is prevented from presenting evidence on the issues that should have been covered in the declaration of disclosure under Family Code section 2107(b)(2).

d. ☐ be granted for good cause his or her request for voluntary waiver of receipt of ☐ preliminary ☐ final declaration of disclosure under Family Code section 2107(b)(3).

e. ☐ for the reasons described below, be ordered to pay money sanctions for failure to comply with disclosure requirements. The amount of the money sanctions should be in an amount sufficient to deter him or her from repeating the conduct or comparable conduct, including reasonable attorney fees, costs incurred, or both, unless the court finds that the noncomplying party acted with substantial justification or that other circumstances make the imposition of the sanction unjust. (Family Code, § 2107(c).)

f. ☐ be granted his or her request to set aside the judgment under Family Code section 2107(d).

g. ☐ be ordered to comply with other, or alternative, relief, requested *(specify):*

2. ☐ FACTS IN SUPPORT of relief requested are *(specify):*

☐ Contained in the attached declaration. (You may use *Attached Declaration* (form MC-031) for this purpose).

I declare under penalty of perjury under the laws of the State of California that the foregoing is true and correct.

Date:

▶

_____
(TYPE OR PRINT NAME)

_____
(SIGNATURE OF APPLICANT)

Page 1 of 1

Form Approved for Optional Use Judicial Council of California FL-316 [Rev. July 1, 2012]	**REQUEST FOR ORDERS REGARDING NONCOMPLIANCE** **WITH DISCLOSURE REQUIREMENTS**	Family Code, § 2107 *www.courts.ca.gov*

For your protection and privacy, please press the Clear This Form button after you have printed the form.

Save This Form   **Print This Form**   **Clear This Form**

Chapter Six

Orders, Spousal Support and Default

Chapter Five discussed the process for preparing an Order subsequent to a formal hearing. It may be likely during the course of the dissolution process that the parties will reach an agreement that needs to be formalized. As previously stated, it is wise to prepare the formal agreement and have it filed with the Court for any of the following reasons: 1) collateral documents that were filed may be served on a third party such as Notice/Order to Withhold Support or Pension/Benefit plans; or 2) for enforcement purposes. These documents are most often referred to as Stipulations & Orders.

Stipulations and Orders

Stipulations

Stipulations are essentially agreements between the parties and are used to memorialize and formalize those agreements as Orders of the Court. At this stage of the dissolution process, they can take two forms: 1) A Stipulation made resolving the issues without, or prior to, a hearing; or 2) a Stipulation that is made subsequent to the hearing. A Stipulation can also be entered post-judgment, which will be further discussed in Chapter Ten.

A Stipulation which is executed prior to a hearing can be done on a Judicial Council form or can be in pleading format. It will be up to the attorney(s) to determine the format to be used. A *Stipulation to Establish or Modify Child Support* (FL-350) is often used if the parties have agreed to child support and related issues. However, it can also be used *only* for child support issues.

If there are additional issues, it is often best to prepare the Stipulation in pleading format. In that instance, as always, it is important to ask the attorney if there is a template or example which can be followed, as it is likely that the paralegal will be the one drafting the Stipulation. For instance, most law firms will have a template containing standard language for adopting a Mediation Recommendation. There may also be specific language that the legislature requires be included with respect to certain issues, such as child custody and child support, or local rules may dictate certain requirements.

It is also helpful to review the Judicial Council forms with respect to custody and support, as they usually contain the specific, required language that **must** be included in all agreements, stipulations, and orders.

The Stipulation that is prepared in conjunction with a hearing is usually prepared at the hearing. Prior to the matter being called, the parties will have an opportunity along, with their attorney(s) to meet (*"meet and confer"*) outside the courtroom to see if they can resolve any of the issues raised in the Request for Hearing or Motion. If they are able to resolve some or all of the issues, they will complete a Stipulation and Order form provided by the Court. In most cases, one of the attorneys will complete the form(s) which follow the same order and format as the Request for Order with subsequent attachments and the Minute Order. Each party and the attorney of record will sign the Stipulation. When the matter is called by the Judge, the parties will present the Stipulation, the Clerk may prepare the Minute Order (may vary by County) based on the Stipulation, the Judge will sign the documents, and the clerk will give each party or their attorney a copy of the Minute Order, if it is prepared, and the filed Stipulation and Order. The Order will also be recorded in the transcript by the Court Reporter.

Child Custody Orders

This Order may be used in a Dissolution when the parties have reached an agreement as to the custody and visitation of the minor children. This form is also used in situations where the parties are separated, and a dissolution has **not** been filed with the Court. As indicated in Chapter Five, the court is required to issue a statement of decision at the request of either party after a custody trial. (CCP§ 632).

Stipulation to Establish or Modify Child Support and Order

As the name of this form (FL-350) infers, this form of agreement may be used during the Dissolution, Legal Separation, Paternity proceeding or after the divorce is final to establish or modify child support. This Stipulation allows the parties to reach an agreement without having to initially appear or return to court to establish or modify child support.

It is always a good idea to attach the Dissomaster™ or Xspouse™ printout to the form so that the court will understand how support was calculated. It should be noted however, that the parties may agree to *other* than guideline support as long as it is in the best interests of the child. The form is fairly complete in that it contains provisions for hardship rebuttals; child care, health care, special-needs costs, and/or travel expenses; a provision naming the party who is responsible for maintaining health insurance for the minor children; a requirement for notification of residence or employment changes; and an Income Withholding for Support provisions.

The form also contains the standard language under FC§ 4053 (See Chapter Three). **Note:** if Child Support is to be collected through the Department of Child Support Services (DCSS), a representative of that office must sign the Stipulation. In the event it is necessary to have the DCSS sign the Stipulation, it is usually best to try to determine who is the person responsible for this case, so that you can telephone ahead of time and then send the documents directly to that person's attention. My experience is that the case load for the Department of Child Support Services is enormous and in the event you send the documents, without naming a specific individual, the document(s) may never be seen again. It is usually best, as stated above, to determine the name of the caseworker or responsible individual. By telephoning ahead of time, the person to whom the case is assigned will be expecting the documents and will hopefully expedite their processing. As a paralegal, it is always a good idea to know how your local county office of the Child Support Services functions and to have a good rapport with them to more easily facilitate the processing of any Orders for which you require signatures.

Mutual Restraining Orders

The parties may agree to certain types of restraining orders with respect to contact, including but not limited to domestic violence, and/or property issues. A stipulation that governs restraining order issues is considered temporary until further order of the Court. The Court must consider mutual restraining orders, TROs and protective orders subject to Family Code §6305, wherein the Court is required to consider **independent** proof to support the mutual orders pursuant to Family Code §§2047 and 2336. These codes require that the court require an appearance of the parties "in the interest of justice."

Stipulation & Order (Pleading)

A sample pleading, as referenced above, can be found at Appendix 6A. In most cases, you will follow a template of standard language utilized by your firm or as dictated by statute or Court rule. The pleading format allows more flexibility to address issues that may not be easily included in a form, or where supplemental information needs to be included pursuant to the Court's Orders.

Wage/Earnings Orders

There are several mechanisms available to obtain a Satisfaction of Judgment for money owed in both civil and family law cases. Some of the other forms used for collecting or enforcing money or property judgments will be discussed in Chapter Ten which deal with enforcement of Orders.

At this point in the proceeding you will primarily be focused on obtaining child and/or spousal support on behalf of the client. *Family Code §5208* exclusively addresses court ordered support. *Family Code §5230* addresses enforcement of child support orders and the *issuance* of wage withholding orders:

(a) When the court orders a party to pay an amount for support or orders a modification of the amount of support to be paid, the court shall include in its order an earnings assignment order for support that orders the employer of the obligor to pay to the obligee that portion of the obligor's earnings due or to become due in the future as will be sufficient to pay an amount to cover both the following:

(1) The amount ordered by the court for support.

(2) An amount which shall be ordered by the court to be paid toward the liquidation of any arrearage.

(b) An earnings assignment order for support shall be issued, and shall be effective and enforceable pursuant to Section 5231, notwithstanding the absence of the name, address, or other identifying information regarding the obligor's employer.

You will note that most Judicial Council forms contain a statement that reference *orders for support* and will contain a statement that an "Income Withholding Order for Support" will be issued. However the *service* of that Order may be stayed, as discussed below. An Order for child support will take priority over other types of wage orders or garnishments, except for taxes.

Previously, in order to collect some of these additional sums, the Court required that different forms be submitted for each type of "support" being requested. The Income Withholding Order for Support (FL-195) was created specifically for obtaining orders to withhold Child Support from the obligor's wages. Each year since it was created, the Judicial Council has made modifications to the form and the form now allows, in addition to current and delinquent child support, for the collection of the following: medical support, spousal support, and "other."

In the case of the type of order you are not required to serve the opposing party once it is served on the employer. In that instance the employer is required to provide a copy to the obligor/employee. Historically, the receipt of a "child support withholding order" was viewed negatively by many employers. There was an implication that the parent was a "dead beat" parent if they had to be garnished in order to support the child(ren). It also created additional work for the employer, particularly small companies, who had to set up special payroll deduction accounts, write additional checks and account for any sums paid out to the obligee spouse.

Family Code § 5241 contains language regarding an employer's obligation to withhold support upon receipt of the Order. In the event the employer willfully fails to withhold support and/or fails to send the withheld support to the obligee, the employer is liable to the obligee for the amount of support that is to be withheld. In other words, an employer may not ignore the Order because there is too much paperwork involved in withholding support or because the employee (obligor) has told the employer that support is being paid directly to the obligee. Once an Order from the Court has been served on the employer, they are required to act on that Order pursuant to FC§ 5241 until they receive further Orders from the court as to a stay, termination or modification.

In some cases the parties will "waive the **service**" of the wage order. This means that the Order to withhold wages will not be served on the obligor's employer. This does not mean that you shouldn't go ahead and get the Order prepared and filed with the Court. Orders which allow this waiver, also state that if the obligor does not pay the ordered support, usually within ten days, that the obligee may then serve the Order on the employer. If you have prepared and filed the Order, this will eliminate further delay in the obligee receiving any support to which they may be entitled. *Family Code § 5260* defines the reasons or "good cause" for which an Order/Notice to Withhold may be stayed, and *Family Code § 5261* provides for the termination of said stay so that the Order may be served. You may utilize Form FL-455, *Stay of Service of Earnings Assignment and Order.*

You should review pages two and three of the Income Withholding for Support, which details about the various compliance information. Of particular importance to the paralegal is the section on **Withholding Limits**. *The Federal Consumer Credit Protection Act 15 U.S.C. § 1673(b)* states that no more than 50% of the obligor's "aggregate disposable weekly earnings" may be withheld by the "employee/obligor's principal place of employment for child support and spousal support."

Aggregate disposal earnings are defined as the gross income less state, federal and local taxes, Social Security and Medicare taxes, and mandatory pension contributions. This is referred to as "net income" and was previously discussed in Chapter Three— "Current Child Support Calculations."

It is, therefore, very important for you to be aware of the obligor's **net** earnings when preparing the Order. In the event that the amount of support ordered in either the Findings & Order or by Stipulation is greater than 50% of the net earnings, the employer may **only** withhold the allowable amount and not the ordered amount. For example:

If the Court order states that the combined child support and spousal support order is set at $1,000 per month and the obligor's net disposable earnings are $900 per month, then the employer is only going to be able to withhold $450 per month. This is not to say that you can't state that the amount to be withheld is $1,000 per month, but that the obligee is only going to receive $450 per month.

> This issue becomes extremely important if you are adding support arrears to the Order. An example of this would be if the Order is as follows: current support—$800; arrears total $1,000; and the obligor's net disposable income is $2,000. Your Order should then reflect the following: $800 per month current support; $200 per month toward the arrears until paid; for a total of $1,000 per month payable to the obligee.

You will also need to complete the Remittance Information on page one of the form to tell the court and the employer the amount to be withheld if the obligor is not paid monthly. Most Courts will require that you complete this information in its entirety, or they are likely to return the form to you unfiled. The same is true for the employer's name and address, as well as the employee's name and Social Security Number for identification purposes.

In the event that your office is representing the obligor, it would be a courtesy to send the client a copy of the Order so the client will know when to expect notification from their employer. As previously stated, if the parties have waived service of the Order, you will simply retain the original filed copy in the client's file (if you have prepared and filed it on behalf of the obligee/client) until such time as it may be necessary, pursuant to FC§ 5261, to serve it on the obligor's employer. It is also a good idea to calendar the date of termination of support so that a timely termination can be filed and served.

Spousal Support

Family Code § 4300 addresses the duty of each spouse to support the other. This section simply states: "Subject to this division, a person shall support the person's spouse." The requirement for reciprocal support is very clear. The Court can even require one spouse to support the other from his/her separate property, subject to the right of reimbursement, in the event there is no community or quasi-community property available. In the event one spouse applies to the County where they reside for assistance, the County, on behalf of the obligee spouse, will bring an action against the obligor spouse for reimbursement and future support of the obligee spouse, if this issue has not been addressed and/or resolved as part of the dissolution process.

As discussed in Chapter Four, Spousal Support may be temporarily ordered in an effort to maintain the status quo during a "pending" dissolution, legal separation or annulment. The *pending* period is from the date the petition is filed until an appeal or the time for appeal has passed. Temporary Spousal Support is typically that amount which is ordered after Request for Hearing or by Stipulation during the pendency of the matter.

Permanent Spousal Support is support which is ordered, typically as part of a Judgment, for either a finite period of time or an infinite period of time, usually with some qualifications and/or conditions. The court is required to review and make specific **factual** findings with respect to the marital standard of living, as well as the assets and debts of the parties. In fact, the court will take this issue under consideration, whether or not they are asked to do so by the moving party.

Family Code § 4320, contains a concise list of circumstances and factors which the court must consider in awarding permanent spousal support. They are (paraphrased) as follows:

(a) The extent to which each party's earning capacity will maintain the standard of living established during the marriage. The court must take into account

(1) what might be required for the supported party to develop or acquire marketable skills and

(2) the extent to which his or her earning capacity is or will be impaired by any periods of unemployment during the marriage to devote time to domestic duties.

(b) The extent to which the supported party contributed to the supporting party's attainment of an education, training, a career position, or a license.

(c) The supporting party's ability to pay, taking into account, his or her earning capacity, earned and unearned income, assets, and standard of living.

(d) Each party's needs based on the standard of living established during the marriage.

(e) Each party's assets (including separate property) and obligations.

(f) The duration of the marriage.

(g) The supported party's ability to be gainfully employed without interfering with the interests of dependent children in his or her custody.

(h) Each party's age and health.

(i) Documented evidence of any history of domestic violence (see FC§ 6211) between the parties, including emotional stress resulting from the violence.

(j) The immediate and specific tax consequences to each party.

(k) The balance of the hardships to each party.

(l) The goal that the supporting party shall be self-supporting within a reasonable period of time.

(m) The criminal conviction of an abusive spouse when the court is reducing or eliminating a spouse support award under FC§ 4325.

(n) Any other factors the court determines are just and equitable.

The Court has an enormous amount of discretion with regard to permanent spousal support orders. Family Code § 4330 states:

(a) In a judgment of dissolution of marriage or legal separation of the parties, the court may order a party to pay for the support of the other party an amount, for a period of time, that the court determines is just and reasonable, based on the standard of living established during the marriage, taking into consideration the circumstances as provided in Chapter 2, commencing with Section 4320.

(b) When making an order for spousal support, the court may advise the recipient of support that he or she should make reasonable efforts to assist in providing for his or her support needs, taking into account the particular circumstances considered by the court pursuant to Section 4320, unless in the case of a marriage of long duration as provided for in Section 4336, the court decides this warning is inadvisable. (See section on *Gavron warning*, below.)

The Court also has the discretion to deny support taking into consideration the circumstances of the supported spouse and what is considered just and equitable. There also numerous court cases on which the court relies to make spousal support determinations. These cases are considered the foundation of spousal support awards and have served to further clarify FC§§ 4320-4330.

Family Code § 4324 was amended effective 1/1/2013: 4324.5(b) precludes an award of Spousal Support to a spouse who has been convicted of a violent sexual felony. It states, in part, "[T]he court must consider the criminal conviction of an abusive spouse under FC§§ 4325 or 4324.5." This revised language is the result of a 2012 case: *Marriage of Freitas*, (2012) CalApp Lexis 1039.

Length of Marriage

As referenced in FC§ 4320(f) duration of the marriage is a factor to be considered. *In re Marriage of Morrison* (1978) 20 C3d 437, 143 CR 139 dealt with the issue of duration of marriage. The trial court determined that the 28-year marriage in Morrison qualified as a "lengthy" marriage. However, the court did not establish the definition of a lengthy marriage. Subsequently, the legislature amended Family Code § 4336(b), which established a rebuttable presumption that a lengthy marriage is a marriage of ten years or more. There is a "burden of proof" requirement in this section and the Court may take into consideration periods of separation during the marriage. The Court also has the discretion to determine that a marriage of less than ten years is a marriage of long duration. Family Code § 4336(a) states that when a marriage has been of long duration, the Court will retain jurisdiction indefinitely, unless the parties agree, in writing, to the contrary or the court reserves jurisdiction with the intent that a change in circumstances can be shown in subsequent proceedings.

The legislature has noted that "Except in the case of a marriage of long duration as described in Section 4336, a 'reasonable period of time' for the purposes of this section generally shall be one-half the length of the marriage. However, nothing in this section is intended to limit the court's discretion to order support for a greater or lesser length of time, based on any other factors listed in this section, Section 4336, and the circumstances of the parties."

The Court also makes the rebuttable assumption that spousal support may be made for one-half the length of the marriage in situations where spousal support is ordered, or where the Court may retain jurisdiction.

Although the obligation of support terminates on either party's death, the Court has jurisdiction to provide funds for the supported party, if the supporting party dies, by including in the support order a provision that there be an annuity or insurance policy purchased in an amount sufficient to meet the needs of the supported party; or requiring the supporting party to establish a trust for the supported party. *Family Code § 4360; In re Marriage of Ziegler* (1989) 207 CA3d 788, 255 CR 100.

In addition to the marital standard of living (FC§ 4320) and the length of the marriage, there are four components the Court considers when determining *long term* spousal support orders: 1) Amount; 2) Substantive Stepdown; 3) Jurisdictional Stepdown; and 4) Reservation of Jurisdiction.

Amount

The amount of spousal support is determined by the factors established in Family Code § 4320 above. Once the court has determined the marital standard of living, it applies the factors in FC§ 4320 when making a finding as to the long term needs of the supported spouse.

Substantive Stepdown

The Court has the discretion to make orders for spousal support whereby adjustments (usually reductions) or modifications will be made, often at specific periodic intervals. The Court will retain jurisdiction to make these adjustments, with the ultimate emphasis on eliminating support entirely in the future. In other words, at some point spousal support will likely be terminated, and the Court will determine the need to retain jurisdiction or alternatively, if jurisdiction will be terminated.

Jurisdictional Stepdown

The substantive and jurisdictional stepdowns are similar. The difference being that the jurisdictional stepdowns are usually established in the initial orders for spousal support which give an estimate of how long the Court's jurisdiction will last.

Reservation of Jurisdiction

A reservation of jurisdiction recognizes that spousal support may or may not presently be necessary, but jurisdiction should not presently be terminated.

Cases relating to Jurisdictional Stepdowns and Reservation of Jurisdiction

In re Marriage of Richmond (1980) 105 CA3d 352, 164 CR 381. This case involves a 16-year marriage. Wife was aged 46. Two years after the judgment was entered, Husband sought a termination due to his unemployment after two months. Wife had a Masters Degree and was a Ph.D. candidate in German literature. The Court determined that her earning potential was low; however, support was ordered for another three years. After three years, spousal support would be forever terminated and jurisdiction would terminate unless prior to that date Wife made a "showing of good cause" to extend spousal support beyond that date.

The *Richmond* Court did not violate the "Morrison" (below) rule against terminating spousal support in a lengthy marriage, as the *Richmond* Court was postponing the support termination until a future date. *Richmond* "orders" do put the supported spouse on notice as to making a good faith effort to become self-sufficient. The burden of proof shifts to the supported spouse to show why support should be continued past the predetermined date.

A *Richmond Order* is often referred to as a typical "stepdown" order. The court will often structure the spousal support agreement with specific reductions in spousal support on specific dates, resulting eventually in support being reduced to zero (0).

The parties will also have to agree whether the court will retain jurisdiction beyond that time. In the event the supported party wishes to extend those dates or request that a reduction not be made pursuant to the order, it is his/her responsibility to file a motion with the court prior to the "stepdown" date. The supported spouse must provide evidence of why there should **not** be a reduction.

In re Marriage of Morrison (1978) 20 C3d 437, 143 CR 139. The Supreme Court ruled that the trial court should not terminate jurisdiction over a long term marriage unless the "record clearly indicates" that the supported party will be able to adequately meet his or her financial needs at the time specified for termination of jurisdiction.

In re Marriage of Rome (1980) 109 CA3d 961, 167 CR 351. The Trial Court ruled that support be paid on a sliding scale based on Husband's earnings. The Court found that it was an "abuse of discretion" since the amount paid to Wife was totally under the control of Husband. The Court determined that there should be periodic reviews to determine the earnings of Husband. This is often referred to as a *Rome Review*.

In re Marriage of Vomacka (1984) 36 C3d 459, 204 CR 568. The Court found that "[O]rders providing for absolute termination of spousal support on a specified date are disfavored and will be overturned as an abuse of discretion unless the record clearly indicates that the supported spouse will be able to adequately meet his or her financial needs at the time selected for termination of jurisdiction." This rule is particularly applicable to lengthy marriages.

The *Vomacka* court also found the following: "[W]here there is an ambiguity in the language of a marital property agreement it must be decided in favor of the right to spousal support." "[L]anguage in a spousal support order suggesting that modification of its terms will be permitted is routinely interpreted as a retention of jurisdiction of the court's fundamental jurisdiction to modify and, upon a proper factual showing, to extend the spousal support provisions contained therein." These provisions should be kept in mind when preparing stipulations and/agreements, as they may affect the client's future right to support or ability to request a modification or termination in the future.

In re Marriage of Berland (1989) 215 CA3d 1257, 264 CR 210. This case discussed the *Richmond* "orders." The court concluded that if the "supported spouse exercises reasonable diligence, he or she will have become self-supporting by the date set for the support payments to end." If the court finds that there was a failure to exercise reasonable diligence to become self-supporting, but that even if reasonable diligence has been exercised the supported spouse would still not have become fully self-supporting, the court possesses the discretion to extend the duration of the order and to fix the support in the amount the supported spouse would have required if reasonable diligence would have been exercised.

Family Code § 4337 states: "A party's spousal support obligation must terminate on either party's death or the supported party's remarriage, unless the parties agree to the contrary in writing." However, of primary importance to the Court in determining at what point, if any, spousal support should be modified or terminated (except upon death or remarriage of the supported party), will be the ability of the supported spouse to meet his or her financial needs at the time of the termination. (Modification of support will be discussed further in Chapter Ten.)

Applicable Case Law and Circumstances for Consideration (FC§ 4320)

1) **Marketable skills**—The party requesting support must provide information as to the marketable skills or lack of those skills. Does the party have any recent marketable skills, when was the last time the party worked and/or what kind of education does the party have? Was there a short interruption in work history, or has the party not worked for a long period of time? Does the party have a high school diploma, GED, college or post graduate education, and/or license or certification? Does the party have any disabilities that would preclude working?

The Court may order a spouse to undergo a vocational review to determine what type of skills the spouse has, what kind of work is available at the skill, experience, and/or education level and if the spouse will need additional training in order to become self-supporting. Or conversely, if the spouse will ever become self-supporting. An order for vocational training requires a noticed motion filed by the supporting party and subsequent order for good cause.

Failure to comply with an order for vocational training could result in sanctions. (Family Code § 4331(a)-(c).)

Failure to exercise due diligence in seeking employment could result in the court denying further support. (*In re Marriage of Mason* (1979) 93 CA3d 215, 155 CR 350.)

2) **Contribution to supporting party's advancement in education, training, career or license.** This circumstance is interpreted broadly and is given much weight by the court in determining long term support. Contributions made by a "homemaker" who was the primary caretaker of the children during the marriage, will be given the same weight as that of an employed spouse who contributed ordinary living expenses. Normally, "credit" for these contributions is subject to *Watts credits* (*In re Marriage of Watts* (1985) 171 Cal App 3d 366) which will be discussed further under division of property.

The Court may also consider whether one spouse worked and made contributions to the education and training of the other spouse (other than ordinary living expenses) is entitled to reimbursement.

For instance, if Wife works as a paralegal while Husband attends law school; Wife pays for books, tuition and other school-related expenses. Wife is entitled to reimbursement. *In Re Marriage of Sullivan* (1984) 37 CA3d 762 (See Appendix 6B.)

3) **Supporting party's ability to pay.** The party's ability to pay is a very important element when considering long term support. If a party who has the ability to earn more, the Court may order support based on the earning capacity, which is also referred to as *imputed in come*, to keep the supporting party from intentionally reducing their earnings. *In re Marriage of Philbin* (1989) 19CA3d 115, 96 CR 408 and *In re Marriage of Everett* (1990) 220 CA3d 846, 269 CR 917. The Courts have long held that the trial court may consider earning capacity, as opposed to actual earnings, only if it finds a **deliberate attempt** on the party of the paying spouse **to avoid financial responsibilities**. If there is a good faith effort to work or find work then the court may not consider earning capacity. This is generally known as the *Philbin Rule*.

Earning capacity is defined in *In re Marriage of Regnery* (1989) 214 CA3d 1367, 263 CR 243 as follows: 1) the ability to work, including such factors as age, occupation, skills, education, health, background, work experience and qualifications; 2) the willingness to work exemplified through good faith efforts, due diligence and meaningful attempts to secure employment; and 3) an opportunity to work which means an employer who is willing to hire. *Regnery* further clarified that "when ability and opportunity are present, and willingness is absent, the court has discretion to apply the earnings capacity standard.

There are numerous cases which relate to this topic. The Court has favorably and consistently ruled in a manner consistent with the fiduciary responsibility of the parties to one another. To that end, the Court will, as long as it is feasible, require the supporting party to continue employment at the standard that was established during the marriage.

On the other hand the Court, makes every effort to be fair to the supporting party. Being fair may require that the tax records and business records, of a self-employed person, for at least five years be used in determining the earning capacity. Actual income must be the basis for the determination. (*In re Marriage of Rosen* (2002) 105 CA4th 808, 130 CR2d 1.) The Court will not require a person to work more hours than they would normally have to work in order to maintain the standard. The Court will not only consider whether a party attempted to find work, but whether work was available in that field and available to the supporting party. The Court may consider whether long term support will affect child support. The Court also must determine, if a modification or termination of spousal support will only minimally reduce the standard of living, that the supporting party may change jobs and reduce income. (*In re Marriage of Meegan* (1992) 11 CA4th 156, 13 CR2d 799.)

4) **Each party's standard of living.** The needs and "station in life" must be considered, rather than just the bare necessities. Thus, the *actual* expenditures of the parties during their marriage will likely be the controlling factor in determining the marital standard of living. The Court also needs to look beyond the actual expenditures, as some parties may habitually live beyond their means, while others may live modestly, yet have substantial savings. A supported party who cohabitates with someone of the opposite sex leads to a rebuttable presumption that there is a decreased need for support pursuant to Family Code §4323. (*In re Marriage of Spiegel* (1972) 26 CA3d 88, 92, 102 CR 613.)

5) **Each party's assets and obligations (including separate property).** *In re Marriage of Epstein* (1979) 24 C3d 76, 154 CR 413 addressed the issue of using separate property for spousal support. The *Epstein* Court held that all assets of a prospective supporting party, whether separate or community to be divided in the marital action, are available sources for long term support. The assets do not have to be in the party's name, but they must be in the party's control. Thus, a child support and other obligations may affect spousal support. The court may also consider actual and potential income, which may include settlements, inheritances, or other windfalls.

In re Marriage of Dick (1993) 15 CA4th 144, 18 CR2d 743 is also a significant case with regard to spousal support, child support and attorney's fees. In *Dick*, husband purposely hid assets, was in arrears for child support and requested a modification (reduction) of spousal support stating that he had no money to pay support and that wife did not need spousal support. The Court is highly unlikely to reduce or terminate any support order when the supporting party is in arrears. It is essentially a penalty for having become delinquent with support payments. The Courts want to send a message that nonpayment of support (child and spousal) is not tolerated and will not be rewarded by reducing or terminating current orders, even if there may be a valid reason to do so.

6) **The duration of the marriage**. The Court cannot solely base its decision to order support on the duration of the marriage, but must include all of the factors of Family Code § 4320.

A marriage of short duration will find the Court hesitant to order support unless there are many other factors such as the age of the children and the ability of the spouse to currently be self-supporting. Short term marriages are those most likely to find the court applying the "rule of thumb" and, if/when support is awarded, ordering support for one-half the length of the marriage. These situations will likely order the supporting party to comply with certain demands, such as obtaining employment once the children have reached a certain age, returning to school, etc. The Court's jurisdiction to continue support beyond that time will be unlikely.

A marriage of medium duration will usually find the court leaning toward retaining jurisdiction, with an open-ended term. The supported party will be admonished (given the *Gavron* warning) that they are required to become self-supporting.

A long term marriage offers the Court the most discretion and latitude based on all of the factors in Family Code § 4320. Unless the Court can clearly show that the supported party has the ability to be self-supporting by a specific date, it is unlikely that the court will establish a clear termination date for spousal support. The Court will likely retain jurisdiction until either party dies or the supported spouse remarries.

7) **Ability to find gainful employment without interfering with the interests of dependent children when those children are in his/her custody**. Although it is the goal of the State of California that a party become self-supporting, the Court also must ensure that the custodial parent is able to attend to the needs of their child. The Court found in *Rosan* (*In re Marriage of Rosan* (1972) 24 CA3d 885, 101 CR 295) that the supported party could defer seeking employment, as she had custody of the two minor children, one of whom had behavioral problems and special needs.

8) **Age and health**. Support cannot be ordered on the basis of age and health alone. (*In re Marriage of Wilson* (1988) 201 CA3d 913, 247 CR 522)

Other criteria as set forth in FC§ 4320 must be considered in conjunction with age and health.

> Discussion #1: A 28-year-old man has developed advanced Multiple Sclerosis. Husband and Wife have been married for 9 years. Is the court likely to order the minimum number of years support or 4.5 years (1/2 the length of the marriage); or would the Court order support for a longer period?

> Discussion #2: A healthy 46-year-old woman, who last worked as a cosmetologist 10 years ago, quit working when the youngest of three children was born. Husband and Wife have been married for 26 years. Wife made approximately $40,000 per year when she last worked. Husband now makes $55,000 per year. What are the various factors that may affect the length of support and potential orders the court could make?

9) **History of Domestic Violence**. Evidence of Domestic Violence must be documented, and include physical and emotional violence and distress. See also FC § 6211.

10) **Tax Consequences**. Spousal support as previously indicated is income to the party receiving it and deductible to the party paying support. This will need to be kept

in mind (usually by using Dissomaster™ or XSpouse™ programs) in determining the tax considerations that long term support may have on either of the parties. Effective January 1, 1989, the Court is required to take tax consequences into consideration.

11) **Hardships**. Hardships must be considered effective January 1, 2002.

12) **Goal to be self-supporting**. Effective January 1, 1997, except for a marriage of long duration as described in Family Code § 4320, a supported party has a reasonable period of time to become self-supporting. Said reasonable time usually is considered to be one-half the length of the marriage. The Court has the discretion to order support for a longer or a shorter period of time, based on the other factors in Family Code § 4320.

The Court is **required** to advise the supported spouse that he/she may be required to become self-supporting, in any spousal support order entered, unless the marriage is of long duration and the court determines the warning is not advisable. *In re Marriage of Gavron* (1988) 203 CA3d 705; 250 CR 148. Said notice **must** be incorporated in all stipulations, agreements, and judgments wherein spousal support is ordered and/or there is a reservation of jurisdiction over the issue of spousal support. There are **no** exceptions to this rule.

Of significance in the *Gavron* case was the court's ruling with respect to giving the supported party notice that they must become self-supporting. The Court ruled in *Gavron* as follows: "We recognize that it is in the best interest of both spouses and of society in general that the supported spouse become self-sufficient. Civil Code § 4801(1)(1)(A) (currently FC§ 4320(n) expressly directs that in determining the amount and duration of spousal support, a court is to consider as a factor the supported spouse's marketable skills and ability to engage in gainful employment. The Legislature intended that all supported spouses who are able to do so should seek employment and to work toward becoming self-supporting ... Nonetheless, the trial court erroneously held that Wife's failure to become employable or to seek training after so many years [shifts] the burden to her to demonstrate her continued need for support in light of her continued inaction in this regard.... Wife ... cannot be penalized now, years later, because of an apparent lack of judicial foresight in not forcing her to focus on the drastic legal and financial consequences of the then-revealed expectation that she become self-sufficient."

In re Marriage of Schaffer (1999) 69 CA4th 801, 81 CR2d 797. The Court applied the language in this section, retroactively. The court denied spousal support to a wife who had unsuccessfully pursued an "unsuitable" career in social work. She did not seek other employment. The Court stated: "The statutory guideline flies in the face of a reading of the material change of circumstance rule that would prevent a trial judge from looking at long-term patterns of job training and employability."

In re Marriage of Khera & Sameer (2012) 206 CA4th 1467, 143 CR3d 81, applied *Gavron* to a previous *Richmond* order, stating that her allegation that the requirement to become self-supporting was an unreasonable expectation; she had shown no attempt to become self-supporting.

13) **Criminal Conviction of Abusive Spouse**. Effective January 1, 2002, Family Code § 4325, raises the rebuttable presumption that if there is criminal conviction for domestic violence, by one spouse against another, within five years before or after filing the dissolution petition, the Court may not make a spousal support award to the abusive spouse. The Court may consider documented evidence of a history of domestic violence, among other things.

The court applied this circumstance in *In re Marriage of Freitas* (2012) Cal App Lexis 1039 stating that the court "properly terminated an order for temporary spousal support to a husband" based on a prior domestic violence conviction (as codified in FC § 4325).

14) **Any other factors the court deems just and equitable.** *In re Marriage of Cosgrove* (1972) 27 CA3d 424, 103 CR 733, states that the court, when addressing long term spousal support, may consider just about anything that bears on "present and prospective matters" relating to the lives and the needs of the parties. The income of a subsequent spouse or nonmarital partner **cannot** be considered when determining spousal support.

In re Marriage of Left (2012) 208 CA4th 1137, 146 CR3d 181, confirms that an *actual* marriage *must* occur and not simply a "marriage-like ceremony" pursuant to FC § 4337.

Some of the considerations and the relative case law are as follows:

Support of third parties, such as education of an adult child (*In re Marriage of Epstein* (1972) 27 CA3d 424, 103 CR 733) and (*In re Marriage of Paul* (1985) 173 CA3d 913, 219 CR 318); education and needs of disabled child (*In re Marriage of Spiegel* (1972) 26 CA3d 88, 102 CR 613.)

Suppression of standard of living during marriage in anticipation of an increased standard on completion of education or training. (*In re Marriage of Watt* (1989) 214 CA3d 340, 262 CR 783.)

Need for household help and/or child care while obtaining education or training in order to become self-supporting. (*Marriage of Ostler & Smith* (1990) 223 CA3d 33, 272 CR 560.)

The court will not allow any modifications or terminations of spousal support when a supporting party is in arrears for child support. (*In re Marriage of Ilas* (1993) 12 CA4th 1630, 16 CR2d 345.)

As previously stated, *In re Marriage of Dick* (1993) 15 CA4th 144, 18 CR2d 743 is also a significant case with regard to spousal support, child support and attorneys fees. *Dick* also deals with the issue of a request for retroactive support. The Court ruled that the supported party may request spousal support retroactively to the date the Petition was filed. The court is **not** mandated to order retroactive support, but is given the discretion to consider it. Most other issues may only be dated back the date the OSC (Request for Order) was filed, spousal support is the exception.

Court Orders & Considerations

As you can probably see based on statutes and some of the case law discussed above Court orders with respect to spousal support can take many forms. Once the above code sections have been applied, the relevant case law reviewed, and the evidence introduced which supports each party's position with respect to standard of living, length of marriage, needs, ability to pay, etc, the court can make any variety of orders based on statute and subsequent case law. There are a number of sample spousal support provisions provided in Appendix 6C for you to utilize, depending upon the type of spousal support agreement made or ordered.

Always remember to draft spousal support documents which include any required provisions, as referenced above, as well as from the perspective that spousal support may undergo frequent modifications or requests for termination.

Default

As stated in Chapter Two, a Respondent's Default may be taken if he or she has not filed a Response within the statutory thirty (30) day period. The court will not, however, allow the Request to Enter Default to be filed until the thirty-first (31st) day after the date the Respondent was served.

At this point, the preliminary disclosure documents must have been served on the opposing party. In most cases if the Default is being taken, your office will be representing the Petitioner and thus serving these documents on the Respondent. There are no exceptions (as seen in Chapter Five) in the preparation and service of the preliminary Disclosure documents.

The second thing that must be determined is whether the Respondent is in "active" military service. The client must be able to declare with absolute certainty, under penalty of perjury, that their spouse is not currently serving in the armed forces. The penalty for making a false declaration and filing the default, is "imprisonment not to exceed one year, a fine not to exceed $1000 or both." (50 USC App § 521(c)). If the person cannot make said declaration with certainty, it will be necessary to make that determination. The Judicial Council in acknowledgment of the large number of men and women serving their country and who are unable to appear before the court may consent to having their default taken and/or they may participate while actively deployed by signing a Declaration and Conditional Waiver of Rights Under Servicemembers' Civil Relief Act of 2003 (SCRA). The form created is FL-141. Inquiries as to the person's military mailing address and I.D. number, or an affidavit certifying that the person is not on active or training duty can be made, by contacting the various branches of the service (locator), as follows:

U.S. ARMY — Commander
U.S. Army Enlisted Records & Evaluations Center
Attn: Locator
8899 East 56th Street
Fort Benjamin Harrison, IN 46249-5301
www.hrc.army.mil.wwl

U.S. AIR FORCE
World Wide Locator
HQ AFMPC/RMIQL
550 "C" Street West, Suite 50
Randolph AFB, TX 78150-4752
(210) 652-5775

U.S. COAST GUARD
Personnel Command Branch
2100 2d Street, S.W.
Washington, DC 20593-0001
Attn: World Wide Locator
(202) 267-0581
locator@comdt.uscg.mil

U.S. NAVY
World Wide Locator

Bureau of Naval Personnel
PERS 312F
5720 Integrity Drive
Millington, TN 38055-3120
(901) 874-3388

U.S. MARINES
World Wide Locator
Commandant of the Marine Corps
Headquarters, USMC
Code MMSB-10
Quantico, VA 22134-5030
(703) 640-3942 or (703) 640-3943

The Servicemembers Civil Relief Act of 2003 (*50 USC App §§ 501-596*) which supercedes Section 101 of the Soldier's and Sailor's Relief Act of 1940 protects persons, in any branch of the military, whether on active duty or training duty from having a default taken against them.

When a Respondent qualifies for protection under the Act, the Court must appoint an attorney to represent the person in the dissolution proceeding. In the event that the Court should grant a default judgment against a person who qualifies for protection under the Act, the Court shall set aside the judgment and reopen the case. The service member will be afforded to the opportunity to respond (defend) if it is determined that the person has been "materially affected" by the taking of the default.

Although the Act states that the "court must appoint an attorney" in most cases the Court will simply reject the Request to Enter Default citing the Act. It is a very fine line as to the Superior Court's jurisdiction to appoint an attorney, when the Respondent has not filed and accepted the court's jurisdiction. Individual state and county courts have little jurisdiction over a person who is in the military, as the service person's lives and actions are governed by federal military codes. It will be necessary to determine the most appropriate method for getting the Respondent to either respond or waive his/her right.

The most common practice in making sure that the Respondent either participates and/or waives his/her right is to contact the Respondent's commanding officer and advise him/her of the pending dissolution. Each member of the military is entitled to basic legal representation for certain matters. In any matters where a person's military benefits (family rights, earnings and retirement) may be affected, the military will afford the person representation through the Judge Advocate General's (JAG) office of that branch of the service. Although a Commander cannot force any personnel to respond to the matter, the Commander can heartily recommend that the service member contact a JAG officer immediately with any legal documents he/she have been served. This is usually enough to get the service member spouse in a position to be "appointed an attorney." In most cases, if there are issues of support and/or benefits subject to the dissolution, the JAG officer will make sure that a Response is filed so that the individual service member's rights are protected, as well as the potential rights of the military.

The proper procedure (for the Respondent), if the Default of a service member as defined in the Act is taken, is for the service member to file a Motion and Application to Vacate or Set Aside the Default, not later than ninety (90) days after the **termination or release** from military service. A service member may waive the protections under the Act, even if **not** represented by legal counsel, by executing an Appearance, Stipulation Waivers form (FL-130) along with form FL-141 as referenced above. The signature on this form must be notarized. (These forms will be discussed further in Chapter Nine.) The Response fee is waived for the service member in this instance. (*Government Code §26857.5*) In this case, the service member is accepting the court's jurisdiction, relinquishing his/her rights under the Act, and basically agreeing that a default can be taken.

It is always advisable to make sure your office is not put in the position of having the Default Judgment vacated or set aside. Your attorney should be able, with utmost certainty, to state that the Respondent is not a service member and if they are, that either the Respondent has filed a Response or their express waiver has been obtained.

Requesting a Default (Completing the Form)

The Request to Enter Default (form) is completed and submitted to the court. A stamped envelope, addressed to the Respondent at the last known address must be submitted to the court along with the "Default" and three copies. One of these copies will be mailed to the Respondent, by the court clerk, in the envelope provided. The clerk will verify before filing and mailing the Default that the Respondent has **not** filed a Response.

Some counties will allow the attorney to schedule a "prove up" hearing in order to obtain the Default. This hearing will require the Petitioner's appearance, at which time they will testify to the facts to which they declared under penalty of perjury on the Petition. The Petitioner will also have to testify that all of the facts in the subsequently submitted documents are true and correct and that the Judgment is fair and equitable.

At the "prove up" hearing, the attorney will need to have the following documents (originals to be retained by the court, as well as copies for the attorney to have for the file and to give the client), and to serve on the Respondent as necessary:

Declaration for Default or Uncontested Dissolution (FL-170)

Income & Expense Declarations (FL-150)

Property Declaration or Schedule of Assets & Debts (FL-160) or (FL-105)

Declaration regarding Service of Final Declaration of Disclosure (FL-141)

Judgment (FL-180) w/and attachments (pleadings or Judicial Council forms)

Notice of Entry of Judgment (FL-190); with two stamped and addressed envelopes.

Child Support Case Registry form (FL-191) (if there are minor children)

Individual counties may also have local forms that must be submitted and/or local rules with which you must comply. Always check your local rules regarding submitting a Request to Enter Default and any subsequent "prove up" hearing.

Due to constraints on courtroom time, many counties prefer not to schedule default or prove up hearings unless it is necessary and expedient to do so. In most cases, once the thirty-one days have elapsed, you may submit all of the above referenced forms, which have been completed and signed by the client, to the Court along with a S.A.S.E. After review by the file examiner, approval by a judge or commissioner, and filing by the clerk, the documents will be returned to your office.

Forms Associated with Topic

Stipulation to Establish or Modify (FL-350)

Stipulation (pleading format)

Request to Enter Default (FL-165)

Preliminary Declaration of Disclosure (FL-140)

(See examples of some forms on the following pages)

Key Terms

- Stipulation & Order
- Notice/Order to Withhold
- Child Support Case Registry
- Gavron Warning
- Philbin Rule
- Richmond Order
- Rome Review
- Jurisdictional Reservation
- Jurisdictional Stepdown
- *Vomacka*
- *Sullivan*
- *Watts*
- *Epstein*

Stipulation to Establish or Modify Child Support and Order

FL-350

ATTORNEY OR PARTY WITHOUT ATTORNEY *(Name, State Bar number, and address):* JOAN CARE-ACTOR, SBN ******** LAW OFFICES OF JOAN CARE-ACTOR 75000 WHY ME LANE, SACRAMENTO, CA 95826 TELEPHONE NO.: 916-5551234 FAX NO. *(Optional):* 916-555-1233 E-MAIL ADDRESS *(Optional):* joan@ care-actorlaw.com ATTORNEY FOR *(Name):* SANDIE SHORES, Petitioner	FOR COURT USE ONLY To keep other people from seeing what you entered on your form, please press the Clear This Form button at the end of the form when finished.

SUPERIOR COURT OF CALIFORNIA, COUNTY OF SACRAMENTO
STREET ADDRESS: 3341 Power Inn Road
MAILING ADDRESS: 3341 Power Inn Road
CITY AND ZIP CODE: Sacramento, CA 95826
BRANCH NAME: Family Law Division

PETITIONER/PLAINTIFF: SANDIE SHORES

RESPONDENT/DEFENDANT: ROCKY SHORES

OTHER PARENT:

STIPULATION TO ESTABLISH OR MODIFY CHILD SUPPORT AND ORDER	CASE NUMBER: 14FLXXXXXXX

1. a. ☐ Mother's net monthly disposable income: $
    Father's net monthly disposable income: $
    -OR-
   b. ☑ A printout of a computer calculation of the parents' financial circumstances is attached.
2. ☑ Percentage of time each parent has primary responsibility for the children: Mother: 70 % Father: 30 %
3. a. ☐ A hardship is being experienced by the mother $ per month because of *(specify):*

    The hardship will last until *(date):*
   b. ☐ A hardship is being experienced by the father $ per month because of *(specify):*

    The hardship will last until *(date):*
4. The amount of child support payable by *(name):* ROCKY SHORES   , referred to as "the parent ordered to pay support," as calculated under the guideline is: $ 1600   per month.
5. ☑ We agree to guideline support.
6. ☐ The guideline amount should be rebutted because of the following:
    a. ☐ We agree to child support in the amount of $ per month; the agreement is in the best interest of the children; the needs of the children will be adequately met by the agreed amount; and application of the guideline would be unjust or inappropriate in this case.
    b. ☐ Other rebutting factors *(specify):*
7. The parent ordered to pay support must pay child support as follows beginning *(date):* XX/01/20XX
   a. BASIC CHILD SUPPORT

Child's name	Monthly amount	Payable to *(name):*
EDDY SHORES	718	SANDIE SHORES
SHELLY SHORES	882	SANDIE SHORES

   Total: $1600   payable ☑ on the first of the month ☐ other *(specify):*
   b. ☐ In addition, the parent ordered to pay support must pay the following:
      (1) ☐ $ per month for child care costs to *(name):*   on *(date):*
      (2) ☐ $ per month for health-care costs not deducted from gross income to *(name):*   on *(date):*
      (3) ☐ $ per month for special educational or other needs of the children to *(name):*   on *(date):*
      (4) ☐ other *(specify):*

   c. **Total monthly child support** payable by the parent ordered to pay support will be: $ 1600.00
   payable ☑ on the first of the month ☐ other *(specify):*

Page 1 of 2

Form Adopted for Mandatory Use Judicial Council of California FL-350 [Rev. July 1, 2010]	STIPULATION TO ESTABLISH OR MODIFY CHILD SUPPORT AND ORDER	Family Code, § 4065 www.courtinfo.ca.gov

Stipulation to Establish or Modify Child Support and Order

FL-350

PETITIONER/PLAINTIFF: SANDIE SHORES	CASE NUMBER:
RESPONDENT/DEFENDANT: ROCKY SHORES	14FLXXXXXXX

8. a. Health insurance will be maintained by *(specify name):* ROCKY SHORES
   The parent ordered to provide health insurance must seek continuation of coverage for the child after the child attains the age when the child is no longer considered eligible for coverage as a dependent under the insurance contract, if the child is incapable of self-sustaining employment because of a physically or mentally disabling injury, illness, or condition and is chiefly dependent upon the parent providing health insurance for support and maintenance.

   b. ☐ A health insurance coverage assignment will issue if health insurance is available through employment or other group plan or otherwise is available at reasonable cost. Both parents are ordered to cooperate in the presentation, collection, and reimbursement of any medical claims.

   c. Any health expenses not paid by insurance will be shared: Mother: %   Father: %

9. a. An earnings assignment order is issued.

   b. ☐ We agree that service of the earnings assignment be stayed because we have made the following alternative arrangements to ensure payment *(specify):*

10. In the event that there is a contract between a party receiving support and a private child support collector, the party ordered to pay support must pay the fee charged by the private child support collector. This fee must not exceed 33 1/3 percent of the total amount in arrears nor may it exceed 50 percent of any fee charged by the private child support collector. The money judgment created by this provision is in favor of the private child support collector and the party receiving support, jointly.

11. ☐ Travel expenses for visitation will be shared: Mother: %   Father: %

12. ☐ We agree that we will promptly inform each other of any change of residence or employment, including the employer's name, address, and telephone number.

13. ☐ Other *(specify):*

14. We agree that we are fully informed of our rights under the California child support guidelines.
15. We make this agreement freely without coercion or duress.
16. The right to support
    a. ☑ has not been assigned to any county, and no application for public assistance is pending.
    b. ☐ has been assigned or an application for public assistance is pending in *(county name):*
    If you checked b., an attorney for the local child support agency must sign below, joining in this agreement.

Date:

▶

_____   _____
(TYPE OR PRINT NAME)   (SIGNATURE OF ATTORNEY FOR LOCAL CHILD SUPPORT AGENCY)

Notice: If the amount agreed to is less than the guideline amount, no change of circumstances need be shown to obtain a change in the support order to a higher amount. If the order is above the guideline, a change of circumstances will be required to modify this order. This form must be signed by the court to be effective.

Date:

SANDIE SHORES   ▶

_____   _____
(TYPE OR PRINT NAME)   (SIGNATURE OF PETITIONER)

Date:

ROCKY SHORES   ▶

_____   _____
(TYPE OR PRINT NAME)   (SIGNATURE OF RESPONDENT)

Date:

JOAN CARE-ACTOR   ▶

_____   _____
(TYPE OR PRINT NAME)   (SIGNATURE OF ATTORNEY FOR PETITIONER)

Date:

CLASS E. ATTORNEY   ▶

_____   _____
(TYPE OR PRINT NAME)   (SIGNATURE OF ATTORNEY FOR RESPONDENT)

THE COURT ORDERS

17. a. ☐ The guideline child support amount in item 4 is rebutted by the factors stated in item 6.

    b. Items 7 through 13 are ordered. All child support payments must continue until further order of the court, or until the child marries, dies, is emancipated, or reaches age 18. The duty of support continues as to an unmarried child who has attained the age of 18 years, is a full-time high school student, and resides with a parent, until the time the child completes the 12th grade or attains the age of 19 years, whichever first occurs. Except as modified by this stipulation, all provisions of any previous orders made in this action will remain in effect.

Date:

_____
JUDGE OF THE SUPERIOR COURT

NOTICE: Any party required to pay child support must pay interest on overdue amounts at the "legal" rate, which is currently 10 percent per year. This can be a large added amount.

FL-350 [Rev. July 1, 2010]   **STIPULATION TO ESTABLISH OR MODIFY**   Page 2 of 2
CHILD SUPPORT AND ORDER

For your protection and privacy, please press the Clear This Form button after you have printed the form. | Save This Form | | Print This Form | | Clear This Form |

Request to Enter Default

FL-165

ATTORNEY OR PARTY WITHOUT ATTORNEY *(Name, State Bar number, and address):* — JOAN CARE-ACTOR, SBN ******* LAW OFFICES OF JOAN CARE-ACTOR 75000 WHY ME LANE SACRAMENTO, CA 95826 TELEPHONE NO.: 916-555-1234 FAX NO. *(Optional):* 916-555-1233 E-MAIL ADDRESS *(Optional):* joan@care-actorlaw.com ATTORNEY FOR *(Name):* SANDY SHORES	To keep other people from seeing what you entered on your form, please press the Clear This Form button at the end of the form when finished.

SUPERIOR COURT OF CALIFORNIA, COUNTY OF SACRAMENTO
STREET ADDRESS: 3341 POWER INN ROAD
MAILING ADDRESS: 3341 POWER INN ROAD
CITY AND ZIP CODE: SACRAMENTO, CA 95826
BRANCH NAME: FAMILY LAW

PETITIONER: SANDY SHORES

RESPONDENT: ROCKY SHORES

REQUEST TO ENTER DEFAULT	CASE NUMBER: 14FLXXXXXX

1. **To the clerk:** Please enter the default of the respondent who has failed to respond to the petition.

2. A completed *Income and Expense Declaration* (form FL-150) or *Financial Statement (Simplified)* (form FL-155)
   ☐ is attached ☐ is not attached.
   A completed *Property Declaration* (form FL-160) ☐ is attached ☐ is not attached
   because *(check at least one of the following):*
   (a) ☑ there have been no changes since the previous filing.
   (b) ☑ the issues subject to disposition by the court in this proceeding are the subject of a written agreement.
   (c) ☐ there are no issues of child, spousal, or partner support or attorney fees and costs subject to determination by the court.
   (d) ☐ the petition does not request money, property, costs, or attorney fees. (Fam. Code, § 2330.5.)
   (e) ☐ there are no issues of division of community property.
   (f) ☐ this is an action to establish parental relationship.

Date:

JOAN CARE-ACTOR
_____
(TYPE OR PRINT NAME)   ▶ _____
                                                        (SIGNATURE OF [ATTORNEY FOR] PETITIONER)

3. **Declaration**
   a. ☐ No mailing is required because service was by publication or posting and the address of the respondent remains unknown.
   b. ☑ A copy of this *Request to Enter Default*, including any attachments and an envelope with sufficient postage, was provided to the court clerk, with the envelope addressed as follows *(address of the respondent's attorney or, if none, the respondent's last known address):*

      ROCKY SHORES, 9600 CHEATER LANE, SACRAMENTO, CA 95816

I declare under penalty of perjury under the laws of the State of California that the foregoing is true and correct.

Date:

SALLY Q. DILIGENT
_____
(TYPE OR PRINT NAME)   ▶ _____
                                                        (SIGNATURE OF DECLARANT)

FOR COURT USE ONLY
☐ *Request to Enter Default* mailed to the respondent or the respondent's attorney on *(date):* ☐ Default entered as requested on *(date):* ☐ Default **not** entered. Reason: Clerk, by _____, Deputy

Page 1 of 2

Form Adopted for Mandatory Use
Judicial Council of California
FL-165 [Rev. January 1, 2005]

REQUEST TO ENTER DEFAULT
(Family Law—Uniform Parentage)

Code of Civil Procedure, §§ 585, 587;
Family Code, § 2335.5
www.courtinfo.ca.gov

Request to Enter Default

CASE NAME (Last name, first name of each party): SANDY SHORES ROCKY SHORES	CASE NUMBER: 14FLXXXXXX

4. **Memorandum of costs**

     a. ☑ Costs and disbursements are waived.

     b. Costs and disbursements are listed as follows:

         (1) ☐ Clerk's fees .... $.................

         (2) ☐ Process server's fees .... $.................

         (3) ☐ Other (specify): ....

                         .... $.................

                         .... $.................

                         .... $ _____

        TOTAL .... $.................

     c. I am the attorney, agent, or party who claims these costs. To the best of my knowledge and belief, the foregoing items of cost are correct and have been necessarily incurred in this cause or proceeding.

I declare under penalty of perjury under the laws of the State of California that the foregoing is true and correct.

Date:

JOAN CARE-ACTOR
          (TYPE OR PRINT NAME)   ▶   (SIGNATURE OF DECLARANT)

5. **Declaration of nonmilitary status.** The respondent is not in the military service of the United States as defined in section 511 et seq. of the Servicemembers Civil Relief Act (50 U.S.C. Appen. § 501 et seq.), and is not entitled to the benefits of such act.

I declare under penalty of perjury under the laws of the State of California that the foregoing is true and correct.

Date:

JOAN CARE-ACTOR
          (TYPE OR PRINT NAME)   ▶   (SIGNATURE OF DECLARANT)

For your protection and privacy, please press the Clear This Form button after you have printed the form.   **Save This Form**   **Print This Form**   **Clear This Form**

Declaration of Disclosure

FL-140

ATTORNEY OR PARTY WITHOUT ATTORNEY *(Name, State Bar number, and address)*: JOAN CARE-ACTOR, SBN XXXXXXX CARE-ACTOR LAW FIRM 75000 WHY ME LANE SACRAMENTO, CA 95826 TELEPHONE NO.: 916-555-1234　　FAX NO.: 916-555-1233 E-MAIL ADDRESS: joan@care-actorlaw.com ATTORNEY FOR *(Name)*: SANDIE SHORES	
SUPERIOR COURT OF CALIFORNIA, COUNTY OF SACRAMENTO STREET ADDRESS: 3341 POWER INN ROAD MAILING ADDRESS: 3341 POWER INN ROAD CITY AND ZIP CODE: SACRAMENTO, CA 95826 BRANCH NAME: FAMILY LAW DIVISION	
PETITIONER: SANDIE SHORES RESPONDENT: ROCKY SHORES OTHER PARENT/PARTY:	
DECLARATION OF DISCLOSURE ✔ Petitioner's ☐ Preliminary ☐ Respondent's ☐ Final	CASE NUMBER: 14FLXXXXXXX

DO NOT FILE DECLARATIONS OF DISCLOSURE OR FINANCIAL ATTACHMENTS WITH THE COURT

In a dissolution, legal separation, or nullity action, both a preliminary and a final declaration of disclosure must be served on the other party with certain exceptions. Neither disclosure is filed with the court. Instead, a declaration stating that service of disclosure documents was completed or waived must be filed with the court (see form FL-141).

- *In summary dissolution cases, each spouse or domestic partner must exchange preliminary disclosures as described in* Summary Dissolution Information *(form FL-810). Final disclosures are not required (see Family Code section 2109).*
- *In a default judgment case that is not a stipulated judgment or a judgment based on a marital settlement agreement, only the petitioner is required to complete and serve a preliminary declaration of disclosure. A final disclosure is not required of either party (see Family Code section 2110).*
- *Service of preliminary declarations of disclosure may not be waived by an agreement between the parties.*
- *Parties who agree to waive final declarations of disclosure must file their written agreement with the court (see form FL-144).*

The petitioner must serve a preliminary declaration of disclosure at the same time as the Petition or within 60 days of filing the Petition. The respondent must serve a preliminary declaration of disclosure at the same time as the Response or within 60 days of filing the Response. The time periods may be extended by written agreement of the parties or by court order (see Family Code section 2104(f)).

Attached are the following:

1. ☒ A completed *Schedule of Assets and Debts* (form FL-142) or ☐ A *Property Declaration* (form FL-160) for *(specify)*:
   ☐ Community and Quasi-Community Property ☐ Separate Property.

2. ☒ A completed *Income and Expense Declaration* (form FL-150).

3. ☒ All tax returns filed by the party in the two years before the date that the party served the disclosure documents.

4. ☒ A statement of all material facts and information regarding valuation of all assets that are community property or in which the community has an interest *(not a form)*.
   PETITIONER HAS NOT COMPLETED A VALUATION OF ALL COMMUNITY ASSETS

5. ☒ A statement of all material facts and information regarding obligations for which the community is liable *(not a form)*.
   PETITIONER HAS NOT COMPLETED DISCOVERY OF THE EXTENT OF OBLIGATIONS

6. ☒ An accurate and complete written disclosure of any investment opportunity, business opportunity, or other income-producing opportunity presented since the date of separation that results from any investment, significant business, or other income-producing opportunity from the date of marriage to the date of separation *(not a form)*.

   Petitioner has had no investment, business or income-producing opportunity since date of separation.

I declare under penalty of perjury under the laws of the State of California that the foregoing is true and correct.

Date:

SANDIE SHORES
_____　　　　　　_____
(TYPE OR PRINT NAME)　　　　　　　　　　　　SIGNATURE

Page 1 of 1

Form Adopted for Mandatory Use Judicial Council of California FL-140 [Rev. July 1, 2013]	**DECLARATION OF DISCLOSURE** **(Family Law)**	Family Code, §§ 2102, 2104, 2105, 2106, 2112 www.courts.ca.gov

For your protection and privacy, please press the Clear This Form button after you have printed the form. | Print this form | Save this form | | Clear this form |

Stipulation to Establish or Modify Child Support and Order

FL-350

ATTORNEY OR PARTY WITHOUT ATTORNEY *(Name, State Bar number, and address)*:	FOR COURT USE ONLY
TELEPHONE NO.: FAX NO. *(Optional)*:	To keep other people from seeing what you entered on your form, please press the Clear This Form button at the end of the form when finished.
E-MAIL ADDRESS *(Optional)*:	
ATTORNEY FOR *(Name)*:	

SUPERIOR COURT OF CALIFORNIA, COUNTY OF

STREET ADDRESS:

MAILING ADDRESS:

CITY AND ZIP CODE:

BRANCH NAME:

PETITIONER/PLAINTIFF:

RESPONDENT/DEFENDANT:

OTHER PARENT:

STIPULATION TO ESTABLISH OR MODIFY CHILD SUPPORT AND ORDER	CASE NUMBER:

1. a. ☐ Mother's net monthly disposable income: $
   Father's net monthly disposable income: $
   -OR-
   b. ☐ A printout of a computer calculation of the parents' financial circumstances is attached.

2. ☐ Percentage of time each parent has primary responsibility for the children: Mother: %   Father: %

3. a. ☐ A hardship is being experienced by the mother $ per month because of *(specify)*:

   The hardship will last until *(date)*:

   b. ☐ A hardship is being experienced by the father $ per month because of *(specify)*:

   The hardship will last until *(date)*:

4. The amount of child support payable by *(name)*:   , referred to as "the parent ordered to pay support," as calculated under the guideline is: $ per month.

5. ☐ We agree to guideline support.

6. ☐ The guideline amount should be rebutted because of the following:
   a. ☐ We agree to child support in the amount of $ per month; the agreement is in the best interest of the children; the needs of the children will be adequately met by the agreed amount; and application of the guideline would be unjust or inappropriate in this case.
   b. ☐ Other rebutting factors *(specify)*:

7. The parent ordered to pay support must pay child support as follows beginning *(date)*:
   a. BASIC CHILD SUPPORT

Child's name	Monthly amount	Payable to *(name)*:

   Total: $ payable ☐ on the first of the month ☐ other *(specify)*:

   b. ☐ In addition, the parent ordered to pay support must pay the following:
   (1) ☐ $ per month for child care costs to *(name)*:   on *(date)*:
   (2) ☐ $ per month for health-care costs not deducted from gross income to *(name)*:   on *(date)*:
   (3) ☐ $ per month for special educational or other needs of the children to *(name)*:   on *(date)*:
   (4) ☐ other *(specify)*:

   c. **Total monthly child support** payable by the parent ordered to pay support will be: $
   payable ☐ on the first of the month ☐ other *(specify)*:

Form Adopted for Mandatory Use
Judicial Council of California
FL-350 [Rev. July 1, 2010]

STIPULATION TO ESTABLISH OR MODIFY CHILD SUPPORT AND ORDER

Page 1 of 2
Family Code, § 4065
www.courtinfo.ca.gov

Stipulation to Establish or Modify Child Support and Order

PETITIONER/PLAINTIFF:	CASE NUMBER:
RESPONDENT/DEFENDANT:	

8. a. Health insurance will be maintained by (specify name):

The parent ordered to provide health insurance must seek continuation of coverage for the child after the child attains the age when the child is no longer considered eligible for coverage as a dependent under the insurance contract, if the child is incapable of self-sustaining employment because of a physically or mentally disabling injury, illness, or condition and is chiefly dependent upon the parent providing health insurance for support and maintenance.

   b. ☐ A health insurance coverage assignment will issue if health insurance is available through employment or other group plan or otherwise is available at reasonable cost. Both parents are ordered to cooperate in the presentation, collection, and reimbursement of any medical claims.

   c. Any health expenses not paid by insurance will be shared: Mother: %   Father: %

9. a. An earnings assignment order is issued.

   b. ☐ We agree that service of the earnings assignment be stayed because we have made the following alternative arrangements to ensure payment (specify):

10. In the event that there is a contract between a party receiving support and a private child support collector, the party ordered to pay support must pay the fee charged by the private child support collector. This fee must not exceed 33 1/3 percent of the total amount in arrears nor may it exceed 50 percent of any fee charged by the private child support collector. The money judgment created by this provision is in favor of the private child support collector and the party receiving support, jointly.

11. ☐ Travel expenses for visitation will be shared: Mother: %   Father: %

12. ☐ We agree that we will promptly inform each other of any change of residence or employment, including the employer's name, address, and telephone number.

13. ☐ Other (specify):

14. We agree that we are fully informed of our rights under the California child support guidelines.

15. We make this agreement freely without coercion or duress.

16. The right to support

   a. ☐ has not been assigned to any county, and no application for public assistance is pending.

   b. ☐ has been assigned or an application for public assistance is pending in (county name):

   If you checked b., an attorney for the local child support agency must sign below, joining in this agreement.

Date:

_____   ► _____
(TYPE OR PRINT NAME)   (SIGNATURE OF ATTORNEY FOR LOCAL CHILD SUPPORT AGENCY)

Notice: If the amount agreed to is less than the guideline amount, no change of circumstances need be shown to obtain a change in the support order to a higher amount. If the order is above the guideline, a change of circumstances will be required to modify this order. This form must be signed by the court to be effective.

Date:

_____   ► _____
(TYPE OR PRINT NAME)   (SIGNATURE OF PETITIONER)

Date: _____   ► _____
(TYPE OR PRINT NAME)   (SIGNATURE OF RESPONDENT)

Date: _____   ► _____
(TYPE OR PRINT NAME)   (SIGNATURE OF ATTORNEY FOR PETITIONER)

Date: _____   ► _____
(TYPE OR PRINT NAME)   (SIGNATURE OF ATTORNEY FOR RESPONDENT)

THE COURT ORDERS

17. a. ☐ The guideline child support amount in item 4 is rebutted by the factors stated in item 6.

   b. Items 7 through 13 are ordered. All child support payments must continue until further order of the court, or until the child marries, dies, is emancipated, or reaches age 18. The duty of support continues as to an unmarried child who has attained the age of 18 years, is a full-time high school student, and resides with a parent, until the time the child completes the 12th grade or attains the age of 19 years, whichever first occurs. Except as modified by this stipulation, all provisions of any previous orders made in this action will remain in effect.

Date: _____

_____
JUDGE OF THE SUPERIOR COURT

> **NOTICE:** Any party required to pay child support must pay interest on overdue amounts at the "legal" rate, which is currently 10 percent per year. This can be a large added amount.

For your protection and privacy, please press the Clear This Form button after you have printed the form. | Save This Form | Print This Form | Clear This Form |

Request to Enter Default

FL-165

ATTORNEY OR PARTY WITHOUT ATTORNEY *(Name, State Bar number, and address)*:	
----	To keep other people from seeing what you entered on your form, please press the Clear This Form button at the end of the form when finished.
TELEPHONE NO.: FAX NO. *(Optional)*:	
E-MAIL ADDRESS *(Optional)*:	
ATTORNEY FOR *(Name)*:	

SUPERIOR COURT OF CALIFORNIA, COUNTY OF

STREET ADDRESS:

MAILING ADDRESS:

CITY AND ZIP CODE:

BRANCH NAME:

PETITIONER:

RESPONDENT:

REQUEST TO ENTER DEFAULT	CASE NUMBER:

1. **To the clerk:** Please enter the default of the respondent who has failed to respond to the petition.

2. A completed *Income and Expense Declaration* (form FL-150) or *Financial Statement (Simplified)* (form FL-155)
   ☐ is attached ☐ is not attached.
   A completed *Property Declaration* (form FL-160) ☐ is attached ☐ is not attached
   because *(check at least one of the following)*:
   (a) ☐   there have been no changes since the previous filing.
   (b) ☐   the issues subject to disposition by the court in this proceeding are the subject of a written agreement.
   (c) ☐   there are no issues of child, spousal, or partner support or attorney fees and costs subject to determination by the court.
   (d) ☐   the petition does not request money, property, costs, or attorney fees. (Fam. Code, § 2330.5.)
   (e) ☐   there are no issues of division of community property.
   (f) ☐   this is an action to establish parental relationship.

Date:

▶

_____   _____
(TYPE OR PRINT NAME)   (SIGNATURE OF [ATTORNEY FOR] PETITIONER)

3. **Declaration**
   a. ☐   No mailing is required because service was by publication or posting and the address of the respondent remains unknown.
   b. ☐   A copy of this *Request to Enter Default*, including any attachments and an envelope with sufficient postage, was provided to the court clerk, with the envelope addressed as follows *(address of the respondent's attorney or, if none, the respondent's last known address)*:

I declare under penalty of perjury under the laws of the State of California that the foregoing is true and correct.

Date:

▶

_____   _____
(TYPE OR PRINT NAME)   (SIGNATURE OF DECLARANT)

FOR COURT USE ONLY
☐ *Request to Enter Default* mailed to the respondent or the respondent's attorney on *(date)*:
☐ Default entered as requested on *(date)*:
☐ Default **not** entered. Reason:
Clerk, by _____ , Deputy

Page 1 of 2

Form Adopted for Mandatory Use Judicial Council of California FL-165 [Rev. January 1, 2005]	**REQUEST TO ENTER DEFAULT** **(Family Law—Uniform Parentage)**	Code of Civil Procedure, §§ 585, 587; Family Code, § 2335.5 www.courtinfo.ca.gov

Request to Enter Default

CASE NAME *(Last name, first name of each party):*	CASE NUMBER:

4. Memorandum of costs

    a. ☐ Costs and disbursements are waived.

    b. Costs and disbursements are listed as follows:

        (1) ☐ Clerk's fees .... $..............................

        (2) ☐ Process server's fees .... $..............................

        (3) ☐ Other *(specify):* .... $..............................

        .... $..............................

        .... $..............................

        .... $ _____

    TOTAL .... $..............................

    c. I am the attorney, agent, or party who claims these costs. To the best of my knowledge and belief, the foregoing items of cost are correct and have been necessarily incurred in this cause or proceeding.

I declare under penalty of perjury under the laws of the State of California that the foregoing is true and correct.

Date:

_____
      (TYPE OR PRINT NAME)

▶ _____
      (SIGNATURE OF DECLARANT)

5. Declaration of nonmilitary status. The respondent is not in the military service of the United States as defined in section 511 et seq. of the Servicemembers Civil Relief Act (50 U.S.C. Appen. § 501 et seq.), and is not entitled to the benefits of such act.

I declare under penalty of perjury under the laws of the State of California that the foregoing is true and correct.

Date:

_____
      (TYPE OR PRINT NAME)

▶ _____
      (SIGNATURE OF DECLARANT)

For your protection and privacy, please press the Clear This Form button after you have printed the form.

    Save This Form   Print This Form   Clear This Form

Declaration of Disclosure

FL-140

ATTORNEY OR PARTY WITHOUT ATTORNEY *(Name, State Bar number, and address)*:	
TELEPHONE NO.: FAX NO. :	
E-MAIL ADDRESS:	
ATTORNEY FOR *(Name)*:	

SUPERIOR COURT OF CALIFORNIA, COUNTY OF
STREET ADDRESS:
MAILING ADDRESS:
CITY AND ZIP CODE:
BRANCH NAME:

| PETITIONER: |
| RESPONDENT: |
| OTHER PARENT/PARTY: |

DECLARATION OF DISCLOSURE		CASE NUMBER:
☐ Petitioner's ☐ Preliminary		
☐ Respondent's ☐ Final		

DO NOT FILE DECLARATIONS OF DISCLOSURE OR FINANCIAL ATTACHMENTS WITH THE COURT

In a dissolution, legal separation, or nullity action, both a preliminary and a final declaration of disclosure must be served on the other party with certain exceptions. Neither disclosure is filed with the court. Instead, a declaration stating that service of disclosure documents was completed or waived must be filed with the court (see form FL-141).

- *In summary dissolution cases, each spouse or domestic partner must exchange preliminary disclosures as described in* Summary Dissolution Information *(form FL-810). Final disclosures are not required (see Family Code section 2109).*
- *In a default judgment case that is not a stipulated judgment or a judgment based on a marital settlement agreement, only the petitioner is required to complete and serve a preliminary declaration of disclosure. A final disclosure is not required of either party (see Family Code section 2110).*
- *Service of preliminary declarations of disclosure may not be waived by an agreement between the parties.*
- *Parties who agree to waive final declarations of disclosure must file their written agreement with the court (see form FL-144).*

The petitioner must serve a preliminary declaration of disclosure at the same time as the Petition or within 60 days of filing the Petition. The respondent must serve a preliminary declaration of disclosure at the same time as the Response or within 60 days of filing the Response. The time periods may be extended by written agreement of the parties or by court order (see Family Code section 2104(f)).

Attached are the following:

1. ☐ A completed *Schedule of Assets and Debts* (form FL-142) or ☐ A *Property Declaration* (form FL-160) for *(specify)*:
   ☐ Community and Quasi-Community Property ☐ Separate Property.

2. ☐ A completed *Income and Expense Declaration* (form FL-150).

3. ☐ All tax returns filed by the party in the two years before the date that the party served the disclosure documents.

4. ☐ A statement of all material facts and information regarding valuation of all assets that are community property or in which the community has an interest *(not a form)*.

5. ☐ A statement of all material facts and information regarding obligations for which the community is liable *(not a form)*.

6. ☐ An accurate and complete written disclosure of any investment opportunity, business opportunity, or other income-producing opportunity presented since the date of separation that results from any investment, significant business, or other income-producing opportunity from the date of marriage to the date of separation *(not a form)*.

I declare under penalty of perjury under the laws of the State of California that the foregoing is true and correct.

Date:

_____   _____
(TYPE OR PRINT NAME)   SIGNATURE

Page 1 of 1

Form Adopted for Mandatory Use Judicial Council of California FL-140 [Rev. July 1, 2013]	**DECLARATION OF DISCLOSURE** **(Family Law)**	Family Code, §§ 2102, 2104, 2105, 2106, 2112 *www.courts.ca.gov*

For your protection and privacy, please press the Clear This Form button after you have printed the form.   [Print this form] [Save this form]   [Clear this form]

Chapter Seven

Division of Property

Division of Property

This section of the Family Code, as well as case law, is almost as complex as custody and visitation. Oftentimes, the parties will be unwilling or unable to objectively focus on this issue. The parties may become manipulative, confrontational and deceptive when it comes to determining what is community property and, therefore, subject to division in the marital action. It will be helpful if the attorney and paralegal have a good understanding of not only the law as it relates to this subject matter, but also be able to understand financial strategies and implications, tax law, business law and entities, research, and the ability to find assets and information.

There are many rules, formulas, presumptions, as well as case law that apply to the division of property. An experienced paralegal will be a valuable asset to the legal team when working in this area of the dissolution process. Research, ferreting out information, obtaining documents and information, reviewing and summarizing the documents seem to just naturally fall into the scope of the paralegal's role. This will leave the attorney time to advocate for the client, as well as work toward a favorable resolution.

While the attorney will ultimately be responsible for making these recommendations to the client and negotiating on his or her behalf it is certainly helpful if the paralegal can grasp why the attorney is making the recommendations and especially how it will ultimately affect the client. What initially, on its face, may seem to be fair and equitable could negatively impact the client in the future and not be in their best interests at all.

The Superior Court of California has exclusive subject matter jurisdiction over the division of property in dissolutions, legal separations and annulments.

Family Code § 2550 provides as follows:

> Except upon the written agreement of the parties, or on oral stipulation of the parties in open court, or as otherwise provided in this division, in a proceeding for dissolution of marriage or for legal separation of the parties, the court shall, either in its judgment of dissolution of the marriage, in its judgment of legal separation of the parties, or at a later time if it expressly reserves jurisdiction to make such a property division, divide the community estate of the parties equally.

The above code section gives the Court a great deal of latitude. It also gives the parties the ability to be very creative in their attempt to obtain the "most favorable settlement," given each party's perspective. Most clients want to "win" and this can result in the parties becoming adversarial, even though California is clearly a *community property* state. Many of you have probably talked to someone who told you that one party took the other party "to the cleaners." Keep in mind that when you are hearing the "facts" from that perspective, you are usually only receiving part of the story. Although the Court can certainly make mistakes or a party will acquiesce in order to get a case resolved without costly litigation, there is always more than meets the eye in these situations. Since the division of community property is very clear, the court relies on the information provided by the parties, and the documentation and evidence that the law firm has obtained. These are applied to statute and case law to reach a just and equitable settlement. Thus the disclosure of all property as previously discussed is very important.

Family Code § 2010(e) gives the Court the ability to "inquire into and render any judgment and make such orders as are appropriate concerning ... the settlement of the property rights of the parties ..."

A party who wants to *win* may try to hide assets or become uncooperative when it comes to disclosing information. While this is not always the case, there may be a perception by one party that the other is not cooperating or disclosing information. However, you are going to encounter situations where a party does try to hide assets and/or information. For example:

> What happens when one party keeps large amounts of cash in a safe in the family home? Over the course of the marriage, it is going to be difficult for a spouse to keep that knowledge from the other. The "unknown" may be the amount that is actually kept in the safe, if the other spouse doesn't really have access. The party who has the cash does not provide the information about the cash in the preliminary disclosure (there is a place for cash on the Schedule of Assets & Debts). This will be a "red flag" for the other party when the cash is not listed. If you are representing that person, you can expect to receive a telephone call telling the attorney (or you as paralegal) that the spouse did not disclose the "large sums of cash" that are kept in the safe.

People have also been known to transfer assets into another person's name, although they may retain control of the asset. This is why discovery is important. If the client tells you that their spouse "keeps large sums of cash" in a safe, or that he/she received a large sum of money but doesn't know where it is, you are most likely going to have to prepare discovery documents requesting the information. As discussed in Chapter Five, Form Interrogatories are a good place to start. Send them to the person and request all of the information allowed in the form. Once the Interrogatories have been answered, you will need to review the information and let the attorney know if the answering party has failed to provide certain information or if the information leads you and the attorney to believe that there is additional information which needs to be provided. The attorney will also want to review the completed form to determine of any other information is missing or what is there does not appear to be correct. Two heads are always better than one. And, the client will also have an opportunity to see the form(s).

> For example, if a credit card statement shows a large pay off, but the checking account doesn't show that a payment of that size was made, you might wonder where the person got the money to make such a large payment. The attorney

then may want you to draft a Demand for Production requesting other specific information and/or Special Interrogatories asking specific questions as they relate to the "missing" information.

When you ask the client for property information, you need to ask for and receive **all** property information—separate, community, quasi-community property and/or a combination of separate and community property. Once you have all the information on the property, it will need to be characterized. "Does one party have a separate property interest in community property" is a frequent question that needs to be resolved. If so, what is the value of the separate property? Does it need to be professionally valued? Tracing, commingling and transmutations are related to the characterization of property, as are liability, control and management. These are all issues that an experienced paralegal will find challenging and interesting.

Marital Property

In California, community and separate property issues, date back to Spanish and Mexican laws which were adopted when California became a state in 1848. The California Constitution guaranteed the separate property rights of individuals and recognized that the legislature needed to devise a statutory scheme to define those rights and responsibilities. The statutes provided that a woman **could** own separate property. However, such separate property could be managed (or mismanaged as the case may be) by her husband. The Husband was given exclusive control and management of **all** community property.

Various laws were enacted over the years wherein the Wife's rights were expanded and which gave her greater control over her separate property. In 1860, the Supreme Court ruled in *In re Marriage of Ransom* (1860) 15 CA 322 that the court had to consider tracing and apportionment as to a Wife's separate property interest, particularly with respect to "passive incomes," such as rent and interest.

Community property rights did not begin changing until the 1950s when wives were given the right to manage and control their earnings. It wasn't until 1975 that men and women were equally given the right to manage and control community property. Is it any wonder that people hesitated to divorce prior to the 1950s?

The "grounds" of irreconcilable differences became effective in 1969.

The 1975 legislative history reflects the fundamental principle that each spouse is entitled to exercise complete management and control over all community property regardless of which spouse was responsible for acquiring the community property. The definition of community property (dating back to the late 1800s) was and remains: "property acquired by the parties during the marriage."

Family Code § 1100 et seq. *Management and Control of Marital Property* contains the concept of equal management and control over the marital property. It provides, in part, as follows:

(a) Except as provided in subdivisions (b), (c), and (d) and Sections 761 and 1103, either spouse has the management and control of the community personal property, whether acquired prior to or on or after January 1, 1975, with the like absolute power of disposition, other than testamentary, as the spouse has of the separate estate of the spouse.

The subject of community property is vast, as recognized by the size of Family Code, Division 7, Sections 2500 et seq.

For the purposes of this text we will focus on the history, rules, case law and presumptions which an average paralegal will encounter within the scope of the work in a typical family law firm. We will cover the most commonly raised issues such as the fiduciary responsibilities of spouses to one another, the characterization of community, separate and quasi-community assets and obligations, and how they are most commonly resolved during the dissolution proceeding.

Keep in mind that there are legislative changes and cases which modify and clarify some of these rules. You will need to remain vigilant through continuing education and other means to keep abreast of the changes concerning the division of property. Additionally, you must be aware that the division of property often interrelates to child and spousal support issues (such as *Duke Orders*) which, on its face, will not always appear to be a just and exactly equitable settlement. The Court will also take into account, the fact that if the parties are willing to agree, in writing, to a settlement which may not be equal, they are entitled to do so, as long as the needs of each party are adequately met and their fiduciary responsibilities are fulfilled. For the more advanced student or family law paralegal, it will be highly beneficial to have a more thorough understanding of the complexity of these issues and any recent changes. The *Rutter Group's Family Law* treatise, written by Judge William Hogoboom and Justice Donald King is an excellent resource. Additionally, the *California Family Law Practice* written by Stephen Adams and Nancy Sevitch is also an excellent reference.

As you begin the dissolution process, it is best to have a clear understanding of the definitions of community, quasi-community and separate property. This will allow the attorney, with your assistance, to determine whether property, real or personal, falls into any of those specific categories, or if the separate property has, in any way, been, transmuted or commingled with community property, or vice-versa.

Community Property

The current definition of Community Property, found in FC§ 760 is:

Except as otherwise provided by statute, all property, real or personal, wherever situated, acquired by a marriage person during the marriage while domiciled in this state is community property.

Quasi-Community Property

Quasi-marital (community) property refers to property acquired by the parties where there is a putative spouse, it also exists where the property would have been considered community if there had been a valid marriage or with property which was acquired by the parties in another state, while they were married and domiciled in that state, whether or not the state is/was a community property state, while the parties resided there.

Quasi-community property is defined in Family Code § 124 as follows:

"Quasi-community property" means all real or personal property, wherever situated, acquired before or after the operative date of this code in any of the following ways:

(a) By either spouse while domiciled elsewhere which would have been community property if the spouse who acquired the property had been domiciled in this state at the time of its acquisition.

(b) In exchange for real or personal property, wherever situated, which would have been community property if the spouse who acquired the property so exchanged had been domiciled in this date at the time of its acquisition.

Separate Property

Separate property as defined in Family Code § 770 is:

(a) Separate property of a married person includes all of the following:

(1) All property owned by the person before marriage.

(2) All property acquired by the person after marriage by gift, bequest, devise or descent.

(3) The rents, issues, and profits of the property described in this section.

(b) A married person may, without the consent of the person's spouse, convey the person's separate property.

Character: Vesting and Title of Property

Once you receive the asset information, the *character, vesting and title* of the property should immediately reviewed.

Vesting is generally defined as the **actual** ownership or the right to receive property that has accrued to the benefit of the individual who is designated as the recipient. In most cases, vesting will apply to employee benefits. Many of these types of benefits will have a named beneficiary. It will be necessary to determine if the employee is **vested** in the plan. You will also want to determine who is the beneficiary of assets such as employee benefits, insurance policies, IRAs, and mutual fund accounts, all of which typically have a named beneficiary.

Title is generally defined as the way the documents of ownership reflect who owns the property. Examples of *title* are: joint tenancy, tenancy in common, tenancy in the entirety, community property, or separate property. Real property deeds are identified by the title, as are motor vehicle registrations. Sometimes "title" and "vesting" will be used interchangeably.

One of the most common pieces of property, or asset, which may have both community and separate property characteristics may be a piece of real property, specifically the family home. An excellent example is as follows:

One of the parties owns a home prior to the marriage, which was purchased using that person's separate funds. Once the parties marry, the mortgage payments are made from the joint (community) bank account. After the parties separate, any payments made by one party, will be considered separate property.

Given the above scenario, it will be necessary to trace the separate and community property interests of each party by applying the above definitions and specific case law to the value of each party's contribution in order to determine the community interest as well as the person's *separate property interest* in the family home. The definitions and application of these concepts will be discussed later in the chapter under Dividing Property.

It is very important to determine the characterization of the property before the attorney can try to propose or the parties negotiate a settlement. It will also be necessary to be familiar with the presumptions concerning the characterization of property. As previously indicated and as will follow in the next section regarding Declarations of Disclosure, it is very important to obtain an accurate list of all of the couple's property, as well as their debts or liabilities.

Once you have obtained a list of the assets and debts, you will need to obtain copies of any documents which reference these items so that you can accurately determine or confirm the *character* (the manner in which title is held) of the asset.

The property could include, but is not limited to:

real property (vacant or improved)

automobiles, boats and trailers, recreational vehicles, airplanes

furniture, furnishings and appliances

bank, credit union, savings and CD accounts

money

stocks (including options), bonds and mutual funds

jewelry and artwork

retirement benefits (pension, IRAs, 401(k), 403(b) and union benefits)

intellectual property

business and business interest

insurance

promissory notes

earnings (including accumulated vacation and sick leave)

Presumptions of Title

California laws *presume* that if the title to the property is held in *joint tenancy* that the property is *owned* by the joint tenants, with a right to survivorship. Common law, and associated case law, have long held that there is a rebuttable presumption that unless evidence is provided to the contrary, property held in joint tenancy reflects the ownership of the property and will determine how the property should be divided (as community property) in the dissolution proceeding.

Property held (titled) by "Jane Doe, as her sole and separate property" indicates the rebuttable presumption is that the property is **owned** by Jane Doe, even if community funds were used to purchase the property.

Property held as follows: Jane Doe, a married woman, as her sole and separate property will also lead to the presumption that the property is **owned** by Jane Doe.

Family Code § 2581 states:

For the purpose of the division of property in a dissolution of marriage or legal separation of the parties, property acquired by the parties during marriage in joint form, including property held in tenancy in common, joint tenancy, or tenancy in the entirety, or as community property, is presumed to be community property. This presumption is a presumption affecting the burden of proof and may be rebutted by either of the following:

(a) A clear statement in the deed or other documentary evidence of title by which the property is acquired that the property is separate property and not community property.

(b) Proof that the parties have made a **written** agreement that the property is separate property.

Family Code § 2640 states:

(a) "Contributions to the acquisition of the property", as used in this section, including down payments, payments for improvements, and payments that reduce the principal loan used to finance the purchase or improvement of the property, but do not include payments of interest on the loan or payments made for maintenance, insurance, or taxation of the property.

(b) In the division of the community estate under this division unless a party has made a written waiver of the right to reimbursement or has signed a writing that has the effect of a waiver, the party shall be reimbursed for the party's contributions to the acquisition of the property to the extent the party traces the contributions to a separate property source. The amount reimbursed shall be without interest or adjustment for change in monetary values and shall not exceed the net value of the property at the time of division.

(c) A party shall be reimbursed for the party's separate property contributions to the acquisition of property of the other spouse's separate property estate during the marriage, unless there has been a transmutation in writing pursuant to Chapter 5 (commencing with Section 850) of Part 2 of Division 4, or a written waiver of the right to reimbursement. The amount reimbursed shall be without interest or adjustment for change in monetary values and may not exceed the net value of the property at the time of the division.

In re Marriage of Lucas (1980) 27 C3d 808, 166 CR 853, established the standard for rebutting the presumption that characterization of the property is community if the title to the property is held in *joint tenancy*. The standard established in *Lucas* requires that evidence of an *agreement* between the spouses must be provided as "*clear and convincing evidence*" in order to establish ownership which is different than what is reflected in the title. The agreement may be oral, but there must be *evidence* and it must be *clear and convincing.*

Civil Code § 4800.1 was also applied to the rebuttable standard to written and oral evidence of an agreement between the parties. However, *In re Marriage of Buol* (1985) 39 C3d 751, 218 CR 31, the court clarified the acquisition of property, as well as property that is *converted* into joint ownership after the date of acquisition. When applying *Buol* you will note that the presumption applies to all types of property and not just real estate. However, the presumption may only be applied during a dissolution or legal separation. Any presumptions with respect to title and ownership upon the **death** of a spouse, or any other joint tenant, will be governed by governed by *Civil Code §682.1* (effective 7/1/2001), *Civil Code §4800.1* and the California Probate Code.

Family Code §2640(c) became operative on January 1, 2005. This statute addresses and clarifies reimbursement of separate property contributions to a spouse's separate property, especially as it relates to "written agreements" and "waiver of rights" to be reimbursed. Specifically, a party **must** be reimbursed for separate property contributions to the other spouse's separate property made during the marriage, "absent written transmutation or waiver of rights" to reimbursement. The statute further indicates that the reimbursement will not include interest or an adjustment for changes in value, nor may the reimbursement exceed the "net value" of the property.

However, the court ruled in 2011 that although a widow was not entitled to her late husband's separate property business, she is entitled to a portion of that part of its increased value that resulted from her husband's community property efforts under FC§1101(b). This is an application of the *Pereira* case law which will be discussed in greater detail later in the chapter. The case that applied *Pereira* in this case is *Patrick v. Alacer Corp.* (2011) 201 CA4th 1326, 136 CR3d 669.

You might then ask the question: What happens if a spouse dies while a dissolution is pending?

> Death terminates a marriage. Therefore, if the death occurs during the pendency of the action, and before the Judgment is entered, the question is moot. The Court has no jurisdiction over the marriage as the marital status has been terminated by death. The property will be disbursed as set forth in the Probate Code.

It is **very** important that married couples carefully consider the manner in which they hold title to property (real and personal). If they intend to keep certain property separate from each other, then the title should be maintained as the person's separate property. In the event they need to place the property in joint tenancy for financial or probate estate reasons, a **written** transmutation agreement should be prepared and executed. This is also a reason why people create pre-nuptial or post-nuptial agreements. These agreements, which will be discussed in Chapter Eleven, memorialize the party's intentions as to separate and community property.

There are also many variations as to how people can transfer, transmute, and commingle separate and community assets. Such actions will require that the title of the property be *traced* through the various transfers and resulting transmutations of the property in order to rebut the presumption that the marital property is either community or that one or the other party may have a separate interest in the property.

As a paralegal, you should be aware of the various entities that may have information available on the title. However, with the changes to some privacy laws, the ability to obtain confidential information may be hampered; it is available but you need to be aware that it may take some additional time to get certain types of information if the opposing party/counsel has not be forthcoming in disclosing the necessary information. Additionally, the paralegal may play a part in transferring the title upon reaching a property settlement once the assets and related encumbrances have been assigned.

Some of these entities include:

County Recorders—real property

Department of Motor Vehicles—Autos, Boats, Trailers, Recreational Vehicles

Department of Housing—Mobile/Modular Homes

Employers, Unions, and Pension Plans—All matters relating to employee benefits

Insurance Companies

Financial Institutions (Checking, Savings, CD, Mutual Funds, and Loans)

Investment Companies and Brokerage Houses

The above is not an exhaustive list but will give you some idea of the various entities you may have to contact to obtain information. The above list will also serve as a reminder that you will need to remind the client, at the conclusion of the dissolution, that they need to contact these entities and change the title/vesting on the assets and/or change the designated beneficiary. This will be discussed further in Chapter Ten.

As discussed above and in Chapter 5, "Discovery," it may be necessary to subpoena documents, send Interrogatories or take the Deposition of the spouse in order to obtain more information or acquire copies of the assets.

Valuation of Property

Once you have obtained the necessary information, the next step will be to determine the value of the assets. Liabilities are more straightforward in as they can usually be evidenced by an invoice or statement which was issued nearest the date of separation or agreed-upon alternate date.

There are many ways by which to value assets. Some of them will be determined by the type of asset. There are individuals and companies who offer their services in valuing assets. Some of these companies may specialize in particular types of assets, while others may offer a wide range of services.

One of the greatest assets you can offer the firm is to keep a database or some other reference source of information at your finger tips should the attorney need this information. As a family law paralegal, I keep a file of names of companies, along with information about the company or individual, including their resume, services provided, and references, if necessary. Included in each company's folder, are the names of previous cases for which we used this person's services, the forms that were required to be submitted (if any) or the types of information that the company will need (which varies by type of asset), the rates charged for valuations, and any other pertinent information.

If you have such information readily available when it is requested, this makes you look really good to the client and the attorney.

Determining a valuation date is important. In most cases, the property will be valued as of the date of separation. The parties can agree to another valuation date, if they choose. However, they will have to mutually agree, usually in writing, to an alternate date to be used for valuation purposes. Alternatively, if the matter is contested, the property will likely be valued (or re-valued) as of the trial date.

As defined above, community property is that property acquired during marriage. Thus, the person valuing the asset will need to know the date of marriage, the date the property was acquired, as well as the date of separation. Always make sure that the evaluator has experience with the type of asset(s) that the client needs to have evaluated.

In the event that one party is asserting a separate property interest, it will be necessary to provide information about the date the person acquired the property, what was paid for the property on that date, and any improvements made to the property before the marriage. There will then essentially be three valuation dates: date of acquisition, date of marriage and date of separation (or alternative agreed-upon post-separation date). Note that the valuation date closest to the date of trial must be used when/if there is a trial. In Re Marriage of Sherman (2005) 133 Cal.App.4th 795, 35 Cal.Rptr.3d 137 states at pages 800–801, that "when an asset increases in value from nonpersonal factors such as inflation or market fluctuations, vernally it is fair that both parties share in the increased values." Likewise, in today's economy losses must also be jointly shared.

If there is a business involved in the marital proceeding, you are most likely going to want to have the business valued by a forensic "expert" in that arena. A business valuation will include, but is not limited to, cash on hand, receivables and payables, tools of the trade and/or equipment, as well as the *goodwill* of the business.

Retirement, pension and employee benefits should be valued by an "actuary" who is an expert in valuing these types of plans. There is some very specific case law with respect to the division of these types of assets. The actuary will need to be well-versed in both the California statutes and the case law that applies. You will also want to provide the actuary with any written information from the pension plan, such as statements, benefit handbooks, etc. Keep in mind that the attorney won't want to have someone who specializes in valuing custom automobiles value a pension or employee benefit plan. Chapter Eight contains more information regarding the division of pension plans.

There is a great deal of additional information that may be requested by an evaluator. It is always best, prior to hiring the evaluator, to have them send or fax you a list of the information that will be needed, along with rates and fees. This saves time and allows you to give the "package" to the client and/or to sit down with the client and obtain the information.

Some assets such as: bank, savings, mutual fund accounts, insurance (whole life where there is cash value), and promissory notes can be quite easily valued. Bank, savings and mutual fund accounts issue monthly or quarterly statements which reflect the actual value of those assets. Insurance and promissory notes may contain an amortization schedule which reflects the payments made against the principal, including interest if applicable, and showing the monthly value of the asset. In the event the client does not have an amortization schedule you may be able to obtain one from the company. If, in the case of a promissory note, the note-holder is an individual, the attorney (or the paralegal) may be able to prepare an amortization schedule using spreadsheet-type software.

Unless the vehicle is unique, valuing automobiles and some other types of motorized vehicles such as boats and recreational vehicles have become quite easy these days. In your case information, the "client" and her spouse possess standard type vehicles. The value range of these vehicles can be easily obtained by knowing the year, make, model, miles and condition. You simply go to a company, such as the Kelly Blue Book website, enter the information and obtain a fairly accurate value. Although the value may not be exact, it will be useful for the purposes of initial settlement discussions. Kelly Blue Book values are also highly recognized by most courts.

The attorney will be in a position to discuss the division of property once the vesting and title to property has been determined, the property has been valued and any applicable property has been traced. This is also the time to decide if a settlement offer will be presented and/or trial will be requested. The updated preliminary or final Declarations of Disclosure should be completed and served on the other party (or the attorney of record) at this point.

Depending upon the size of the martial estate, there may be numerous ways of dividing the property.

Declarations of Disclosure

Family Code §§ 2100–2113 requires each party to serve *preliminary declarations of disclosure* or in the case of a default judgment, the Petitioner is required to comply with the disclosure rules. Specifically, FC§ 721 states that each party has a **fiduciary duty** as to (1) all activities affecting assets or liabilities of the other party from the date that a binding resolution of their disposition is reached until they are actually distributed; and (2) all issues relating to child or spousal support and attorney fees, from the date of separation until the date of a binding resolution of all issues relating to support and fees. Family Code §§ 1100–1103 contains the definitions for the rights and obligations of spouses to each other as to the management and control over the marital property.

The California Legislature determined that certain protections are required for the parties with respect to disclosure of their marital assets and debts. Family Code § 2100 became effective January 1, 1993. This statute established very strict and specific requirements as to the disclosure of **all** property including community and quasi-community assets as well as all liabilities.

Family Code § 2100, is as follows:

The Legislature finds and declares the following:

(a) It is the policy of the State of California (1) to marshal, preserve, and protect community and quasi community assets and liabilities that exist at the date of separation so as to avoid dissipation of the community estate prior to distribution; (2) to ensure fair and sufficient child and spousal support awards, and (3) to achieve a division of community and quasi community assets and liabilities on the dissolution of marriage or nullity of marriage or legal separation of the parties as provided under California law.

(b) Sound public policy further favors the reduction of the adversarial nature of marital dissolution and the attendant costs by fostering full disclosure and cooperative discovery.

(c) In order to promote this public policy, a full and accurate disclosure of all assets and liabilities in which one or both parties have or may have an interest must be made in the early stages of a proceeding for dissolution of marriage or legal separation of the parties, regardless of the characterization as community or separate, together with a disclosure of all income and expenses of the parties. Moreover, each party has a continuing duty to update and augment that disclosure to the extent there have been any material changes so that at the time the parties enter into an agreement for the resolution of any of these issues, or at the time of trial on the issues, each party will have a full and complete knowledge of the relevant underlying facts as is reasonably possible under the circumstances of the case.

Family Code § 2102 requires the parties to disclose any activities that may affect the assets and debts. Such activities may include investment opportunities, business opportunities and activities, or any other type of income-producing activity on the part of either spouse. The parties have a duty to continue to disclose, update and augment the disclosures if there are any material changes which occur after the date of separation and up to the time the property is distributed. (*Family Code § 2102(a)*.) The party may simply amend the preliminary disclosure or serve an updated Schedule of Assets and Debts and/or Income & Expense Declarations. A party may also be able to complete and serve a simplified *Financial Statement* (FL-155), provided the party qualifies under the requirements stated on both the form and in the form's instructions. As set forth in Section 2100(c) (above), whenever there is a material change, there is a "duty to update and augment that disclosure" up until the time of a written agreement or trial.

The preliminary declaration of disclosure (Form FL-140) and required forms (Income & Expense Declaration and Schedule of Assets & Debts) should be served concurrently with the Petition or within sixty (60) days of filing the Petition (FL§ 2104 as amended in 2013) and as previously discussed. (A separate Proof of Service by Mail (FL-335) needs to be used for proper service.) The paralegal should therefore work with the client and the attorney to collect the information on separate property and community and quasi-community property as early as possible in the proceedings. Of note, is the additional requirement that the declarant's tax returns for the previous two (2) years be included in the preliminary declaration of disclosure.

The paralegal should have a clear understanding of the code sections which provide a strict and detailed description of the disclosure of the property owned or controlled by each party. It was the Legislature's intent to minimize the party's motivation and ability to hide, undervalue, or by any other means keep the other from having "full disclosure" to any and all assets to which they may be entitled. This is an area of the process where a paralegal can be an invaluable asset to the firm. Diligence in gathering and reporting the initial disclosures, a well as supplemental documents cannot be overstated.

The preliminary declaration of disclosure is prepared under penalty of perjury. It must be accompanied by both a completed Schedule of Assets and Debts and a completed Income & Expense Declarations. The Declaration and accompanying documents are served on the Respondent and/or exchanged if the Respondent has filed a Response. The *preliminary* declaration is **not** filed with the court, unless the Court orders that it be filed. However a proof of service indicating that the disclosure documents were served must be filed with the court.

A pleading form can be sent to the other party advising of the statutory requirements. (Appendix 7A-1) A letter may also be sent to the client requesting the disclosure information and advising them of the statutory requirements and the need to provide the information to the attorney and to disclose same to the other party. (Appendix 7A-2).

The Schedule of Assets and Debts should contain as much specific information as is known to the client. He or she must declare, to the best of his/her knowledge, a description of the asset and any liability on that asset. For instance, real property information should include the address and parcel number, if known, the estimated fair market value, as well as the mortgage or any other liens against the property. Please note, however, that it is not imperative at the preliminary stage of the proceeding that all property be precisely valued. For the purposes of disclosure at this stage, you may work with the client and a realtor to obtain recent "comparables" for properties in the neighborhood which have recently been listed for sale or sold or by researching other and similar types of property on the Internet. You can often find vehicles (automobiles, trailers, boats), tools, collectibles, and other items for sale, which may give the client an idea of the approximate value of the assets.

It may be difficult at this preliminary stage for the client to obtain certain types of information such as loan balances, values of insurance policies, annuities, investments, etc. if they are not in possession of the names, account numbers or passwords required to obtain the information. These documents are often the basis for determining what additional information you may need to get from the other party or for which you will have to prepare a subpoena, as discussed in Chapter Five—Hearings, Discovery and Disclosure.

At this stage, each party must also serve an Income & Expense Declaration (I&E) on the other party. The exception would be if this had been recently served and there were no changes. For instance, if an I&E was filed and served along with the Petition and a Request for Order and provided that the client has not recently had employment terminated or began working (change in circumstances), then it is not necessary to prepare a new I&E to be served with the preliminary declaration of disclosure. A copy of the recently filed I&E can be attached.

It is critical, even in uncontested cases, that the parties comply with the preliminary declarations of disclosure. Family Code § 2107(d) provides that if a court enters a judgment where the parties have not complied with the disclosure requirements, then the judgment must be set aside.

In re Marriage of Brewer & Federici (2001) 93 CA4th 1334, 113 CR2d 849, found that "a spouse who fails to disclose information when he or she is in a superior position to obtain information and records from which an asset can be valued, breached the continuing duty to update and augment information." In that case, Wife stated that the value of her pension plan was "unknown" which constituted a breach of fiduciary duty. Therefore, if the Respondent's Default will be taken, the Petitioner is **required** to comply with the preliminary declarations of disclosure and may waive the final disclosure by virtue of the Respondent's non-appearance.

The Petitioner must declare these facts, under penalty of perjury, on the Declaration for Default or Uncontested Dissolution or Legal Separation. (Form FL-170).

Family Code § 2107(d) was added in 2001 based on *In re Marriage of McLaughlin* (2000) 82 CA 4th 327, 98 CR2d 136, wherein the Court ruled that "failure to comply is *not* harmless error" to enter the judgment without complying with the disclosure rules, unless prejudice can be shown. The legislature enacted the disclosure rules so that judgments would not be set aside when the party(ies) did not disclose all of their income, assets and debts. *McLaughlin* thus created a loophole, which the legislature closed by creating Family Code § 2107(d). As indicated In Chapter 5, with the amending of FC§ 2104, FC§ 2107 was also amended to address non-compliance with the required disclosure of property. Subsequently, the Judicial Council created a new form to be used to remedy the non-compliance as previously discussed.

The parties are also required to serve a *final* declaration of disclosure when they will/ have entered into a settlement agreement which addresses property and support or if the matter has been set for trial. If the matter will go to trial, the parties **must** prepare and serve a Final Declaration of Disclosure, an updated Schedule of Assets and Debts with valuations and supporting documentation and an updated Income & Expense Declaration at least forty-five (45) days prior to trial. **All** of these documents **must** be filed with the court. The attorney representing the party may sign the Declaration Regarding

Service of Final Declaration of Disclosure, however, the client, must sign the Declaration of Disclosure and all attachments such as the Schedule of Assets & Debts and the Income & Expense Declarations.

Effective January 1, 2005, a party who is providing information of a personal and/or confidential nature (such as date of birth, social security number, and account number(s)) may request that the court allow the redaction of that information. (FC§ 2024.6.) An Ex Parte Application & Order to Seal Financial Forms (FL-316) may be completed. The information must be provided to the opposing party. However, that code section, with respect to sealing financial documents was found to be unconstitutional in 2006, *In Re Marriage of Burkle* (2006) 135 Cal.App.4th 1045, 37 Cal.Rptr.3d 805. The attorney will need to review any subsequent challenges to this statute and case law to determine whether a client can request that the documents be redacted and/or sealed. Confidentiality is one reason why, until trial, this information is not provided to the court, rather is only exchanged between the parties. Once submitted to the court, the information, unless the Application to Seal is submitted and approved, is public information.

The parties may specifically waive service of the *final declaration of disclosure*, **provided they have complied with the preliminary disclosures**, and where there has been no material change. Regardless of whether service is waived, a *Declaration regarding Service of Final Declaration of Disclosure* (FL-141) must be completed, served, and filed.

To waive the disclosure within their Marital Settlement Agreement as of January 1, 2002, the parties must both sign, under penalty of perjury, a separate *Stipulation and Waiver of Final Declaration of Disclosure* (Form FL-144), pursuant to Family Code § 2105. This method may only be used in matters where a Response has been filed and the parties have reached an agreement. The Stipulation and Waiver cannot be utilized when the Respondent's Default is being taken or the matter is proceeding to trial.

Dividing Property

Now that you have a feel for the manner by which property may be owned and the process used to determine the value, it is time to review further some of the statutes and case law which may be applied when determining separate property interest asserted in the community assets, as well as reimbursements or credits which may be due the respective party.

This is the time when the issues truly become complex and the parties will have the most difficulty in being objective about how the property will be divided. While there may be a sense of California being a community state, and therefore, property will be divided "50/50," there are also financial and psychological values placed on the assets, which often make it difficult for spouses to be objective. We will also review what is truly "community." For example wedding rings and other jewelry, a car, or other tangible property given for a birthday or an anniversary, a monetary gift given by one of the party's parent(s), may be perceived as gifts and therefore as separate property. But are they really? Your instructor will discuss these concepts with you in greater detail.

The division of property is essentially a business transaction. However, the attorney will often have a difficult time trying to convey that concept to the client when the client has an emotional attachment or when the person feels he/she is "getting the short end of the stick" in financial terms.

We will also return to the discussion of transmutation, commingling and tracing of separate property, as you learn to apply the various statutes and case law to the division of property. This will enable you to have a clearer concept of the permeation of property.

Chapter Two contained a basic definition of separate property. California Family Code § 770 contains the definition of separate property of a married person, as follows:

(a) Separate property of a married person includes all of the following:

(1) All property owned by the person before marriage.

(2) All property owned by the person after marriage by gift, bequest, devise, or descent.

(3) The rents, issues, and profits of the property described in this section.

Transmutation, Commingling, Tracing of Property

Transmutation

Transmutation is the result of an agreement, between the parties, to change the status of an asset from either separate to community or community to separate property. Family Code § 850 provides as follows:

Subject to Family Code §§ 851 to 853, inclusive, married persons may, by agreement or transfer, with or without consideration, do any of the following:

(a) Transmute community property to separate property of either spouse.

(b) Transmute separate property of either spouse to community property.

(c) Transmute separate property of one spouse to separate property of the other spouse.

As previously indicated, oral agreements must be proven. Family Code § 852 was enacted to disallow an oral agreement, which is what is referred to as a "pillow talk" agreement with respect to real and personal property. Effective on the date of enactment this code section states:

(a) A transmutations of real or personal property that is made, joined in, consented to, or accepted by the spouse whose interest in the property is adversely affected.

Thus "pillow talk" agreements after that date are not allowed, but agreements made prior to the enactment of the statute are acceptable upon proof. The Court confirmed Family Code § 853 in 2005, *In Re Marriage of Benson* (2005) 36 CA4th 1096, 32 Cal.Rptr.3d 471, wherein they held that an "oral bargain to transmute community property is an inadequate substitute for 'express declaration.'"

As previously indicated, Family Code § 2640(c) became operative January 1, 2005, which states that separate property contributions to the other spouse's separate property is subject to reimbursement regardless of having a written agreement.

The legislature further clarified the transmutation and characterization of "personal" gifts such as jewelry, in FC§ 852(c), which states:

(c) This section does not apply to a gift between spouses of clothing, wearing apparel, jewelry, or other tangible articles of a personal nature that is used solely or principally by the spouse to whom the gift is made and that is not substantial in value taking into account the circumstances of the marriage.

The above section, when applied to the type of gifts given to a spouse on birthdays, anniversaries, and other special days clearly indicates that these items are considered gifts and **not** community property. The key to this section is the term "substantial in value." Thus most earrings, necklaces, and bracelets, the value of which is, for example, a few hundred dollars, would be the separate property of the spouse who received them.

> If a Wife "buys" a new Mercedes Benz for her Husband as an anniversary gift and the parties combined net income is $80,000 per year, this item is clearly **not** a gift. The car would be considered a community asset because it has "substantial value," especially when compared to the party's economic means.

Another key to determining whether the "gift" is or is not community property is if the community assets will have any continued contribution to the item. In this instance, although the Wife gave the vehicle to the Husband, she also went to the dealership and made the choice of make and model. Most likely she also made a down-payment using funds from a community bank account, and the successive monthly loan payments would probably be made out of the community checking account.

> On the other hand, if you had the same scenario and the party's combined annual income was $2 million per year, then presumably, you would have an easier job of convincing the court the vehicle was a gift.

The court still has the discretion of applying FC§ 842 in determining whether the asset was a gift, if the property was transmuted to separate property, or if it should still be considered community property. A vehicle is a wonderful example to use in this scenario, because the Court will also apply the concept of "used solely or principally by the spouse to whom the gift was made." Regardless of the annual income of the parties, if the vehicle was a high end Sport Utility Vehicle purchased primarily to transport the family, the children and their friends, to events, activities and on vacations, the Court may interpret this to mean it is a "family" car and not used primarily by one spouse. A BMW Sport Coupe (two-seater, convertible) would more likely be considered a vehicle purchased for primary use solely by one spouse, provided the income level is high enough to make such a gift or the spouse has separate property from which such a purchase could be made.

In Re Marriage of Starkman (2005) 129 Ca4th 659, 28 Cal.Rptr.3d 639, held that the transfer of separate property to a revocable trust "with boilerplate language" that transfers all property to community property is not sufficient to transmute the property from separate to community.

Some parties will find that due to the previous financial difficulties of one spouse, their joint credit is affected. Consider the following scenario:

> Wife has very poor credit from previous marriage. (She may have even filed bankruptcy.) Wife and new spouse want to purchase a home. New Spouse has excellent credit. They contact a lender to be "pre-qualified" for a loan. The lender tells them that because of Wife's poor credit rating, they will only qualify for a lesser value home or that the interest rate will be higher. However, because of New Spouse's income and great credit, he can qualify for the home they really want and at an excellent rate. The parties discuss the financial ramifications and decide that the loan will be taken solely in New Spouse's name. Because New

Spouse is "financing" the home, his name will be placed on the deed, during the transaction. Wife's name will not be on the deed, but the parties have agreed that once the loan transaction is complete and the deed recorded, they will have a new deed prepared, put both of their names on the *title*, and have the new deed recorded. The loan transaction is complete and the deed is recorded. It is now five years later and the parties are divorcing. They failed to have a new deed prepared and recorded with both of their names on the *title*.

Based on what you know about the presumption of title and transmutation—Who owns the property? What other information might you need to make any separate or community property determinations? (Hint: consider the down payment and subsequent payments of principal, interest, insurance and taxes.)

Tracing

The above scenario will lead to tracing. The Wife is most likely to argue that her name "should have been on the deed," that her name was simply omitted because of the financial implications, and that it was always their "intention" that the home be community property. New Spouse contends that only his name was on the deed, therefore, the property is his.

Was the property transmuted? If so, how?

Does the ownership of the property need to be traced?

Conversely, the concept of tracing will also allow a party to rebut the presumption that property acquired during the marriage is community in nature or that a portion of the asset is separate in nature and that the "ratio" of that party's separate interest in the community asset must be allocated. The determination of a person's separate interest in a community asset, along with any increase in value of that asset, is referred to as *apportionment*.

It should be fairly clear that transmutations of property should be made in some form of written instrument such as an agreement, or a pre-nuptial or a post-nuptial agreement, etc. This is to prevent transmutation and commingling, without informed consent, which could lead to litigation and the need to trace the (separate and/or community) ownership of the assets.

In general, tracing will require a determination of the source of the funds used in acquiring and/or maintaining the asset. Depending upon the determination of a separate property contribution to the community, it may be necessary to calculate whether there was any appreciation on the separate property, if there was appreciation upon the part of the community, or both.

The following are some different scenarios resulting in different characterizations of separate property contributions:

1) One party owns a vehicle prior to marriage. About six months after the marriage, the party sells the vehicle and places the money in a money market account solely in his/her name. This property is the separate property of that individual.

2) One party owns a house prior to marriage. One year after the marriage, the parties decide to remodel the family home. They refinance the property and take out a home equity loan. The separate property interest, and appreciated value, will have to be traced and apportioned.

3) Post-separation, one party makes payments on the party's community credit cards. That person is entitled to reimbursement for paying the other party's (50%) of the community debt.

Each of the scenarios will be discussed below in greater detail relative to the various case laws decisions. As you can probably see there is great potential for "commingling" or unknowingly "transmuting" separate and community property. There is also a great deal of case law which is used by the Court as a guideline in apportioning the separate and community values.

The following are other examples of how married couples may easily commingle funds or assets, which could initially be characterized as separate property.

(1) One party receives an inheritance and places the money in a joint savings account or uses the funds to make improvements on real property;

(2) When separate property is sold and the proceeds placed in any community asset, without executing an agreement;

(3) When a party receives any kind of "lump sum" settlement for a personal injury, worker's compensation, employee benefit(s);

(4) When one party's parent(s) offer money for a down-payment or purchase of any type of property, without obtaining a promissory note or a specific notation that the "gift" is only to their child and not a gift to the married couple.

Assets to which a party may assert a separate or community interest, include the following:

(A) Personal Injury Awards. Family Code § 2603 states as follows:

(a) Community estate personal injury damages as used in this section means all money or other property received or to be received by a person in full satisfaction of a judgment for damages for the person's personal injuries or pursuant to an agreement for the settlement or compromise of a claim for the damages, if the cause of action for the damages arose during the marriage but is not separate property as described in Section 781, unless the money or other property has been commingled with other assets of the community estate.

(b) Community estate personal injury damages shall be assigned to the party who suffered the injuries unless the court, after taking into account the economic condition and needs of each party, the time that has elapsed since the recovery of the damages or the accrual of the cause of action, and all other facts of the case, determine that the interest of justice require another disposition. In such a case, the community estate personal injury damages shall be assigned to the respective parties in such proportions as the court determines to be just, except that at least one-half of the damages shall be assigned to the party who suffered the injuries.

(B) Employment Benefits. Employment benefits are comprised of many different forms of compensation: earnings, deferred compensation, pension/retirement plans, vacation pay, bonuses, stock options, and other "fringe benefits."

I encourage you to review FC§§ 2600-2604 as they relate to "Special Rules for Division of Community Estate" to see some of the other ways the court may apply the statutes diving property. Specifically, one of the newest applications relates to Domestic Violence judgments. The following is one excerpt:

FC§ 2603.5. The court may, if there is a judgment for civil damages for an act of domestic violence perpetrated by one spouse against the other spouse, enforce that judgment against the abusive spouse's share of community property, if a proceeding for dissolution of marriage or legal separation of the parties is pending prior to the entry of final judgment.

As defined by *Black's Law Dictionary* earnings are "equivalent to income" and are considered to be the "fruit or reward of labor; the fruits of the proper skill, experience and industry; the gains of a person derived from his services or labor without the aid of capital ..."

California Courts have long held that all earnings or compensation earned as a result of services performed, if performed during the marriage, are community property.

Income derived from ownership of a business or as major a shareholder of a corporation is not considered earnings because the capital or the accumulations of the business or corporation, are usually reinvested in the business. However, Accounts Receivable, are most often considered earnings. If the business owner, or the corporate shareholder receives a salary, then that person's salary is considered compensation. There are always variations and exceptions to these rules. Should you find that the client owns a business or is a sole or the primary shareholder in a corporation, additional research on the applicable case law will need to be done. A 2011 probate case which cited FC§ 1101 speaks to this application. The *Patrick* case, which cited *Pereira* (discussed later in this chapter) that addresses the application of personal efforts used to increase community assets.

Pension and retirement benefits, deferred compensation, and vacation pay are all considered earnings as they are "deferred" earnings or compensation that will be paid later. Bonuses, are also considered community property, even if they aren't paid until after the date of separation, as long as they were accumulated during the marriage.

As a family law paralegal, you should become familiar with the different types of plans and retirement benefits. Most will fall into two categories: defined contribution plans or defined benefit plans. You will also need to be familiar with whether an employee contributes (along with the employer) to the plan or if the employee has to be *vested* in the plan in order to receive any compensation upon retirement. In most cases, there is a presumption that any and all pension and retirement benefits accumulated during the marriage are community property.

As a paralegal, you will also need to make sure that the pension or retirement plan is *joined* as previously discussed in Chapter Two. You will also need to make sure that any documents subsequent to the division of community interest in the plan be prepared. Domestic Relations Orders (DROs) will be discussed in more detail in Chapter Ten.

Most pension and retirement plans will be divided based on the "time rule." The time rule is generally defined as: one-half the value of the community asset which is based on the date of marriage (or employment) to the date of separation. If one or both parties have pension plans ("the Plan"), and they have decided to simply divide the Plan(s) based on the time rule, it will not be necessary to have the Plan(s) valued. It will, however, be necessary to *join* the respective Plans. This will essentially delay the distribution of this asset until the respective party retires. At the time of retirement, the Plan Administrator will make the appropriate divisions based on the "time rule," and each party will receive their share through the Plan.

An alternative to the time rule is that the employee spouse retains all of his or her interest in the pension, in exchange for or by "buying out" the non-employee spouse. This will require that the Plan be valued to be able to determine what asset(s) or the amount of "buy-out" by the employee spouse for the community property interest of the non-employee spouse. This is a very complicated valuation, and only an expert should be retained to make such valuations.

More information regarding the dividing of pension/retirement plans will be discussed in Chapter 10.

(C) Disability Pay. Generally defined as compensation for income lost by a diminished ability to earn, inability to perform job functions, or premature retirement.

It is very clear that any disability paid post-separation is that person's separate property. It is less clear as to the community interest in disability pay during marriage. The Court has the discretion to decide if the disability pay is earnings and compensation and thus community property or if disability pay should be considered a personal injury settlement, in which case, it will usually be considered separate property regardless of the date of injury. The Court often considers whether the disabled spouse received a "lump sum" cash settlement, which is to compensate the disabled employee for their inability to work and/or achieve the same income they would have if they had continued to be able to work at that job. That portion may likely not be considered community property.

(D) Gifts and Inheritances: Family Code § 770(a)(2), states: that property received by "gift, bequest, devise, or descent" constitutes separate property. A gift is something that is given or transferred to a person without *compensation* or receiving anything in return. An inheritance is a "gift" that is made subsequent to a death. A gift can be made to a spouse, as previously discussed. In most cases, however, the issue considered under this code section are gifts given by third parties to one or both of the spouses. See the following examples:

1) Wedding gift—owned 50/50 by each party; community property. (Although some parties will argue that gifts from "their" friends and family were gifts intended specifically for that person—it is still a community gift.)

2) Gift from an employer—may actually be a "bonus" or reward and be considered community property.

3) Gift of $10,000 payable to John & Jane Doe from Jane's parent(s).

It is often necessary to learn the intent of the person making the gift. Was the gift intended for only one spouse? Was it clearly stated? For example was the check in example three made out solely to John Doe and did it say gift to John Doe, or was it made out to John & Jane Doe and say for "down-payment" on home.

Oftentimes parents of one or both parties will "loan" money to their children. Many times, the parents will anticipate "forgiving" the loan at some point. In other words, they will never press for repayment and the money is most likely classified as a *gift*. However, what if the money was truly a loan and a Promissory Note was executed? Was the Note signed by both parties making them equally responsible for payment of the loan? In this situation, the intent is clear.

(E) Education and Training Contributions. Family Code § 2641 provides for the community reimbursement for all contributions made to the education and training of a party that has substantially enhanced that party's earning capacity.

This means that if one spouse continues to work and support a spouse (and family if they have one) while the other spouse goes to school to receive an advanced education, degree, and/or professional license, the supporting party is entitled to reimbursement for all education related costs during that time. The party is not, though there are exceptions to most rules, able to claim a right to "substantially benefit" from the community contributions to the education or training of the student spouse.

When one spouse sacrifices his/her own education or training to allow the other spouse the opportunity to receive advanced or specialized education and training, that spouse does so with the expectation that, he or she will benefit from higher earnings once the education or training is complete. The Court must determine *if* there was a period of time when the supporting spouse did benefit, if not, the spouse may be entitled to some claim. In most cases, although the Court has a great deal of discretion and latitude in the reimbursements to be considered, the supporting spouse will only be entitled to the reimbursement and **not** the enhanced earning capacity.

See *In re Marriage of Sullivan* (1984) 37 CA3d 762, which is the controlling case, which is summarized at Appendix 6B. Also see Family Code § 2641.

(F) Business Interests. This area was previously discussed under earnings and compensation, with respect to that area. However, it will often be necessary to value a business, particularly when the business owner/spouse(s) is technically the "employer" of one or both spouses. Valuation of a business should include: inventory, machinery, desks, copy machines, computer, printers, fax machines and other business-related equipment and tools, accounts receivable, accounts payable, cash on hand, contingency fees, pending contracts for work in progress, and *goodwill*.

Goodwill is that on-going business which represents future patronage. Most businesses have an expectation that they will have repeat business. They will want to continue a good business relationship so that people will want to again purchase their goods and services. The business owners also want these customers to recommend the business to their family, friends, neighbors, and co-workers who may need the services. Word-of-mouth is very powerful advertising and is considered goodwill. Goodwill is dependent upon the efforts, energy and labor of the business owner, in this case the owner/spouse. If a spouse is a sole proprietor or has a controlling interest in a business, it will need to be valued. The value will be considered, in most cases, community property.

The Court has had to make a ruling clarifing some of the assets that may not be recognized as community property, particularly with regard to the engagement of business. *In Re Marriage of McTiernan & Dubrow* (2005) 133 Cal.App.4th 1090, 35 Cal.Rptr.3d 287 held that career assets "such as celebrity or executive goodwill" are **not** recognized as career assets unless "the holder is engaged in a business or profession." However, in *Patrick v. Alacer* (2011) 201 CA4th 1326, 136 CR3d 669, the court ruled that under FC§ 1101, *Pereira v. Pereira* (1909) 156 C 1, 103 P 488 should be applied (apportioned) because the "husband's efforts in the company during marriage were community efforts."

Family Code § 1101 provides for the obligations of a spouse operating a community business. This code section should be reviewed when considering the fiduciary duty of the spouses, including but not limited to situations where there is a family business. An important consideration is which spouse has the "primary management and control" of the business or the business interest.

(G) Rents, Incomes & Profits. Family Code § 770 states, in part: "rents, issues and profits of the property" (FC§ 770(a)(3) constitute separate property. The rents, issues and profits flow from the separate property of the spouses and are therefore the separate property of that spouse.

It is very clear, however, when a person has a bank account prior to the marriage and that account is retained solely in that person's name, all income (interest) derived from that account will continue to be that person's separate property.

Conversely, many couples today maintain their separate bank accounts after they are married and create their own unique method of paying separate and community debts. One party may pay the mortgage out of his/her account while the other pays for food, utilities, and other community liabilities out of his/her account. Or, the couple comes up with some pro rata formula which each of them then contributes into a joint account and out of which the community liabilities are paid. While this may seem like it simplifies matters, it can actually make it more difficult—absent property to which title is affixed or a post-marital agreement—to clearly determine ownership and community contributions.

Of primary importance in this section is to research the asset(s) to uncover not only the current characterization of the assets, but also any contributions, transmutations, or commingling that might have occurred during the marriage. As stated above, all profits from an asset will retain the character of the asset. However, as you have seen from this section, parties often commingle or change the character of an asset without realizing they are doing so. Based on Family Code § 770, the same rule can be applied to community property. Any "rents, issues and profits" which flow from community assets, will be deemed community assets.

Were community assets used to "finance" an individual project? Examples are as follows:

Intellectual property, such as artwork, recordings, publications all may have happened as the result of it being created during the marriage or alternatively, some community funds were contributed. If so, then the community would be entitled to royalties and earnings on sales of the property.

Gambling or lottery winnings would be considered community if the money to "fund" the initial cash outlay was taken from the joint checking account.

(H) Quasi-community and Quasi-marital property. Quasi-community and/or marital property are essentially the same. The are generally defined as property which, except for the occurrence of some particular event or circumstances, would otherwise be treated as community property.

Family Code § 2660 provides for the division of property located outside of California, as follows:

(a) Except as provided in subdivision (b), if the property subject to division includes real property situated in another state, the Court shall, if possible, divide the community property and quasi community property as provided in this division ["Division of Property"—Sections 2500–2660] in such a manner that it is not necessary to change the nature of the interest held in the real property situated in another state.

(b) If it is not possible to divide the property in the same manner provided for in subdivision (a), the Court may do any of the following in order to effect a division of the property as provided for in this division:

(1) Require the parties to execute conveyances or take other actions with respect to the real property situated in the other state as are necessary.

(2) Award to the party who would have been benefited by the conveyances or other actions the money value of the interest in the property that the party would have received if the conveyances had been executed or other actions taken.

Quasi-marital property is property, except through some extenuating circumstance such as a void or voidable marriage, which was acquired during the marriage. The property owned by the parties to an invalid marriage (an "innocent" or "putative spouse") is quasi-marital property. Since the putative spouse enjoys the same rights as a legal spouse, any property acquired during that time would be divided as though it were community property, subject to the debts and liabilities as they would be under the definition of community property.

Family Code § 2251 provides as follows:

(a) If a determination is made that a marriage is void or voidable and the Court finds that either party or both parties believed in good faith that the marriage was valid, the court shall:

(1) Declare the party or parties to have the status of a putative spouse.

(2) If the division of property is in issue, divide, in accordance with Division 7 (commencing with section 2550), that property acquired during the union which would have been community property or quasi-community property if the union had not been void or voidable.

Thus, all quasi-community and quasi-marital property, for all practical purposes, is considered community property.

Liabilities

The liabilities or debts of the parties must also be determined and allocated during the process of determining the characterization of property.

Family Code § 900 et seq. provides guidelines for dealing with the debts of the marriage, as well as rules for reimbursement, if either party pays community debts after the date of separation. Family Code § 910 sets forth the guidelines for the pay-off of community and separate debts, as follows:

(a) Except as otherwise expressly provided by statute, the community estate is liable for a debt incurred by either spouse before or during marriage, regardless of which spouse has the management and control of the property and regardless of whether one or both spouses are parties to the debt or to a judgment for the debt. **Note:** the above section specifically states that debts accrued prior to the marriage, may be considered community debt. (See FC§ 915 below.)

(b) "During marriage" for purposes of this section does not include the period during which the spouses are living separate and apart before a judgment of dissolution of marriage or legal separation of the parties.

Family Code § 911 does protect the earnings of a spouse that are earned "during marriage" from liability for debts incurred by the current spouse before the current marriage. To ensure protection under this section, the spouse who wishes to protect his/

her earnings must place the money where the other spouse does not have control over the money and assure that the money is not commingled with community funds. Once the funds are commingled, the right to protection is lost. If commingled, this would be the one time that a current spouse could be obligated for child support for a child who is not his/her child.

Family Code § 915 states:

(a) For the purpose of this part, a child or spousal support obligation of a married person that does not arise out of the marriage shall be treated as a debt incurred before marriage, regardless of whether a court order for support is made or modified before or during marriage and regardless of whether any installment payment on the obligation accrues before or during marriage.

Generally, a spouse's separate property is liable for only the debts incurred prior to and during the marriage. Nor, is the spouse liable for their spouses separate debt acquired prior to marriage (except as above). There are exceptions as to when a spouse can become liable for "some" of his/her spouse's debt. Family Code §§ 913-914 provide:

Family Code § 913. (a) The separate property of a married person is liable for a debt incurred by the person before or during marriage.

(b) Except as otherwise provided by statute:

(1) The separate property of a married person is not liable for a debt incurred by the person's spouse before or during marriage.

(2) The joinder or consent of a married person to an encumbrance of community estate property to secure payment of a debt incurred by the person's spouse does not subject the person's separate property to liability for the debt unless the person also incurred the debt.

Family Code § 914. (a) Notwithstanding Section 913, a married person is personally liable for the following debts incurred by the person's spouse during marriage:

(1) A debt incurred for necessaries of life of the person's spouse while the spouses are living together.

(2) Except as provided in Section 4302, a debt incurred for common necessaries of life of the person's spouse while the spouses are living separately.

(b) The separate property of a married person may be applied to the satisfaction of a debt for which the person is personally liable pursuant to this section. If separate property is so applied at a time when nonexempt property in the community estate or separate property of the person's spouse is available but is not applied to the satisfaction of the debt, the married person is entitled to reimbursement to the extent such property was available.

(c) (1) Except as provided in paragraph (2), the statute of limitations set forth in Section 366.2 of the Code of Civil Procedure shall apply if the spouse for whom the married person is personally liable dies.

(2) If the surviving spouse had actual knowledge of the debt prior to expiration of the period set forth in Section 366.2 and the personal representative of the deceased spouse's estate failed to provide the creditor asserting the claim under this section with a timely written notice of the probate administration of the estate in the manner provided for pursuant to Section 9050 of the Probate Code, the statute of limitations set forth in Section 337 or 339, as applicable, shall apply.

Note that FC§ 914(a) above references the fiduciary responsibility to a spouse and the obligation to pay spousal support.

Division of Property; Debt Responsibility

The parties will either reach an agreement regarding their community and/or separate property division, or the Court will make a ruling regarding the division of property, and a Judgment will be entered.

California is a community property state. Therefore, all assets must be divided equally. This also means that debts should be divided equally. In most cases, it is advisable to allocate a debt to the party who receives the asset. The Court cannot, however, make orders that directly affect creditors. The creditor may attempt to collect the debt from either party regardless of whom it was assigned in the dissolution of marriage and even though it is now considered the separate property of the person receiving it.

Since most married couples carry substantial debt, especially credit cards, this is a very touchy area and is not easily resolved.

In the event a party who was assigned a debt fails to pay the debt, the Legislature has put some safeguards in place. Family Code § 916, provides as follows:

(a) Notwithstanding any other provision of this chapter, after division of community and quasi-community property pursuant to Division 7 (commencing with Section 2500):

(1) The separate property owned by a married person at the time of the division and the property received by the person in the division is liable for a debt incurred by the person before or during marriage and the person is personally liable for the debt, whether or not the debt was assigned for payment by the person's spouse in the division.

(2) The separate property owned by a married person at the time of the division and the property received by the person in the division is not liable for a debt incurred by the person's spouse before or during marriage, and the person is not personally liable for the debt, unless the debt was assigned for payment by the person in the division of property. Nothing in this paragraph affects the liability of property for the satisfaction of a lien on the property.

(3) The separate property owned by a married person at the time of the division and the property received by the person in the division is liable for a debt incurred by that person's spouse before or during marriage, and the person is personally liable for the debt, if the debt was assigned for payment by the person in the division of property. If a money judgment for the debt is entered after the division, the property is not subject to enforcement of the judgment and the judgment may not be enforced against the married person, unless the person is made a party to the judgment for the purposes of this paragraph.

(b) If the property of a married person is applied to the satisfaction of a money judgment pursuant to subdivision (a) for a debt incurred by a person that is assigned for payment by the person's spouse, the person has a right of reimbursement from the person's spouse to the extent of the property applied, with interest at the legal rate, and may recover reasonable attorney fees incurred in enforcing the right of reimbursement.

Family Code § 2620–2627 also establishes guidelines for allocating community debts, as follows:

Section 2620(c) The debts for which the community estate is liable which are unpaid at the time of trial, or for which the community estate becomes liable after trial, shall be confirmed or divided.

Section 2621 Debts incurred by either spouse before the date of marriage shall be confirmed without offset to the spouse who incurred the debt.

Section 2622 (a) Debts incurred by either spouse after the date of marriage but prior to the date of separation shall be divided as set forth in Section 2550 to 2552, inclusive and Sections 2601 to 2604, inclusive.

Section 2622 (b) To the extent that community debts exceed the total community and quasi community assets, the excess of debt shall be assigned as the Court deems just and equitable, taking into account factors such as the parties' relative ability to pay.

Section 2623 Debts incurred by either spouse after the date of separation but before the entry of judgment of dissolution or a legal separation shall be confirmed as follows:

(a) Debts incurred by either spouse for the common necessities of life of either spouse or the necessities of life of the children of the marriage for whom support may be ordered, in the absence of a court order or a written agreement for support or for the payment of these debts, shall be confirmed to either spouse according to the parties' respective needs and abilities to pay at the time the debt was incurred.

(b) Debts incurred by either spouse for non necessities of that spouse or children of the marriage for whom support may be ordered shall be confirmed without offset to the spouse who incurred the debt.

Section 2624 Debts incurred by either spouse after entry of judgment of dissolution of marriage but before termination of the parties' marital status or after the entry of judgment of legal separation of the parties shall be confirmed without offset to the spouse who incurred the debt.

Section 2625 Notwithstanding sections 2620 to 2624, inclusive, all separate debts, including those debts incurred by a spouse during marriage and before the date of separation that were not incurred for the benefit of the community, shall be confirmed without offset to the spouse who incurred the debt.

The above sections are very clear and straightforward. Of significant note is the Court's ability to deviate from the standard "equal" division, where economic need dictates, or where an "innocent" spouse must be reimbursed due to the inappropriate use of community funds by a spouse. The Court is also given the discretion to allocate debts to a spouse when there is a "negative" balance of the marital estate, which would lead to economic hardship on the part of one spouse or where it affects the needs of the party's children, and when the other has more ability to pay. In some cases the "negative" balance may potential lead to bankruptcy, which will be discussed in greater detail in Chapter 10.

While the above code sections may be straightforward, there is also case law that has evolved over the years and has applied those statutes to the various circumstances of the parties.

Many of the property settlements with which you will be involved will be fairly simple. The average family will have a home which is highly mortgaged, two vehicles both with debt, possibly a boat or recreational vehicle also with debt, medium priced furniture and furnishings, employee benefits such as retirement and a few additional assets such as a mutual fund or other investment. This situation is fairly simple to divide. Having obtained all of the information concerning the marital property, you can simply create a spreadsheet which reflects the property and the client's wishes as to *who gets what*.

As you review the following information and scenarios please be aware that the author has utilized "net" value rather than fair market value (FMV) for ease in understanding. As a paralegal, you will be using both FMV and the "net" values (net = FMV minus debt) when assisting with the allocation of property within the dissolution process.

A **very** simple division would be as follows:

Asset	Net Value
House	100,000
Vehicle #1	15,000
Vehicle #2	20,000
Furniture	5,000
Total	**140,000**

$140,000 divided by 2 = $70,000 to Husband; $70,000 to Wife

In the above division of property, it is *assumed* that all property is liquidated and that each party will get one-half or $70,000.

However, very few marital situations are resolved in that manner. Sample spreadsheets can be found at Appendix 7A. You will note that each spreadsheet contains more assets, less the liabilities, and, therefore, adds to the complexity of the division of property. The first spreadsheet assumes that each spouse will take certain items of community property in order to achieve an "equal" division. For the purposes of this text, these spread sheets are very simple and contain *round* numbers.

Cases having more property, separate property interests in community property, businesses, retirement plans, and other assets which must be valued will add to the complexity of the matter. This will also contribute to the emotional attachments to the items and issues. If you have clients with more complex property issues, the attorney will need to work closely with the client and make various suggestions as to how the property can be divided, while accomplishing two things: 1) the client's wants and needs; and 2) the equal division of property as set forth in the Family Code, while attempting to achieve harmony between two individuals who no longer wish to be married to each other.

There are also spreadsheet programs available for the attorney to use. The significance of these spreadsheets is that they may be used to incorporate any tax considerations into the calculations. As issues become more complex in nature, the tax consequences may change for the party receiving a certain asset. For instance, the spouse receiving the house, will be able to deduct mortgage and property taxes when the annual tax returns are prepared. Thus, it may be more beneficial for one party to receive the tax benefits than the other.

An example would be if Husband were to receive the house because he is more able to make the payments, then he would also be able to claim the deductions. If Wife has primary physical custody of the two children and only works part time, it may be more beneficial for Husband to claim the dependents on his taxes. This scenario may actually reduce Husband's taxable earnings, in which case Child Support may be higher. (Note: the attorney must be the one to work with these various methods of achieving what is best for the client, as well as what will be ultimately acceptable to the other party and the court.)

There will also be cases where one party may want or need to keep an asset with a higher value, as shown in the following example:

> Wife is a dentist, she cannot give her professional license or her business to another individual who does not have a license in that profession. Let us say you have a business valuation completed and the family home appraised. Now, add this information to the equation from above (assuming these numbers are strictly community values) and see what happens:

Asset	Net Value	Husband	Wife
House	100,000	100,000	
Vehicle #1	15,000	15,000	
Vehicle #2	20,000		20,000
Dental Practice	200,000		200,000
Furniture	5,000	2,500	2,500
Total	340,000	117,500	222,500

An alternative example would be:

> Wife has $105,000 **more** community assets than Husband [222,500–117,500] based on the above division of property. Therefore, Wife owes $105,000 to Husband in order to make an equal division of property. (This is referred to as an "equalizing payment.") Wife can pay the Husband in cash (if she has it or by taking out a loan) or by executing a Promissory Note, wherein she makes periodic payments to Husband.

You will note in the above examples that the "net value" was used for items having equity. Remember that credit card debt, for which the parties will not be able to "see" any asset, will make the division of property and the outcomes more complex, especially in light of current bankruptcy laws. Remember that debts must be included in the "real life" application of these allocations and they are always a negative (minus) on the spreadsheet.

The parties may agree, or the Court may order, the postponement of the distribution of certain property. A *Duke Order* or Delayed Sale of Family home, would be such an instance, as long as one of the parties requests it.

The value of an asset may change during the pendency of the matter. Once the parties separate, it may take them at least a year to reach an agreement or have the matter set for trial. It is not uncommon for the period of time to be even longer. A new property valuation may be necessary if it has been a long time, or for some reason the property has had an extraordinary increase or decrease in value. The same may be true if the parties have agreed or the Court has ordered the postponement and the retention of the jurisdiction over certain property or the entire marital estate.

Clients may attempt to decrease the value of or under value, an asset. In the above scenario, Wife could potentially encumber her dental practice, drive away patients, or not make any attempt to collect co-pays, insurance reimbursements and other receivables. The same could be true for a spouse who remains in the family home. That person could potentially diminish the value by not making certain repairs or maintaining the property.

The Court has recognized the temptation to diminish the value of a community asset or assets. Family Code § 2552 provides that "the court shall value the assets and liabilities as near as practicable to the time of trial ... unless upon 30 days notice by the moving party to the other party, the court for good cause shown [values] all or any portion of the assets and liabilities at a date after separation and before trial to accomplish an equal division of the community estate of the parties in an equitable manner." This statute gives a party the ability to request that the valuation date be used is the date of separation as opposed to date of trial, which would be prior to the spouse's deliberate mismanagement of the property. Keep in mind, that each spouse has a fiduciary responsibility to each other and to maintain the property.

Complex Division Issues and Remedies

The above situations are fairly simple and straight forward. There may be issues of transmutation or commingling of separate and community property, which will result in the need to trace the various changes in the characterization of the property. Once the tracing is complete, it will be necessary to *apportion* the various separate and community property interests. There are several "landmark" cases which family law practitioners and the Courts use to determine apportionment of certain types of assets. Some of these cases are as follows:

Pereira & *Van Camp*

The use of community property to improve separate property is a common question. Specifically, time, energy, skill, talent and labor, are considered "valuable" community assets. What are the ramifications of one spouse utilizing his/her time, energy, skill, talent and labor in increasing the separate property of the spouse?

The Courts have developed two formulas to resolve these types of issues, known as *Pereira* and *Van Camp*. *In re Marriage of Pereira* (1909) 156 C1 103 is used to determine an increase in value as a result of the labors and effort of a spouse. *In re Marriage of Van Camp* (1921) 53 CA 17, 199 P 885 is used to determine a *natural* tendency for an asset to increase, which is outside the control of the owner.

An example of the applications of these cases would be as follows:

Pereira would be applied if the spouse used considerable time and energy during the marriage to increasing the stock portfolio over and above its normal rate of return.

> One spouse owns, on the date of marriage, a stock portfolio valued at $20,000. During the five-year marriage, the value of the portfolio increases to $200,000.

> It would appear, on its face, that the party increased the value of the portfolio by $180,000. However, consideration must be made for the "normal" rate of return, which would be considered separate property, and the "above-normal" difference would be considered community property. Each spouse would re-

ceive one-half of the increase in the value. The original amount owned by the spouse on the date of marriage would also have to be deducted.

Van Camp utilizes the concept of the "value" of the spouse's labor and effort.

Using the same figures above, the court might apply *Van Camp* to determine that the value of the spouse's labor would be $12,000 per year, then $12,000 x 5 years of marriage would equal $60,000. Thus, $60,000 would be deducted from the current $200,000 value of the portfolio, less $20,000 initial value for a community value of $120,000.

You should note, that these applications are similar but there is no specific determination as to which method to use. In most instances, the Courts do lean toward the use of *Pereira*, if there is a question as to which application should be made. The attorney will decide which case is the most advantageous to the client and develop that argument for trial. As indicated earlier the court itself applied *Periera* in a probate case, related to a previous dissolution judgment. Specifically, the probate court was asked to apply FC§1101(b) wherein the former wife claimed the value of husband's company stock was increased in value due to his community efforts. The court found that the former wife was entitled to an increased community interest of over $3M. *Patrick v. Alacer Corp* (2011) 201 CA4th 1326, 136 CR3d 669.

Epstein & Watts

Family Code §910 et seq. provides for the right of reimbursement relating to either community or separate property. Specifically, this is community property that is used to satisfy a separate property debt and for debts incurred to pay for the "necessities of life." As you will recall, Family Code §2641 provides for the reimbursement of community contributions to a spouse's education and training, as well as reimbursement rights pursuant to Family Code §2640, and spousal support considerations.

The Court makes the presumption that if a spouse makes a contribution of separate property toward a community asset, then it is considered a *gift*. The spouse making the *gift* must rebut the presumption by providing evidence of a written agreement, which has been signed by the other spouse. The case most commonly applied to the situation wherein a spouse uses separate property to maintain, or improve, community assets after the date of separation is *In re Marriage of Epstein* (1979) 24 C3d 76. This case is well recognized as the "controlling legal application" and what is commonly known as *Epstein Credits*.

The *Epstein* court found that a spouse making post-separation contributions should be allowed to be reimbursed for those amounts unless the spouses had agreed, in writing, that the spouse would **not** be reimbursed. The Court found that the contributions made should be considered a *gift* absent said written agreement. Family Code §2640(b) may be applicable in that the agreement must be in writing, rather than oral, except in those situations where the new section (FC§2640(c)) may be applied.

One of the most common scenarios for the application of *Epstein Credits* is as follows:

Husband remains in family home post separation. Husband makes the mortgage payments (referred to as a "pay-down" of the mortgage). Husband would then assert his right for reimbursement applying for *Epstein Credits*. Based on the above case, however, absent written agreement, the Court may deny Husband's request. Husband is certainly going to protest, stating that the payments were certainly **not** to be considered a *gift* to the community.

It is usually advisable in this instance, while the matter is pending, to have a Stipulation (agreement) signed by the parties stating that Husband is paying the mortgage, and he will receive credit for those payments.

There is also a question as to whether the payments would be considered *support* in the event it was the Wife who remained in the family home, and Husband had been ordered to pay support.

The second concept, when applied to the above scenario, requires the court to look at the payments made by the spouse who remains in the home is to establish that he/she is "enjoying exclusive use" of the home or other asset. (This same concept could be applied to a vehicle.) In that event, the Court is required to consider the *fair rental value* of the asset, which is then applied to the payment. If that is the case, then the request for *Epstein Credits* will be denied. However, *In re Marriage of Watts* (1985) 171 Cal App 3d 366 will be applied. The Court provided in *Watts* that the spouse exercising exclusive control over an asset should be assessed a "usage" charge against the *credit*.

The following is an example:

> Husband ("in spouse") is given exclusive use of the family home after the date of separation. The mortgage on the home is $500 per month. The rental value is $1,500 per month. Wife ("out spouse") is entitled to $750 per month or one-half of the fair rental value. However, the "in spouse" is realizing a $1,000 per month *use value excess*. Based on the ruling in *Watts* the "out spouse" would argue that she is entitled to $500 per month in *Watts* charges.

Within family law concepts, agreements and decisions, *Watts* is considered the "flip side" of *Epstein* and therefore these two cases are often referenced together.

Moore/Marsden

One of the most common areas of apportionment is a separate property contribution to the family home. The application of apportionment with respect to the purchase of real property is that until the mortgage is paid in full, the parties really don't own the home. They own only a portion and the lender owns the rest (and usually the most). This particular issue of apportionment is even more complex, in that the attorney (and his or her paralegal) need to understand that when purchasing property on credit, the amount of the ownership changes each month. It is not a static amount. The "credit" can only be made on any *principal* paid and not toward the interest. Additionally, the owner/debtor is actually paying more than the value of the property (at the loan's inception), since they are paying primarily interest on the loan. The reduction of principal is minimal in the early stage of the loan. The apportionment does not include any improvements made at a later time or any natural appreciation in value.

For example:

> If you purchase a car for $20,000; make a down payment of $5,000; and finance the rest for a five year period at the rate of $520 per month, the total amount paid for the car upon the completion of the contract is $23,720. (Of the $520 monthly payment, most will be interest for the first two years of the loan, meaning the actual price paid for the vehicle is not significantly reduced.)

In re Marriage of Moore (1980) 28 C3d 366 established the guidelines for the application of applying only principal that has been paid down. The *Marsden* court stated that interest, tax and insurance payments must be disregarded when calculating a separate property interest.

The formula most commonly used is referred to as "*Moore/Marsden.*" *In re Marriage of Marsden* (1982) 130 CA3d 426 led to the creation of a *formula* to be used by the Court in determining the separate and community property allocation, including the appreciation of the value of the separate property.

The following is a synopsis of the *Marsden* case:

> Mr. Marsden purchased a home prior to marriage for the sum of $38,300. He made an $8,300 down payment and signed a promissory note for the balance of $30,000. His monthly payments resulted in $7,000 paid toward the principal as of the date of his marriage to Mrs. Marsden. The fair market value on the date of marriage was $65,000, which was an increase of $26,700. During the course of the marriage and prior to separation, the *community* paid down the *principal* on the loan in the amount of $9,200. The property also continued to appreciate and had a fair market value of $182,500 at the time of trial. The property had appreciated by $117,500. Additionally, Mr. Marsden made a $655 post-separation mortgage payment. On the date of the trial, the balance due on the mortgage was $13,145.

The court calculated the separate property interest of Mr. Marsden, and the community property interest, as follows:

Down Payment	$8,300
Principal Paydown	$20,800

$29,100 ÷ $38,300 = .7598 = 75.98%

Community Paydown	$9,200
Purchase Price of House	$38,300

$9,200 ÷ $38,300 = .2402 = 24.02% or,

Simpler calculation: 100% − 75.98% = 24.02%

You must also calculate the appreciation in value that occurred. That amount is calculated as follows:

$117,500 × 75.98% = $89,276.50 — Separate Property

$117,500 × 24.02% = $28,223.50 — Community Property

The current net fair market of the house can be determined simply by subtracting the current fair market value, less the current debt:

$182,500 − $13,145 = $169,355

The respective values of the parties' interests are calculated as follows:

Mr. Marsden's Separate Property Interest

Down Payment $8,300.00

Loan Paydown (Prior to Marriage) $7,000.00

Loan Paydown (Post Separation) $655.00

Appreciation (Pre-Marital) $26,700.00

75.98% Marital Appreciation $89,276.50

Total **$131,931.50**

Community Share

Loan Paydown (During Marriage) $9,200.00

24.02% Marital Appreciation $28,223.50

Total **$37,423.50**

Mrs. Marsden's share is one-half of the community share or $18,711.75.

The two cases (*Moore* and *Marsden*) have been *merged* as one theory of law to be applied to a review of separate and community property interests.

Keep in mind that Family Code § 2581 provides the presumption that if the title to the property, which is owned prior to the marriage, is subsequently transferred into joint tenancy after marriage, the property is community property. The first task to be accomplished prior to applying *Moore/Marsden*, is to rebut the presumption that the property should be characterized solely as community property. As indicated above, the most obvious manner by which to retain a separate interest is to memorialize the agreement in writing.

In re Marriage of Delaney (2003) 111CA4th 991, 4 CR3d 378 changed, in some situations, whether or not *Moore/Marsden* will be applied. The Court held that if the spouse owned property prior to marriage and the spouse alleges undue influence, the burden shifts to the spouse who was put on the title to establish that the transfer was done freely and voluntarily as well as made with full knowledge of the transaction's effect on the separate property. The community property presumption could be overcome by proof of agreement or an understanding "to the contrary." The proof does not need to be in writing (although that would always be the preferred method and the "gold standard.")

Delaney also invoked the fiduciary responsibility provisions of Family Code § 721. There must be evidence that one spouse had disadvantaged the other in an interspousal property transaction.

Your instructor will provide you with details for dividing the community property in your case study as well as for creating a spreadsheet. Sample spreadsheets are found at Appendix 7B. This exercise will be helpful in creating a fair and equitable division of property in order to prepare the Marital Settlement Agreement.

Forms Associated with Topic

Declaration of Disclosure (FL-140)

Schedule of Debts and Assets (FL-142)

Declaration regarding Service of Final Declaration of Disclosure (FL-141)

Proof of Service by Mail (FL-335)

(See examples of some forms on the following pages)

Key Terms

- Final Declaration of Disclosure
- Fiduciary Duty
- Community Property
- Separate Property
- Quasi-Community Property
- Quasi-Marital Property
- Real Property
- Personal Property
- Apportionment
- Tracing
- Commingling
- Transmutation
- Pension, Retirement, Employee Benefits
- The "Time Rule"
- *Pereira & Van Camp*
- *Moore/Marsden*
- *Epstein & Watts*
- Inheritance, Bequest, Gift, and Devise
- Alternate Valuation Date
- Vesting
- Title

Notes

1: The author has found that one of the best sources for staying current on all family law issues and changes is the annual *Practice Under the California Family Code*, published by the Continuing Education of the Bar. It is usually available by February of each year and it contains a section at the beginning of the book called "Selected Developments." This is a summary of recent case law and changes in the family code. It does not cover every change but will have the most relevant topics about which the family law practitioner should be aware.

The volume also contains a list of family law forms, a list of statutes which relate to family law, and a Table of Cases.

This book is an excellent desk reference and provides helpful insight on completing Judicial Council forms as well as sample pleadings and other documents utilized by family law practitioners and their paralegals.

2: A resource for more advanced and complex issues relative to California Family Law. It is a four-volume series titled *Complex Issues in California Family Law* and is published by Lexis-Nexis. The four volumes, which address the "tough issues facing today's California family law practitioners" according to the publisher. The volumes are divided into the following topics: 1) Fiduciary Duties—Nature and Effect; 2) Fiduciary Duties—A Practical Approach; 3) Transmutations; and 4) Family Law Tracings.

Declaration Regarding Service of Declaration of Disclosure

FL-141

ATTORNEY OR PARTY WITHOUT ATTORNEY *(Name, State Bar number, and address)*:	
JOAN CARE-ACTOR, SBN ******* LAW OFFICES OF JOAN CARE-ACTOR 75000 WHY ME LANE SACRAMENTO, CA 95826	

TELEPHONE NO.: 916-555-1234   FAX NO.: 916-555-1233
E-MAIL ADDRESS: joan@care-actorlaw.com
ATTORNEY FOR *(Name)*: SANDIE SHORES, PETITIONER

SUPERIOR COURT OF CALIFORNIA, COUNTY OF SACRAMENTO
STREET ADDRESS: 3341 POWER INN ROAD
MAILING ADDRESS: 3341 POWER INN ROAD
CITY AND ZIP CODE: SACRAMENTO, CA 95826
BRANCH NAME: FAMILY LAW

PETITIONER: SANDIE SHORES
RESPONDENT: ROCKY SHORES
OTHER PARENT/PARTY:

DECLARATION REGARDING SERVICE OF DECLARATION OF DISCLOSURE AND INCOME AND EXPENSE DECLARATION [x] Petitioner's [ ] Preliminary [ ] Respondent's [x] Final	CASE NUMBER: 14FLXXXXXXX

1. I am the [x] attorney for [x] petitioner [ ] respondent in this matter.

2. [x] Petitioner's [ ] Respondent's *Preliminary Declaration of Disclosure* (form FL-140), current* *Income and Expense Declaration* (form FL-150), completed *Schedule of Assets and Debts* (form FL-142) or *Community and Separate Property Declarations* (form FL-160) with appropriate attachments, all tax returns filed by the party in the two years before service of the preliminary disclosures, and all other required information under Family Code section 2104 were served on:

   [x] the other party   [ ] the other party's attorney   by   [ ] personal service   [x] mail
   [ ] Other *(specify):*
   on *(date):* XX/XX/2014

3. [ ] Petitioner's [ ] Respondent's *Final Declaration of Disclosure* (form FL-140), current* *Income and Expense Declaration* (form FL-150), completed *Schedule of Assets and Debts* (form FL-142) or *Community or Separate Property Declarations* (form FL-160) with attachments, and the material facts and information required by Family Code section 2105 were served on:

   [ ] the other party   [ ] other party's attorney   by   [ ] personal service   [ ] mail
   [ ] Other *(specify):*
   on *(date):*

4. [x] Service of [x] Petitioner's [ ] Respondent's [ ] preliminary [x] final declaration of disclosure
   [x] current income and expense declaration has been waived as follows:
   a. [x] The parties agreed to waive final declaration of disclosure requirements under Family Code section 2105(d).
      (Form FL-144 may be used for this purpose.) The waiver [ ] was filed on *(date):*
      [x] is being filed at the same time as this form.
   b. [ ] The party has failed to comply with disclosure requirements, and the court has granted the request for voluntary waiver of receipt under Family Code section 2107 on *(date):*
   c. [ ] This is a default proceeding that does not include a stipulated judgment or settlement agreement. Petitioner waives final disclosure requirements under Family Code section 2110.

*Current is defined as completed within the past three months providing no facts have changed. (Cal. Rules of Court, rule 5.260.)

I declare under penalty of perjury under the laws of the State of California that the foregoing is true and correct.

Date:

JOAN CARE-ACTOR   ▶
_____   _____
(TYPE OR PRINT NAME)   SIGNATURE

NOTE: File this document with the court.
Do not file a copy of the Preliminary or Final Declaration of Disclosure or any attachments to either declaration of disclosure with this document.

Page 1 of 1

Form Adopted for Mandatory Use
Judicial Council of California
FL-141 [Rev. July 1, 2013]

DECLARATION REGARDING SERVICE OF DECLARATION OF DISCLOSURE AND INCOME AND EXPENSE DECLARATION
(Family Law)

Family Code, §§ 2102, 2104, 2105, 2106, 2112
www.courts.ca.gov

For your protection and privacy, please press the Clear This Form button after you have printed the form. | Print this form | Save this form | | Clear this form |

Declaration of Disclosure

FL-140

ATTORNEY OR PARTY WITHOUT ATTORNEY *(Name, State Bar number, and address):* JOAN CARE-ACTOR, SBN XXXXXXX CARE-ACTOR LAW FIRM 75000 WHY ME LANE SACRAMENTO, CA 95826 TELEPHONE NO.: 916-555-1234 FAX NO.: 916-555-1233 E-MAIL ADDRESS: joan@care-actorlaw.com ATTORNEY FOR *(Name):* SANDIE SHORES	

SUPERIOR COURT OF CALIFORNIA, COUNTY OF SACRAMENTO
STREET ADDRESS: 3341 POWER INN ROAD
MAILING ADDRESS: 3341 POWER INN ROAD
CITY AND ZIP CODE: SACRAMENTO, CA 95826
BRANCH NAME: FAMILY LAW DIVISION

PETITIONER: SANDIE SHORES
RESPONDENT: ROCKY SHORES
OTHER PARENT/PARTY:

DECLARATION OF DISCLOSURE		CASE NUMBER:
✓ Petitioner's ☐ Preliminary		14FLXXXXXXX
☐ Respondent's ☐ Final		

DO NOT FILE DECLARATIONS OF DISCLOSURE OR FINANCIAL ATTACHMENTS WITH THE COURT

In a dissolution, legal separation, or nullity action, both a preliminary and a final declaration of disclosure must be served on the other party with certain exceptions. Neither disclosure is filed with the court. Instead, a declaration stating that service of disclosure documents was completed or waived must be filed with the court (see form FL-141).

- *In summary dissolution cases, each spouse or domestic partner must exchange preliminary disclosures as described in Summary Dissolution Information (form FL-810). Final disclosures are not required (see Family Code section 2109).*
- *In a default judgment case that is not a stipulated judgment or a judgment based on a marital settlement agreement, only the petitioner is required to complete and serve a preliminary declaration of disclosure. A final disclosure is not required of either party (see Family Code section 2110).*
- *Service of preliminary declarations of disclosure may not be waived by an agreement between the parties.*
- *Parties who agree to waive final declarations of disclosure must file their written agreement with the court (see form FL-144).*

The petitioner must serve a preliminary declaration of disclosure at the same time as the Petition or within 60 days of filing the Petition. The respondent must serve a preliminary declaration of disclosure at the same time as the Response or within 60 days of filing the Response. The time periods may be extended by written agreement of the parties or by court order (see Family Code section 2104(f)).

Attached are the following:

1. ☒ A completed *Schedule of Assets and Debts* (form FL-142) or ☐ A *Property Declaration* (form FL-160) for *(specify):*
   ☐ Community and Quasi-Community Property ☐ Separate Property.

2. ☒ A completed *Income and Expense Declaration* (form FL-150).

3. ☒ All tax returns filed by the party in the two years before the date that the party served the disclosure documents.

4. ☒ A statement of all material facts and information regarding valuation of all assets that are community property or in which the community has an interest *(not a form).*
   PETITIONER HAS NOT COMPLETED A VALUATION OF ALL COMMUNITY ASSETS

5. ☒ A statement of all material facts and information regarding obligations for which the community is liable *(not a form).*
   PETITIONER HAS NOT COMPLETED DISCOVERY OF THE EXTENT OF OBLIGATIONS

6. ☒ An accurate and complete written disclosure of any investment opportunity, business opportunity, or other income-producing opportunity presented since the date of separation that results from any investment, significant business, or other income-producing opportunity from the date of marriage to the date of separation *(not a form).*
   Petitioner has had no investment, business or income-producing opportunity since date of separation.

I declare under penalty of perjury under the laws of the State of California that the foregoing is true and correct.

Date:

SANDIE SHORES
_____
(TYPE OR PRINT NAME) SIGNATURE

Page 1 of 1

Form Adopted for Mandatory Use Judicial Council of California FL-140 [Rev. July 1, 2013]	**DECLARATION OF DISCLOSURE** **(Family Law)**	Family Code, §§ 2102, 2104, 2105, 2106, 2112 *www.courts.ca.gov*

For your protection and privacy, please press the Clear This Form button after you have printed the form. | Print this form | Save this form | Clear this form

Schedule of Assets and Debts

To keep other people from seeing what you entered on your form, please press the Clear This Form button at the end of the form when finished.

THIS FORM SHOULD NOT BE FILED WITH THE COURT

FL-142

ATTORNEY OR PARTY WITHOUT ATTORNEY *(Name and Address):*	TELEPHONE NO.: 916-555-1234

JOAN CARE-ACTOR,   SBN ********

75000 WHY ME LANE

SACRAMENTO, CA 95826
ATTORNEY FOR *(Name):* SANDIE SHORES

SUPERIOR COURT OF CALIFORNIA, COUNTY OF
SACRAMENTO

PETITIONER: SANDIE SHORES

RESPONDENT: ROCKY SHORES

SCHEDULE OF ASSETS AND DEBTS ☑ Petitioner's ☐ Respondent's	CASE NUMBER: 14FLxxxxxx

— INSTRUCTIONS —

List all your known community and separate assets or debts. Include assets even if they are in the possession of another person, including your spouse. If you contend an asset or debt is separate, put P (for Petitioner) or R (for Respondent) in the first column (separate property) to indicate to whom you contend it belongs.

All values should be as of the date of signing the declaration unless you specify a different valuation date with the description. For additional space, use a continuation sheet numbered to show which item is being continued.

ITEM NO. ASSETS DESCRIPTION	SEP. PROP	DATE ACQUIRED	CURRENT GROSS FAIR MARKET VALUE	AMOUNT OF MONEY OWED OR ENCUMBRANCE
1. REAL ESTATE *(Give street addresses and attach copies of deeds with legal descriptions and latest lender's statement.)*			$	$
11155 Turtle Dove Court, Folsom, CA		2008	300,000	150,000
5555 Wilderness Lane, Mokulemne Hill, CA		2010	80,000	-0-
2. HOUSEHOLD FURNITURE, FURNISHINGS, APPLIANCES *(Identify.)* Children's Bedroom furniture (2 sets); master bedroom furniture, living room, family room and dining room furniture. Kitchen table and chairs, barstools, appliances, lawn care equipment, and other miscellaneous furnishings, decorative items and small appliances.		various	$10,000	-0-
3. JEWELRY, ANTIQUES, ART, COIN COLLECTIONS, etc. *(Identify.)* Garnet Necklace and Earnings	W	2011	Unknown	-0-

Page 1 of 4

Form Approved for Optional Use
Judicial Council of California
FL-142 [Rev. January 1, 2005]

SCHEDULE OF ASSETS AND DEBTS
(Family Law)

Code of Civil Procedure, §§ 2030(c), 2033.5
www.courtinfo.ca.gov

Schedule of Assets and Debts

ITEM NO.	ASSETS DESCRIPTION	SEP. PROP	DATE ACQUIRED	CURRENT GROSS FAIR MARKET VALUE	AMOUNT OF MONEY OWED OR ENCUMBRANCE
				$	$
4.	VEHICLES, BOATS, TRAILERS *(Describe and attach copy of title document.)*				
	2001 Honda motorcycle	H	2001	Unknown	-0-
	2010 Dodge Pick-Up	H	2013	$30,000	$28,000
	2005 Dodge Caravan		2007	$3,000	-0-
5.	SAVINGS ACCOUNTS *(Account name, account number, bank, and branch. Attach copy of latest statement.)*				
	Bank of America		2003	$10,000	-0-
	Golden One Credit Union		2004	500	-0-
6.	CHECKING ACCOUNTS *(Account name and number, bank, and branch. Attach copy of latest statement.)*				
7.	CREDIT UNION, OTHER DEPOSIT ACCOUNTS *(Account name and number, bank, and branch. Attach copy of latest statement.)*				
	Golden One Credit Union		2004	varies	-0-
8.	CASH *(Give location.)*				
	In Pocket				
9.	TAX REFUND				
	Unknown				
10.	LIFE INSURANCE WITH CASH SURRENDER OR LOAN VALUE *(Attach copy of declaration page for each policy.)*				
	None				

Schedule of Assets and Debts

ITEM NO.	ASSETS DESCRIPTION	SEP. PROP	DATE ACQUIRED	CURRENT GROSS FAIR MARKET VALUE	AMOUNT OF MONEY OWED OR ENCUMBRANCE
11.	STOCKS, BONDS, SECURED NOTES, MUTUAL FUNDS *(Give certificate number and attach copy of the certificate or copy of latest statement.)* 10 Shares Microsoft		2008	$ $500	$ -0-
12.	RETIREMENT AND PENSIONS *(Attach copy of latest summary plan documents and latest benefit statement.)* CalPERS		on-going	Unknown	-0-
13.	PROFIT - SHARING, ANNUITIES, IRAS, DEFERRED COMPENSATION *(Attach copy of latest statement.)* California State Employees Deferred Comp		on-going	Unknown	-0-
14.	ACCOUNTS RECEIVABLE AND UNSECURED NOTES *(Attach copy of each.)* None				
15.	PARTNERSHIPS AND OTHER BUSINESS INTERESTS *(Attach copy of most current K-1 form and Schedule C.)* None				
16.	OTHER ASSETS None				
17.	TOTAL ASSETS FROM CONTINUATION SHEET				
18.	TOTAL ASSETS			$ XXXXX	$ XXXXXX

Schedule of Assets and Debts

ITEM NO.	DEBTS—SHOW TO WHOM OWED	SEP. PROP.	TOTAL OWING	DATE INCURRED
			$	
19. STUDENT LOANS *(Give details.)* None				
20. TAXES *(Give details.)* None				
21. SUPPORT ARREARAGES *(Attach copies of orders and statements.)* None				
22. LOANS—UNSECURED *(Give bank name and loan number and attach copy of latest statement.)* None				
23. CREDIT CARDS *(Give creditor's name and address and the account number. Attach copy of latest statement.)* Discover CitiCard Bank Americard			$5,000 $5,000 $8,000	various various various
24. OTHER DEBTS *(Specify.):* Loan from parents for attorney's fees			$8,000	Dec 2013
25. TOTAL DEBTS FROM CONTINUATION SHEET				
26. TOTAL DEBTS			$ XXXXX	

27. ☐ *(Specify number):* _____ pages are attached as continuation sheets.

I declare under penalty of perjury under the laws of the State of California that the foregoing is true and correct.

Date:

SANDY SHORES
(TYPE OR PRINT NAME)   ▶   (SIGNATURE OF DECLARANT)

FL-142 [Rev. January 1, 2005]   **SCHEDULE OF ASSETS AND DEBTS**
                                                                  (Family Law)   Page 4 of 4

For your protection and privacy, please press the Clear This Form button after you have printed the form.   **Save This Form**   **Print This Form**   **Clear This Form**

Declaration Regarding Service of Declaration of Disclosure

FL-141

ATTORNEY OR PARTY WITHOUT ATTORNEY *(Name, State Bar number, and address):*	
TELEPHONE NO.: FAX NO. :	
E-MAIL ADDRESS:	
ATTORNEY FOR *(Name):*	

SUPERIOR COURT OF CALIFORNIA, COUNTY OF
STREET ADDRESS:
MAILING ADDRESS:
CITY AND ZIP CODE:
BRANCH NAME:

PETITIONER:
RESPONDENT:
OTHER PARENT/PARTY:

DECLARATION REGARDING SERVICE OF DECLARATION OF DISCLOSURE AND INCOME AND EXPENSE DECLARATION ☐ Petitioner's ☐ Preliminary ☐ Respondent's ☐ Final	CASE NUMBER:

1. I am the ☐ attorney for ☐ petitioner ☐ respondent in this matter.

2. ☐ Petitioner's ☐ Respondent's *Preliminary Declaration of Disclosure* (form FL-140), current* *Income and Expense Declaration* (form FL-150), completed *Schedule of Assets and Debts* (form FL-142) or *Community and Separate Property Declarations* (form FL-160) with appropriate attachments, all tax returns filed by the party in the two years before service of the preliminary disclosures, and all other required information under Family Code section 2104 were served on:

   ☐ the other party ☐ the other party's attorney   by ☐ personal service ☐ mail
   ☐ Other *(specify):*
   on (date):

3. ☐ Petitioner's ☐ Respondent's *Final Declaration of Disclosure* (form FL-140), current* *Income and Expense Declaration* (form FL-150), completed *Schedule of Assets and Debts* (form FL-142) or *Community or Separate Property Declarations* (form FL-160) with attachments, and the material facts and information required by Family Code section 2105 were served on:

   ☐ the other party ☐ other party's attorney   by ☐ personal service ☐ mail
   ☐ Other *(specify):*
   on (date):

4. ☐ Service of ☐ Petitioner's ☐ Respondent's ☐ preliminary ☐ final   declaration of disclosure
   ☐ current income and expense declaration has been waived as follows:

   a. ☐ The parties agreed to waive final declaration of disclosure requirements under Family Code section 2105(d.).
      (Form FL-144 may be used for this purpose.) The waiver ☐ was filed on *(date):*
      ☐ is being filed at the same time as this form.

   b. ☐ The party has failed to comply with disclosure requirements, and the court has granted the request for voluntary waiver of receipt under Family Code section 2107 on *(date):*

   c. ☐ This is a default proceeding that does not include a stipulated judgment or settlement agreement. Petitioner waives final disclosure requirements under Family Code section 2110.

*Current is defined as completed within the past three months providing no facts have changed. (Cal. Rules of Court, rule 5.260.)

I declare under penalty of perjury under the laws of the State of California that the foregoing is true and correct.

Date:

▶

_____   _____
(TYPE OR PRINT NAME)   SIGNATURE

NOTE: File this document with the court. Do not file a copy of the Preliminary or Final Declaration of Disclosure or any attachments to either declaration of disclosure with this document.

Page 1 of 1

Form Adopted for Mandatory Use
Judicial Council of California
FL-141 [Rev. July 1, 2013]

DECLARATION REGARDING SERVICE OF DECLARATION OF DISCLOSURE AND INCOME AND EXPENSE DECLARATION
(Family Law)

Family Code, §§ 2102, 2104, 2105, 2106, 2112
www.courts.ca.gov

For your protection and privacy, please press the Clear This Form button after you have printed the form.   Print this form   Save this form   Clear this form

Declaration of Disclosure

FL-140

ATTORNEY OR PARTY WITHOUT ATTORNEY *(Name, State Bar number, and address)*: TELEPHONE NO.: FAX NO. : E-MAIL ADDRESS: ATTORNEY FOR *(Name)*:	
SUPERIOR COURT OF CALIFORNIA, COUNTY OF STREET ADDRESS: MAILING ADDRESS: CITY AND ZIP CODE: BRANCH NAME:	
PETITIONER: RESPONDENT: OTHER PARENT/PARTY:	

DECLARATION OF DISCLOSURE ☐ Petitioner's ☐ Preliminary ☐ Respondent's ☐ Final	CASE NUMBER:

DO NOT FILE DECLARATIONS OF DISCLOSURE OR FINANCIAL ATTACHMENTS WITH THE COURT

In a dissolution, legal separation, or nullity action, both a preliminary and a final declaration of disclosure must be served on the other party with certain exceptions. Neither disclosure is filed with the court. Instead, a declaration stating that service of disclosure documents was completed or waived must be filed with the court (see form FL-141).

* *In summary dissolution cases, each spouse or domestic partner must exchange preliminary disclosures as described in Summary Dissolution Information (form FL-810). Final disclosures are not required (see Family Code section 2109).*
* *In a default judgment case that is not a stipulated judgment or a judgment based on a marital settlement agreement, only the petitioner is required to complete and serve a preliminary declaration of disclosure. A final disclosure is not required of either party (see Family Code section 2110).*
* *Service of preliminary declarations of disclosure may not be waived by an agreement between the parties.*
* *Parties who agree to waive final declarations of disclosure must file their written agreement with the court (see form FL-144).*

The petitioner must serve a preliminary declaration of disclosure at the same time as the Petition or within 60 days of filing the Petition. The respondent must serve a preliminary declaration of disclosure at the same time as the Response or within 60 days of filing the Response. The time periods may be extended by written agreement of the parties or by court order (see Family Code section 2104(f)).

Attached are the following:

1. ☐ A completed *Schedule of Assets and Debts* (form FL-142) or ☐ A *Property Declaration* (form FL-160) for *(specify)*: ☐ Community and Quasi-Community Property ☐ Separate Property.

2. ☐ A completed *Income and Expense Declaration* (form FL-150).

3. ☐ All tax returns filed by the party in the two years before the date that the party served the disclosure documents.

4. ☐ A statement of all material facts and information regarding valuation of all assets that are community property or in which the community has an interest *(not a form)*.

5. ☐ A statement of all material facts and information regarding obligations for which the community is liable *(not a form)*.

6. ☐ An accurate and complete written disclosure of any investment opportunity, business opportunity, or other income-producing opportunity presented since the date of separation that results from any investment, significant business, or other income-producing opportunity from the date of marriage to the date of separation *(not a form)*.

I declare under penalty of perjury under the laws of the State of California that the foregoing is true and correct.

Date:

_____
(TYPE OR PRINT NAME)   SIGNATURE

Page 1 of 1

Form Adopted for Mandatory Use Judicial Council of California FL-140 [Rev. July 1, 2013]	**DECLARATION OF DISCLOSURE** **(Family Law)**	Family Code, §§ 2102, 2104, 2105, 2106, 2112 www.courts.ca.gov

For your protection and privacy, please press the Clear This Form button after you have printed the form.   [Print this form]   [Save this form]   [Clear this form]

Schedule of Assets and Debts

To keep other people from seeing what you entered on your form, please press the Clear This Form button at the end of the form when finished.

THIS FORM SHOULD NOT BE FILED WITH THE COURT

FL-142

ATTORNEY OR PARTY WITHOUT ATTORNEY *(Name and Address)*:	TELEPHONE NO.:

ATTORNEY FOR *(Name)*:

SUPERIOR COURT OF CALIFORNIA, COUNTY OF

PETITIONER:

RESPONDENT:

SCHEDULE OF ASSETS AND DEBTS ☐ Petitioner's ☐ Respondent's	CASE NUMBER:

—— INSTRUCTIONS ——

List all your known community and separate assets or debts. Include assets even if they are in the possession of another person, including your spouse. If you contend an asset or debt is separate, put P (for Petitioner) or R (for Respondent) in the first column (separate property) to indicate to whom you contend it belongs.

All values should be as of the date of signing the declaration unless you specify a different valuation date with the description. For additional space, use a continuation sheet numbered to show which item is being continued.

ITEM NO.	ASSETS DESCRIPTION	SEP. PROP	DATE ACQUIRED	CURRENT GROSS FAIR MARKET VALUE	AMOUNT OF MONEY OWED OR ENCUMBRANCE
1.	REAL ESTATE *(Give street addresses and attach copies of deeds with legal descriptions and latest lender's statement.)*			$	$
2.	HOUSEHOLD FURNITURE, FURNISHINGS, APPLIANCES *(Identify.)*				
3.	JEWELRY, ANTIQUES, ART, COIN COLLECTIONS, etc. *(Identify.)*				

Page 1 of 4

Form Approved for Optional Use
Judicial Council of California
FL-142 [Rev. January 1, 2005]

SCHEDULE OF ASSETS AND DEBTS
(Family Law)

Code of Civil Procedure, §§ 2030(c), 2033.5
www.courtinfo.ca.gov

Schedule of Assets and Debts

ITEM NO.	ASSETS DESCRIPTION	SEP. PROP	DATE ACQUIRED	CURRENT GROSS FAIR MARKET VALUE	AMOUNT OF MONEY OWED OR ENCUMBRANCE
				$	$
4.	VEHICLES, BOATS, TRAILERS *(Describe and attach copy of title document.)*				
5.	SAVINGS ACCOUNTS *(Account name, account number, bank, and branch. Attach copy of latest statement.)*				
6.	CHECKING ACCOUNTS *(Account name and number, bank, and branch. Attach copy of latest statement.)*				
7.	CREDIT UNION, OTHER DEPOSIT ACCOUNTS *(Account name and number, bank, and branch. Attach copy of latest statement.)*				
8.	CASH *(Give location.)*				
9.	TAX REFUND				
10.	LIFE INSURANCE WITH CASH SURRENDER OR LOAN VALUE *(Attach copy of declaration page for each policy.)*				

Schedule of Assets and Debts

ITEM NO.	ASSETS DESCRIPTION	SEP. PROP	DATE ACQUIRED	CURRENT GROSS FAIR MARKET VALUE	AMOUNT OF MONEY OWED OR ENCUMBRANCE
11.	STOCKS, BONDS, SECURED NOTES, MUTUAL FUNDS *(Give certificate number and attach copy of the certificate or copy of latest statement.)*			$	$
12.	RETIREMENT AND PENSIONS *(Attach copy of latest summary plan documents and latest benefit statement.)*				
13.	PROFIT - SHARING, ANNUITIES, IRAS, DEFERRED COMPENSATION *(Attach copy of latest statement.)*				
14.	ACCOUNTS RECEIVABLE AND UNSECURED NOTES *(Attach copy of each.)*				
15.	PARTNERSHIPS AND OTHER BUSINESS INTERESTS *(Attach copy of most current K-1 form and Schedule C.)*				
16.	OTHER ASSETS				
17.	TOTAL ASSETS FROM CONTINUATION SHEET				
18.	TOTAL ASSETS			$	$

SCHEDULE OF ASSETS AND DEBTS
(Family Law)

Schedule of Assets and Debts

ITEM NO.	DEBTS—SHOW TO WHOM OWED	SEP. PROP.	TOTAL OWING	DATE INCURRED
19. STUDENT LOANS *(Give details.)*			$	
20. TAXES *(Give details.)*				
21. SUPPORT ARREARAGES *(Attach copies of orders and statements.)*				
22. LOANS—UNSECURED *(Give bank name and loan number and attach copy of latest statement.)*				
23. CREDIT CARDS *(Give creditor's name and address and the account number. Attach copy of latest statement.)*				
24. OTHER DEBTS *(Specify.):*				
25. TOTAL DEBTS FROM CONTINUATION SHEET				
26. TOTAL DEBTS			$	

27. ☐ *(Specify number):* _____ pages are attached as continuation sheets.

I declare under penalty of perjury under the laws of the State of California that the foregoing is true and correct.

Date:

_____ ▶ _____
(TYPE OR PRINT NAME)   (SIGNATURE OF DECLARANT)

For your protection and privacy, please press the Clear This Form button after you have printed the form.   **Save This Form**   **Print This Form**   **Clear This Form**

Chapter Eight

Judgments and Resolutions

It is now time to finalize the dissolution of marriage or legal separation. Provided all disclosures and documents have been completed and served as required, the exact process will depend upon the wants and needs of the client as well as exactly where you are in the time-line.

The soonest the marital status can be terminated is six months, plus one day from the date the Respondent was served. If the Respondent was served and 31 days have passed without a Response being filed and served, the Respondent's Default can be taken. The parties may also have reached an agreement at this point. If so, a marital settlement agreement can be submitted, provided all of the necessary Disclosure has been completed. Remember that a legal separation does not terminate the marital status so there is no six-month waiting period.

This Chapter will address the various ways the marital status can be terminated in a Dissolution. Legal separation does not terminate marital status, but the same process can be used to finalize a Judgment for Legal Separation. There are several ways the matter can be resolved and we will review the various types of resolutions. Finally, the judgment for dissolution of the parties will be obtained using the case facts you have been provided. The case study, utilized in this text, is considered a simple, uncontested divorce.

Bifurcation — Request for Separate Trial

Bifurcation is generally defined as: The division or separation of issues, wherein the termination of the martial status is separated from the other issues such as division of property, custody and support.

Family Code §2337 provides the Court with authority to grant an "early trial on the issue of dissolution of status of marriage." If the Respondent has filed a Response and upon the request of one or both parties, the court may sever (or alter) from the "normal" progression the issue of the status of the marriage, leaving all other matters to be tried or resolved at a later time. Such matters may include, but are not limited to, child custody and support, spousal support, and the division of property. This Code section also provides "protections" for the party who is **not** requesting the bifurcation. The most common "protection" is that if the "requesting" party should die before the matter goes to trial, the non-requesting party will be afforded the same benefits afforded a spouse of the decedent.

Health insurance is an important protection, particularly to a "supported" spouse. A Judgment of Dissolution and resulting termination of marital status normally will automatically terminate health insurance benefits for the non-employee spouse. However, Family Code § 2337 provides that the requesting party must maintain the non-requesting party's health insurance to insure that the non-requesting party does not suffer due to the early termination of the marital status. COBRA benefits may be available; however, the non-employee spouse must be made aware of this benefit and complete the applicable documents. If your office is representing the non-employee spouse, you will want to make sure that the court documents reference how this will be handled and the attorney may also want to have the client or the paralegal contact the insurance company to obtain the required forms and information.

There are many reasons why either of the parties may request a bifurcation. The complexity of issues, particularly the valuation and division of property, may take time. Several years may pass before the issues can be resolved or the case is in a position to be set the matter for trial. In that situation, the parties may simply wish to move on with terminating the marital status. One or both of the parties may want to remarry even though the issues have not been settled.

Once the "six-month waiting period" has passed, a party may be ready to move on and/or one or the other party may want to marry another person. A bifurcation **cannot** be granted until **after** the six-month period.

The two methods to achieve the bifurcation are: 1) applying to the Court or 2) written agreement of the parties.

Request for Separate Trial

The requesting party must file a Request for Order (FL-300) along with an Application for Separate Trial (FL-315). The requesting party must also provide a written declaration. To allow the non-requesting party time to prepare for the trial, the Application for Separate Trial requires a longer time for service of this type of motion. The form also requires the requesting party to have complied with all Disclosure rules. At the hearing the Judge will decide whether the marital status may be 1) terminated; 2) set for trial; or 3) if the termination may be delayed, pending the requesting party's compliance with the Court's orders. The Courts will retain jurisdiction over all other issues.

If the client is the requesting party and the attorney is fairly certain that the Judge will grant the Orders it is always a good idea to have the following forms ready: Declaration for Default/Uncontested Dissolution (FL-170), Judgment (FL-180), and Notice of Entry of Judgment (FL-190), along with the required envelopes (which will be discussed later in the chapter) for the attorney to take to the hearing.

You should also review the local rules to determine whether the court has any specific requirements to which your office (or the client) will have to comply before obtaining a hearing date and serving the other party.

Written Agreement for Bifurcation

The parties may sign a written stipulation (agreement) stating that they agree to have an early termination of the marital status. In that event, you will need to make sure that **each party's** Preliminary Declaration of Disclosure has been prepared and served on the other party. If there is a pension plan involved in the matter, the plan **must** be joined prior to the preparation of the agreement and the agreement must state that the Plan has been joined. Additionally, others holding assets subject to division, which may affect the rights of the supported spouse, must be notified and/or joined. Any previous Orders made by the court, such as custody and visitation or child support orders should be re-iterated in the agreement. It will also be necessary to confirm that insurance policies are maintained. The attorney should carefully review the conditions set forth in FC§ 2337 (set forth in its entirety below) to make sure that the client has complied and that all pertinent issues are addressed within the agreement, especially those concerning any potential liabilities and the indemnification of same.

The Court may require that if there are mutual "conduct" restraining orders or TROs to be incorporated in the bifurcation agreement, that the parties must appear and have the agreement entered on the record. (For more information, see Chapter Nine.)

Family Code § 2337 states in pertinent part:

The court may impose upon a party any of the following conditions on granting a severance of the issue of the dissolution of the status of the marriage, and in case that party's death, an order of any of the following conditions continues to be binding upon the party's estate:

(1) The party shall indemnify and hold the other party harmless from any taxes, reassessments, interest, and penalties payable by the other party if the dissolution of the marriage before the division of the parties' community estate results in a taxable event to either of the parties by reason of the ultimate division of their community estate, which taxes would not have been payable if the parties were still married at the time the division was made.

(2) Until judgment has been entered on all remaining issues and has become final, the party shall maintain all existing health and medical insurance coverage for the other party and the minor children as named dependents, so long as the party is legally able to do so. At the time the party is no longer legally eligible to maintain the other party as a named dependent under the existing health and medical policies, the party or the party's estate shall, at the party's sole expense, purchase and maintain health and medical insurance coverage that is comparable to the existing health and medical insurance coverage. If comparable insurance coverage is not obtained, the party or the party's estate is responsible for the health and medical expenses incurred by the other party that would have been covered by the insurance coverage, and shall indemnify and hold the other party harmless from any adverse consequences resulting from the lack of insurance.

(3) Until judgment has been entered on all remaining issues and has become final, the party shall indemnify and hold the other party harmless from any adverse consequences resulting to the other party if the bifurcation results in a termination of the other party's right to a probate homestead in the residence in which the other party resides at the time the severance was granted.

(4) Until judgment has been entered on all remaining issues and has become final, the party shall indemnify and hold the other party harmless from any adverse consequences resulting to the other party if the bifurcation results in the loss of the rights of the other party to a probate family allowance as the surviving spouse of the party.

(5) Until judgment has been entered on all remaining issues and has become final, the party shall indemnify and hold the other party harmless from any adverse con-

sequences resulting to the other party if the bifurcation results in the loss of the other party's rights to pension benefits, elections, or survivors' benefits under the party's pension or retirement plan to the extent that the other party would have been entitled to those benefits or elections as the surviving spouse of the party.

(6) Prior to entry of judgment terminating status, both of the following must occur:

(A) The party's retirement or pension plan shall be joined as a party to the proceeding for the dissolution.

(B) If applicable, an order pursuant to Section 2610 shall be entered with reference to the defined benefit or similar plan pending the ultimate resolution of the distribution of benefits under the employee benefit plan.

(7) The party shall indemnify and hold the other party harmless from any adverse consequences if the bifurcation results in the loss of rights to social security benefits or elections to the extent the other party would have been entitled to those benefits or elections as the surviving spouse of the party.

(8) Any other conditions the court deems just and equitable.

Default Judgment

If the Respondent does not file a Response within the thirty (30) days as required, the Petitioner may take the Respondent's Default. As a result, the Petitioner may bring the matter to conclusion, without any participation on the part of the Respondent. There are, however, many procedures with which the Petitioner must comply in order to bring the dissolution to conclusion.

First, the Petitioner will want to make sure that the original Proof of Service and the Request to Enter Default have been filed with the court. The Petitioner's Preliminary Declarations of Disclosure, including his/her Income & Expense Declarations (FL-150) and a Schedule of Assets and Debts (FL-142) must be served on the Respondent pursuant to FC§ 2104. The Court will not allow the final documents to be reviewed by the Judge, approved and filed unless these two requirements are completed. You will file the Petitioner's Declaration Regarding Service of Declaration of Disclosure (FL-141) with the Court, as well as a Proof of Service by Mail (FL-335) for the documents with the Court. The Income & Expense and the Schedule of Assets & Debts do not have to be filed. Please review the previous chapters that discuss both the preparation and service of the Preliminary Declarations of Disclosure as well as requirements and procedures for taking a person's default. As previously indicated, if the party upon whom the Default is being taken is in the active military service, additional restrictions may be in place and specific procedures must be followed.

Once you have prepared, served and/or filed the documents as stated above, you can prepare a "Default Judgment." The Default Judgment will be less complex than a Marital Settlement Agreement (MSA) because it is **not** an agreement. It is simply a legal document that sets forth the resolution of the issues in the divorce, such as custody, visitation, support and the division of property. In the event any previous orders have been made, they will need to be incorporated into the Default Judgment. The Default Judgment **must** contain an equal division of assets and liabilities. The client may not request that he or she be awarded **all** of the assets and that **all** the debts be given to the spouse.

California is a community property state. Although you may be taking the Respondent's default, the Court still has a duty to make sure that the property is divided equally among the parties.

The Declaration for Default or Uncontested Dissolution or Legal Separation (FL-170) must be completed. A Property Declaration (FL-160) indicating the equal division of property **must** be completed and submitted, as well. If there is separate property, you will also need to prepare a Property Declaration for any separate property listed on the Petition.

Remember that any issues listed on the Petition must also be included in the Default Judgment. Items of property must be listed in the Property Declaration(s) and must also be included in the Default Judgment.

A Judgment (FL-180) will be the "face sheet" for the Default Judgment. A sample Default Judgment (Appendix 8A) is included for your reference. In the event there is a family home or other asset that needs to be divided or transferred, the appropriate "legal descriptions" of those documents must be included in the Default Judgment. Once the Default Judgment is entered by the Court, you may need to obtain a certified copy from the Court and have the certified copy of the Judgment filed with the County Recorder, in the County where the property is located.

> For example: If there is a family home and a retirement of equal value and Wife will get the home and Husband the retirement in the Default Judgment, you must include the legal description of the home within the Judgment. You will also want to include the specific name of the pension plan. Once the Judgment is entered and you have obtained a certified copy, you can record the Judgment with the County Recorder. This will accomplish the transfer of title of the real property (home) to Wife. You can also mail a copy of the certified Judgment to the pension plan, so that the plan administrator knows that Wife has relinquished all interest in Husband's retirement.

A Notice of Entry of Judgment (FL-190) will be prepared and submitted along with the "final" documents. (These are listed below.) You will also need to provide self-addressed, stamped envelopes to the Court so that the clerk can mail copies of the Entry of Judgment to your office (on behalf of the Petitioner) and to the Respondent. This will be the only document that the Respondent will receive letting him or her know that the Judgment has been entered. The Court is not required to provide the Respondent with a copy of the actual Default Judgment.

You will also need to submit any collateral documents relating to any orders made in the Judgment, such as Income Withholding for Support, Child Support Case Registry form, Joinders for the Pension Plan, etc.

The completed "final" package **must** contain the following documents:

Declaration for Default/Uncontested Dissolution or Legal Separation (FL-170)

Property Declaration(s) (FL-160)

Judgment (face sheet) (FL-180) with Default Judgment (pleading) attached

Notice of Entry of Judgment (FL-190) with envelopes

Child Support Case Registry (FL-191)

If the client wishes to have child and/or spousal support paid through Respondent's wages, you should also submit an Income Withholding for Support (FL-196) with the documents.

You will provide the Court with the original and at least two copies of each of the above documents. You will also provide a large postage paid and addressed envelope for the return of the "final" package to your office. In addition, you need to provide the Court with a self-addressed, postage paid envelope for each party so that the Court can mail a copy of the Notice of Entry of Judgment to the parties or their attorney(s) of record.

In the event you work in a pro bono clinic or frequently with pro se clients, it is common to use many of the Judicial Council forms as attachments to the Judgment face sheet to avoid having to prepare documents, particularly if the client requests the Judgment at a "prove up" hearing. It is easier to prepare forms, wherein the boxes can be checked and/or changed as needed in court, than have to return to the office or risk that the party will never complete the process if it is not user-friendly. Many of the forms that are used for the Findings and Order can also be used for the Judgment. There are a few exceptions, such as the Property Order Attachment to Judgment (FL-345) which must be used. Review each form carefully to determine which form is appropriate should you find your skills being used in these situations.

Contested Dissolution: Setting Matter for Trial

Any time the parties cannot reach an agreement, the matter is considered contested and should be set for trial. The first two matters that need to be handled at this point are: 1) make sure that **all** Preliminary Declarations of Disclosure have been served on the opposing party; and 2) check the local rules to determine what forms must be completed, how to set the matter for trial, and any other specific requirements of the Court.

Most Courts will have their own *"At Issue Memorandum"* which must be completed and served on the other party and then filed with the Court. Most Courts will want to know if you have complied with the Preliminary Declarations of Disclosure, Family Mediation (if there are minor children) and any other local rules. The Court may also want to know what attempts you have made to reach an agreement and if you have conferred with the other party (or attorney of record) to obtain mutually available dates for a Settlement Conference and Trial.

You are now on the **fast track**. Depending upon how quickly the local Court sets matters for trial, you will want to make sure that you have enough time to finish any discovery, file motions to compel any documents that you have not received, and/or take the deposition of a party or an expert. The **final** Declarations of Disclosure will have to be completed, served and filed with the Court. Much like civil matters, most Courts have local rules governing the time lines for the exchange and filing of these documents prior to the trial date. In most instances, you will want to have Disclosures done at least 45 days prior to trial, unless local rules or Code of Civil Procedures requires a different time line.

Some Courts will have a *Trial Setting Conference*. If that is the case, you will want to confer with the opposing counsel (or their paralegal) about dates for the Trial Setting Conference. Once you have that date, you will need to make sure the attorney's calendar is current so that he or she will know the dates available for the trial. Contact the client and make sure there are no conflicts, such as a large project, work travel or vacation plans that might interfere with potential dates. Most Courts do not like to reschedule Trial Dates without express agreement of the parties. Don't cause yourself and the attorney a lot of extra time and/or work by not having the attorney and the client prepared to set a date for trial. During a Trial Setting Conference, the Judge will usually ask what matters are "at issue." The Judge wants to get a feel for the amount of time that the trial will take. The attorney will also need to make an assessment as to how much time to set aside for trial and trial preparation. In most counties where a Trial Setting Conference is held, the Court will require you to prepare and serve a Memorandum of Issues at least ten (10) days prior to the conference. The Court has the ability to reset the Trial Setting Conference for a future date if you have not complied with any local rule in this respect.

As you become a more experienced family law paralegal, you will be able to work closely with the attorney to determine the amount of time necessary for trial. You will learn which causes are highly contested and which issues are most likely to remain unresolved at the time of trial. Your average case will likely only take only a day or less. However, if there is extensive property and/or experts will be called to testify, it may be necessary to request more than one day for trial. Most parties will be able to settle most aspects of their case without the need to go to trial. Oftentimes, it is just one issue over which they cannot agree. Most commonly, it will be child custody or support.

Once the matter has been set for trial, you will want to carefully review your timeline to make sure that you comply with all rules in the Code of Civil Procedure, as well as with local rules. It is also a good idea to prepare a trial time-line and checklist so that all dates are calendared and the attorney is aware of those dates. Do not jeopardize the client's right to admit evidence or to be heard by not completing all the necessary preparatory work, or by not giving proper notice to the opposing party and the Court.

In most counties, the client will have to attend a *Mandatory* Settlement Conference. That Settlement Conference is a type of court-ordered mediation. Again, review your local rules to determine the number of days (court or calendar) **prior** to the Settlement Conference or Trial that the client's Settlement Conference Statement (or Statement of Issues) must be submitted and if there are particular forms or formats to follow. (See the following section for more information about the Statement of Issues.)

Both the parties are **required** to attend the Settlement Conference. Most Settlement Conferences will involve the parties, their attorneys and two "pro tem" judges, who will try to assist the parties in resolving their differences. A Settlement Conference is a means to resolve the issues without having to go forward with a trial.

If the parties have reached an agreement, at the conclusion of the Settlement Conference, they will be brought before the Judge and the Stipulation will be read into the Court's record. The Court transcript will be available or alternatively a Minute Order or Stipulation will be prepared as per each Court's custom and rules. The parties will sign the Stipulation before the Judge. It then becomes a binding agreement and an enforceable Order. The attorney will still want you to prepare a formal Order for circulation and signatures. This is called a Stipulated Judgment.

If the parties have reached an agreement on some of the issues, only those specific items will be read into the Court's record (Minute Order or will be part of the transcript), and the parties will be required to go forward with the trial on the remaining issues. Alternatively, if the parties have been unable to resolve **all** of their issues, the parties will go forward with the trial, as previously set, unless the Court deems it necessary to have the Trial moved to a later date. In that event, the Court will usually require one of the attorneys to prepare a Notice of Trial, which will be served on the other party and will be filed with the Court, along with a Proof of Service (of the Trial Notice). Check your local rules to determine whether any other types of orders may be made that require the parties to comply with mediation or another manner of resolving their differences without having to go to trial.

Settlement Conference Statements — Trial Briefs

The Statement of Issues and Contentions ("Statement") may also be referred to as a Settlement Conference or Pre-Trial Brief, depending upon the Court's local rules. Most local rules will outline the contents of the Statement. The Statement will usually contain all the jurisdictional facts, the information regarding the party's children, support, assets and debts, and any other relative facts and issues. The Statement should also contain any previous orders made such as: Orders After Hearing, Stipulation & Orders, which were adopted, etc. The Statement should reiterate all issues that have been resolved and outline which issues remain at issue. (A Sample Statement of Issues is included as Appendix 8B.) You will want to confirm that you comply with any specific format that is required by the Court. As with the hearing process, the Court usually prefers the issues to be presented in the same order as they were listed on the original Petition.

In most cases in family law matters, the Statement of Issues and the Trial Brief will be very similar documents. You may prepare either a Supplemental Statement of Issues or a Trial Brief prior to Trial, in the event there is additional information, expert testimony, evidence that requires clarification, or additional relevant case law that may affect the client's position. Again, check your local rules, as well as the wishes of your attorney as to which documents need to be prepared.

The Trial Brief may also include additional documentation. At this point, the attorney may want you to prepare a Trial Notebook to be used at trial. Unless otherwise requested, the trial will be before a judge. It is **not** a jury trial.

Disclosure of Documents, Experts, Motions

You will want to carefully review the applicable Code of Civil Procedure sections that related to pre-trial motions, exchange of expert witness lists and the documents. As previously discussed, Family Code § 2024 et seq. provides the requirements for the exchange and disclosure of **all** financial documents of the parties.

As always, consult any local rules that may affect disclosures, experts and pre-trial.

Of primary concern is allowing enough time to complete all disclosure documents to anticipate the exchange of expert witness information, and any motions that need to be filed. In other words, always allow yourself enough time to be prepared and ready for trial.

Stipulated Judgment, Judgment on the Reserved Issues

A Marital Settlement Agreement, Stipulated Judgment, and Judgment on the Reserved Issues are somewhat similar documents. However, they serve different purposes, depending upon how the matter(s) has/have been resolved.

A Marital Settlement Agreement (MSA) is an agreement by the parties and is usually prepared as the result of an **uncontested** dissolution. Even if the Respondent files a Response, as long the parties reach an amicable resolution without having appeared at a trial, the matter is considered uncontested. Chapter Ten will discuss the MSA in greater detail.

Stipulated Judgment

A Stipulated Judgment is prepared as the result of the parties having been through a Settlement Conference or the Trial process. It is used for **contested** matters. The Minute Order and the facts read into the Court's record at Settlement Conference and/or the Trial will be the foundation for the Stipulated Judgment. The Stipulated Judgment will contain the jurisdictional facts and the manner in which all issues raised in the Petition have been resolved, either by the parties stipulating and/or by the Court's order. The parties may add additional information, as necessary, as long as both parties agree to any additional language. Both parties will need to sign the Stipulated Judgment and the attorney or attorneys, will sign to "approve as to form and content." The Stipulated Judgment (pleading) will be attached to the Judgment (face sheet) (FL-180) and it will be submitted to the Court for the Judge's signature and filing.

Upon its execution, the Stipulated Judgment becomes an enforceable Order upon its execution. Any related documents, such as an Income Withholding for Support, DROs, Deeds, etc. should always be prepared, signed and submitted, as necessary, along with the Stipulated Judgment.

A Notice of Entry of Judgment (FL-190) must be submitted to the Court with the Stipulated Judgment, as well as self-addressed, postage paid envelopes to be mailed to the parties or their attorney(s) of record. If there are minor children from the marriage, a Child Support Case Registry form must also be submitted for the Court's information.

You do not need to submit any other forms, such as those that would be submitted along with an MSA, with a Stipulated Judgment as those forms are in lieu of the declarations and jurisdiction facts which are read into the record at the Settlement Conference and/or Trial. Any other forms, such as Declaration Regarding Service of Final Declaration of Disclosure, will have been submitted prior to trial.

Judgment on the Reserved Issues

A Judgment on the Reserved Issues will follow the same format as a Stipulated Judgment but is used when the marital status has been previously terminated by Bifurcation. As you will recall, during the Bifurcation process, the parties only agreed to terminate their marital status and to indemnify and hold each other harmless. The resolution of the remaining issues was *reserved* until a later time.

At such time as the parties have reached an agreement or a Settlement Conference and/or Trial has occurred, the document that is prepared at that point is called a Judgment (or Agreement) on the Reserved Issues.

Once again, the Judgment (or Agreement) on the Reserved Issues, should follow the same format as the MSA or the Minute Order/Transcript, which are essentially in the same order. This document will reiterate the jurisdictional facts, reiterate the previous orders made with respect to the marital status, outline any other orders that may have been made in the Stipulation or Order to Bifurcate, and set forth the resolution of the remaining issues.

The Judgment is signed by both of the parties, "approved as to form and content" by the attorney(s), submitted to the Judge and, when signed by the Judge, will be filed by the clerk of the court.

A Judgment face sheet (form FL-180) **is not** submitted with a Judgment on the Reserved Issues as it was previously submitted during the Bifurcation process. A Notice of Entry of Judgment (form FL-190) may be submitted, but check your local court rules to determine if the court mandates this form. (Since the Judgment face sheet was already provided with the termination of marital status it will not be filed again.)

If the Judgment is an Agreement, and a Settlement Conference or Trial was not held, you will need to prepare a Declaration Regarding Service of Final Declaration of Disclosure (FL-141) form, with Proof of Service, and submit it to the Court with the document. You will also want to make sure that the other party has submitted their Final Declaration by requesting a **filed** copy for your records, since they will have served your office with an unfiled copy. Alternatively, you may request that the other party's attorney provide a copy of the document to your office for submission with the other documents. This will assure that the entire document package will not be returned because the other party has not complied and will forestall any delay in the processing of the documents and the entry of the judgment.

Again, you will want to have prepared, signed, and submitted along with the Judgment any of the applicable documents, including: Income Withholding for Support, Child Support Case Registry, DRO, etc.

Notice Regarding Health Care Responsibilities and Modification of Child Support Attachment

Effective January 1, 2000, (FL-192): Notice Regarding Rights and Responsibilities — Health Care Costs and Reimbursement Procedures/Information Sheet on Changing a Child Support Order **must** be attached to **all** Judgments if there are minor children of the marriage. Do not forget to attach these forms and include them in the final page count for the document.

Alternative Dispute Resolution

Some parties will find that Alternative Dispute Resolution (ADR) or Collaborative Law Practice methods can be helpful in assisting the parties to a resolution to the division of property. Family Court Services and Private Mediation are for resolving custody and visitation issues. There are many attorneys who have incorporated ADR or Collaborative Practice, usually by means of mediation of property and support issues, into their practice. In most cases, your local bar association will have a list of the attorneys who are well-versed in the mediation process. As indicated in Chapter Two, FC§ 2013 defines the collaborative law practice and subsequent legislative enactments (expected to be codified in 2008) will provide procedures for collaborative family law practice.

An attorney/mediator typically meets with the parties as many times as necessary to review the property and support issues, review valuation reports and other related information, and finally to work with the parties to reach an amicable resolution.

The ADR/Collaborative process does not allow the attorney/mediator to represent either party. The attorney/mediator may prepare the Martial Settlement Agreement once the parties reach an agreement. However, if the parties are unable to reach an agreement, or refuse to sign the agreement, they will each need to seek separate legal counsel to continue with the litigation process. The Collaborative Practice was discussed previously and is usually decided upon at the commencement of the matter.

In an attempt to keep the matter out of court, it is also becoming more common for attorneys who are representing the respective parties to suggest that they retain a third party, attorney/mediator, to assist them. Clients are also becoming more savvy and may request this type of resolution in order to avoid costly litigation and court fees or to feel they are using their fees more cost-effectively by retaining an attorney/mediator. Remember, that an attorney representing a client is that person's **advocate**. While the attorney can certainly encourage and recommend that a client compromise, if the client does not take the attorney's advice, the attorney has no other option but to become adversarial on behalf of the client. Those positions lead to litigation. Alternatively, the attorney may feel that his or her client does not have sound legal footing, and therefore, knows that mediation of the matter may result in a better resolution for the client. Mediation is often the "best of both worlds."

Once the parties, if they are represented by counsel, have completed the mediation process with a third party, a report or summary of the resolved issues will be prepared and forwarded to their respective attorneys. One of the attorneys will then prepare the Marital Settlement Agreement for review by and signature of the parties.

In the event that the client does wish to pursue ADR/Collaborative Law, all property valuations will need to be completed as well as all Declarations of Disclosure. The mediator will want to have available all of this documentation in order to fully assist the parties. You will want to contact the attorney/mediator, once the parties have agreed to a specific individual, and determine his/her requirements, which could include, such items as: up-front retainer, signed agreement, disclosure information provided prior to the first meeting, copies of previously filed documents that related to the issues to be resolved, and any other pertinent information requested by the mediator.

You will also want to let the client know of the attorney/mediator's requirements so that they are fully prepared for the meeting with the attorney/mediator.

Preparation of Property Spread Sheet

As previously indicated in Chapter Seven, under the division of property, the community assets and liabilities must be divided in order to create an equal division of property. The basis for this division will be a spreadsheet, similar to those described in Chapter Seven.

The spreadsheet is often a proposal to demonstrate to each party that the property was divided equally or 50/50. The same spreadsheet can also attached as an exhibit to the marital settlement agreement or may be used as a basis for the Property Declaration which would be submitted to the Court in the event of a Default Judgment. Most people respond to this type of document as it is hard to argue with "the numbers," if the property has been accurately and fairly valued.

As set forth in the provisions for division of property in the Family Code, the parties may agree to a settlement that is less than equal as long as the needs of the parties are met. The agreement must be in writing and signed by both parties.

It is always best to have the spreadsheet prepared and agreed upon by the parties before preparing the Marital Settlement Agreement (MSA). It will be much easier to prepare the MSA if you know in advance who is getting what, in addition to the custody, support and other related orders. The spreadsheet will also help you make sure that all related details are covered completely.

For example, if the parties are going to divide the pension plan equally, it is always best to have the Domestic Relations Order (DRO) ready to be signed at the same time as the MSA. If one party is going to retain the family home, an Interspousal Transfer Deed should be executed along with a Preliminary Change of Ownership Report so that it can be submitted to the County Recorder. A copy of the executed Interspousal Deed should also be incorporated in the MSA.

Depending upon the type of employee benefit/pension plan, the non-employee spouse may have an option to receive their share in a lump sum, upon the maturation or retirement of the employee spouse, or may receive their share on the date the employee spouse becomes eligible to receive their benefit, even if he/she does not retire. See Chapter Ten for more information on employee benefit/pension plans and DROs.

Nunc Pro Tunc

In the family law setting you will occasionally come across people who thought they were divorced and really are not. FC§ 2346(a), (c) state that when a judgment of dissolution ought to have been or was granted but, by mistake, inadvertence or negligence, the judgment either was not entered or was not entered as early as was possible, the court may "cause the judgment to be signed, filed, and entered at the earliest date it could have been entered."

This can happen for a number of reasons:

1) Many years ago a Final Judgment had to be submitted after an Interlocutory was filed with the court. If the Final Judgment was not submitted after the appropriate "waiting period," the person's marital status was not actually terminated;

2) If the marital status is reserved as part of the Judgment and then neither of the parties files a motion or a Judgment on the Reserved Issues to have the marital status terminated; or,

3) One (or both) of the parties thought the Judgment had been entered on a specific date (perhaps the date it was filed/entered and not the date listed as the termination of marital status date).

Parties to any of the above situations can arrive in the law office and inform the attorney that they have remarried and have essentially committed bigamy because they didn't know they weren't divorced.

The remedy for this situation, if applicable, is to request that the Court enter the Judgment *Nunc Pro Tunc* or "before the fact." Essentially the client is asking that the date of termination of marital status be "back-dated."

If the attorney advises the client, that this option is available, a Judgment will need to be entered, with the appropriate boxes on the Judgment (FL-180) form.

In some cases, you will have to file a Motion requesting that the Judgment be entered and serve it on the other party. Or, perhaps the other party can be contacted and will stipulate to the Judgment to Terminate Marital Status. The Judgment then would be entered on a date prior to the date of the marriage to another person.

The Court may enter a nunc pro tunc judgment in the event a decision was rendered, but one of the parties dies before the judgment becomes final. The judgment would then be entered as of the date of the decision, or pre-date the spouse's death.

Forms Associated with Topic

Declaration for Default Uncontested Dissolution (FL-170)

Appearance Stipulation & Waivers (if Respondent filed Response) (FL-130)

Stipulation Regarding Waiver of Final Declaration of Disclosure (FL-141)

Judgment (face sheet) (FL-180)

Notice of Rights and Responsibilities—Health Care Costs and Reimbursement Procedures/Information Sheet on Changing a Child Support Order (FL-192)

Notice of Entry of Judgment (FL-190)

(See examples of some forms on the following pages)

Key Terms

- Alternate Dispute Resolution
- Collaborative Practice
- Bifurcation
- Default Judgment
- Stipulated Judgment
- Marital Settlement Agreement
- Judgment on the Reserved Issues
- At Issue Memorandum
- Nunc Pro Tunc

Declaration for Default or Uncontested Dissolution or Legal Separation

	FL-170
ATTORNEY OR PARTY WITHOUT ATTORNEY *(Name, State Bar number, and address):* JOAN CARE-ACTOR, SBN ****** LAW OFFICES OF JOAN CARE-ACTOR 75000 WHY ME LANE, SACRAMENTO, CA 95826 TELEPHONE NO.: 916-555-1234 FAX NO. *(Optional):* 916-555-1233 E-MAIL ADDRESS *(Optional):* joan@ care-actorlaw.com ATTORNEY FOR *(Name):* SANDIE SHORES, PETITIONER	*FOR COURT USE ONLY* To keep other people from seeing what you entered on your form, please press the Clear This Form button at the end of the form when finished.

SUPERIOR COURT OF CALIFORNIA, COUNTY OF SACRAMENTO
STREET ADDRESS: 3341 POWER INN ROAD
MAILING ADDRESS: 3341 POWER INN ROAD
CITY AND ZIP CODE: SACRAMENTO, CA 95826
BRANCH NAME: FAMILY LAW

PETITIONER: SANDIE SHORES

RESPONDENT: ROCKY SHORES

DECLARATION FOR DEFAULT OR UNCONTESTED ☑ DISSOLUTION ☐ LEGAL SEPARATION	CASE NUMBER: 14FLXXXXXXX

(NOTE: Items 1 through 12 apply to both dissolution and legal separation proceedings.)

1. I declare that if I appeared in court and were sworn, I would testify to the truth of the facts in this declaration.

2. I agree that my case will be proven by this declaration and that I will not appear before the court unless I am ordered by the court to do so.

3. All the information in the ☐ amended ☑ *Petition* ☐ *Response* is true and correct.

4. **Type of case** *(check a, b, or c):*

   a. ☐ **Default without agreement**

      (1) No response has been filed and there is no written agreement or stipulated judgment between the parties;

      (2) The default of the respondent was entered or is being requested, and I am not seeking any relief not requested in the petition; and

      (3) The following statement is true *(check one):*

         (A) ☐ There are no assets or debts to be disposed of by the court.

         (B) ☐ The community and quasi-community assets and debts are listed on the **completed** current *Property Declaration* (form FL-160), which includes an estimate of the value of the assets and debts that I propose to be distributed to each party. The division in the proposed *Judgment* (form FL-180) is a fair and equal division of the property and debts, or if there is a negative estate, the debts are assigned fairly and equitably.

   b. ☐ **Default with agreement**

      (1) No response has been filed and the parties have agreed that the matter may proceed as a default matter without notice; and

      (2) The parties have entered into a written agreement regarding their property and their marriage or domestic partnership rights, including support, the original of which is being or has been submitted to the court. I request that the court approve the agreement.

   c. ☑ **Uncontested**

      (1) Both parties have appeared in the case; and

      (2) The parties have entered into a written agreement regarding their property and their marriage or domestic partnership rights, including support, the original of which is being or has been submitted to the court. I request that the court approve the agreement.

5. **Declaration of disclosure** *(check a, b, or c):*

   a. ☐ Both the petitioner and respondent have filed, or are filing concurrently, a *Declaration Regarding Service of Declaration of Disclosure* (form FL-141) and an *Income and Expense Declaration* (form FL-150).

   b. ☐ This matter is proceeding by default. I am the petitioner in this action and have filed a proof of service of the preliminary *Declaration of Disclosure* (form FL-140) with the court. I hereby waive receipt of the final *Declaration of Disclosure* (form FL-140) from the respondent.

   c. ☑ This matter is proceeding as an uncontested action. Service of the final *Declaration of Disclosure* (form FL-140) is mutually waived by both parties. A waiver provision executed by both parties under penalty of perjury is contained on the *Stipulation and Waiver of Final Declaration of Disclosure* (form FL-144), in the settlement agreement or proposed judgment or another, separate stipulation.

Page 1 of 3

Form Adopted for Mandatory Use
Judicial Council of California
FL-170 [Rev. July 1, 2012] **DECLARATION FOR DEFAULT OR UNCONTESTED
DISSOLUTION OR LEGAL SEPARATION
(Family Law)** Family Code, § 2336
www.courts.ca.gov

Declaration for Default or
Uncontested Dissolution or Legal Separation

FL-170

PETITIONER: SANDIE SHORES	CASE NUMBER:
RESPONDENT: ROCKY SHORES	14FLXXXXXXX

6. [✔] **Child custody and visitation (parenting time)** should be ordered as set forth in the proposed *Judgment* (form FL-180).

    a. [✔] The information in *Declaration Under Uniform Child Custody Jurisdiction and Enforcement Act* (UCCJEA) (form FL-105)
        [ ] has [✔] has not changed since it was last filed with the court. *(If changed, attach updated form.)*

    b. [ ] There is an existing court order for custody/parenting time in another case in *(county)*:
        The case number is *(specify)*:

    c. [ ] The current custody and visitation (parenting time) previously ordered in this case, or current schedule is *(specify)*:
        [ ] Contained on Attachment 6c.

    d. [✔] Facts in support of requested judgment (*In a default case, state your reasons below*):
        [✔] Contained on Attachment 6d.

        AS SET FORTH IN THE JUDGMENT/MARITAL SETTLEMENT AGREEMENT SUBMITTED TO THE COURT CONCURRENTLY.

7. [✔] **Child support** should be ordered as set forth in the proposed *Judgment* (form FL-180).

    a. If there are minor children, check and complete item (1) if applicable and item (2) or (3):

        (1) [ ] Child support is being enforced in another case in *(county)*:
            The case number is *(specify)*:

        (2) [✔] The information in the child support calculation attached to the proposed judgment is correct based on my personal knowledge.

        (3) [ ] I request that this order be based on the [ ] petitioner's [ ] respondent's earning ability. The facts in support of my estimate of earning ability are *(specify)*:
            [ ] Continued on Attachment 7a(3).

    b. Complete items (1) and (2) regarding public assistance.

        (1) I [ ] am receiving [✔] am not receiving [ ] intend to apply for public assistance for the child or children listed in the proposed order.

        (2) To the best of my knowledge, the other party [ ] is [✔] is not receiving public assistance.

    c. [ ] The petitioner [ ] respondent is presently receiving public assistance, and all support should be made payable to the local child support agency at the address set forth in the proposed judgment. A representative of the local child support agency has signed the proposed judgment.

8. **Spousal, Partner, and Family Support** (*If a support order or attorney fees are requested, submit a completed* Income and Expense Declaration *(form FL-150) unless a current form is on file. Include your best estimate of the other party's income. Check at least one of the following.*)

    a. [ ] I knowingly give up forever any right to receive spousal or partner support.

    b. [ ] I ask the court to reserve jurisdiction to award spousal or partner support in the future to *(name)*:

    c. [ ] I ask the court to terminate forever spousal or partner support for: [ ] petitioner [ ] respondent.

    d. [✔] Spousal support or domestic partner support should be ordered as set forth in the proposed *Judgment* (form FL-180) based on the factors described in:
        [ ] *Spousal or Partner Support Declaration Attachment* (form FL-157)
        [✔] written agreement
        [ ] attached declaration (*Attachment 8d.*)

    e. [ ] Family support should be ordered as set forth in the proposed *Judgment* (form FL-180).

    f. [ ] Other *(specify)*:

Declaration for Default or
Uncontested Dissolution or Legal Separation

FL-170

PETITIONER: SANDIE SHORES	CASE NUMBER:
RESPONDENT: ROCKY SHORES	14FLXXXXXXX

9. ☐ **Parentage** of the children of the petitioner and respondent born prior to their marriage or domestic partnership should be ordered as set forth in the proposed *Judgment* (form FL-180).

    a. ☐ A Voluntary Declaration of Paternity is attached.

    b. ☐ Parentage was previously established by the court in *(county)*:
        The case number is *(specify)*:

    ☐ Written agreement of the parties attached here or to the *Judgment* (form FL-180).

10. ☑ **Attorney fees** should be ordered as set forth in the proposed *Judgment* (form FL-180)
    ☐ facts in support in form FL-319
    ☐ other *(specify facts below)*:

11. ☐ The judgment should be entered nunc pro tunc for the following reasons *(specify)*:

12. ☐ The petitioner ☐ respondent requests restoration of his or her former name as set forth in the proposed *Judgment* (form FL-180).

13. There are irreconcilable differences that have led to the irremediable breakdown of the marriage or domestic partnership, and there is no possibility of saving the marriage or domestic partnership through counseling or other means.

14. This declaration may be reviewed by a commissioner sitting as a temporary judge, who may determine whether to grant this request or require my appearance under Family Code section 2336.

STATEMENTS IN THIS BOX APPLY ONLY TO DISSOLUTIONS

15. If this is a dissolution of marriage or of a domestic partnership created in another state, the petitioner and/or the respondent have been residents of this county for at least three months and of the state of California for at least six months continuously and immediately preceding the date of the filing of the petition for dissolution of marriage or domestic partnership.

16. I ask that the court grant the request for a judgment for dissolution of marriage or domestic partnership based on irreconcilable differences and that the court make the orders set forth in the proposed *Judgment* (form FL-180) submitted with this declaration.

17. ☐ This declaration is for the termination of **marital or domestic partner status only.** I ask the court to reserve jurisdiction over all issues whose determination is not requested in this declaration.

THIS STATEMENT APPLIES ONLY TO LEGAL SEPARATIONS

18. I ask that the court grant the request for a judgment for legal separation based on irreconcilable differences and that the court make the orders set forth in the proposed *Judgment* (form FL-180) submitted with this declaration.

I understand that a judgment of legal separation does not terminate a marriage or domestic partnership and that I am still married or a partner in a domestic partnership.

---

19. ☐ Other *(specify)*:

I declare under penalty of perjury under the laws of the State of California that the foregoing is true and correct.

Date:

SANDIE SHORES ▶

(TYPE OR PRINT NAME)	(SIGNATURE OF DECLARANT)

FL-170 [Rev. July 1, 2012]

DECLARATION FOR DEFAULT OR UNCONTESTED DISSOLUTION OR LEGAL SEPARATION
(Family Law)

Page 3 of 3

For your protection and privacy, please press the Clear This Form button after you have printed the form.

| Print This Form | Save This Form | Clear This Form |

Appearance, Stipulations, and Waivers

ATTORNEY OR PARTY WITHOUT ATTORNEY *(Name, State Bar number, and address)*:
JOAN CARE-ACTOR, SBN ******
CARE-ACTOR LAW FIRM
75000 WHY ME LANE
SACRAMENTO, CA 95826
TELEPHONE NO.: 916-555-1234   FAX NO. *(Optional)*: 916-555-1233
E-MAIL ADDRESS *(Optional)*: joan@careactorlaw.com
ATTORNEY FOR *(Name)*: SANDIE SHORES, PETITIONER

> To keep other people from seeing what you entered on your form, please press the Clear This Form button at the end of the form when finished.

SUPERIOR COURT OF CALIFORNIA, COUNTY OF SACRAMENTO
STREET ADDRESS: 3341 POWER INN ROAD
MAILING ADDRESS: 3341 POWER INN ROAD
CITY AND ZIP CODE: SACRAMENTO, CA 95826
BRANCH NAME: FAMILY LAW

PETITIONER: SANDIE SHORES
RESPONDENT: ROCKY SHORES

APPEARANCE, STIPULATIONS, AND WAIVERS

CASE NUMBER: 14FLXXXXXXX

1. **Appearance by respondent** *(you must choose one)*:
   a. [✔] By filing this form, I make a general appearance.
   b. [ ] I have previously made a general appearance.
   c. [ ] I am a member of the military services of the United States of America. I have completed and attached to this form *Declaration and Conditional Waiver of Rights Under the Servicemembers Civil Relief Act of 2003* (form FL-130(A)).

2. **Agreements, stipulations, and waivers** *(choose all that apply)*:
   a. [✔] The parties agree that this cause may be decided as an uncontested matter.
   b. [✔] The parties waive their rights to notice of trial, a statement of decision, a motion for new trial, and the right to appeal.
   c. [✔] This matter may be decided by a commissioner sitting as a temporary judge.
   d. [✔] The parties have a written agreement that will be submitted to the court, or a stipulation for judgment will be submitted to the court and attached to *Judgment (Family Law)* (form FL-180).
   e. [✔] None of these agreements or waivers will apply unless the court approves the stipulation for judgment or incorporates the written settlement agreement into the judgment.
   f. [ ] This is a parentage case, and both parties have signed an *Advisement and Waiver of Rights Re: Establishment of Parental Relationship* (form FL-235) or its equivalent.

3. **Other** *(specify)*:

Date:
SANDY SHORES
(TYPE OR PRINT NAME)   ▶   (SIGNATURE OF PETITIONER)

Date:
ROCKY SHORES
(TYPE OR PRINT NAME)   ▶   (SIGNATURE OF RESPONDENT)

Date:
JOAN CARE-ACTOR
(TYPE OR PRINT NAME)   ▶   (SIGNATURE OF ATTORNEY FOR PETITIONER)

Date:
SAM E. SPADE
(TYPE OR PRINT NAME)   ▶   (SIGNATURE OF ATTORNEY FOR RESPONDENT)

Page 1 of 1

Form Approved for Optional Use
Judicial Council of California
FL-130 [Rev. January 1, 2011]

APPEARANCE, STIPULATIONS, AND WAIVERS
(Family Law—Uniform Parentage—Custody and Support)

Government Code, § 70673
www.courtinfo.ca.gov

For your protection and privacy, please press the Clear This Form button after you have printed the form.   Save This Form   Print This Form   Clear This Form

Stipulation and Waiver of Final Declaration of Disclosure

FL-144

ATTORNEY OR PARTY WITHOUT ATTORNEY *(Name, State Bar number, and address)*:	
JOAN CARE-ACTOR, SBN ****** LAW OFFICES OF JOAN CARE-ACTOR 75000 WHY ME LANE SACRAMENTO, CA 95826 TELEPHONE NO.: 916-555-1234 FAX NO. *(Optional)*: 916-555-1233 E-MAIL ADDRESS *(Optional)*: joan@care-actorlaw.com ATTORNEY FOR *(Name)*: SANDIE SHORES, Petitioner	To keep other people from seeing what you entered on your form, please press the Clear This Form button at the end of the form when finished.

SUPERIOR COURT OF CALIFORNIA, COUNTY OF SACRAMENTO
STREET ADDRESS: 3341 POWER INN ROAD
MAILING ADDRESS: 3341 POWER INN ROAD
CITY AND ZIP CODE: SACRAMENTO, CA 95826
BRANCH NAME: FAMILY LAW

PLAINTIFF/ PETITIONER: SANDIE SHORES
DEFENDANT/ RESPONDENT: ROCKY SHORES
OTHER:

STIPULATION AND WAIVER OF FINAL DECLARATION OF DISCLOSURE	CASE NUMBER: 14FLXXXXXX

1. Under Family Code section 2105(d), the parties agree to waive the requirements of Family Code section 2105(a) concerning the final declaration of disclosure.

2. The parties agree as follows:

   a. We have complied with Family Code section 2104, and the preliminary declarations of disclosure have been completed and exchanged.

   b. We have completed and exchanged a current *Income and Expense Declaration* (form FL-150) that includes all material facts and information on each party's earnings, accumulations, and expenses.

   c. We have fully complied with Family Law section 2102 and have fully augmented the preliminary declarations of disclosure, including disclosure of all material facts and information on

      (1) the characterization of all assets and liabilities,

      (2) the valuation of all assets that are community property or in which the community has an interest, and

      (3) the amounts of all community debts and obligations.

   d. Each of the parties enters into this waiver knowingly, intelligently, and voluntarily.

   e. Each party understands that this waiver does not limit the legal disclosure obligations of the parties but rather is a statement under penalty of perjury that those obligations have been fulfilled.

   f. The parties also understand that if they do not comply with these obligations, the court will set aside the judgment.

The petitioner and respondent declare under penalty of perjury under the laws of the State of California that the foregoing is true and correct.

Date:

SANDIE SHORES
_____
(TYPE OR PRINT NAME)   (SIGNATURE OF PETITIONER)

ROCKY SHORES
_____
(TYPE OR PRINT NAME)   (SIGNATURE OF RESPONDENT)

Page 1 of 1

Form Approved for Optional Use Judicial Council of California FL-144 [Rev. January 1, 2007]	STIPULATION AND WAIVER OF FINAL DECLARATION OF DISCLOSURE	Family Code, §§ 2102, 2104, 2105(d) www.courtinfo.ca.gov

For your protection and privacy, please press the Clear This Form button after you have printed the form.   **Save This Form**   **Print This Form**   **Clear This Form**

Judgment

FL-180

ATTORNEY OR PARTY WITHOUT ATTORNEY *(Name, State Bar number, and address):*	FOR COURT USE ONLY
JOAN CARE-ACTOR, SBN ******** LAW OFFICES OF JOAN CARE-ACTOR TELEPHONE NO.: 916-555-1234 FAX NO. *(Optional):* 916-555-1233 E-MAIL ADDRESS *(Optional):* joan@ care-actorlaw.com ATTORNEY FOR *(Name):* SANDIE SHORES, PETITIONER	To keep other people from seeing what you entered on your form, please press the Clear This Form button at the end of the form when finished.

SUPERIOR COURT OF CALIFORNIA, COUNTY OF SACRAMENTO
STREET ADDRESS: 3341 POWER INN ROAD
MAILING ADDRESS: 3341 POWER INN ROAD
CITY AND ZIP CODE: SACRAMENTO, CA 95826
BRANCH NAME: FAMILY LAW DIVISION

MARRIAGE OR PARTNERSHIP OF
PETITIONER: SANDIE SHORES

RESPONDENT: ROCKY SHORES

JUDGMENT	CASE NUMBER:

[✔] **DISSOLUTION** [ ] **LEGAL SEPARATION** [ ] **NULLITY**
  [ ] **Status only**
  [ ] **Reserving jurisdiction over termination of marital or domestic partnership status**
  [ ] **Judgment on reserved issues**
Date marital or domestic partnership status ends:
	14FLXXXXXX

1. [ ] This judgment [ ] contains personal conduct restraining orders [ ] modifies existing restraining orders.
   The restraining orders are contained on page(s)   of the attachment. They expire on *(date):*

2. This proceeding was heard as follows: [✔] Default or uncontested [✔] By declaration under Family Code section 2336
   [ ] Contested [ ] Agreement in court
   a. Date: Dept.:   Room:
   b. Judicial officer *(name):*   [ ] Temporary judge
   c. [ ] Petitioner present in court   [ ] Attorney present in court *(name):*
   d. [ ] Respondent present in court   [ ] Attorney present in court *(name):*
   e. [ ] Claimant present in court *(name):*   [ ] Attorney present in court *(name):*
   f. [ ] Other *(specify name):*

3. The court acquired jurisdiction of the respondent on *(date):*   XX/XX/2014
   a. [✔] The respondent was served with process.
   b. [ ] The respondent appeared.

THE COURT ORDERS, GOOD CAUSE APPEARING

4. a. [✔] Judgment of dissolution is entered. Marital or domestic partnership status is terminated and the parties are restored to the status of single persons
       (1) [✔] on *(specify date):* ENTRY OF JUDGMENT
       (2) [ ] on a date to be determined on noticed motion of either party or on stipulation.
   b. [ ] Judgment of legal separation is entered.
   c. [ ] Judgment of nullity is entered. The parties are declared to be single persons on the ground of *(specify):*

   d. [ ] This judgment will be entered nunc pro tunc as of *(date):*
   e. [ ] Judgment on reserved issues.
   f. The [ ] petitioner's [ ] respondent's former name is restored to *(specify):*
   g. [ ] Jurisdiction is reserved over all other issues, and all present orders remain in effect except as provided below.
   h. [✔] This judgment contains provisions for child support or family support. Each party must complete and file with the court a *Child Support Case Registry Form* (form FL-191) within 10 days of the date of this judgment. The parents must notify the court of any change in the information submitted within 10 days of the change, by filing an updated form. The *Notice of Rights and Responsibilities—Health-Care Costs and Reimbursement Procedures and Information Sheet on Changing a Child Support Order* (form FL-192) is attached.

Page 1 of 2

JUDGMENT
(Family Law)

Judgment

CASE NAME *(Last name, first name of each party):*	CASE NUMBER:
IN RE MARRIAGE OF SHORES, SANDIE & ROCKY	14FLXXXXXX

4. i. ☑ The children of this marriage or domestic partnership are:

    (1) ☑   Name   Birthdate

                EDDY SHORES   5/1/2005

                SHELLY SHORES   10/15/2009

    (2) ☐   Parentage is established for children of this relationship born prior to the marriage or domestic partnership

  j. ☑ Child custody and visitation (parenting time) are ordered as set forth in the attached

    (1) ☑   Settlement agreement, stipulation for judgment, or other written agreement which contains the information required by Family Code section 3048(a).

    (2) ☐   *Child Custody and Visitation Order Attachment* (form FL-341).

    (3) ☐   *Stipulation and Order for Custody and/or Visitation of Children* (form FL-355).

    (4) ☐   Previously established in another case. Case number: Court:

  k. ☑ Child support is ordered as set forth in the attached

    (1) ☑   Settlement agreement, stipulation for judgment, or other written agreement which contains the declarations required by Family Code section 4065(a).

    (2) ☐   *Child Support Information and Order Attachment* (form FL-342).

    (3) ☐   *Stipulation to Establish or Modify Child Support and Order* (form FL-350).

    (4) ☐   Previously established in another case. Case number: Court:

  l. ☑ Spousal, domestic partner, or family support is ordered:

    (1) ☐   Reserved for future determination as relates to ☐ petitioner ☐ respondent

    (2) ☐   Jurisdiction terminated to order spousal or partner support to ☐ petitioner ☐ respondent

    (3) ☐   As set forth in the attached *Spousal, Partner, or Family Support Order Attachment* (form FL-343).

    (4) ☑   As set forth in the attached settlement agreement, stipulation for judgment, or other written agreement.

    (5) ☐   Other *(specify):*

  m. ☑ Property division is ordered as set forth in the attached

    (1) ☑   Settlement agreement, stipulation for judgment, or other written agreement.

    (2) ☐   *Property Order Attachment to Judgment* (form FL-345).

    (3) ☐   Other *(specify):*

  n. ☑ Attorney fees and costs are ordered as set forth in the attached

    (1) ☑   Settlement agreement, stipulation for judgment, or other written agreement.

    (2) ☐   *Attorney Fees and Costs Order* (form FL-346).

    (3) ☐   Other *(specify):*

  o. ☐ Other *(specify):*

Each attachment to this judgment is incorporated into this judgment, and the parties are ordered to comply with each attachment's provisions. Jurisdiction is reserved to make other orders necessary to carry out this judgment.

Date:

5. Number of pages attached: _____XX_____

                             JUDICIAL OFFICER

                    ☐ SIGNATURE FOLLOWS LAST ATTACHMENT

NOTICE

Dissolution or legal separation may automatically cancel the rights of a spouse or domestic partner under the other spouse's or domestic partner's will, trust, retirement plan, power of attorney, pay-on-death bank account, transfer-on-death vehicle registration, survivorship rights to any property owned in joint tenancy, and any other similar property interest. It does not automatically cancel the rights of a spouse or domestic partner as beneficiary of the other spouse's or domestic partner's life insurance policy. You should review these matters, as well as any credit cards, other credit accounts, insurance policies, retirement plans, and credit reports, to determine whether they should be changed or whether you should take any other actions.

A debt or obligation may be assigned to one party as part of the dissolution of property and debts, but if that party does not pay the debt or obligation, the creditor may be able to collect from the other party.

An earnings assignment may be issued without additional proof if child, family, partner, or spousal support is ordered.

Any party required to pay support must pay interest on overdue amounts at the "legal rate," which is currently 10 percent.

For your protection and privacy, please press the Clear This Form button after you have printed the form.

[Print This Form]   [Save This Form]   [Clear This Form]

Notice of Entry of Judgment

FL-190

ATTORNEY OR PARTY WITHOUT ATTORNEY *(Name, State Bar number, and address):* JOAN CARE-ACTOR, SBN ******* LAW OFFICES OF JOAN CARE-ACTOR 75000 WHY ME LANE SACRAMENTO, CA 95826 TELEPHONE NO.: 916-555-1234 FAX NO. *(Optional):* 916-555-1233 E-MAIL ADDRESS *(Optional):* joan@care-actorlaw.com ATTORNEY FOR *(Name):* SANDIE SHORES, PETITIONER	To keep other people from seeing what you entered on your form, please press the Clear This Form button at the end of the form when finished.

SUPERIOR COURT OF CALIFORNIA, COUNTY OF SACRAMENTO
STREET ADDRESS: 3341 POWER INN ROAD
MAILING ADDRESS: 3341 POWER INN ROAD
CITY AND ZIP CODE: SACRAMENTO, CA 95826
BRANCH NAME: FAMILY LAW

PETITIONER: SANDIE SHORES

RESPONDENT: ROCKY SHORES

NOTICE OF ENTRY OF JUDGMENT	CASE NUMBER: 14FLXXXXXX

You are notified that the following judgment was entered on *(date):*

1. ☑ Dissolution
2. ☐ Dissolution—status only
3. ☐ Dissolution—reserving jurisdiction over termination of marital status or domestic partnership
4. ☐ Legal separation
5. ☐ Nullity
6. ☐ Parent-child relationship
7. ☐ Judgment on reserved issues
8. ☐ Other *(specify):*

Date: _____

Clerk, by _____, Deputy

—NOTICE TO ATTORNEY OF RECORD OR PARTY WITHOUT ATTORNEY—

Under the provisions of Code of Civil Procedure section 1952, if no appeal is filed the court may order the exhibits destroyed or otherwise disposed of after 60 days from the expiration of the appeal time.

STATEMENT IN THIS BOX APPLIES ONLY TO JUDGMENT OF DISSOLUTION
Effective date of termination of marital or domestic partnership status *(specify):*
WARNING: Neither party may remarry or enter into a new domestic partnership until the effective date of the termination of marital or domestic partnership status, as shown in this box.

CLERK'S CERTIFICATE OF MAILING

I certify that I am not a party to this cause and that a true copy of the *Notice of Entry of Judgment* was mailed first class, postage fully prepaid, in a sealed envelope addressed as shown below, and that the notice was mailed
at *(place):* _____, California, on *(date):* _____

Date: _____

Clerk, by _____, Deputy

Name and address of petitioner or petitioner's attorney
JOAN CARE-ACTOR, CARE-ACTOR FIRM
75000 WHY ME LANE
SACRAMENTO, CA 95826

Name and address of respondent or respondent's attorney
SAM E. SPADE, SPADE LAW FIRM
99999 DEFENSE COURT,
SACRAMENTO, CA 95826

Page 1 of 1

Form Adopted for Mandatory Use Judicial Council of California FL-190 [Rev. January 1, 2005]	**NOTICE OF ENTRY OF JUDGMENT** **(Family Law—Uniform Parentage—Custody and Support)**	Family Code, §§ 2338, 7636, 7637 www.courtinfo.ca.gov

For your protection and privacy, please press the Clear This Form button after you have printed the form.

Save This Form   Print This Form   Clear This Form

Notice of Rights and Responsibilities

FL-192

NOTICE OF RIGHTS AND RESPONSIBILITIES

Health-Care Costs and Reimbursement Procedures

IF YOU HAVE A CHILD SUPPORT ORDER THAT INCLUDES A PROVISION FOR THE REIMBURSEMENT OF A PORTION OF THE CHILD'S OR CHILDREN'S HEALTH-CARE COSTS AND THOSE COSTS ARE NOT PAID BY INSURANCE, THE LAW SAYS:

1. Notice. You must give the other parent an itemized statement of the charges that have been billed for any health-care costs not paid by insurance. You must give this statement to the other parent within a reasonable time, but no more than 30 days after those costs were given to you.

2. Proof of full payment. If you have already paid all of the uninsured costs, you must (1) give the other parent proof that you paid them and (2) ask for reimbursement for the other parent's court-ordered share of those costs.

3. Proof of partial payment. If you have paid only your share of the uninsured costs, you must (1) give the other parent proof that you paid your share, (2) ask that the other parent pay his or her share of the costs directly to the health-care provider, and (3) give the other parent the information necessary for that parent to be able to pay the bill.

4. Payment by notified parent. If you receive notice from a parent that an uninsured health-care cost has been incurred, you must pay your share of that cost within the time the court orders; or if the court has not specified a period of time, you must make payment (1) within 30 days from the time you were given notice of the amount due, (2) according to any payment schedule set by the health-care provider, (3) according to a schedule agreed to in writing by you and the other parent, or (4) according to a schedule adopted by the court.

5. Disputed charges. If you dispute a charge, you may file a motion in court to resolve the dispute, but only if you pay that charge before filing your motion.

If you claim that the other party has failed to reimburse you for a payment, or the other party has failed to make a payment to the provider after proper notice has been given, you may file a motion in court to resolve the dispute. The court will presume that if uninsured costs have been paid, those costs were reasonable. The court may award attorney fees and costs against a party who has been unreasonable.

6. Court-ordered insurance coverage. If a parent provides health-care insurance as ordered by the court, that insurance must be used at all times to the extent that it is available for health-care costs.

a. **Burden to prove.** The party claiming that the coverage is inadequate to meet the child's needs has the burden of proving that to the court.

b. **Cost of additional coverage.** If a parent purchases health-care insurance in addition to that ordered by the court, that parent must pay all the costs of the additional coverage. In addition, if a parent uses alternative coverage that costs more than the coverage provided by court order, that parent must pay the difference.

7. Preferred health providers. If the court-ordered coverage designates a preferred health-care provider, that provider must be used at all times consistent with the terms of the health insurance policy. When any party uses a health-care provider other than the preferred provider, any health-care costs that would have been paid by the preferred health provider if that provider had been used must be the sole responsibility of the party incurring those costs.

Page 1 of 2

NOTICE OF RIGHTS AND RESPONSIBILITIES
Health-Care Costs and Reimbursement Procedures

Family Code, §§ 4062, 4063
www.courtinfo.ca.gov

Notice of Rights and Responsibilities

INFORMATION SHEET ON CHANGING A CHILD SUPPORT ORDER

General Information
The court has just made a child support order in your case. This order will remain the same unless a party to the action requests that the support be changed (modified). An order for child support can be modified only by filing a motion to change child support and serving each party involved in your case. If both parents and the local child support agency (if it is involved) agree on a new child support amount, you can complete, have all parties sign, and file with the court a *Stipulation to Establish or Modify Child Support and Order* (form FL-350) or *Stipulation and Order (Governmental)* (form FL-625).

When a Child Support Order May Be Modified
The court takes several things into account when ordering the payment of child support. First, the number of children is considered. Next, the net incomes of both parents are determined, along with the percentage of time each parent has physical custody of the children. The court considers both parties' tax filing status and may consider hardships, such as a child of another relationship. An existing order for child support may be modified when the net income of one of the parents changes significantly, the parenting schedule changes significantly, or a new child is born.

Examples
- You have been ordered to pay $500 per month in child support. You lose your job. You will continue to owe $500 per month, plus 10 percent interest on any unpaid support, unless you file a motion to modify your child support to a lower amount and the court orders a reduction.
- You are currently receiving $300 per month in child support from the other parent, whose net income has just increased substantially. You will continue to receive $300 per month unless you file a motion to modify your child support to a higher amount and the court orders an increase.
- You are paying child support based upon having physical custody of your children 30 percent of the time. After several months it turns out that you actually have physical custody of the children 50 percent of the time. You may file a motion to modify child support to a lower amount.

How to Change a Child Support Order
To change a child support order, you must file papers with the court. *Remember:* You must follow the order you have now.

What forms do I need?
If you are asking to change a child support order open with the local child support agency, you must fill out one of these forms:
- FL-680, *Notice of Motion (Governmental)* or FL-683 *Order to Show Cause (Governmental)* **and**
- FL-684, *Request for Order and Supporting Declaration (Governmental)*

If you are asking to change a child support order that is **not** open with the local child support agency, you must fill out one of these forms:
- FL-301, *Notice of Motion* or FL-300, *Order to Show Cause* **and**
- FL-310, *Application for Order and Supporting Declaration* **or**
- FL-390, *Notice of Motion and Motion for Simplified Modification of Order for Child, Spousal, or Family Support*

You must also fill out one of these forms:
- FL-150, *Income and Expense Declaration* or FL-155, *Financial Statement (Simplified)*

What if I am not sure which forms to fill out?
Talk to the family law facilitator at your court.

After you fill out the forms, file them with the court clerk and ask for a hearing date. Write the hearing date on the form. The clerk will ask you to pay a filing fee. If you cannot afford the fee, fill out these forms, too:
- Form FW-001, *Application for Waiver of Court Fees and Costs*
- Form FW-003, *Order on Application for Waiver of Court Fees and Costs*

You must serve the other parent. If the local child support agency is involved, serve it too.
This means someone 18 or over—**not you**—must serve the other parent copies of your filed court forms at least **16 court days** before the hearing. Add **5 calendar days** if you serve by mail within California (see Code of Civil Procedure section 1005 for other situations). **Court days** are weekdays when the court is open for business (Monday through Friday except court holidays). **Calendar days** include all days of the month, including weekends and holidays. To determine court and calendar days, go to *www.courtinfo.ca.gov/selfhelp/courtcalendars/*.

The server must also serve blank copies of these forms:
- FL-320, *Responsive Declaration to Order to Show Cause or Notice of Motion* **and** FL-150, *Income and Expense Declaration*, **or**
- FL-155, *Financial Statement (Simplified)*
Then the server fills out and signs a *Proof of Service* (form FL-330 or FL-335). Take this form to the clerk and file it.

Go to your hearing and ask the judge to change the support. Bring your tax returns from the last two years and your last two months' pay stubs. The judge will look at your information, listen to both parents, and make an order. After the hearing, fill out:
- FL-340, *Findings and Order After Hearing* **and**
- FL-342, *Child Support Information and Order Attachment*

Need help?
Contact the family law facilitator in your county or call your county's bar association and ask for an experienced family lawyer.

Judgment Checklist—Dissolution/Legal Separation

	FL-182
ATTORNEY OR PARTY WITHOUT ATTORNEY *(Name, State Bar number, and address)*: —JOAN CARE-ACTOR SBN ******* LAW OFFICES OF JOAN CARE-ACTOR 75000 WHY ME LANE SACRAMENTO, CA 95826 TELEPHONE NO.: 916-555-1234 FAX NO. *(Optional)*: 916-555-1233 E-MAIL ADDRESS *(Optional)*: joan@ care-actorlaw.com ATTORNEY FOR *(Name)*: SANDIE SHORES, PETITIONER	*FOR COURT USE ONLY* To keep other people from seeing what you entered on your form, please press the Clear This Form button at the end of the form when finished.
SUPERIOR COURT OF CALIFORNIA, COUNTY OF SACRAMENTO STREET ADDRESS: 3341 POWER INN ROAD MAILING ADDRESS: 3341 POWER INN ROAD CITY AND ZIP CODE: SACRAMENTO, CA 95826 BRANCH NAME: FAMILY LAW	
PETITIONER: SANDIE SHORES RESPONDENT: ROCKY SHORES	

JUDGMENT CHECKLIST— DISSOLUTION/LEGAL SEPARATION	CASE NUMBER: 14FLXXXXXX

This judgment checklist is a list of documents that a court may require to complete a default or uncontested judgment. The checklist may be filed along with your judgment, but is not required. If the forms or other documents have already been filed, you should check the boxes indicating that they have been previously filed. Unless listed otherwise on this form, when you file a document with the court, you should submit an original and 2 copies. One copy is for you and one is for the other party. There are three types of default and uncontested judgments:

- **Default With No Agreement (no response and no written agreement)**
- **Default With Agreement (no response, but there is a written agreement)**
- **Uncontested Case (response filed, or other appearance by respondent, and a written agreement)**

1. ☐ **DEFAULT WITH NO AGREEMENT (no response and no written agreement)**
   (Please check the box by each document being filed)   Previously Filed

   a. ☐ *Proof of Service of Summons* (form FL-115) or other proof of service   ☐

   b. ☐ *Request to Enter Default* (form FL-165), with a stamped envelope addressed to respondent and the court   ☐
   clerk's address as the return address

   c. ☐ Petitioner's *Declaration Regarding Service of Declaration of Disclosure* (form FL-141)   ☐

   d. ☐ *Declaration for Default or Uncontested Dissolution or Legal Separation* (form FL-170)

   e. ☐ *Judgment* (form FL-180) *(5 copies)*

   f. ☐ *Notice of Entry of Judgment* (form FL-190)

   g. ☐ 2 stamped envelopes of sufficient size and with sufficient postage to return the *Judgment* and *Notice of Entry of Judgment*, one envelope addressed to petitioner and the other to respondent.

   If there are minor children of the marriage or domestic partnership:

   h. ☐ *Declaration Under Uniform Child Custody Jurisdiction and Enforcement Act (UCCJEA)* (form FL-105).   ☐
   (A new form must be filed if there have been any changes since the one most recently filed.)

   i. ☐ Petitioner's *Income and Expense Declaration* (form FL-150) or *Financial Statement (Simplified)* (form   ☐
   FL-155). *(Needed unless one has been filed within the past 90 days and there have been no changes since then.)*

   j. ☐ Computer printout of guideline child support *(optional)*

   k. ☐ *Notice of Rights and Responsibilities and Information Sheet on Changing a Child Support Order* (form FL-192). This may be attached by the petitioner or by the court.

Form Approved for Optional Use
Judicial Council of California
FL-182 [New July 1, 2012]   **JUDGMENT CHECKLIST—
DISSOLUTION/LEGAL SEPARATION**   Cal. Rules of Court, rule 5.405
www.courts.ca.gov

Judgment Checklist—Dissolution/Legal Separation

FL-182

PETITIONER: SANDIE SHORES	CASE NUMBER:
RESPONDENT: ROCKY SHORES	14FLXXXXXX

Previously Filed

  l.   Child Support Order

      ☐   *Stipulation to Establish or Modify Child Support and Order* (form FL-350) *(attach to* Judgment*), or*

      ☐   *Child Support Information and Order Attachment* (form FL-342) *(attach to* Judgment*), or*

      ☐   Written agreement containing declarations required by Family Code section 4065(a) *(attach to* Judgment*)*

  m. ☐   *Income Withholding for Support* (form FL-195/OMB No. 0970-0154)

  n. ☐   *Child Custody and Visitation* (Parenting Time) *Order Attachment* (form FL-341) or other proposed written order containing the information required by Family Code 3048(a) *(attach to* Judgment*)*

If spousal/partner support is requested, the marriage/partnership is over 10 years in duration, or termination of spousal/partner support for the respondent is requested:

  o. ☐   *Spousal or Partnership Support Declaration Attachment* (form FL-157)

  p. ☐   *Income and Expense Declaration* (form FL-150) *(Needed unless a current financial declaration has been filed within the past 90 days and there have been no changes since then.)*   ☐

  q. ☐   *Spousal, Partner, or Family Support Order Attachment* (form FL-343) or other proposed written order *(attach to* Judgment*)*

If assets or debts need to be divided or assigned:

  r. ☐   *Property Declaration* (form FL-160)   ☐

  s. ☐   *Property Order Attachment to Judgment* (form FL-345) or other proposed written order *(attach to* Judgment*)*

If attorney fees and costs are requested:

  t. ☐   *Request for Attorney Fees and Costs* (form FL-319)

  u. ☐   *Attorney Fees and Costs Order Attachment* (form FL-346) or other proposed written order *(attach to* Judgment*)*

2. ☑ **DEFAULT WITH AGREEMENT (no response and a written agreement)**

  a. ☑   *Proof of Service of Summons* (form FL-115) or other proof of service   ☑

  b. ☑   *Request to Enter Default* (form FL-165), with a stamped envelope addressed to respondent and the court clerk's address as the return address   ☑

  c. ☑   Petitioner's *Declaration Regarding Service of Declaration of Disclosure* (form FL-141) (preliminary)   ☐

  d.   Declaration Regarding Service of Final Declaration of Disclosure   ☐

      ☐   Petitioner's *Declaration Regarding Service of Declaration of Disclosure* (form FL-141) (final) or

      ☑   *Stipulation and Waiver of Final Declaration of Disclosure* (form FL-144) or

      ☐   Separately filed waiver or waiver included in a written agreement under Family Code section 2105(d)

  e. ☑   *Declaration for Default or Uncontested Dissolution or Legal Separation* (form FL-170)

  f. ☑   Written agreement of the parties. Respondent's signature on the agreement must be notarized. *(attach to* Judgment.*)*

  g. ☑   *Judgment* (form FL-180) *(5 copies)*

  h. ☑   *Notice of Entry of Judgment* (form FL-190)

  i. ☑   2 stamped envelopes of sufficient size and with sufficient postage to return the *Judgment* and *Notice of Entry of Judgment*, one envelope addressed to petitioner and the other to respondent

If there are minor children of the marriage or domestic partnership:

  j. ☑   *Declaration Under Uniform Child Custody Jurisdiction and Enforcement Act (UCCJEA)* (form FL-105). *(A new form must be filed if there have been any changes since the one most recently filed.)*   ☑

  k. ☐   *Income and Expense Declaration* (form FL-150) or *Financial Statement (Simplified)* (form FL-155). *(Needed unless one has been filed within the past 90 days and there have been no changes since then.)*

Judgment Checklist—Dissolution/Legal Separation

					FL-182
PETITIONER: SANDIE SHORES			CASE NUMBER:		
RESPONDENT: ROCKY SHORES			14FLXXXXXX		

Previously Filed

l. ☐ Computer printout of guideline child support *(optional)*.

m. ☑ *Notice of Rights and Responsibilities and Information Sheet on Changing a Child Support Order* (form FL-192). This may be attached by the petitioner or by the court.

n. Child Support Order

  ☐ *Stipulation to Establish or Modify Child Support and Order* (form FL-350) *(attach to Judgment)*, or

  ☐ *Child Support Information and Order Attachment* (form FL-342) *(attach to Judgment)*, or

  ☑ Written agreement containing declarations required by Family Code section 4065(a) *(attach to Judgment)*

o. ☑ *Income Withholding for Support* (form FL-195/OMB No. 0970-0154)

p. ☑ *Child Custody and Visitation Order Attachment* (form FL-341) or written agreement containing the information required by Family Code section 3048(a) *(attach to Judgment)*

3. ☐ **UNCONTESTED CASE (Response filed, or other appearance by respondent, and a written agreement)**

   a. ☐ *Proof of Service of Summons* (form FL-115) or other proof of service if you want to use the date of service as the beginning of the six-month waiting period.   ☐

   b. ☐ *Appearance, Stipulations, and Waivers* (form FL-130)   ☐

   c. ☐ Respondent's filing fee, if first appearance, unless respondent has a fee waiver or is currently on active duty in the military   ☐

   d. ☐ *Declaration Regarding Service of Declaration of Disclosure* (**both** petitioner's and respondent's preliminary) (form FL-141)   ☐

   e. Declaration Regarding Service of Final Declaration of Disclosure   ☐

     ☐ *Declaration Regarding Service of Declaration of Disclosure* (**both** petitioner's and respondent's final) (form FL-141), or

     ☐ *Stipulation and Waiver of Final Declaration of Disclosure* (form FL-144), or

     ☐ Separately filed waiver or waiver included in a written agreement under Family Code section 2105(d)

   f. ☐ *Declaration for Default or Uncontested Dissolution or Legal Separation* (form FL-170)

   g. ☐ Written agreement of the parties *(attach to Judgment)*

   h. ☐ *Judgment* (form FL-180) *(5 copies)*

   i. ☐ *Notice of Entry of Judgment* (form FL-190)

   j. ☐ 2 stamped envelopes of sufficient size and with sufficient postage to return the *Judgment* and *Notice of Entry of Judgment*, one envelope addressed to petitioner and the other to respondent

If there are minor children of the marriage or domestic partnership:

   k. ☐ *Declaration Under Uniform Child Custody Jurisdiction and Enforcement Act (UCCJEA)* (form FL-105). *(A new form must be filed if there have been any changes since the one most recently filed.)*   ☐

   l. ☐ Computer printout of guideline child support *(optional)*

   m. ☐ *Notice of Rights and Responsibilities and Information Sheet on Changing a Child Support Order* (form FL-192). This may be attached by either party or by the court.

   n. Child Support Order

     ☐ *Stipulation to Establish or Modify Child Support and Order* (form FL-350) *(attach to Judgment)* or

     ☐ *Child Support Information and Order Attachment* (form FL-342) *(attach to Judgment)*, or

     ☐ Written agreement which includes declarations required by Family Code section 4065(a) *(attach to Judgment)*

   o. ☐ *Income Withholding for Support* (form FL-195/OMB No. 0970-0154)

   p. ☐ *Child Custody and Visitation Order Attachment* (form FL-341) or written agreement containing the information required by Family Code section 3048(a) *(attach to Judgment)*

    JUDGMENT CHECKLIST– DISSOLUTION/LEGAL SEPARATION

For your protection and privacy, please press the Clear This Form button after you have printed the form. | Print This Form | Save This Form | Clear This Form |

Declaration for Default or
Uncontested Dissolution or Legal Separation

FL-170

ATTORNEY OR PARTY WITHOUT ATTORNEY *(Name, State Bar number, and address)*:	*FOR COURT USE ONLY*
	To keep other people from seeing what you entered on your form, please press the Clear This Form button at the end of the form when finished.

TELEPHONE NO.:   FAX NO. *(Optional)*:
E-MAIL ADDRESS *(Optional)*:
ATTORNEY FOR *(Name)*:

SUPERIOR COURT OF CALIFORNIA, COUNTY OF
STREET ADDRESS:
MAILING ADDRESS:
CITY AND ZIP CODE:
BRANCH NAME:

PETITIONER:

RESPONDENT:

DECLARATION FOR DEFAULT OR UNCONTESTED ☐ **DISSOLUTION** ☐ **LEGAL SEPARATION**	CASE NUMBER:

(NOTE: Items 1 through 12 apply to both dissolution and legal separation proceedings.)

1. I declare that if I appeared in court and were sworn, I would testify to the truth of the facts in this declaration.

2. I agree that my case will be proven by this declaration and that I will not appear before the court unless I am ordered by the court to do so.

3. All the information in the ☐ amended ☐ *Petition* ☐ *Response* is true and correct.

4. **Type of case** *(check a, b, or c):*

    a. ☐ **Default without agreement**

        (1) No response has been filed and there is no written agreement or stipulated judgment between the parties;

        (2) The default of the respondent was entered or is being requested, and I am not seeking any relief not requested in the petition; and

        (3) The following statement is true *(check one):*

            (A) ☐ There are no assets or debts to be disposed of by the court.

            (B) ☐ The community and quasi-community assets and debts are listed on the **completed** current *Property Declaration* (form FL-160), which includes an estimate of the value of the assets and debts that I propose to be distributed to each party. The division in the proposed *Judgment* (form FL-180) is a fair and equal division of the property and debts, or if there is a negative estate, the debts are assigned fairly and equitably.

    b. ☐ **Default with agreement**

        (1) No response has been filed and the parties have agreed that the matter may proceed as a default matter without notice; and

        (2) The parties have entered into a written agreement regarding their property and their marriage or domestic partnership rights, including support, the original of which is being or has been submitted to the court. I request that the court approve the agreement.

    c. ☐ **Uncontested**

        (1) Both parties have appeared in the case; and

        (2) The parties have entered into a written agreement regarding their property and their marriage or domestic partnership rights, including support, the original of which is being or has been submitted to the court. I request that the court approve the agreement.

5. **Declaration of disclosure** *(check a, b, or c):*

    a. ☐ Both the petitioner and respondent have filed, or are filing concurrently, a *Declaration Regarding Service of Declaration of Disclosure* (form FL-141) and an *Income and Expense Declaration* (form FL-150).

    b. ☐ This matter is proceeding by default. I am the petitioner in this action and have filed a proof of service of the preliminary *Declaration of Disclosure* (form FL-140) with the court. I hereby waive receipt of the final *Declaration of Disclosure* (form FL-140) from the respondent.

    c. ☐ This matter is proceeding as an uncontested action. Service of the final *Declaration of Disclosure* (form FL-140) is mutually waived by both parties. A waiver provision executed by both parties under penalty of perjury is contained on the *Stipulation and Waiver of Final Declaration of Disclosure* (form FL-144), in the settlement agreement or proposed judgment or another, separate stipulation.

Page 1 of 3

Form Adopted for Mandatory Use Judicial Council of California FL-170 [Rev. July 1, 2012]	**DECLARATION FOR DEFAULT OR UNCONTESTED DISSOLUTION OR LEGAL SEPARATION** **(Family Law)**	Family Code, § 2338 www.courts.ca.gov

Declaration for Default or
Uncontested Dissolution or Legal Separation

PETITIONER:	CASE NUMBER:
RESPONDENT:	

6. ☐ **Child custody and visitation (parenting time)** should be ordered as set forth in the proposed *Judgment* (form FL-180).

    a. ☐ The information in *Declaration Under Uniform Child Custody Jurisdiction and Enforcement Act* (UCCJEA) (form FL-105)
        ☐ has ☐ has not changed since it was last filed with the court. *(If changed, attach updated form.)*

    b. ☐ There is an existing court order for custody/parenting time in another case in *(county)*:
        The case number is *(specify)*:

    c. ☐ The current custody and visitation (parenting time) previously ordered in this case, or current schedule is *(specify)*:
        ☐ Contained on Attachment 6c.

    d. ☐ Facts in support of requested judgment *(In a default case, state your reasons below)*:
        ☐ Contained on Attachment 6d.

7. ☐ **Child support** should be ordered as set forth in the proposed *Judgment* (form FL-180).

    a. If there are minor children, check and complete item (1) if applicable and item (2) or (3):

      (1) ☐ Child support is being enforced in another case in *(county)*:
          The case number is *(specify)*:

      (2) ☐ The information in the child support calculation attached to the proposed judgment is correct based on my
          personal knowledge.

      (3) ☐ I request that this order be based on the ☐ petitioner's ☐ respondent's earning ability. The facts in support
          of my estimate of earning ability are *(specify)*:
          ☐ Continued on Attachment 7a(3).

    b. Complete items (1) and (2) regarding public assistance.

      (1) I ☐ am receiving ☐ am not receiving ☐ intend to apply for public assistance for the child or children
         listed in the proposed order.

      (2) To the best of my knowledge, the other party ☐ is ☐ is not receiving public assistance.

    c. ☐ The petitioner ☐ respondent is presently receiving public assistance, and all support should be made
        payable to the local child support agency at the address set forth in the proposed judgment. A representative of the local
        child support agency has signed the proposed judgment.

8. **Spousal, Partner, and Family Support** *(If a support order or attorney fees are requested, submit a completed* Income and
Expense Declaration *(form FL-150) unless a current form is on file. Include your best estimate of the other party's income.
Check at least one of the following.)*

    a. ☐ I knowingly give up forever any right to receive spousal or partner support.

    b. ☐ I ask the court to reserve jurisdiction to award spousal or partner support in the future to *(name)*:

    c. ☐ I ask the court to terminate forever spousal or partner support for: ☐ petitioner ☐ respondent.

    d. ☐ Spousal support or domestic partner support should be ordered as set forth in the proposed *Judgment* (form FL-180)
       based on the factors described in:
       ☐ *Spousal or Partner Support Declaration Attachment* (form FL-157)
       ☐ written agreement
       ☐ attached declaration *(Attachment 8d.)*

    e. ☐ Family support should be ordered as set forth in the proposed *Judgment* (form FL-180).

    f. ☐ Other *(specify)*:

FL-170 [Rev. July 1, 2012]   **DECLARATION FOR DEFAULT OR UNCONTESTED
DISSOLUTION OR LEGAL SEPARATION
(Family Law)**   Page 2 of 3

Declaration for Default or
Uncontested Dissolution or Legal Separation

	FL-170
PETITIONER:	CASE NUMBER:
RESPONDENT:	

9. ☐ **Parentage** of the children of the petitioner and respondent born prior to their marriage or domestic partnership should be ordered as set forth in the proposed *Judgment* (form FL-180).

    a. ☐ A Voluntary Declaration of Paternity is attached.

    b. ☐ Parentage was previously established by the court in *(county):*

        The case number is *(specify):*

    ☐ Written agreement of the parties attached here or to the *Judgment* (form FL-180).

10. ☐ **Attorney fees** should be ordered as set forth in the proposed *Judgment* (form FL-180)

    ☐ facts in support in form FL-319

    ☐ other *(specify facts below):*

11. ☐ The judgment should be entered nunc pro tunc for the following reasons *(specify):*

12. ☐ The petitioner ☐ respondent requests restoration of his or her former name as set forth in the proposed *Judgment* (form FL-180).

13. There are irreconcilable differences that have led to the irremediable breakdown of the marriage or domestic partnership, and there is no possibility of saving the marriage or domestic partnership through counseling or other means.

14. This declaration may be reviewed by a commissioner sitting as a temporary judge, who may determine whether to grant this request or require my appearance under Family Code section 2336.

STATEMENTS IN THIS BOX APPLY ONLY TO DISSOLUTIONS

15. If this is a dissolution of marriage or of a domestic partnership created in another state, the petitioner and/or the respondent have been residents of this county for at least three months and of the state of California for at least six months continuously and immediately preceding the date of the filing of the petition for dissolution of marriage or domestic partnership.

16. I ask that the court grant the request for a judgment for dissolution of marriage or domestic partnership based on irreconcilable differences and that the court make the orders set forth in the proposed *Judgment* (form FL-180) submitted with this declaration.

17. ☐ This declaration is for the termination of **marital or domestic partner status only.** I ask the court to reserve jurisdiction over all issues whose determination is not requested in this declaration.

THIS STATEMENT APPLIES ONLY TO LEGAL SEPARATIONS

18. I ask that the court grant the request for a judgment for legal separation based on irreconcilable differences and that the court make the orders set forth in the proposed *Judgment* (form FL-180) submitted with this declaration.

I understand that a judgment of legal separation does not terminate a marriage or domestic partnership and that I am still married or a partner in a domestic partnership.

---

19. ☐ Other *(specify):*

I declare under penalty of perjury under the laws of the State of California that the foregoing is true and correct.

Date:

▶

(TYPE OR PRINT NAME)	(SIGNATURE OF DECLARANT)

DECLARATION FOR DEFAULT OR UNCONTESTED DISSOLUTION OR LEGAL SEPARATION (Family Law)

For your protection and privacy, please press the Clear This Form button after you have printed the form.

[Print This Form] Save This Form [Clear This Form]

Appearance, Stipulations, and Waivers

FL-130

ATTORNEY OR PARTY WITHOUT ATTORNEY *(Name, State Bar number, and address)*:	To keep other people from seeing what you entered on your form, please press the Clear This Form button at the end of the form when finished.
TELEPHONE NO.: FAX NO. *(Optional)*: E-MAIL ADDRESS *(Optional)*: ATTORNEY FOR *(Name)*:	

SUPERIOR COURT OF CALIFORNIA, COUNTY OF
STREET ADDRESS:
MAILING ADDRESS:
CITY AND ZIP CODE:
BRANCH NAME:

PETITIONER:

RESPONDENT:

APPEARANCE, STIPULATIONS, AND WAIVERS	CASE NUMBER:

1. **Appearance by respondent** *(you must choose one)*:

   a. ☐ By filing this form, I make a general appearance.

   b. ☐ I have previously made a general appearance.

   c. ☐ I am a member of the military services of the United States of America. I have completed and attached to this form *Declaration and Conditional Waiver of Rights Under the Servicemembers Civil Relief Act of 2003* (form FL-130(A)).

2. **Agreements, stipulations, and waivers** *(choose all that apply)*:

   a. ☐ The parties agree that this cause may be decided as an uncontested matter.

   b. ☐ The parties waive their rights to notice of trial, a statement of decision, a motion for new trial, and the right to appeal.

   c. ☐ This matter may be decided by a commissioner sitting as a temporary judge.

   d. ☐ The parties have a written agreement that will be submitted to the court, or a stipulation for judgment will be submitted to the court and attached to *Judgment (Family Law)* (form FL-180).

   e. ☐ None of these agreements or waivers will apply unless the court approves the stipulation for judgment or incorporates the written settlement agreement into the judgment.

   f. ☐ This is a parentage case, and both parties have signed an *Advisement and Waiver of Rights Re: Establishment of Parental Relationship* (form FL-235) or its equivalent.

3. **Other** *(specify)*:

Date: _____

_____   ▶ _____
(TYPE OR PRINT NAME)   (SIGNATURE OF PETITIONER)

Date: _____

_____   ▶ _____
(TYPE OR PRINT NAME)   (SIGNATURE OF RESPONDENT)

Date: _____

_____   ▶ _____
(TYPE OR PRINT NAME)   (SIGNATURE OF ATTORNEY FOR PETITIONER)

Date: _____

_____   ▶ _____
(TYPE OR PRINT NAME)   (SIGNATURE OF ATTORNEY FOR RESPONDENT)

Form Approved for Optional Use
Judicial Council of California
FL-130 [Rev. January 1, 2011]

APPEARANCE, STIPULATIONS, AND WAIVERS
(Family Law—Uniform Parentage—Custody and Support)

Government Code, § 70673
www.courtinfo.ca.gov

For your protection and privacy, please press the Clear This Form button after you have printed the form.

Save This Form   Print This Form   Clear This Form

Stipulation and Waiver of Final Declaration of Disclosure

FL-144

ATTORNEY OR PARTY WITHOUT ATTORNEY (Name, State Bar number, and address):	To keep other people from seeing what you entered on your form, please press the Clear This Form button at the end of the form when finished.
TELEPHONE NO.: FAX NO. (Optional):	
E-MAIL ADDRESS (Optional):	
ATTORNEY FOR (Name):	

SUPERIOR COURT OF CALIFORNIA, COUNTY OF
STREET ADDRESS:
MAILING ADDRESS:
CITY AND ZIP CODE:
BRANCH NAME:

PLAINTIFF/ PETITIONER:
DEFENDANT/ RESPONDENT:
OTHER:

STIPULATION AND WAIVER OF FINAL DECLARATION OF DISCLOSURE	CASE NUMBER:

1. Under Family Code section 2105(d), the parties agree to waive the requirements of Family Code section 2105(a) concerning the final declaration of disclosure.

2. The parties agree as follows:

   a. We have complied with Family Code section 2104, and the preliminary declarations of disclosure have been completed and exchanged.

   b. We have completed and exchanged a current *Income and Expense Declaration* (form FL-150) that includes all material facts and information on each party's earnings, accumulations, and expenses.

   c. We have fully complied with Family Law section 2102 and have fully augmented the preliminary declarations of disclosure, including disclosure of all material facts and information on

      (1) the characterization of all assets and liabilities,

      (2) the valuation of all assets that are community property or in which the community has an interest, and

      (3) the amounts of all community debts and obligations.

   d. Each of the parties enters into this waiver knowingly, intelligently, and voluntarily.

   e. Each party understands that this waiver does not limit the legal disclosure obligations of the parties but rather is a statement under penalty of perjury that those obligations have been fulfilled.

   f. The parties also understand that if they do not comply with these obligations, the court will set aside the judgment.

The petitioner and respondent declare under penalty of perjury under the laws of the State of California that the foregoing is true and correct.

Date:

_____   _____
(TYPE OR PRINT NAME)   (SIGNATURE OF PETITIONER)

_____   _____
(TYPE OR PRINT NAME)   (SIGNATURE OF RESPONDENT)

Page 1 of 1

Form Approved for Optional Use Judicial Council of California FL-144 [Rev. January 1, 2007]	**STIPULATION AND WAIVER OF FINAL DECLARATION OF DISCLOSURE**	Family Code, §§ 2102, 2104, 2105(d) www.courtinfo.ca.gov

For your protection and privacy, please press the Clear This Form button after you have printed the form.   Save This Form   Print This Form   Clear This Form

Judgment

FL-180

ATTORNEY OR PARTY WITHOUT ATTORNEY *(Name, State Bar number, and address):*	FOR COURT USE ONLY
TELEPHONE NO.: FAX NO. *(Optional):*	To keep other people from seeing what you entered on your form, please press the Clear This Form button at the end of the form when finished.
E-MAIL ADDRESS *(Optional):*	
ATTORNEY FOR *(Name):*	

SUPERIOR COURT OF CALIFORNIA, COUNTY OF
    STREET ADDRESS:
    MAILING ADDRESS:
    CITY AND ZIP CODE:
    BRANCH NAME:

MARRIAGE OR PARTNERSHIP OF
    PETITIONER:

    RESPONDENT:

JUDGMENT

CASE NUMBER:

☐ **DISSOLUTION**   ☐ **LEGAL SEPARATION**   ☐ **NULLITY**

    ☐ **Status only**
    ☐ **Reserving jurisdiction over termination of marital or domestic partnership status**
    ☐ **Judgment on reserved issues**
Date marital or domestic partnership status ends:

1. ☐ This judgment ☐ contains personal conduct restraining orders ☐ modifies existing restraining orders.
   The restraining orders are contained on page(s)   of the attachment. They expire on *(date):*

2. This proceeding was heard as follows: ☐ Default or uncontested ☐ By declaration under Family Code section 2336
       ☐ Contested ☐ Agreement in court
   a. Date: Dept.:   Room:
   b. Judicial officer *(name):*   ☐ Temporary judge
   c. ☐ Petitioner present in court   ☐ Attorney present in court *(name):*
   d. ☐ Respondent present in court   ☐ Attorney present in court *(name):*
   e. ☐ Claimant present in court *(name):*   ☐ Attorney present in court *(name):*
   f. ☐ Other *(specify name):*

3. The court acquired jurisdiction of the respondent on *(date):*
   a. ☐ The respondent was served with process.
   b. ☐ The respondent appeared.

THE COURT ORDERS, GOOD CAUSE APPEARING

4. a. ☐ Judgment of dissolution is entered. Marital or domestic partnership status is terminated and the parties are restored to the status of single persons
       (1) ☐ on *(specify date):*
       (2) ☐ on a date to be determined on noticed motion of either party or on stipulation.
   b. ☐ Judgment of legal separation is entered.
   c. ☐ Judgment of nullity is entered. The parties are declared to be single persons on the ground of *(specify):*

   d. ☐ This judgment will be entered nunc pro tunc as of *(date):*
   e. ☐ Judgment on reserved issues.
   f. The ☐ petitioner's ☐ respondent's former name is restored to *(specify):*
   g. ☐ Jurisdiction is reserved over all other issues, and all present orders remain in effect except as provided below.
   h. ☐ This judgment contains provisions for child support or family support. Each party must complete and file with the court a *Child Support Case Registry Form* (form FL-191) within 10 days of the date of this judgment. The parents must notify the court of any change in the information submitted within 10 days of the change, by filing an updated form. The *Notice of Rights and Responsibilities—Health-Care Costs and Reimbursement Procedures and Information Sheet on Changing a Child Support Order* (form FL-192) is attached.

Form Adopted for Mandatory Use
Judicial Council of California
FL-180 [Rev. July 1, 2012]

JUDGMENT
(Family Law)

Family Code, §§ 2024, 2340, 2343, 2346
www.courts.ca.gov

Judgment

FL-180

CASE NAME (Last name, first name of each party):	CASE NUMBER:

4. i. ☐ The children of this marriage or domestic partnership are:

    (1) ☐   Name   Birthdate

    (2) ☐   Parentage is established for children of this relationship born prior to the marriage or domestic partnership

  j. ☐ Child custody and visitation (parenting time) are ordered as set forth in the attached

    (1) ☐   Settlement agreement, stipulation for judgment, or other written agreement which contains the information required by Family Code section 3048(a).

    (2) ☐   *Child Custody and Visitation Order Attachment* (form FL-341).

    (3) ☐   *Stipulation and Order for Custody and/or Visitation of Children* (form FL-355).

    (4) ☐   Previously established in another case. Case number: Court:

  k. ☐ Child support is ordered as set forth in the attached

    (1) ☐   Settlement agreement, stipulation for judgment, or other written agreement which contains the declarations required by Family Code section 4065(a).

    (2) ☐   *Child Support Information and Order Attachment* (form FL-342).

    (3) ☐   *Stipulation to Establish or Modify Child Support and Order* (form FL-350).

    (4) ☐   Previously established in another case. Case number: Court:

  l. ☐ Spousal, domestic partner, or family support is ordered:

    (1) ☐   Reserved for future determination as relates to ☐ petitioner ☐ respondent

    (2) ☐   Jurisdiction terminated to order spousal or partner support to ☐ petitioner ☐ respondent

    (3) ☐   As set forth in the attached *Spousal, Partner, or Family Support Order Attachment* (form FL-343).

    (4) ☐   As set forth in the attached settlement agreement, stipulation for judgment, or other written agreement.

    (5) ☐   Other *(specify):*

  m. ☐ Property division is ordered as set forth in the attached

    (1) ☐   Settlement agreement, stipulation for judgment, or other written agreement.

    (2) ☐   *Property Order Attachment to Judgment* (form FL-345).

    (3) ☐   Other *(specify):*

  n. ☐ Attorney fees and costs are ordered as set forth in the attached

    (1) ☐   Settlement agreement, stipulation for judgment, or other written agreement.

    (2) ☐   *Attorney Fees and Costs Order* (form FL-346).

    (3) ☐   Other *(specify):*

  o. ☐ Other *(specify):*

Each attachment to this judgment is incorporated into this judgment, and the parties are ordered to comply with each attachment's provisions. Jurisdiction is reserved to make other orders necessary to carry out this judgment.

Date: _____

5. Number of pages attached: _____

                                     JUDICIAL OFFICER
                            ☐ SIGNATURE FOLLOWS LAST ATTACHMENT

NOTICE

Dissolution or legal separation may automatically cancel the rights of a spouse or domestic partner under the other spouse's or domestic partner's will, trust, retirement plan, power of attorney, pay-on-death bank account, transfer-on-death vehicle registration, survivorship rights to any property owned in joint tenancy, and any other similar property interest. It does not automatically cancel the rights of a spouse or domestic partner as beneficiary of the other spouse's or domestic partner's life insurance policy. You should review these matters, as well as any credit cards, other credit accounts, insurance policies, retirement plans, and credit reports, to determine whether they should be changed or whether you should take any other actions.

A debt or obligation may be assigned to one party as part of the dissolution of property and debts, but if that party does not pay the debt or obligation, the creditor may be able to collect from the other party.

An earnings assignment may be issued without additional proof if child, family, partner, or spousal support is ordered.

Any party required to pay support must pay interest on overdue amounts at the "legal rate," which is currently 10 percent.

For your protection and privacy, please press the Clear This Form button after you have printed the form.

[Print This Form]   [Save This Form]   [Clear This Form]

Notice of Entry of Judgment

FL-190

ATTORNEY OR PARTY WITHOUT ATTORNEY *(Name, State Bar number, and address):*	To keep other people from seeing what you entered on your form, please press the Clear This Form button at the end of the form when finished.

TELEPHONE NO.:   FAX NO. *(Optional):*
E-MAIL ADDRESS *(Optional):*
ATTORNEY FOR *(Name):*

SUPERIOR COURT OF CALIFORNIA, COUNTY OF
STREET ADDRESS:
MAILING ADDRESS:
CITY AND ZIP CODE:
BRANCH NAME:

PETITIONER:

RESPONDENT:

NOTICE OF ENTRY OF JUDGMENT	CASE NUMBER:

You are notified that the following judgment was entered on *(date):*

1. ☐ Dissolution
2. ☐ Dissolution—status only
3. ☐ Dissolution—reserving jurisdiction over termination of marital status or domestic partnership
4. ☐ Legal separation
5. ☐ Nullity
6. ☐ Parent-child relationship
7. ☐ Judgment on reserved issues
8. ☐ Other *(specify):*

Date:

Clerk, by _____, Deputy

—NOTICE TO ATTORNEY OF RECORD OR PARTY WITHOUT ATTORNEY—

Under the provisions of Code of Civil Procedure section 1952, if no appeal is filed the court may order the exhibits destroyed or otherwise disposed of after 60 days from the expiration of the appeal time.

STATEMENT IN THIS BOX APPLIES ONLY TO JUDGMENT OF DISSOLUTION
Effective date of termination of marital or domestic partnership status *(specify):*
WARNING: Neither party may remarry or enter into a new domestic partnership until the effective date of the termination of marital or domestic partnership status, as shown in this box.

CLERK'S CERTIFICATE OF MAILING

I certify that I am not a party to this cause and that a true copy of the *Notice of Entry of Judgment* was mailed first class, postage fully prepaid, in a sealed envelope addressed as shown below, and that the notice was mailed

at *(place):*   , California,   on *(date):*

Date:

Clerk, by _____, Deputy

Name and address of petitioner or petitioner's attorney	Name and address of respondent or respondent's attorney

Page 1 of 1

Form Adopted for Mandatory Use Judicial Council of California FL-190 [Rev. January 1, 2005]	**NOTICE OF ENTRY OF JUDGMENT** (Family Law—Uniform Parentage—Custody and Support)	Family Code, §§ 2338, 7636,7637 www.courtinfo.ca.gov

For your protection and privacy, please press the Clear This Form button after you have printed the form.

[Save This Form]   [Print This Form]   [Clear This Form]

Judgment Checklist—Dissolution/Legal Separation

FL-182

ATTORNEY OR PARTY WITHOUT ATTORNEY *(Name, State Bar number, and address)*:	FOR COURT USE ONLY
TELEPHONE NO.: FAX NO. *(Optional)*: E-MAIL ADDRESS *(Optional)*: ATTORNEY FOR *(Name)*:	

SUPERIOR COURT OF CALIFORNIA, COUNTY OF

STREET ADDRESS:

MAILING ADDRESS:

CITY AND ZIP CODE:

BRANCH NAME:

PETITIONER:

RESPONDENT:

JUDGMENT CHECKLIST— DISSOLUTION/LEGAL SEPARATION	CASE NUMBER:

This judgment checklist is a list of documents that a court may require to complete a default or uncontested judgment. The checklist may be filed along with your judgment, but is not required. If the forms or other documents have already been filed, you should check the boxes indicating that they have been previously filed. Unless listed otherwise on this form, when you file a document with the court, you should submit an original and 2 copies. One copy is for you and one is for the other party. There are three types of default and uncontested judgments:

- **Default With No Agreement (no response and no written agreement)**
- **Default With Agreement (no response, but there is a written agreement)**
- **Uncontested Case (response filed, or other appearance by respondent, and a written agreement)**

1. ☐ **DEFAULT WITH NO AGREEMENT (no response and no written agreement)**
   (Please check the box by each document being filed)   Previously Filed

   a. ☐ *Proof of Service of Summons* (form FL-115) or other proof of service   ☐

   b. ☐ *Request to Enter Default* (form FL-165), with a stamped envelope addressed to respondent and the court   ☐
   clerk's address as the return address

   c. ☐ Petitioner's *Declaration Regarding Service of Declaration of Disclosure* (form FL-141)   ☐

   d. ☐ *Declaration for Default or Uncontested Dissolution or Legal Separation* (form FL-170)

   e. ☐ *Judgment* (form FL-180) *(5 copies)*

   f. ☐ *Notice of Entry of Judgment* (form FL-190)

   g. ☐ 2 stamped envelopes of sufficient size and with sufficient postage to return the *Judgment* and *Notice of Entry of Judgment*, one envelope addressed to petitioner and the other to respondent.

   If there are minor children of the marriage or domestic partnership:

   h. ☐ *Declaration Under Uniform Child Custody Jurisdiction and Enforcement Act (UCCJEA)* (form FL-105).   ☐
   (A new form must be filed if there have been any changes since the one most recently filed.)

   i. ☐ Petitioner's *Income and Expense Declaration* (form FL-150) or *Financial Statement (Simplified)* (form   ☐
   FL-155). *(Needed unless one has been filed within the past 90 days and there have been no changes since then.)*

   j. ☐ Computer printout of guideline child support *(optional)*

   k. ☐ *Notice of Rights and Responsibilities and Information Sheet on Changing a Child Support Order* (form FL-192). This may be attached by the petitioner or by the court.

Page 1 of 3

Judgment Checklist—Dissolution/Legal Separation

FL-182

PETITIONER:	CASE NUMBER:
RESPONDENT:	

Previously Filed

l. Child Support Order

☐ *Stipulation to Establish or Modify Child Support and Order* (form FL-350) *(attach to* Judgment*), or*

☐ *Child Support Information and Order Attachment* (form FL-342) *(attach to* Judgment*), or*

☐ Written agreement containing declarations required by Family Code section 4065(a) *(attach to* Judgment*)*

m. ☐ *Income Withholding for Support* (form FL-195/OMB No. 0970-0154)

n. ☐ *Child Custody and Visitation* (Parenting Time) *Order Attachment* (form FL-341) or other proposed written order containing the information required by Family Code 3048(a) *(attach to* Judgment*)*

If spousal/partner support is requested, the marriage/partnership is over 10 years in duration, or termination of spousal/partner support for the respondent is requested:

o. ☐ *Spousal or Partnership Support Declaration Attachment* (form FL-157)

p. ☐ *Income and Expense Declaration* (form FL-150) *(Needed unless a current financial declaration has been filed within the past 90 days and there have been no changes since then.)*   ☐

q. ☐ *Spousal, Partner, or Family Support Order Attachment* (form FL-343) or other proposed written order *(attach to* Judgment*)*

If assets or debts need to be divided or assigned:

r. ☐ *Property Declaration* (form FL-160)   ☐

s. ☐ *Property Order Attachment to Judgment* (form FL-345) or other proposed written order *(attach to* Judgment*)*

If attorney fees and costs are requested:

t. ☐ *Request for Attorney Fees and Costs* (form FL-319)

u. ☐ *Attorney Fees and Costs Order Attachment* (form FL-346) or other proposed written order *(attach to* Judgment*)*

2. ☐ **DEFAULT WITH AGREEMENT (no response and a written agreement)**

a. ☐ *Proof of Service of Summons* (form FL-115) or other proof of service   ☐

b. ☐ *Request to Enter Default* (form FL-165), with a stamped envelope addressed to respondent and the court clerk's address as the return address   ☐

c. ☐ Petitioner's *Declaration Regarding Service of Declaration of Disclosure* (form FL-141) (preliminary)   ☐

d. Declaration Regarding Service of Final Declaration of Disclosure   ☐

   ☐ Petitioner's *Declaration Regarding Service of Declaration of Disclosure* (form FL-141) (final) or

   ☐ *Stipulation and Waiver of Final Declaration of Disclosure* (form FL-144) or

   ☐ Separately filed waiver or waiver included in a written agreement under Family Code section 2105(d)

e. ☐ *Declaration for Default or Uncontested Dissolution or Legal Separation* (form FL-170)

f. ☐ Written agreement of the parties. Respondent's signature on the agreement must be notarized. *(attach to* Judgment.*)*

g. ☐ *Judgment* (form FL-180) *(5 copies)*

h. ☐ *Notice of Entry of Judgment* (form FL-190)

i. ☐ 2 stamped envelopes of sufficient size and with sufficient postage to return the *Judgment* and *Notice of Entry of Judgment,* one envelope addressed to petitioner and the other to respondent

If there are minor children of the marriage or domestic partnership:

j. ☐ *Declaration Under Uniform Child Custody Jurisdiction and Enforcement Act (UCCJEA)* (form FL-105). *(A new form must be filed if there have been any changes since the one most recently filed.)*   ☐

k. ☐ *Income and Expense Declaration* (form FL-150) or *Financial Statement (Simplified)* (form FL-155). *(Needed unless one has been filed within the past 90 days and there have been no changes since then.)*

Judgment Checklist — Dissolution/Legal Separation

FL-182

PETITIONER:	CASE NUMBER:
RESPONDENT:	

Previously Filed

l. ☐ Computer printout of guideline child support *(optional).*

m. ☐ *Notice of Rights and Responsibilities and Information Sheet on Changing a Child Support Order* (form FL-192). This may be attached by the petitioner or by the court.

n. Child Support Order

    ☐ *Stipulation to Establish or Modify Child Support and Order* (form FL-350) *(attach to* Judgment*)*, or

    ☐ *Child Support Information and Order Attachment* (form FL-342) *(attach to* Judgment*)*, or

    ☐ *Written agreement containing declarations required by Family Code section 4065(a) (attach to* Judgment*)*

o. ☐ *Income Withholding for Support* (form FL-195/OMB No. 0970-0154)

p. ☐ *Child Custody and Visitation Order Attachment* (form FL-341) or written agreement containing the information required by Family Code section 3048(a) *(attach to* Judgment*)*

3. ☐ **UNCONTESTED CASE (Response filed, or other appearance by respondent, and a written agreement)**

a. ☐ *Proof of Service of Summons* (form FL-115) or other proof of service if you want to use the date of service ☐
    as the beginning of the six-month waiting period.

b. ☐ *Appearance, Stipulations, and Waivers* (form FL-130) ☐

c. ☐ Respondent's filing fee, if first appearance, unless respondent has a fee waiver or is ☐
    currently on active duty in the military

d. ☐ *Declaration Regarding Service of Declaration of Disclosure* (**both** petitioner's and ☐
    respondent's preliminary) (form FL-141)

e. Declaration Regarding Service of Final Declaration of Disclosure ☐

    ☐ *Declaration Regarding Service of Declaration of Disclosure* (**both** petitioner's and
    respondent's final) (form FL-141), or

    ☐ *Stipulation and Waiver of Final Declaration of Disclosure* (form FL-144), or

    ☐ Separately filed waiver or waiver included in a written agreement under Family Code section 2105(d)

f. ☐ *Declaration for Default or Uncontested Dissolution or Legal Separation* (form FL-170)

g. ☐ Written agreement of the parties *(attach to* Judgment*)*

h. ☐ *Judgment* (form FL-180) *(5 copies)*

i. ☐ *Notice of Entry of Judgment* (form FL-190)

j. ☐ 2 stamped envelopes of sufficient size and with sufficient postage to return the *Judgment* and *Notice of Entry of Judgment*, one envelope addressed to petitioner and the other to respondent

If there are minor children of the marriage or domestic partnership:

k. ☐ *Declaration Under Uniform Child Custody Jurisdiction and Enforcement Act (UCCJEA)* (form FL-105). ☐
    (A new form must be filed if there have been any changes since the one most recently filed.)

l. ☐ Computer printout of guideline child support *(optional)*

m. ☐ *Notice of Rights and Responsibilities and Information Sheet on Changing a Child Support Order* (form FL-192). This may be attached by either party or by the court.

n. Child Support Order

    ☐ *Stipulation to Establish or Modify Child Support and Order* (form FL-350) *(attach to* Judgment*)* or

    ☐ *Child Support Information and Order Attachment* (form FL-342) *(attach to* Judgment*)*, or

    ☐ *Written agreement which includes declarations required by Family Code section 4065(a) (attach to* Judgment*)*

o. ☐ *Income Withholding for Support* (form FL-195/OMB No. 0970-0154)

p. ☐ *Child Custody and Visitation Order Attachment* (form FL-341) or written agreement containing the information required by Family Code section 3048(a) *(attach to* Judgment*)*

Chapter Nine

Agreements and Finalization of the Dissolution

You are now ready to bring the *uncontested* dissolution to a conclusion. At any time after the 31st day (default date) from the date the Respondent was served, the *final* documents may be submitted to the court for approval and filing.

One important factor to keep in mind is that the marital status is not terminated until the appropriate documents have been submitted to the Court. Many clients will be under the erroneous assumption that they are automatically divorced six months after the documents are filed with the court. As previously discussed, the six-month period starts from the **date of service** not the date of filing. Second, the six-month "waiting period" does not automatically grant divorced status to a person. Without the request of the party or parties, the Court **will not** make any further orders.

To terminate the marital status, the parties must either Bifurcate (as discussed in Chapter Eight, if the six-month period has already expired) or they must make sure that all of their documents are submitted to the court for filing and for entry of Judgment prior to the six-month period. The waiting period includes an additional day, just as the Default period did. (See Chapter Eight—Judgments and Resolutions.)

The Judgment may be entered any time after the 31st day after service and prior to six months, plus one day period, however, the marital status **cannot be terminated in a Dissolution of Marriage** any sooner than the **six months plus one day.** You will find it is necessary to remind the client that he/she is not divorced unless the paperwork is submitted. Clients *assume* that the Court enters the Judgment *automatically* after the "waiting period." If the final documents are submitted **after** the six-month period, the marital status will be terminated on the date of the **Entry of Judgment.** In the case of a Judgment for Legal Separation there is **no** six-month "waiting period," because there is no termination of marital status. The same is true of an annulment, because the marriage is void or voidable by the annulment and did "not exist."

In an uncontested dissolution or legal separation the most common method is to prepare a Marital Settlement Agreement (MSA) for the parties to execute. The MSA is a legal and binding contract between the parties. That means that any of the provisions made in the agreement are legally enforceable, if either of the parties fails to comply with any portion of the agreement.

A very simple MSA is included at the end of the chapter. (**Note: this sample is strictly for informational purposes and should not be construed as legal advice or as all inclusive for every dissolution proceeding.**) The MSA should mirror the issues raised in the Petition. As indicated in Chapter Two, any items checked on the Petition must be included and resolved within the Agreement. The format should also follow the same order as the other orders discussed in previous chapters. In other words, the Court wants to see the issues in this matter set forth in the following order:

Child Custody & Visitation

Child Support (including health care, day care and other matters that involve the children)

Spousal Support

Property Division

Attorney Fees

Any other orders relating to the marriage

The above list encompasses the major issues or topics. Within each of those topics, there will be certain language that the attorney will want to include. There will also be some boilerplate-type contractual language. For example, as previously indicated, the court requires certain language regarding jurisdiction to be included in custody and visitation orders. Child support requires certain acknowledgments on the part of the parties, as well as language indicating when support terminates (upon majority or other factors). Spousal support, if ordered, in most cases requires a "Gavron" warning as well as dates of termination, review or other qualifying conditions. Property issues may require language regarding taxes and the execution of documents to effectuate transfers. Some language is statutory while some is required for contractual and enforcement purposes.

The Marital Settlement Agreement (MSA) will usually be attached to the Judgment (face sheet) (FL-180) and should be incorporated by reference, if attached. You will, however, want to be aware of any preferences of the attorney and/or firm. Also, check local rules for the Court's specific requirements, if any. Some firms will actually create two different documents or **contracts:** 1) Judgment that contains the jurisdictional facts; and 2) a separate MSA wherein all the issues are resolved. In that case, you will want to ask your supervising attorney for an example of how the attorney likes the documents prepared or if there is a template available on the firm's computer network. Some firms use the pleading format while some prefer a more contractual tone. Remember to check the appropriate boxes on the form to specify in the MSA whether this is a dissolution or a legal separation. Again, a Judgment for Legal Separation **does not terminate the martial status of the parties**, although it may contain all of the other resolution of issues as would a Dissolution Judgment.

You will also need to determine if a party's signature needs to be notarized or if the firm has such a requirement. Some counties may require a signature to be notarized if the party is unrepresented. Other counties may require that the parties' signatures be notarized, regardless of whether they are represented.

The Judicial Council has also made it easier for *pro se* litigants to complete the dissolution process. You will recall, that when the Findings & Order After Hearing was prepared, you attached Judicial Council forms relating to the each issue raised. These same forms may be attached to the Judgment (FL-180) and the appropriate boxes will be checked. While these forms are available, you will find that most attorneys will want to use pleading format rather than the Judicial Council form(s), so they can customize each issue addressed. The forms frequently don't allow for anything other than checking the boxes, nor do they contain some of the contractual boilerplate language needed in the event the agreement must be enforced.

You will also want to attach any exhibits that relate to any of the issues and matters within the agreement. Such exhibits may include, but are not limited to, Family Court Services recommendations, Domestic Violence Orders, and/or Deeds or Interspousal Transfers. Also, you **must** attach a Notice Regarding Health Care Rights and Responsibilities—Health Care Costs and Reimbursements/Information Sheet on Changing a Child Support Order (FL-192), whenever there are minor children.

It is always wise to include and/or attach any previously made orders to the Agreement, because it may be necessary to enforce the MSA at some future date. It is much simpler for the Court to issue enforcement orders when the orders are contained in the Agreement that the client wishes to enforce.

> For instance, if the parties agreed that one of them would receive the house and signed an Interspousal Transfer Deed along with the MSA. However, the party who received the house has failed to record the deed with the County Recorder. In that event, your office could obtain a certified copy of the Judgment with MSA and have the entire document recorded with the County Recorder. This would effectuate the transfer of the property. These matters will be discussed in greater detail in Chapter Ten. However, you want to keep these points in mind when preparing the initial agreement, because it will take less time and make any orders easier to enforce at a later date, should it be necessary to do so.

In order to complete the dissolution process, the following documents **must** be submitted as the "final package" to the court.

Declaration Regarding Service of Final Declaration of Disclosure (FL-141) and Proof of Service (FL-335)

Declaration for Default or Uncontested Dissolution or Legal Separation (FL-141)

Judgment (face sheet) (FL-180) with Marital Settlement Agreement and attachments

Notice of Entry of Judgment (FL-190)

A Request to Enter Default (FL-165) and Proof of Service of Summons (FL-115) would be included, if these forms have not previously been filed with the court.

If the Respondent filed a Response, an Appearance Stipulation and Waiver (FL-130) must be signed and included in the "final package" along with the Respondent's Declaration Regarding Service of Final Declaration of Disclosure. If the Respondent did not file a Response, but is signing the Marital Settlement Agreement, most Courts will require that the Respondent pay their "first appearance" fee, which would have to be submitted with the documents.

As previously discussed, the parties may agree to **waive service** of the Final Declaration of Disclosure. However, the form must be completed and the parties must execute a Stipulation and Waiver of Final Declaration of Disclosure (FL-144). The appropriate box on both the Declaration regarding Service of Final Declaration of Disclosure and the Declaration for Default or Uncontested Dissolution/Legal Separation must be checked stating the parties have complied with all Preliminary Declarations of Disclosure.

As always, check the local rules to determine if any other documents, local forms, or other information must be submitted with the documents listed above.

In the event either or both of the parties are *pro se* the following documents must be notarized prior to submitting them to the Court. In the event the documents are not notarized, the Court will reject the documents without filing. This can cause undue delay in the entry of judgment. The documents are:

Appearance, Stipulation & Waiver (FL-130) (if applicable as above)

Marital Settlement Agreement

Always submit stamped, addressed envelope(s) so that the Notice of Entry of Judgment can be returned to the law firm. In the event you need a certified copy of any document, it is always less expensive and more expedient to determine the cost of any certified copies and submit a check with the documents. If you are submitting a check or requesting any special processing, you should send a cover letter to the court so that the clerk understands what you are asking and so that the request is less likely to be misplaced.

If your office is submitting the Judgment with Martial Settlement Agreement or Stipulated Judgment in an uncontested matter, you will also need to serve a copy of the Judgment on the other party. You will need to prepare a Proof of Service by Mail, and send the Judgment and any other applicable documents to the other party or to their attorney of record. You will then file the proof of service with the court.

Note: While there is no statutory requirement that a copy of a Default Judgment be served on the Respondent always check the local rules to confirm any requirements with respect to the Default Judgment.

You should also be aware of the fact that parties will often realize that the end of the year is quickly approaching and suddenly want to be divorced before the end of the year. This is often so that their tax filing status will be "single" when they begin the new year. In that event, you need to be aware of the "normal" amount of time it takes the Court to process the final dissolution packages. Although some Court's also feel the need to clear desks before the end of the year and will more rapidly process the documents, if there are any "deficiencies" that the Court finds in your documents, they may send them back to you without adequate time to clear the deficiencies and get the Judgment entered before the end of the year. All of these potential problems should be considered when determining if it is even feasible to have all of the paperwork completed, signed, plus submitted and have the Judgment "entered" before the end of the year.

Transfers of Property Pursuant to Judgment

One of the most valuable tasks of a paralegal can perform is the detail work. As you have seen through the dissolution/legal separation process, a paralegal is instrumental in working with the clients to obtain and access information, to participate in the valuation process, in organizing information, and in generally streamlining the entire process.

As a family law paralegal, you will likely possess the most intimate knowledge about the client's property and personal issues. Armed with this information, it is likely that you will be the one to assist the client in assuring that any property (real or personal) is transferred as required in the Judgment (Default, Stipulated, or MSA).

Examples of property requiring transfer, and a good basis for preparing a check-list, will be:

Real Property — Deeds (including family home, vacation/time share, etc.)

Vehicles (trucks, automobiles, motorcycles, boats, trailers, recreational vehicles, etc.)

Modular Homes (HUD transfers)

Employee Benefits

Insurance on personal items

Insurance Account and Beneficiary changes

It is always a good idea to have any documents needed to transfer title prepared and ready for a signature at the time the agreement is executed. All property which is titled or owned in some manner usually has certain types of documents that need to be executed in order to transfer title. Property which has a beneficiary will also require a change in beneficiary upon the change of marital status, unless the agreement says otherwise.

It is also helpful to keep a file (hard copy and/or on the computer) of the various types of documents that you can give to the client to transfer title as well as the requirements and guidelines for making transfers. In most cases, California exempts an assessment fee on any property (real or personal) pursuant to a dissolution of marriage. For instance, there is no transfer tax on real property, vehicles, and other types of property because the transfer is not a *sale*. However, there may be a processing fee for the transfer such as a recording fee for real property or a registration fee for vehicles. Some jurisdictions outside of California require fees for making transfers of property. You may need to learn if there are any exceptions to this rule. Thus, if the parties own a time-share in Hawaii or Nevada, you will want to check to see if there are any transfer assessments and/or fees associated with the transfer of the property from one party to the other.

You will want to ask the attorney if there is any particular language that should be included on transfers to state specifically that the transfer is "not a sale" or that the property is transferring pursuant to a dissolution of marriage and is being transferred to the person as their "sole and separate property." Also, it is a good idea to ask the attorney if there is other language that may be appropriate.

For vehicle transfers, although an actual pink slip has to be signed, there are other forms which can be down-loaded from the DMV website. These are Notice of Transfer and Release of Liabilities, Odometer Reading, Power of Attorney, and other documents which are required to effectuate the transfer.

Most firms will have access to, or will have created a database of certain types of deeds for use in certain situations. If you are starting from scratch, you might want to contact a Title Company, to obtain copies of various types of deeds: Quitclaim Deed, Grant Deed, Interspousal Transfer Deed, Trust Deed, and any applicable language for changing the title on the property. Additionally, if your office placed a Lis Pendens, or notice of a pending lawsuit affecting title to the property on real property (as discussed in Chapter Two) it will need to be released once the MSA and/or a new Deed have been executed and prior to filing the new Deed transferring title.

Whenever a property carries an insurance policy, the "owner" of the insurance policy will need to be changed, when the property title is changed. Thus, property insurance, auto insurance, special riders on jewelry, etc., will need to be changed. You may need to assist the client with obtaining the change in beneficiary forms in order to make these changes.

Examples of documents or property which require beneficiary changes are: wills, trusts, IRA's, mutual funds, insurance policies, and other assets which are contractual in nature, with the company who maintains the account (or contract).

Ex Parte Application (Request) to Restore Former Name

Some clients will request that their former (maiden or unmarried) name be restored as part of the Dissolution process. This can be accomplished by completing the portion on the Petition that requests that the former name be restored. Previously, this was requested primarily by a woman who took her husband's name upon marriage. However, today some men take their wife's name upon marriage and thus, the court has removed the gender specific reference on Judicial Council forms. Other married persons have never taken their spouse's name and have continued to be known by their birth name or maiden name throughout the duration of the marriage.

A party who has changed his/her name upon marriage may be undecided as to a name change at the time the Petition is filed; or, the person might want to wait until the child(ren) are older so that he/she continue to have the same name as the child(ren) to avoid confusion.

If the party has indicated on the Petition that he/she wishes to have his/her former name restored, the Judgment should reflect this request and provide the name which will be restored on the Judgment face sheet. It will then be necessary to obtain a certified copy of the **entire** Judgment as this document will be required by all entities who will be responsible for changing the name such as: social security, administration, department of motor vehicles, banks and financial institutions, professional certifications, credit card companies, etc.

There is another mechanism for a person to restore a former name that is less complicated or that can be done at any time after the Judgment has been entered. This is accomplished by completing an Ex Parte Application to Restore Former Name (FL-395). This form simply states what the party's "married" or current name is when the Judgment was entered and what name should be restored. The person usually will have to pay a fee as well as the costs for as many certified copies as necessary. The Judge will sign the "Order," the clerk will file and certify the copy(ies) and the form will be mailed to the requesting party. That person can then go to Social Security, DMV, the bank, etc., with this one page certified document, rather than the entire Judgment and complete the process of changing the name.

Many family law practitioners tell their clients at the beginning of the process that they recommend the ex parte procedure over requesting the name change as part of the Petition and the Judgment. The form can be completed and signed by the client when the client is signing all of the other documents of the "final package," and it can then be submitted to the Court for processing and certification. Alternatively, the form can also be submitted once the Judgment has been entered and returned.

This method is preferable because of confidentiality issues as the Judgment usually contains confidential information that is not needed to be filed as part of the public record in order to change a person's name.

Notice of Withdrawal of Attorney of Record

Once your office has received the filed/endorsed Judgment, or in some cases a certified copy if one has been requested, and you have served a copy of same on the other party, or their attorney, and you have tied up any loose ends, you should prepare a Notice of Withdrawal of Attorney of Record (FL-960). This document puts the other party and the Court on notice that any subsequent documents (such as motions or enforcement orders) must be served directly on the party as a *pro se*. The party always has the option of again retaining your office, if matters arise that require representation. However, this will avoid speaking on behalf of a client, who is technically not the client once the Judgment is entered. It will also keep the client from incurring any attorney fees, because the attorney is not "representing" the client in that phase of the case.

The Notice is prepared and served on both the client and the other party/attorney and then filed with the Court.

Historically, clients have retained attorneys to assist them during the family law process. After the matter is concluded, the client may file a pro se motion, such as for enforcement or to modify child support. At the hearing, the Judge may ask the party why the attorney has not appeared, because according to the Court's files, the law firm is still "on record" as representing the client. Filing a Notice of Withdrawal will confirm to the Court that the firm is no longer representing the client.

At this time many attorneys send the client a "closing letter." The "closing letter" will serve as a means of thanking the client for the opportunity to represent them. It may also serve as a reminder of any items the client needs to finish alone such as changes in beneficiaries or refinancing vehicle(s), etc. This reminder also memorializes who is responsible for any additional tasks, so that if at a later date, the client states that your office was supposed to complete a transfer or other task on the client's behalf, you have on file a written document indicating that the client was responsible, not the firm. The closing letter should also state the firm's **retention and destruction of records policy** as it eliminates having to locate the client when the time comes to destroy the file. Sending such a letter spells out to the client the exact status of his/her situation while at the same time, protects the attorney from potential malpractice issues.

The closing letter is also a good method of confirming that you can now close the file on this matter.

Appeal of Judgment

In most cases, as part of their MSA the parties will mutually agree to **waive** any and all right to "move for a new trial" and/or appeal the settlement of their case. There are, however, instances when a party feels that the Judgment should be vacated or set aside. Also, if there was a trial, one party may file a *Motion for a New Trial* or a *Motion to Vacate and Enter Different Judgment* or a *Motion to Vacate and Set Aside the Judgment*.

Common grounds for these motions are as follows:

New Trial—CCP§§ 657–657.1 and the ruling in the case: *Fomco, Inc. v. Joe Maggio, Inc* (1961) 55 C2d 162, 166 10 CR 462, 464, which held that Defendants were not entitled to a new trial on the ground of newly discovered evidence because Defendants failed to show reasonable diligence to produce the evidence at the trial.

Motion to Vacate and Enter Different Judgment: Is usually requesting that the "facts or case law" be reviewed again, thus requesting a review of the decision based on "judicial error." (*CCP§ 663*)

Motion to Vacate and Set Aside Judgment: In most cases this request will be due to a default judgment being entered as a result of "mistake, inadvertence, surprise, or excusable neglect." (*CCP§ 473*)

Such errors (mistake, inadvertence, surprise or excusable neglect) as referenced in CCP§ 473 may include:

Error of the Party

Error of the Attorney

A party may make a Motion for a New Trial as follows: (1) 15 days after the clerk mails, or the moving party serves, the notice of entry of Judgment, or (2) 180 days after the entry of Judgment. (*CCP§ 659*). Either of these motions must contain a declaration stating the "grounds" for the request and must be accompanied by Points and Authorities.

Motions to Vacate to Enter a Different Judgment or to Set Aside the Judgment must be filed as follows: "within a reasonable time" but "in no case exceeding six months after the judgment, dismissal, order or proceeding was taken." (CCP §473(b)) The general rule is that the six-month time period commences with the entry of default, **not** from the entry of Judgment.

It should be noted that if a party files an appeal (or any motion referenced above), the marital status will be considered final on the date entered by the Judgment, unless the appeal is objecting to the date of termination of the marital status.

Forms Associated with Topic

Income Withholding for Support (FL-195)

Child Support Case Registry (FL-191)

Ex Parte Request to Restore Former Name (FL-395)

Notice of Withdrawal of Attorney of Record (FL-960)

(See examples of some forms on the following pages)

Key Terms

- Stipulated Judgment
- Notice of Withdrawal of Attorney of Record
- Termination of Marital Status
- Waiting Period
- Final Dissolution/Legal Separation Package
- Ex Parte Request to Restore Former Name
- Appeal of Judgment
- Motion to Vacate and Enter a Different Judgment
- Motion to Vacate and Set Aside Judgment
- Motion for New Trial

Income Withholding for Support

FL-195

INCOME WITHHOLDING FOR SUPPORT

☑ ORIGINAL INCOME WITHHOLDING ORDER/NOTICE FOR SUPPORT (IWO)
☐ AMENDED IWO
☐ ONE-TIME ORDER/NOTICE FOR LUMP SUM PAYMENT
☐ TERMINATION of IWO   Date: _____

☐ Child Support Enforcement (CSE) Agency ☐ Court ☑ Attorney ☐ Private Individual/Entity (Check One)

NOTE: This IWO must be regular on its face. Under certain circumstances you must reject this IWO and return it to the sender (see IWO instructions http://www.acf.hhs.gov/programs/cse/newhire/employer/publication/publication.htm - forms). If you receive this document from someone other than a State or Tribal CSE agency or a Court, a copy of the underlying order must be attached.

State/Tribe/Territory _____   Remittance Identifier (include w/payment) _____
City/County/Dist./Tribe _____   Order Identifier _____
Private Individual/Entity _____   CSE Agency Case Identifier _____

State of California   RE: SHORES, ROCKY BLUFF
Employer/Income Withholder's Name   Employee/Obligor's Name (Last, First, Middle)
                                               XXX-XX-XXXX

Employer/Income Withholder's Address   Employee/Obligor's Social Security Number
700 P Street, Sacramento, CA 95814   SHORES, SANDIE BEECH
                                               Custodial Party/Obligee's Name (Last, First, Middle)

Employer/Income Withholder's FEIN _____

Child(ren)'s Name(s) (Last, First, Middle)   Child(ren)' s Birth Date(s)
EDDY WADE SHORES   5/1/05
SHELLY PEBBLES SHORES   10/15/09

ORDER INFORMATION: This document is based on the support or withholding order from _____ (State/Tribe). You are required by law to deduct these amounts from the employee/obligor's income until further notice.

$ 1600 _____ Per MONTH _____ current child support
$_____ Per _____ past-due child support - **Arrears greater than 12 weeks?** ☐ Yes ☐No
$_____ Per _____ current cash medical support
$_____ Per _____ past-due cash medical support
$ 700 _____ Per MONTH _____ current spousal support
$_____ Per _____ past-due spousal support
$_____ Per _____ other (must specify) _____.
for a **Total Amount to Withhold** of $ 2,600.00 _____ per MONTH _____.

AMOUNTS TO WITHHOLD: You do not have to vary your pay cycle to be in compliance with the *Order Information*. If your pay cycle does not match the ordered payment cycle, withhold one of the following amounts:
$ _____ per weekly pay period $ _____ per semimonthly pay period (twice a month)
$ _____ per biweekly pay period (every two weeks) $ 2600.00 _____ per monthly pay period
$ _____ **Lump Sum Payment:** Do not stop any existing IWO unless you receive a termination order.

REMITTANCE INFORMATION: If the employee/obligor's principal place of employment is California _____ (State/Tribe), you must begin withholding no later than the first pay period that occurs __10__ days after the date of receipt . Send payment within 10 _____ working days of the pay date. If you cannot withhold the full amount of support for any or all orders for this employee/obligor, withhold up to __50__ % of disposable income for all orders. If the employee/obligor's principal place of employment is not__ California ____ (State/Tribe), obtain withholding limitations, time requirements, and any allowable employer fees at http://www.acf.hhs.gov/programs/cse/newhire/employer/contacts/contact_map.htm for the employee/obligor's principal place of employment.

Document Tracking Identifier _____

1

Income Withholding for Support

FL-195

For electronic payment requirements and centralized payment collection and disbursement facility information (State Disbursement Unit [SDU]), see http://www.acf.hhs.gov/programs/cse/newhire/employer/contacts/contact_map.htm.

Include the *Remittance Identifier* **with the payment** and if necessary this FIPS code: _____

Remit payment to _Sandie Shores, 11155 Turtle Dove Court, Folsom, CA 95630_____(SDU/Tribal Order Payee)
at _____(SDU/Tribal Payee Address)

☐ **Return to Sender [Completed by Employer/Income Withholder].** Payment must be directed to an SDU in accordance with 42 USC §666(b)(5) and (b)(6) or Tribal payee (see Payments to SDU below). If payment is not directed to an SDU/Tribal Payee or this IWO is not regular on its face, you *must* check this box and return the IWO to the sender.

Signature of Judge/Issuing Official (if required by State or Tribal law): _____
Print Name of Judge/Issuing Official: _____
Title of Judge/Issuing Official: _____
Date of Signature: _____

If the employee/obligor works in a State or for a Tribe that is different from the State or Tribe that must issued this order, a copy of this IWO must be provided to the employee/obligor.
☐ If checked, the employer/income withholder must provide a copy of this form to the employer/obligor.

ADDITIONAL INFORMATION FOR EMPLOYERS/INCOME WITHHOLDERS

State-specific contact and withholding information can be found on the Federal Employer Services website located at:
http://www.acf.hhs.gov/programs/cse/newhire/employer/contacts/contact_map.htm

Priority: Withholding for support has priority over any other legal process under State law against the same income (USC 42 §666(b)(7)). If a Federal tax levy is in effect, please notify the sender.

Combining Payments: When remitting payments to an SDU or Tribal CSE agency, you may combine withheld amounts from more than one employee/obligor's income in a single payment. You must, however, separately identify each employee/obligor's portion of the payment.

Payments to SDU: You must send child support payments payable by income withholding to the appropriate SDU or to a Tribal CSE agency. If this IWO instructs you to send a payment to an entity other than an SDU (e.g., payable to the custodial party, court, or attorney), you must check the box above and return this notice to the sender. Exception: If this IWO was sent by a Court, Attorney, or Private Individual/Entity and the initial order was entered before January 1, 1994 or the order was issued by a Tribal CSE agency, you must follow the "Remit payment to" instructions on this form.

Reporting the Pay Date: You must report the pay date when sending the payment. The pay date is the date on which the amount was withheld from the employee/obligor's wages. You must comply with the law of the State (or Tribal law if applicable) of the employee/obligor's principal place of employment regarding time periods within which you must implement the withholding and forward the support payments.

Multiple IWOs: If there is more than one IWO against this employee/obligor and you are unable to fully honor all IWOs due to Federal, State, or Tribal withholding limits, you must honor all IWOs to the greatest extent possible, giving priority to current support before payment of any past-due support. Follow the State or Tribal law/procedure of the employee/obligor's principal place of employment to determine the appropriate allocation method.

Lump Sum Payments: You may be required to notify a State or Tribal CSE agency of upcoming lump sum payments to this employee/obligor such as bonuses, commissions, or severance pay. Contact the sender to determine if you are required to report and/or withhold lump sum payments.

Liability: If you have any doubts about the validity of this IWO, contact the sender. If you fail to withhold income from the employee/obligor's income as the IWO directs, you are liable for both the accumulated amount you should have withheld and any penalties set by State or Tribal law/procedure. _____
_____

Anti-discrimination: You are subject to a fine determined under State or Tribal law for discharging an employee/obligor from employment, refusing to employ, or taking disciplinary action against an employee/obligor because of this IWO.

_____

OMB Expiration Date – 05/31/2014. The OMB Expiration Date has no bearing on the termination date of the IWO; it identifies the version of the form currently in use. 2

Income Withholding for Support

FL-195

Employer's name: _____ Employer FEIN: _____

Employee/Obligor's Name: _____

CSE Agency Case Identifier: _____ Order Identifier _____

Withholding Limits: You may not withhold more than the lesser of: 1) the amounts allowed by the Federal Consumer Credit Protection Act (CCPA) (15 U.S.C. 1673(b)); or 2) the amounts allowed by the State or Tribe of the employee/obligor's principal place of employment (see *REMITTANCE INFORMATION*). Disposable income is the net income left after making mandatory deductions such as: State, Federal, local taxes; Social Security taxes; statutory pension contributions; and Medicare taxes. The Federal limit is 50% of the disposable income if the obligor is supporting another family and 60% of the disposable income if the obligor is not supporting another family. However, those limits increase 5% - to 55% and 65% - if the arrears are greater than 12 weeks. If permitted by the State or Tribe, you may deduct a fee for administrative costs. The combined support amount and the fee may not exceed the limit indicated in this section.

For Tribal orders, you may not withhold more than the amounts allowed under the law of the issuing Tribe. For Tribal employers/income withholder who receive a State IWO, you may not withhold more than the lesser of the limit set by the law of the jurisdiction in which the employer/income withholder is located or the maximum amount permitted under section 303(d) of the CCPA (15 U.S.C. 1673 (b)).

Depending upon applicable State law or Tribal law, you may need to also consider the amounts paid for health care premiums in determining disposable income and applying appropriate withholding limits.

Arrears greater than 12 weeks? If the *Order Information* does not indicate that the arrears are greater than 12 weeks, then the Employer should calculate the CCPA limit using the lower percentage.

Additional Information: _____
_____
_____
_____

NOTIFICATION OF EMPLOYMENT TERMINATION OR INCOME STATUS: If this employee/obligor never worked for you or you are no longer withholding income for this employee/obligor, an employer must promptly notify the CSE agency and/or the sender by returning this form to the address listed in the Contact information below:

☐   This person has never worked for this employer nor received periodic income.

☐   This person no longer works for this employer nor receives periodic income.

Please provide the following information for the employee/obligor:

Termination date: _____Last known phone number: _____

Last known address_____
_____

Final payment date to SDU/Tribal Payee: _____ Final payment amount:_____

New employer's name: _____

New employer's address: _____

CONTACT INFORMATION

To Employer/Income Withholder: If you have any questions, contact <u>Joan Care-Actor, Attorney at Law</u> (Issuer name) by phone at <u>916-555-1234</u> , by fax at <u>916-555-1233</u> , by email or website at: <u>joan@care-actorlaw.com</u> .

Send termination notice and other correspondence to: <u>Sandie Shores, 11155 Turtle Dove Court, Folsom, CA 95630</u>
_____ (Issuer address).

To Employer/Obligor: If the employee/obligor has questions, contact <u>Joan Care-Actor, Attorney at Law</u> (Issuer name) by phone at<u>916-555-1234</u> , by fax at <u>916-555-1233</u> , by email or website at: <u>joan@care-actorlaw.com</u> .

IMPORTANT: The person completing this form is advised that the information may be shared with the employee/obligor.   3

| For your protection and privacy, please press the Clear This Form button after you have printed the form. | **Save This Form** | **Print This Form** | **Clear This Form** |

Child Support Case Registry Form

FL-191

ATTORNEY OR PARTY WITHOUT ATTORNEY *(Name, State Bar number, and address):*	
JOAN CARE-ACTOR, SBN ******* LAW OFFICES OF JOAN CARE-ACTOR 75000 WHY ME LANE SACRAMENTO, CA 95826 TELEPHONE NO.: 916-555-1234 FAX NO. *(Optional):* 916-555-1233 E-MAIL ADDRESS *(Optional):* joan@care-actorlaw.com ATTORNEY FOR *(Name):* SANDIE SHORES, PETITIONER	To keep other people from seeing what you entered on your form, please press the Clear This Form button at the end of the form when finished.

SUPERIOR COURT OF CALIFORNIA, COUNTY OF SACRAMENTO
STREET ADDRESS: 3341 POWER INN ROAD
MAILING ADDRESS: 3341 POWER INN ROAD
CITY AND ZIP CODE: SACRAMENTO, CA 95826
BRANCH NAME: FAMILY LAW

PETITIONER/PLAINTIFF: SANDIE SHORES

RESPONDENT/DEFENDANT: ROCKY SHORES

OTHER PARENT:

CHILD SUPPORT CASE REGISTRY FORM	CASE NUMBER:
[✔] Mother [ ] First form completed [ ] Father [ ] Change to previous information	14FLXXXXXX

THIS FORM WILL NOT BE PLACED IN THE COURT FILE. IT WILL BE MAINTAINED IN A CONFIDENTIAL FILE WITH THE STATE OF CALIFORNIA.

Notice: Pages 1 and 2 of this form must be completed and delivered to the court along with the court order for support. Pages 3 and 4 are instructional only and do not need to be delivered to the court. If you did not file the court order, you must complete this form and deliver it to the court within 10 days of the date on which you received a copy of the support order. Any later change to the information on this form must be delivered to the court on another form within 10 days of the change. It is important that you keep the court informed in writing of any changes of your address and telephone number.

1. Support order information *(this information is on the court order you are filing or have received).*
   a. Date order filed: XX/XX/2014
   b. [✔] Initial child support or family support order   [ ] Modification
   c. Total monthly base current child or family support amount ordered for children listed below, plus any monthly amount ordered payable on past-due support:

Child Support:	Family Support:	Spousal Support:
(1) [✔] Current base child support: $1600 [ ] Reserved order [ ] $0 (zero) order	[ ] Current base family support: $ [ ] Reserved order [ ] $0 (zero) order	[✔] Current spousal support: $700 [ ] Reserved order [ ] $0 (zero) order
(2) [ ] Additional monthly support: $	[ ] Additional monthly support: $	
(3) [ ] Total past-due support: $	[ ] Total past-due support: $	[ ] Total past-due support: $
(4) [ ] Payment on past-due support: $	[ ] Payment on past-due support: $	[ ] Payment on past-due support: $
(5) Wage withholding was [ ] ordered [ ] ordered but stayed until *(date):*		

2. Person required to pay child or family support *(name):* ROCKY SHORES
   Relationship to child *(specify):* FATHER

3. Person or agency to receive child or family support payments *(name):* SANDIE SHORES
   Relationship to child *(if applicable):* MOTHER

TYPE OR PRINT IN INK

Child Support Case Registry Form

PETITIONER/PLAINTIFF: **SANDIE SHORES**	CASE NUMBER:
RESPONDENT/DEFENDANT: **ROCKY SHORES**	**14FLXXXXXX**
OTHER PARENT:	

4. The child support order is for the following children:

Child's name	Date of birth	Social security number
a. EDDY WADE SHORES	5/1/2005	XXX-XX-XXXX
b. SHELLY PEBBLES SHORES	10/15/2009	XXX-XX-XXXX
c.		

☐ Additional children are listed on a page attached to this document.

You are required to complete the following information about yourself. You are not required to provide information about the other person, but you are encouraged to provide as much as you can. This form is confidential and will not be filed in the court file. It will be maintained in a confidential file with the State of California.

5. Father's name: **ROCKY WADE SHORES**

  a. Date of birth: XX/XX/XXXX

  b. Social security number: XXX-XX-XXXX

  c. Street address:

    6900 CHEATER LANE

  City, state, zip code:

  SACRAMENTO, CA 95816

  d. Mailing address:

  SAME AS ABOVE

  City, state, zip code:

  e. Driver's license number:

  BXXXXXXXX

  State:

  CALIFORNIA

  f. Telephone number:

  916-555-XXXX

  g. ☑ Employed ☐ Not employed ☐ Self-employed

  Employer's name:

  STATE OF CALIFORNIA
  DEPARTMENT OF TRANSPORTATION

  Street address:
  700 P STREET

  City, state, zip code:
  SACRAMENTO, CA 95814

  Telephone number:
  916-XXX-XXXX

6. Mother's name: **SANDIE BEECH SHORES**

  a. Date of birth: XX/XX/XXXX

  b. Social security number: XXX-XX-XXXX

  c. Street address:

    11155 TURTLE DOVE COURT

  City, state, zip code:

  FOLSOM, CA 95630

  d. Mailing address:

  SAME AS ABOVE

  City, state, zip code:

  e. Driver's license number:

  CXXXXXXXX

  State:

  CALIFORNIA

  f. Telephone number:

  916-555-XXXX

  g. ☐ Employed ☑ Not employed ☐ Self-employed

  Employer's name:

  N/A

  Street address:

  City, state, zip code:

  Telephone number:

7. ☐ A restraining order, protective order, or nondisclosure order due to domestic violence is in effect.

  a. The order protects: ☐ Father ☐ Mother ☐ Children

  b. From: ☐ Father ☐ Mother

  c. The restraining order expires on *(date):*

I declare under penalty of perjury under the laws of the State of California that the foregoing is true and correct.

Date:

JOAN CARE-ACTOR
      (TYPE OR PRINT NAME)

▶

      (SIGNATURE OF PERSON COMPLETING THIS FORM)

Child Support Case Registry Form

INFORMATION SHEET FOR CHILD SUPPORT CASE REGISTRY FORM
(Do NOT deliver this Information Sheet to the court clerk.)

Please follow these instructions to complete the *Child Support Case Registry Form* (form FL-191) if you do not have an attorney to represent you. Your attorney, if you have one, should complete this form.

Both parents must complete a *Child Support Case Registry Form*. The information on this form will be included in a national database that, among other things, is used to locate absent parents. When you file a court order, you must deliver a completed form to the court clerk along with your court order. If you did not file a court order, you must deliver a completed form to the court clerk **WITHIN 10 DAYS** of the date you received a copy of your court order. If any of the information you provide on this form changes, you must complete a new form and deliver it to the court clerk within 10 days of the change. The address of the court clerk is the same as the one shown for the superior court on your order. This form is confidential and will not be filed in the court file. It will be maintained in a confidential file with the State of California.

INSTRUCTIONS FOR COMPLETING THE *CHILD SUPPORT CASE REGISTRY FORM* (TYPE OR PRINT IN INK):

If the top section of the form has already been filled out, skip down to number 1 below. If the top section of the form is blank, you must provide this information.

Page 1, first box, top of form, left side: Print your name, address, telephone number, fax number, and e-mail address, if any, in this box. Attorneys must include their State Bar identification numbers.

Page 1, second box, top of form, left side: Print the name of the county and the court's address in this box. Use the same address for the court that is on the court order you are filing or have received.

Page 1, third box, top of form, left side: Print the names of the petitioner/plaintiff, respondent/defendant, and other parent in this box. Use the same names listed on the court order you are filing or have received.

Page 1, fourth box, top of form, left side: Check the box indicating whether you are the mother or the father. If you are the attorney for the mother, check the box for mother. If you are the attorney for the father, check the box for father. Also, if this is the first time you have filled out this form, check the box by "First form completed." If you have filled out form FL-191 before, and you are changing any of the information, check the box by "Change to previous information."

Page 1, first box, right side: Leave this box blank for the court's use in stamping the date of receipt.

Page 1, second box, right side: Print the court case number in this box. This number is also shown on the court papers.

Instructions for numbered paragraphs:

1. a. Enter the date the court order was filed. This date is shown in the "COURT PERSONNEL: STAMP DATE RECEIVED HERE" box on page 1 at the top of the order on the right side. If the order has not been filed, leave this item blank for the court clerk to fill in.

   b. If the court order you filed or received is the first child or family support order for this case, check the box by "Initial child support or family support order." If this is a change to your order, check the box by "Modification."

   c. Information regarding the amount and type of support ordered and wage withholding is on the court order you are filing or have received.

      (1) If your order provides for any type of current support, check all boxes that describe that support. For example, if your order provides for both child and spousal support, check both of those boxes. If there is an amount, put it in the blank provided. If the order says the amount is reserved, check the "Reserved order" box. If the order says the amount is zero, check the "$0 (zero) order" box. Do not include child care, special needs, uninsured medical expenses, or travel for visitation here These amounts will go in (2). Do NOT complete the Child Support Case Registry form if you receive spousal support only.

      (2) If your order provides for a set monthly amount to be paid as additional support for such needs as child care, special needs, uninsured medical expenses or travel for visitation check the box in Item 2 and enter the monthly amount. For example, if your order provides for base child support and in addition the paying parent is required to pay $300 per month, check the box in item 2 underneath the "Child Support" column and enter $300. Do NOT check this box if your order provides only for a payment of a percentage, such as 50% of the childcare.

Child Support Case Registry Form

(3) If your order determined the amount of past due support, check the box in Item 3 that states the type of past due support and enter the amount. For example, if the court determined that there was $5000 in past due child support and $1000 in past due spousal support, you would check the box in item 3 in the "Child Support" column and enter $5000 and you would also check the box in item 3 in the "Spousal Support" column and enter $1000.

(4) If your order provides for a specific dollar amount to be paid towards any past due support, check the box in Item 4 that states the type of past due support and enter the amount. For example, the court ordered $350 per month to be paid on the past due child support, you would check the box in Item 4 in the "Child Support" column and enter $350.

(5) Check the "ordered" box if wage withholding was ordered with no conditions. Check the box "ordered but stayed until" if wage withholding was ordered but is not to be deducted until a later date. If the court delayed the effective date of the wage withholding, enter the specific date. Check only one box in this item.

2. a. Write the name of the person who is supposed to pay child or family support.
   b. Write the relationship of that person to the child.

3. a. Write the name of the person or agency supposed to receive child or family support payments.
   b. Write the relationship of that person to the child.

4. List the full name, date of birth, and social security number for each child included in the support order. If there are more than five children included in the support order, check the box below item 4e and list the remaining children with dates of birth and social security numbers on another sheet of paper. Attach the other sheet to this form.

The local child support agency is required, under section 466(a)(13) of the Social Security Act, to place in the records pertaining to child support the social security number of any individual who is subject to a divorce decree, support order, or paternity determination or acknowledgment. This information is mandatory and will be kept on file at the local child support agency.

Top of page 2, box on left side: Print the names of the petitioner/plaintiff, respondent/defendant, and other parent in this box. Use the same names listed on page 1.

Top of page 2, box on right side: Print your court case number in this box. Use the same case number as on page 1, second box, right side.

You are required to complete information about yourself. If you know information about the other person, you may also fill in what you know about him or her.

5. If you are the father in this case, list your full name in this space. See instructions for a–g under item 6 below.

6. If you are the mother in this case, list your full name in this space.

   a. List your date of birth.

   b. Write your social security number.

   c. List the street address, city, state, and zip code where you live.

   d. List the street address, city, state, and zip code where you want your mail sent, if different from the address where you live.

   e. Write your driver's license number and the state where it was issued.

   f. List the telephone number where you live.

   g. Indicate whether you are employed, not employed, self-employed, or by checking the appropriate box. If you are employed, write the name, street address, city, state, zip code, and telephone number where you work.

7. If there is a restraining order, protective order, or nondisclosure order, check this box.

   a. Check the box beside each person who is protected by the restraining order.

   b. Check the box beside the parent who is restrained.

   c. Write the date the restraining order expires. See the restraining order, protective order, or nondisclosure order for this date.

If you are in fear of domestic violence, you may want to ask the court for a restraining order, protective order, or nondisclosure order.

You must type or print your name, fill in the date, and sign the *Child Support Case Registry Form* under penalty of perjury. When you sign under penalty of perjury, you are stating that the information you have provided is true and correct.

For your protection and privacy, please press the Clear This Form button after you have printed the form.

Save This Form   **Print This Form**   **Clear This Form**

Ex Parte Application for Restoration of Former Name

FL-395

ATTORNEY OR PARTY WITHOUT ATTORNEY *(Name and Address):*	TELEPHONE NO.:

_ JOAN CARE-ACTOR, SBN ******
LAW OFFICES OF JOAN CARE-ACTOR
75000 WHY ME LANE
SACRAMENTO, CA 95826

ATTORNEY FOR *(Name):* SANDIE SHORES, PETITIONER

SUPERIOR COURT OF CALIFORNIA, COUNTY OF SACRAMENTO
STREET ADDRESS: 3341 POWER INN ROAD
MAILING ADDRESS: 3341 POWER INN ROAD
CITY AND ZIP CODE: SACRAMENTO, CA 95826
BRANCH NAME: FAMILY LAW

MARRIAGE OF SHORES
PETITIONER: SANDIE SHORES

RESPONDENT: ROCKY SHORES

EX PARTE APPLICATION FOR RESTORATION OF FORMER NAME AFTER ENTRY OF JUDGMENT AND ORDER	CASE NUMBER: 14FLXXXXXX

To keep other people from seeing what you entered on your form, please press the Clear This Form button at the end of the form when finished.

APPLICATION

1. A judgment of dissolution or nullity was entered on *(date):* XX/XX/2014

2. Applicant now requests that his or her former name be restored. The applicant's former name is *(specify):*

   SANDIE RAE BEECH

Date:

_____   ▶ _____
SANDIE SHORES
(TYPE OR PRINT NAME)   (SIGNATURE OF APPLICANT)
                                          (USE CURRENT NAME)

ORDER

3. IT IS ORDERED that applicant's former name is restored to *(specify):*

   SANDIE RAE BEECH

Date:

_____
JUDICIAL OFFICER

[SEAL]

CLERK'S CERTIFICATE

I certify that the foregoing is a true and correct copy of the original on file in my office.

Date: Clerk, by _____, Deputy

Page 1 of 1

Form Adopted for Mandatory Use
Judicial Council of California
FL-395 [Rev. January 1, 2003]

**EX PARTE APPLICATION FOR RESTORATION OF FORMER NAME
AFTER ENTRY OF JUDGMENT AND ORDER
(Family Law)**

Family Code, § 2080
www.courtinfo.ca.gov

For your protection and privacy, please press the Clear This Form button after you have printed the form.

Save This Form | Print This Form | Clear This Form

Notice of Withdrawal of Attorney of Record

FL-960

ATTORNEY OR PARTY WITHOUT ATTORNEY *(Name, state bar number, and address):* JOAN CARE-ACTOR, SBN ******* LAW OFFICES OF JOAN CARE-ACTOR 75000 WHY ME LANE SACRAMENTO, CA 95826 TELEPHONE NO.: 916-555-1234 FAX NO.: 916-555-1233 ATTORNEY FOR *(Name):* SANDIE SHORES, PETITIONER	To keep other people from seeing what you entered on your form, please press the Clear This Form button at the end of the form when finished.

SUPERIOR COURT OF CALIFORNIA, COUNTY OF SACRAMENTO
STREET ADDRESS: 3341 POWER INN ROAD
MAILING ADDRESS: 3341 POWER INN ROAD
CITY AND ZIP CODE: SACRAMENTO, CA 95826
BRANCH NAME: FAMILY LAW

PETITIONER/PLAINTIFF: SANDIE SHORES

RESPONDENT/DEFENDANT: ROCKY SHORES

NOTICE OF WITHDRAWAL OF ATTORNEY OF RECORD	CASE NUMBER: 14FLXXXXX

1. In accordance with the provisions of section 285.1 of the Code of Civil Procedure, I withdraw as Attorney of Record for: SANDIE SHORES
   ☑ Petitioner ☐ Respondent

2. The final judgment of dissolution, legal separation, nullity, parentage, or postjudgment order was entered on *(specify date):* XX/XX/2014 and no motions or other proceedings are pending at this time.

3. The last known address for the ☑ Petitioner ☐ Respondent is:
   11155 TURTLE DOVE COURT, FOLSOM, CA 95630

4. The last known telephone number for the ☑ Petitioner ☐ Respondent is: 916-555-XXXX

5. I mailed a copy of this *Notice of Withdrawal* to ☑ Petitioner ☐ Respondent at the address set forth in item 3.

I declare under penalty of perjury under the laws of the State of California that the foregoing is true and correct.

Date:

_____   ▶   _____
JOAN CARE-ACTOR   (SIGNATURE)
(TYPE OR PRINT NAME)

WARNING
This form may not be used after a status-only judgment.

Page 1 of 2

Form Adopted for Mandatory Use Judicial Council of California FL-960 [Rev. January 1, 2003]	**NOTICE OF WITHDRAWAL OF ATTORNEY OF RECORD**	Code of Civil Procedure, § 285.1 www.courtinfo.ca.gov

Notice of Withdrawal of Attorney of Record

	CASE NUMBER:
PETITIONER/PLAINTIFF: SANDIE SHORES	
RESPONDENT/DEFENDANT: ROCKY SHORES	14FLXXXXX

PROOF OF SERVICE BY ☐ **PERSONAL SERVICE** ☐ **MAIL**

1. At the time of service I was at least 18 years of age and **not a party to this legal action.**

2. I served a copy of the *Notice of Withdrawal of Attorney of Record* as follows *(check either a. or b. below)*:

   a. ☐ **Personal service.** I personally delivered the *Notice of Withdrawal of Attorney of Record* as follows:
   (1) Name of person served:
   (2) Address where served:

   (3) Date served:
   (4) Time served:

   b. ☐ **Mail.** I deposited the *Notice of Withdrawal of Attorney of Record* in the United States mail, in a sealed envelope with postage fully prepaid. The envelope was addressed and mailed as follows:
   (1) Name of person served:
   (2) Address:

   (3) Date of mailing:
   (4) Place of mailing *(city and state)*:
   (5) I am a resident of or employed in the county where the *Notice* was mailed.

   c. My residence or business address is *(specify)*:

   d. My phone number is *(specify)*:

I declare under penalty of perjury under the laws of the State of California that the foregoing is true and correct.

Date:

▶

_____   _____
(TYPE OR PRINT NAME)   (SIGNATURE OF PERSON SERVING NOTICE)

For your protection and privacy, please press the Clear This Form button after you have printed the form. | Save This Form | Print This Form | Clear This Form |

Income Withholding for Support

To keep other people from seeing what you entered on your form, please press the Clear This Form button at the end of the form when finished.

FL-195

INCOME WITHHOLDING FOR SUPPORT

☐ **ORIGINAL INCOME WITHHOLDING ORDER/NOTICE FOR SUPPORT (IWO)**
☐ **AMENDED IWO**
☐ **ONE-TIME ORDER/NOTICE FOR LUMP SUM PAYMENT**
☐ **TERMINATION of IWO**   Date: _____

☐ Child Support Enforcement (CSE) Agency   ☐ Court   ☐ Attorney   ☐ Private Individual/Entity   (Check One)

NOTE: This IWO must be regular on its face. Under certain circumstances you must reject this IWO and return it to the sender (see IWO instructions http://www.acf.hhs.gov/programs/cse/newhire/employer/publication/publication.htm - forms). If you receive this document from someone other than a State or Tribal CSE agency or a Court, a copy of the underlying order must be attached.

State/Tribe/Territory _____   Remittance Identifier (include w/payment) _____
City/County/Dist./Tribe _____   Order Identifier _____
Private Individual/Entity _____   CSE Agency Case Identifier _____

_____   RE: _____
Employer/Income Withholder's Name   Employee/Obligor's Name (Last, First, Middle)

_____   _____
Employer/Income Withholder's Address   Employee/Obligor's Social Security Number

_____   Custodial Party/Obligee's Name (Last, First, Middle)

_____

Employer/Income Withholder's FEIN _____

Child(ren)'s Name(s) (Last, First, Middle)   Child(ren)' s Birth Date(s)
_____   _____
_____   _____
_____   _____
_____   _____
_____   _____

ORDER INFORMATION: This document is based on the support or withholding order from _____ (State/Tribe). You are required by law to deduct these amounts from the employee/obligor's income until further notice.
$_____ Per _____ current child support
$_____ Per _____ past-due child support - **Arrears greater than 12 weeks?** ☐ Yes ☐No
$_____ Per _____ current cash medical support
$_____ Per _____ past-due cash medical support
$_____ Per _____ current spousal support
$_____ Per _____ past-due spousal support
$_____ Per _____ other (must specify) _____.
for a **Total Amount to Withhold** of $_____ per _____.

AMOUNTS TO WITHHOLD: You do not have to vary your pay cycle to be in compliance with the *Order Information*. If your pay cycle does not match the ordered payment cycle, withhold one of the following amounts:
$_____ per weekly pay period $_____ per semimonthly pay period (twice a month)
$_____ per biweekly pay period (every two weeks) $_____ per monthly pay period
$_____ **Lump Sum Payment:** Do not stop any existing IWO unless you receive a termination order.

REMITTANCE INFORMATION: If the employee/obligor's principal place of employment is _____ (State/Tribe), you must begin withholding no later than the first pay period that occurs _____ days after the date of_____ . Send payment within _____ working days of the pay date. If you cannot withhold the full amount of support for any or all orders for this employee/obligor, withhold up to _____% of disposable income for all orders. If the employee/obligor's principal place of employment is not_____ (State/Tribe), obtain withholding limitations, time requirements, and any allowable employer fees at http://www.acf.hhs.gov/programs/cse/newhire/employer/contacts/contact_map.htm for the employee/obligor's principal place of employment.

Document Tracking Identifier _____   1

Income Withholding for Support

FL-195

For electronic payment requirements and centralized payment collection and disbursement facility information (State Disbursement Unit [SDU]), see http://www.acf.hhs.gov/programs/cse/newhire/employer/contacts/contact_map.htm.

Include the *Remittance Identifier* with the payment and if necessary this FIPS code: _____

Remit payment to _____(SDU/Tribal Order Payee)
at _____(SDU/Tribal Payee Address)

☐ **Return to Sender [Completed by Employer/Income Withholder].** Payment must be directed to an SDU in accordance with 42 USC §666(b)(5) and (b)(6) or Tribal payee (see Payments to SDU below). If payment is not directed to an SDU/Tribal Payee or this IWO is not regular on its face, you *must* check this box and return the IWO to the sender.

Signature of Judge/Issuing Official (if required by State or Tribal law): _____
Print Name of Judge/Issuing Official: _____
Title of Judge/Issuing Official: _____
Date of Signature: _____

If the employee/obligor works in a State or for a Tribe that is different from the State or Tribe that must issued this order, a copy of this IWO must be provided to the employee/obligor.
☐ If checked, the employer/income withholder must provide a copy of this form to the employer/obligor.

ADDITIONAL INFORMATION FOR EMPLOYERS/INCOME WITHHOLDERS

State-specific contact and withholding information can be found on the Federal Employer Services website located at:
http://www.acf.hhs.gov/programs/cse/newhire/employer/contacts/contact_map.htm

Priority: Withholding for support has priority over any other legal process under State law against the same income (USC 42 §666(b)(7)). If a Federal tax levy is in effect, please notify the sender.

Combining Payments: When remitting payments to an SDU or Tribal CSE agency, you may combine withheld amounts from more than one employee/obligor's income in a single payment. You must, however, separately identify each employee/obligor's portion of the payment.

Payments to SDU: You must send child support payments payable by income withholding to the appropriate SDU or to a Tribal CSE agency. If this IWO instructs you to send a payment to an entity other than an SDU (e.g., payable to the custodial party, court, or attorney), you must check the box above and return this notice to the sender. Exception: If this IWO was sent by a Court, Attorney, or Private Individual/Entity and the initial order was entered before January 1, 1994 or the order was issued by a Tribal CSE agency, you must follow the "Remit payment to" instructions on this form.

Reporting the Pay Date: You must report the pay date when sending the payment. The pay date is the date on which the amount was withheld from the employee/obligor's wages. You must comply with the law of the State (or Tribal law if applicable) of the employee/obligor's principal place of employment regarding time periods within which you must implement the withholding and forward the support payments.

Multiple IWOs: If there is more than one IWO against this employee/obligor and you are unable to fully honor all IWOs due to Federal, State, or Tribal withholding limits, you must honor all IWOs to the greatest extent possible, giving priority to current support before payment of any past-due support. Follow the State or Tribal law/procedure of the employee/obligor's principal place of employment to determine the appropriate allocation method.

Lump Sum Payments: You may be required to notify a State or Tribal CSE agency of upcoming lump sum payments to this employee/obligor such as bonuses, commissions, or severance pay. Contact the sender to determine if you are required to report and/or withhold lump sum payments.

Liability: If you have any doubts about the validity of this IWO, contact the sender. If you fail to withhold income from the employee/obligor's income as the IWO directs, you are liable for both the accumulated amount you should have withheld and any penalties set by State or Tribal law/procedure. _____
_____
_____

Anti-discrimination: You are subject to a fine determined under State or Tribal law for discharging an employee/obligor from employment, refusing to employ, or taking disciplinary action against an employee/obligor because of this IWO.

OMB Expiration Date – 05/31/2014. The OMB Expiration Date has no bearing on the termination date of the IWO; it identifies the version of the form currently in use.

Income Withholding for Support

FL-195

Employer's name: _____ Employer FEIN: _____
Employee/Obligor's Name: _____
CSE Agency Case Identifier: _____ Order Identifier _____

Withholding Limits: You may not withhold more than the lesser of: 1) the amounts allowed by the Federal Consumer Credit Protection Act (CCPA) (15 U.S.C. 1673(b)); or 2) the amounts allowed by the State or Tribe of the employee/obligor's principal place of employment (see *REMITTANCE INFORMATION*). Disposable income is the net income left after making mandatory deductions such as: State, Federal, local taxes; Social Security taxes; statutory pension contributions; and Medicare taxes. The Federal limit is 50% of the disposable income if the obligor is supporting another family and 60% of the disposable income if the obligor is not supporting another family. However, those limits increase 5% - to 55% and 65% - if the arrears are greater than 12 weeks. If permitted by the State or Tribe, you may deduct a fee for administrative costs. The combined support amount and the fee may not exceed the limit indicated in this section.

For Tribal orders, you may not withhold more than the amounts allowed under the law of the issuing Tribe. For Tribal employers/income withholder who receive a State IWO, you may not withhold more than the lesser of the limit set by the law of the jurisdiction in which the employer/income withholder is located or the maximum amount permitted under section 303(d) of the CCPA (15 U.S.C. 1673 (b)).

Depending upon applicable State law or Tribal law, you may need to also consider the amounts paid for health care premiums in determining disposable income and applying appropriate withholding limits.

Arrears greater than 12 weeks? If the *Order Information* does not indicate that the arrears are greater than 12 weeks, then the Employer should calculate the CCPA limit using the lower percentage.

Additional Information: _____
_____
_____
_____

NOTIFICATION OF EMPLOYMENT TERMINATION OR INCOME STATUS: If this employee/obligor never worked for you or you are no longer withholding income for this employee/obligor, an employer must promptly notify the CSE agency and/or the sender by returning this form to the address listed in the Contact information below:

☐   This person has never worked for this employer nor received periodic income.

☐   This person no longer works for this employer nor receives periodic income.

Please provide the following information for the employee/obligor:

Termination date: _____ Last known phone number: _____
Last known address_____
_____

Final payment date to SDU/Tribal Payee: _____ Final payment amount:_____
New employer's name: _____
New employer's address: _____

CONTACT INFORMATION

To Employer/Income Withholder: If you have any questions, contact _____ (Issuer name)
by phone at _____, by fax at_____, by email or website at:_____ .

Send termination notice and other correspondence to: _____
_____ (Issuer address).

To Employer/Obligor: If the employee/obligor has questions, contact _____ (Issuer name)
by phone at _____, by fax at_____, by email or website at:_____.

IMPORTANT: The person completing this form is advised that the information may be shared with the employee/obligor.   3

| For your protection and privacy, please press the Clear This Form button after you have printed the form. | Save This Form | Print This Form | Clear This Form |

Child Support Case Registry Form

FL-191

ATTORNEY OR PARTY WITHOUT ATTORNEY *(Name, State Bar number, and address)*:	
	To keep other people from seeing what you entered on your form, please press the Clear This Form button at the end of the form when finished.

TELEPHONE NO.:   FAX NO. *(Optional)*:

E-MAIL ADDRESS *(Optional)*:

ATTORNEY FOR *(Name)*:

SUPERIOR COURT OF CALIFORNIA, COUNTY OF

STREET ADDRESS:

MAILING ADDRESS:

CITY AND ZIP CODE:

BRANCH NAME:

PETITIONER/PLAINTIFF:

RESPONDENT/DEFENDANT:

OTHER PARENT:

CHILD SUPPORT CASE REGISTRY FORM	CASE NUMBER:
☐ Mother ☐ First form completed	
☐ Father ☐ Change to previous information	

THIS FORM WILL NOT BE PLACED IN THE COURT FILE. IT WILL BE MAINTAINED IN A CONFIDENTIAL FILE WITH THE STATE OF CALIFORNIA.

Notice: Pages 1 and 2 of this form must be completed and delivered to the court along with the court order for support. Pages 3 and 4 are instructional only and do not need to be delivered to the court. If you did not file the court order, you must complete this form and deliver it to the court within 10 days of the date on which you received a copy of the support order. Any later change to the information on this form must be delivered to the court on another form within 10 days of the change. It is important that you keep the court informed in writing of any changes of your address and telephone number.

1. Support order information *(this information is on the court order you are filing or have received)*.

    a. Date order filed:

    b. ☐ Initial child support or family support order   ☐ Modification

    c. Total monthly base current child or family support amount ordered for children listed below, plus any monthly amount ordered payable on past-due support:

Child Support:	Family Support:	Spousal Support:
(1) ☐ Current base child support: $ ☐ Reserved order ☐ $0 (zero) order	☐ Current base family support: $ ☐ Reserved order ☐ $0 (zero) order	☐ Current spousal support: $ ☐ Reserved order ☐ $0 (zero) order
(2) ☐ Additional monthly support: $	☐ Additional monthly support: $	
(3) ☐ Total past-due support: $	☐ Total past-due support: $	☐ Total past-due support: $
(4) ☐ Payment on past-due support: $	☐ Payment on past-due support: $	☐ Payment on past-due support: $
(5) Wage withholding was ☐ ordered ☐ ordered but stayed until *(date)*:		

2. Person required to pay child or family support *(name)*:

    Relationship to child *(specify)*:

3. Person or agency to receive child or family support payments *(name)*:

    Relationship to child *(if applicable)*:

TYPE OR PRINT IN INK

Form Adopted for Mandatory Use
Judicial Council of California
FL-191 [Rev. July 1, 2005]

CHILD SUPPORT CASE REGISTRY FORM

Page 1 of 4
Family Code, § 4014
www.courtinfo.ca.gov

Child Support Case Registry Form

PETITIONER/PLAINTIFF:	CASE NUMBER:
RESPONDENT/DEFENDANT:	
OTHER PARENT:	

4. The child support order is for the following children:

	Child's name	Date of birth	Social security number
a.			
b.			
c.			

☐ Additional children are listed on a page attached to this document.

You are required to complete the following information about yourself. You are not required to provide information about the other person, but you are encouraged to provide as much as you can. This form is confidential and will not be filed in the court file. It will be maintained in a confidential file with the State of California.

5. Father's name:

   a. Date of birth:

   b. Social security number:

   c. Street address:

      City, state, zip code:

   d. Mailing address:

      City, state, zip code:

   e. Driver's license number:

      State:

   f. Telephone number:

   g. ☐ Employed ☐ Not employed ☐ Self-employed

      Employer's name:

      Street address:

      City, state, zip code:

      Telephone number:

6. Mother's name:

   a. Date of birth:

   b. Social security number:

   c. Street address:

      City, state, zip code:

   d. Mailing address:

      City, state, zip code:

   e. Driver's license number:

      State:

   f. Telephone number:

   g. ☐ Employed ☐ Not employed ☐ Self-employed

      Employer's name:

      Street address:

      City, state, zip code:

      Telephone number:

7. ☐ A restraining order, protective order, or nondisclosure order due to domestic violence is in effect.

   a. The order protects: ☐ Father ☐ Mother ☐ Children

   b. From: ☐ Father ☐ Mother

   c. The restraining order expires on (date):

I declare under penalty of perjury under the laws of the State of California that the foregoing is true and correct.

Date:

▶

_____
(TYPE OR PRINT NAME)

_____
(SIGNATURE OF PERSON COMPLETING THIS FORM)

Child Support Case Registry Form

INFORMATION SHEET FOR CHILD SUPPORT CASE REGISTRY FORM
(Do NOT deliver this Information Sheet to the court clerk.)

Please follow these instructions to complete the *Child Support Case Registry Form* (form FL-191) if you do not have an attorney to represent you. Your attorney, if you have one, should complete this form.

Both parents must complete a *Child Support Case Registry Form*. The information on this form will be included in a national database that, among other things, is used to locate absent parents. When you file a court order, you must deliver a completed form to the court clerk along with your court order. If you did not file a court order, you must deliver a completed form to the court clerk **WITHIN 10 DAYS** of the date you received a copy of your court order. If any of the information you provide on this form changes, you must complete a new form and deliver it to the court clerk within 10 days of the change. The address of the court clerk is the same as the one shown for the superior court on your order. This form is confidential and will not be filed in the court file. It will be maintained in a confidential file with the State of California.

INSTRUCTIONS FOR COMPLETING THE *CHILD SUPPORT CASE REGISTRY FORM* (TYPE OR PRINT IN INK):

If the top section of the form has already been filled out, skip down to number 1 below. If the top section of the form is blank, you must provide this information.

<u>Page 1, first box, top of form, left side</u>: Print your name, address, telephone number, fax number, and e-mail address, if any, in this box. Attorneys must include their State Bar identification numbers.

<u>Page 1, second box, top of form, left side</u>: Print the name of the county and the court's address in this box. Use the same address for the court that is on the court order you are filing or have received.

<u>Page 1, third box, top of form, left side</u>: Print the names of the petitioner/plaintiff, respondent/defendant, and other parent in this box. Use the same names listed on the court order you are filing or have received.

<u>Page 1, fourth box, top of form, left side</u>: Check the box indicating whether you are the mother or the father. If you are the attorney for the mother, check the box for mother. If you are the attorney for the father, check the box for father. Also, if this is the first time you have filled out this form, check the box by "First form completed." If you have filled out form FL-191 before, and you are changing any of the information, check the box by "Change to previous information."

<u>Page 1, first box, right side</u>: Leave this box blank for the court's use in stamping the date of receipt.

<u>Page 1, second box, right side</u>: Print the court case number in this box. This number is also shown on the court papers.

Instructions for numbered paragraphs:

1. a. Enter the date the court order was filed. This date is shown in the "COURT PERSONNEL: STAMP DATE RECEIVED HERE" box on page 1 at the top of the order on the right side. If the order has not been filed, leave this item blank for the court clerk to fill in.

   b. If the court order you filed or received is the first child or family support order for this case, check the box by "Initial child support or family support order." If this is a change to your order, check the box by "Modification."

   c. Information regarding the amount and type of support ordered and wage withholding is on the court order you are filing or have received.

   (1) If your order provides for any type of current support, check all boxes that describe that support. For example, if your order provides for both child and spousal support, check both of those boxes. If there is an amount, put it in the blank provided. If the order says the amount is reserved, check the "Reserved order" box. If the order says the amount is zero, check the "$0 (zero) order" box. Do not include child care, special needs, uninsured medical expenses, or travel for visitation here These amounts will go in (2). Do NOT complete the Child Support Case Registry form if you receive spousal support only.

   (2) If your order provides for a set monthly amount to be paid as additional support for such needs as child care, special needs, uninsured medical expenses or travel for visitation check the box in Item 2 and enter the monthly amount. For example, if your order provides for base child support and in addition the paying parent is required to pay $300 per month, check the box in item 2 underneath the "Child Support" column and enter $300. Do NOT check this box if your order provides only for a payment of a percentage, such as 50% of the childcare.

Child Support Case Registry Form

(3) If your order determined the amount of past due support, check the box in Item 3 that states the type of past due support and enter the amount. For example, if the court determined that there was $5000 in past due child support and $1000 in past due spousal support, you would check the box in item 3 in the "Child Support" column and enter $5000 and you would also check the box in item 3 in the "Spousal Support" column and enter $1000.

(4) If your order provides for a specific dollar amount to be paid towards any past due support, check the box in Item 4 that states the type of past due support and enter the amount. For example, the court ordered $350 per month to be paid on the past due child support, you would check the box in Item 4 in the "Child Support" column and enter $350.

(5) Check the "ordered" box if wage withholding was ordered with no conditions. Check the box "ordered but stayed until" if wage withholding was ordered but is not to be deducted until a later date. If the court delayed the effective date of the wage withholding, enter the specific date. Check only one box in this item.

2. a. Write the name of the person who is supposed to pay child or family support.
   b. Write the relationship of that person to the child.

3. a. Write the name of the person or agency supposed to receive child or family support payments.
   b. Write the relationship of that person to the child.

4. List the full name, date of birth, and social security number for each child included in the support order. If there are more than five children included in the support order, check the box below item 4e and list the remaining children with dates of birth and social security numbers on another sheet of paper. Attach the other sheet to this form.

The local child support agency is required, under section 466(a)(13) of the Social Security Act, to place in the records pertaining to child support the social security number of any individual who is subject to a divorce decree, support order, or paternity determination or acknowledgment. This information is mandatory and will be kept on file at the local child support agency.

Top of page 2, box on left side: Print the names of the petitioner/plaintiff, respondent/defendant, and other parent in this box. Use the same names listed on page 1.

Top of page 2, box on right side: Print your court case number in this box. Use the same case number as on page 1, second box, right side.

You are required to complete information about yourself. If you know information about the other person, you may also fill in what you know about him or her.

5. If you are the father in this case, list your full name in this space. See instructions for a–g under item 6 below.

6. If you are the mother in this case, list your full name in this space.

   a. List your date of birth.
   b. Write your social security number.
   c. List the street address, city, state, and zip code where you live.
   d. List the street address, city, state, and zip code where you want your mail sent, if different from the address where you live.
   e. Write your driver's license number and the state where it was issued.
   f. List the telephone number where you live.
   g. Indicate whether you are employed, not employed, self-employed, or by checking the appropriate box. If you are employed, write the name, street address, city, state, zip code, and telephone number where you work.

7. If there is a restraining order, protective order, or nondisclosure order, check this box.

   a. Check the box beside each person who is protected by the restraining order.
   b. Check the box beside the parent who is restrained.
   c. Write the date the restraining order expires. See the restraining order, protective order, or nondisclosure order for this date.

If you are in fear of domestic violence, you may want to ask the court for a restraining order, protective order, or nondisclosure order.

You must type or print your name, fill in the date, and sign the *Child Support Case Registry Form* under penalty of perjury. When you sign under penalty of perjury, you are stating that the information you have provided is true and correct.

For your protection and privacy, please press the Clear This Form button after you have printed the form.

Save This Form | Print This Form | | Clear This Form |

Ex Parte Application for Restoration of Former Name

FL-395

ATTORNEY OR PARTY WITHOUT ATTORNEY *(Name and Address)*:	TELEPHONE NO.:	To keep other people from seeing what you entered on your form, please press the Clear This Form button at the end of the form when finished.
ATTORNEY FOR *(Name)*:		

SUPERIOR COURT OF CALIFORNIA, COUNTY OF
STREET ADDRESS:
MAILING ADDRESS:
CITY AND ZIP CODE:
BRANCH NAME:

MARRIAGE OF
PETITIONER:

RESPONDENT:

EX PARTE APPLICATION FOR RESTORATION OF FORMER NAME AFTER ENTRY OF JUDGMENT AND ORDER	CASE NUMBER:

APPLICATION

1. A judgment of dissolution or nullity was entered on *(date)*:

2. Applicant now requests that his or her former name be restored. The applicant's former name is *(specify)*:

Date:

_____
(TYPE OR PRINT NAME)

▶ _____
(SIGNATURE OF APPLICANT)
(USE CURRENT NAME)

ORDER

3. IT IS ORDERED that applicant's former name is restored to *(specify)*:

Date:

_____
JUDICIAL OFFICER

[SEAL]

CLERK'S CERTIFICATE

I certify that the foregoing is a true and correct copy of the original on file in my office.

Date: _____   Clerk, by _____, Deputy

Page 1 of 1

Form Adopted for Mandatory Use Judicial Council of California FL-395 [Rev. January 1, 2003]	EX PARTE APPLICATION FOR RESTORATION OF FORMER NAME AFTER ENTRY OF JUDGMENT AND ORDER (Family Law)	Family Code, § 2080 www.courtinfo.ca.gov

For your protection and privacy, please press the Clear This Form button after you have printed the form.

Save This Form | Print This Form | | Clear This Form |

Notice of Withdrawal of Attorney of Record

FL-960

ATTORNEY OR PARTY WITHOUT ATTORNEY *(Name, state bar number, and address):*	
TELEPHONE NO.: FAX NO.:	To keep other people from seeing what you entered on your form, please press the Clear This Form button at the end of the form when finished.
ATTORNEY FOR *(Name):*	

SUPERIOR COURT OF CALIFORNIA, COUNTY OF
STREET ADDRESS:
MAILING ADDRESS:
CITY AND ZIP CODE:
BRANCH NAME:

PETITIONER/PLAINTIFF:

RESPONDENT/DEFENDANT:

NOTICE OF WITHDRAWAL OF ATTORNEY OF RECORD	CASE NUMBER:

1. In accordance with the provisions of section 285.1 of the Code of Civil Procedure, I withdraw as Attorney of Record for:
   ☐ Petitioner   ☐ Respondent

2. The final judgment of dissolution, legal separation, nullity, parentage, or postjudgment order was entered on *(specify date):*
   and no motions or other proceedings are pending at this time.

3. The last known address for the   ☐ Petitioner   ☐ Respondent   is:

4. The last known telephone number for the   ☐ Petitioner   ☐ Respondent   is:

5. I mailed a copy of this *Notice of Withdrawal* to   ☐ Petitioner   ☐ Respondent   at the address set forth in item 3.

I declare under penalty of perjury under the laws of the State of California that the foregoing is true and correct.

Date:

▶

_____   _____
(TYPE OR PRINT NAME)   (SIGNATURE)

WARNING
This form may not be used after a status-only judgment.

Page 1 of 2

Form Adopted for Mandatory Use
Judicial Council of California
FL-960 [Rev. January 1, 2003]

NOTICE OF WITHDRAWAL OF ATTORNEY OF RECORD

Code of Civil Procedure, § 285.1
www.courtinfo.ca.gov

Notice of Withdrawal of Attorney of Record

| PETITIONER/PLAINTIFF: | CASE NUMBER: |
| RESPONDENT/DEFENDANT: | |

PROOF OF SERVICE BY ☐ PERSONAL SERVICE ☐ MAIL

1. At the time of service I was at least 18 years of age and **not a party to this legal action.**

2. I served a copy of the *Notice of Withdrawal of Attorney of Record* as follows *(check either a. or b. below):*
   a. ☐ **Personal service.** I personally delivered the *Notice of Withdrawal of Attorney of Record* as follows:
      (1) Name of person served:
      (2) Address where served:

      (3) Date served:
      (4) Time served:

   b. ☐ **Mail.** I deposited the *Notice of Withdrawal of Attorney of Record* in the United States mail, in a sealed envelope with postage fully prepaid. The envelope was addressed and mailed as follows:
      (1) Name of person served:
      (2) Address:

      (3) Date of mailing:
      (4) Place of mailing *(city and state):*
      (5) I am a resident of or employed in the county where the *Notice* was mailed.

   c. My residence or business address is *(specify):*

   d. My phone number is *(specify):*

I declare under penalty of perjury under the laws of the State of California that the foregoing is true and correct.

Date:

▶

_____
(TYPE OR PRINT NAME)

_____
(SIGNATURE OF PERSON SERVING NOTICE)

For your protection and privacy, please press the Clear This Form button after you have printed the form.

Save This Form Print This Form Clear This Form

Chapter Ten

Post-Judgment Enforcement, Modifications, and Other Considerations

Post-Judgment Enforcement and Modification

The entry of **any** Judgment is closely followed by the enforcement of that Judgment. In family law, you have to consider enforcement while the client and his/her spouse negotiate a settlement. The effects of property settlements on child support and spousal support are considerations when drafting the agreement as they may lead to enforcement or modifications after the entry of the Judgment. For example, a spouse's *ability to pay* must carefully be considered in all aspects of a family law settlement. Otherwise, one or both of the parties will be caught in the position of not being able to meet obligations.

In the event a party does not *voluntarily* comply with the Court's orders, the California legislature has created a variety of statutory enforcement mechanisms. You will find as a family law paralegal that most parties will attempt to voluntarily comply with the Court's orders by turning over property, paying support and other obligations as set forth in the Judgment or in any other Orders made. However, there are always exceptions such as the taking of a Default of the Respondent. In that case, the Respondent is less likely to cooperate in any aspect at the conclusion of the case when he or she did not participate during the pendency of the matter. Asking that person to turn over property *voluntarily* or to sign documents or pay obligations will **not** be likely.

Alternatively, a party may have every intention of voluntarily complying with the obligations, agreements and any Orders made. As we all know, life and reality often get in the way of our everyday lives.

Imagine the sudden reality of a parent who has not received support and has two children to feed, a mortgage or rent payment due, car payment, utilities, gas and repairs and child care provider bills. To top it off, various creditors are calling asking for payment on obligations that were to be assumed by the former spouse as part of the settlement. How is the parent going to make ends meet if the other parent is not meeting obligations?

With this in mind Family Code § 290 states: "A judgment or order made or entered pursuant to this code may be enforced by the Court by execution, the appointment of a receiver, or contempt, or by such other order as the Court in its discretion determines from time to time to be necessary." The Court has broad discretion when dealing with enforcement methods in family law matters.

Family Code § 291 addresses property enforcement and renewal of judgments. FC§§ 4500 et. seq. addresses enforcement of support orders. Pursuant to CCP § 580 a property judgment must be renewed every ten (10) years in the event it hasn't been satisfied. However, support orders are subject to different enforcement and renewal requirements and will depend upon several different factors for the Court to consider. Thus, FC§§ 4500 et. seq. should be reviewed in its entirety when asking the Court for enforcement of support orders, particularly arrearages.

For example an award of a house in a dissolution judgment was subject to the 10-year rule. While an equalization payment was considered a money judgment and was not subject to the 10-year rule. Thus, there were different rules for essentially the same community property which could be detrimental to one party depending upon the manner in which the parties agreed to the division of said property. If the obligee did not renew the judgment, he or she could potentially lose the opportunity to claim property to which they were entitled. This amendment takes into consideration the unique situations common in family law.

This Chapter will discuss the various avenues and mechanisms for enforcing the orders made in the Marital Settlement Agreement or Stipulated Judgment. In most cases, unless otherwise stated, an application to the Court should take the form of a Notice of Motion (FL-301) with a supporting declaration. However, a Request for Order may also be used. In most cases, the declaration will be a declaration under penalty of perjury on the part of the "applicant" or moving party, along with any supporting documentation or evidence. In other cases, specific Judicial Council forms will need to be used as indicated below and in the various Family Code Sections governing the enforcement application. (See Chapter 4 re: Motions and Hearings and Documents.)

This Chapter will also discuss the various ways the parties may modify orders made, particularly those relating to child custody and visitation, as well as support issues. In order to reinforce the client's ability to modify or enforce an order as expeditiously and as easily as the law will allow always be wary when drafting agreements to insure that all "the i's are dotted" and "the t's crossed."

Enforcement

The enforcement of a Judgment or an Order may be as simple as serving an Income Withholding for Support (FL-195) on the obligor's employer. Alternatively, it may be as complex as having to prove to the Court that the obligor has substantial arrearages and/ or is in contempt of the court's order. In the event the obligor is unable to comply with the Court's orders it may also be necessary to place liens of the obligor's earnings, property, retirement and any other asset that person may own.

The California legislature has made it very clear that support must be paid. Family Code § 4500 et seq. provides that: "An order for child, family or spousal support that is made, entered, or enforceable in this state is enforceable under this Code, whether or not the order was made and entered pursuant to the Code." While there are many civil statutes that provide for enforcement of all types of money judgments, the Family Code is unique in that it has provides for a lesser time-consuming and less costly means of enforcing support orders.

There are numerous Judicial Council forms which can be used in addition to or in conjunction with a Motion or Request for Order to enforce the receipt of support and/ or collect arrearages. These include:

Earning Assignment Order for Spousal Support (FL-435); which is used for withholding **only** spousal support from the supporting spouse's wages.

Application to Determine Arrearages (FL-490); which is attached to a Motion or Request for Order and is used for detailing the amounts of child and/or spousal support paid and in default.

Declaration of Payment History (FL-420) and Payment History Attachment (FL-421); Judicial Council forms (similar to a spreadsheet) showing amounts due, amounts paid, amounts in default and total amount due. The declarant may also ask for interest on the amounts due.

An *Ex Parte Application to Issue, Modify or Terminate Earnings Assignment Order* (FL-430) is the form that may be used in family law cases where the obligor is substantially in arrears and/or if there are monies owed to the other spouse that is not specifically designated for support (child, family, and spousal). If you need to collect support arrears and/or other monies, such as an equalization payment, you will need to file a Motion with the Court requesting that the Court issue the Ex Parte Application for Earnings Assignment Order. You **must** document all monies paid, the balance due, interest, and any attempts to collect those monies in your motion. Once the Court grants the Order, you will want to submit the Earnings Assignment and Order for the Judge's signature. It will then be served on the obligor's employer by the Sheriff of the county where the obligor's employer is located.

When requesting these types of orders, you will also need to keep in mind, that the law may state that certain types of "liens" have priority over others. For example, support and taxes will always have priority over any other types of monies due. It is conceivable that the client may never see the money owed through an Earnings Order if it is for something other than support. Additionally, the obligor may have more than one child support obligation such as support due from a child of another relationship; therefore, the obligee may not receive the full amount of the money owed.

The *Income Withholding for Support* (FL-195) is specific to Family Law and is used to collect current support as well as any established arrears. Directions for completing this form are included on the form.

Family Code § 5208 provides exclusive enforcement of court-ordered support. As you have seen in the numerous forms that you have completed, the imposition of this enforcement mechanism is incorporated into **every** order that contains support orders, usually by the statement "[a]n earnings assignment order for support shall be issued" as found in FC§ 5230.

Family Code § 5230 states as follows:

(a) When the court orders a party to pay an amount for support or orders a modification of the amount of support to be paid, the court shall include in its order an earnings assignment order for support that orders the employer of the obligor to pay to the obligee that portion of the obligor's earnings due or to become due in the future as will be sufficient to pay an amount to cover both of the following:

(b)(1) The amount ordered by the court for support.

(2) An amount which shall be ordered by the court to be paid toward the liquidation of any arrearage.

(c) An earnings assignment order for support shall be issued, and shall be effective and enforceable pursuant to Section 5231, notwithstanding the absence of the name, address, or other identifying information regarding the obligor's employer.

The enactment of Family Code § 5230 makes the issuance of the earnings assignment **mandatory** and out of the control of either party or the Court. The Court may, for "good cause," or upon agreement of the parties stay the **service** of the Income Withholding for Support. As previously indicated, even though the parties may agree to a "stay" by not serving the Order at the present time, it should still be obtained in the event the party fails to make the support payments as obligated. The Order may then be served. FC§ 5260 specifically allows this to happen. In the event a stay is granted, the stay will be terminated by court order or upon the obligor's failure to make timely payments. The obligee simply prepares and files a declaration with the court stating that a payment was not timely made. Upon receipt of the filed declaration and signed Order by the Judge, the earnings assignment can be served on the obligor's employer.

In the past, there was a negative connotation against the employee when an employer received an Order to withhold any support from the employee's earnings it gave the *appearance* that the obligor parent was a "dead beat" and was not taking care of parental responsibilities. Additionally, the withholding order created additional paperwork for the employer who had to create a separate account to hold the funds until disbursement. The enactment of Family Code §§ 5230–5260 removed any discretion as to the **issuance** of the earnings assignment and took away the negative perception. Additionally, Family Code § 5290 states that "no employer shall use any assignment authorized by this chapter as grounds for refusing to hire a person or for discharging or taking disciplinary action against an employee. An employer who engages in the conduct prohibited by this section may be assessed a civil penalty of a maximum of Five Hundred Dollars ($500.00)." Thus the previous negative connotations with regard to wage withholding orders have been removed and wage withholding orders have become commonplace in most marital and paternity proceedings where support is ordered.

Upon the receipt of the filed Income Withholding for Support the employer is served with the document unless there is a stay of service in place. The obligor must be provided with a copy within ten (10) days of receipt by the employer. The employer must also provide the obligor/employee with a copy of a *Request for Hearing re: Earnings Assignment* (FL-450). This form provides the obligor with instructions as to how to modify or terminate a support order. The obligor cannot simply tell the employer that the support is not owed because the Order can only be changed by further order of the court. The employer must send the withheld support to the obligee within ten days of the date the obligor/employee is paid, unless otherwise specified in the Order.

A business or person if who knowingly assists a child support obligor in evading or avoiding unpaid child support obligations can be assessed civil penalties. Additionally, Civil Code § 1714.4 and § 1714.41 address the problem of unpaid child support arrears. The legislature addressed the time-consuming and costly collection of unpaid child support by holding not only the obligor responsible, but employers and others who help a person avoid having to pay support. The civil penalty can be up to three times the "value of the assistance provided." The amount can be the fair market value of the obligor's hidden assets, not to exceed the total amount of the child support owed by the obligor.

Knowingly assisting is defined in this code section and includes: failing to timely file the appropriate forms when a new employee is hired, or when the employer, individual, or entity knew or should have know of the child support obligation.

Additionally, Family Code §§ 5610–5616 regulate private child support collection. The law requires that court-approved agreements and court orders issued on or after January 1, 2010, include a separate money judgment for fees that may be incurred to collect child support. The law does not apply to attorneys who are addressing issues of ongoing child support or support arrearage during the course of a family law proceeding.

Of special note are support orders made prior to July 1, 1990. It is unlikely that you will have to comply with these special statutes as most of the children who were subject to these orders will have reached majority. However, if you should be involved in an Order that was entered prior to that date and which has not been modified since that date, any wage assignment(s) issued are subject to the application process that was in effect at the time. An application (request) must be made to the court by the obligee, in writing and signed under penalty of perjury, stating that the obligor is in default of support payments by at least one month. Upon receipt of the application, the court will issue the Order/Notice to Withhold or which should be submitted along with the application to expedite the process, without notice to the obligor.

Any time an order for support is made, an Income Withholding for Support should be filed with the Court. The service of the document will depend upon whether or not its service is stayed. Any time the amount of support is changed a **new** order should be prepared and filed with the court and then served on the employer, if applicable. This includes any reductions in support amounts as well as a termination of support, which would then require an Ex parte Application to Issue, Modify or Terminate and Earnings Assignment Order (FL-430). Since the employer must comply with any orders received, a letter or phone call, whether from the obligor or obligee, will not be sufficient to change an existing order. An employer will not want to risk the penalties involved by not complying with a Court Order. Upon termination of a support order, you will simply fill out the new Income Withholding for Support and submit it to the Court, along with the corresponding order indicating that the amount to be withheld is zero (–0–).

Also remember that a new Child Support Case Registry form (FL-191) must be submitted with any new or modified support order.

Family Code §§ 4550–4573, provide that every judgment and/or order made with respect to child support may require the obligor parent to deposit up to one (1) year's child support. This is known as a *Child Support Security Deposit*. The required amount must be deposited by the obligor parent into an interest-bearing account at a financial institution that: 1) does business in California; 2) has a trust department; and 3) is federally insured. The money in such an account may only be withdrawn by Court order and is used "exclusively to guarantee the monthly payment of child support."

To access these funds, the obligee parent must apply to the court, in writing and under penalty of perjury, that the obligor is at least ten (10) days late with the support payment. The Court may then authorize the bank to disburse the funds necessary to bring any child support obligation current. The Court may also order the obligor to replenish any ordered funds disbursed, as appropriate.

Promissory Notes, Deeds of Trust, and Liens on Property

A Promissory Note ("Note") with Deed of Trust securing a party's interest in the family home may need to be executed along with the MSA or Stipulated Judgment. This can occur when one party has agreed to pay the other a payment to equalize a settlement, often the interest in the family home. For instance, Wife keeps the family home but is unable to refinance the property and "cash out" Husband given her current financial situation. The parties may agree to a specific amount for an "equalizing payment" to be made at a future date, which may be a time specific or upon the sale or refinancing of the property. The original Note should be kept by Husband, and the Deed of Trust is recorded with the County Recorder. The Deed of Trust is a lien on Husband's behalf and will have to be satisfied along with the mortgage and any other liens that would be paid off as a result of a sale or refinance of the property. The parameters of this agreement and all the documents should **always** be referenced in the MSA or Stipulated Judgment in order to be able to use the appropriate family law enforcement procedures.

An additional consideration in drafting the MSA or Stipulated Judgment is whether a specific date should be required for the payoff of the Note and Deed of Trust. If a date specific is not incorporated in the MSA or Stipulated Judgment, it could be years before the party holding the Note will receive that equalizing payment from the settlement. A significant consideration is that the "out spouse" who holds the Note still has his/her name on the mortgage. If the firm is representing the "out spouse," it may not be in that party's best interest to have this type of arrangement.

> What if the "in spouse" fails to make the mortgage payments and the "out spouse" now wants to purchase another piece of property. The out spouse's credit may be negatively impacted making it difficult, if not impossible, to purchase other property. Again, such potential "down the road" problems must be considered when the parties are in settlement discussions or at trial as well as prior to putting the agreement in writing and making it a formal order of the Court.

Abstracts

An *Abstract of Support Judgment* (FL-480) is very much like an Abstract of Judgment. However, it is used specifically for support arrears. The Judicial Council has developed a specific declaration form which must accompany the obligee's request in order for the Court to issue the Abstract of Support Judgment.

Pursuant to Civil Code of Procedure §4502, a Judgment, and thus an Abstract, is effective for ten (10) years and must be renewed after that time the application for renewal must be made *before* the expiration date. Note that although Family Code §2126 and CCP §580 were amended to provide that family law Judgments do not have to be renewed after ten years, the Abstract will need to be renewed. Therefore, calendaring becomes important if your office has prepared the Abstract on behalf of the client. Support is excepted from this statute, which is why a specific Judicial Council form was created.

Family Code §4506 sets forth the information or the items needed for the Court to issue an Abstract. They are as follows:

(1) The title of the court where the judgment is entered and the cause and number of the proceeding.

(2) The date of entry of the judgment and of any renewal of the judgment.

(3) Where the judgment and any renewals are entered in the records of the court.

(4) The name and last known address of the party ordered to pay support.

(5) The name and address of the party to whom support payments are ordered to be paid.

(6) The last four digits of the social security number, birth date, and driver's license number of the party to whom support payments are to be paid. If any of those numbers are not known to the party to whom support payments are to be paid, that fact shall be indicated on the abstract of the court judgment.

(7) Whether a stay of enforcement has been ordered by the court and, if so, the date the stay ends.

(8) The date of issuance of the abstract.

(9) Any other information deemed reasonable and appropriate by the Judicial Council.

An *Abstract of Judgment* (EJ-001) may be issued by the Court to deal with property (real or personal) issues that have not been resolved by the parties. An Abstract is a document that is issued by the Court certifying that one party has an obligation to the other party.

There are a number of collection purposes when an Abstract of Judgment may be appropriate:

1) When a party owes money to the other for an equalizing payment;

2) When one party has agreed to pay a community debt and did not comply;

3) To enforce a Promissory Note or other Order for payment.

The examples above are some of the more common reasons why an Abstract of Judgment may be necessary.

In applying these examples, let's presume #2. Wife is ordered to pay a debt to a department store and does not. Husband pays the bill in order to protect his credit since his name is also on the account and it cannot be closed ... neither can his name be removed until the balance is paid in full. Based on the Judgment (Agreement) of the parties, Husband is entitled to reimbursement by Wife for having paid said bill. However, Wife has no available cash, but as part of the settlement, she kept the house. Husband may file an Abstract with the Court, along with a declaration, and supporting documentation (copies of receipts, invoices, checks) as to why he is requesting the Abstract. Upon receipt of the filed Abstract, Husband can record the Abstract with the County where the Wife resides (location of the property). At such time as Wife refinances the house or sells the house, the Abstract will be treated as a lien, and the "debt" to Husband will be paid as part of the escrow process.

In some instances, you may also find it necessary to file a certified copy of the **entire** Judgment for Dissolution with the County Clerk as an Abstract (or lien) against any obligor's property.

This is a very effective method of collecting monies owed, provided the obligor is not in a hurry to get the money. Obligors have had to pay any number of types of obligations when they come into money. Financial institutions and lenders look for Abstracts and other types of liens during a loan process. Even the California State Lottery will search for liens for taxes, child support arrears, and any other debtor obligations, prior to distributing any Lottery winnings. Abstracts and liens must be satisfied first.

Writs

A *Writ of Execution* can be used in family law to collect money or personal property. This form is often used to collect money in civil matters, but it may not be as effective in family law matters. There are two reasons for this: 1) other mechanisms specific to family law exist which the court prefers; and 2) a Writ is usually served on a financial institution. Unless you can, without a doubt, confirm that the obligor has substantial funds in an account, usually a Writ of Execution is a waste of time and money. A person, who is unable to pay support or other financial obligations relating to a divorce, is unlikely to have sufficient money to fulfill an obligation through a Writ. Writs and other obligations also carry with them a priority as to payment. Obligations for taxes and support will have first priority with all others following after. If a party has been ordered to pay attorney fees, and has not done so, the attorney may request that the Court issue a Writ. The Writ can be served on the obligor's employer or a financial institution where the obligor has an account. If the obligor has an ongoing child support order, that order is going to take priority and may not allow enough for the attorney to be paid. Add to that scenario a tax lien and support orders from children of other relationships, and the attorney is unlikely to receive any payments, at least not in the immediate future.

A *Writ of Possession* is used specifically for obtaining personal property in the possession of another person.

The court will need to be provided with the following documents in order to issue the Writ:

Application for Writ of Possession (CD-100)

Notice of Application for Writ of Possession (CD-110)

Order for Writ of Possession (CD-120)

Writ of Possession (CD-130)

A copy of the Judgment or Order entered by the Court to which the other party has not complied, needs to be attached to the Application. The Notice should be served as referenced on the Notice of Application. This process does not require a court appearance.

A Writ fee must be paid to the Court. All of the documentation will be submitted to the Court Clerk. It will then be verified, approved, and issued (not filed).

A Writ will be more effective if filed and then served by a Deputy Sheriff who is demanding that a party having possession of an automobile or other property turn over the property and sign the appropriate document(s) to make any necessary transfers.

Contempt

Contempt is specifically mentioned in Family Code §290 as a means of enforcing an Order. This method, however, is the least liked by most Judges, as it is **quasi-criminal** in nature, and can lead to the arrest and a jail sentence for the obligor. Therefore, contempt should be used as a **last resort**, especially since there are several other ways of enforcing an Order that are discussed in this Chapter.

Contempt is both civil and criminal in nature, thus the quasi-criminal designation. It is civil in nature in that it is used to compel a party to comply with the court's order. It is criminal in that there is a penalty meant to punish the party, known as the citee, for their knowledge, the ability to comply, and yet, their "willful disobedience" of the Order. Due to the potential criminal penalties for finding contempt, the Courts and, ultimately the legislature, have created some very specific requirements for any allegations of contempt.

The Court found in *Albrecht v. Superior Court (Laird)* (1982) 132 CA 3d 612, as follows:

[a]lthough, the order to show cause in re contempt arises out of the main civil action, the contempt proceeding itself is separate and distinct. It is a quasi-criminal proceeding, and may result in a fine or jail sentence, or both.

Thus, a contempt proceeding in the context of a domestic relations action is uniquely situated. It has attributes of a new, criminal matter, yet is also a principal means of enforcing the court's orders, as the court exercises its continuing jurisdiction over the parties and subject matter.

The facts to be proven by the moving party must contain four elements:

1) The existence of a lawful order;

2) The citee had knowledge of the order;

3) The citee had the ability to comply with the order; and

4) The willful disobedience of the order by the citee.

An Order to Show Cause and Affidavit for Contempt (FL-410) form must be completed and filed with the court and a hearing date requested. You should carefully review the *Information Sheet for Order to Show Cause and Affidavit of Facts Constituting Contempt* (pages three and four of the documents), which will provide you with the information needed to complete, file and serve the Contempt documents. (A sample declaration is included as Appendix 10A.)

Due to the quasi-criminal nature of the proceeding, the following rights are afforded the citee:

1) The citee must be personally served the Order to Show Cause for Contempt.

2) The citee may request that an attorney be present at the hearing.

3) The evidence must be proven beyond a reasonable doubt.

Once the moving party has submitted evidence of the four prima facie elements, listed above; the burden of proof shifts to the citee to defend his or her actions by proving that the order was either invalid or ambiguous, that the citee did not have the ability to pay or comply with the order, that the moving party's conduct was such that citee could not comply with the order, or that the statute of limitations has been exceeded.

The penalties for **each** contempt charge are: Five (5) days in jail, a fine of $1,000, or both. There can be one or more contempt charges, depending upon the number of instances that the citee violated each of the prima facie elements.

For example, an obligor who is ordered to pay child support and day care expenses in the amount of $1,000 per month on the first day of each and every month; and who has failed to make said support/day care payments for twelve months, may be charged with twelve counts if they are found in contempt. Each count could result in five days jail or 60 days in jail, and a fine of $12,000 ($1,000 for each count). The citee would still also owe the actual amount owed of $1,000 per month, plus interest, at the legal rate of ten percent (10%) per annum.

The statute of limitations on contempt cases, is set forth in Code of Civil Procedure § 1218.5, and is as follows:

"If the contempt alleged is the failure to pay child, family, or spousal support, the period of limitations for commencing a contempt action is three years from the date that the payment was due. If the action before the court is enforcement of another order under the Family Code, the period of limitations for commencing a contempt action is two years from the time that the alleged contempt occurred."

Based on the above, if the moving party brings a contempt action five years (60 months) for nonpayment of support, the moving party may only request a contempt order for the previous three years or 36 months. The Court may find that the citee is obligated to pay support for the entire five years, however, the contempt or quasi-criminal penalties will only be assessed for the 36-month period.

The Department of Child Support Services (DCSS) has replaced the County District Attorney's office as the "collection" agency for child support. The DCSS will collect child support, without question, when a party applies for some type of government assistance (Welfare, TANF, Social Security, etc.). Upon application for any of these subsidies, the DCSS will be notified, a case will be opened and the other parent or spouse will be held responsible for the support of their child. (See Chapter Three regarding obligations for support.)

The DCSS will collect through wages or other income such as tax refunds, lottery winnings or the Department may place a lien on real or personal property that is owned by the obligor. (See Family Code § 5206 for the definition of earnings.) Remember the definition of "earnings" is very broad and the DCSS has far-reaching powers to intercept income, when necessary.

If a client is having difficulty collecting support for him/herself and/or the children, and there is a current support Order with the Court, the obligee may contact the DCSS and request that a file be opened in order to collect the support. Private law firms often recommend this avenue if the obligee is on the verge of filing contempt, but may have trouble providing that the obligor has the ability to pay or that the non-payment is willful. While it may take several months for the DCSS to begin collecting any support, as previously stated, the support arrears, with interest, will continue to accrue.

The DCSS has many more options available to collect support than do attorneys in the private sector. Despite potential delays, DCSS may be the best approach for the client, as it is likely during this time period that the client is not going to see any support being paid anyway. It is certainly a difficult situation when a client is not receiving any support as ordered, and the money is needed for the necessities of life. It may be hard for the client to hold out for a long period of time. The obligee may certainly file a Request for Order with the Court if he/she cannot file for contempt and request enforcement. This will also take time, and if an attorney is retained, will cost money. Utilizing the services of DCSS is often the most cost-effective method, if not the only option left to the supported party.

All support orders made through the DCSS, whether through public assistance or private request, will incur interest if not paid in full when due. Thus support arrears can become quite large and take many years to pay if the obligor is not making timely payments. However, there is no statute of limitations as to what is owed for support unless it is established through a Contempt proceeding. In fact, there have been instances when children have reached majority and the obligor's income is attached or a lien paid many years later, providing a substantial payment of back support and interest to the obligee parent.

Support through public assistance will be paid by the DCSS to the obligee parent, whether or not the obligor is making the payment. DCSS will then collect the ongoing support, arrears, plus any interest as soon as the Department is able to garnish the obligor's wages or upon satisfaction of a lien. Support, which is established through Court Order and where the obligee requests that a case be opened with the DCSS, will not be paid by the Department. However, DCSS will do its best to collect the ordered support for the individual. In the event DCSS cannot collect, the arrears and interest (compounded) will continue to grow until such time as it is collected.

Family Code § 4583 provides that child support arrears may be collected "at any time within the period otherwise specified for the enforcement of such a judgment, notwithstanding the fact that the child has attained the age of 18 years."

Family Code § 4502 provides that orders for child, family or spousal support are enforceable "until paid in full."

Family Code § 291 provides that:

291. (a) A money judgment or judgment for possession or sale of property that is made or entered under this code, including a judgment for child, family, or spousal support, is enforceable until paid in full or otherwise satisfied.

(b) A judgment described in this section is exempt from any requirement that a judgment be renewed. Failure to renew a judgment described in this section has no effect on the enforceability of the judgment.

(c) A judgment described in this section may be renewed pursuant to Article 2 (commencing with Section 683.110) of Chapter 3 of Division 1 of Title 9 of Part 2 of the Code of Civil Procedure. An application for renewal of a judgment described in this section, whether or not payable in installments, may be filed:

(1) If the judgment has not previously been renewed as to past due amounts, at any time.

(2) If the judgment has previously been renewed, the amount of the judgment as previously renewed and any past due amount that became due and payable after the previous renewal may be renewed at any time after a period of at least five years has elapsed from the time the judgment was previously renewed.

(d) In an action to enforce a judgment for child, family, or spousal support, the defendant may raise, and the court may consider, the defense of laches only with respect to any portion of the judgment that is owed to the state.

(e) Nothing in this section supersedes the law governing enforcement of a judgment after the death of the judgment creditor or judgment debtor.

(f) On or before January 1, 2008, the Judicial Council shall develop self-help materials that include: (1) a description of the remedies available for enforcement of a judgment under this code, and (2) practical advice on how to avoid disputes relating to the enforcement of a support obligation. The self-help materials shall be made available to the public through the Judicial Council self-help Internet Web site.

(g) As used in this section, "judgment" includes an order.

This concept is known as laches. Laches are designed to limit the recovery of a person who waits too long in seeking to enforce their rights. The person asserting laches as a defense must prove that they are prejudiced in some way by the delay in enforcement. Thus, it is important that a party move to establish arrearages within a reasonable timeframe to thwart a defense of laches. It should be noted, however, that once arrears are established even if there is ongoing support, if the ongoing support is not paid, it will be considered arrears immediately after the date it is due. Therefore, once the obligee has notified the Court that the obligor is in default and the obligor has had an opportunity to be heard, it is not necessary for the obligee to repeatedly return to court to reestablish arrears.

In re Marriage of Fellows, (2006) 39 C4th 179. The Court held that Family Code § 4502(c) may be applied **retroactively** to child support arrearage. The defense of laches is barred under Family Code § 4.

Other Types of Liens, Judgments, and Enforcement

A Notice of Delinquency may be used to establish arrears and to create significant penalties for the obligor. Family Code § 4722 provides for civil penalties for child support delinquency as follows:

(a) Any person with a court order for child support, the payments on which are more than 30 days in arrears, may file and then serve a notice of delinquency, as described in this chapter.

(b) Except as provide in Section 4726, and subject to Section 4727, any amount of child support specified in a notice of delinquency that remains unpaid for more than 30 days after the notice of delinquency has been filed and served shall incur a penalty of 6 percent of the delinquent payment for each month that it remains unpaid, up to a maximum of 72 percent of the unpaid balance due.

Yes you read correctly, "72 percent," which is a significant amount of interest on a support order and a great incentive to pay any past due support.

A *Notice of Delinquency* (form FL-485) must be prepared stating the amount of support that is due, the payments made, the arrears, and the amount that will incur the penalty. (*Family Code § 4722*). The Notice must be served on the obligor who then has 30 days to either pay the delinquent amount or file a motion to determine the arrears and determine whether penalties should be applied.

Child support orders may also be collected by attaching an obligor's retirement or employee benefit plan by utilizing the *Attachment to Qualified Domestic Relations Order (Earnings Assignment Order for Support)* form (FL-461).

Additionally, the Judicial Council has established a form, *Application and Order for Heath Insurance Coverage* (FL-470) which may be served on an employer to determine available health care benefits. This form also notifies the employer that the employer is required, by Court Order, to maintain the child(ren) on the employee's health insurance, which may include dental and vision. If the employee is required to pay premium(s), or any portion, of said insurance premium, the payment will be withheld from the employee's pay. As indicated under the section on wage assignments for support, the employer will be notified directly, and the employee/obligor cannot change the order without setting the matter for a hearing before the Court. The employer is required to comply with this Order upon receipt.

Sister State Judgments and Uniform Interstate Family Support Act

Because people may divorce in another state and then relocate to California, The Uniform Interstate Family Support Act is significant in that people may divorce in another state and then relocate to California and need to modify support orders. Family Code § 4900 et seq. provides for the enforcement of support with respect to the Uniform Interstate Family Support Act (UIFSA). The UIFSA is applicable in all 50 states as well as in the District of Columbia, Puerto Rico, and the U.S. Virgin Islands. The introduction to the *Uniform Interstate Family Support Act* (UIFSA) located at Chapter 6 of the Family Code, (1996) contains a table providing the corollary statutes in each state as well as the dates they became effective.

Family Code § 4900 provides the mechanism for "registering" a support Order in California. The purpose of the UIFSA, as preceded by the Uniform Reciprocal Enforcement of Support Act (URESA), is to "improve and to make uniform the law with respect thereto" and thus allow each state to "reciprocate" in enforcing support orders.

In order to enforce a support order using the UIFSA, a Registration of Foreign Support Order must be filed with the California county where the obligee is now living. In most cases, the California Court having jurisdiction will require a certified copy of the Order from the other state. It is always a good idea to review Family Code § 4900 et seq. to determine the exact requirements prior to the filing of the Registration of Foreign Support. It will simplify matters greatly if you already have original certified copy(ies) of the Order(s) in the file, which will be submitted to the court. The name and address of the obligor, the obligee and the children will also need to be provided to the Court. The obligor will be notified of the pending action and will have an opportunity to contest the California court's jurisdiction. Upon receipt of an objection, the Court will set the matter for hearing. If the obligor does not object, the order is confirmed and is enforceable as though the original order had been issued in California.

It is not necessary to file support orders in another county in California unless there is an order for support through the Department of Child Support Services (DCSS), pursuant to Family Code Section 17400. In that circumstance, the "registration" will be filed by the DCSS, rather than the obligee. Family Code § 5600 et seq. provides the procedures for an "intercounty" registration of support orders.

Family Code §§ 3426 and 3457 also provide for the registration of out-of-state custody orders. The same process may be followed as is registering a support order. A Registration of Out-Of-State Custody Order (JCC form FL-580) and a Request for Hearing Regarding Registration of Out-Of-State Custody Decree (JCC form FL585) must be completed with the required documents, filed with the court and a hearing requested.

See Appendix 10B for the forms and information required.

Modifications

Child Custody & Visitation

Modification of child custody and visitation orders can occur for as many reasons as there are families. A change can occur because the custodial parent wishes to move away with the children or an older child may request that they be allowed to live primarily with one parent. These are very simple reasons, but the modification and enforcement of custody and visitation orders are usually anything but simple. More complex issues could include a child refusing to go to a parent's house for visitation; the parties not being able to agree on a day care provider, doctor, counselor or other professional to whom the child has been referred; one or both of the parties being referred to counseling, for drug/alcohol testing or other professional assistance in order to have custody or visitation and has refused to go; the parties disagreeing on school, religious upbringing, extra-curricular activities; the child doesn't get along with the stepparent; or, other related issues. The list goes on and on.

If the parties cannot agree to a modification of custody and visitation, they must attend some form of mediation to determine what is in the best interests of the child(ren). Additionally, the Court may refuse to hear a matter within six (6) months of orders made, unless there is a *significant* change in circumstances.

Unless a client is requesting ex parte orders due to domestic violence, the California Courts require that the parties attend mediation prior to "litigating" any changes in custody and visitation, regardless of whether they have previously attended meditation. If a client wishes to seek a modification of a custody and/or visitation, the appropriate forms should be submitted to the Court requesting a referral to Family Court Services or alternatively submitting a Petition and Order for Private Mediation. (See Chapter Four for additional information on this process, as it is the same and also consult your Local Rules.)

The parties can agree in writing in the manner provided in the MSA/Judgment to any changes, usually by Stipulation & Order. The Stipulation would simply be filed with the Court, signed by the Judge, and then filed with the Court. Once filed, it becomes an enforceable Order. Note changes in custody and visitation may impact child support. That issue should be addressed, whenever possible, while negotiating any changes in custody and/or time share.

Case law has established some guidelines with respect to what defines "in the best interest of the child" in cases where a custodial parent wishes to move away from the area. While it is assumed that a custodial parent has the right to change the residence of the child, the right to relocate, if it is determined **not** to be in the best interests of the child may be questioned by the court.

A family law practitioner may be called upon to request visitation for a grandparent of a child subject to family law proceedings. Family Code § 3104(b), as amended in 2007, sets forth the guidelines for *third party* rights. The standard required for all grandparent visitation petitions is whether the grandparent and grandchild have a "preexisting relationship" and that the order granting visitation is in the best interest of the child to continue on-going contact. The statute reads as follows:

§ 3014(b) A petition for visitation under this section may not be filed while the natural or adoptive parents are married, unless one or more the following circumstances exist:

(1) The parents are currently living separately and apart on a permanent or indefinite basis;

(2) One of the parents has been absent for more than one month without the other spouse knowing the whereabouts of the absent spouse;

(3) One of the parents joins in the petition with the grandparents;

(4) The child is not residing with either parent;

(5) The child has been adopted by a stepparent.

Petitions for visitation by a grandparent of an adopted child is discussed in Chapter Eleven.

Relocation

Family Code § 3024 addresses the notice requirements that must be given to a non-custodial parent if the custodial parent wishes to relocate with the child(ren). It states:

> In making an order for custody, if the court does not consider it inappropriate, the court may specify that a parent shall notify the other parent if the other parent plans to change the residence of the child for more than 30 days, unless there is a prior written agreement to the removal. The notice shall be given before the contemplated move, by mail, return receipt requested, postage pre-paid, to the last known address of the parent to be notified. A copy of the notice shall also be sent to that parent's counsel of record. To the extent feasible, the notice shall be provided within a minimum of 45 days before the proposed change of residence so as to allow for time for mediation of a new agreement concerning custody.

Based on the above statute, **all** Judgments should contain some form of the "notice requirement" as set forth above in order to make the obligation to give notice clear to any party considering moving with the children.

There have been a number of cases that have significantly impacted the ability of a parent to relocate with the children. These cases are typically referred to as "move-away" cases. The Courts, and particularly the California Appellate Court, have always tried to base their decision on what is in the best interests of the child(ren). However, they have vacillated on what constitutes the basis for what is in the best interests of the child, as opposed to the need for frequent and continuing contact.

The first case to actually establish criteria for "move-away" cases was *In re Marriage of McGinnis* (1992) 7 CA4th 473. *McGinnis* established that a change to custody [and visitation] can only be made for "**imperative**" reasons and that a change in custody is "the exception, not the rule." The *McGinnis* ruling also established a three-prong test to utilize when a parent is requesting a change in custody, as follows:

1) adequate notice must be given

2) "meaningful" mediation must be completed

3) the parents have been given an opportunity for an outside evaluation

Additionally, the *McGinnis* Court, placed the burden of proof on the party requesting the relocation by stating the following in their decision:

> The State of California has a strong public policy in protecting ... stable custody arrangements ... It is well established that the courts are reluctant to order a

change of custody and will not do so except for imperative reasons; that it is desirable that there be an end of litigation and undesirable to change the child's established mode of living ... We hold that these same rules apply to a "move away" when a shared parenting arrangement is working ... In such situations, the burden of proof is upon the "move away" parent to demonstrate that the move is in the best interests of the children, i.e. that it is "essential and expedient" and for an "imperative reason."

In 1996, the California Supreme Court issued a definitive statement as to the move-away issue which took into account the three-prong test established in *McGinnis*. If you practice in the area of family law, it is highly recommended that you read *In re Marriage of Burgess* (1996) 13 CA4th 25, 51 CR2d 444, in its entirety.

In summary, The *Burgess* Court stated the following:

1) Family Code § 7501 must be considered. This code section specifically states that there is a "presumptive right" of the custodial parent to change the residence of the minor children, as long as the change will not be prejudicial to **their** rights or welfare. (Note ... this refers to the "children's rights and welfare" and **not** the parents.)

2) The burden of proof created by previous case law (*McGinnis* and others), wherein the relocating party had to prove that the move was "necessary," "expedient," "essential," or imperative where not necessary.

3) The previously applied policy of "frequent and continuous contact" is not meant to be so constraining that the presumptive right of the relocating party is inhibited. Although the relocation may result in less frequent contact with the non-custodial parent, it will be necessary to create a new schedule that will result in the same time-share with the children.

4) A change in circumstances and a review of what is the best interests of the child based on relocation is more important than the current or previously ordered custodial arrangement.

5) If the move is simply meant to frustrate the visitation of the non-custodial parent, then the custodial parent's actions may be reason enough for the court to modify a custody arrangement.

6) All move-away cases need to be evaluated individually and solely on what is in the best interests of the child(ren) of the specific case.

There are three recent cases which have reinforced the *Burgess* Court's ruling: *In re Marriage of Campos* (2003) 108 CA4th 839, *In re Marriage of Abrams* (2003) 105 CA4th 979, and *In re Marriage of LaMusga* (2004) 32 Cal. 4th 1072. The Court held that the non-custodial parent is entitled to an evidentiary hearing on whether relocation is detrimental or in the best interests of the child. They also stated that the non-custodial parent has the burden of establishing that the relocation is detrimental.

In re Marriage of Abargil (2003) 106 CA4th 1294, dealt with relocation to a foreign country. The Court held that the party wishing to relocate must show that the parenting rights of the non-custodial parent can be preserved in light of "cultural, transportation, and financial" issues. The *Abargil* Court also imposed additional conditions which must be met in a "international" relocation, as follows: 1) the custodial parent was ordered to post a financial bound to assure compliance with the orders; 2) only California has jurisdiction to modify the orders; and 3) the California order must be registered with the foreign authorities before leaving the state.

In re Marriage of LaMusga (2004) 32 Cal. 4th 1072. The Court stated with respect to the application of *Burgess* "we conclude that just as a custodial parent does not have to establish that a planned move is 'necessary,' neither does the noncustodial parent have to establish that a change of custody is 'essential' to prevent detriment to the children from the planned move. Rather, the noncustodial parent bears the initial burden of showing that the proposed relocation of the children's residence would cause detriment to the children, requiring a reevaluation of the children's custody. The likely impact of the proposed move on the noncustodial parent's relationship with the children is a relevant factor in determining whether the move would cause detriment to the children and, when considered in light of all of the relevant factors, may be sufficient to justify a change in custody. If the noncustodial parent makes such an initial showing of detriment, the court must perform the delicate and difficult task of determining whether a change in custody is in the best interests of the children."

Osgood v. Landon (2005) 127 CA4th 425, the Court upheld the *LaMusga* finding that requires a non-custodial parent to prove that the relocation would be detrimental to the child. The trial court's Order per missing a custodial mother to move from California to Tennessee was proper as the non-custodial father did not show that the move would cause detriment to the child.

Custody and Visitation Modifications

The process for requesting a change in custody and/or visitation or for relocation is the Request for Order procedure. Keep in mind that it is best to have completed the mediation process prior to filing the Request for Order. (See Chapter Four for this procedure.) If the client is moving away, you will also need to be aware of the notice requirements outlined in *McGinnis/Burgess*, and make sure they are met prior to filing the Request for Order. The party moving away will have the burden of proof which should be established as early on as possible. The mediator and/or evaluator's opinion(s) will carry great weight with the court.

In the event the parties have not been able to reach an agreement through the mediation process, and/or one or both of the parties do not like the Judge's ruling at the Request for Order, the matter may be set for trial. In this event, you will want to follow the basic trial procedures with regard to notice, documents, witnesses, etc.

Note that in 2006 the court ruled, in two cases, with respect to termination of a parent's rights. The law firm may encounter individuals who wish to terminate a parent's rights due to lack of contact or payment of support. The court ruled that it is against public policy to terminate one parent's rights unless there is a "contemplated stepparent or second parent adoption." *Marriage of Jackson* (2006) 136 CA4th 980, 39 CR3d 365; *Kristine M. v. David P.* (2006) 135 CA4th 783, 37 CR3d 748.

A recent case, and situation of note, is the effect a parent's deployment may have on changes to a custody/visitation order. Specifically, the legislature amended FC § 3047, effective 1/1/13, to clarify the effect of a party's deployment and the actions that must be taken in the event of deployment or return from deployment. In this situation, you will want to review the statute to determine what steps must be taken in order to modify the current orders.

Child Support Modification and Enforcement

Child Support may also require modification or enforcement for many reasons: a party is not paying the support as previously ordered, a party's financial situation has changed, a child has moved in with the other parent, the time share has changed, or the child has reached majority.

Family Code §§ 3047, 3651, 3653, 17440, and 17560 include criteria and requirements for parents ordered to pay child support who were on active duty in the U.S. Military. These sections provide that a parent who is on active duty (including the National Guard) and who are deployed out of state are afforded special accommodation regarding modification of child support orders. A specific set of guidelines has been established. These code sections should be reviewed prior to filing a modification for child support in these situations.

If they can agree to the change in support, the parties may file a Stipulation & Order with the Court. The Stipulation may be a Judicial Council form *Stipulation to Establish or Modify Child Support Order* (FL-350). (This form was previously reviewed under the Order to Show Cause in Chapter Four.) Alternatively, a pleading Stipulation & Order may be prepared, signed and filed. This avenue may be more appropriate when the parties are modifying any additional issue(s) or portion(s) of the Judgment in addition to modifying Child Support.

As with modifications for custody and visitation, the Court does not want to have the parties filing motions or appearing more frequently than every six (6) months unless there is a *significant* change in circumstances. A good way to determine if there is a change in circumstances, particularly for the obligor, is to serve a *Request for Production of an Income & Expense Declaration After Judgment* (FL-396), before filing for a modifcation.

The Judicial Council form is served with an Income & Expense Declaration. This form requests that the party, on whom the document is served, provide copies of pay stubs and/or tax returns, as well as complete the I&E within **sixty (60) days of service**. A noncompliance may result in being found in contempt by the court. Once received from the obligor, the attorney can utilize the child support software to determine if there would be a change in the amount of ordered support.

When a parent remarries, the other parent may assume that means child support should automatically increase and therefore be modified because there is now another parent to help support the child. As you previously have noted from the variations of information during the support discussion of the class, that is not necessarily the case. Keep in mind that a "new spouse" is not responsible for the support of children who are not his/her own, and that two incomes may place a married couple into a different tax bracket. Remarriage may actually reduce support. This new "family" may also give birth to a new child, in which case, the obligor parent is also now responsible for the support and care of this new child, further reducing the child support payments to the children of another marriage or relationship. The supported party may actually be "opening a can of worms" by bringing up this issue. The attorney will want to use the support calculation software and weigh the pros and cons with the client.

> If the amount would increase, the supported party has to decide at what amount the support level would increase enough to spend the money to return to court. If the increase is $20 per month, is it worth spending approximately

$2,000 (this amount will vary depending upon the hourly rate in your area of the state and by law firm) to retain an attorney, file the Request for Order, go to court, and enforce a new order. Not to mention that this kind of behavior does nothing to endear the supported party to someone with whom they already may not have the best relationship.

The proper procedure for modification or termination of a child support order is by filing a Request for Order with the court and then requesting a hearing.

While child support and visitation are closely tied due to the time share calculation, ordinarily a parent cannot be "punished" for nonpayment of child support by the withholding of visitation. A custodial parent may try to use this tactic, but it is frowned upon by the Courts. There is one case, however, where the Court made an exception to this practice. The extenuating circumstance in that case was the risk that Father would take the children to his native Greece and not return with them. This is **not**, however, considered to be a controlling case.

Another situation may be when a parent loses his or her job or attempts to hide or reduce earnings in order to reduce child support. As discussed in Chapter Three, the court may input income for a parent who *knowingly* attempts to reduce their income. The court ruled in *Marriage of Sorge* (2012) 202 CA4th 626, 134 CR3d 751 that the court may input the income of a supporting parent on the basis of business assets and does not need to consider business losses if deemed to be use as a means of reducing his fiduciary responsibility to his children.

In re Marriage of Economou (1990) 224 Cal. App. 3d 466. The Court gave sole legal and physical custody to Mother after Father failed to pay support, failed to surrender his passports during periods of visitation, and failed to divide the community assets with Wife. The Court restricted his visitation as a result stating that: he is "deceitful, untrustworthy and likely to detain the children ... cannot be trusted; his word is worthless. He is more than a cad and a bounder, he is a con and a thief ..."

Judicial Council form (FL-460) *Qualified Domestic Relations Order for Support* (*Earnings Assignment Order for Support*) may also be used to enforce a child support order on a person's retirement in the event the person has retired or is delinquent, and the supported party has no other means to *attach* the supporting party's earnings.

Always remember when reviewing a current support order to determine whether or not the Department of Child Support Services (formerly District Attorney) is involved in the collection of support. If DCSS is, any subsequent modifications will need to be noticed to the Department.

Spousal Support Modifications/Terminations

Spousal support can be enforced or terminated for several different. Most common may be the need to enforce an order whereby the supported party must become self-supporting. As discussed in Chapter Six, usually there will be an Order for the supported party to become self-supporting at a future date. Usually, the supported party will be given a time frame in which to meet that requirement or to show the court why the party has been unable to do so. (Richmond, Rome, and Gavron cases.)

Thus, if a supported party has been unable to complete education or find suitable employment, the party may file a motion requesting that the Court extend spousal support. Conversely, if the supporting party has been paying support and it is determined that the supported party has not finished his/her education or training and has willfully failed to comply with the Court's orders to become self-supporting, then depending upon the language of the Judgment, the supporting spouse may request that the support be terminated.

If such language was included in the Judgment, cohabitation with a person of the opposite sex may be grounds for requesting that spousal support be terminated. Also, if cohabitation was not specifically stated in the Judgment, the supporting party may move to terminate based on an "inference" that support should terminate if the supported ex-spouse is being supported by another individual.

Recently the Court ruled on a similar question. In *In re Marriage of Left* (2012) 208 CA4th 1137, 146 CR3d 181, the court stated that because Family Code § 4337 requires a legal marriage to terminate support, a supported spouse who has merely gone through a "marriage-like ceremony" cannot have their support terminated.

Marriage of Shaughnessy (2006) 139 CA4th 1225. The Court of Appeals held that the trial court may consider monetary gifts given to a supported spouse from a third party when setting spousal support. Additionally, they upheld the precedent that requires that a supported spouse make good faith efforts to become self-support. The failure to do may "constitute a change in circumstances" warranting a modification of spousal support.

The same process is used to enforce, modify or terminate spousal support that is used in other matters. A Request for Order and supporting documents are filed and served on the other party, these include:

Request for Order (FL-300) or Notice of Motion (FL-301), with applicable attachments

Written declarations, previous orders, exhibits and documentation

Duke Orders

It may be necessary to enforce orders with respect to the "Delayed Sale of Family Home." If the "in spouse" has not made arrangements to either purchase the family home on his/her own or to cooperate with the "out spouse" in listing the property for sale once the youngest child has reached majority (or whatever order is made in the Judgment), it may be necessary to enforce those orders so that the "out spouse" can receive any community property interest he/she may have in the property.

A Request for Order is filed and served reiterating the orders made in the Judgment and describing how and/or why the "in spouse" has not complied with those orders. The moving party requests the type of relief that the party would like the Court to order. The moving party will, in most cases, ask for attorney fees to enforce said Order.

Other Considerations

Bankruptcy

There are three types of Bankruptcies (Chapters) that may be filed by individuals. For the most part, your office will encounter possible *Chapter Seven* bankruptcy filings as they relate to Family Law. Occasionally, you may have to consider a business (Chapter 11) filing if one of the parties owns or is a partner in a business entity.

For the purposes of family law, you will need to have some basic information that may impact the division of property and the enforcement of any Judgment entered as these items apply to any community debt. A *Chapter Seven* allows the discharge of some types of consumer debts. Child and spousal support (alimony), back taxes, and student loans are **not** dischargeable in any type of personal bankruptcy.

11 U.S.C. § 523(a)(15) was amended and is effective October 15, 2005. The statutes, as amended, eliminate the need for a non-debtor spouse to file a complaint to determine dischargeability of the debt. Thus, a property settlement agreement which provides for **domestic obligations** will become **non-dischargeable** by operation of law. The priority accorded to domestic obligations (support) is a first priority unsecured claim, over everything other than administrative expenses, as set forth in Section 507(a)(1).

A debtor must be current with all support obligations before a Chapter 13 can be confirmed. If the debtor falls behind, post-petition, the Chapter 13 petition may be dismissed. (Bankruptcy § 1307(c)(11)).

A new section, Section 101(14A) was added to define **domestic obligations** as "any debt payable or recoverable to or by a spouse, former spouse, guardian or governmental unit, owed or recoverable for alimony, support or maintenance, whether or not expressly designated, and payable or recoverable to or by a spouse, former spouse, guardian or governmental unit."

County of Sacramento v. Foross (*In re Marriage of Foross*) (1999) 9th Cir BAP, 242 BR 692 states that "interest accruing on nondischargeable child and spousal support obligations after filing bankruptcy is also nondischargeable." This case occurred prior to the 2005 changes, but the holding is consistent with the new laws.

Prior to these amendments, any bankruptcy which was filed by either party would "*stay*" the dissolution proceedings. However, the automatic stay has been expanded to expressly state that custody, domestic violence, determinations of domestic support obligations, and dissolution of marriage proceedings (except as they may affect property of the bankruptcy estate) are not subject to automatic stay. If the dissolution proceeding involves a property settlement, then the stay will be imposed. Additionally, previous bankruptcy laws allowed one spouse to file bankruptcy on community debts that they were to have paid as part of the dissolution. Thus, "sticking" their spouse with the debt and potential collections issues. The new law does not allow a spouse to discharge the debt, making the other party responsible.

In re Marriage of Lynn (2002) 101 Cal. App. 4th 120, Cal. Rptr. 2d 611 addressed the issue of a modification of support when one party discharged community debt or, in this case, an equalization payment in a bankruptcy. The Court found that if the party filing bankruptcy discharged the community debt, the party now had more disposable income upon which to base an increase in support. The Court has long held that if there is a "material change" in the parties' economic circumstances resulting from a discharge in bankruptcy, the Court has the authority to consider that a modification of support. (See Family Code § 4812 and *In re Marriage of Clements* (1982) 134 CA3d 737, 184 CR 756.)

In the event either party to the dissolution or legal separation being handled by your office decides to file bankruptcy, you will want to make sure read the current law and determine if there has been any case law subsequent to the October 15, 2005, changes, and/or the attorney schould contact the bankruptcy attorney retained.

While the Marital Settlement Agreement is a contract between the parties resolving all of their marital issues, and, thus, is binding on them, it is not binding on a creditor. Therefore, if one party agrees to pay off certain debts as part of the marital settlement and that party files bankruptcy or simply stops making payments on those debts, the creditor is going to go after the other party because the other party's name is also on the debt. As previously stated, even though there is a "contract" between the parties, an account cannot be closed … neither can a name be removed from an account until the balance is paid in full.

In fact, the court found *In re Marriage of Williams* (1984) 157 Cal App 3d 1215, 203 CR 909, that one spouse may file bankruptcy and discharge the debt the spouse acquired as part of the marital settlement. The Court stated as follows:

> "Despite the obvious inequities of permitting one spouse who has assumed a share of the community property debts incident to a dissolution to subsequently discharge those debts and leave the non bankrupt spouse liable, in apparent derogation of the otherwise equal division of community property, the practice is well recognized and not one easily circumvented by the trial courts."

Keep in mind that if a party is ordered to pay attorney fees as part of the Judgment, those fees could also be included in any bankruptcy filing. Therefore, the client and the attorney may suffer the adverse effects of a spouse who files a bankruptcy subsequent to the Judgment being entered.

Mejia v. Reed (2003) 31 C4th 657, 3 CR3d 390. The Court held that transfers between spouses in a dissolution or legal separation settlement (MSA) are subject to the Uniform Fraudulent Transfer Act (UFTA) as set forth in Civil Code § 3439–3439.12. In particular, the division of property (including debts) does not allow for an opportunity to defraud creditors. A creditor may attack the Judgment (MSA) and move to have the transfer of the property set aside. Although in *Mejia* the creditor owed child support arrears, which the court determined were **not** subject to the UFTA, the Court was concerned that a party to a dissolution could be held responsible for paying a debt which was transferred to the party's spouse, when the spouse knowingly does not intend to pay the debt.

Thus, you can see the bankruptcy issue and/or the non-payment of marital debts may cause a significant impact on the other party. As previously discussed in Chapter Nine, an attorney must carefully advise his or her client as to the potential ramifications of either party taking a debt or debts which the party will be unable to pay.

Additionally, Federal and State Courts have ruled over the years that payments for support are **not** dischargeable and payments for property settlement are dischargeable. Thus if there is any ambiguity in the Judgment, the Court will usually find that a payment to be made to a spouse is dischargeable. The California Appellate Court found in *Smalley v. Smalley* (1959) 176 Cal.App 2d 374 as follows:

It is true ... that an alimony judgment or a judgment which can properly be construed as being for alimony is not affected by a discharge in bankruptcy. However ... where the parties have entered into a property settlement agreement whereby payments are thereafter to be made to the wife, not for support but in settlement of property rights, the discharge in bankruptcy of the husband discharges the debt.

Likewise, the Federal Court found in *Shaver v. Shaver* (1984, Ninth Circuit) 736 F2d 1314, the following:

Because of the federal interests reflected in the Bankruptcy Act, the courts look to federal law to determine whether an obligation is "actually in the nature of ... support" and is therefore nondischargeable ... "[R]egardless of how a state may choose to define 'alimony' a federal court, for purposes of applying the federal bankruptcy laws, is not bound to a label that a state affixes to an award, and that consistent with the objectives of federal bankruptcy policy, the substance of the award must govern." In determining whether an obligation is intended for support of a former spouse, the court must look beyond the language of the decree to the intent of the parties and to the substance of the obligation ... The courts that have considered this issue have used several factors to aid in the characterization of the debt. If an agreement fails to provide explicitly for spousal support, a court may presume that a so-called "property settlement" is intended for support when the circumstances of the case indicate that the recipient spouse needs support ... Factors indicating that support is necessary include the presence of minor children and an imbalance in the relative income of the parties ... Similarly, if an obligation terminates on the death or remarriage of the recipient spouse, a court may be included to classify the agreement as one of support. The court will look also to [the] nature and duration of the obligation to determine whether it is intended as support.

The parties may still, however, wish to file bankruptcy jointly prior to filing for divorce or legal separation, which may dispose of the debts (subject to the filing chapter's rules). In fact, this may be the best avenue for parties who have a high debt ratio and who will ultimately file for divorce. This avenue may simplify or complicate the division of community property and debts during the dissolution proceeding. The attorney should be made aware of a client's debt ratio early on in the proceeding so that a discussion of these options can be held with the client.

Taxes

As previously discussed, spousal support is deductible by the party paying support and considered income to the party receiving it. The IRS requires that the following criteria be met for payments to be considered "alimony":

1. The payment must be made in cash or its equivalent;

2. The payment must be received by or on behalf of the payee spouse pursuant to a divorce or separation instrument;

3. Neither spouse may opt out of alimony treatment for purposes of federal income taxes;

4. Spouses cannot be members of the same household at the time payment is made;

5. The obligation to make spousal support payments must terminate upon the recipient's death;

6. The payor and the recipient cannot file joint income tax returns; and

7. If any portion of the payment is considered to be child support, even if it is not actually designated as child support, that portion cannot be treated as alimony.

In order to protect the client, the IRS must be informed of how much of the payment is child support if the Order is for family support or some other category.

With respect to Child Support, the party who has the largest time share is the party entitled to the exemption for the child(ren) on their taxes unless otherwise agreed, in writing, by the parties. Thus, if each party is going to claim a tax deduction for one child on their taxes, they **must** state that in the Agreement and it will be honored by the State of California with regard to State taxes. The IRS has new rules (effective 2005) that establish who may claim the child, in some cases, if the time share is 50/50, the IRS gives the deduction to the higher earner. There are several new rules and you will want to work closely with the attorney and/or CPA in determining who is entitled to the exemption, the filing status of the client and other tax issues, in you are involved in this issue. The parties must complete the appropriate forms required by the IRS indicating that they have waived their right to claim a child on their taxes, if the are the party who is entitled to the exemption.

It is always a challenge when people who can't get along in marriage both decide to deduct the child(ren) regardless of what the parties have agreed. If one party decides to immediately file and then the other files "claiming" the child(ren), the IRS will send a notice that the deduction cannot be allowed, even if that party was entitled to claim the deduction(s). When people file their taxes without using a tax preparer and do so electronically, the IRS will not "catch" this *error* until after the fact. It may then be necessary to file a motion on behalf of the party who has the "right" to claim the children as dependents, either to force the other party to amend his/her tax return or to pay the custodial parent the amount they would have been entitled as an exemption on his/her taxes. Always make sure that language is included in the Judgment detailing exactly who and how the exemptions are to be made. This is not only to remind the parties of who may claim the exemption(s) but also for enforcement purposes should the matter have to go back before the court at a later date. The documents must be properly prepared to indicate the exemption is not a "sale or other taxable event" or taxes may be imposed. As referenced above, the IRS had made a number of changes and interpretation of the filing status and a parent's right to exemption(s) may have changed.

Another consideration is the transfer of property from one spouse to another. In California, as long as the transfer of property is "incident to" a dissolution of marriage, there is no "gain" in the transfer. For example, if Wife signs an Interspousal Transfer Deed transferring the property to Husband, even if the fair market value of the property has tripled since the date of purchase, there are no *capitol gains taxes* assessed on the property.

As previously stated, government liens whether for local, state and/or federal taxes, support arrears collected through the Department of Child Support Services, or any other types of liens are **not** dischargeable through bankruptcy. Generally liens are collected through wage garnishments and may take priority over support. Liens will always take priority over other types of monies owed.

Many states, including California, have implemented other mechanisms to "encourage" debtors to pay off these liens. These enforcement mechanisms may result in the loss of licenses—driver's license as well as professional license(s). The loss of a license to drive and/or to act in a professional capacity, such as an architect, attorney, doctor, psychologist, realtor, and any other professions which require licensure, may impact that person's ability to earn a living. Thus, there is a great deal of pressure to make payment on these types of liens in order to be able to continue to go about one's personal and professional business.

Domestic Relations Orders

Most large and many mid-size to smaller employers offer some type of employee benefit. The most common benefit, other than health insurance, is some type of retirement plan. These types of plans will vary greatly among employers. Various pension plans include, but are not limited to, Defined benefit plans; 401(k); 403(b); and Deferred Compensation.

The Retirement Equity Act (REA) and the (federal) Employees Retirement Income & Security Act of 1974 (ERISA) provide federal statutes covering the division of employee retirement and pension plans. These statutes mandate that the state courts, which may make orders impacting retirement and pension plans, utilize a Domestic Relations Order (DRO) as the device for dividing these plans. (This may also be referred to by some pension plans as a *Qualified Domestic Relations Order*.)

In Re Marriage of Gilmore (1981) 29 C3d 418, 174 Cal.Rptr. 493 held that a non-employee spouse has a right to receive pension benefits at the time the employee is eligible to retire, even if he/she does not. It is referred to as a *Gilmore Election*.

The Retirement and Equity Action of 1984 (29 U.S.C. § 1056(d)(3)(E)(I)) recognized the *Gilmore* Election for all private retirement plans. California State law requires that Sacramento County Employee Retirements System (SCERS), California Public Employees Retirement System (CalPERS) and State Teachers Retirement System (STRS), and the Judge's Retirement System plans pay a non-employee spouse directly under a *Gilmore* election. A DRO and Joinder are required. The employee must pay the non-employee spouse if the employee spouse's plan does not provide for a *Gilmore* election. Potential tax consequences should be reviewed with an accountant and/or tax attorney, as the Tax Court has several pending cases regarding the assignment of income under a *Gilmore* election.

Many retirement and pension plans are administered by a third party administrator. Others, such as the California Public Employees Retirement System (CalPERS), are administered in-house. Some of the retirement and pension plans have their own "fill-in-the-blank" type DROs which they will require that you use. Others may send a copy of another Order which has been redacted, while still others will require that the law firm create their own DRO.

The difficulty in drafting a DRO from scratch is that each plan will have its own definitions and requirements, which may be only slightly different from other plans. If you do not have a copy of the entire employee handbook, pension book or other documents governing the manner by which the retirement is disbursed, it will be difficult to draft such a document. The potential malpractice occurs when important information is omitted from a DRO, and a non-employee spouse may lose their rights to any community portion of the retirement or pension plan and/or finds themself paying taxes on the earnings because the document was not reviewed by a tax attorney and/or accountant.

CalPERS is a good example of a pension plan which has three "templates" that they will provide upon receipt of a Joinder (Summons). The attorney and client will need to review the templates to determine which is the appropriate option for the client. The first one contemplates a division of the employee and non-employee community interest; the second one contemplates a non-employee spouse establishing a separate account and/or roll-over of the community portion into his/her own plan; and the third would be used if the employee spouse is already or about to be retired.

Pension plans for Railroad Employees, Federal Employees, Postal Employees, and many other government agencies, such as county and city pension plans, have also developed the same kinds of templates, which are always best to follow. Once the Plan has acknowledged receipt of the Joinder, it is best to ask if they have a template to be used, if one is not automatically sent to you. Some plans will provide you with a disk, while others may have the documents available through the Plan's website, or they may even provide a redacted Order. Inasmuch as the Plan cannot give legal advise, the attorney may want to confirm that the client is protected from unnecessary taxes and/or waiving any options to which they are entitled.

Employee Unions, Railroad employees, and the Armed Forces may have other specific documents that will need to be completed and served on those plan's administrators. Although you may serve a Joinder on these types of entities, your office may receive a letter stating the plan cannot be "joined" in the matter, but acknowledging that there is a community interest in the "employee-spouse's" retirement benefits.

Some retirement plans will simply be divided by Stipulation or by providing the plan administrator with a certified copy of the Judgment stating the exact amount to which the non-employee spouse is entitled. This is because these plans are not the types of plans where an employer "matches" the amount placed in the account by the employee. Plans that are matched must have an actuarial valuation determined because the value is not determined by the "present" value, but based on the value at the time the employee spouse retires. Plans that are not matched, such as Deferred Compensation Plans, have a "present" value which will, usually be based on the date of separation, unless the parties agree to using another valuation date. In most cases, these values can be determined simply by looking at a monthly or quarterly statement received from the plan administrator.

In some cases it will be important to determine if the employee is required to be "vested" in the plan. Vesting is generally defined as the length of employment that must be met in order to establish "ownership" rights to the retirement fund. In other words, did the employee spouse have to work for a period of six months or five years (or any other plan requirement) before the employee spouse can contribute, receive, and/or the employer will match the contribution?

As previously indicated in Chapter Seven, once you know there is a retirement plan of any type involved in the action, you should start gathering the information early to determine the type of plan and what type of DRO will need to be prepared. Many law firms are also securing the services of attorneys who draft DROs as their main source of clientele. You will want to check with the attorney as to who will prepare the DRO. This information is included in the enforcement chapter because it is often an area where the parties retain jurisdiction and do not complete the DRO process, and/or further work needs to be completed post-judgment rather than during the dissolution process.

You may also discover that 20+ years ago many attorneys simply included a provision in the Judgment stating that each party would receive one-half of the retirement of husband/wife according to the "time rule." It is now time for the employee spouse to retire and the non-employee spouse is entitled to receive one-half community share. In those cases, family law attorneys and paralegals often find themselves trying to determine if the employee spouse has actually retired; where the person is currently living; if he/she has already retired and is collecting the **entire** share of the retirement while the non-employee spouse has not received any share and is, therefore, owed money by the former spouse; and any number of other circumstances. Thus, it may be necessary to file a Motion requesting that the employee spouse participate in providing information about the retirement, whether the employee spouse has received any retirement or are about to retire, and if the employee spouse has received any retirement which should have rightfully gone to the former spouse to determine how that amount is going to be repaid.

Keeping track of retirement information is an area of the family law practice where a paralegal can be a "hero." By simply maintaining a database, file and/or templates for various contacts, forms, and types of DROs and other retirement requirements and information the paralegal can save both time and money. Information regarding the names of actuaries who value the various plans and who will also draft DROs will also come in handy. The paralegal will perform an invaluable service for the client and the firm when it is time to complete the procedures required in this area of the law if they have a list of resources at their fingertips.

Forms Associated with Topic

Request for Order (FL-300) and Application to Determine Arrearages (FL-490)

Payment History Attachment (FL-421)

Declaration of Payment History (FL-420)

Abstract of Support Judgment (FL-480)

Summons (Joinder) (FL-375)

Pleading on Joinder—Employees Benefit Plan (FL-370)

Request for Joinder of Employees Benefit Plan Order (FL-372)

Notice and Appearance and Response of Employees Benefit Plan (FL-374)

(See examples of some forms on the following pages)

Key Terms

- Wage Assignment Order
- Order/Notice to Withhold Support
- Equalizing Payment
- Contempt
- Quasi-Criminal
- Abstract of Support
- Abstract of Judgment

- Writ
- Domestic Relations Order (DRO)
- Joinder
- Bankruptcy
- Citee
- Department of Child Support Services (DCSS)
- Laches
- *McGinnis*
- *Burgess*
- Sister State Judgment
- Defined Benefit Plan
- Gilmore Election

Request for Order

ATTORNEY OR PARTY WITHOUT ATTORNEY *(Name, State Bar number, and address):* JOAN CARE-ACTOR, SBN ******** LAW OFFICES OF JOAN CARE-ACTOR 75000 WHY ME LANE SACRAMENTO, CA 95826 TELEPHONE NO.: 916-555-1234　FAX NO. *(Optional):* 916-555-1233 E-MAIL ADDRESS *(Optional):* joan@ care-actorlaw.com ATTORNEY FOR *(Name):* SANDIE SHORES, PETITIONER	**FOR COURT USE ONLY** To keep other people from seeing what you entered on your form, please press the Clear This Form button at the end of the form when finished.

SUPERIOR COURT OF CALIFORNIA, COUNTY OF SACRAMENTO
STREET ADDRESS: 3341 POWER INN ROAD
MAILING ADDRESS: 3341 POWER INN ROAD
CITY AND ZIP CODE: SACRAMENTO, CA 95826
BRANCH NAME: FAMILY LAW

PETITIONER/PLAINTIFF: SANDIE SHORES
RESPONDENT/DEFENDANT: ROCKY SHORES
OTHER PARENT/PARTY:

REQUEST FOR ORDER	☐ MODIFICATION	☐ Temporary Emergency Court Order	CASE NUMBER: 14FLXXXXXX
☐ Child Custody ☑ Child Support ☑ Attorney Fees and Costs	☐ Visitation ☑ Spousal Support	☑ Other *(specify):* ARREARS	

1. TO *(name):* ROCKY SHORES

2. A hearing on this *Request for Order* will be held as follows: **If child custody or visitation is an issue in this proceeding, Family Code section 3170 requires mediation before or at the same time as the hearing (see item 7.)**

a. Date:	Time:	☐ Dept.:		☐ Room.:

b. Address of court ☑ same as noted above ☐ other *(specify):*

3. Attachments to be served with this *Request for Order:*
   a. A **blank** *Responsive Declaration* (form FL-320)
   b. ☑ Completed *Income and Expense Declaration* (form FL-150) and a **blank** *Income and Expense Declaration*
   c. ☐ Completed *Financial Statement (Simplified)* (form FL-155) and a **blank** *Financial Statement (Simplified)*
   d. ☐ Points and authorities
   e. ☑ Other *(specify):* PAYMENT HISTORY

Date:

JOAN CARE-ACTOR
_____
(TYPE OR PRINT NAME)

▶

_____
(SIGNATURE)

☐ COURT ORDER

4. ☐ YOU ARE ORDERED TO APPEAR IN COURT AT THE DATE AND TIME LISTED IN ITEM 2 TO GIVE ANY LEGAL REASON WHY THE ORDERS REQUESTED SHOULD NOT BE GRANTED.

5. ☐ Time for ☐ service ☐ hearing is shortened. Service must be on or before *(date):*

6. Any responsive declaration must be served on or before *(date):*

7. The parties are ordered to attend mandatory custody services as follows:

8. ☐ You are ordered to comply with the *Temporary Emergency Court Orders* (form FL-305) attached.

9. ☐ Other *(specify):*

Date: _____

_____
JUDICIAL OFFICER

To the person who received this *Request for Order:* If you wish to respond to this *Request for Order*, you must file a *Responsive Declaration to Request for Order* (form FL-320) and serve a copy on the other parties at least nine court days before the hearing date unless the court has ordered a shorter period of time. You do not have to pay a filing fee to file the *Responsive Declaration to Request for Order* (form FL-320) or any other declaration including an *Income and Expense Declaration (form FL-150)* or *Financial Statement (Simplified)* (form FL-155).

Page 1 of 4
 Form Adopted for Mandatory Use
 Judicial Council of California
 FL-300 [Rev. July 1, 2012]
 REQUEST FOR ORDER
 Family Code, §§ 2045, 2107, 6224, 6226, 6320–6326, 6380–6383
 Government Code, § 26826 <br> www.courts.ca.gov

Request for Order

PETITIONER/PLAINTIFF: SANDIE SHORES RESPONDENT/DEFENDANT: ROCKY SHORES OTHER PARENT/PARTY:	CASE NUMBER: 14FLXXXXXX

REQUEST FOR ORDER AND SUPPORTING DECLARATION

☑ **Petitioner** ☐ **Respondent** ☐ **Other Parent/Party**   requests the following orders:

1. ☐ CHILD CUSTODY   ☐ **To be ordered pending the hearing**
   a. Child's name and age   b. Legal custody to (name of person who   c. Physical custody to (name of
                                     makes decisions about health, education, etc.)   person with whom child will live)

   d. ☐ As requested in form   ☐ Child Custody and Visitation Application Attachment (form FL-311)
                               ☐ Request for Child Abduction Prevention Orders (form FL-312)
                               ☐ Children's Holiday Schedule Attachment (form FL-341(C))
                               ☐ Additional Provisions—Physical Custody Attachment (form FL-341(D))
                               ☐ Joint Legal Custody Attachment (form FL-341(E))
                               ☐ Other (Attachment 1d)

   e. ☐ Modify existing order
      (1) filed on (date):
      (2) ordering (specify):

2. ☐ CHILD VISITATION (PARENTING TIME)   ☐ **To be ordered pending the hearing**
   a. As requested in: (1) ☐ Attachment 2a   (2) ☐ Child Custody and Visitation Application Attachment (form FL-311)
                        (3) ☐ Other (specify):
   b. ☐ Modify existing order
      (1) filed on (date):
      (2) ordering (specify):

   c. ☐ One or more domestic violence restraining/protective orders are now in effect. (Attach a copy of the orders if you
         have one.) The orders are from the following court or courts (specify county and state):
      (1) ☐ Criminal: County/state: (3) ☐ Juvenile: County/state:
            Case No. (if known):   Case No. (if known):
      (2) ☐ Family: County/state: (4) ☐ Other: County/state:
            Case No. (if known):   Case No. (if known):

3. ☐ CHILD SUPPORT (An earnings assignment order may be issued.)
   a. Child's name and age   b. ☐ I request support based on the   c. Monthly amount requested (if not by guideline)
                                       child support guidelines $

   d. ☐ Modify existing order
      (1) filed on (date):
      (2) ordering (specify):

**Notice: The court is required to order child support based on the income of both parents. It normally continues until the
child is 18. You must supply the court with information about your finances by filing an *Income and Expense Declaration*
(form FL-150) or a *Financial Statement (Simplified)* (form FL-155). Otherwise, the child support order will be based on
information about your income that the court receives from other sources, including the other parent.**

Request for Order

PETITIONER/PLAINTIFF: SANDIE SHORES RESPONDENT/DEFENDANT: ROCKY SHORES OTHER PARENT/PARTY:	CASE NUMBER: 14FLXXXXXX

4. ☐ SPOUSAL OR PARTNER SUPPORT *(An earnings assignment order may be issued.)*

    a. ☐   Amount requested *(monthly):* $ c. ☐   Modify existing order

    b. ☐   Terminate existing order   (1) filed on *(date):*

        (1) filed on *(date):*   (2) ordering *(specify):*

        (2) ordering *(specify):*

    d. ☐   The *Spousal or Partner Support Declaration Attachment* (form FL-157) is attached *(for modification of spousal or partner support after judgment only)*

    e.   An *Income and Expense Declaration* (form FL-150) must be attached

5. ☑ ATTORNEY FEES AND COSTS are requested on *Request for Attorney Fees and Costs Order Attachment* (form FL-319) or a declaration that addresses the factors covered in that form. An *Income and Expense Declaration* (form FL-150) must be attached. A *Supporting Declaration for Attorney Fees and Costs Order Attachment* (form FL-158) or a declaration that addresses the factors covered in that form must also be attached.

6. ☐ PROPERTY RESTRAINT   ☐   **To be ordered pending the hearing**

    a.   The ☐ petitioner ☐ respondent ☐ claimant   is restrained from transferring, encumbering, hypothecating, concealing, or in any way disposing of any property, real or personal, whether community, quasi-community, or separate, except in the usual course of business or for the necessities of life.

         ☐   The applicant will be notified at least five business days before any proposed extraordinary expenditures, and an accounting of such will be made to the court.

    b. ☐   Both parties are restrained and enjoined from cashing, borrowing against, canceling, transferring, disposing of, or changing the beneficiaries of any insurance or other coverage, including life, health, automobile, and disability, held for the benefit of the parties or their minor children.

    c. ☐   Neither party may incur any debts or liabilities for which the other may be held responsible, other than in the ordinary course of business or for the necessities of life.

7. ☐ PROPERTY CONTROL   ☐   **To be ordered pending the hearing**

    a. ☐   The petitioner ☐ respondent   is given the exclusive temporary use, possession, and control of the following property that we own or are buying *(specify):*

    b. ☐   The petitioner ☐ respondent   is ordered to make the following payments on liens and encumbrances coming due while the order is in effect:

         Debt   Amount of payment   Pay to

8. ☑ OTHER RELIEF *(specify):*

    RESPONDENT, ROCKY SHORES, IS DELINQUENT AND IN ARREARS FOR CHILD SUPPORT AND SPOUSAL SUPPORT. A DECLARATION REGARDING ARREARS AND PAYMENT HISTORY IS ATTACHED. I AM ALSO REQUESTING ATTORNEYS FEES AND COSTS RELATED TO THIS HEARING.

NOTE: To obtain domestic violence restraining orders, you must use the forms *Request for Order (Domestic Violence Prevention)* (form DV-100), *Temporary Restraining Order (Domestic Violence)* (form DV-110), and *Notice of Court Hearing (Domestic Violence)* (form DV-109).

Request for Order

	CASE NUMBER:
PETITIONER/PLAINTIFF: SANDIE SHORES	14FLXXXXXX
RESPONDENT/DEFENDANT: ROCKY SHORES	
OTHER PARENT/PARTY:	

9. ☐ **I request** that time for service of the *Request for Order* and accompanying papers be shortened so that these documents may be served no less than *(specify number):*   days before the time set for the hearing. I need to have this order shortening time because of the facts specified in item 10 or the attached declaration.

10. ☑ FACTS IN SUPPORT of orders requested and change of circumstances for any modification are *(specify):*
     ☑ Contained in the attached declaration. (*You may use* Attached Declaration *(form MC-031) for this purpose. The attached declaration must not exceed 10 pages in length unless permission to file a longer declaration has been obtained from the court.*)

RESPONDENT WAS ORDERED TO PAY CHILD SUPPORT AND SPOUSAL SUPPORT COMMENCING ON
_____. WE AGREED TO STAY THE INCOME WITHHOLDING ORDER. SINCE THAT
TIME, RESPONDENT HAS FAILED TO TIMELY MAKE PAYMENTS AS AND FOR SAID SUPPORT.

I AM REQUESTING THAT THE COURT ESTABLISH THE ARREARS THAT ARE OWED BY RESPONDENT,
SUBJECT TO VERIFICATION ON THE PAYMENT HISTORY INFORMATION ATTACHED AND
INCORPORATED HEREIN.

I ALSO REQUEST THAT THE COURT NOT ALLOW THE INCOME WITHHOLDING OLDER TO BE STAYED
AND THAT IT BE SERVED ON RESPONDENT'S EMPLOYER IMMEDIATELY UPON APPROVAL AND
FILING WITH THE COURT.

ADDITIONALLY, BECAUSE I HAVE HAD TO INCUR ATTORNEY'S FEES AND COSTS TO BRING THIS
MATTER BEFORE THE COURT, I AM REQUESTING THAT RESPONDENT ALSO BE ORDERED TO PAY
MY ATTORNEY'S FEES AND COSTS.

I declare under penalty of perjury under the laws of the State of California that the foregoing is true and correct.

Date:

SANDIE SHORES
_____   ►   _____
     (TYPE OR PRINT NAME)   (SIGNATURE OF APPLICANT)

Requests for Accommodations
Assistive listening systems, computer-assisted real-time captioning, or sign language interpreter services are available if you ask at least five days before the proceeding. Contact the clerk's office or go to *www.courts.ca.gov/forms* for *Request for Accommodations by Persons With Disabilities and Response* (form MC-410). (Civil Code, § 54.8.)

For your protection and privacy, please press the Clear This Form button after you have printed the form.

     Save This Form | **Print This Form** | **Clear This Form**

Application to Determine Arrearages

To keep other people from seeing what you entered on your form, please press the Clear This Form button at the end of the form when finished.

FL-490

PETITIONER: SANDIE SHORES
RESPONDENT: ROCKY SHORES
OTHER PARENT/PARTY:

CASE NUMBER:
14FLXXXXXX

APPLICATION TO DETERMINE ARREARAGES
Attachment to *Request for Order* (form FL-300)

- [✔] Child support
- [✔] Spousal or partner support
- [ ] Family support
- [ ] Medical support
- [ ] Unreimbursed expenses
- [ ] Unreimbursed medical expenses
- [ ] Other *(specify):*

1. I ask that arrearages be determined in this case.

2. I have attached *(check all that apply):*
   a. [✔] a *Declaration of Payment History* (FL-420)
   b. [✔] a *Payment History Attachment* (FL-421)
   c. [ ] Other *(specify):*

3. [✔] I ask that the support arrearage be changed as follows:
   a. [ ] I have already paid [ ] some [ ] all of the support ordered. Proof of payment is attached.
   b. [✔] The children for whom support is to be paid were living with me full time for the period from XX/XX/XXXX
      to PRESENT   . I provided all of their support during that period. I am attaching a detailed declaration
      explaining these facts and supporting documentation, including any proof that the children were living with me.
   c. [ ] Other *(specify):*

4. [ ] I have previously asked the other parent for payment and provided the other parent with an itemized statement of the
      unreimbursed [ ] childcare expense [ ] medical expense *(Attach copies of all bills being claimed and proof of any
      payments that you have made on these bills.)*

5. [✔] Attorney fees and costs a. [✔] Fees b. [✔] Costs
      Income and Expense Declaration (form FL- 150) is attached.

6. Facts in support of the relief requested are *(specify):*
   [ ] contained in the attached declaration.

I declare under penalty of perjury under the laws of the State of California that the foregoing is true and correct.

Date:

SANDIE SHORES
(TYPE OR PRINT NAME)

▶

(SIGNATURE OF DECLARANT)

- [✔] Petitioner/Plaintiff
- [ ] Attorney
- [ ] Respondent/Defendant
- [ ] Other *(specify):*

NOTICE: This form must be attached to *Request for Order* (FL-300)

NOT A COURT ORDER

Page   of

Form Adopted for Mandatory Use
Judicial Council of California
FL-490 [Rev. July 1, 2013]

APPLICATION TO DETERMINE ARREARAGES

Family Code, §§ 4720-4732
www.courts.ca.gov

For your protection and privacy, please press the Clear This Form button after you have printed the form.

Save This Form   Print This Form   Clear This Form

Payment History Attachment

To keep other people from seeing what you entered on your form, please press the Clear This Form button at the end of the form when finished.

FL-421

PETITIONER/PLAINTIFF: SANDIE SHORES	CASE NUMBER:
RESPONDENT/DEFENDANT: ROCKY SHORES	14FLXXXXX
OTHER PARENT:	

PAYMENT HISTORY FOR *(check one):*

☑ Child   ☑ Spousal   ☐ Family   ☐ Medical   ☐ Unreimbursed child care
☐ Unreimbursed medical   ☐ Other *(specify):*

Year 2014

	AMOUNT ORDERED	AMOUNT PAID	AMOUNT ORDERED	AMOUNT PAID	AMOUNT ORDERED	AMOUNT PAID
January	2300	800				
February	2300	-0-				
March	2300	-0-				
April	2300	-0-				
May	2300	-0-				
June	2300	-0-				
July	2300	-0-				
August	2300	-0-				
September	2300	-0-				
October						
November						
December						
TOTAL	20,700	800				

Year _____   Year _____   Year _____

	AMOUNT ORDERED	AMOUNT PAID	AMOUNT ORDERED	AMOUNT PAID	AMOUNT ORDERED	AMOUNT PAID
January						
February						
March						
April						
May						
June						
July						
August						
September						
October						
November						
December						
TOTAL						

Page 1 of _____

Form Approved for Optional Use
Judicial Council of California
FL-421 [Rev. July 1, 2003]

PAYMENT HISTORY ATTACHMENT
(Family Law—Governmental—Uniform Parentage Act)

Family Code, §§ 5230.5,
17524 (a), 17526(c)

www.courtinfo.ca.gov

Payment History Attachment

INSTRUCTIONS FOR COMPLETING PAYMENT RECORD

You must complete a separate *Payment History Attachment* form for each type of support paid. Enter the year, list the amount ordered, and the amount paid for each month during that year. If the amounts repeat in a column, you can use an arrow as shown in the example below. Add the amounts in each column to get the yearly totals. Enter the totals at the bottom.

Attach additional sheets and supporting documents (bills, receipts, and other proof of expense) as necessary.

[X] Child

Year 2000   Year 2001

	AMOUNT ORDERED	AMOUNT PAID	AMOUNT ORDERED	AMOUNT PAID
January	100	0	100	100
February				0
March				
April		100		100
May		100		0
June		100		
July		0		
August				100
September				100
October		100		0
November				
December				
TOTAL	**1,200**	**600**	**1,200**	**400**

[X] Spousal

	AMOUNT ORDERED	AMOUNT PAID
January	100	0
February		
March		
April		100
May		100
June		100
July		0
August		
September		
October		100
November		
December		
TOTAL	**1,200**	**600**

UNREIMBURSED CHILD CARE, MEDICAL, OR OTHER EXPENSES:

You must complete a separate *Payment History Attachment* form for each type of unreimbursed expense. If you have more than one bill, receipt, and other proof of expense per month use an additional declaration page (form MC-031) or separate page. **1.)** Itemize each expense; **2.)** attach proof of bill or payment; **3.)** mark each bill or payment with an Exhibit # _____; **4.)** group the bills, receipts, and other proof of expense in chronological order for each month; and **5.)** enter the total bills, receipts, and other proof of expense for each month. If your court order did not state a specific due date for reimbursement, then include that amount in the month that the expense was incurred.

[X] Unreimbursed child care expenses   **[X] Unreimbursed medical expenses**

Year 2001

	AMOUNT ORDERED	AMOUNT PAID
January	50% ($200)	0
February	50% ($200)	100
March	50% ($200)	0
April	50% ($200)	50
May		
June		
July		
August		
September		
October		
November		
December		
TOTAL	**$400**	**150**

Year 2001

	AMOUNT ORDERED	AMOUNT PAID
January	50% ($200)	0
February		
March	50% ($200)	0
April	50% ($75)	0
May		
June		
July		
August		
September		
October		
November		
December		
TOTAL	**$237.50**	**0**

Form MC-031

Petitioner/Plaintiff Defendant/Respondent	CASE NUMBER

I request reimbursement for 50% of these expenses, which are supported by copies of bills, receipts, and other proof of expense.

01/04/01	Dr. Adams	$45.00	Exhibit A
01/08/01	Dr. Lee, D.D.S.	$155.00	Exhibit B
02/15/01	AB X-ray Inc.	$200.00	Exhibit C
04/26/01	Kids Therapy	$75.00	Exhibit D

Child care expenses:

01/02	ABC School	50% ($200)	
02/02	ABC School	50% ($200)	— Exhibit E
03/02	ABC School	50% ($200)	
04/02	ABC School	50% ($200)	

I declare under penalty of perjury under the laws of the State of California that the foregoing is true and correct.

....
(TYPE OR PRINT NAME)   (SIGNATURE OF DECLARANT)

Form MC-031   **ATTACHED DECLARATION**

FL-421 [Rev. July 1, 2003]

PAYMENT HISTORY ATTACHMENT
(Family Law—Governmental—Uniform Parentage Act)

For your protection and privacy, please press the Clear This Form button after you have printed the form.

[Save This Form]   [Print This Form]   [Clear This Form]

Declaration of Payment History

FL-420

ATTORNEY OR PARTY WITHOUT ATTORNEY *(Name, state Bar number, and address)* or GOVERNMENTAL AGENCY *(under Family Code, §§ 17400, 17406)*:	
JOAN CARE-ACTOR, SBN ******* LAW OFFICES OF JOAN CARE-ACTOR 75000 WHY ME COURT SACRAMENTO, CA 95826 TELEPHONE NO.: 916-555-1234 FAX NO. *(Optional)*: 916-555-1233 E-MAIL ADDRESS *(Optional)*: joan@care-actorlaw.com ATTORNEY FOR *(Name)*: SANDIE SHORES, PETITIONER	To keep other people from seeing what you entered on your form, please press the Clear This Form button at the end of the form when finished.

SUPERIOR COURT OF CALIFORNIA, COUNTY OF SACRAMENTO
STREET ADDRESS: 3341 POWER INN COURT
MAILING ADDRESS: 3341 POWER INN COURT
CITY AND ZIP CODE: SACRAMENTO, CA 95826
BRANCH NAME: FAMILY LAW

PETITIONER/PLAINTIFF: SANDIE SHORES
RESPONDENT/DEFENDANT: ROCKY SHORES
OTHER PARENT:

DECLARATION OF PAYMENT HISTORY	CASE NUMBER: 14FLXXXXXX

1. Declaration of *(name)*: SANDIE SHORES

2. Based on my records or my recollection, I declare that the information on the attached pages showing the amounts ordered and the amounts paid are true and correct for the following obligations *(check all that apply)*:

    a. ☑ Child support   d. ☐ Medical support   g. ☐ Other *(specify)*:
    b. ☑ Spousal support   e. ☐ Unreimbursed medical expenses
    c. ☐ Family support   f. ☐ Unreimbursed child care expenses

3. Number of pages attached: 1

I declare under penalty of perjury under the laws of the State of California that the foregoing is true and correct.

Date:

_____   ▶ _____
SANDIE SHORES
(TYPE OR PRINT NAME)   (SIGNATURE OF DECLARANT)

SUPPORT ARREARAGE SUMMARY

This summary is for arrearage for the periods specified in the attached pages.
Interest is calculated through *(specify date)*: 9/1/14

	Principal:	Interest *(optional)*:	Total Arrearage:
CHILD SUPPORT:	$ 1600	$	$ 13,200
SPOUSAL SUPPORT:	$ 700	$	$ 6,300
FAMILY SUPPORT:	$	$	$
MEDICAL SUPPORT:	$	$	$
UNREIMBURSED MEDICAL EXPENSES:	$	$	$
UNREIMBURSED CHILD CARE EXPENSES:	$	$	$
OTHER *(specify)*:	$	$	$

NOTICE: Interest that is not calculated is not waived

Date: Submitted by:

_____   ▶ _____
JOAN CARE-ACTOR
(TYPE OR PRINT NAME)   (SIGNATURE)

Details of the arrearage statement, consisting of *(specify number)* 1 pages, are attached.   Page 1 of 1

Form Adopted for Mandatory Use Judicial Council of California FL-420 [Rev. January 1, 2003]	**DECLARATION OF PAYMENT HISTORY** (Family Law—Governmental—Uniform Parentage Act)	Family Code, §§ 5230.5, 17524(a), 17526(c) www.courtinfo.ca.gov

For your protection and privacy, please press the Clear This Form button after you have printed the form.

Save This Form   Print This Form   Clear This Form

Abstract of Support Judgment

FL-480

ATTORNEY OR PARTY WITHOUT ATTORNEY *(Name and address):* ☑ Recording requested by and return to: JOAN CARE-ACTOR, SBN ******** LAW OFFICES OF JOAN CARE-ACTOR 75000 WHY ME COURT SACRAMENTO, CA 95826 TELEPHONE NO.: 916-555-1234 ☑ ATTORNEY FOR ☑ JUDGMENT CREDITOR ☐ ASSIGNEE OF RECORD	**FOR RECORDER'S USE ONLY** To keep other people from seeing what you entered on your form, please press the Clear This Form button at the end of the form when finished.

SUPERIOR COURT OF CALIFORNIA, COUNTY OF SACRAMENTO
STREET ADDRESS: 3341 POWER INN ROAD
MAILING ADDRESS: 3341 POWER INN ROAD
CITY AND ZIP CODE: SACRAMENTO, CA 95826
BRANCH NAME: FAMILY LAW

PETITIONER/PLAINTIFF: SANDY SHORES

RESPONDENT/DEFENDANT: ROCKY SHORES

ABSTRACT OF SUPPORT JUDGMENT	CASE NUMBER: 14FLXXXXXXX

1. The ☑ judgment creditor ☐ assignee of record
applies for an abstract of a support judgment and represents the following:
   a. Judgment debtor's
      name and last known address

      ⌐ ROCKY SHORES
        6900 CHEATER LANE
        SACRAMENTO, CA 95816

      ⌐
   b. Driver's license no. and state: BXXXXXXXX   ☐ Unknown
   c. Social security number: XXX-XX-9999 *(provide only last four digits)*   ☐ Unknown
   d. Birth date: XX/XX/XXXX   ☐ Unknown

   Date:

   JOAN CARE-ACTOR
   _____
   (TYPE OR PRINT NAME)

   ▶ _____
   (SIGNATURE OF APPLICANT OR ATTORNEY)

FOR COURT USE ONLY

2. I CERTIFY that the judgment entered in this action contains an order for payment of spousal, family, or child support.

3. Judgment creditor *(name):*
   SANDIE SHORES
   whose address appears on this form above the court's name.

4. ☑ The support is ordered to be paid to the following county officer *(name and address):*
   SACRAMENTO COUNTY SHERIFF
   CIVIL DIVISION
   3341 POWER INN ROAD
   SACRAMENTO, CA 95826

[SEAL]

This abstract issued on
(date):

5. Judgment debtor *(full name as it appears in judgment):*
   ROCKY SHORES

6. a. A judgment was entered on *(date):* XX/XX/XXXX
   b. Renewal was entered on *(date):*
   c. Renewal was entered on *(date):*

7. ☑ An execution lien is endorsed on the judgment as follows:
   a. Amount: $ 19,900
   b. In favor of *(name and address):*
      SANDIE SHORES
      11155 TURTLE DOVE CT.
      FOLSOM, CA 95630

8. A stay of enforcement has
   a. ☑ not been ordered by the court.
   b. ☐ been ordered by the court effective until *(date):*

9. ☐ This is an installment judgment.

Clerk, by _____, Deputy

Page 1 of 1

Form Adopted for Mandatory Use
Judicial Council of California
FL-480 [Rev. January 1, 2011]

ABSTRACT OF SUPPORT JUDGMENT

Code of Civil Procedure, §§ 488.480, 674,
697.320, 700.190
www.courtinfo.ca.gov

For your protection and privacy, please press the Clear This Form button after you have printed the form.

Save This Form   Print This Form   Clear This Form

Summons (Joinder)

FL-375

ATTORNEY OR PARTY WITHOUT ATTORNEY *(Name, state bar number, and address):* JOAN CARE-ACTOR, SBN ******* LAW OFFICES OF JOAN CARE-ACTOR 75000 WHY ME LANE, SACRAMENTO, CA 95826 TELEPHONE NO. *(Optional):* 916-555-1234 FAX NO. *(Optional):* 916-555-1233 E-MAIL ADDRESS *(Optional):* joan@care-actorlaw.com ATTORNEY FOR *(Name):* SANDIE SHORES, PETITION	To keep other people from seeing what you entered on your form, please press the Clear This Form button at the end of the form when finished.

SUPERIOR COURT OF CALIFORNIA, COUNTY OF SACRAMENTO
STREET ADDRESS: 3341 POWER INN ROAD
MAILING ADDRESS: 3341 POWER INN ROAD
CITY AND ZIP CODE: SACRAMENTO, CA 95826
BRANCH NAME: FAMILY LAW

MARRIAGE OF SHORES

PETITIONER: SANDIE SHORES

RESPONDENT: ROCKY SHORES

CLAIMANT: CALIFORNIA PUBLIC EMPLOYEES RETIREMENT SYSTEM

SUMMONS (JOINDER)	CASE NUMBER: 14FLXXXXXX

NOTICE! You have been sued. The court may decide against you without your being heard unless you respond within 30 days. Read the information below.	**¡AVISO!** Usted ha sido demandado. El tribunal puede decidir contra Ud. sin audiencia a menos que Ud. responda dentro de 30 dias. Lea la información que sigue.
If you wish to seek the advice of an attorney in this matter, you should do so promptly so that your response or pleading, if any, may be filed on time.	Si Usted desea solicitar el consejo de un abogado en este asunto, debería hacerlo inmediatamente, de esta manera, su respuesta o alegación, si hay alguna, puede ser registrada a tiempo.

1. [✔] TO THE [ ] PETITIONER [ ] RESPONDENT [✔] CLAIMANT
A pleading has been filed under an order joining *(name of claimant):* CALIFORNIA PUBLIC EMPLOYEES RETIRMENT SYSTEM
as a party in this proceeding. If you fail to file an appropriate pleading within **30** days of the date this summons is served on you, your default may be entered and the court may enter a judgment containing the relief requested in the pleading, court costs, and such other relief as may be granted by the court, which could result in the garnishment of wages, taking of money or property, or other relief.

2. [✔] TO THE CLAIMANT EMPLOYEE BENEFIT PLAN
A pleading on joinder has been filed under the clerk's order joining *(name of employee benefit plan):* CALIFORNIA PUBLIC EMPLOYEES RETIREMENT SYSTEM
as a party claimant in this proceeding. If the employee benefit plan fails to file an appropriate pleading within **30** days of the date this summons is served on it, a default may be entered and the court may enter a judgment containing the relief requested.

Dated: Clerk, By   , Deputy

3. NOTICE TO THE PERSON SERVED: You are served
   a. [ ] As an individual.
(SEAL)
   b. [ ] As (or on behalf of) the person sued under the fictitious name of:

   c. [✔] On behalf of:

     Under: [ ] CCP 416.10 (Corporation)   [ ] CCP 416.60 (Minor)
            [ ] CCP 416.20 (Defunct Corporation)   [ ] CCP 416.70 (Incompetent)
            [ ] CCP 416.40 (Association or Partnership)   [ ] CCP 416.90 (Individual)
            [ ] Other: [✔] FC 2062 (Employee Benefit Plan)

   d. [ ] By personal delivery on *(date):*

Page 1 of 2

Form Adopted for Mandatory Use
Judicial Council of California
FL-375 [Rev. January 1, 2003]
       SUMMONS (JOINDER)   www.courtinfo.ca.gov.

Summons (Joinder)

PROOF OF SERVICE—SUMMONS (JOINDER)
(Use separate proof of service for each person served)

1. I served the

  a. *Summons and (1)* ☑ Request for Joinder of Employee Benefit Plan and Order, Pleading on Joinder-Employee Benefit Plan, blank Notice of Appearance and Response of Employee Benefit Plan

  (2) ☐ *Notice of Motion and Declaration for Joinder* (3) ☐ Order re Joinder
  (4) ☑ *Pleading on Joinder (specify title):*
  (5) ☐ Other:

  b. On *(name of party or claimant):* CALIFORNIA PUBLIC EMPLOYEES RETIREMENT SYSTEM
  c. By serving (1) ☑ Party or claimant. (2) ☐ Other *(name and title or relationship to person served):*

  d. ☑ By delivery at ☐ home   ☑ business (1) Date of:
  (2)   Time of: (3) Address:

  e. ☐ By mailing (1) Date of: (2) Place of:

2. Manner of service: *(check proper box)*
  a. ☐ **Personal service.** By personally delivering copies. (CCP 415.10)
  b. ☑ **Substituted service on corporation, unincorporated association (including partnership), or public entity.** By leaving, during usual office hours, copies in the office of the person served with the person who apparently was in charge and thereafter mailing (by first-class mail, postage prepaid) copies to the person served at the place where the copies were left. (CCP 41 5.20(a))
  c. ☐ **Substituted service on natural person, minor, incompetent, or candidate.** By leaving copies at the dwelling house, usual place of abode, or usual place of business of the person served in the presence of a competent member of the household or a person apparently in charge of the office or place of business, at least 18 years of age, who was informed of the general nature of the papers, and thereafter mailing (by first-class mail, postage prepaid) copies to the person served at the place where the copies were left. (CCP 415.20(b)) **(Attach separate declaration or affidavit stating acts relied on to establish reasonable diligence in first attempting personal service.)**
  d. ☐ **Mail and acknowledgment service.** By mailing (by first-class mail or airmail) copies to the person served, together with two copies of the form of notice and acknowledgment and a return envelope, postage prepaid, addressed to the sender. (CCP 415.30) **(Attach completed acknowledgment of receipt.)**
  e. ☐ **Certified or registered mail service.** By mailing to address outside California (by registered or certified airmail with return receipt requested) copies to the person served. (CCP 415.40) **(Attach signed return receipt or other evidence of actual delivery to the person served.)**
  f. ☐ Other *(specify code section):*
    ☐ Additional page is attached.

3. The notice to the person served (item 3 on the copy of the summons served) was completed as follows (CCP 412.30, 415.10, and 474):
  a. ☐ As an individual.
  b. ☐ As the person sued under the fictitious name of:
  c. ☑ On behalf of:
    Under: ☐ CCP 416.10 (Corporation)   ☐ CCP 416.60 (Minor)
           ☐ CCP 416.20 (Defunct Corporation) ☐ CCP 416.70 (Incompetent)
           ☐ CCP 416.40 (Association or   ☐ CCP 416.90 (Individual)
                partnership)   ☑ FC 2062 (Employee Benefit Plan)
  d. By personal delivery on *(date):*

4. At the time of service I was at least 18 years of age and not a party to this action.
5. Fee for service: $ -0-............
6. Person serving
  a. ☑ Not a registered California process server.
  b. ☐ Registered California process server.
  c. ☐ Exempt from registration under Bus. & Prof. Code 22350(b).
  d. ☐ California sheriff, marshal, or constable.

  e. Name, address, telephone number, and, if applicable, county of registration and number:

    SALLIE Q. DILIGENT
    LAW OFFICES OF JOAN CARE-ACTOR
    75000 WHY ME LANE
    SACRAMENTO, CA 95826

I declare under penalty of perjury that the foregoing is true and correct and that this declaration is executed on *(date):*   at *(place):*
                    , California.

(For California sheriff, marshal, or constable use only)
I certify that the foregoing is true and correct and that this certificate is executed on *(date):*
at *(place):*   , California.

_____   _____
(Signature)   (Signature)

FL-375 [Rev. January 1, 2003]   **SUMMONS (JOINDER)**   Page 2 of 2

For your protection and privacy, please press the Clear This Form button after you have printed the form.

Save This Form   Print This Form   Clear This Form

Pleading on Joinder Employee Benefit Plan

<table>
<tr>
<td colspan="2">

ATTORNEY OR PARTY WITHOUT ATTORNEY *(Name, state bar number, and address):*
JOAN CARE-ACTOR, SBN *******
LAW OFFICES OF JOAN CARE-ACTOR
75000 WHY ME LANE, SACRAMENTO, CA 95826
  TELEPHONE NO.: 916-555-1234   FAX NO. *(Optional):* 916-555-1233
E-MAIL ADDRESS *(Optional):* joan@care-actorlaw.com
  ATTORNEY FOR *(Name):* SANDIE SHORES, PETITIONER

FL-370

To keep other people from seeing what you entered on your form, please press the Clear This Form button at the end of the form when finished.

</td>
</tr>
</table>

SUPERIOR COURT OF CALIFORNIA, COUNTY OF SACRAMENTO
STREET ADDRESS: 3341 POWER INN ROAD
MAILING ADDRESS: 3341 POWER INN ROAD
CITY AND ZIP CODE: SACRAMENTO, CA 95826
BRANCH NAME: FAMILY LAW

MARRIAGE OF
PETITIONER: SANDIE SHORES

RESPONDENT: ROCKY SHORES

CLAIMANT: CALIFORNIA PUBLIC EMPLOYEE RETIREMENT SYSTEM

PLEADING ON JOINDER—EMPLOYEE BENEFIT PLAN	CASE NUMBER: 14FLXXXXXX

TO THE CLAIMANT: You have been joined as a party claimant in this proceeding because an interest is claimed in the employee benefit plan that is or may be subject to disposition by this court. The party who obtained the order for your joinder declares:

1. Information concerning the employee covered by the plan:
   a. Name: ROCKY SHORES
   b. Employer *(name):* STATE OF CALIFORNIA - DEPARTMENT OF TRANSPORTATION
   c. ☐ Name of labor union representing employee:
   d. ☑ Employee identification number: SSN: XXX-XX-XXXX
   e. Other *(specify):*

2. Petitioner's

   a. ☑ Attorney *(name, address, and telephone number):*
       JOAN CARE-ACTOR, LAW OFFICES OF JOAN CARE-ACTOR
       75000 WHY ME LANE, SACRAMENTO, CA 95826
       916-555-1234
   b. ☐ Address and telephone number, if unrepresented by an attorney:

3. Respondent's
   a. ☑ Attorney *(name, address, and telephone number):*

   b. Address and telephone number, if unrepresented by an attorney:
      6900 CHEATER LANE, SACRAMENTO, CA 95826
      916-555-XXXX

Form Adopted for Mandatory Use
Judicial Council of California
FL-370 [Rev. January 1, 2003]

PLEADING ON JOINDER—EMPLOYEE BENEFIT PLAN

Page 1 of 2
Family Code, §§ 2060–2065
www.courtinfo.ca.gov

Pleading on Joinder Employee Benefit Plan

PETITIONER: SANDIE SHORES	CASE NUMBER:
RESPONDENT: ROCKY SHORES	14FLXXXXXX

4. Petition for dissolution ☑ and response states
   a. Date of marriage: JUNE 20, 2003
   b. Date of separation: AUGUST 30, 2014

5. ☐ Response states
   a. Date of marriage:
   b. Date of separation:

6. Judgment
   a. ☐ has not been entered
   b. ☑ was entered on *(date):* XX/XX/2015
     (1) ☑ and disposes of each spouse's interest in the employee benefit plan.
     (2) ☐ and does not dispose of each spouse's interest in the employee benefit plan.

7. The following relief is sought:
   a. ☑ An order determining the nature and extent of both employee and nonemployee spouse's interest in employee's benefits under the plan.
   b. ☑ An order restraining claimant from making benefit payments to employee spouse pending the determination and disposition of nonemployee spouse's interest, if any, in employee's benefits under the plan.
   c. ☑ An order directing claimant to notify nonemployee spouse when benefits under the plan first become payable to employee.
   d. ☑ An order directing claimant to make payment to nonemployee spouse of said spouse's interest in employee's benefits under the plan when they become payable to employee.
   e. ☑ Other *(specify):*
     ALL SUCH OTHER ORDERS THAT MAY BE CONSISTENT WITH THE QUALIFIED DOMESTIC RELATIONS ORDER (QDRO) TO BE SUBMITTED PURSUANT TO THE PLAN'S REQUIRED ADMINISTRATION.

   f. Such other orders as may be appropriate.

Dated:

▸

_____
(SIGNATURE OF ☑ ATTORNEY FOR)

☑ PETITIONER   ☐ RESPONDENT

SANDIE SHORES
(TYPE OR PRINT NAME)

For your protection and privacy, please press the Clear This Form button after you have printed the form.

Save This Form   **Print This Form**   **Clear This Form**

Request for Joinder of Employee Benefit Plan and Order

FL-372

ATTORNEY OR PARTY WITHOUT ATTORNEY *(Name, state bar no., and address)*:

ATTORNEY OR PARTY WITHOUT ATTORNEY *(Name, state bar no., and address)*:
JOAN CARE-ACTOR, SBN ******
LAW OFFICES OF JOAN CARE-ACTOR
75000 WHY ME LANE
SACRAMENTO, CA 95826
TELEPHONE NO.: 916-555-1234   FAX NO. *(Optional)*: 916-555-1233
E-MAIL ADDRESS *(Optional)*: joan@care-actorlaw.com
ATTORNEY FOR *(Name)*: SANDIE SHORES, PETITIONER

To keep other people from seeing what you entered on your form, please press the Clear This Form button at the end of the form when finished.

SUPERIOR COURT OF CALIFORNIA, COUNTY OF SACRAMENTO
STREET ADDRESS: 3341 POWER INN ROAD
MAILING ADDRESS: 3341 POWER INN ROAD
CITY AND ZIP CODE: SACRAMENTO, CA 95826
BRANCH NAME: FAMILY LAW

MARRIAGE OF
PETITIONER: SANDIE SHORES

RESPONDENT: ROCKY SHORES

CLAIMANT: California Public Employee Retirement System

REQUEST FOR JOINDER OF EMPLOYEE BENEFIT PLAN AND ORDER	CASE NUMBER: 14FXXXXXX

TO THE CLERK
1. Please join as a party claimant to this proceeding *(specify name of employee benefit plan)*:
CALIFORNIA STATE EMPLOYEE RETIREMENT SYSTEM (CalPERS)

2. The pleading on joinder is submitted with this application for filing.

Dated:

▶ _____
(SIGNATURE OF ☐ ATTORNEY FOR)
☑ PETITIONER ☐ RESPONDENT

JOAN CARE-ACTOR
(TYPE OR PRINT NAME)

ORDER OF JOINDER

3. IT IS ORDERED
    a. The claimant listed in item 1 is joined as a party claimant to this proceeding.
    b. The pleading on joinder be filed.
    c. Summons be issued.
    d. Claimant be served with a copy of the pleading on joinder, a copy of this request for joinder and order, the summons, and
    a blank *Notice of Appearance and Response of Employee Benefit Plan* (form FL-374).

Dated:

Clerk, By _____, Deputy

Page 1 of 1

Form Adopted for Mandatory Use Judicial Council of California FL-372 [Rev. January 1, 2003]	**REQUEST FOR JOINDER OF EMPLOYEE BENEFIT PLAN AND ORDER**	Family Code, §§ 2010, 2021, 2060–2065, 2070–2074 www.courtinfo.ca.gov

For your protection and privacy, please press the Clear This Form button after you have printed the form.

Save This Form | Print This Form | | Clear This Form |

Notice of Appearance and Response
of Employee Benefit Plan

FL-374

ATTORNEY OR PARTY WITHOUT ATTORNEY (Name, state bar number and address):	To keep other people from seeing what you entered on your form, please press the Clear This Form button at the end of the form when finished.

TELEPHONE NO. (Optional):   FAX NO. (Optional):
E-MAIL ADDRESS (Optional):
ATTORNEY FOR (Name):

SUPERIOR COURT OF CALIFORNIA, COUNTY OF
STREET ADDRESS:
MAILING ADDRESS:
CITY AND ZIP CODE:
BRANCH NAME:

MARRIAGE OF
PETITIONER:

RESPONDENT:

CLAIMANT:

CASE NUMBER:

NOTICE OF APPEARANCE ☐ **AND RESPONSE
OF EMPLOYEE BENEFIT PLAN**

1. An appearance in this proceeding is entered by claimant employee benefit plan (name):

2. Service on claimant may be made as follows

   a. ☐ Attorney for claimant (name, address, and telephone number):

   b. ☐ Other (name, title, address, and telephone number):

3. ☐ Claimant responds to the pleading on joinder and states that the allegations of the pleadings are

   a. ☐ correct

   b. ☐ incorrect as set forth in ☐ attachment 3b or ☐ as follows (specify):

Dated:

Claimant

_____
(TYPE OR PRINT NAME)

By _____
(SIGNATURE)

Page 1 of 1

Form Adopted for Mandatory Use
Judicial Council of California
FL-374 [Rev. January 1, 2003]

**NOTICE OF APPEARANCE AND RESPONSE
OF EMPLOYEE BENEFIT PLAN**

Family Code, §§ 80, 2010, 2021,
2060–2065, 2070–2074
www.courtinfo.ca.gov

For your protection and privacy, please press the Clear This Form button after you have printed the form.

Save This Form | Print This Form | Clear This Form

Chapter Eleven

Other Family Law Matters

Family law encompasses several areas other than the Dissolution and Legal Separation process. However, as a family law paralegal, you will find at least sixty percent (60%) of your time, if not more, will be spent in that arena, depending on your firm's area of expertise.

You will also need to be familiar with family law-related matters listed below as you may either be involved in these processes or may encounter them as part of a dissolution or legal separation matter. In the event you also work in any of these areas of family law, I encourage you to take continuing education courses to help you to have a better understanding of the nuances of these types of cases, as well as any changes made in those areas of law:

Guardianship

Conservatorship

Emancipation

Paternity/Child Custody & Support Orders

Adoption

Pre-Nuptial and Post-Nuptial Agreements

Guardianship

In most cases, the actual guardianship procedure will be heard in the probate court rather than family law Courts. Very often, family law practitioners will take on these types of cases. The primary reason you should be familiar with the guardianship process is that more and more parents are unable to care for their children. In order for another person to provide for the care, support, and education of a minor child, it may be necessary for that person to be appointed as a guardian of the child(ren).

The Courts are reporting a significant increase in the number of grandparents who are requesting that they be appointed as guardians. When a grandparent, or other individual, has been appointed as a guardian, that person is entitled to request child support from the natural parents. Thus, your office may be involved in obtaining, modifying or enforcing child support orders which are made subsequent to the guardianship process. Alternatively, a natural parent may be seeking visitation rights to the natural child from the guardian.

Often support related to custody of a grandparent or other family member will be initiated and maintained through DCSS, but the representation may be where an occasional support order originated through a family law attorney. Thus, you should at least have a general knowledge of this area of law.

These types of cases are fairly complex due to the potential termination of parental rights. You will want to review closely the Family Code Sections dealing with the termination of parental rights, some of which will be covered under "Adoption" later in this chapter. In most cases, a grandparent or other family member, who seeks to be appointed as guardian of a minor, will have to obtain the written consent of both natural parents (or the natural mother and presumed father) or seek a court order terminating the parental rights. The Court is very reluctant to terminate the parental rights of a parent unless it can be proved that is in the best interests of the child(ren) or that it would be detrimental to the child to have the parent(s) actively involved in the child's life. For example, not paying child support is simply not enough for a termination of parental rights. The child's welfare must be at risk. Or, the natural parent(s) may freely acknowledge they cannot care for the child and will willingly consent to the guardianship. Another situation may be where a parent has sole legal and physical custody is deployed. In that event, if the other parent is unable and/or unwilling to have custody, the custodial parent may wish to have a guardian appointed to provide stability and legal standing to take care of all of the child's needs during that deployment. Such needs may include, but are not limited to, enrollment in school, sports or other activities, medical attention, counseling, and any other needs the guardian deems appropriate under the circumstances.

Parents may need to seek the services of a family law practitioner to represent their rights and protect their interests in an action filed by a person seeking guardianship of their child.

The Court may appoint a Guardian Ad Litem to protect a child's interests. That topic is beyond the scope of this text.

Conservatorship

A Conservatorship is generally used to protect the rights of persons who are unable to support or care for themselves, or to protect their own rights. Examples are, a person with a severe physical or mental handicap or a person who is in a coma.

Conservatorship proceedings are primarily a function of the probate court and governed by Probate Code. Similar to the guardianship process, a conservator may be appointed for a child if the parents are dissolving the marriage, or are requesting post-judgment enforcement or modification which may relate to family law matters. In the event the child is unable to support him or herself due to physical or mental disability, the issue of a child's conservatorship may continue past the age of majority and, therefore, and in some cases, relate to family law.

Emancipation

Although you will rarely be involved in the process of emancipation, this is another area of law with which you should be familiar. The primary reason most law firms do not represent minors who wish to be emancipated is there isn't usually any money to be made. It is a process that most minors will proceed through on their own or with the assistance of a legal clinic.

Emancipation of Minors Law can be found in Family Code §§ 7000 through 7143. The statutes provide that children may be recognized as an adult, even though they have not reached the age of eighteen. There are some very specific conditions that must be met before the court will grant a Petition for Emancipation.

A child will be considered an adult whenever any of the following occur (*Family Code § 7002*):

(a) The person has entered into a valid marriage, whether or not the marriage has been dissolved.

(b) The person is on active duty with the armed forces of the United States.

(c) The person has received a declaration of emancipation pursuant to Section 7122.

The child must be at least 14 years old to petition for emancipation. In the Petition, the child must state, under penalty of perjury, that he or she is willing to live (or is currently living) separate from the parent(s). The child must also prove, to the court's satisfaction, that he or she is able to support him/herself, manage his/her own finances, and that the support is obtained through lawful means and not through criminal activity. An Income & Expense form (FL-150) must be filed with the Petition.

The Petition for Emancipation must be served on the parents or guardian and any other person who may be entitled to custody of the child. Once the Petition is filed, the court clerk will send a copy to the District Attorney.

Upon approval by the Court, the Order for Emancipation is entered and the child is declared emancipated and has all adult privileges and responsibilities. Any child support that was previously ordered for the support of that now emancipated child is automatically terminated.

An emancipated child will be considered an adult and is subject to the following: (*Family Code § 7050*)

An emancipated minor shall be considered as being an adult for the following purposes:

(a) The minor's rights to support by the minor's parent.

(b) The right of the minor's parents to the minor's earnings and to control the minor.

(c) The application of Sections 300 and 601 of the Welfare and Institutions Code.

(d) Ending all vicarious and imputed liability of the minor's parents or guarding for the minor's torts. Nothing in this section affects any liability of a parent, guardian, spouse, or employer imposed by the Vehicle Code, or any vicarious liability that arises from an agency relationship.

(e) The minor's capacity to do any of the following:

(1) Consent to medical, dental, or psychiatric care, without parental consent, knowledge or liability.

(2) Enter into a binding contract, or give a delegation of power.

(3) Buy, sell, lease, encumber, exchange or transfer an interest in real or personal property, including, but not limited to share of stock in a domestic or foreign corporation or a membership in a nonprofit corporation.

(4) Sue or be sued in the minor's own name.

(5) Compromise, settle, arbitrate or otherwise adjust a claim, action or proceeding by or against the minor.

(6) Make or revoke a will.

(7) Make a gift, outright or in trust.

(8) Convey or release contingent or expectant interests in property, including marital property rights and any right of survivorship incident to joint tenancy, and consent to a transfer, encumbrance, or gift of marital property.

(9) Exercise or release the minor's powers and donee of a power of appointment unless the creating instrument otherwise provides.

(10) Create for the minor's own benefit or for the benefit of others a revocable or irrevocable trust.

(11) Revoke a revocable trust.

(12) Elect to take under or against a will.

(13) Renounce or disclaim any interest acquired by testate or intestate succession or by inter vivos transfer, including exercise of a right to surrender the right to revoke a revocable trust.

(14) Make an election referred to in Section 13502 of, or an election and agreement referred to in Section 13501 of the Probate Code.

(15) Establish the minor's own residence.

(16) Apply for a work permit pursuant to Section 49110 of the Education Code, without the request of the minor's parents.

(17) Enroll in a school or college.

A Declaration of Emancipation may be voided or rescinded. The emancipation could be voided, for example, if the minor is unable to support him or herself. It may also be rescinded if the Court finds that the declaration was false or fraudulently filed. Upon the Order being voided or rescinded, the child's parents are once again liable for the child's actions and support. However, any contractual obligations made or performed during the period of emancipation are not affected by the order of recision. (See Family Code §§ 7130—7135.)

One of the frequently asked questions is: Can I get my child emancipated? This is a common question when a parent is having problems with the child. For instance the child may be running around late at night, keeping bad company, failing to attend school and do their school work, drinking or taking drugs, as well as showing signs of criminal behavior, etc.

A parent cannot emancipate a child. Parents are responsible for the child's education, health and welfare until the child is 18. A child who petitions the court to be emancipated must notify his or her parents of the intention, but the child must also meet the conditions as set forth in FC§7122. The court must also find that it is in the minor's best interests to be emancipated (*Family Code § 7120*). You may have heard this colloquially referred to a "divorcing" one's parents.

Given the above circumstances, if a child is considered uncontrollable, has no means of support, and is just not getting along with the parents, it is highly unlikely the Court will find that it is in the child's best interest to be emancipated. Based on this same logic, the Court will not find that it is in the child's best interests for a parent to emancipate his or her child, just because the parent(s) has lost control of the child.

Paternity/Child Custody and Support Orders

As previously indicated, a valid marriage does not need to exist for there to be custody and support orders to be made regarding minor children. Either natural parent, Mother or Father, may petition the Court to establish the paternity of the child(ren) and to obtain orders for custody, visitation, and child support and other related orders.

Family Code § 7570, states as follows:

• The Legislature hereby finds and declares as follows:

(a) There is a compelling state interest in establishing paternity for all children. Establishing paternity is the first step toward a child support award, which, in turn, provides children with equal rights and access to benefits, including, but not limited to, social security, health insurance, survivors' benefits, military benefits, and inheritance rights. Knowledge of family medical history is often necessary for correct medical diagnosis and treatment. Additionally, knowing one's father is important to a child's development.

(b) A simple system allowing for establishment of voluntary paternity will result in a significant increase in the ease of establishing paternity, a significant increase in paternity establishment, an increase in the number of children who have greater access to child support and other benefits, and a significant decrease in the time and money required to establish paternity due to the removal of the need for a lengthy and expensive court process to determine and establish paternity and is in the public interest.

(See Family Code §§ 7591–7577 for more information on the recording of "live" births and voluntary declarations of paternity.)

Family Code §§ 7630—7643 contain the specifics required for determining paternity as set forth in Chapter 4 of the Uniform Parentage Act.

The first condition of paternity that must be considered is the "presumption of paternity."

Family § 7540 states: "Except as provided in Section 7541, the child of a wife cohabitating with her husband, who is not impotent or sterile, is conclusively presumed to be a child of the marriage."

Family Code § 7541 should be reviewed carefully as it relates to the time limitations a child, the child's mother, and the *presumed* father have to request that a blood test be ordered to determined the paternity of a child. While FC§ 7541 references blood tests, in most cases, a DNA "swab test" will be the type of test administered to determine paternity. Most testing laboratories use the "swab test" as it is quicker, less invasive and easier to obtain, particularly on a small child. There are testing facilities that regularly perform the DNA tests. It takes 10 to 14 days to receive the results and can cost $500 or more.

Family Code § 7541–7551 states as follows:

(a) Notwithstanding Section 7540, if the court finds that the conclusions of all the experts, as disclosed by the evidence based on blood tests performed pursuant to

Chapter 2 (commencing with Section 7550), are that the husband is not the father of the child, the question of paternity of the husband shall be resolved accordingly.

(b) The notice of motion for blood tests under this section may be filed not later than two years from the child's date of birth by the husband, or for the purposes of establishing paternity by the presumed father or the child through or by the child's guardian ad litem. As used in this subdivision, "presumed father" has the meaning given in Sections 7611 and 7612.

(c) The notice of motion for blood tests under this section may be filed by the mother of the child not later than two years from the child's date of birth if the child's biological father has filed an affidavit with the court acknowledging paternity of the child.

(d) The notice of motion for blood tests pursuant to this section shall be supported by a declaration under oath submitted by the moving party stating the factual basis for placing the issue of paternity before the court.

(e) Subdivision (a) does not apply, and blood tests may not be used to challenge paternity, in any of the following cases:

(1) A case that reached final judgment of paternity on or before September 30, 1980.

(2) A case coming within Section 7613.

(3) A case in which the wife, with the consent of the husband, conceived by means of a surgical procedure.

Family Code § 7550 states as follows:

This chapter may be cited as the Uniform Act on Blood Tests to Determine Paternity.

Family Code § 7551 states as follows:

In a civil action or proceeding in which paternity is a relevant fact, the court may upon its own initiative or upon suggestion made by or on behalf of any person who is involved, and shall upon motion of any party to the action or proceeding made at a time so as not to delay the proceedings unduly, order the mother, child, and alleged father to submit to genetic tests. If a party refuses to submit to the tests, the court may resolve the question of paternity against that party or enforce its order if the rights of others and the interests of justice so required. A party's refusal to submit to the tests is admissible in evidence in any proceeding to determine paternity. For the purposes of this chapter, "genetic tests" means any genetic test that is generally acknowledged as reliable by accreditation bodies designated by the United States Secretary of Health and Human Services.

Family Code commending at Section 7600 is referred to as *The Uniform Parentage Act*. One of the important sections of this chapter is the codified definition of a natural parent. Specifically, FC§ 7601 states:

Family Code § 7601. (a) "Natural parent" as used in this code means a nonadoptive parent established under this part, whether biologically related to the child or not.

(b) "Parent and child relationship" as used in this part means the legal relationship existing between a child and the child's natural or adoptive parents incident to which the law confers or imposes rights, privileges, duties, and obligations. The term includes the mother and child relationship and the father and child relationship.

(c) This part does not preclude a finding that a child has a parent and child relationship with more than two parents.

(d) For purposes of state law, administrative regulations, court rules, government policies, common law, and any other provision or source of law governing the rights, protections, benefits, responsibilities, obligations, and duties of parents, any reference to two parents shall be interpreted to apply to every parent of a child where that child has been found to have more than two parents under this part.

Historically, the Courts presumed that the "sanctity of marriage" should be upheld whenever possible. Thus the Court's presumption that if a man and woman are married, the child is "presumed" to be a child of the marriage, and the Husband is the *presumed* father.

Another important definition with respect to the child and who is the presumed natural parent(s) is FC § 7611, which states:

Family Code § 7611. A person is presumed to be the natural parent of a child if the person meets the conditions provided in Chapter 1 (commencing with Section 7540) or Chapter 3 (commencing with Section 7570) of Part 2 or in any of the following subdivisions:

(a) The presumed parent and the child's natural mother are or have been married to each other and the child is born during the marriage, or within 300 days after the marriage is terminated by death, annulment, declaration of invalidity, or divorce, or after a judgment of separation is entered by a court.

(b) Before the child's birth, the presumed parent and the child's natural mother have attempted to marry each other by a marriage solemnized in apparent compliance with law, although the attempted marriage is or could be declared invalid, and either of the following is true:

(1) If the attempted marriage could be declared invalid only by a court, the child is born during the attempted marriage, or within 300 days after its termination by death, annulment, declaration of invalidity, or divorce.

(2) If the attempted marriage is invalid without a court order, the child is born within 300 days after the termination of cohabitation.

(c) After the child's birth, the presumed parent and the child's natural mother have married, or attempted to marry, each other by a marriage solemnized in apparent compliance with law, although the attempted marriage is or could be declared invalid, and either of the following is true:

(1) With his or her consent, the presumed parent is named as the child's parent on the child's birth certificate.

(2) The presumed parent is obligated to support the child under a written voluntary promise or by court order.

(d) The presumed parent receives the child into his or her home and openly holds out the child as his or her natural child.

(e) If the child was born and resides in a nation with which the United States engages in an Orderly Departure Program or successor program, he acknowledges that he is the child's father in a declaration under penalty of perjury, as specified in Section 2015.5 of the Code of Civil Procedure. This subdivision shall remain in effect only until January 1, 1997, and on that date shall become inoperative.

(f) The child is in utero after the death of the decedent and the conditions set forth in Section 249.5 of the Probate Code are satisfied.

7611.5. Where Section 7611 does not apply, a man shall not be presumed to be the natural father of a child if either of the following is true:

(a) The child was conceived as a result of an act in violation of Section 261 of the Penal Code and the father was convicted of that violation.

(b) The child was conceived as a result of an act in violation of Section 261.5 of the Penal Code, the father was convicted of that violation, and the mother was under the age of 15 years and the father was 21 years of age or older at the time of conception.

The above presumptions created in FC§ 7611, are rebuttable. They do, however, create the basis for establishing the paternity of a child. The most conclusive way to determine paternity is through blood (DNA) testing.

Paternity can be established by the Mother, the *presumed* Father, or the child. The paternity process is utilized to determine the identity of the Father, thus naming him as the true natural father and not just the presumed father.

A man who is not the natural father, but one who may attempt to prove he is the "presumed" father may file an action with the court establishing paternity. In the past, it was possible to be named the "presumed" father. As a result the natural father could not actually claim his status as the natural father until the presumed father died.

Another important part of this chapter is the following section:

Family Code § 7632. Regardless of its terms, an agreement between an alleged father or a presumed parent and the other parent or child does not bar an action under this chapter.

Family Code § 7541 does allow the Court the ability to "ignore" the presumption if blood test evidence shows that the Husband is not the biological father. This code section and previous case law were put to test in *Brian C v. Ginger K.* (2000) 77 Cal App 4th 1198, 92 CR2d 294.

In that case, the California Court of Appeal remanded the case back to the trial court because they presumed that the Husband was the father, without considering the evidence indicating that another man was the biological father.

The Court must stay within the requirements of FC§ 7541 which requires that both the child's mother and the *presumed* father file the action within two years of the child's birth.

The Department of Child Support Services (DCSS) also has the ability to request that Paternity be established. The Department's primary motivation is to obtain child support from the presumed or natural father so that the Mother and/or child will not be seeking or receiving public assistance or to request reimbursement for public funds and services provided.

Family Code § 7558 states:

(a) This section applies only to cases where support enforcement services are being provided by the local child support agency pursuant to Section 17400.

(b) In any civil action or proceeding in which paternity is a relevant fact, and in which the issue of paternity is contested, the local child support agency may issue an administrative order requiring the mother, child, and the alleged father to submit to genetic testing if any of the following conditions exist:

(1) The person alleging paternity has signed a statement under penalty of perjury that sets forth facts that establish a reasonable possibility of the requisite sexual conduct between the mother and the alleged father.

(2) The person denying paternity has signed a statement under penalty of perjury that sets forth facts that establish a reasonable possibility of the nonexistence of the requisite sexual contact between the parties.

(3) The alleged father has filed an answer in the action or proceeding in which paternity is a relevant fact and has requested that genetic tests be performed.

(4) The mother and the alleged father agree in writing to submit to genetic tests.

(c) Notwithstanding subdivision (b), the local child support agency may not order an individual to submit to genetic tests if the individual has been found to have good cause for failure to cooperate in the determination of paternity pursuant to Section 11477 of the Welfare and Institutions Code.

(d) The local child support agency shall pay the costs of any genetic tests that are ordered under subdivision (b), subject to the county obtaining a court order for reimbursement from the alleged father if paternity is established under Section 7553.

(e) Nothing in this section prohibits any person who has been ordered by the local child support agency to submit to genetic tests pursuant to this section from filing a notice of motion with the court in the action or proceeding in which paternity is a relevant fact seeking relief from the local child support agency's order to submit to genetic tests. In that event, the court shall resolve the issue of whether genetic tests should be ordered as provided in Section 7551. If any person refuses to submit to the tests after receipt of the administrative order pursuant to this section and fails to seek relief from the court from the administrative order either prior to the scheduled tests or within 10 days after the tests are scheduled, the court may resolve the question of paternity against that person or enforce the administrative order if the rights of others or the interest of justice so require. Except as provided in subdivision (c), a person's refusal to submit to tests ordered by the local child support agency is admissible in evidence in any proceeding to determine paternity if a notice of motion is not filed within the time-frames specified in this subdivision.

(f) If the original test result creates a rebuttable presumption of paternity under Section 7555 and the result is contested, the local child support agency shall order an additional test only upon request and advance payment of the contestant.

Family Code §7630 sets forth the conditions under which the child, the child's mother and the *presumed* father may bring a paternity action, as follows:

Family Code §7630.

(a) A child, the child's natural parent, a person presumed to be the child's parent under subdivision (a), (b), or (c) of Section 7611, an adoption agency to whom the child has been relinquished, or a prospective adoptive parent of the child may bring an action as follows:

(1) At any time for the purpose of declaring the existence of the parent and child relationship presumed under subdivision (a), (b), or (c) of Section 7611.

(2) For the purpose of declaring the nonexistence of the parent and child relationship presumed under subdivision (a), (b), or (c) of Section 7611 only if the action is brought within a reasonable time after obtaining knowledge of relevant facts.

After the presumption has been rebutted, parentage of the child by another person may be determined in the same action, if that person has been made a party.

(b) Any interested party may bring an action at any time for the purpose of determining the existence or nonexistence of the parent and child relationship presumed under subdivision (d) or (f) of Section 7611.

(c) Except as to cases coming within Chapter 1 (commencing with Section 7540) of Part 2, an action to determine the existence of the parent and child relationship may be brought by the child or personal representative of the child, the Department of Child Support Services, the parent or the personal representative or a parent of that parent if that parent has died or is a minor, a man alleged or alleging himself to be the father, or the personal representative or a parent of the alleged father if the alleged father has died or is a minor.

(d) (1) If a proceeding has been filed under Chapter 2 (commencing with Section 7820) of Part 4, an action under subdivision (a) or (b) shall be consolidated with that proceeding. The parental rights of the presumed parent shall be determined as set forth in Sections 7820 to 7829, inclusive.

(2) If a proceeding pursuant to Section 7662 has been filed under Chapter 5 (commencing with Section 7660), an action under subdivision (c) shall be consolidated with that proceeding. The parental rights of the alleged natural father shall be determined as set forth in Section 7664.

(3) The consolidated action under paragraph (1) or (2) shall be heard in the court in which the proceeding under Section 7662 or Chapter 2 (commencing with Section 7820) of Part 4 is filed, unless the court finds, by clear and convincing evidence, that transferring the action to the other court poses a substantial hardship to the petitioner. Mere inconvenience does not constitute a sufficient basis for a finding of substantial hardship. If the court determines there is a substantial hardship, the consolidated action shall be heard in the court in which the parentage action is filed.

(e) (1) If any prospective adoptive parent who has physical custody of the child, or any licensed California adoption agency that has legal custody of the child, has not been joined as a party to an action to determine the existence of a parent and child relationship under subdivision (a), (b), or (c), or an action for custody by the alleged natural father, the court shall join the prospective adoptive parent or licensed California adoption agency as a party upon application or on its own motion, without the necessity of a motion for joinder. A joined party shall not be required to pay a fee in connection with this action.

(2) If a person brings an action to determine parentage and custody of a child who he or she has reason to believe is in the physical or legal custody of an adoption agency, or of one or more persons other than the child's parent who are prospective adoptive parents, he or she shall serve his or her entire pleading on, and give notice of all proceedings to, the adoption agency or the prospective adoptive parents, or both.

(f) A party to an assisted reproduction agreement may bring an action at any time to establish a parent and child relationship consistent with the intent expressed in that assisted reproduction agreement.

(g) (1) In an action to determine the existence of the parent and child relationship brought pursuant to subdivision (b), if the child's other parent has died and there are no existing court orders or pending court actions involving custody or guardian-ship of the child, then the persons having physical custody of the child shall be served with notice of the proceeding at least 15 days prior to the hearing, either by mail or in any manner authorized by the court. If any person identified as having physical custody of the child cannot be located, the court shall prescribe the manner of giving notice.

(2) If known to the person bringing the parentage action, relatives within the sec-ond degree of the child shall be given notice of the proceeding at least 15 days prior to the hearing, either by mail or in any manner authorized by the court. If a person identified as a relative of the second degree of the child cannot be located, or his or her whereabouts are unknown or cannot be ascertained, the court shall prescribe the manner of giving notice, or shall dispense with giving notice to that person.

(3) Proof of notice pursuant to this subdivision shall be filed with the court before the proceeding to determine the existence of the parent and child relationship is heard.

The Paternity action will require that a Petition to Establish Parental Relationship (FL-200) be filed with the Court. As previously indicated, the Petition can be filed by the *presumed* father, the child, or the child's mother. The child's petition may be filed by a person who is appointed as a guardian ad litem for the child or by DCSS. The Petition can also be filed before the child's birth.

The cost for filing the Petition is usually the same as for a Dissolution or Legal Sepa-ration.

The Petition will have to be served on the other parent along with a Summons (FL-210), as well as any interested parties, such as the Department of Child Support Services.

In the event the Petitioner is requesting custody and/or visitation with the child, it would be in that party's best interest to request Mediation at the same time as the Peti-tion is filed. If the child is already born, the Court is going to want to know if the parties have been to mediation to attempt to work out the custody and parenting arrange-ments. The same process for requesting mediation that is used in the Dissolution process is used in Paternity. (See Chapter Four.)

If a voluntary declaration of paternity has already been signed by both of the parents, that declaration should be attached to the petition. If the DNA testing has been com-pleted, the test results should also be attached to the Petition. This will expedite the matter and will provide the required evidence for the Court. Effective 1/1/13 the legisla-ture amended FC § 7960 and added FC § 7962 to further define terms associated with and when assisted reproduction (surrogacy) is involved. Specifically, the legislature de-fined terms such as "intended parent," "surrogate," and "nonattorney surrogacy facilita-tor," among others to assist the courts and practitioners in this area of law. These statutes apply to both paternity as well as adoption cases.

However, if the parties are in dispute about the paternity, custody and visitation or any other issues relating to the paternity of the child(ren), either party may file a Re-quest for Order with the court requesting that certain orders be made. The Request can ask that the other party be ordered to comply with such matters as obtaining the blood test, attending mediation, etc.

The basic process for this matter will follow the same pattern as other family law ac-tion. Interim orders can be made subsequent to the hearing and a Judgment for Paternity can be obtained. Such Judgment will memorialize either the agreement of the parties or the Stipulated Judgment entered pursuant to trial or other decision of the court.

Your Instructor will discuss the forms relative to Uniform Parentage required for completion of process as listed below:

Petition to Establish Parental Relationship (Uniform Parentage): FL-200

Summons (Uniform Parentage for Custody and Support): FL-210

Response to Petition to Establish Parental Relationship: FL 220

Declaration for Default or Uncontested Judgment: FL-230

Advisement and Waiver of Rights re: Establishment of Parental Rights: FL-235

Stipulation for Entry of Judgment re: Establishment of Parental Relationship: FL-240

Judgment: FL-250

Other applicable forms:

Request for Hearing to Set Aside Voluntary Declaration of Paternity: FL-280

Responsive Declaration to Application to Set Aside Voluntary Declaration of Paternity: FL-285

Petition for Custody and Support of Minor Children

This process was developed in situations where the parties have not or prefer not to file for a dissolution or legal separation but need to establish the custody and support of their minor children. This procedure may also be used in situations where the child's parents are the same sex, and a Domestic Partnership has not been established.

This may be the appropriate procedure to use in the event your firm is retained to establish the custody and support of a minor child of a same-sex relationship. Note though, the laws are rapidly changing in this area of the law. The Court's primary concern is for the welfare and best interests of the children involved in **any** relationship. You will want to make sure that you stay current with both the statutory amendments and the related Judicial Council forms as they change and evolve.

The forms needed to begin the custody and/or support process are as follows:

Summons (Uniform Parentage — Petition for Custody and Support): FL-210

Petition for Custody and Support of Minor Children: FL-260

Response to Petition for Custody and Support of Minor Children: FL-270

Proof of Service of Summons (Family Law, Uniform Parentage, Custody and Support): FL-115

As with Dissolution and the other types of remedies we have discussed throughout this book, you will need to complete the Summons and Petition and have the Respondent served. It may also be necessary to file a Request for Order. The client will likely be required to go through the established mediation process. If you have questions, consult Chapter Four and your local rules as the process will be essentially the same.

Non-Marital Relationships

Domestic Partnership

California was the first state to create and institute a domestic partnership program, which allows the individuals meeting the criteria, to enjoy some, but not all, of the benefits of married persons. Vermont has created the **civil union relationship** which gives same-sex relationships the same support and property rights that would apply to traditional marriages.

Massachusetts was the first state, in 2004, to codify that definition of marriage which is not consisted with the Defense of Marriage Act (DOMA). As you are probably aware, several other States have recently rewritten their statutes as to the definition of marriage or more specifically who can marry. Additionally, California's recent ballot initiative to confirm the DOMA—marriage is between only one man and one woman—was struck down by the California Supreme Court in 2012. Then the United States Supreme Court in 2013 struck down the DOMA definition. (*Perry v. Brown* 9th Cir 2012, 671, F3d 1052) However, as of the writing of this text the California Legislature has not revised Family Code § 300 to reflect this decision. Thus the current statutes still reflect that marriage is between a man and a woman. A paralegal working in family law will want to keep a vigilant watch for the revision and adoption of revised language for FC § 300.

Thus a disclaimer ... without knowing how the California Legislature will revise this definition and how it will affect the process, procedures, and particularly the forms involved in family law, the author has proceeded with presenting the information based on all statutes and rules in effect as of January 1, 2014.

Likewise, it is unclear if or how Domestic Partnership relationships and dissolutions of same may be affected. It is possible that little related to Domestic Partnerships will be affected because this is a method of establishing a legal relationship between two people whether heterosexual or same-sex. The most likely result will be that same-sex couples who have established Domestic Partnerships may go through the process of dissolving them in order to avail themselves of the ability to marry.

Two individuals of the same sex may wish to live together as "Domestic Partners," as defined in Family Code § 298, however a Domestic Partnership is not exclusive to same-sex couples. It may also be established by heterosexual couples who choose to cohabitate but not to marry.

Family Code § 297 sets forth the requirements for domestic partnership. They are:

- The parties share a common residence;
- They are jointly responsible for each other's basic living expenses incurred during the domestic partnership;
- Neither is married, nor are they a member of another domestic partnership;
- They are not related by blood;
- They are at least 18 years of age;
- They are both members of the same sex *or* they are over the age of 62 and meet the eligibility criteria under Title II or Title XVI of the Social Security Act;
- They are both capable of consenting;

- Neither has previously filed a Declaration of Domestic Partnership with the Secretary of State, and that partnership has not been terminated as set forth in Family Code § 299.

Both parties must sign the Declaration of Domestic Partnership (which is available on the California Secretary of State website) before a notary public and the document must be filed with the California Secretary of State.

Family Code § 299 provides that if the parties wish to terminate their relationship, they must execute a Notice of Termination of Domestic Partnership before a notary public and file said Termination with the California Secretary of State.

Please note: The above statutes also provide that the Domestic Partnership can be established for a man and woman, over the age of 62, who are eligible to receive Social Security under Title II (as defined in 42 U.S.C. § 402(a) old age insurance benefits) or Title XVI (as defined in 42 U.S. C. § 1381 for aged individuals). This provision was included for two reasons: 1) A widowed spouse who remarries prior to the age of 60 will forfeit her Social Security benefits to which she would otherwise be entitled; and 2) a cohabitating partner cannot be held responsible for paying the other person's hospital and/or Medicaid bills.

Some of the benefits of establishing a domestic partnership are: health and other insurance benefits through one's employment; ability to visit the partner at the hospital, and use of "family" sick leave or bereavement leave. Most of the benefits are applicable to employment. A domestic partnership does not, in all cases, allow a partner to be considered a "surviving spouse" under the probate code in California. However, several laws in this area have been amended to include domestic partnerships. Thus, domestic partners will want to take title of property as joint tenants, have wills, and name each other as beneficiaries on retirement accounts and other assets if they wish the survivor of the partnership to be entitled to the property as though the partner were a spouse.

The primary means for determining a division of property for persons who are cohabitating is through civil remedies. As more people are cohabitating or do not qualify as Domestic Partners under FC§ 297 et seq., family law practitioners find that they are drafting more cohabitation agreements. A cohabitation agreement can be created for any unmarried persons who wish to reside together. The Bureau of Census defines "unmarried-couple households" as "people of the opposite sex sharing living quarters," however, cohabitation agreements can certainly be created for homosexual couples also. Any couple who contemplates cohabitation should have a mechanism for dealing with financial issues and property acquired during the relationship.

Cohabitation agreements or contracts should always contain the same elements of any well-drafted contract: offer, acceptance, and consideration. The parties must also have the intent to make the contract. These agreements are similar in nature to prenuptial and post-nuptial agreements which will be discussed later in this Chapter. A sample co-habitation agreement is included as Appendix 11F.

Family Code § 299 provides as follows:

299. (a) A registered domestic partnership may be terminated without filing a proceeding for dissolution of domestic partnership by the filing of a Notice of Termination of Domestic Partnership with the Secretary of State pursuant to this section, provided that all of the following conditions exist at the time of the filing:

(1) The Notice of Termination of Domestic Partnership is signed by both registered domestic partners.

(2) There are no children of the relationship of the parties born before or after registration of the domestic partnership or adopted by the parties after registration of the domestic partnership, and neither of the registered domestic partners, to their knowledge, is pregnant.

(3) The registered domestic partnership is not more than five years in duration.

(4) Neither party has any interest in real property wherever situated, with the exception of the lease of a residence occupied by either party which satisfies the following requirements:

(A) The lease does not include an option to purchase.

(B) The lease terminates within one year from the date of filing of the Notice of Termination of Domestic Partnership.

(5) There are no unpaid obligations in excess of the amount described in paragraph (6) of subdivision (a) of Section 2400, as adjusted by subdivision (b) of Section 2400, incurred by either or both of the parties after registration of the domestic partnership, excluding the amount of any unpaid obligation with respect to an automobile.

(6) The total fair market value of community property assets, excluding all encumbrances and automobiles, including any deferred compensation or retirement plan, is less than the amount described in paragraph (7) of subdivision (a) of Section 2400, as adjusted by subdivision (b) of Section 2400, and neither party has separate property assets, excluding all encumbrances and automobiles, in excess of that amount.

(7) The parties have executed an agreement setting forth the division of assets and the assumption of liabilities of the community property, and have executed any documents, title certificates, bills of sale, or other evidence of transfer necessary to effectuate the agreement.

(8) The parties waive any rights to support by the other domestic partner.

(9) The parties have read and understand a brochure prepared by the Secretary of State describing the requirements, nature, and effect of terminating a domestic partnership.

(10) Both parties desire that the domestic partnership be terminated.

(b) The registered domestic partnership shall be terminated effective six months after the date of filing of the Notice of Termination of Domestic Partnership with the Secretary of State pursuant to this section, provided that neither party has, before that date, filed with the Secretary of State a notice of revocation of the termination of domestic partnership, in the form and content as shall be prescribed by the Secretary of State, and sent to the other party a copy of the notice of revocation by first-class mail, postage prepaid, at the other party's last known address. The effect of termination of a domestic partnership pursuant to this section shall be the same as, and shall be treated for all purposes as, the entry of a judgment of dissolution of a domestic partnership.

(c) The termination of a domestic partnership pursuant to subdivision (b) does not prejudice nor bar the rights of either of the parties to institute an action in the superior court to set aside the termination for fraud, duress, mistake, or any other ground recognized at law or in equity. A court may set aside the termination of domestic partnership and declare the termination of the domestic partnership null and void upon proof that the parties did not meet the requirements of subdivision (a) at the time of the filing of the Notice of Termination of Domestic Partnership with the Secretary of State.

(d) The superior courts shall have jurisdiction over all proceedings relating to the dissolution of domestic partnerships, nullity of domestic partnerships, and legal separation of partners in a domestic partnership. The dissolution of a domestic partnership, nullity of a domestic partnership, and legal separation of partners in a domestic partnership shall follow the same procedures, and the partners shall possess the same rights, protections, and benefits, and be subject to the same responsibilities, obligations, and duties, as apply to the dissolution of marriage, nullity of marriage, and legal separation of spouses in a marriage, respectively, except as provided in subdivision (a), and except that, in accordance with the consent acknowledged by domestic partners in the Declaration of Domestic Partnership form, proceedings for dissolution, nullity, or legal separation of a domestic partnership registered in this state may be filed in the superior courts of this state even if neither domestic partner is a resident of, or maintains a domicile in, the state at the time the proceedings are filed.

Family Code § 299.2. A legal union of two persons of the same sex, other than a marriage, that was validly formed in another jurisdiction, and that is substantially equivalent to a domestic partnership as defined in this part, shall be recognized as a valid domestic partnership in this state regardless of whether it bears the name domestic partnership.

As you can see, the legislature has provided a mechanism for "registered" Domestic Partners to resolve their issues of custody, support and property, within the family court system, provided that they registered **after** January 1, 2005. You will note that the legislature specifically warns that if the parties were registered prior to that date and wish to benefit from this new legislation, they must have terminated their partnership by December 31, 2004, and then filed a new Declaration after January 1, 2005.

The legislature also dealt with partnerships where there aren't any issues that related to children, support or the division of property, much as in the Summary Dissolution, the partners may still file a Notice of Termination of Domestic Partnership pursuant to Family Code § 299 et seq.

The Judicial Council created mandatory forms to be used, as of January 1, 2005, for terminating Domestic Partnerships. They are Petition—Domestic Partnership (FL-103) and Response—Domestic Partnership (FL-123). These forms look very similar to and contain much the same information as a Petition—Dissolution of Marriage. Should you be involved in the process of terminating a Domestic Partnership, once the Petition is filed, you will need to serve the Summons and Petition and file the Proof of Service of Summons (FL-115). You will then follow the same process and procedures, as well as use the same forms, including the Judgment and Notice of Entry of Judgment (FL-190), that are used for the dissolution of marriage process.

The California courts heard numerous cases in 2006 and 2007 regarding the application of rights and benefits in Domestic Partnerships. The following are several cases which are precedent-setting and of which the family law paralegal will need to be aware.

In re Elisa B v. Superior Court (2005) 37 C4th 108, 33 CR3d 46

Lesbian mother meets the presumed parent criteria of Family Code § 7611(d) by receiving child born to her partner into her home and openly holding them out as her natural children. Considered "second mother."

Kristine H. v. Lisa R. (2005) 37 C4th 156, 33 CR3d 81

Lesbian mother was estopped from challenging the validity of a judgment of parentage to which she had stipulated.

K.M. v. E.G. (2005) 37 C4th 130, 33 CR3d 81

The woman who provided an ovum to impregnate her lesbian partner and the partner who bore the child are parents to the child.

L.M. v. M.G. (2012) 208 CA4th 133, 145 CR3d 97

The trial court ruled that the former same-sex partner of a woman who had adopted a child during the partners' relationship was the second parent of the child under FC §7611(d).

The following code sections were amended in 2006 and 2007 to with respect to Domestic Partnerships:

Education Code §§ 22007.5, 22171, 22650, 22651, 24300.6, 24307, 25000.9, 26002.5, 261401; Government Code §§ 22771, 22775, 22818 and 22819; Probate Code §§ 1900, 1901, and 2351.5.

The following code sections were added:

Government Code §§ 21291.5, 21626.5, and 31760.7

The following code sections were repealed:

Government Code §§ 22818.5, 22887, 22887.5, 22903, 22903.5 and 22929

The existing law provided that the term "spouse" includes registered domestic partners for the purposes of retirement benefits under the Teachers' Retirement Law. SB973 clarified that a registered domestic partner "will be treated in the same manner as a spouse." This law also requires that the member's spouse or the registered domestic partner must sign the form used by the Teacher's Retirement System when the member is taking a preretirement election. The law also states that a spouse or registered domestic partner is prohibited from receiving a distribution from CalPERS upon separation of employment until certain conditions are met.

Additionally, the rights and duties of married couples are extended to registered domestic partners under the Public Employees' Medical and Hospital Care Act. It also extends retirement allowance elections under the County Employees Retirement Law of 1937 to include registered domestic partners, provided specific criteria are met. The capacity of a conservatee has been expanded from only married partners to both married and domestic partnerships.

Revenue and Tax Code §62 (Property Tax Reassessment) was amended to include reassessment exemptions for transfers to a domestic partner or upon the death of a domestic partner.

Family Code §297.5 and R&T Code §§ 17024.5 and 18521 have been amended to allow domestic partners to file either joint or separate state income tax returns. FC§297.5(g) was deleted as a result of this amendment. Earned income may now be considered community property for the purposes of state income tax. Note that Federal law continues to prohibit the filing of joint tax returns for domestic partners under the Defense of Marriage Act.

Look for additional amendments, changes, and new statutory language in light of recent case law and pending changes related to the definition of marriage.

Adoption

For a family law paralegal and for the Courts, Adoptions are the "good part" of this area of practice. While dissolution and its related aspects deal with dividing the family, adoptions bring families together.

You may want to review Judicial Council form ADOPT-050 "How to Adopt a Child in California" before you begin the adoption process.

When someone wants to adopt, the first determination to be made is: "**is the child 'free' to be adopted?"**

> For example: Is a mother placing the child for adoption? If so, has the *presumed* father been informed and has he waived his rights to paternity of the child? Or, has he (or will he) file an objection to the adoption?

Family Code §§ 7660–7661 provide the criteria for assessing the parental rights of the *presumed* father and whether those parental rights can be terminated so that the child is "free" to be adopted.

> What if the mother does not know who the natural father is, or if she knows his identity, does not know where to find him? In that case, the Uniform Parentage Act (Family Code § 7600 et seq.) will be used to identify, locate and terminate the parental rights of the father so that the adoption may go forward. Mothers sometimes do not put the Father's name on the child's Birth Certificate. This is irrelevant, as far as the Court is concerned, the Father, or the *presumed father,* must be notified if the child will be placed for adoption.

Family Code § 7662–7663 provide the parameters for a Petition to Terminate Parental Rights. These code sections also provide instructions for the Department of Social Services, or any other agency recognized by the Court, to complete an inquiry into the request for adoption as well as for the termination of parental rights.

Family Code § 7662 states:

7662. (a) If a mother relinquishes for or consents to, or proposes to relinquish for or consent to, the adoption of a child, or if a child otherwise becomes the subject of an adoption proceeding, the agency or person to whom the child has been or is to be relinquished, or the mother or the person having physical or legal custody of the child, or the prospective adoptive parent, shall file a petition to terminate the parental rights of the alleged father, unless one of the following occurs:

> (1) The alleged father's relationship to the child has been previously terminated or determined not to exist by a court.

> (2) The alleged father has been served as prescribed in Section 7666 with a written notice alleging that he is or could be the biological father of the child to be adopted or placed for adoption and has failed to bring an action for the purpose of declaring the existence of the father and child relationship pursuant to subdivision (c) of Section 7630 within 30 days of service of the notice or the birth of the child, whichever is later.

> (3) The alleged father has executed a written form developed by the department to waive notice, to deny his paternity, relinquish the child for adoption, or consent to the adoption of the child.

(b) The alleged father may validly execute a waiver or denial of paternity before or after the birth of the child, and once signed, no notice of, relinquishment for, or consent to adoption of the child shall be required from the alleged father for the adoption to proceed.

(c) All proceedings affecting a child under Divisions 8 (commencing with Section 3000) to 11 (commencing with Section 6500), inclusive, and Parts 1 (commencing with Section 7500) to 3 (commencing with Section 7600), inclusive, of this division, other than an action brought pursuant to this section, shall be stayed pending final determination of proceedings to terminate the parental rights of the alleged father pursuant to this section.

(d) Nothing in this section may limit the jurisdiction of the court pursuant to Part 3 (commencing with Section 6240) and Part 4 (commencing with Section 6300) of Division 10 with respect to domestic violence orders.

Family Code § 7663 states:

(a) In an effort to identify all alleged fathers and presumed parents, the court shall cause inquiry to be made of the mother and any other appropriate person by one of the following:

(1) The State Department of Social Services.

(2) A licensed county adoption agency.

(3) The licensed adoption agency to which the child is to be relinquished.

(4) In the case of a stepparent adoption, the licensed clinical social worker or licensed marriage and family therapist who is performing the investigation pursuant to Section 9001, if applicable. In the case of a stepparent adoption in which no licensed clinical social worker or licensed marriage and family therapist is performing the investigation pursuant to Section 9001, the board of supervisors may assign those inquiries to a licensed county adoption agency, the county department designated by the board of supervisors to administer the public social services program, or the county probation department.

(b) The inquiry shall include all of the following:

(1) Whether the mother was married at the time of conception of the child or at any time thereafter.

(2) Whether the mother was cohabiting with a man at the time of conception or birth of the child.

(3) Whether the mother has received support payments or promises of support with respect to the child or in connection with her pregnancy.

(4) Whether any person has formally or informally acknowledged or declared his or her possible parentage of the child.

(5) The names and whereabouts, if known, of every person presumed or man alleged to be the parent of the child, and the efforts made to give notice of the proposed adoption to each person identified.

(c) The agency that completes the inquiry shall file a written report of the findings with the court.

Family Code § 7664 states:

(a) If, after the inquiry, the biological father is identified to the satisfaction of the court, or if more than one man is identified as a possible biological father, notice of the proceeding shall be given in accordance with Section 7666. If any alleged biological father fails to appear or, if appearing, fails to claim parental rights, his parental rights with reference to the child shall be terminated.

(b) If the biological father or a man representing himself to be the biological father claims parental rights, the court shall determine if he is the biological father. The court shall then determine if it is in the best interest of the child that the biological father retain his parental rights, or that an adoption of the child be allowed to proceed. The court, in making that determination, may consider all relevant evidence, including the efforts made by the biological father to obtain custody, the age and prior placement of the child, and the effects of a change of placement on the child.

(c) If the court finds that it is in the best interest of the child that the biological father should be allowed to retain his parental rights, the court shall order that his consent is necessary for an adoption. If the court finds that the man claiming parental rights is not the biological father, or that if he is the biological father it is in the child's best interest that an adoption be allowed to proceed, the court shall order that the consent of that man is not required for an adoption. This finding terminates all parental rights and responsibilities with respect to the child.

Family Code § 7665 states:

If, after the inquiry, the court is unable to identify the biological father or any possible biological father and no person has appeared claiming to be the biological father and claiming custodial rights, the court shall enter an order terminating the unknown biological father's parental rights with reference to the child.

The primary factor to be considered by the Court, is what is in the best interest of the child(ren). Family Codes §§ 7800–7801 addresses what is in the best interests of the child.

Family Code § 7800 states:

The purpose of this part is to serve the welfare and best interest of a child by providing the stability and security of an adoptive home when those conditions are otherwise missing from the child's life.

Family Code § 7801 states:

This part shall be liberally construed to serve and protect the interests and welfare of the child.

Family Code § 7802 states:

A proceeding may be brought under this part for the purpose of having a minor child declared free from the custody and control of either or both parents.

There are specific references in the Family Code to termination of a parent's rights due to lack of contact with the child(ren) for over one year and/or non-payment of child support. The Court will usually go to great lengths to **not** terminate the parental rights of a natural parent, in hopes that the parent will become more active in the child's life. Read the following code section carefully, to determine the legislative intent, what evidence must be provided, and what determination the Court must make before it will allow the adoption to take place.

Family Code § 8604 provides as follows:

(a) Except as provided in subdivision (b), a child having a presumed father under Section 7611 may not be adopted without the consent of the child's birth parents, if living. The consent of a presumed father is not required for the child's adoption unless he became a presumed father as described in Chapter 1 (commencing with Section 7540) or Chapter 3 (commencing with Section 7570) of Part 2 of Division 12, or subdivision (a), (b), or (c) of Section 7611 before the mother's relinquishment or consent becomes irrevocable or before the mother's parental rights have been terminated.

(b) If one birth parent has been awarded custody by judicial order, or has custody by agreement of both parents, and the other birth parent for a period of one year willfully fails to communicate with and to pay for the care, support, and education of the child when able to do so, then the birth parent having sole custody may consent to the adoption, but only after the birth parent not having custody has been served with a copy of a citation in the manner provided by law for the service of a summons in a civil action that requires the birth parent not having custody to appear at the time and place set for the appearance in court under Section 8718, 8823, 8913, or 9007.

(c) Failure of a birth parent to pay for the care, support, and education of the child for the period of one year or failure of a birth parent to communicate with the child for the period of one year is prima facie evidence that the failure was willful and without lawful excuse. If the birth parent or parents have made only token efforts to support or communicate with the child, the court may disregard those token efforts.

Family Code § 8606 does provide for an adoption to take place without the birth parent(s) consent. Those criteria are as follows:

Notwithstanding Sections 8604 and 8605, the consent of a birth parent is not necessary in the following cases:

(a) Where the birth parent has been judicially deprived of the custody and control of the child (1) by a court order declaring the child to be free from the custody and control of either or both birth parents pursuant to Part 4 (commencing with Section 7800) of Division 12 of this code, or Section 366.25 or 366.26 of the Welfare and Institutions Code, or (2) by a similar order of a court of another jurisdiction, pursuant to a law of that jurisdiction authorizing the order.

(b) Where the birth parent has, in a judicial proceeding in another jurisdiction, voluntarily surrendered the right to the custody and control of the child pursuant to a law of that jurisdiction providing for the surrender.

(c) Where the birth parent has deserted the child without provision for identification of the child.

(d) Where the birth parent has relinquished the child for adoption as provided in Section 8700.

(e) Where the birth parent has relinquished the child for adoption to a licensed or authorized child-placing agency in another jurisdiction pursuant to the law of that jurisdiction.

The above Family Code Sections relate to adoption of minors and there are three methods of adopting a **minor**. These methods are: Agency, Independent and Stepparent adoptions. They are covered as Division 13, Part I, of the Family Code.

As a Family Law paralegal, you will most frequently be involved in Stepparent Adoptions of minor children. Therefore, that area will be covered more thoroughly than Agency and Independent adoptions.

You may find yourself working for an adoption agency or for a practitioner who handles independent adoptions. These types of adoptions are quite specialized and often require more documentation. The agency or practitioner may also have some specific guidelines and processes that they prefer to utilize. You should check with your supervising attorney first to determine what needs to be done for these types of cases. Practitioners who find themselves working with Agency adoptions, will usually let the agency prepare most of the documentation and will provide information and assistance as needed.

Additionally, as you may have read or heard on the news, these types of adoptions may require a "waiting" period before the child(ren) are formally declared as adopted by the "new" parents, or they may be disputed by birth parent(s) after the adoption has been finalized. Thus, many family law practitioners prefer not to deal with these types of adoptions. They can be time-consuming and emotionally draining. Such "media" type cases are usually the exception and not the rule, and an Adoption will be a very rewarding experience for any person working in this area of law.

The cost (filing fee) for an Adoption is quite reasonable—currently $25. However, depending upon the type of adoption the investigation fees, contractual and/or medical fees may be significant. In addition, there are usually minimal costs for certified copies of the Order, new Birth Certificates, etc.

Third Party Rights

Family Code § 3104(b) addresses a grandparent's right to file a petition for visitation when a child has been adopted by a stepparent.

Prior to the enactment of this statute, a grandparent had difficulty petitioning the court for visitation if the parents were divorced, while it was relatively simple if the natural parent had died. The statute essentially had two different standards for what was in the best interest of the child. This amendment provides that the standard should be the same regardless of whether the natural parent is deceased or has relinquished their parental rights. The standard required for all grandparent visitation petitions is whether the grandparent and grandchild have a "preexisting relationship" and that it is in the best interest of the child to continue the on-going contact.

Section 3104 was drafted to balance the often-conflicting values of parental autonomy an the child's interest in having a relationship with grandparents. (*Practice Under the California Family Code: Case and Legislation Highlights*, 2007, Continuing Education of the Bar, George Seide, Esq.) The "presumption that grandparent visitation is not in the best interest of the grandchild if both parents in an intact marriage object to that visitation remains unchanged." *Ibid.*

Controlling cases that lead to the enactment of this statute are:

Troxel v. Granville (2000) 530 U.S. 57, 147 L.Ed 2d 49, 120 S.Ct. 2054

Marriage of Harris (2004) 34 C4th 210, 17 CR 3d 842

Lopez v. Martinez (2000) 85 CA4th 279, 102 CR 2d 71

A more recent case in 2012 involved the adoption of a child by a same-sex couple; this case, is of interest and can be found at *L.M. v. M.G.* (2012) 208 CA4th 133, 145 CR3d 97.

Family Code § 3014(b) provides reference to the statutory guidelines governing a grandparent's right to file a petition for visitation when a child has been adopted by a stepparent, as discussed in Chapter Ten.

Agency Adoptions

In most instances, an agency will take care of all the required documentation, evidence and other information that is needed to complete the adoption process. The child will be *relinquished* to the agency by the birth mother. Family Code §8700 specifically grants the ability of the birth parent(s) to relinquish the child into the care of a licensed adoption agency. Once a child is placed in the agency's care, the agency will obtain the consents from the mother and presumed father and make sure that the child is "free" to be adopted. Alternatively, the agency will try to locate the presumed father to obtain his consent.

The agency's job is to place the child with adoptive parents. The birth parents may also name the person(s) who wish to adopt the child. The natural parent may specify a friend, sibling, other family member, or any other person as the adoption parent(s). Those persons will be subject to the same scrutiny as any other adoptive parent. Family Code §8700 et seq. sets forth the guidelines for designating specific person(s) to adopt the child through the licensed agency, including adoptions by foster parents and other caregivers.

You will want to make sure to use the current Judicial Council forms required for adoptions. It is also advisable to review local rules to determine if a particular county's Superior Court requires the use of the Judicial Council forms in all types of adoptions or if the Court prefers pleading forms for some types of adoptions and JCC forms for others. For your reference, the two formats are provided in this chapter.

An investigation of the adoptive parents is required for all persons wishing to adopt a minor child. A "home study" will be performed and the parties must be finger-printed to determine if there is any criminal history on the part of any adoptive parent. The home study will also include background information on the adoptive parents such as dates of birth, social security numbers, current and previous residences, current and previous employment, current earnings, any other children or persons who are residing in the home, schools that the child(ren) will be attending, the adoptive parents religious affiliation, if any, and any other information the investigator feels is relevant to the adoption.

An issue which may arise and which will need to be dealt with is whether the child is a Native American. If the child has Native American heritage, the tribe to which the child belongs must be notified of any request to adopt the child(ren). Because there are "tribal rights" which will need to be addressed if this is the case. (See: Indian Welfare Act, 25 U.S.C. §1901 et seq. for the Federal regulations governing adoptions of an Indian child and Family Code §8620.) The Tribal affiliation must be identified, and each family member must be notified. This issue **must be** addressed prior to going forward with any adoption proceedings. There are specific Judicial Council forms which were created and became mandatory effective January 1, 2005, to use for adoptions which involve a Native American child:

Adoption of an Indian Child (ADOPT-220)

Notice of Voluntary Adoption Proceedings for an Indian Child (ADOPT-226)

Parent of Indian Child Agrees to End Parental Rights (ADOPT-225)

The form ADOPT-220 is attached to the Petition for Adoption (ADOPT-200). The Notice is served by certified mail and all certified confirmations must be filed with the Court. The Judge must certify that the parent appeared and understands the significance of giving up the legal rights of the child, and of the tribe, and is doing so without duress or coercion.

The report will be prepared containing information as to whether the natural parents have consented to the adoption, and if not, why the consents have not been secured. The report will also contain information on the fingerprint results and will contain a recommendation to the Court as to whether the prospective adoptive parents should be allowed to adopt the child(ren).

If the report states that the adoption is **not** recommended, the parties should contact the agency and/or their attorney and decide how to go forward with the adoption or if the matter should be dropped.

Once a report with a positive recommendation has been received by the agency and/or attorney, the matter will be set for hearing. The prospective adoptive parents and the child(ren) will attend the hearing, at which time, the Judge will enter the Decree and Order for Adoption. The Decree and Order will also state whether the name of the child(ren) is to be changed. As you will see from the Judicial Council forms, the Petitioner(s) have the option of leaving the child's name or changing it. The Judge will make the Orders based on the original pleading (or prayer) of the adopting parents.

Independent Adoption

Family Code §§ 8800–8823 provide the instructions for Independent Adoptions. Independent adoptions are those which are arranged by individual parties with the prospective parents, usually with the assistance of an attorney. If you are working in a firm who does Independent adoptions, you will want to become very familiar with these code sections as well as with your firm's procedures for working on these types of cases. The practitioner who works in the arena of Independent adoptions is often referred to as an Adoption Facilitator.

In most cases, the birth mother or parents will make the initial contact with the prospective parent(s). The attorney will then prepare all of the documents for the agreement. As discussed in the section above, the adoptive parents must be interviewed by the county or other agency that is mandated to perform investigative evaluations for adoptions.

The investigator will submit a report to the Court along with their recommendation. Once the child is born and the prospective parents have been approved by the Court, the Court will issue a decree for the adoption at the subsequent hearing.

Independent Adoptions are most often contractual in nature. The birth parent may agree to adopt in exchange for medical and hospital expenses relative to the pregnancy and birth of the child. Alternatively, the adoptive parent(s) may pay a fee to the birth mother (and/or father). Independent Adoptions may also include contractual agreements between a surrogate mother who is "carrying" the child for a Mother who is unable to carry her own child to term.

If your firm does Independent Adoptions, as a paralegal, you will likely be involved in drafting the contract between the parties.

You should review the sections of the Family Code covering adoptions as they have been changed with regard to the "sealing" or records and the children's ability to obtain information about their birth parents when they turn eighteen.

Stepparent Adoption

As a family law paralegal, the stepparent adoption is the process in which you will most likely be involved. This type of adoption will typically occur when a stepparent has bonded with the spouse's children, where the natural parent does not have any significant part in the child(ren)'s life, and/or where the stepparent wishes to treat the child as his/her own, including but not limited to last name and rights as an heir. As indicated in Family Code §8604, if a parent has wilfully not contacted a child for at least a year and where the parent has not paid in support, the Court **may** terminate the parental rights of that parent.

Stepparent adoptions guidelines can be found in Family Code §§9000–9007.

When the parents come to your office stating that the stepparent wants to adopt the child(ren), the first thing you will want to do is to determine if you can locate the biological parent. As previously indicated, the child must be considered "free" to be adopted. As part of the adoption process, a Petition for Termination of Parental Rights will have to be filed with the Court. A hearing date will be set and a Citation (notice to appear) will also need to be issued by the Clerk. It will then be served on the parent. The biological parent is given an opportunity either to consent or to object. In the event the biological parent objects, the parent can request a court-appointed attorney for legal representation. If the parent fails to appear at the hearing the Judge can terminate the parental rights based on what the Court feels is in the best interests of the child(ren). Examples of the forms needed to Terminate Parental Rights are found at Appendix 11A–C.

As previously indicated in Chapter Ten, the court ruled in 2006 that it is against public policy to terminate one parent's rights unless there is a "contemplated stepparent or second parent adoption." *Marriage of Jackson* (2006) 136 CA4th 980, 39 CR3d 365; *Kristine M. v. David P.* (2006) 135 CA4th 783, 37 CR3d 748.

Keep in mind that some Judges will interpret FC§8604 very strictly with regard to terminating parental rights. They will go to great lengths to require that the parent whose rights will be terminated be given proper notice. As set forth in CCP§415.10 (Service of Summons) as discussed in Chapter Two, "Types of Service," if a person cannot be located the person may be served by publication in the county where he/she were last known to reside. It has been my experience that when it comes to terminating parental rights, Judges are reluctant to allow a Citation to be published. If this is the case, the client may have to enroll the services of a private investigator to locate the natural parent. This can be time-consuming and costly, especially if you are dealing with parents who do not want to be found, because he/she has warrants for their arrest, owe taxes and/or child support arrears. Such person may be doing everything in their power **not** to be found.

Immediately after the filing of the Request for Adoption and the Agreement of Adoption if the child is over the age of twelve (12) years, with the Court, you should contact the agency in your county which completes the investigation process. In some Counties, the Court will automatically forward a copy of the Petition to that agency. In other Counties, it will be your responsibility to take care of this step. You will want to check your local rules to determine the proper procedure.

Even if the Court forwards the Petition to the agency, it is always a good idea to follow up and make sure the agency received it. This will also give you the opportunity to determine which case-worker will be visiting the family and preparing the report. It also allows you to introduce yourself to the various case workers in the agency and open communications with them. It is often helpful for the caseworker to also have a contact person at the law firm in the event they run into problems such as not being able to contact the family for the interview. You may also need to provide more information, such as the contact and background information for the biological parent, as the investigator will be required to attempt contact with that person. This contact will also give you the opportunity to determine how long it is taking the agency to complete the investigative process and write the report. It is always best if you can give the client a time-frame for when the hearing might be held and the subsequent order issued. You don't want to set a hearing date and notice all "interested" parties, only to find out that the investigative report will not be complete until after the hearing date. This causes undue stress on the client.

Imagine clients who contact your office in June to complete the stepparent adoption, hoping that by the time the child goes to school in August and/or for soccer sign-ups, they will have a new birth certificate showing the adoptive parent's name and the child's new name. You prepare all the necessary documents: Petition for Adoption, Consents, Petition for Termination, Citation, etc. and set the matter for hearing for July. You serve all of the documents as required and the natural parent even signs the consent. However, the investigator is so far behind that he or she can't even schedule an appointment to meet the family until early September.

The clients are going to be very anxious and upset because they believed that it will all be done when school started. Although they will be disappointed, it is much better to inform them from the beginning about the procedures and the time frame for the process, so they won't be calling you daily asking about the report. It will also keep them from being angry at you and your office for the delay. The above scenario is also one where everything goes smoothly. Imagine the delay, disappointment and anxiety if you are unable to locate the natural parent and that person files an objection or finds some other way of delaying the procedure.

At the end of the chapter you will find both the Judicial Council forms and the pleading forms for the Adoption as follows: Adoption Request: ADOPT-200; Adoption Agreement: ADOPT-210; Adoption Order: ADOPT-215. An optional form Adoption Expenses (ADOPT-230) may also be used as needed. Also included are the pleading forms for these documents in the event your particular county has a preference for a certain type of pleading in their local rules. Also included is a Citation, a Petition for Termination of Parental Rights and an Order Determining the Child Free for Adoption.

As discussed under Agency adoption, the stepparent adoption investigative report will contain the same type of information. The report will, likewise, contain a recommendation as to whether or not the stepparent should be allowed to adopt the child(ren). The report will also contain information as to whether the Petition to Terminate Parental Rights was filed and properly served, if the natural parent has been contacted to sign the consent, and/or if the investigator anticipates that the natural parent will file an objection or plans to **not** appear at the hearing. The stepparent is responsible for paying for the report and will be billed when the report is complete. The stepparent should be made aware of this so the bill doesn't catch them by surprise. It is always a good idea to ask the investigator what the "going rate" is for the reports so that you can advise the stepparent, who will in turn, budget for this expense.

Upon receipt of a copy of the Report, a hearing date should be scheduled. In most cases the original will have been sent to the Court. The clients should be notified of the date, time and department where the hearing will be taking place. The child(ren) should also be present at the hearing. If an adoptive child is over the age of twelve (12), the

Judge will ask that the child(ren) to sign the Consent during the hearing. The family should be dressed nicely for the occasion as the Judge will be pleased to have a group picture taken on the "happy" day in his or her chambers.

At this stage, one of the paralegal's functions is to make sure that all of the documents have been submitted and that the attorney takes enough copies of the consents to be signed in the Judge's chambers, as well as the Decree and Order. The attorney will also want to take a firm check, or request that the client bring their checkbook, so that **certified** copies of the Order can be obtained while at the courthouse. This will eliminate time later when obtaining a certified copy in order to change the birth certificate. There may also be others, such as the child's school, who will require that you provide them with a copy of the certified Order.

You will also want to make sure that the forms required by the Department of Health Services, Vital Statistics Division are completed correctly and signed by the parents so that the **new** birth certificate can be issued in a timely manner.

Other Considerations When Adopting a Minor

In situations where there is a contractual agreement between the parties, or where a family member is adopting the child, the parties may agree to allow contact between the adopted child and the natural parent(s). In that case, a Contract After Adoption Agreement (ADOPT-310) should be completed and filed with the Court.

In some situations, the parties to the adoption may need to either enforce, change or terminate the contractual agreement. There are three forms created by the Judicial Council for those situations. They are as follows: Request to Enforce, Change, End Contract After Adoption Agreement (ADOPT-315); Answer to Request to Enforce, Change, End Contract After Adoption Agreement (ADOPT-320); and, Judge's Order to Enforce Change, End Contract After Adoption Agreement (ADOPT-325). All of the forms are very "user friendly" and give detail as to what is required for this procedure. Essentially, a hearing will be set, the parties will be noticed, evidence will be presented at the hearing, culminating with the Judge making Orders, which will either enforce, change or terminate the contract.

Adult Adoption

The final type of adoption is an "adult" adoption, rather than the adoption of minors in the various ways discussed above. This method of adoption is found in the Family Code Chapter 13, Part II (FC §§ 9300-9340).

One might find it odd that there is a process for Adult adoptions. There are actually a number of reasons why an adult would adopt another "adult." Most adults will adopt a "child" whom they have raised as if the child were their own in order to formalize their familial relationship. A child who was raised by a stepparent, and who was unable to obtain consent from the natural parent, can simply wait until the "child" is over the age of 18 and able to consent him/herself. The child then receives all the rights of a "child" of that person including the right to be an heir to the parent's estate. Another advantage of the adoption at this stage is to receive health and other employee benefits of the adoptive parent. Additionally, in the types of adoptions of a minor, as described above, the adult must be at least ten (10) years older than the minor. This is not true in adult adoptions. The adoptive parent must simply be **older** than the adoptee.

An example of an adult adoption may involve the following scenario:

Mother has two children from a previous marriage and remarries. The step-father wishes to adopt the children, but the natural father refuses to consent to the adoption although he has little contact with the children and has never paid support. While married and while the children are under 18, the step-father can include his wife and the children on his health, dental and vision plan through his place of employment. However, once the child turns 18 and is no longer in high school, the step-father often cannot continue to carry the child(ren) on his health plan. (There are some exceptions allowed on various plans and the plan administrator should be consulted by the parent to determine when the "child" is no longer eligible.) The Mother and step-father want the child(ren) to attend college, but are concerned that the child may not be covered by health insurance while he/she is attending college. The parents and child agree that they have a long-standing familial relationship and that it is in everyone's best interest that the step-father adopt the child(ren) so that the relationship can continue. The adoption will also allow "father" to continue to maintain the child(ren) on his insurance plan(s) until the child(ren) has completed college or turned 23, whichever occurs first. (Again, the plan administrator should be consulted to determine the exact parameters for coverage for a child attending college, as plans could differ.)

Adult adoptions involve a much simpler process than adoptions of a minor. The significant differences are: 1) the adoptive parent does not have to be **more** than 10 years older than the adoptee (person they are adopting), they only have to be older; 2) both the adoptive parent and the adoptee will sign an adoption agreement and consents; and 3) the adoptee may, but does not have to, change his/her name and/or the birth certificate.

Note: If the adoptee is married, that person's spouse must also sign a consent.

Family Code §9320 et seq. provide the criteria and instructions for obtaining an adult adoption.

(Note: the code section below also contains provisions for adopting a person who is developmentally disabled.)

(a) An adult may adopt another adult who is younger, except the spouse of the prospective adoptive parent, by an adoption agreement approved by the court, as provided in this chapter.

(b) The adoption agreement shall be in writing, executed by the prospective adoptive parent and the proposed adoptee, and shall state that the parties agree to assume toward each other the legal relationship of parent and child and to have all of the rights and be subject to all of the duties and responsibilities of that relationship.

Family Code §9327 states:

(a) The prospective adoptive parent and the proposed adoptee may file in the county in which either person resides a petition for approval of the adoption agreement.

(b) The petition for approval of the adoption agreement shall state all of the following:

(1) The length and nature of the relationship between the prospective adoptive parent and the proposed adoptee.

(2) The degree of kinship, if any.

(3) The reason the adoption is sought.

(4) A statement as to why the adoption would be in the best interest of the prospective adoptive parent, the proposed adoptee, and the public.

(5) The names and addresses of any living birth parents or adult children of the proposed adoptee.

(6) Whether the prospective adoptive parent or the prospective adoptive parent's spouse has previously adopted any other adult and, if so, the name of the adult, together with the date and place of the adoption.

Family Code § 9322 states:

When the petition for approval of the adoption agreement is filed, the court clerk shall set the matter for hearing.

Family Code § 9323 states:

The court may require notice of the time and place of the hearing to be served on any other interested person and any interested person may appear and object to the proposed adoption.

Family Code § 9324 states:

Both the prospective adoptive parent and the proposed adoptee shall appear at the hearing in person, unless an appearance is impossible, in which event an appearance may be made for either or both of the persons by counsel, empowered in writing to make the appearance.

Family Code § 9325 states:

No investigation or report to the court by any public officer or agency is required, but the court may require the county probation officer or the department to investigate the circumstances of the proposed adoption and report thereon, with recommendations, to the court before the hearing.

Family Code § 9326 states:

The prospective adoptive parent shall mail or personally serve notice of the hearing and a copy of the petition to the director of the regional center for the developmentally disabled, established pursuant to Chapter 5 (commencing with Section 4620) of Division 4.5 of the Welfare and Institutions Code, and to any living birth parents or adult children of the proposed adoptee, at least 30 days before the day of the hearing on an adoption petition in any case in which both of the following conditions exist:

(a) The proposed adoptee is an adult with developmental disabilities.

(b) The prospective adoptive parent is a provider of board and care, treatment, habilitation, or other services to persons with developmental disabilities or is a spouse or employee of a provider.

Note: The above code section states the "adoptive parent shall mail or personally serve." As a matter of technicality, the adoptive parent will cause to be served the necessary documents. As in all legal matters, a party to the action cannot serve, but must have someone else serve for them.

Family Code § 9327 states:

If the prospective adoptive parent is a provider of board and care, treatment, habilitation, or other services to persons with developmental disabilities, or is a spouse or employee of a provider, and seeks to adopt an unrelated adult with developmental disabilities, the regional center for the developmentally disabled notified pursuant to Section 9326 shall file a written report with the court regarding the suitability of the proposed adoption in meeting the needs of the proposed adoptee and regarding any known previous adoption by the prospective adoptive parent.

Family Code § 9328 states:

(a) At the hearing the court shall examine the parties, or the counsel of any party not present in person.

(b) If the court is satisfied that the adoption will be in the best interests of the persons seeking the adoption and in the public interest and that there is no reason why the petition should not be granted, the court shall approve the adoption agreement and make an order of adoption declaring that the person adopted is the child of the adoptive parent. Otherwise, the court shall withhold approval of the agreement and deny the petition.

(c) In determining whether or not the adoption of any person pursuant to this part is in the best interests of the persons seeking the adoption or the public interest, the court may consider evidence, oral or written, whether or not it is in conformity with the Evidence Code.

The Judicial Council adoption forms, in most cases, are not practical for Adult Adoptions and the court will prefer that you use the pleading format. You should, therefore, check your local rules or with the Clerk at the Court to determine whether the Court requires Judicial Council forms, pleading forms, or a combination of the two.

If your office handles any type of adoption you should carefully read and be familiar with the Family Code Sections which relate to adoptions. The statutes can be found in their entirety at Division 13. Review the local rules, as well as the Judicial Council forms for frequent changes. See Appendix 11 B–F for Adoption (pleading) forms.

Pre-Marital and Post-Marital Agreements

Pre-Marital and Post-Marital Agreements are similar in nature to the Marital Settlement Agreement. Their purpose is to create a contract which incorporates the rights, remedies and manner in which property is to be distributed upon the dissolution of the marriage of the parties. Many people's response to the concept of these agreements is to question why "get married" if you are already deciding how the property is going to be divided?

First, let's discuss the concept of these agreements or contracts. A premarital agreement is simply an agreement which is executed prior to the marriage. A post-marital agreement is one that is executed after the marriage has taken place.

Premarital agreements are governed by Family Code § 1600 et seq, known as the Uniform Pre-marital Agreement Act ("UPAA"). The UPAA specifically states that it does not "promote" dissolution of marriage. The agreement's purpose is to protect and maintain property that is to be considered the separate property of an individual spouse. It also places limitations on what property may be considered community property once the parties are married and begin acquiring property as a couple. There are also other considerations such as the fiduciary responsibilities of spouses to each other, as discussed in Chapter Four. Waivers of child support and spousal support are not allowed (see *Bonds* and *Pendleton & Fireman* exceptions below) as they are against public policy.

Post-marital agreements are essentially the same as the pre-marital agreements. The only difference is that once the parties are married, there is a "higher" standard of fiduciary responsibility owed a spouse than there is to a potential spouse. While either party may change the characterization of any of their property, at any time and in any manner, a post-marital agreement will require that when the parties wish to change the character of any property, causing a transmutation of the property (see Chapter Seven), then they **must** do so in writing. These types of agreements make it imperative that any changes in property conform with the agreement, or the changes are unlikely to be upheld, should the parties seek a divorce later.

Both types of agreements are primarily governed in the same manner as would a "normal" contract. However, in certain instances, the Family Code must be considered where any provisions of the contact would violate public policy, such as child support and spousal support. The statutes which must be considered in these instances are Family Code §§ 720, 4300 and 4301.

Of primary importance in drafting either of these agreements, is the fact that **full and complete** disclosure **must** be made by each party. That is, both parties **must** provide a complete listing of **all** of their assets and debts and income to each other. Oftentimes, attorneys will require that each party prepare an Income & Expense Declaration and a Schedule of Assets and Debts and provide it to (or even serve it) on the other party.

Back to the question of why get married if you are already going to "divide" the property. These agreements do not infer that the parties will **never** have any community property. They are simply created to specify any property that may be considered strictly separate by that individual as he/she enters the marriage or receives non-marital property. Also, it does not mean that at a later date the property cannot be liquidated by the spouse or that it cannot be transmuted and changed to community property. The agreement is to require that the parties transfer property in the correct manner in order to protect their interests should they eventually divorce.

In today's world, these agreements are becoming more common. Consider the following:

> Husband and Wife have both previously been married and have children from those previous marriages. When they met, each party had a home. They each received certain assets from their previous marriages as well have accumulated assets along the way since that time. Regardless of their actual "wealth," they want to make sure that their children inherit what they are entitled to should they pass away. Rather than place everything into a big pot as community property, they want to maintain some sense of what is separate for the sake of their respective children.

> What if one party has children and the other doesn't? The party who has children will want **his/her** separate property to be inherited eventually by his/her children.

The party who does not have children wants his/her property to go to whomever he/she determines should have it. If all the property is considered community property and the party without children dies first, that property will likely go to the spouse. Upon the second spouse's death, the property would go to his/her children. This may be what the spouses want, but what if it isn't and they have not executed a Will or Trust to specify their wishes.

Once married, the couple may begin to attain additional property as community property, which, upon divorce or death, will be treated as community property by either family law or the probate code, whichever applies. However, the property that was maintained as separate property will either be retained by that individual upon a divorce or will be distributed pursuant to the spouse's will or the laws of intestate succession.

The parties are also free to transmute the property, but they must do so knowingly and in writing so that there is never a question as to a future interest or the reason that the property was transferred. For instance, if each spouse liquidates stocks or other assets at an equal rate and then the spouses purchase a vacation home, as community property, they have reduced their respective separate property assets in favor of community property. They will have to do so, knowingly and in writing.

It is **always** against public policy to waive child support. (See Chapter Three and the responsibility as set forth in FC§ 3900 with regard to support of one's children.) Spousal support has historically held the same result. However, case law has changed the way the court interprets whether spousal support can be waived.

Family Code § 1610 et seq states as follows:

(a) "Premarital agreement" means an agreement between prospective spouses made in contemplation of marriage and to be effective upon marriage.

(b) "Property" means an interest, present or future, legal or equitable, vested or contingent, in real or personal property, including income and earnings.

Family Code § 1611 states:

A premarital agreement shall be in writing and signed by both parties. It is enforceable without consideration.

Family Code § 1612 states:

(a) Parties to a premarital agreement may contract with respect to all of the following:

(1) The rights and obligations of each of the parties in any of the property of either or both of them whenever and wherever acquired or located.

(2) The right to buy, sell, use, transfer, exchange, abandon, lease, consume, expend, assign, create a security interest in, mortgage, encumber, dispose of, or otherwise manage and control property.

(3) The disposition of property upon separation, marital dissolution, death, or the occurrence or nonoccurrence of any other event.

(4) The making of a will, trust, or other arrangement to carry out the provisions of the agreement.

(5) The ownership rights in a disposition of the death benefit from a life insurance policy.

(6) The choice of law governing the construction of the agreement.

(7) Any other matter, including their personal rights and obligations, not in violation of public policy or a statute imposing a criminal penalty.

(b) The right of a child to support may not be adversely affected by a premarital agreement.

(c) Any provision in a premarital agreement regarding spousal support, including, but not limited to, a waiver of it, is not enforceable if the party against whom enforcement of the spousal support provision is sought was not represented by independent counsel at the time the agreement containing the provision was signed, or if the provision regarding spousal support is unconscionable at the time of enforcement. An otherwise unenforceable provision in a premarital agreement regarding spousal support may not become enforceable solely because the party against whom enforcement is sought was represented by independent counsel.

As set forth in Family Code § 6413, a premarital agreement becomes effective upon marriage.

Family Code § 6414, states:

After marriage, a premarital agreement may be amended or revoked only by a written agreement signed by the parties. The amended agreement or the revocation is enforceable without consideration.

Family Code § 6415, states:

(a) A premarital agreement is not enforceable if the party against whom enforcement is sought proves either of the following:

(1) That party did not execute the agreement voluntarily.

(2) The agreement was unconscionable when it was executed and, before execution of the agreement, all of the following applied to that party: (A) That party was not provided a fair, reasonable, and full disclosure of the property or financial obligations of the other party. (B) That party did not voluntarily and expressly waive, in writing, any right to disclosure of the property or financial obligations of the other party beyond the disclosure provided. (C) That party did not have, or reasonably could not have had, an adequate knowledge of the property or financial obligations of the other party.

(b) An issue of unconscionability of a premarital agreement shall be decided by the court as a matter of law.

(c) For the purposes of subdivision (a), it shall be deemed that a premarital agreement was not executed voluntarily unless the court finds in writing or on the record all of the following:

(1) The party against whom enforcement is sought was represented by independent legal counsel at the time of signing the agreement or, after being advised to seek independent legal counsel, expressly waived, in a separate writing, representation by independent legal counsel.

(2) The party against whom enforcement is sought had not less than seven calendar days between the time that party was first presented with the agreement and advised to seek independent legal counsel and the time the agreement was signed.

(3) The party against whom enforcement is sought, if unrepresented by legal counsel, was fully informed of the terms and basic effect of the agreement as well

as the rights and obligations he or she was giving up by signing the agreement, and was proficient in the language in which the explanation of the party's rights was conducted and in which the agreement was written. The explanation of the rights and obligations relinquished shall be memorialized in writing and delivered to the party prior to signing the agreement. The unrepresented party shall, on or before the signing of the premarital agreement, execute a document declaring that he or she received the information required by this paragraph and indicating who provided that information.

(4) The agreement and the writings executed pursuant to paragraphs (1) and (3) were not executed under duress, fraud, or undue influence, and the parties did not lack capacity to enter into the agreement.

(5) Any other factors the court deems relevant.

The Court found in *Hill v. Dittmer* (2011) 202 CA4th 1046, 136 CR3d 700 that the "five findings" established when Family Code § 1615 was amended in 2002 are not retroactive to agreements made prior to that time.

There are two cases which have had a significant impact upon the way pre-marital agreements and post-marital agreements are drafted and what information **must** be included. These two cases are primarily responsible for the amendments, and five findings referenced above, that occurred in 2002.

In re Marriage of Bonds (2000) 24 C4th 1, 99 CR2d 252

Family Code § 1615 governs the enforceability of premarital agreements. FC§ 1615(c)(4) specifically states that "none of the writings can be executed under duress, fraud, or undue influence." The Courts, prior to *Bonds*, interpreted the time frame for "duress" and "undue influence" to be at least six months prior to the marriage. Full disclosure of all assets is imperative in pre and post marital agreements for them to be enforceable.

The Court considered the following factors in *Bonds*:

1) how many days prior to the marriage was the agreement executed;

2) did the party know about the agreement in advance;

3) did the party have an opportunity to have independent counsel review the agreement;

4) was full disclosure made;

5) was there a "confidential" relationship (were the parties already co-habitating)

One of the specific questions in *Bonds* was whether the earnings and/or contributions to earnings made by one spouse can be considered the sole and separate property of that party. The specific reference to the contract follows:

10. CONTROL AND EARNINGS OF BOTH HUSBAND AND WIFE DURING MARRIAGE. We agree that all the earnings and accumulations resulting from the other's personal services, skill, efforts and work, together with all property acquired with funds and income derived therefrom, shall be the separate property of that spouse.

The Court spent a great deal of time reviewing the above portion of the contract as it would mean that Susann (Sun) Bonds would have no community interest in Barry Bonds' very large contract with the San Francisco Giants. The Court also went into great detail about the evidence that was provided by either party's attorney and how it related to the decision. Upon reviewing the case, you will have some feel for the amount of time and effort that goes into this type of case, should a pre-marital agreement be contested.

The Court made the following determinations:

- Was the party "against whom the agreement is asserted" represented by legal counsel or, after being advised in writing to seek such counsel, in a separate writing expressly waived such representation;

- Did the party have an opportunity to review the document for at least seven calendar days before it was signed; and,

- If the party was unrepresented, were the party fully informed in writing, in a language in which the party was proficient, of the terms and basic effects of the agreement and made written acknowledgment of the receipt and understanding of this information.

Family Code § 1615(c) was amended in 2001, and the amended language of this statute overrules much of the *Bonds* decision. Also, there is a question of whether this ruling and the subsequent statute changes apply to agreements made after January 1, 1986, and the Uniform Premarital Agreement Act.

In re Marriage of Pendleton & Fireman (2000) 24 C4th 39, 99 CR2d 278

The Trial Court ruled that the premarital agreement, which waived spousal support, was unenforceable as it is against public policy. The Supreme Court held that if the parties voluntarily enter into a premarital agreement, wherein spousal support is waived, and they are fully aware of the effects of that waiver and agreement, there is no violation of public policy. The Court held that public policy is **not** "violated by permitting enforcement of a waiver of spousal support executed by intelligent, well-educated persons, each of whom is self-sufficient in property and earning ability, and both of whom had the advice of counsel regarding their rights and obligations as marital partners at the time they executed the waiver."

The result of *Pendleton & Fireman* for family law practitioners who draft pre or post marital agreements is that when a waiver of spousal support is included, it is necessary to specifically establish on what basis support was waived. For example, do the spouses own property and/or have earning sufficient capacity of their own.

The *Pendleton & Fireman* case also discussed the common law assumption that dissolving a marriage is against public policy and thus, whether or not premarital agreements encouraged people to dissolve their marriage. The Court found that "permanency is no longer a dominant characteristic of marriage" and, therefore, premarital agreements do not necessarily "promote divorce."

A 2006 case also addressed issues with respect to post-marital agreements. *Marriage of Burkle* (2006) 139 CA4th 712, 43 CR3d 181 held that a post nuptial agreement does not require statutory disclosures as do pre-nuptial, marital settlement and separation agreements.

Many family law practitioners draft pre-marital and post-marital agreements. In drafting these agreements, however, the practitioner needs to be very careful in reviewing the UPAA and the above cited cases. Some of the things that you are going to want to make sure are done correctly follows:

1) Full Disclosure—Make sure that **each** party completes and exchanges all asset, debt, and income information. Judicial Council form FL-150, Income & Expense Declarations; and FL-142, Schedule of Assets and Debts, may be used. The attorney will advise you concerning the method he or she prefers to complete the disclosure process.

2) Coercion or Duress—How much notice was given to each party to review the document prior to the marriage. The Court has historically questioned agreements that were signed weeks, days, or hours prior to the marriage ceremony. It can easily be construed by the Court as duress, if a party signed the agreement just before the marriage took place. As a result the Court has long held that the parties should have a proposed pre-marital agreement for review at least six (6) months prior to the date of marriage. More recently however, the Court has considered seven (7) days to be the standard as to the party's knowledge of the agreement and the opportunity to meet with independent counsel to review the agreement.

3) Attorney Review—Did the party (who did not cause the agreement to be drafted) have ample opportunity to have an attorney review and discuss the agreement with the party? Did the party know what he/she was signing? Did the attorney advise the party of the ramifications of signing the agreement and waiving certain rights? Did that attorney sign the agreement stating that he/she reviewed and discussed the agreement with the party? Or, did the attorney refuse to sign the agreement, and if so why?

4) Did the party knowingly waive the right to have an attorney review the agreement?

5) Was there a waiver of spousal support? If so, does the party (or parties) have property and or a means of support if a dissolution of marriage should take place?

It may also be in the firm's best interest to document all the time and effort that was utilized in drafting such an agreement should the "contract" be questioned and the firm should also disclose the time spent in making sure the client and "other party" was aware of the contents and ramifications of the signing the agreement.

During the period when both *Bonds* and *Pendleton* were being considered by the Supreme Court, many practitioners were hesitant to draft these types of agreements until the decisions were reported. Attorneys were not sure how the Courts' decisions were going to affect the drafting of future contracts. Both decisions were issued on the **same** day and neither changed the true nature of pre-marital and post-marital agreements. These cases simply reiterated the care that must be taken in disclosure as well as clarifying the responsibilities and the standards under which each party will be held should they divorce after having signed a pre or post-marital agreement.

In re Marriage of Rosendale (2004) S126908 (G031925; 119 CA.4th, 1202, 15 CR3d, 137; Orange County Superior Court; 00D000542.) dealt with the issue of premarital agreements, as follows:

Petition for review after the Court of Appeal affirmed in part and reversed in part an order in a marital dissolution action. This case includes the following issue: May a waiver of spousal support in a premarital agreement be found unenforceable on the ground that enforcement of the waiver would be unconscionable at the time enforcement of the waiver is sought, when (1) the waiver is contained in an agreement entered into before the effective date of the recently enacted Family Code section 1612, subdivision (c), (2) the waiver was negotiated by the parties, and (3) both parties to the premarital agreement were represented by counsel?

Additionally, in *Rosendale*, the Court of Appeal interpreted a provision for a payment on dissolution as being unrelated to spousal support and not a lump sum intended as an "alternative" method of providing spousal support. The court also addressed the retroactivity of *Pendleton & Fireman* and the effect of the 2002 amendment to Family Code § 1612. For more information on *Bonds* please see Appendix 11-J.

A sample pre-marital agreement is included as Appendix 11-I. ***Please note that this is only an example and should not be construed as legal advice. An attorney should be consulted prior to drafting any pre-marital or post-marital agreement.***

Some of the forms referenced in areas of law discussed in this chapter are contained at the end of the chapter for your reference. Others can be found in the Appendix, as referenced.

Forms Associated with Topic

Petition—Domestic Partnership (FL-103)

Response—Domestic Partnership (FL-123)

Judgment (FL-180)

Adoption Request (FL-200)

Adoption Agreement (FL-210)

Adoption Order (FL-215)

Joint Petition for Summary Dissolution of Marriage (FL-800)

Notice of Revocation of Petition for Summary Dissolution (FL-830)

Request for Judgment, Judgment of Dissolution of Marriage, and Notice of Entry Judgment (FL-820)

(See examples of some forms on the following pages)

Key Terms

- Guardianship
- Conservatorship
- Emancipation
- Domestic Partnership
- Adult Adoption
- Agency Adoption
- Stepparent Adoption
- Independent Adoption
- Paternity
- Premarital Agreement
- Post-marital Agreement
- *Marriage of Bonds*

- *Marriage of Pendleton & Fireman*
- Unconscionability
- Fiduciary Responsibility
- Cohabitation Agreement
- Termination of Parental Rights

Petition—Domestic Partnership/Marriage

FL-103

ATTORNEY OR PARTY WITHOUT ATTORNEY *(Name, State Bar number, and address):*	FOR COURT USE ONLY
	To keep other people from seeing what you entered on your form, please press the Clear This Form button at the end of the form when finished.

TELEPHONE NO. :   FAX NO. *(Optional):*

E-MAIL ADDRESS *(Optional):*

ATTORNEY FOR *(Name):*

SUPERIOR COURT OF CALIFORNIA, COUNTY OF

STREET ADDRESS:

MAILING ADDRESS:

CITY AND ZIP CODE:

BRANCH NAME:

☐ DOMESTIC PARTNERSHIP OF   ☐ MARRIAGE OF

PETITIONER:

RESPONDENT:

PETITION FOR	☐ AMENDED	CASE NUMBER:
☐ Dissolution of ☐ Domestic Partnership ☐ Marriage		
☐ Legal Separation of ☐ Domestic Partnership ☐ Marriage		
☐ Nullity of ☐ Domestic Partnership ☐ Marriage		

NOTICE: If petitioner and respondent are of the same sex, use this form. If petitioner and respondent are of the opposite sex and are *not* also domestic partners, use form FL-100.

1. STATISTICAL FACTS
   a. ☐ (1) Registration date of domestic partnership with the California Secretary of State or other state equivalent:
       (2) Date of separation:
       (3) Time from date of registration of domestic partnership to date of separation *(specify):*   Years   Months
   b. ☐ (1) Date of marriage: (2) Date of separation:
       (3) Time from date of marriage to date of separation *(specify):*   Years   Months

2. RESIDENCE *(check all that apply)*
   a. ☐ Our domestic partnership was established in California. Neither of us has to be a resident or have a domicile in California to dissolve our partnership here.
   b. ☐ Our domestic partnership was established in a place other than California. ☐ Petitioner ☐ Respondent has been a resident of the state of California for at least six months and of this county for at least three months immediately preceding the filing of this *Petition.*
   c. ☐ We are the same sex and are married. ☐ We are the opposite sex and are married. We are also domestic partners. ☐ Petitioner ☐ Respondent has been a resident of the state of California for at least six months and of this county for at least three months immediately preceding the filing of this *Petition.*
   d. ☐ We are the same sex and were married in California but are not residents of California. Neither of us lives in a state or nation that will dissolve the marriage. This case is filed in the county in which we married.
       Petitioner's residence *(state or nation):*   Respondent's residence *(state or nation):*

3. DECLARATION REGARDING MINOR CHILDREN *(include children of this relationship born or adopted prior to or during this domestic partnership or marriage)*
   a. ☐ There are no minor children.
   b. ☐ The minor children are

Child's name	Birthdate	Age	Sex

☐ Continued on Attachment 3b.

   c. If there are minor children of the petitioner and respondent, a completed *Declaration Under Uniform Child Custody Jurisdiction and Enforcement Act (UCCJEA)* (form FL-105) must be attached.

NOTICE: You may redact (black out) social security numbers from any written material filed with the court in this case other than a form used to collect child or partner support.

Form Adopted for Mandatory Use
Judicial Council of California
FL-103 [Rev. January 1, 2013]

PETITION—DOMESTIC PARTNERSHIP/MARRIAGE
(Family Law)

Page 1 of 2

Family Code, §§ 297, 299, 2320, 2330
www.courts.ca.gov

Petition—Domestic Partnership/Marriage

Petitioner:	CASE NUMBER:
Respondent:	

4. DECLARATION REGARDING SEPARATE PROPERTY AS CURRENTLY KNOWN
   a. ☐ There are no such assets or debts subject to disposition by the court in this proceeding.
   b. ☐ All such assets and debts listed are listed in ☐ *Property Declaration* (form FL-160) ☐ Attachment 4b
   and should be confirmed as petitioner's or respondent's separate property as indicated in form FL-160 or Attachment 4b.

5. DECLARATION REGARDING COMMUNITY AND QUASI-COMMUNITY ASSETS AND DEBTS AS CURRENTLY KNOWN
   a. ☐ There are no such assets or debts subject to disposition by the court in this proceeding.
   b. ☐ All such assets and debts are listed in ☐ *Property Declaration* (form FL-160) ☐ Attachment 5b
   and should be divided between petitioner and respondent as indicated in form FL-160 or Attachment 5b.

6. **Petitioner requests**
   a. ☐ dissolution of the ☐ domestic partnership ☐ marriage based on
      (1) ☐ irreconcilable differences. (Fam. Code, § 2310(a).)   (2) ☐ incurable insanity. (Fam. Code, § 2310(b).)
   b. ☐ legal separation of the ☐ domestic partnership ☐ marriage based on
      (1) ☐ irreconcilable differences. (Fam. Code, § 2310(a).)   (2) ☐ incurable insanity. (Fam. Code, § 2310(b).)
   c. ☐ nullity of void ☐ domestic partnership ☐ marriage based on
      (1) ☐ incest. (Fam. Code, § 2200.)   (2) ☐ bigamy. (Fam. Code, § 2201.)
   d. ☐ nullity of voidable ☐ domestic partnership ☐ marriage based on
      (1) ☐ petitioner's age at time of registration of domestic   (3) ☐ unsound mind. (Fam. Code, § 2210(c).)
          partnership or marriage. (Fam. Code, § 2210(a).)   (4) ☐ fraud. (Fam. Code, § 2210(d).)
      (2) ☐ prior existing marriage or domestic partnership.   (5) ☐ force. (Fam. Code, § 2210(e).)
          (Fam. Code, § 2210(b).)   (6) ☐ physical incapacity. (Fam. Code, § 2210(f).)

7. **Petitioner requests** that the court grant the above relief and make injunctive (including restraining) and other orders as follows:

	Petitioner	Respondent	Joint	Other
a. Legal custody of children to	☐	☐	☐	☐
b. Physical custody of children to	☐	☐	☐	☐
c. Child visitation granted to	☐	☐		☐

   As requested in form: ☐ FL-311 ☐ FL-312 ☐ FL-341(C) ☐ FL-341(D) ☐ FL-341(E) ☐ Attachment 7c.
   d. ☐ Determination of parentage of any children born to the petitioner and respondent prior to the domestic partnership or
      marriage.

| e. Attorney fees and costs payable by .... | ☐ | ☐ | | |
| f. Partner or spousal support payable to .... | ☐ | ☐ | | |

   g. ☐ Terminate the court's jurisdiction (ability) to award partner or spousal support to respondent.
   h. ☐ Determine property rights.
   i. ☐ Restore petitioner's former name *(specify):*
   j. ☐ Other *(specify):*
      ☐ Continued on Attachment 7j.

8. **Child support:** If there are minor children who were born to or adopted by the petitioner and respondent before or during this domestic partnership or marriage, the court will make orders for the support of the children on request and submission of financial forms by the requesting party. An earnings assignment may be issued without further notice. Any party required to pay support must pay interest on overdue amounts at the "legal" rate, which is currently 10 percent.

9. I HAVE READ THE RESTRAINING ORDERS ON THE BACK OF THE SUMMONS, AND I UNDERSTAND THAT THEY APPLY TO ME WHEN THIS PETITION IS FILED.

I declare under penalty of perjury under the laws of the State of California that the foregoing is true and correct.

Date: _____   ▶ _____

_____   _____
(TYPE OR PRINT NAME)   (SIGNATURE OF PETITIONER)

Date: _____   ▶ _____

_____   _____
(TYPE OR PRINT NAME)   (SIGNATURE OF ATTORNEY FOR PETITIONER)

NOTICE: Dissolution or legal separation may automatically cancel the rights of a domestic partner or spouse under the other domestic partner's or spouse's will, trust, retirement plan, power of attorney, pay-on-death bank account, survivorship rights to any property owned in joint tenancy, and any other similar thing. It does not automatically cancel the right of a domestic partner or spouse as beneficiary of the other partner's or spouse's life insurance policy. You should review these matters, as well as any credit cards, other credit accounts, insurance polices, retirement plans, and credit reports, to determine whether they should be changed or whether you should take any other actions. However, some changes may require the agreement of your partner or spouse or a court order (see Fam. Code, §§ 231–235).

FL-103 [Rev. January 1, 2013]   **PETITION—DOMESTIC PARTNERSHIP/MARRIAGE**   Page 2 of 2
                                                    (Family Law)

For your protection and privacy, please press the Clear This Form
button after you have printed the form.   [Save This Form] [Print This Form] [Clear This Form]

Response—Domestic Partnership/Marriage

FL-123

ATTORNEY OR PARTY WITHOUT ATTORNEY *(Name, State Bar number, and address)*:	FOR COURT USE ONLY
TELEPHONE NO.: FAX NO. *(Optional)*: E-MAIL ADDRESS *(Optional)*: ATTORNEY FOR *(Name)*:	To keep other people from seeing what you entered on your form, please press the Clear This Form button at the end of the form when finished.

SUPERIOR COURT OF CALIFORNIA, COUNTY OF
STREET ADDRESS:
MAILING ADDRESS:
CITY AND ZIP CODE:
BRANCH NAME:

☐ **DOMESTIC PARTNERSHIP OF**   ☐ **MARRIAGE OF**
PETITIONER:

RESPONDENT:

RESPONSE ☐ and **REQUEST FOR** ☐ **AMENDED**	CASE NUMBER:
☐ **Dissolution of** ☐ **Domestic Partnership** ☐ **Marriage** ☐ **Legal Separation of** ☐ **Domestic Partnership** ☐ **Marriage** ☐ **Nullity of** ☐ **Domestic Partnership** ☐ **Marriage**	

> **NOTICE: Use this form to respond to** *Petition—Domestic Partnership/Marriage* **(form FL-103).**

1. STATISTICAL FACTS
   a. ☐ (1) Registration date of domestic partnership with the California Secretary of State or other state equivalent:
      (2) Date of separation:
      (3) Time from date of registration of domestic partnership to date of separation *(specify):*   Years   Months
   b. ☐ (1) Date of marriage: (2) Date of separation:
      (3) Time from date of marriage to date of separation *(specify):*   Years   Months

2. RESIDENCE *(check all that apply)*
   a. ☐ Our domestic partnership was established in California. Neither of us has to be a resident or have a domicile in California to dissolve our partnership here.
   b. ☐ Our domestic partnership was established in a place other than California. ☐ Petitioner ☐ Respondent has been a resident of the state of California for at least six months and of this county for at least three months immediately preceding the filing of this *Petition.*
   c. ☐ We are the same sex and are married. ☐ We are the opposite sex and are married. We are also domestic partners. ☐ Petitioner ☐ Respondent has been a resident of the state of California for at least six months and of this county for at least three months immediately preceding the filing of this *Petition.*
   d. ☐ We are the same sex and were married in California but are not residents of California. Neither of us lives in a state or nation that will dissolve the marriage. This case is filed in the county in which we married.
      Petitioner's residence *(state or nation):*   Respondent's residence *(state or nation):*

3. DECLARATION REGARDING MINOR CHILDREN *(include children of this relationship born or adopted prior to or during this domestic partnership or marriage)*
   a. ☐ There are no minor children.
   b. ☐ The minor children are

Child's name	Birthdate	Age	Sex

   ☐ Continued on Attachment 3b.
   c. If there are minor children of the petitioner and the respondent, a completed *Declaration Under Uniform Child Custody Jurisdiction and Enforcement Act (UCCJEA)* (form FL-105) must be attached.

> **NOTICE: You may redact (black out) social security numbers from any written material filed with the court in this case other than a form used to collect child or partner support.**

Form Adopted for Mandatory Use
Judicial Council of California
FL-123 [Rev. January 1, 2013]
RESPONSE—DOMESTIC PARTNERSHIP/MARRIAGE
(Family Law)
Family Code, §§ 299, 308, 2020
www.courts.ca.gov

Response—Domestic Partnership/Marriage

Petitioner: Respondent:	CASE NUMBER:

4. DECLARATION REGARDING SEPARATE PROPERTY AS CURRENTLY KNOWN
   a. ☐ There are no such assets or debts subject to disposition by the court in this proceeding.
   b. ☐ All such assets and debts listed are listed in ☐ *Property Declaration* (form FL-160) ☐ Attachment 4b
   and should be confirmed as petitioner's or respondent's separate property as indicated in form FL-160 or Attachment 4b.

5. DECLARATION REGARDING COMMUNITY AND QUASI-COMMUNITY ASSETS AND DEBTS AS CURRENTLY KNOWN
   a. ☐ There are no such assets or debts subject to disposition by the court in this proceeding.
   b. ☐ All such assets and debts are listed in ☐ *Property Declaration* (form FL-160) ☐ Attachment 5b
   and should be divided between petitioner or respondent as indicated in form FL-160 or Attachment 5b.

6. ☐ **Respondent contends** that there is not a valid domestic partnership, marriage, or equivalent.

7. ☐ **Respondent denies** the grounds stated in item 6 of the petition.

8. **Respondent requests**
   a. ☐ dissolution of the ☐ domestic partnership ☐ marriage   based on
      (1) ☐ irreconcilable differences. (Fam. Code, § 2310(a).)   (2) ☐ incurable insanity. (Fam. Code, § 2310(b).)
   b. ☐ legal separation of the ☐ domestic partnership ☐ marriage   based on
      (1) ☐ irreconcilable differences. (Fam. Code, § 2310(a).)   (2) ☐ incurable insanity. (Fam. Code, § 2310(b).)
   c. ☐ nullity of void ☐ domestic partnership ☐ marriage   based on
      (1) ☐ incest. (Fam. Code, § 2200.)   (2) ☐ bigamy. (Fam. Code, § 2201.)
   d. ☐ nullity of voidable ☐ domestic partnership ☐ marriage   based on
      (1) ☐ respondent's age at time of registration of domestic   (3) ☐ unsound mind. (Fam. Code, § 2210(c).)
          partnership or marriage. (Fam. Code, § 2210(a).)   (4) ☐ fraud. (Fam. Code, § 2210(d).)
      (2) ☐ prior existing marriage or domestic partnership.   (5) ☐ force. (Fam. Code, § 2210(e).)
          (Fam. Code, § 2210(b).)   (6) ☐ physical incapacity. (Fam. Code, § 2210(f).)

9. **Respondent requests** that the court grant the above relief and make injunctive (including restraining) and other orders as follows:

	Petitioner	Respondent	Joint	Other
a. Legal custody of children to	☐	☐	☐	☐
b. Physical custody of children to	☐	☐	☐	☐
c. Child visitation granted to	☐	☐		☐

   As requested in form: ☐ FL-311 ☐ FL-312 ☐ FL-341(C) ☐ FL-341(D) ☐ FL-341(E) ☐ Attachment 9c.

   d. ☐ Determination of parentage of any children born to the petitioner and respondent prior to the domestic partnership or marriage.

e. Attorney fees and costs payable by	☐	☐
f. Partner or spousal support payable to	☐	☐

   g. ☐ Terminate the court's jurisdiction (ability) to award partner or spousal support to the petitioner.
   h. ☐ Determine property rights.
   i. ☐ Restore respondent's former name *(specify):*
   j. ☐ Other *(specify):*
      ☐ Continued on Attachment 9j.

10. **Child support:** If there are minor children who were born to or adopted by the petitioner and respondent before or during this domestic partnership or marriage, the court will make orders for the support of the children on request and submission of financial forms by the requesting party. An earnings assignment may be issued without further notice. Any party required to pay support must pay interest on overdue amounts at the "legal" rate, which is currently 10 percent.

I declare under penalty of perjury under the laws of the State of California that the foregoing is true and correct.

Date:

_____   ▶ _____
(TYPE OR PRINT NAME)   (SIGNATURE OF RESPONDENT)

Date:

_____   ▶ _____
(TYPE OR PRINT NAME)   (SIGNATURE OF ATTORNEY FOR RESPONDENT)

The original response must be filed in the court with proof of service of a copy on petitioner.

FL-123 [Rev. January 1, 2013]   **RESPONSE—DOMESTIC PARTNERSHIP/MARRIAGE**   Page 2 of 2
                                                (Family Law)

Save This Form   Print This Form   Clear This Form

Judgment

ATTORNEY OR PARTY WITHOUT ATTORNEY *(Name, State Bar number, and address):*	FOR COURT USE ONLY
TELEPHONE NO.: FAX NO. *(Optional):* E-MAIL ADDRESS *(Optional):* ATTORNEY FOR *(Name):*	To keep other people from seeing what you entered on your form, please press the Clear This Form button at the end of the form when finished.

SUPERIOR COURT OF CALIFORNIA, COUNTY OF
STREET ADDRESS:
MAILING ADDRESS:
CITY AND ZIP CODE:
BRANCH NAME:

MARRIAGE OR PARTNERSHIP OF
PETITIONER:

RESPONDENT:

JUDGMENT ☐ **DISSOLUTION** ☐ **LEGAL SEPARATION** ☐ **NULLITY** ☐ Status only ☐ Reserving jurisdiction over termination of marital or domestic partnership status ☐ Judgment on reserved issues Date marital or domestic partnership status ends:	CASE NUMBER:

1. ☐ This judgment ☐ contains personal conduct restraining orders ☐ modifies existing restraining orders.
The restraining orders are contained on page(s) of the attachment. They expire on *(date):*

2. This proceeding was heard as follows: ☐ Default or uncontested ☐ By declaration under Family Code section 2336
☐ Contested ☐ Agreement in court
   a. Date: Dept.: Room:
   b. Judicial officer *(name):* ☐ Temporary judge
   c. ☐ Petitioner present in court ☐ Attorney present in court *(name):*
   d. ☐ Respondent present in court ☐ Attorney present in court *(name):*
   e. ☐ Claimant present in court *(name):* ☐ Attorney present in court *(name):*
   f. ☐ Other *(specify name):*

3. The court acquired jurisdiction of the respondent on *(date):*
   a. ☐ The respondent was served with process.
   b. ☐ The respondent appeared.

THE COURT ORDERS, GOOD CAUSE APPEARING
4. a. ☐ Judgment of dissolution is entered. Marital or domestic partnership status is terminated and the parties are restored to the status of single persons
   (1) ☐ on *(specify date):*
   (2) ☐ on a date to be determined on noticed motion of either party or on stipulation.
   b. ☐ Judgment of legal separation is entered.
   c. ☐ Judgment of nullity is entered. The parties are declared to be single persons on the ground of *(specify):*

   d. ☐ This judgment will be entered nunc pro tunc as of *(date):*
   e. ☐ Judgment on reserved issues.
   f. The ☐ petitioner's ☐ respondent's former name is restored to *(specify):*
   g. ☐ Jurisdiction is reserved over all other issues, and all present orders remain in effect except as provided below.
   h. ☐ This judgment contains provisions for child support or family support. Each party must complete and file with the court a *Child Support Case Registry Form* (form FL-191) within 10 days of the date of this judgment. The parents must notify the court of any change in the information submitted within 10 days of the change, by filing an updated form. The *Notice of Rights and Responsibilities—Health-Care Costs and Reimbursement Procedures and Information Sheet on Changing a Child Support Order* (form FL-192) is attached.

Form Adopted for Mandatory Use
Judicial Council of California
FL-180 [Rev. July 1, 2012]

JUDGMENT
(Family Law)

Family Code, §§ 2024, 2340,
2343, 2346
www.courts.ca.gov

Judgment

CASE NAME (Last name, first name of each party):	CASE NUMBER:

4. i. ☐ The children of this marriage or domestic partnership are:

    (1) ☐ Name   Birthdate

    (2) ☐ Parentage is established for children of this relationship born prior to the marriage or domestic partnership

  j. ☐ Child custody and visitation (parenting time) are ordered as set forth in the attached

    (1) ☐ Settlement agreement, stipulation for judgment, or other written agreement which contains the information required by Family Code section 3048(a).

    (2) ☐ *Child Custody and Visitation Order Attachment* (form FL-341).

    (3) ☐ *Stipulation and Order for Custody and/or Visitation of Children* (form FL-355).

    (4) ☐ Previously established in another case. Case number: Court:

  k. ☐ Child support is ordered as set forth in the attached

    (1) ☐ Settlement agreement, stipulation for judgment, or other written agreement which contains the declarations required by Family Code section 4065(a).

    (2) ☐ *Child Support Information and Order Attachment* (form FL-342).

    (3) ☐ *Stipulation to Establish or Modify Child Support and Order* (form FL-350).

    (4) ☐ Previously established in another case. Case number: Court:

  l. ☐ Spousal, domestic partner, or family support is ordered:

    (1) ☐ Reserved for future determination as relates to ☐ petitioner ☐ respondent

    (2) ☐ Jurisdiction terminated to order spousal or partner support to ☐ petitioner ☐ respondent

    (3) ☐ As set forth in the attached *Spousal, Partner, or Family Support Order Attachment* (form FL-343).

    (4) ☐ As set forth in the attached settlement agreement, stipulation for judgment, or other written agreement.

    (5) ☐ Other *(specify):*

  m. ☐ Property division is ordered as set forth in the attached

    (1) ☐ Settlement agreement, stipulation for judgment, or other written agreement.

    (2) ☐ *Property Order Attachment to Judgment* (form FL-345).

    (3) ☐ Other *(specify):*

  n. ☐ Attorney fees and costs are ordered as set forth in the attached

    (1) ☐ Settlement agreement, stipulation for judgment, or other written agreement.

    (2) ☐ *Attorney Fees and Costs Order* (form FL-346).

    (3) ☐ Other *(specify):*

  o. ☐ Other *(specify):*

Each attachment to this judgment is incorporated into this judgment, and the parties are ordered to comply with each attachment's provisions. Jurisdiction is reserved to make other orders necessary to carry out this judgment.

Date:

5. Number of pages attached: _____

JUDICIAL OFFICER
SIGNATURE FOLLOWS LAST ATTACHMENT

NOTICE

Dissolution or legal separation may automatically cancel the rights of a spouse or domestic partner under the other spouse's or domestic partner's will, trust, retirement plan, power of attorney, pay-on-death bank account, transfer-on-death vehicle registration, survivorship rights to any property owned in joint tenancy, and any other similar property interest. It does not automatically cancel the rights of a spouse or domestic partner as beneficiary of the other spouse's or domestic partner's life insurance policy. You should review these matters, as well as any credit cards, other credit accounts, insurance policies, retirement plans, and credit reports, to determine whether they should be changed or whether you should take any other actions.

A debt or obligation may be assigned to one party as part of the dissolution of property and debts, but if that party does not pay the debt or obligation, the creditor may be able to collect from the other party.

An earnings assignment may be issued without additional proof if child, family, partner, or spousal support is ordered.

Any party required to pay support must pay interest on overdue amounts at the "legal rate," which is currently 10 percent.

JUDGMENT
(Family Law)

For your protection and privacy, please press the Clear This Form button after you have printed the form.

| Print This Form | Save This Form | Clear This Form |

Adoption Request

ADOPT-200 **Adoption Request**

Clerk stamps date here when form is filed.

If you are adopting more than one child, fill out an adoption request for each child.

(1) Your name(s) *(adopting parent(s)):*

a. _____

b. _____

Relationship to child: _____

Street address: _____

City: _____ State: _____ Zip: _____

Telephone number: _____

Lawyer *(if any): (Name, address, telephone numbers, and State Bar number):*

_____

_____

_____

Fill in court name and street address:

Superior Court of California, County of

Court fills in case number when form is filed.

Case Number:

(2) I/We filed this *Adoption Request* in this court because it is in the county *(check all that apply):*

☐ Where the adopting parent(s) reside;

☐ Where the child was born or resides at the time of filing;

☐ Where an office of the agency that placed the child for adoption is located;

☐ Where an office of the department or public adoption agency that is investigating the petition is located;

☐ Where a placing birth parent or parents resided when the adoptive placement agreement, consent, or relinquishment was signed;

☐ Where a placing birth parent or parents resided when the petition was filed;

☐ Where the child was freed for adoption.

(If the child is a dependent of the court, the Adoption Request must be filed in the county where the child was freed for adoption or the county where the adopting parent(s) reside(s). See Fam. Code, § 8714.)

(3) Type of adoption *(check one):*

☐ Agency *(name):* _____

    ☐ Relative   ☐ Nonrelative

☐ Joinder will be filed.   ☐ Joinder is being filed at same time as this *Adoption Request.*

☐ Tribal customary adoption
(attach tribal customary adoption order)

☐ Independent
    ☐ Relative   ☐ Nonrelative

☐ Intercountry *(name of agency):*

_____

☐ This adoption may be subject to the Hague Adoption Convention *(form ADOPT-216 must be filed with this request).*

☐ Stepparent

(To be completed by the clerk of the superior court if a hearing date is available.)

Hearing Date Hearing is set for:

Date: _____

Time: _____

Dept.: _____ Room: _____

Name and address of court if different from above:

_____

To the person served with this request: If you do not come to this hearing, the judge can order the adoption without your input.

Judicial Council of California, www.courts.ca.gov
Revised January 1, 2014, Mandatory Form
Family Code, §§ 170–180, 7822, 7892.5, 8601.5,
8604, 8606, 8700, 8714, 8714.5, 8802, 8900–8905,
8908–8912, 8919, 8924, 8925, 9000, 9208;
Welfare and Institutions Code, §§ 366.24, 16119;
Cal. Rules of Court, rules 5.480–5.487, 5.730

Adoption Request

ADOPT-200, Page 1 of 5
→

Adoption Request

Your name: _____

(4) Information about the child:

   a. The child's new name will be:

   _____

   b. ☐ Boy ☐ Girl

   c. Date of birth: _____ Age: ____

   d. Child's address *(if different from yours)*:

     Street: _____

     City: _____ State: ____ Zip: _____

   e. Place of birth *(if known)*:

     City: _____

     State: _____ Country: _____

   f. If the child is 12 or older, does the child agree to the adoption? ☐ Yes ☐ No

   g. Date child was placed in your physical care:

     _____

(5) Child's name before adoption *(Fill out ONLY if this is an independent, stepparent, or tribal customary adoption)*:

_____

(6) Does the child have a legal guardian? ☐ Yes ☐ No

(If yes, attach a copy of the Letters of Guardianship and fill out below):

   a. Date guardianship ordered: _____

   b. County: _____

   c. Case number: _____

(7) Is the child a dependent of the court? ☐ Yes ☐ No

(If yes, fill out below):

   Juvenile case number: _____

   County: _____

(8) Child may have Indian ancestry: ☐ Yes ☐ No

   a. Whether you answered "Yes" or "No," you must fill out and attach *Indian Child Inquiry Attachment* (form ICWA-010(A)) and *Parental Notification of Indian Status* (form ICWA-020) or other proof that ICWA inquiry has been completed in accordance with rule 5.481(a).

   b. If you answered "Yes," you must also fill out and attach *Adoption of Indian Child* (form ADOPT-220) if, after notice, it is determined that ICWA does apply to the child.

(9) Names of birth parents, if known:

   a. Mother: _____

   b. Father: _____

(10) **If this is an agency adoption:**

   a. I/We have received information about the Adoption Assistance Program, the Regional Center, mental health services available through Medi-Cal or other programs, and federal and state tax credits that might be available.
   ☐ Yes ☐ No

   b. All persons with parental rights agree that the child should be placed for adoption by the California Department of Social Services or a county adoption agency or a licensed adoption agency (Fam. Code, § 8700) and have signed a relinquishment form approved by the California Department of Social Services, and the time to revoke the relinquishment has expired or been waived.
   ☐ Yes ☐ No *(If no, list the name and relationship to child of each person who has not signed the relinquishment form or whose time to revoke the relinquishment has not expired or been waived)*:

_____

_____

Adoption Request

Your name: _____

---

c. This is a tribal customary adoption under Welfare and Institutions Code section 366.24. Parental rights have been modified under and in accordance with the attached tribal customary adoption order, and the child has been ordered placed for adoption. ☐ Yes ☐ No

d. This is an adoption conducted under the requirements of the Hague Adoption Convention and the child will be moving or has already moved with the adopting parent(s) to another Hague Convention member country at the conclusion of this adoption. ☐ Yes ☐ No If yes, child will be moving or has moved to *(name of country):* _____ and adopting parent(s): ☐ seek(s) a California adoption ☐ will be petitioning for a Hague Adoption Certificate ☐ will be seeking a Hague Custody Declaration.

(11) If this is an independent adoption:

a. A copy of the Independent Adoptive Placement Agreement from the California Department of Social Services is attached. (This is required in most independent adoptions; see Fam. Code, § 8802.) ☐ Yes ☐ No

b. All persons with parental rights agree to the adoption and have signed the Independent Adoptive Placement Agreement or consent on the appropriate California Department of Social Services form. ☐ Yes ☐ No *(If no, list the name and relationship to child of each person who has not signed the agreement form):*

_____

c. I/We will file promptly with the department or delegated county adoption agency the information required by the department in the investigation of the proposed adoption. ☐ Yes ☐ No

(12) If this is a stepparent adoption:

a. The birth parent *(name):* _____ ☐ has signed a consent ☐ will sign a consent

b. The birth parent *(name):* _____ ☐ has signed a consent ☐ will sign a consent

c. The adopting parents were married on **or** The domestic partnership was registered on *(date):* _____ *(For court use only. This does not affect social worker's recommendation. There is no waiting period.)*

(13) ☐ There is no presumed or biological father because the child was conceived by artificial insemination using semen provided to a medical doctor or a sperm bank. (Fam. Code, § 7613.)

(14) Contact after adoption

Contact After Adoption Agreement (form ADOPT-310) ☐ is attached ☐ will not be used

☐ will be filed at least 30 days before the adoption hearing ☐ is undecided at this time.

☐ This is a tribal customary adoption. Postadoption contact is governed by the attached tribal customary adoption order.

(15) Consent for adoption is not necessary because *(complete all sections that apply to your adoption):*

a. ☐ The consent of the ☐ birth parent ☐ presumed father is not necessary because *(check the applicable reasons under Fam. Code, § 8606):*

(1) ☐ The parent has been judicially deprived of the custody and control of the child.

(2) ☐ The parent has voluntarily surrendered the right to custody and control of the child in a judicial proceeding in another jurisdiction, under a law of that jurisdiction providing for the surrender.

(3) ☐ The parent has deserted the child without providing information to identify the child.

(4) ☐ The parent has relinquished the child under Family Code section 8700.

(5) ☐ The parent has relinquished the child for adoption to a licensed or authorized child-placing agency in another jurisdiction.

Adoption Request

Your name: _____

Case Number: _____

b. ☐ A court ended the parental rights of:

Name: _____ Relationship to child: _____ on *(date):* _____

Name: _____ Relationship to child: _____ on *(date):* _____

(Enter the date of the court order ending parental rights and attach a copy of the order.)

c. ☐ The child is the subject of a tribal customary adoption order under Welfare and Institutions Code section 366.24, which has modified the parental rights of:

Name: _____ Relationship to child: _____ on *(date):* _____

Name: _____ Relationship to child: _____ on *(date):* _____

Name: _____ Relationship to child: _____ on *(date):* _____

(Attach a copy of the order.)

d. ☐ I/We will ask the court to end the parental rights of *(attach copy of* Petition to Terminate Parental Rights *or* Application for Freedom From Parental Custody, *if filed):*

Name: _____ Relationship to child: _____

Name: _____ Relationship to child: _____

e. ☐ Adopting parent has custody of the child by court order or by agreement with the other parent, and each of the following persons with parental rights has not contacted the child and has not paid for the child's care, support, and education for one year or more when able to do so. (Fam. Code, § 8604(b).)

Name: _____ Relationship to child: _____

Name: _____ Relationship to child: _____

Name: _____ Relationship to child: _____

f. ☐ The child has been abandoned as follows:

    (1) ☐ The child has been left by the child's parent or parents with no way to identify the child.

    (2) ☐ The child has been left in the custody of another person by both parents or the sole parent for six months without providing for the child's support, or without communication from the parent or parents, with the intent to abandon the child.

    (3) ☐ One parent has left the child in the care and custody of the other parent for one year or longer without providing for the child's support or without communication from the parent, with the intent to abandon the child.

(If any of the above boxes were checked, adopting parent must also check item 15(d) and file an Application for Freedom from Parental Custody. *See Fam. Code, § 7822(a).)*

g. ☐ The consent of the presumed father is not required because he did not become a presumed father before the mother's relinquishment or consent became irrevocable or the mother's parental rights were terminated. (Fam. Code, § 8604(a).)

h. ☐ Each of the following persons with parental rights has died:

Name: _____ Relationship to child: _____

Name: _____ Relationship to child: _____

Adoption Request

	Case Number:
Your name: _____	

(16) Suitability for adoption

Each adopting parent:

a. Is at least 10 years older than the child or meets the criteria in Family Code section 8601(b);

b. Will treat the child as his or her own;

c. Will support and care for the child;

d. Has a suitable home for the child; *and*

e. Agrees to adopt the child.

(17) ☐ I/We ask the court to approve the adoption and to declare that the adopting parents and the child have the legal relationship of parent and child, with all the rights and duties of this relationship, including the right of inheritance.

☐ I/We ask the court to date its order approving the adoption as of an earlier date *(date):* _____ for the following reason (Fam. Code, § 8601.5):

_____

_____

_____

(Enter a date no earlier than the date parental rights were ended.)

☐ This is a tribal customary adoption. I/We ask the court to approve the adoption and to declare that the adopting parents and the child have the legal relationship of parent and child, with all of the rights and duties stated in the attached tribal customary adoption order and in accordance with Welfare and Institutions Code section 366.24.

(18) If a lawyer is representing you in this case, he or she must sign here:

Date: _____   _____   ▶ _____

  Type or print your name   *Signature of attorney for adopting parent(s)*

(19) I declare under penalty of perjury under the laws of the State of California that the information in this form and all its attachments is true and correct to my knowledge. This means that if I lie on this form, I am guilty of a crime.

Date: _____   _____   ▶ _____

  Type or print your name   *Signature of adopting parent*

Date: _____   _____   ▶ _____

  Type or print your name   *Signature of adopting parent*

NOTICE—ACCESS TO AFFORDABLE HEALTH INSURANCE: Do you or someone in your household need affordable health insurance? If so, you should apply for Covered California. Covered California can help reduce the cost you pay toward high-quality affordable health care. For more information, visit www.coveredca.com. Or call Covered California at 1-800-300-1506 (English) or 1-800-300-0213 (Spanish).

For your protection and privacy, please press the Clear This Form button after you have printed the form.   [**Print this form**] [**Save this form**]   [**Clear this form**]

Adoption Agreement

ADOPT-210 Adoption Agreement	*Clerk stamps date here when form is filed.*

(1) Your name (adopting parent):

    a. _____

    b. _____

    Relationship to child: _____

    Address *(skip this if you have a lawyer)*:

    Street: _____

    City: _____ State: _____ Zip: _____

    Telephone number: (___)_____

    Lawyer *(if any): (Name, address, telephone number, and State Bar number):* _____

    _____

    _____

    _____

Fill in court name and street address:

Superior Court of California, County of

Fill in case number if known:

Case Number:

(2) Child's name before adoption: _____

    Child's name after adoption: _____

    Date of birth: _____ Age: _____

(3) I am the child listed in **(2)** and I agree to the adoption. *(Sign at the hearing in front of the judge. Not required in the case of a tribal customary adoption under Welf. & Inst. Code, § 366.24.)*

Date: _____   _____   ▶ _____
               Type or print your name   *Signature of child (child must sign at hearing if 12 or older; optional if child is under 12)*

(4) *If there is only **one** adopting parent, read and sign below. Sign at the hearing in front of the judge.*

    a. I am the adopting parent listed in **(1)**, and I agree that the child will:

        (1) Be adopted and treated as my legal child *(Fam. Code § 8612(b)) and*

        (2) Have the same rights as a natural child born to me, including the right to inherit my estate.

Date: _____   _____   ▶ _____
               Type or print your name   *Signature of adopting parent (sign at hearing)*

    b. I am married to, or the registered domestic partner of, the adopting parent listed in **(1)**, and I agree to his or her adoption of the child.

Date: _____   _____   ▶ _____
               Type or print your name   *Signature of spouse or registered domestic partner (may be signed before hearing)*

Judicial Council of California, www.courts.ca.gov
Revised January 1, 2011, Mandatory Form
Family Code, §§ 8602–8606, 8612, 9003; Welfare and
Institutions Code, § 366.24; Cal. Rules of Court, rule 5.730

Adoption Agreement

ADOPT-210, Page 1 of 2
→

Adoption Agreement

<table>
<tr><td>Your name: _____</td><td>Case Number:</td></tr>
</table>

(5) *If there are **two** adopting parents, read and sign below. Sign at the hearing in front of the judge.*
We are the adopting parents listed in **(1)** , and we agree that the child will:
(a) Be adopted and treated as our legal child *(Fam. Code. § 8612(b))* and
(b) Have the same rights as a natural child born to us, including the right to inherit our estate.

I agree to the other parent's adoption of the child.

Date: _____   _____   ▶ _____
                     Type or print your name   *Signature of adopting parent (sign at hearing)*

I agree to the other parent's adoption of the child.

Date: _____   _____   ▶ _____
                     Type or print your name   *Signature of adopting parent (sign at hearing)*

(6) *If this is a tribal customary adoption, read and sign below. Sign at the hearing in front of the judge.*
I/we are the adopting parents listed in **(1)**, and I/we agree that the child will:
a. Be adopted and treated as my/our legal child *(Fam. Code. § 8612(b))* and
b. Have the same rights and duties stated in the tribal customary adoption order dated _____ *(copy attached)*.
If two adopting parents, we agree to the other parent's adoption of the child.

Date: _____   _____   ▶ _____
                     Type or print your name   *Signature of adopting parent (sign at hearing)*

Date: _____   _____   ▶ _____
                     Type or print your name   *Signature of adopting parent (sign at hearing)*

(7) *For stepparent adoptions only:*
If you are the legal parent of the child listed in **(2)***, read and sign below. Sign at the hearing in front of the judge.*
I am the legal parent of the child and am the spouse or registered domestic partner of the adopting parent listed in
(1), and I agree to his or her adoption of my child.

Date: _____   _____   ▶ _____
                     Type or print your name   *Signature of legal parent (sign at hearing)*

(8) **Executed:**

Date: _____   ▶ _____
                                                    Judge (or Judicial Officer)

Adoption Order

ADOPT-215   **Adoption Order**

Clerk stamps date here when form is filed.

1 Your name *(adopting parent(s))*:

a. _____

b. _____

Relationship to child: _____

Street address: _____

City: _____ State: _____ Zip: _____

Daytime telephone number: _____

Lawyer *(if any): (Name, address, telephone number, and State*

Bar number): _____

_____

_____

Fill in court name and street address:

Superior Court of California, County of

2 Child's name after adoption: _____

First Name: _____

Middle Name: _____

Last Name: _____

Date of birth: _____ Age: _____

Place of birth *(if known):* _____

City: _____ State: _____ Country: _____

Court fills in case number when form is filed.

Case Number:

3 Name of adoption agency *(if any):* _____

4 Hearing date: _____

Dept.: _____ Div.: _____ Rm.: _____ Judicial Officer: _____

Clerk's office telephone number: _____

5 People present at the hearing:

☐ Adopting parent(s)   ☐ Lawyer for adopting parent(s)

☐ Child   ☐ Child's lawyer

☐ Parent keeping parental rights: _____

☐ Other people present *(list each name and relationship to child):*

a. _____

b. _____

If there are more names, attach a sheet of paper, write "ADOPT-215, Item 5" at the top, and list the additional names and each person's relationship to child.

Judge will fill out section below.

6 The judge finds that the child *(check all that apply):*

a. ☐ Is 12 or older and agrees to the adoption

b. ☐ Is under 12

c. ☐ This is a tribal customary adoption and the child's consent is not required.

7 The judge has reviewed the report and other documents and evidence and finds that each adopting parent:

a. Is at least 10 years older than the child or meets the criteria in Fam. Code, § 8601(b)

b. Will treat the child as his or her own

c. Will support and care for the child

d. Has a suitable home for the child *and*

e. Agrees to adopt the child

Judicial Council of California, www.courts.ca.gov
Revised July 1, 2013, Mandatory Form
Family Code, §§ 8601.5, 8612, 8714, 8714.5,
8900, 8900.5, 8902, 8912, 9000;
Welfare and Institutions Code, § 366.24;
Cal. Rules of Court, rule 5.730

Adoption Order

Adoption Order

Your name: _____

Case Number: _____

---

(8) ☐ This case is an adoption by a relative petitioned under Family Code section 8714.5.
   ☐ The adopting relative   ☐ The child, who is 12 or older,   has requested that the child's name
   before adoption be listed on this order. (Fam. Code, § 8714.5(g).)
   The child's name before adoption was:
   First Name:_____   Middle Name:_____   Last Name:_____

(9) ☐ The child is an Indian child. The judge finds that this adoption meets the placement requirements of the
   Indian Child Welfare Act or that there is good cause to give preference to these adopting parents. The clerk
   will fill out **(14)** below.

(10) ☐ The judge approves the *Contact After Adoption Agreement* (ADOPT-310)
   ☐ As submitted   ☐ As amended on ADOPT-310

(11) This is a tribal customary adoption, The tribal customary adoption order of the _____

   tribe dated _____ containing _____ pages and attached hereto is fully incorporated into this order of adoption.

(12) ☐ This is an adoption under the Hague Adoption Convention. *Verification of Compliance with Hague Adoption
   Convention Attachment* (form ADOPT-216) is attached and fully incorporated into this order.

(13) The judge believes the adoption is in the child's best interest and orders this adoption.
   The child's name after adoption will be:
   First Name:_____   Middle Name:_____   Last Name:_____

   The adopting parent or parents and the child are now parent and child under the law, with all the rights and duties
   of the parent-child relationship or, in the case of a tribal customary adoption, all the rights and duties set out in the
   tribal customary adoption order and Welfare and Institutions Code section 366.24.

   ☐ The judge believes it will serve public policy and the best interest of the child to grant the request of the
   adopting parent or parents for the court to make this order effective as of *(date):* _____ .

Date: _____
   (Date of Signature)   _____
                                                  Judge (or Judicial Officer)

Clerk will fill out section below.

---

(14) Clerk's Certificate of Mailing
For the adoption of an Indian child, the Clerk certifies:
I am not a party to this adoption. I placed a filed copy of:

☐ *Adoption Request* (ADOPT-200)   ☐ *Adoption of Indian Child* (ADOPT-220)
☐ *Adoption Order* (ADOPT-215)   ☐ *Contact After Adoption Agreement* (ADOPT-310)

in a sealed envelope, marked "Confidential" and addressed to:
   Chief, Division of Social Services
   Bureau of Indian Affairs
   1849 C Street, NW
   Mail Stop 310-SIB
   Washington, DC 20240
The envelope was mailed by U.S. mail, with full postage, from:
Place: _____   on *(date):* _____
Date: _____   Clerk, by: _____ , Deputy

Revised July 1, 2013   **Adoption Order**   **ADOPT-215**, Page 2 of 2

For your protection and privacy, please press the Clear
This Form button after you have printed the form.   [Print this form]   [Save this form]   [Clear this form]

Joint Petition for Summary Dissolution

		FL-800
ATTORNEY OR PARTY WITHOUT ATTORNEY *(Name, State Bar number, and address):*		
TELEPHONE NO.: FAX NO. : E-MAIL ADDRESS: ATTORNEY FOR *(Name)*:		

SUPERIOR COURT OF CALIFORNIA, COUNTY OF
STREET ADDRESS:
MAILING ADDRESS:
CITY AND ZIP CODE:
BRANCH NAME:

MARRIAGE OR PARTNERSHIP OF
PETITIONER 1:
PETITIONER 2:

JOINT PETITION FOR SUMMARY DISSOLUTION	CASE NUMBER:
☐ MARRIAGE ☐ DOMESTIC PARTNERSHIP	

We petition for a summary dissolution of marriage, registered domestic partnership, or both and declare that all the following conditions exist on the date this petition is filed with the court:

1. We have read and understand the *Summary Dissolution Information* booklet (form FL-810).

2. a. ☐ We were married on *(date):*

   b. ☐ We registered as domestic partners on *(date):*

3. ☐ We separated on *(date):*

4. Less than five years have passed between the date of our marriage and/or registration of our domestic partnership and the date of our separation.

5. a. ☐ One of us has lived in California for at least six months and in the county of filing for at least the three months preceding the date of filing. Or we are only asking to end a domestic partnership registered in California.

   b. ☐ We are the same sex and were married in California but are not residents of California. Neither of us lives in a place that will allow us to divorce. We are filing this case in the county in which we married.

6. There are no minor children who were born of our relationship before or during our marriage or domestic partnership or adopted by us during our marriage or domestic partnership. Neither one of us, to our knowledge, is pregnant.

7. Neither of us has an interest in any real property anywhere. **(You may have a lease for a residence in which one of you lives. It must terminate within a year from the date of filing this petition. The lease must not include an option to purchase.)**

8. Except for obligations with respect to cars, on obligations incurred by either or both of us during our marriage or domestic partnership, we owe no more than $6,000.

9. The total fair market value of community property assets, not including what we owe on those assets and not including cars, is less than $40,000.

10. Neither of us has separate property assets, not including what we owe on those assets and not including cars, in excess of $40,000.

11. We each have filled out and given the other an *Income and Expense Declaration* (form FL-150).

12. We have complied with the preliminary disclosure requirements as follows:

    a. We each have disclosed information about the value and division of our property by filling out and giving each other copies of the documents listed in 1 or 2 below (specify):

       (1) ☐ The worksheets on pages 7, 9, and 11 of the *Summary Dissolution Information* booklet (form FL-810).

       (2) ☐ A *Declaration of Disclosure* (form FL-140), a *Schedule of Assets and Debts* (form FL-142), or *Property Declaration (form FL-160)*, and all attachments to these forms.

    b. We have told each other in writing about any investment, business, or other income-producing opportunities that came up after we were separated based on investments made or work done during the marriage or domestic partnership and before our separation.

    c. We have exchanged all tax returns each of us has filed within the two years before disclosing the information described in 12a.

Page 1 of 2

Form Adopted for Mandatory Use
Judicial Council of California
FL-800 [Rev. July 1, 2013]

JOINT PETITION FOR SUMMARY DISSOLUTION
(Family Law—Summary Dissolution)

Family Code, § 299, 2109, 2320, 2400-2406
www.courts.ca.gov

Joint Petition for Summary Dissolution

FL-800

PETITIONER 1:	CASE NUMBER:
PETITIONER 2:	

13. *(Check whichever statement is true.)*

    a. ☐ We have no community assets or liabilities.

    b. ☐ We have signed an agreement listing and dividing all our community assets and liabilities and have signed all the papers necessary to carry out our agreement. A copy of our agreement is attached to the *Judgment of Dissolution and Notice of Entry of Judgment* (form FL-825).

14. Irreconcilable differences have caused the irremediable breakdown of our marriage and/or domestic partnership, and each of us wishes to have the court dissolve our marriage and/or domestic partnership without our appearing before a judge.

15. a. ☐ Petitioner 1 desires to have his or her former name restored. That name is *(specify):*

    b. ☐ Petitioner 2 desires to have his or her former name restored. That name is *(specify):*

16. We each give up our rights to appeal and to move for a new trial after the effective date of our *Judgment of Dissolution.*

17. **Each of us forever gives up any right to spousal or partner support from the other.**

18. We each agree to keep the court and each other informed of any change of mailing address or phone number occurring within six months from the filing of this joint petition using the *Notice of Change of Address or Other Contact Information* (form MC-040).

19. We are submitting the original and three copies of the proposed *Judgment of Dissolution and Notice of Entry of Judgment* (form FL-825) and two stamped envelopes together with this petition. One envelope is addressed to Petitioner 1 and the other to Petitioner 2.

20. We agree that this matter may be determined by a commissioner sitting as a temporary judge.

21. **Mailing address of Petitioner 1**
    Name:
    Address:

    City:
    State:
    Zip Code:

22. **Mailing address of Petitioner 2**
    Name:
    Address:

    City:
    State:
    Zip Code:

23. Number of pages attached: _____

I declare under penalty of perjury under the laws of the State of California that the foregoing and all attached documents are true and correct.

Date:

I declare under penalty of perjury under the laws of the State of California that the foregoing and all attached documents are true and correct.

Date:

_____
(SIGNATURE OF PETITIONER 1)

_____
(SIGNATURE OF PETITIONER 2)

NOTICES

Your marriage and/or domestic partnership will end six months from the date of filing this joint petition. Both petitioners will receive a stamped copy from the court of the *Judgment of Dissolution and Notice of Entry of Judgment* **(from FL-825) stating the effective date of your dissolution. Until the effective date specified on form FL-825 for the dissolution of your marriage and/or domestic partnership, either one of you can stop this joint petition by filing a** *Notice of Revocation of Petition for Summary Dissolution* **(form FL-830). If you stop this joint petition, you will STILL be married or in a domestic partnership.**

Dissolution may automatically cancel the rights of a spouse or domestic partner under the other spouse's or domestic partner's will, trust, retirement plan, power of attorney, pay-on-death bank account, transfer-on-death vehicle registration, survivorship rights to any property owned in joint tenancy, and any other similar instrument. It does not automatically cancel the rights of a spouse or domestic partner as beneficiary of the other spouse's or domestic partner's life insurance policy. You should review these matters, as well as any credit card accounts, other credit accounts, insurance policies, and credit reports to determine whether they should be changed or whether you should take any other actions. However, some changes may require the agreement of your spouse or domestic partner or a court order. (See Fam. Code, §§ 231–235.)

For your protection and privacy, please press the Clear This Form button after you have printed the form.

[Print this form]   [Save this form]   [Clear this form]

Notice of Revocation of Petition for Summary Dissolution

FL-830

PARTY WITHOUT ATTORNEY OR ATTORNEY (Name, State Bar number, and address):	FOR COURT USE ONLY
	To keep other people from seeing what you entered on your form, please press the Clear This Form button at the end of the form when finished.

TELEPHONE NO.:   FAX NO. (Optional):

E-MAIL ADDRESS (Optional):

ATTORNEY FOR (Name):

SUPERIOR COURT OF CALIFORNIA, COUNTY OF

STREET ADDRESS:

MAILING ADDRESS:

CITY AND ZIP CODE:

BRANCH NAME:

MARRIAGE OR DOMESTIC PARTNERSHIP OF

PETITIONER 1:

PETITIONER 2:

NOTICE OF REVOCATION OF JOINT PETITION FOR SUMMARY DISSOLUTION	CASE NUMBER:

Notice is given that the undersigned terminates the summary dissolution proceedings and revokes the *Joint Petition for Summary Dissolution* (form FL-800) filed on *(date):*

I declare under penalty of perjury under the laws of the State of California that the foregoing is true and correct.

Date:

_____
(TYPE OR PRINT NAME)

▶ _____
(SIGNATURE OF DECLARANT)

Complete this notice. Submit the original and two copies to the court clerk's office. If the effective date of the judgment has not yet occurred, the clerk will notify you that this notice of revocation has been filed by completing the certificate below.

Name and address of Petitioner 1   Name and address of Petitioner 2

CLERK'S CERTIFICATE OF MAILING (For court use only)

I certify that I am not a party to this cause and that a copy of the foregoing was mailed first class, postage fully prepaid, in a sealed envelope as shown above, and that the mailing of the foregoing and execution of this certificate occurred at

(place):   California, on

Date: Clerk, by _____ , Deputy

NOTICE

If the clerk's certificate of mailing above has been dated and signed by the clerk, this summary dissolution case is ended. You are still married and/or domestic partners. If you still want to get divorced, you will have to file a regular divorce case using the *Petition—Marriage* (form FL-100) or *Petition—Domestic Partnership* (form FL-103).

Page 1 of 1

Form Adopted for Mandatory Use
Judicial Council of California
FL-830 [Rev. January 1, 2012]

**NOTICE OF REVOCATION OF PETITION
FOR SUMMARY DISSOLUTION
(Family Law—Summary Dissolution)**

Family Code § 2402
www.courts.ca.gov

For your protection and privacy, please press the Clear This Form button after you have printed the form.   **Save This Form**   **Print This Form**   **Clear This Form**

Request for Judgment, Judgment of Dissolution of Marriage, and Notice of Entry of Judgment

FL-820

PARTY WITHOUT ATTORNEY OR ATTORNEY *(Name, State Bar number, and address)*:	**FOR COURT USE ONLY**
TELEPHONE NO.: FAX NO. *(Optional)*: E-MAIL ADDRESS *(Optional)*: ATTORNEY FOR *(Name)*:	To keep other people from seeing what you entered on your form, please press the Clear This Form button at the end of the form when finished.

SUPERIOR COURT OF CALIFORNIA, COUNTY OF
STREET ADDRESS:
MAILING ADDRESS:
CITY AND ZIP CODE:
BRANCH NAME:

MARRIAGE OF
HUSBAND:
WIFE:

REQUEST FOR JUDGMENT, JUDGMENT OF DISSOLUTION OF MARRIAGE, AND NOTICE OF ENTRY OF JUDGMENT	CASE NUMBER:

1. The *Joint Petition for Summary Dissolution* (form FL-800) was filed on *(date)*:
    (Use this form ONLY if the Joint Petition for Summary Dissolution *(form FL-800) was filed before January 1, 2011. If it was filed after January 1, 2011, use* Judgment of Dissolution and Notice of Entry of Judgment *(form FL-825) instead.)*

2. No notice of revocation has been filed, and the parties have not become reconciled.

3. I request that judgment of dissolution of marriage be
    a. ☐ entered to be effective now.
    b. ☐ entered to be effective (nunc pro tunc) as of *(date)*:
        for the following reason:

I declare under penalty of perjury under the laws of the State of California that the foregoing is true and correct.
Date:

▶

_____
(TYPE OR PRINT NAME)

_____
(SIGNATURE OF HUSBAND OR WIFE)

4. Husband ☐   Wife ☐   who did **not** request that his or her own former name be restored when he or she signed the joint petition, now requests that it be restored. The applicant's former name is:

Date:

▶

_____
(TYPE OR PRINT NAME)

_____
(SIGNATURE OF PARTY WISHING TO HAVE HIS OR HER NAME RESTORED)

(For Court Use Only)
JUDGMENT OF DISSOLUTION

THE COURT ORDERS

5. A judgment of dissolution of marriage will be entered, and the parties are restored to the status of unmarried persons.
    a. ☐ The judgment of dissolution of marriage will be entered nunc pro tunc as of *(date)*:
    b. ☐ Wife's former name is restored *(specify)*:
    c. ☐ Husband's former name is restored *(specify)*:
Husband and wife must comply with any agreement attached to the petition.

Date:

_____
JUDICIAL OFFICER

Page 1 of 2

Form Adopted for Mandatory Use
Judicial Council of California
FL-820 [Rev. January 1, 2012]

**REQUEST FOR JUDGMENT, JUDGMENT OF DISSOLUTION
OF MARRIAGE, AND NOTICE OF ENTRY OF JUDGMENT
(Family Law—Summary Dissolution)**

Family Code, § 2403
www.courts.ca.gov

Request for Judgment, Judgment of Dissolution of Marriage, and Notice of Entry of Judgment

HUSBAND:	CASE NUMBER:
WIFE:	

NOTICE: Dissolution may automatically cancel the rights of a spouse under the other spouse's will, trust, retirement benefit plan, power of attorney, pay-on-death bank account, transfer-on-death vehicle registration, survivorship rights to any property owned in joint tenancy, and any other similar instrument. It does not automatically cancel the rights of a spouse as beneficiary of the other spouse's life insurance policy. You should review these matters, as well as any credit cards, other credit accounts, insurance policies, retirement benefit plans, and credit reports, to determine whether they should be changed or whether you should take any other actions.

NOTICE OF ENTRY OF JUDGMENT

6. You are notified that a judgment of dissolution of marriage was entered on *(date)*:

Date: Clerk, by _____, Deputy

CLERK'S CERTIFICATE OF MAILING

I certify that I am not a party to this cause and that a true copy of the *Notice of Entry of Judgment* was mailed first class, postage fully prepaid, in a sealed envelope addressed as shown below, and that the notice was mailed

at *(place):*   California,

on *(date):*

Date: Clerk, by _____, Deputy

HUSBAND'S ADDRESS   WIFE'S ADDRESS

FL-820 [Rev. January 1, 2012]

For your protection and privacy, please press the Clear This Form button after you have printed the form.

| Save This Form | Print This Form | Clear This Form |

Judgment of Dissolution and Notice of Entry of Judgment

FL-825

PARTY WITHOUT ATTORNEY OR ATTORNEY *(Name, State Bar number, and address):*	FOR COURT USE ONLY
TELEPHONE NO.: FAX NO. *(Optional):* E-MAIL ADDRESS *(Optional):* ATTORNEY FOR *(Name):*	To keep other people from seeing what you entered on your form, please press the Clear This Form button at the end of the form when finished.

SUPERIOR COURT OF CALIFORNIA, COUNTY OF

STREET ADDRESS:

MAILING ADDRESS:

CITY AND ZIP CODE:

BRANCH NAME:

MARRIAGE OR DOMESTIC PARTNERSHIP OF

PETITIONER 1:

PETITIONER 2:

JUDGMENT OF DISSOLUTION AND NOTICE OF ENTRY OF JUDGMENT ☐ **MARRIAGE** ☐ **DOMESTIC PARTNERSHIP**	CASE NUMBER:

Use this form ONLY if the *Joint Petition for Summary Dissolution* (form FL-800) was filed after January 1, 2011. If the *Joint Petition for Summary Dissolution* was filed before January 1, 2011, use *Request for Judgment, Judgment of Dissolution, and Notice of Entry of Judgment* (form FL-820) instead.

1. THE COURT ORDERS

    a. A judgment of dissolution of marriage and/or domestic partnership will be entered, and the parties are restored to the status of single persons, effective *(date):*

    b. ☐ The former name of Petitioner 1 is restored *(specify):*

    c. ☐ The former name of Petitioner 2 is restored *(specify):*

    Both petitioners must comply with any agreement attached to this judgment.

Date: _____   _____

                                                      JUDICIAL OFFICER

NOTICE: Dissolution may automatically cancel the rights of a spouse or domestic partner under the other spouse or domestic partner's will, trust, retirement benefit plan, power of attorney, pay-on-death bank account, transfer-on-death vehicle registration, survivorship rights to any property owned in joint tenancy, and any other similar instrument. It does not automatically cancel the rights of a spouse or domestic partner as beneficiary of the other spouse's or domestic partner's life insurance policy. You should review these matters, as well as any credit cards, other credit accounts, insurance policies, retirement benefit plans, and credit reports to determine whether they should be changed or whether you should take any other actions.

NOTICE OF ENTRY OF JUDGMENT

2. You are notified that a judgment of dissolution of

    a. ☐ marriage

    b ☐ domestic partnership

    was entered on *(date):*

Date: _____   Clerk, by _____, Deputy

The date the judgment of dissolution is entered is NOT the date your divorce or termination of your domestic partnership is final. For the effective date of the dissolution of your marriage and/or domestic partnership, see the date in item 1a.

Page 1 of 2

Form Adopted for Mandatory Use
Judicial Council of California
FL-825 [New January 1, 2012]

JUDGMENT OF DISSOLUTION AND NOTICE OF ENTRY OF JUDGMENT
(Family Law—Summary Dissolution)

Family Code, § 2403
www.courts.ca.gov

Judgment of Dissolution and Notice of Entry of Judgment

PETITIONER 1:	CASE NUMBER:
PETITIONER 2:	

CLERK'S CERTIFICATE OF MAILING

I certify that I am not a party to this cause and that a true copy of the *Judgment of Dissolution* and *Notice of Entry of Judgment* was mailed first class, postage fully prepaid, in a sealed envelope addressed as shown below, and that the notice was mailed

at *(place):*   California,

on *(date):*

Date: Clerk, by _____ , Deputy

ADDRESS OF PETITIONER 1   ADDRESS OF PETITIONER 2

**JUDGMENT OF DISSOLUTION AND
NOTICE OF ENTRY OF JUDGMENT
(Family Law—Summary Dissolution)**

For your protection and privacy, please press the Clear This Form button after you have printed the form.

| Save This Form | Print This Form | Clear This Form |

Appendix

Contents

Disclaimer: These forms and examples are for reference only and should not be construed as legal advice. Anyone using this information should consult an attorney to determine if laws, Rules of Court, or local rules have been updated or changed requiring an alternative format or specific language to be included when preparing these documents for the client and/or court. The author does not accept any responsibility for the examples and work product used herein. These examples are provided only for ease in understanding the concepts presented in this book.

1A *Marvin v. Marvin*

MARVIN v MARVIN
18 Cal.3d 660, 557 P.2d 106, 134 Cal. Rptr. 815 (1976)

During the past 15 years, there has been a substantial increase in the number of couples living together without marrying. Such non-marital relationships lead to legal controversy when one partner dies or the couple separates.

........Plaintiff avers that in October 1964 she and defendant "entered into an oral agreement" that while "the parties lived together they would combine their efforts and earnings and would share equally and all property accumulated as a result of their efforts whether individual or combined." Furthermore, they agreed to "hold themselves out to the general public as husband and wife" and that "plaintiff would further render her services as a companion, homemaker, housekeeper and cook to.....defendant."

Shortly thereafter plaintiff agreed to "give up her lucrative career as an entertainer [and] singer" in order to "devote her full time to defendant....as a companion, homemaker, housekeeper and cook", in return defendant agreed to "provide for all of plaintiff's financial support and needs for the rest of her life."

Plaintiff alleges that she lived with defendant from October of 1964 through May 1970 and fulfilled her obligations under the agreement. During this period the parties as a result of their efforts and earnings acquired in defendant's name substantial real and personal property, including motion picture rights worth over $1 million. In May of 1970, however, defendant compelled plaintiff to leave his household. He continued to support plaintiff until November 1971, but thereafter refused to provide further support. On the basis of these allegations plaintiff asserts two causes of action. The first, for declaratory relief, asks the court to determine her contract and property rights; the second seeks to impose a constructive trust upon one half of the property acquired during the course of the relationship......

In the case before us, plaintiff, basing her cause of action in contract.....maintains that the trail court erred in denying her a trial on the merits of her contention. Although that court did not specify the ground for its conclusion that plaintiff's contractual allegations stated no cause of action, defendant offers some four theories to sustain the ruling.....

Defendant first and principally relies on the contention that the alleged contract is so closely related to the supposed "immoral" character of the relationship between plaintiff and himself that the enforcement of the contract would violate public policy. He points to cases asserting that a contract been nonmarital partners is unenforceable if it is "involved in" an illicit relationship.....A review of the numerous California decisions concerning contracts between nonmarital partners, however, reveals that the courts have not employed such broad and uncertain standards to strike down contracts. The decisions instead disclose a narrower and more precise standard: a contract between nonmarital partners is unenforceable only to the extent that it explicitly rests upon the

1A *Marvin v. Marvin*

immoral and illicit consideration of meretricious sexual services....

Although the past decisions however over the issue in the somewhat wispy form of the figures of a Chagall painting, we can abstract from those decisions a clear and simple rule. The fact that a man and a woman live together without marriage, and engage in a sexual relationship, does not in itself invalidate agreements between them relating to their earnings, property, or expenses. Neither is such an agreement invalid merely because the parties may have contemplated the creation or continuation of a nonmarital relationship when they entered into it. Agreements between nonmarital partners fail only to the extent that they rest upon a consideration of meretricious sexual services. Thus the rule asserted by defendant that a contract fails if it is "involved in"or made "in contemplation" of a nonmarital relationship, cannot be reconciled with the decisions.

The three cases cited by defendant which have declined to enforce contracts between nonmarital partners involved consideration that was expressly founded upon an illicit sexual services [sic].....

The principle that a contract between nonmarital partners will be enforced unless expressly and inseparably based upon an illicit consideration of sexual services not only represents the distillation of the decisional law, but also offers a far more precise and workable standard than that advocated by defendant.....

In summary, we base our opinion on the principle that adults who voluntarily live together and engagte in sexual relations are nonetheless as competent as any other person to contract respecting their earnings and property rights. Of course, they cannot lawfully contract to pay for the performance of sexual services, for such a contract is, in essence, an agreement for prostitution and unlawful for that reason. But they may agree to pool their earnings and to hold all property acquired during the relationship in accord with the law governing community property; conversely, they may agree that each partner's earnings and the property acquired from those earnings remain the separate property of the earning partner. So long as the agreement does not rest upon illicit meretricious consideration, the parties may order their economic affairs as they chose, and no policy precludes the courts from enforcing such agreements.

In the present instance, plaintiff alleges that the parties agreed to pool their earnings, that they contracted to share equally in all property acquired, and that defendant agreed to support plaintiff. The terms of the contract as alleged do not rest upon any unlawful consideration. We therefore conclude that the complaint furnishes a suitable basis upon which the trial court can order declaratory relief.....The trial court consequently erred in granting defendant's motion for judgment on the pleadings.....

As we have noted, both causes of action in plaintiff's complaint allege and express contract; neither assert any basis for relief independent from the contract. In In re Marriage of Cary, *supra*, 34 Cal. App. 3d 345, however, the Court of Appeal held that, in view of the policy of The Family Code Act, property accumulated by nonmarital partners in an actual family relationship

1A *Marvin v. Marvin*

should be divided equally. Upon examining the *Cary* opinion, the parties to the present case realized that plaintiff's alleged relationship with defendant might arguably support a cause of action independent of any express contract between spouses.

Reviewing the prior decisions which had denied relief to the homemaking partner, the Court of Appeal reasoned that those decisions rested upon a policy of punishing persons guilty of cohabitation without marriage. The Family Law Act, the court observed, aimed to eliminate fault or guilt as a basis for dividing marital property. But once fault or guilt is excluded, the court reasoned, nothing distinguishes the property rights of a nonmarital "spouse" from those of a putative spouse. Since the latter is entitled to half the "quasi-marital property'"......, the Court of Appeal concluded that, giving effect to the policy of the Family Law Act, a nonmarital cohabitator should also be entitled to half the property accumulated during an "actual family relationship."

Cary met with a mixed reception in other appellate districts. In Estate of Atherley, *supra* 44 Cal. App. 3d 758, the Fourth District agreed with *Cary* that under the Family Law Act a nonmarital partner in an actual family relationship enjoys the same right to an equal division of property as a putative spouse. In Beckman v Mayhew, *supra*, 49 Cal App. 3d 529, however, the Third District rejected *Cary* on the ground that the Family Law Act was not intended to change California law dealing with nonmarital relationships. If *Cary* is interpreted as holding that the Family Law Act requires an equal division of property accumulated in non marital "actual family relationships," then we agree with Beckman v Mayhew that *Cary* distends the act......

But although we reject the reasoning of *Cary* and *Atherley*, we share the perception of the *Cary* and *Atherley* courts that the application of former precedent in the factual setting of those cases would work an unfair distribution of the property accumulated by the couple.....

The principal reason why the pre-*Cary* decisions result in an unfair distribution of property inheres in the court's refusal to permit a nonmarital partner to assert rights based upon accepted principles of implied contract or equity. We have examined the reasons advanced to justify this denial of relief, and find that none have merit.....

First, we note that the cases denying relief do not rest their refusal upon any theory of "punishing" a "guilty" partner. Indeed, to the extent that denial of relief "punishes" one partner, it necessarily rewards the other by permitting him to retain a disproportionate amount of the property. Concepts of "guilt" thus cannot justify an unequal division of property between two equally "guilty" persons.

Other reason advanced in the decision fare no better. The principal argument seems to be that "[equitable]" considerations arising from the reasonable expectation of.....benefits attending the status of marriage....are not present [in nonmarital relationships]." (Vallera v Vallera, *supra*, 21 Cal.2d at p. 685.) But, although parties to a nonmarital relationship obviously cannot have based any expectations upon the belief that they were married, other expectations and equitable considerations remain. The parties, may well expect that property will be divided in accord with

1A *Marvin v. Marvin*

the parties' own tacit understanding and that in the absence of such understanding the courts will fairly apportion property accumulated through mutual effort. We need not treat nonmarital partners as putatively married persons in order to apply principals of implied contract, or extend equitable remedies; we need to treat them only as we do any other unmarried persons......

......The argument that granting remedies to the nonmarital partners would discourage marriage must fail; as *Cary* pointed out, "with equal or greater force the point might be made that the pre-1970 rule was calculated to cause the income-producing partner to avoid marriage and thus retain the benefit of all of his or her accumulated earnings." (34 Ca. App.3d at p. 353.) Although we recognize the well-established public policy to foster and promote the institution of marriage.....perpetuation of judicial rules which result in an inequitable distribution of property accumulated during a nonmarital relationship is neither a just nor an effective way of carrying out that policy.

In summary, we believe that the prevalence of nonmarital relationships in modern society and the social acceptance of them, marks this as a time when our courts should by no means apply the doctrine of the unlawfulness of the so-called meretricious relationship to the instant case. As we have explained, the nonenforceability of agreements expressly providing for meretricious conduct rested upon the fact that such conduct, as the word suggests, pertained to and encompassed prostitution. To equate the nonmarital relationship of today to such a subject matter is to do violence to an accepted and wholly different practice.

We are aware that many young couples live together without the solemnization of marriage, in order to make sure that they can successfully later undertake marriage. This trial period, preliminary to marriage, serves as some assurance that the marriage will not subsequently end in dissolution to the harm of both parties. We are aware, as we have stated, of the pervasiveness of nonmarital relationships in other situations.

The mores of society have indeed changed so radically in regard to cohabitation that we cannot impose a standard based on alleged moral considerations that have apparently been so widely abandoned by so many. Lest we be misunderstood, however, we take this occasion to point out that the structure of society itself largely depends upon the institution of marriage, and nothing we have said in this opinion should be taken to derogate from that institution. The joining of the man and woman in marriage is at once the most socially productive and individually fulfilling relationship that one can enjoy in the course of a lifetime.

We conclude that the judicial barriers that may stand in the way of a policy based upon fulfillment of the reasonable expectations of the parties to a nonmarital relationship should be removed. As we have explained, the courts now hold that express agreements will be enforced unless they rest on an unlawful meretricious consideration. We add that in the absence of an express agreement, the courts may look to a variety of other remedies in order to protect the parties' lawful expectations.

The courts may inquire into the conduct of the parties to determine whether that conduct

1A *Marvin v. Marvin*

demonstrates an implied contract or implied agreement of partnership or joint venture...or some other tacit understanding between the parties. The courts may, when appropriate, employ principles of constructive trust...or resulting trust.....Finally, a nonmarital partner may recover in quantum meruit for the reasonable value of household services rendered less the reasonable value of support received if he can show that he rendered services with the expectation of monetary reward.

Since we have determined that plaintiff's complaint states a cause of action for breach of an express contract, and, as we have explained, can be amended to state a cause of action independent of allegations of express contract, we must conclude the trial court erred in granting defendant a judgment on the pleadings. The judgment is reversed and the cause remanded for further proceedings consistent with the views expressed herein.

2A Client Information/Intake — Example

CLIENT INFORMATION

PERSONAL FACTS:

CLIENT'S FULL NAME: _____
CURRENT ADDRESS: _____
TELEPHONE NUMBERS: _____HOME; _____WORK; _____CELL
DATE MOVED TO ADDRESS: _____; DATE OF RESIDENCE IN CALIFORNIA:_____
DATE OF RESIDENCE IN _____ COUNTY: _____
PREVIOUS ADDRESS: _____
DATE OF BIRTH: _____; SOCIAL SECURITY NUMBER: _____
DRIVER'S LICENSE NUMBER & STATE OF ISSUE: _____
EMPLOYER - NAME: _____
ADDRESS:_____
DATE EMPLOYMENT BEGAN: _____POSITION/TITLE: _____

SPOUSE'S FULL NAME:_____
CURRENT ADDRESS: _____
TELEPHONE NUMBERS: _____HOME; _____WORK; _____CELL
DATE MOVED TO ADDRESS: _____; DATE OF RESIDENCE IN CALIFORNIA:_____
DATE OF RESIDENCE IN _____ COUNTY: _____
PREVIOUS ADDRESS: _____
DATE OF BIRTH: _____; SOCIAL SECURITY NUMBER: _____
DRIVER'S LICENSE NUMBER & STATE OF ISSUE: _____
EMPLOYER - NAME: _____
ADDRESS:_____
DATE EMPLOYMENT BEGAN: _____POSITION/TITLE:_____

DATE OF MARRIAGE: _____ LOCATION OF MARRIAGE:_____
DATE OF SEPARATION: _____

CHILDREN (UNDER THE AGE OF 18 AND RESIDING AT HOME) OF THIS MARRIAGE/RELATIONSHIP:

CHILD'S NAME   DATE OF BIRTH   SOCIAL SECURITY NUMBER

_____   _____   _____

_____   _____   _____

_____   _____   _____

_____   _____   _____
[add pages if more than four children]

2A Client Information/Intake — Example

PLACE OF BIRTH AND WITH WHOM DO EACH OF THE CHILDREN CURRENTLY RESIDE

CHILD'S NAME	PLACE OF BIRTH	RESIDE W/ MOTHER OR FATHER	SINCE (DATE)
_____	_____	_____	_____
_____	_____	_____	_____
_____	_____	_____	_____
_____	_____	_____	_____

LIST ANY MINOR CHILDREN FOR WHOM YOU ARE FINANCIALLY RESPONSIBLE (NOT LISTED ABOVE); THEIR AGE AND WHERE THEY RESIDE

_____	_____	_____	_____
_____	_____	_____	_____
_____	_____	_____	_____

<u>**REAL PROPERTY**</u>:

_____
Address

Title Held: _____

Date Purchased: _____ Date last re-financed: _____

Fair Market Value: _____ As of (date): _____ Approximate Debt: _____

_____
Address

Title Held: _____

Date Purchased: _____ Date last re-financed: _____

Fair Market Value: _____ As of (date): _____ Approximate Debt: _____

_____
Address

2A Client Information/Intake — Example

Title Held: _____

Date Purchased: _____   Date last re-financed: _____

Fair Market Value: _____ As of (date): _____ Approximate Debt: _____

VEHICLES (Automobiles, Trailers, Recreational Vehicles, Motorcyles, etc.)

Year	Make	Model	FMV	Debt

Year	Make	Model	FMV	Debt

Year	Make	Model	FMV	Debt

Year	Make	Model	FMV	Debt

BANK ACCOUNTS (Checking, Savings, Credit Union, CD)

Financial Institution	Branch	Account Number	Approximate Balance

Financial Institution	Branch	Account Number	Approximate Balance

Financial Institution	Branch	Account Number	Approximate Balance

Financial Institution	Branch	Account Number	Approximate Balance

Financial Institution	Branch	Account Number	Approximate Balance

2A Client Information/Intake — Example

OTHER ACCOUNTS (Stocks, Bonds, Mutual Funds)

Financial Institution	Branch	Account Number	Approximate Balance
Financial Institution	Branch	Account Number	Approximate Balance
Financial Institution	Branch	Account Number	Approximate Balance
Financial Institution	Branch	Account Number	Approximate Balance

PENSION & BENEFIT PLANS (457, 409(b) 401(k), etc.)

Name of Plan	Type of Plan	Date Started	Vested	Husband/Wife
Name of Plan	Type of Plan	Date Started	Vested Husband/Wife	
Name of Plan	Type of Plan	Date Started	Vested Husband/Wife	
Name of Plan	Type of Plan	Date Started	Vested Husband/Wife	

OTHER ASSETS

2A Client Information/Intake — Example

DEBTS & OBLIGATIONS

Company   Account #   Balance Due:

_____   _____   _____

_____   _____   _____

_____   _____   _____

_____   _____   _____

_____   _____   _____

_____   _____   _____

_____   _____   _____

DO YOU OWE ANY ONE (OTHER THAN LISTED ABOVE) MONEY; OR DOES ANYONE OWE YOU MONEY? If so, list

_____   _____   _____

_____   _____   _____

_____   _____   _____

_____   _____   _____

SEPARATE PROPERTY

Type of Property   Husband/Wife Location of Property

_____   _____   _____

_____   _____   _____

_____   _____   _____

_____   _____   _____

INCOME (Client's and if known for the other party)

2A Client Information/Intake—Example

WIFE'S MONTHLY GROSS INCOME (Please provide a copy of pay stubs for the past two months and/or tax returns for the past two years)

_____

HUSBAND'S MONTHLY GROSS INCOME (Please provide a copy of pay stubs for the past two months and/or tax returns for the past two years)

_____

<u>AVERAGE MONTHLY EXPENSES</u> (OR ATTACH AN INCOME & EXPENSE DECLARATON)

Mortgage/Rent: _____
      Principal: _____
      Interest: _____
      Taxes: _____
      Insurance: _____
      Maintenance: _____

Food & Household Supplies: _____
Food - Eating Out: _____
Laundry/Cleaning _____
Utilities: _____
Telephone: _____
Clothing: _____
Auto (Gas/Oil/Repairs) _____
Insurance (not medical) _____
Child Care: _____
Entertainment: _____
Incidentals: _____
Avg Monthly Credit Cards: _____
Other (list) _____
                     _____
                     _____
                     _____

3A Points & Authorities for Motion to Quash

POINTS AND AUTHORITIES IN SUPPORT OF

RESPONDENT'S MOTION TO QUASH PROCEEDING

1. The Court does not have jurisdiction over the status of the marriage of the parties because neither Petitioner nor Respondent is currently domiciled in California.

In order for a court to acquire jurisdiction to dissolve a marriage, the court must have jurisdiction of the marital "res" and such jurisdiction is acquired by a valid domicile of either party within the forum state. [William v. North Carolina (1942) 317 U.S. 287].

2. The Court may not exercise personal jurisdiction over Respondent because Respondent is not domiciled within California, was not personally served with process in California, has not consented to California jurisdiction, and has no "contacts" with the State of California.

Respondent is domiciled in Cleveland, Ohio. He/she was not served with process in California, but was served by mail in Cleveland, Ohio, where he/she resides. Respondent does not consent to California jurisdiction and will be filing for a dissolution of marriage in the State of Ohio, which is the proper forum for this matter. [Burnham v. Superior Court (Burnham) (1990) 495 U.S. 604, 110 S. Ct 2105; International Shoe Co. v. Washington (1977) 433 U.S. 186].

3A Points & Authorities for Motion to Quash

1   3. <u>Where a court lacks jurisdiction over a party, a motion to quash summons is the</u>

2 <u>appropriate method of obtaining relief.</u>

3   Respondent has filed a Motion to Quash Summons as the California Court lacks

4 jurisdiction over him/her. There is no jurisdiction to have this matter come before the court

5 in California, therefore, Respondent is requesting the court for relief herein. <u>California</u>

6 <u>Rules of Court, Rule 1234</u>

7

8

9

10

11

12

13

14

15

16

17

18

19

20

21

22

23

24

25

26

27

28

3B Declaration for Motion to Quash

1   **DECLARATION OF** _____

2   **IN SUPPORT OF MOTION TO QUASH PROCEEDING**

3

4   I, _____, declare:

5   I am named in the within proceeding as Respondent. A Summons was served on me,

6 together with a copy of the Petition for Dissolution, on _____, ____. The Petition

7 in this proceeding was filed by Petitioner on _____, _____.

8   I am now, and for the past _____ (___) years been married to Petitioner. We were

9 married in Las Vegas, Nevada on _____, and ever since that date have been

10 residents of the State of Ohio. Neither Petitioner nor I have ever resided in any other place than

11 our family home located at _____, Cleveland, Ohio, from the date of our

12 marriage until or about _____. On _____, Petitioner moved out

13 of the family residence, and her whereabouts have been unknown to me since that date. I still do

14 not know where he/she is residing.

15   I as served with process in this proceeding by mail with a return receipt requested on

16 _____, _____. Other than a short stop-over at the Los Angeles International Airport

17 on _____, _____, for our honeymoon and while on route to Maui, Hawaii, I have

18 never been within the State of California and do not transact business within the State of

19 California.

20   Our minor children reside in Cleveland, Ohio. All of our property acquired during our

21 marriage is located in the State of Ohio. To my personal knowledge, Petitioner can only have

22 been staying in the State of California since _____, _____, as I have obtained a

23 copy of his/her, and the children's, airline tickets purchased via the internet. At this time, he/she

24 does not satisfy the residence requirement of California law to pursue a dissolution proceeding

25 there.

26   I am attaching the following documents to this declaration as evidence that I am <u>not</u>

27 domiciled in California and that Petitioner does not meet the residency requirements which

28 would enable him/her to file for a dissolution in California:

3B Declaration for Motion to Quash

1   1) Tax returns, filed jointly, for the years ____, _____, and ____;

2   2) Voter's registration for the county of _____, State of Ohio;

3   3) Copy of airline tickets purchased by Petitioner on _____, for he/she and the children

4 leaving Ohio on _____ ,_____ and arriving in California on _____ ,_____.

5 This ticket confirms that as of _____, _____, Petitioner was still in Ohio and could

6 not have established residency in California;

7   4) School records of children showing they were enrolled in _____ School as of

8 _____, _____;

9   5) Copies of joint accounts, vehicle registrations, deed, and other property held jointly by

10 Petitioner and I in the State of Ohio;

11   6) Grocery receipts, clothing purchases, and other purchases made by Petitioner on or

12 about _____, _____, indicating that those purchases were made in Ohio by

13 Petitioner.

14   Petitioner requests that the Court Quash Petitioner's Summons and Petition filed in this

15 county, finding in favor of Respondent, based upon the above Declaration and the Points &

16 Authorities as attached an incorporated herein.

17   I declare under penalty of perjury under the laws of the State of California that the

18 foregoing is true and correct.

19 Dated:_____   /s/_____

20

21

22

23

24

25

26

27

28

3C Motion Declaration Samples

MOTION TO QUASH THE PROCEEDING:

#13. Other Relief: To change venue to Ventura County (California Rules of Court, Rule 1235).

#14. Facts in Support: The parties have resided at all times during their marriage in the County of Ventura; Respondent is a resident of that County, but Petitioner moved to Orange County in the past 40 days. All of the parties' community property is located in Ventura County; the minor children of the parties reside in Ventura County and attend school there. Respondent intends to seek permanent legal and physical custody of the parties' minor children, and intends to call, if needed, two school teachers of the minor children who reside in Ventura County.

MOTION TO CHANGE VENUE:

#13. Other Relief: To Quash the Proceeding (California Rules of Court, Rule 1230(a)(2)), on the ground that there is another action pending between the parties for the same cause.

#14. Facts in Support: There is another action pending between Petitioner and Respondent in the Superior Court of California Ventura County, action No._____, entitled "Marriage of Petitioner _____, and Respondent _____." That action is at issue, a Response having been filed by Respondent in that action, the same party named as Respondent in this action. Petitioner has moved her residence since the filing of the Ventura County proceeding; Respondent was and still is a resident of the County of Ventura, and the court of that county has jurisdiction of the matters involved in the dissolution of the marriage of the parties.

3C Motion Declaration Samples

MOTION TO STAY OR DISMISS:

#13. Other Relief: To stay or dismiss the proceedings herein on ground that the State of California is an inconvenient forum (California Code of Civil Procedure Section 410.30).

#14. Facts: contained in attached declaration.

3D Child Support Formal Report

Xspouse 2004-2-CA   *Page 1*

Formal Report   **Monthly figures**

Figures on this page exclude effects of guideline support.

		Father	Mother
CHILDREN			
Supported children of this relationship		1	0
Husband's visitation of children with wife		0.00%	
Wife's visitation of children with husband			0.00%
INCOME			
Tax filing status		HH/MLA	HH/MLA
Number of federal exemptions		2	1
Wage and salary income		6000	1500
Self-employment income		0	0
Other federally taxable income		0	0
Other non-taxable income		0	0
TOTAL GUIDELINE INCOME		6000	1500
TANF and child support received from other relationships		0	0
New spouse income on joint return		0	0
EXPENSES			
Deductible support paid re other relationships	B	0	0
Non-deductible support paid re other relationships	G	0	0
Health insurance premiums	B	0	0
Recurring other medical, dental and drug expenses	T	0	0
Recurring property taxes paid	T	0	0
Recurring interest expense	T	0	0
Recurring charitable contribution deductions	T	0	0
Recurring miscellaneous expenses	T	0	0
Union dues required for employment	B	0	0
Mandatory retirement/pension contributions	B	0	0
Hardship deductions	G	0	0
Other discretionary guideline deductions	G	0	0
Child care expenses, this relationship	B	0	0
Total guideline deductions, excluding taxes		0	0
COMPUTATIONS (BEFORE SUPPORT)			
State income tax (prorated in the case of MFJ)		224	0
Federal income tax (prorated in the case of MFJ)		772	65
FICA		459	115
Federal self-employment tax		0	0
State employment taxes		68	18
Total taxes		1523	197
TOTAL GUIDELINE DEDUCTIONS		1523	197
NET GUIDELINE INCOME BEFORE SUPPORT		4477	1303

Time: *Date:*

3D Child Support Formal Report

Xspouse 2004-2-CA   *Page 2*

Formal Report   **Monthly figures**

Guideline spousal support is based on adjusted nets

	Guideline	Proposed
COMBINED CASH FLOW		
Combined net spendable income	5988	5918
Percent change	0%	-1%
FATHER'S CASH FLOW		
After-tax cost (-) or benefit (+) of payment	-407	-455
Net spendable income after support	4070	4022
Percent of combined net spendable income	68%	68%
Percent of total tax savings	0%	68%
Total taxes after credits	1144	1285
Value of dependency exemptions	185	191
Number of withholding allowances	10	9
Net wage paycheck	4739	4668
State marginal bracket	8%	9%
Federal marginal bracket	25%	25%
Combined marginal bracket	31%	32%
MOTHER'S CASH FLOW		
After-tax cost (-) or benefit (+) of payment	616	593
Net spendable income after support	1918	1896
Percent of combined net spendable income	32%	32%
Percent of total tax savings	0%	32%
Total taxes after credits	368	297
Value of dependency exemptions	100	100
Number of withholding allowances	0	0
Net wage paycheck	1205	1205
State marginal bracket	2%	2%
Federal marginal bracket	15%	15%
Combined marginal bracket	17%	17%

Time: *Date:*

3D Child Support Formal Report

Xspouse 2004-2-CA

Page 3

Formal Report

Monthly figures

Guideline spousal support is based on adjusted nets

Support Summary

GUIDELINE SUPPORT

Addons	0	
Child support	326	mother pays
Spousal support	1113	father pays
Total support	787	father pays

PROPOSED SETTLEMENT

Child support	0	
Spousal support	693	father pays
Total support	693	father pays
Saving	-70	

Comments

On page 1, the lines marked G affect guideline directly, lines marked T affect taxes directly and guideline indirectly through changes in tax, and lines marked B affect both guideline and taxes directly.

Proposed column minimizes taxes, then splits the enlarged net spendable income in the same proportion as the guideline allocation.

Proposed column assumes that Mother releases 0 exemptions via IRS Form 8332.

Spousal Support formula: S.Clara SS

Tax year:

Time:

Date:

3E Child Support Calculations — 6 Examples

Xspouse 2004-2-CA

2004   **Findings and Rebuttals**

Income	Father	Mother	Child care expenses allocated	Equally
Gross income	5000	1500		
Net disposable income	3426	1717		
Filing status	SINGLE	HH/MLA		
Number of exemptions	1	3		
Total deductions	1574	-217		
New spouse/significant other income	0	0		

Allocation

	Father	Mother
Amount allocated for child support	1644	824

	Custodial Time		Child Care		Presumed CS	
	Father	Mother	Father	Mother		
All children	20.00 %	80.00 %	0	0	1151	father pays
	20.00 %	80.00 %	0	0	423	father pays
	20.00 %	80.00 %	0	0	728	father pays

Tax	Father	Mother
Federal income tax	813	-349
FICA	383	115
Self-employment tax	0	0
State income tax	270	0
State disability insurance	59	18

Other Deductions		
Mandatory union dues	0	0
Mandatory retirement	0	0
Health insurance	50	0
Child and spousal support paid other relationships	0	0
Hardship	0	0
Other guideline deductions	0	0

Totals		
Total taxes	1524	-217
Total other deductions	50	0
Total taxes + other deductions	1574	-217

3E Child Support Calculations—6 Examples

Xspouse 2004-2-CA

2004   Findings and Rebuttals

Income	Father	Mother	Child care expenses allocated	Equally
Gross Income	5000	1500		
Net disposable income	3226	1717		
Filing status	SINGLE	HH/MLA		
Number of exemptions	1	3		
Total deductions	1774	-217		
New spouse/significant other income	0	0		

Allocation

	Father	Mother
Amount allocated for child support	1574	838

	Custodial Time		Child Care		Presumed CS	
	Father	Mother	Father	Mother		
All children	22.00 %	78.00 %	0	0	1043	father pays
	22.00 %	78.00 %	0	0	382	father pays
	22.00 %	78.00 %	0	0	662	father pays

Tax	Father	Mother
Federal income tax	813	-349
FICA	383	115
Self-employment tax	0	0
State income tax	270	0
State disability insurance	59	18

Other Deductions		
Mandatory union dues	50	0
Mandatory retirement	100	0
Health insurance	100	0
Child and spousal support paid other relationships	0	0
Hardship	0	0
Other guideline deductions	0	0

Totals		
Total taxes	1524	-217
Total other deductions	250	0
Total taxes + other deductions	1774	-217

3E Child Support Calculations—6 Examples

Xspouse 2004-2-CA

2004   **Findings and Rebuttals**

Income	Father	Mother	Child care expenses allocated	Equally
Gross income	5000	1500		
Net disposable income	3384	1717		
Filing status	<-MFJ	HH/MLA		
Number of exemptions	2	3		
Total deductions	1616	-217		
New spouse/significant other income	0	0		

Allocation

	Father	Mother
Amount allocated for child support	1651	838

	Custodial Time		Child Care		Presumed CS	
	Father	Mother	Father	Mother		
All children	22.00 %	78.00 %	0	0	1104	father pays
	22.00 %	78.00 %	0	0	404	father pays
	22.00 %	78.00 %	0	0	699	father pays

Tax	Father	Mother
Federal income tax	703	-349
FICA	383	115
Self-employment tax	0	0
State income tax	222	0
State disability insurance	59	18

Other Deductions		
Mandatory union dues	50	0
Mandatory retirement	100	0
Health insurance	100	0
Child and spousal support paid other relationships	0	0
Hardship	0	0
Other guideline deductions	0	0

Totals		
Total taxes	1366	-217
Total other deductions	250	0
Total taxes + other deductions	1616	-217

3E Child Support Calculations — 6 Examples

Xspouse 2004-2-CA

2004   **Findings and Rebuttals**

Income	Father	Mother	Child care expenses allocated	Equally
Gross income	5000	1500		
Net disposable income	3393	1717		
Filing status	<-MFJ	HH/MLA		
Number of exemptions	2	3		
Total deductions	1607	-217		
New spouse/significant other income	0	0		

Allocation

	Father	Mother
Amount allocated for child support	1656	838

	Custodial Time		Child Care		Presumed CS	
	Father	Mother	Father	Mother		
All children	22.00 %	78.00 %	0	0	1107	father pays
	22.00 %	78.00 %	0	0	406	father pays
	22.00 %	78.00 %	0	0	701	father pays

Tax	Father	Mother
Federal income tax	694	-349
FICA	383	115
Self-employment tax	0	0
State income tax	222	0
State disability insurance	59	18

Other Deductions		
Mandatory union dues	50	0
Mandatory retirement	100	0
Health insurance	100	0
Child and spousal support paid other relationships	0	0
Hardship	0	0
Other guideline deductions	0	0

Totals		
Total taxes	1357	-217
Total other deductions	250	0
Total taxes + other deductions	1607	-217

3E Child Support Calculations—6 Examples

Xspouse 2004-2-CA

2004   **Findings and Rebuttals**

Income	Father	Mother	Child care expenses allocated	Equally
Gross income	5000	1500		
Net disposable income	3015	1717		
Filing status	<-MFJ	HH/MLA		
Number of exemptions	3	3		
Total deductions	1986	-217		
New spouse/significant other income	0	0		

Allocation

	Father	Mother
Amount allocated for child support	1471	838

	Custodial Time		Child Care		Presumed CS	
	Father	Mother	Father	Mother		
All children	22.00 %	78.00 %	0	0	963	father pays
	22.00 %	78.00 %	0	0	377	father pays
	22.00 %	78.00 %	0	0	586	father pays

Tax	Father	Mother
Federal income tax	605	-349
FICA	383	115
Self-employment tax	0	0
State income tax	208	0
State disability insurance	59	18
Other Deductions		
Mandatory union dues	50	0
Mandatory retirement	100	0
Health insurance	100	0
Child and spousal support paid other relationships	0	0
Hardship	482	0
Other guideline deductions	0	0
Totals		
Total taxes	1254	-217
Total other deductions	732	0
Total taxes + other deductions	1986	-217

3E Child Support Calculations—6 Examples

Xspouse 2004-2-CA

Findings and Rebuttals

Income	Father	Mother		
			Child care expenses allocated	Equally
Gross income	5000	1500		
Net disposable income	3453	1717		
Filing status	SINGLE	HH/MLA		
Number of exemptions	1	3		
Total deductions	1547	-217		
New spouse/significant other income	0	0		

Allocation		
Amount allocated for child support	2058	1023

	Custodial Time		Child Care		Presumed CS	
	Father	Mother	Father	Mother		
All children	49.00 %	51.00 %	0	0	548	father pays
	49.00 %	51.00 %	0	0	180	father pays
	49.00 %	51.00 %	0	0	368	father pays

Tax	Father	Mother
Federal income tax	813	-349
FICA	383	115
Self-employment tax	0	0
State income tax	243	0
State disability insurance	59	18

Other Deductions		
Mandatory union dues	0	0
Mandatory retirement	0	0
Health insurance	50	0
Child and spousal support paid other relationships	0	0
Hardship	0	0
Other guideline deductions	0	0

Totals		
Total taxes	1497	-217
Total other deductions	50	0
Total taxes + other deductions	1547	-217

3F Child Support Calculations — Example

Xspouse 2004-2-CA

2004   **Findings and Rebuttals**

Income	Father	Mother	Child care expenses allocated	Equally
Gross income	5000	3000		
Net disposable income	3453	2700		
Filing status	SINGLE	HH/MLA		
Number of exemptions	1	3		
Total deductions	1547	300		
New spouse/significant other income	0	0		

Allocation

	Father	Mother
Amount allocated for child support	2058	1609

	Custodial Time		Child Care		Presumed CS	
	Father	Mother	Father	Mother		
All children	49.00 %	51.00 %	0	0	261	father pays
	49.00 %	51.00 %	0	0	75	father pays
	49.00 %	51.00 %	0	0	186	father pays

Tax	Father	Mother
Federal income tax	813	35
FICA	383	230
Self-employment tax	0	0
State income tax	243	0
State disability insurance	59	35

Other Deductions		
Mandatory union dues	0	0
Mandatory retirement	0	0
Health insurance	50	0
Child and spousal support paid other relationships	0	0
Hardship	0	0
Other guideline deductions	0	0

Totals		
Total taxes	1497	300
Total other deductions	50	0
Total taxes + other deductions	1547	300

4A(a) Request for Domestic Violence Restraining Order (DV-100)

DV-100	**Request for Domestic Violence Restraining Order**

Clerk stamps date here when form is filed.

You must also complete Form CLETS-001, Confidential CLETS Information and give it to the clerk when you file this Request.

To keep other people from seeing what you entered on your form, please press the Clear This Form button at the end of the form when finished.

(1) Name of person asking for protection:

_____ Age: _____

Your lawyer in this case *(if you have one)*:

Name: _____ State Bar No.: _____

Firm Name: _____

Address *(If you have a lawyer for this case, give your lawyer's information. If you do not have a lawyer and want to keep your home address private, give a different mailing address instead. You do not have to give your telephone, fax, or e-mail.):*

Address: _____

City: _____ State: _____ Zip: _____

Telephone: _____ Fax: _____

E-Mail Address: _____

Fill in court name and street address:

Superior Court of California, County of

Clerk fills in case number when form is filed.

Case Number:

(2) Name of person you want protection from:

_____

Description of person you want protection from:

Sex: ☐ M ☐ F Height: _____ Weight: _____ Hair Color: _____ Eye Color: _____

Race: _____ Age: _____ Date of Birth: _____

Address *(if known):* _____

City: _____ State: _____ Zip: _____

(3) Do you want an order to protect family or household members? ☐ Yes ☐ No

If yes, list them:

Full name	Sex	Age	Lives with you?	Relationship to you
_____	_____	_____	☐ Yes ☐ No	_____
_____	_____	_____	☐ Yes ☐ No	_____
_____	_____	_____	☐ Yes ☐ No	_____

☐ *Check here if you need more space. Attach a sheet of paper and write "DV-100, Protected People" for a title.*

(4) What is your relationship to the person in (2)? *(Check all that apply):*

a. ☐ We are now married or registered domestic partners.

b. ☐ We used to be married or registered domestic partners.

c. ☐ We live together.

d. ☐ We used to live together.

If you do not have one of these relationships, the court may not be able to consider your request. Read DV-500-INFO for help.

e. ☐ We are related by blood, marriage, or adoption (specify relationship): _____

f. ☐ We are dating or used to date, or we are or used to be engaged to be married.

g. ☐ We are the parents together of a child or children under 18:

Child's Name: _____ Date of Birth: _____

Child's Name: _____ Date of Birth: _____

Child's Name: _____ Date of Birth: _____

☐ *Check here if you need more space. Attach a sheet of paper and write "DV-100, Children Under 18" for a title.*

h. ☐ We have signed a Voluntary Declaration of Paternity for our child or children. *(Attach a copy if you have one).*

This is not a Court Order.

Judicial Council of California, www.courts.ca.gov
Revised January 2, 2012, Mandatory Form
Family Code, § 6200 et seq.

Request for Domestic Violence Restraining Order
(Domestic Violence Prevention)

DV-100, Page 1 of 5
→

4A(a) Request for Domestic Violence Restraining Order (DV-100)

Case Number:

---

⑤ Other Court Cases

a. Have you or any other person named in item ③ been involved in another court case with the person in ②?

  ☐ No ☐ Yes *If yes, check each kind of case and indicate where and when each was filed:*

Kind of Case	County or Tribe Where Filed	Year Filed	Case Number *(if known)*
☐ Divorce, Nullity, Legal Separation			
☐ Civil Harassment			
☐ Domestic Violence			
☐ Criminal			
☐ Juvenile, Dependency, Guardianship			
☐ Child Support			
☐ Parentage, Paternity			
☐ Other *(specify):* _____			

  ☐ *Check here if you need more space. Attach a sheet of paper and write "DV-100, Other Court Cases" for a title.*

b. Are there any domestic violence restraining/protective orders now (criminal, juvenile, family)?

  ☐ No ☐ Yes *If yes, attach a copy if you have one.*

Check the orders you want. ☑

⑥ ☐ Personal Conduct Orders

I ask the court to order the person in ② not to do the following things to me or anyone listed in ③:

a. ☐ Harass, attack, strike, threaten, assault (sexually or otherwise), hit, follow, stalk, molest, destroy personal property, disturb the peace, keep under surveillance, or block movements

b. ☐ Contact, either directly or indirectly, in any way, including but not limited to, by telephone, mail or e-mail or other electronic means

The person in ② will be ordered not to take any action to get the addresses or locations of any protected person unless the court finds good cause not to make the order.

⑦ ☐ Stay-Away Order

a. I ask the court to order the person in ② to stay at least _____ yards away from *(check all that apply):*

  ☐ Me   ☐ My vehicle
  ☐ My home   ☐ The children's school or child care
  ☐ My job or workplace   ☐ Each person listed in ③
  ☐ My school   ☐ Other *(specify):* _____

b. If the person listed in ② is ordered to stay away from all the places listed above, will he or she still be able to get to his or her home, school, job, workplace, school, or vehicle? ☐ Yes ☐ No *(If no, explain):*

_____

⑧ ☐ Move-Out Order

(If the person in ② lives with you and you want that person to stay away from your home, you must ask for this move-out order)

I ask the court to order the person in ② to move out from and not return to *(address):*

_____

I have the right to live at the above address because (explain): _____

_____

This is not a Court Order.

4A(a) Request for Domestic Violence Restraining Order (DV-100)

Case Number:

⑨ Guns or Other Firearms and Ammunition

I believe the person in ② owns or possesses guns, firearms, or ammunition. ☐ Yes ☐ No ☐ I don't know

If the judge approves the order, the person in ② will be ordered not to own, possess, purchase or receive a firearm or ammunition. The person will be ordered to sell to a gun dealer or turn in to law enforcement any guns or firearms that he or she owns or possesses.

⑩ ☐ Record Unlawful Communications

I ask for the right to record communications made to me by the person in ② that violate the judge's orders.

⑪ ☐ Animals: Possession and Stay-Away Order

I ask for the sole possession, care, and control of the animals listed below. I ask the court to order the person in ② to stay at least _____ yards away from and not take, sell, transfer, encumber, conceal, molest, attack, strike, threaten, harm, or otherwise dispose of the following animals:_____

_____

I ask for the animals to be with me because: _____

_____

⑫ ☐ Child Custody and Visitation

a. ☐ I do not have a child custody or visitation order and I want one.

b. ☐ I have a child custody or visitation order and I want it changed.

If you ask for orders, you must fill out and attach Form DV-105, Request for Child Custody and Visitation Orders.

You and the other parent may tell the court that you want to be legal parents of the children (use Form DV-180, Agreement and Judgment of Parentage).

⑬ ☐ Child Support *(Check all that apply):*

a. ☐ I do not have a child support order and I want one.

b. ☐ I have a child support order and I want it changed.

c. ☐ I now receive or have applied for TANF, Welfare, CalWORKS, or Medi-Cal.

If you ask for child support orders, you must fill out and attach Form FL-150, Income and Expense Declaration *or Form FL-155,* Financial Statement (Simplified).

⑭ ☐ Property Control

I ask the court to give *only* me temporary use, possession, and control of the property listed here:

_____

⑮ ☐ Debt Payment

I ask the court to order the person in ② to make these payments while the order is in effect:

☐ *Check here if you need more space. Attach a sheet of paper and write "DV-100, Debt Payment" for a title.*

Pay to: _____ For: _____ Amount: $_____ Due date: _____

⑯ ☐ Property Restraint

I am married to or have a registered domestic partnership with the person in ②. I ask the judge to order that the person in ② not borrow against, sell, hide, or get rid of or destroy any possessions or property, except in the usual course of business or for necessities of life. I also ask the judge to order the person in ② to notify me of any new or big expenses and to explain them to the court.

This is not a Court Order.

4A(a) Request for Domestic Violence Restraining Order (DV-100)

Case Number: _____

(17) ☐ **Spousal Support**

I am married to or have a registered domestic partnership with the person in ② and no spousal support order exists. I ask the court to order the person in ② to pay spousal support. *(You must fill out, file, and serve Form FL-150,* Income and Expense Declaration, *before your hearing).*

(18) ☐ **Lawyer's Fees and Costs**

I ask that the person in ② pay some or all of my lawyer's fees and costs.
You must complete, file and serve Form FL-150, Income and Expense Declaration *before your hearing.*

(19) ☐ **Payments for Costs and Services**

I ask the court to order the person in ② to pay the following:
You can ask for lost earnings or your costs for services caused directly by the person in ② *(damaged property, medical care, counseling, temporary housing, etc.). You must bring proof of these expenses to your hearing.*

Pay to: _____ For: _____ Amount: $_____

Pay to: _____ For: _____ Amount: $_____

(20) ☐ **Batterer Intervention Program**

I ask the court to order the person listed in ② to go to a 52-week batterer intervention program and show proof of completion to the court.

(21) ☐ **Other Orders**

What other orders are you asking for?_____
_____
_____

☐ *Check here if you need more space. Attach a sheet of paper and write "DV-100, Other Orders" for a title.*

(22) ☐ **Time for Service (Notice)**

The papers must be personally served on the person in ② *at least five days before the hearing, unless the court orders a shorter time for service. If you want there to be fewer than five days between service and the hearing, explain why below. For help, read Form DV-200-INFO, "What Is Proof of Personal Service?"*

_____
_____
_____

(23) **No Fee to Serve (Notify) Restrained Person**

If you want the sheriff or marshal to serve (notify) the restrained person about the orders for free, ask the court clerk what you need to do.

(24) **Court Hearing**

The court will schedule a hearing on your request. If the judge does not make the orders effective right away ("temporary restraining orders"), the judge may still make the orders after the hearing. If the judge does not make the orders effective right away, you can ask the court to cancel the hearing. Read Form DV-112, *Waiver of Hearing on Denied Request for Temporary Restraining Order* for more information.

This is not a Court Order.

4A(a) Request for Domestic Violence Restraining Order (DV-100)

Case Number:

(25) Describe Abuse

Describe how the person in (2) abused you. Abuse means to intentionally or recklessly cause or attempt to cause bodily injury to you; or to place you or another person in reasonable fear of imminent serious bodily injury; or to molest, attack, hit, stalk, threaten, batter, harass, telephone, or contact you; or to disturb your peace; or to destroy your personal property. Abuse can be spoken, written, or physical. (For a complete definition, see Family Code §§ 6203, 6320).

a. Date of most recent abuse: _____

b. Who was there? _____

c. Describe how the person in (2) abused you or your children: _____
_____
_____
_____
_____
_____
_____

☐ *Check here if you need more space. Attach a sheet of paper and write "DV-100, Recent Abuse" for a title.*

d. Did the person in (2) use or threaten to use a gun or any other weapon? ☐ No ☐ Yes *(If yes, describe):*
_____

e. Describe any injuries: _____
_____

f. Did the police come? ☐ No ☐ Yes
If yes, did they give you or the person in (2) an Emergency Protective Order? ☐ Yes ☐ No ☐ I don't know
Attach a copy if you have one.
The order protects ☐ you   or   ☐ the person in (2)

g. **Has the person in (2) abused you (or your children) other times?**
If yes, ☐ check here and use Form DV-101, Description of Abuse *or a sheet of paper to describe any previous abuse.*

(26) Other Persons to Be Protected

The persons listed in item (3) need an order for protection because *(describe):* _____
_____
_____

(27) Number of pages attached to this form, if any: _____

I declare under penalty of perjury under the laws of the State of California that the information above is true and correct.

Date: _____

▶
_____   _____
Type or print your name   *Sign your name*

Date: _____

▶
_____   _____
Lawyer's name, if you have one   *Lawyer's signature*

This is not a Court Order.

For your protection and privacy, please press the Clear This Form button after you have printed the form.   Save This Form   Print This Form   Clear This Form

4A(b) Notice of Hearing (DV-109)

DV-109	**Notice of Court Hearing**

Clerk stamps date here when form is filed.

① Name of Person Asking for Order:

_____

Your lawyer in this case *(if you have one):*
Name:_____ State Bar No.: _____
Firm Name: _____
Address *(If you have a lawyer for this case, give your lawyer's information. If you do not have a lawyer and want to keep your home address private, give a different mailing address instead. You do not have to give your telephone, fax, or e-mail.):*
Address:_____
City:_____ State: _____ Zip:_____
Telephone: _____ Fax:_____
E-Mail Address: _____

To keep other people from seeing what you entered on your form, please press the Clear This Form button at the end of the form when finished.

Fill in court name and street address:
Superior Court of California, County of

② Name of Person to Be Restrained:

_____

The court will fill out the rest of this form.

Clerk fills in case number when form is filed.
Case Number:

③ Notice of Court Hearing

A court hearing is scheduled on the request for restraining orders against the person in ②.

	Name and address of court if different from above:

Hearing Date → Date: _____ Time: _____ _____
Dept.: _____ Room: _____ _____
_____

④ Temporary Restraining Orders (any orders granted are attached on Form DV-110)

a. Temporary restraining orders for personal conduct, stay away, and protection of animals, as requested in Form DV-100, *Request for Domestic Violence Restraining Order,* are:

(1) ☐ All **granted** until the court hearing

(2) ☐ All **denied** until the court hearing *(specify reasons for denial in (b)):*

(3) ☐ Partly **granted** and partly **denied** until the court hearing *(specify reasons for denial in (b)):*

b. Requested temporary restraining orders for personal conduct, stay away, and protection of animals are denied because:

(1) ☐ The facts as stated in form DV-100 do not show reasonable proof of a past act or acts of abuse. (Family Code, §§ 6320 and 6320.5)

(2) ☐ The facts do not describe in sufficient detail the most recent incidents of abuse, such as what happened, the dates, who did what to whom, or any injuries or history of abuse.

(3) ☐ Further explanation of reason for denial, or reason not listed above:

_____
_____
_____

This is a Court Order.

Judicial Council of California, www.courts.ca.gov
Revised January 1, 2012, Mandatory Form
Family Code, § 242. Approved by DOJ

Notice of Court Hearing
(Domestic Violence Prevention)

DV-109, Page 1 of 3
→

4A(b) Notice of Hearing (DV-109)

Case Number:

---

5 **Service of Documents and Time for Service—for Person in** ①

At least ☐ **five or** ☐ ___ **days before the hearing,** someone age 18 or older—**not you or anyone else to be protected**—must personally give (serve) a court's file-stamped copy of this form (DV-109, *Notice of Court Hearing*) to the person in ② along with a copy of all the forms indicated below:

a. Form DV-100, *Request for Domestic Violence Restraining Order,* (file-stamped) with applicable attachments

b. ☐ Form DV-110, *Temporary Restraining Order* (file-stamped) with applicable attachments **if granted by the judge**

c. Form DV-120, *Response to Request for Domestic Violence Restraining Order* (blank form)

d. Form DV-250, *Proof of Service by Mail* (blank form)

e. ☐ Other *(specify):* _____

Date: _____   _____

Judicial Officer

Right to Cancel Hearing: Information for the Person in ❶

- If item ④(a)(2) or ④(a)(3) is checked, the judge has denied some or all of the temporary orders you requested until the court hearing. The judge may make the orders you want after the court hearing. You can keep the hearing date, or you can cancel your request for orders so there is no court hearing.

- If you want to cancel the hearing, use Form DV-112, *Waiver of Hearing on Denied Request for Temporary Restraining Order.* Fill it out and file it with the court as soon as possible. You may file a new request for orders, on the same or different facts, at a later time.

- If you cancel the hearing, do not serve the documents listed in item ⑤ on the other person.

- If you want to keep the hearing date, you must have all of the documents listed in item ⑤ served on the other person within the time listed in item ⑤.

- At the hearing, the judge will consider whether denial of any requested orders will jeopardize your safety and the safety of children for whom you are requesting custody or visitation.

- You must come to the hearing if you want the judge to make restraining orders or continue any orders already made. If you cancel the hearing or do not come to the hearing, any restraining orders made on Form DV-110 will end on the date of the hearing.

To the Person in ❶

- The court cannot make the restraining orders after the court hearing unless the person in ② has been personally given (served) a copy of your request and any temporary orders. To show that the person in ② has been served, the person who served the forms must fill out a proof of service form. Form DV-200, *Proof of Personal Service* may be used.

- For information about service, read Form DV-210-INFO, *What Is "Proof of Personal Service"?*

- If you are unable to serve the person in ② in time, you may ask for more time to serve the documents. Read Form DV-115-INFO, *How to Ask for a New Hearing Date.*

This is a Court Order.

4A(b) Notice of Hearing (DV-109)

Case Number:

To the Person in ❷

- If you want to respond in writing, mail a copy of your completed Form DV-120, *Response to Request for Domestic Violence Restraining Order*, to the person in ① and file it with the court. You cannot mail Form DV-120 yourself. Someone age 18 or older—**not you**—must do it.

- To show that the person in ① has been served by mail, the person who mailed the forms must fill out a proof of service form. Form DV-250, *Proof of Service by Mail*, may be used. File the completed form with the court before the hearing and bring it with you to the hearing.

- For information about responding to a restraining order and filing your answer, read Form DV-120-INFO, *How Can I Respond to a Request for Domestic Violence Restraining Order?*.

- Whether or not you respond in writing, go to the court hearing if you want the judge to hear from you before making orders. You may tell the judge why you agree or disagree with the orders requested. You may bring witnesses and other evidence.

- **At the hearing, the judge may make restraining orders against you that could last up to five years.**

- **The judge may also make other orders about your children, child support, spousal support, money, and property and may order you to turn in or sell any firearms that you own or possess.**

 Request for Accommodations
Assistive listening systems, computer-assisted real-time captioning, or sign language interpreter services are available if you ask at least five days before the hearing. Contact the clerk's office or go to *www.courts.ca.gov/forms* for *Request for Accommodations by Persons With Disabilities and Response* (Form MC-410). (Civil Code, § 54.8.)

(Clerk will fill out this part.)

—Clerk's Certificate—

Clerk's Certificate
[seal]

I certify that this *Notice of Court Hearing* is a true and correct copy of the original on file in the court.

Date: _____ Clerk, by_____, Deputy

This is a Court Order.

Revised January 1, 2012

Notice of Court Hearing
(Domestic Violence Prevention)

DV-109, Page 3 of 3

For your protection and privacy, please press the Clear This Form button after you have printed the form.

Save This Form | Print This Form | Clear This Form

4A(c) Temporary Restraining Order (DV-110)

DV-110   **Temporary Restraining Order**

Person in ① must complete items ①, ②, and ③ only.

① Name of Protected Person:

_____

Your lawyer in this case *(if you have one):*
Name: _____ State Bar No.: _____
Firm Name: _____
Address *(If you have a lawyer for this case, give your lawyer's*
information. If you do not have a lawyer and want to keep your home
address private, give a different mailing address instead. You do not have
to give your telephone, fax, or e-mail.):
Address: _____
City: _____ State: _____ Zip: _____
Telephone: _____ Fax: _____
E-Mail Address: _____

② Name of Restrained Person:

_____

Description of restrained person:

Sex: ☐ M ☐ F Height: _____ Weight: _____ Hair Color: _____ Eye Color: _____
Race: _____ Age: _____ Date of Birth: _____
Address *(if known):* _____
City: _____ State: _____ Zip: _____
Relationship to protected person: _____

Clerk stamps date here when form is filed.

> To keep other people from seeing what you entered on your form, please press the Clear This Form button at the end of the form when finished.

Fill in court name and street address:

Superior Court of California, County of

Clerk fills in case number when form is filed.

Case Number:

---

③ ☐ Additional Protected Persons

In addition to the person named in ①, the following persons are protected by temporary orders as indicated in items
⑥ and ⑦ *(family or household members):*

Full name	Relationship to person in ①	Sex	Age
_____	_____	_____	_____
_____	_____	_____	_____
_____	_____	_____	_____

☐ *Check here if there are additional protected persons. List them on an attached sheet of paper and write,*
"DV-110, Additional Protected Persons" as a title.

The court will complete the rest of this form.

④ Expiration Date
This order expires at the date and time of the hearing below:

Hearing Date: _____ Time: _____ ☐ a.m. ☐ p.m.

This is a Court Order.

Judicial Council of California, www.courts.ca.gov
Revised January 1, 2012, Mandatory Form
Family Code, § 6200 et seq.
Approved by DOJ

Temporary Restraining Order
(CLETS—TRO)
(Domestic Violence Prevention)

DV-110, Page 1 of 5

4A(c) Temporary Restraining Order (DV-110)

Case Number: _____

(5) ☐ **Criminal Protective Order**
    a. ☐ A criminal protective order on Form CR-160, *Criminal Protective Order–Domestic Violence*, is in effect.
        Case Number: _____ County: _____ Expiration Date: _____
    b. ☐ No information has been provided to the judge about a criminal protective order.

To the person in ❷

The court has granted the temporary orders checked below. If you do not obey these orders, you can be arrested and charged with a crime. You may be sent to jail for up to one year, pay a fine of up to $1,000, or both.

(6) **Personal Conduct Orders**   ☐ Not requested   ☐ Denied until the hearing   ☐ Granted as follows:
    a. You must **not** do the following things to the person in ① and ☐ persons in ③:
        ☐ Harass, attack, strike, threaten, assault (sexually or otherwise), hit, follow, stalk, molest, destroy personal property, disturb the peace, keep under surveillance, or block movements
        ☐ Contact, either directly or indirectly, in any way, including but not limited to, by telephone, mail, e-mail or other electronic means
        ☐ Take any action, directly or through others, to obtain the addresses or locations of the persons in ① and ③. *(If this item is not checked, the court has found good cause not to make this order.)*
    b. Peaceful written contact through a lawyer or process server or another person as needed to serve Form DV-120 *(Response to Request for Domestic Violence Restraining Order)* or other legal papers is allowed and does not violate this order.
    c. ☐ Exceptions: Brief and peaceful contact with the person in ①, and peaceful contact with children in ③, as required for court-ordered visitation of children, is allowed unless a criminal protective order says otherwise.

(7) **Stay-Away Order**   ☐ Not requested   ☐ Denied until the hearing   ☐ Granted as follows:
    a. You **must** stay at least *(specify):* _____ yards away from:
        ☐ The person in ①   ☐ School of person in ①
        ☐ The persons in ③   ☐ The children's school or child care
        ☐ Home of person in ①   ☐ Other *(specify):* _____
        ☐ The job or workplace of person in ①   _____
        ☐ Vehicle of person in ①   _____
    b. ☐ Exceptions: Brief and peaceful contact with the person in ①, and peaceful contact with children in ③, as required for court-ordered visitation of children, is allowed unless a criminal protective order says otherwise.

(8) **Move-Out Order**   ☐ Not requested   ☐ Denied until the hearing   ☐ Granted as follows:
You must take only personal clothing and belongings needed until the hearing and move out immediately from *(address):* _____

This is a Court Order.

4A(c) Temporary Restraining Order (DV-110)

Case Number:

(9) No Guns or Other Firearms or Ammunition

a. You cannot own, possess, have, buy or try to buy, receive or try to receive, or in any other way get guns, other firearms, or ammunition.

b. You must:
- Sell to a licensed gun dealer or turn in to a law enforcement agency any guns or other firearms within your immediate possession or control. This must be done within 24 hours of being served with this order.
- File a receipt with the court within 48 hours of receiving this order that proves guns have been turned in or sold. (You may use Form DV-800, *Proof of Firearms Turned In or Sold*, for the receipt.)

c. ☐ The court has received information that you own or possess a firearm.

(10) Record Unlawful Communications   ☐ **Not requested**   ☐ **Denied until the hearing**   ☐ **Granted as follows:**

The person in (1) can record communications made by you that violate the judge's orders.

(11) Care of Animals   ☐ **Not requested**   ☐ **Denied until the hearing**   ☐ **Granted as follows:**

The person in (1) is given the sole possession, care, and control of the animals listed below. The person in (2) must stay at least _____ yards away from and not take, sell, transfer, encumber, conceal, molest, attack, strike, threaten, harm, or otherwise dispose of the following animals: _____

(12) Child Custody and Visitation   ☐ **Not requested**   ☐ **Denied until the hearing**   ☐ **Granted as follows:**

You and the person in (1) must follow the orders listed in attached Form DV-140, *Child Custody and Visitation Order*. The parent with temporary custody of the child must not remove the child from California until a noticed hearing *(Family Code Section 3063)*.

(13) Child Support

Not ordered now but may be ordered after a noticed hearing.

(14) Property Control   ☐ **Not requested**   ☐ **Denied until the hearing**   ☐ **Granted as follows:**

Until the hearing, *only* the person in (1) can use, control, and possess the following property and things:

_____

(15) Debt Payment   ☐ **Not requested**   ☐ **Denied until the hearing**   ☐ **Granted as follows:**

The person in (2) must make these payments until this order ends:

Pay to: _____ For: _____ Amount: $_____ Due date:_____
Pay to: _____ For: _____ Amount: $_____ Due date:_____

(16) Property Restraint   ☐ **Not requested**   ☐ **Denied until the hearing**   ☐ **Granted as follows:**

If the people in (1) and (2) are married to each other or are registered domestic partners,

☐ the person in (1)   ☐ the person in (2) must not transfer, borrow against, sell, hide, or get rid of or destroy any property, including animals, except in the usual course of business or for necessities of life. In addition, each person must notify the other of any new or big expenses and explain them to the court. *(The person in* (2) *cannot contact the person in* (1) *if the court has made a "no contact" order.)*

Peaceful written contact through a lawyer or a process server or other person for service of legal papers related to a court case is allowed and does not violate this order.

This is a Court Order.

4A(c) Temporary Restraining Order (DV-110)

Case Number:

(17) Spousal Support
Not ordered now but may be ordered after a noticed hearing.

(18) Lawyer's Fees and Costs
Not ordered now but may be ordered after a noticed hearing.

(19) Payments for Costs and Services
Not ordered now but may be ordered after a noticed hearing.

(20) Batterer Intervention Program
Not ordered now but may be ordered after a noticed hearing.

(21) Other Orders ☐ Not requested ☐ Denied until the hearing ☐ Granted as follows:

_____

_____

_____

☐ Check here if there are additional orders. List them on an attached sheet of paper and write "DV-110, other Orders" as a title.

(22) No Fee to Serve (Notify) Restrained Person
If the sheriff serves this order, he or she will do it for free.

Date: _____   _____
                                          Judge (or Judicial Officer)

Warnings and Notices to the Restrained Person in ②

You Cannot Have Guns, Other Firearms or Ammunition

You cannot own, have, possess, buy or try to buy, receive or try to receive, or otherwise get guns, other firearms, or ammunition while this order is in effect. If you do, you can go to jail and pay a $1,000 fine. You must sell to a licensed gun dealer or turn in to a law enforcement agency any guns or other firearms that you have or control as stated in item ⑨ above. The court will require you to prove that you did so.

If You Do Not Obey This Order, You Can Be Arrested and Charged With a Crime

- It is a felony to take or hide a child in violation of this order.
- If you travel to another state or to tribal lands or make the protected person do so, with the intention of disobeying this order, you can be charged with a federal crime.
- If you do not obey this order, you can go to jail or prison and/or pay a fine.

Service of Order by Mail

If the judge makes a restraining order at the hearing, which has the same orders as in this form, you will get a copy of that order by mail at your last known address, which is written in ②. If this address is not correct, or to know if the orders were made permanent, contact the court.

This is a Court Order.

4A(c) Temporary Restraining Order (DV-110)

Case Number:

Child Custody, Visitation, and Support

- **Child custody and visitation:** If you do not go to the hearing, the judge can make custody and visitation orders for your children without hearing from you.
- **Child support:** The judge can order child support based on the income of both parents. The judge can also have that support taken directly from your paycheck. Child support can be a lot of money, and usually you have to pay until the child is age 18. File and serve a *Financial Statement* (Simplified) (Form FL-155) or an *Income and Expense Declaration* (Form FL-150) so the judge will have information about your finances.
- **Spousal support:** File and serve an *Income and Expense Declaration* (Form FL-150) so the judge will have information about your finances. Otherwise, the court may make support orders without hearing from you.

Instructions for Law Enforcement

This order is effective when made. It is enforceable by any law enforcement agency that has received the order, is shown a copy of the order, or has verified its existence on the California Law Enforcement Telecommunications System (CLETS). If the law enforcement agency has not received proof of service on the restrained person, and the restrained person was not present at the court hearing, the agency shall advise the restrained person of the terms of the order and then shall enforce it. Violations of this order are subject to criminal penalties.

Arrest Required If Order Is Violated

If an officer has probable cause to believe that the restrained person had notice of the order and has disobeyed the order, the officer must arrest the restrained person. (Penal Code, §§ 836(c)(1), 13701(b).) A violation of the order may be a violation of Penal Code section 166 or 273.6.

Certificate of Compliance With VAWA

This temporary protective order meets all "full faith and credit" requirements of the Violence Against Women Act, 18 U.S.C. § 2265 (1994) (VAWA) upon notice of the restrained person. This court has jurisdiction over the parties and the subject matter; the restrained person has been or will be afforded notice and a timely opportunity to be heard as provided by the laws of this jurisdiction. **This order is valid and entitled to enforcement in each jurisdiction throughout the 50 states of the United States, the District of Columbia, all tribal lands, and all U.S. territories, commonwealths, and possessions and shall be enforced as if it were an order of that jurisdiction.**

(Clerk will fill out this part.)

—Clerk's Certificate—

Clerk's Certificate
[seal]

I certify that this *Temporary Restraining Order* is a true and correct copy of the original on file in the court.

Date: _____   Clerk, by _____ , Deputy

This is a Court Order.

For your protection and privacy, please press the Clear This Form button after you have printed the form.   Save This Form   Print This Form   Clear This Form

4A(d) Response to Request for Domestic Violence Restraining Order (DV-120)

DV-120 | **Response to Request for Domestic Violence Restraining Order**

Clerk stamps date here when form is filed.

(1) Name of Person Asking for Protection:
(See Form DV-100, item (1)):
_____

(2) Your Name:
_____

Your lawyer in this case *(if you have one)*:
Name: _____ State Bar No.: _____
Firm Name: _____
Address *(If you have a lawyer for this case, give your lawyer's information. If you do not have a lawyer and want to keep your home address private, give a different mailing address instead. You do not have to give your telephone, fax, or e-mail.):*
Address: _____
City: _____ State: _____ Zip: _____
Telephone: _____ Fax: _____
E-Mail Address: _____

> To keep other people from seeing what you entered on your form, please press the Clear This Form button at the end of the form when finished.

Fill in court name and street address:
Superior Court of California, County of

Fill in case number:
Case Number:

(3) Use this form to respond to the *Request for Domestic Violence Restraining Order* (Form DV-100)

- Fill out this form and take it to the court clerk.
- Have the person in (1) served by mail with a copy of this form and any attached pages. (See Form DV-250, *Proof of Service by Mail.)*
- For more information, read Form DV-120-INFO, *How Can I Respond to Request for Domestic Violence Restraining Order?*

> **The judge will consider your Response at the hearing.**
> Write your hearing date, time, and place from Form DV-109, *Notice of Court Hearing,* item (3) here:
>
> **Hearing Date** → Date: _____ Time: _____
> Dept.: _____ Room: _____
>
> **You must obey the orders in Form DV-110, *Temporary Restraining Order,* until the hearing.** At the hearing, the court may make restraining orders against you that could last up to 5 years and could be renewed.

(4) ☐ Relationship to Person Asking for Protection
    a. ☐ I agree to the relationship listed in item (4) on Form DV-100.
    b. ☐ I do not agree to the relationship listed in item (4) on Form DV-100. *(Specify your reasons in item 23, page 4 of this form.)*

(5) ☐ Other Protected People
    a. ☐ I agree to the order requested.
    b. ☐ I do not agree to the order requested. *(Specify your reasons in item 23, page 4 of this form.)*

(6) ☐ Personal Conduct Order
    a. ☐ I agree to the order requested.
    b. ☐ I do not agree to the order requested. *(Specify your reasons in item 23, page 4 of this form.)*

This is not a Court Order.

Judicial Council of California, www.courts.ca.gov
Revised January 1, 2012, Mandatory Form
Family Code, § 6200 et seq.

Response to Request for Domestic Violence Restraining Order
(Domestic Violence Prevention)

DV-120, Page 1 of 4
→

4A(d) Response to Request for Domestic Violence Restraining Order (DV-120)

Case Number:

⑦ ☐ **Stay-Away Orders**
    a. ☐ I agree to the order requested.
    b. ☐ I do not agree to the order requested. *(Specify your reasons in item 23, page 4 of this form.)*

⑧ ☐ **Move-Out Order**
    a. ☐ I agree to the order requested.
    b. ☐ I do not agree to the order requested. *(Specify your reasons in item 23, page 4 of this form.)*

⑨ ☐ **Turn In Guns or Other Firearms**
    If you were served with Form DV-110, Temporary Restraining Order, you must turn in any guns or firearms in your immediate possession or control. You must file a receipt with the court from a law enforcement agency or a licensed gun dealer within 48 hours after you received Form DV-110.
    a. ☐ I do not own or have any guns or firearms.
    b. ☐ I ask for an exemption from the firearms prohibition under Family Code § 6389(h) because
        (specify): _____
    c. ☐ I have turned in my guns and firearms to law enforcement or sold them to a licensed gun dealer.
    d. ☐ A copy of the receipt showing that I turned in or sold my firearms
        ☐ is attached   ☐ has already been filed with the court.

⑩ ☐ **Record Unlawful Communications Order**
    a. ☐ I agree to the order requested.
    b. ☐ I do not agree to the order requested. *(Specify your reasons in item 23, page 4 of this form.)*

⑪ ☐ **Animals: Possession and Stay-Away Order**
    a. ☐ I agree to the order requested.
    b. ☐ I do not agree to the order requested. *(Specify your reasons in item 23, page 4 of this form.)*

⑫ ☐ **Child Custody and Visitation Order**
    a. ☐ I agree to the order requested.
    b. ☐ I do not agree to the order requested. *(Specify your reasons in item 23, page 4 of this form.)*
    c. ☐ I am not the parent of the child listed in Form DV-105, *Request for Child Custody and Visitation Orders.*
    d. ☐ I ask for the following custody order *(specify):*

    e. ☐ I do ☐ I do not agree to the orders requested to limit the child's travel as listed in Form DV-108,
        Request for Order: No Travel with Children.
    You and the other parent may tell the court that you want to be legal parents of the children (use Form DV-180, Agreement and Judgment of Parentage).

⑬ ☐ **Child Support Order** *(Check all that apply):*
    a. ☐ I agree to the order requested.
    b. ☐ I do not agree to the order requested. *(Specify your reasons in item 23, page 4 of this form.)*
    c. ☐ I agree to pay guideline child support.
    Whether or not you agree to pay support, you must fill out, serve, and file Form FL-150, Income and Expense Declaration or FL-155, Financial Statement.

This is not a Court Order.

4A(d) Response to Request for Domestic Violence Restraining Order (DV-120)

Case Number:

(14) ☐ **Property Control Order**
    a. ☐ I agree to the order requested.
    b. ☐ I do not agree to the order requested. *(Specify your reasons in item 23, page 4 of this form.)*

(15) ☐ **Debt Payment Order**
    a. ☐ I agree to the order requested.
    b. ☐ I do not agree to the order requested. *(Specify your reasons in item 23, page 4 of this form.)*

(16) ☐ **Property Restraint Order**
    a. ☐ I agree to the order requested.
    b. ☐ I do not agree to the order requested. *(Specify your reasons in item 23, page 4 of this form.)*

(17) ☐ **Spousal Support Order**
    a. ☐ I agree to the order requested.
    b. ☐ I do not agree to the order requested. *(Specify your reasons in item 23, page 4 of this form.)*
    Whether or not you agree, you must fill out, serve, and file Form FL-150, Income and Expense Declaration.

(18) ☐ **Lawyer's Fees and Costs**
    a. ☐ I agree to the order requested.
    b. ☐ I do not agree to the order requested. *(Specify your reasons in item 23, page 4 of this form.)*
    c. ☐ I request the court to order payment of my lawyer's fees and costs.
    Whether or not you agree, you must fill out, serve, and file Form FL-150, Income and Expense Declaration.

(19) ☐ **Payments for Costs and Services**
    a. ☐ I agree to the order requested.
    b. ☐ I do not agree to the order requested. *(Specify your reasons in item 23, page 4 of this form.)*

(20) ☐ **Batterer Intervention Program**
    a. ☐ I agree to the order requested.
    b. ☐ I do not agree to the order requested. *(Specify your reasons in item 23, page 4 of this form.)*

(21) ☐ **Other Orders** *(see item 21 on Form DV-100)*
    a. ☐ I agree to the order requested.
    b. ☐ I do not agree to the order requested. *(Specify your reasons in item 23, page 4 of this form.)*

(22) ☐ **Out-of-Pocket Expenses**
    I ask the court to order payment of my out-of-pocket expenses because the temporary restraining order was issued without enough supporting facts. The expenses are:
    Item:_____ Amount: $_____ Item: _____ Amount: $_____
    You must fill out, serve, and file Form FL-150, Income and Expense Declaration.

This is not a Court Order.

4A(d) Response to Request for Domestic Violence Restraining Order (DV-120)

Case Number:

---

(23) ☐ **Reasons I do not agree to the orders requested**

Explain your answers to each of the orders requested *(give specific facts and reasons):*

☐ *Check here if there is not enough space below for your answer. Put your complete answer on an attached sheet of paper and write, "DV-120, Reasons I Do Not Agree" as a title.*

_____

_____

_____

_____

_____

_____

_____

_____

_____

_____

_____

_____

_____

_____

_____

_____

_____

_____

_____

_____

_____

_____

_____

_____

_____

(24) Number of pages attached to this form, if any: _____

I declare under penalty of perjury under the laws of the State of California that the information above is true and correct.

Date: _____

_____   ▶ _____
Type or print your name   *Sign your name*

Date: _____

_____   ▶ _____
Lawyer's name, if you have one   *Lawyer's signature*

This is not a Court Order.

**Response to Request for Domestic Violence
Restraining Order**
(Domestic Violence Prevention)

For your protection and privacy, please press the Clear This Form button after you have printed the form.

Save This Form | Print This Form | Clear This Form

4A(e) Restraining Order After Hearing (DV-130)

DV-130 | **Restraining Order After Hearing (Order of Protection)**

Clerk stamps date here when form is filed.

To keep other people from seeing what you entered on your form, please press the Clear This Form button at the end of the form when finished.

(1) Name of Protected Person:

_____

Your lawyer in this case *(if you have one):*
Name: _____ State Bar No.: _____
Firm Name: _____
Address *(If you have a lawyer for this case, give your lawyer's information. If you do not have a lawyer and want to keep your home address private, give a different mailing address instead. You do not have to give your telephone, fax, or e-mail.):*
Address: _____
City: _____ State: _____ Zip: _____
Telephone: _____ Fax: _____
E-Mail Address: _____

Fill in court name and street address:
Superior Court of California, County of

(2) Name of Restrained Person:

_____

Description of restrained person:

Fill in case number:
Case Number:

Sex: ☐ M ☐ F Height: _____ Weight: _____ Hair Color: _____ Eye Color: _____
Race: _____ Age: _____ Date of Birth: _____
Mailing Address *(if known):* _____
City: _____ State: _____ Zip: _____
Relationship to protected person: _____

(3) ☐ Additional Protected Persons
In addition to the person named in (1), the following persons are protected by orders as indicated in item (6) and (7) *(family or household members):*

Full name	Relationship to person in (1)	Sex	Age
_____	_____	_____	_____
_____	_____	_____	_____
_____	_____	_____	_____

☐ *Check here if there are additional protected persons. List them on an attached sheet of paper and write, "DV-130, Additional Protected Persons" as a title.*

(4) Expiration Date
The orders, except as noted below, end on

(date): _____ at *(time):* _____ ☐ a.m. ☐ p.m. or ☐ midnight

- *If no date is written, the restraining order ends three years after the date of the hearing in item (5)(a).*
- *If no time is written, the restraining order ends at midnight on the expiration date.*
- *Note: Custody, visitation, child support, and spousal support orders remain in effect after the restraining order ends. Custody, visitation and child support orders usually end when the child is 18.*
- *The court orders are on pages 2, 3, 4 and 5 and attachment pages (if any).*

This order complies with VAWA and shall be enforced throughout the United States. See page 5.

This is a Court Order.

Judicial Council of California, www.courts.ca.gov
Revised January 1, 2012, Mandatory Form
Family Code, § 6200 et seq.
Approved by DOJ

**Restraining Order After Hearing (CLETS—OAH)
(Order of Protection)
(Domestic Violence Prevention)**

DV-130, Page 1 of 6
→

4A(e) Restraining Order After Hearing (DV-130)

Case Number:

⑤ Hearings

a. The hearing was on *(date)*:_____ with *(name of judicial officer)*:_____

b. These people were at the hearing *(check all that apply)*:

☐ The person in ①   ☐ The lawyer for the person in ① *(name)*: _____

☐ The person in ②   ☐ The lawyer for the person in ② *(name)*: _____

c. ☐ The people in ① and ② must **return to court** on *(date)*:_____

at *(time)*:_____ ☐ a.m. ☐ p.m.   to review *(specify issues)*:_____

_____

To the person in ❷

The court has granted the orders checked below. Item ⑨ is also an order. If you do not obey these orders, you can be arrested and charged with a crime. You may be sent to jail for up to one year, pay a fine of up to $1,000, or both.

⑥ ☐ Personal Conduct Orders

a. The person in ② must **not** do the following things to the protected people in ① and ③:

☐ Harass, attack, strike, threaten, assault (sexually or otherwise), hit, follow, stalk, molest, destroy personal property, disturb the peace, keep under surveillance, or block movements.

☐ Contact, either directly or indirectly, by any means, including, but not limited to, by telephone, mail, e-mail or other electronic means.

☐ Take any action, directly or through others, to obtain the addresses or locations of any protected persons. *(If this item is not checked, the court has found good cause not to make this order.)*

b. Peaceful written contact through a lawyer or process server or another person as needed to serve legal paper is allowed and does not violate this order.

c. ☐ Exceptions: Brief and peaceful contact with the person in ①, and peaceful contact with children in ③, as required for court-ordered visitation of children, is allowed unless a criminal protective order says otherwise.

⑦ ☐ Stay-Away Order

a. The person in ② **must** stay at least *(specify)*: _____ yards away from:

☐ The person in ①   ☐ School of person in ①
☐ The persons in ③   ☐ The children's school or child care
☐ Home of person in ①   ☐ Other *(specify)*: _____
☐ The job or workplace of person in ①   _____
☐ Vehicle of person in ①   _____

b. ☐ Exceptions: Brief and peaceful contact with the person in ① and peaceful contact with children in ③, as required for court-ordered visitation of children, is allowed unless a criminal protective order says otherwise.

⑧ ☐ Move-Out Order

The person in ② must move out immediately from *(address)*: _____

This is a Court Order.

4A(e) Restraining Order After Hearing (DV-130)

Case Number:

(9) No Guns or Other Firearms or Ammunition

    a. The person in ② cannot own, possess, have, buy or try to buy, receive or try to receive, or in any other way get guns, other firearms, or ammunition.

    b. The person in ② must:

       • Sell to a licensed gun dealer or turn in to a law enforcement agency any guns or other firearms within his or her immediate possession or control. This must be done within 24 hours of being served with this order.

       • File a receipt with the court within 48 hours of receiving this order that proves guns have been turned in or sold. *(Form DV-800*, Proof of Firearms Turned In or Sold, *may be used for the receipt.)*

    c. ☐ The court has received information that the person in ② owns or possesses a firearm.

(10) ☐ Record Unlawful Communications

The person in ① has the right to record communications made by the person in ② that violate the judge's orders.

(11) ☐ Animals: Possession and Stay-Away

The person in ① is given the sole possession, care, and control of the animals listed below. The person in ② must stay at least _____ yards away from and not take, sell, transfer, encumber, conceal, molest, attack, strike, threaten, harm, or otherwise dispose of the following animals: _____
_____

(12) ☐ Child Custody and Visitation

Child custody and visitation are ordered on the attached Form DV-140, *Child Custody and Visitation Order* or *(specify other form):* _____

(13) ☐ Child Support

Child support is ordered on the attached Form FL-342, *Child Support Information and Order Attachment* or *(specify other form):* _____

(14) ☐ Property Control

Only the person in ① can use, control, and possess the following property:_____
_____

(15) ☐ Debt Payment

The person in ② must make these payments until this order ends:

Pay to: _____ For:_____ Amount: $ _____ Due date:_____
Pay to: _____ For:_____ Amount: $ _____ Due date:_____
Pay to: _____ For:_____ Amount: $ _____ Due date:_____

    ☐ *Check here if more payments ordered. Attach a sheet of paper and write, "DV-130, Debt Payments" as a title.*

(16) ☐ Property Restraint

The ☐ person in ① ☐ person in ② must not transfer, borrow against, sell, hide, or get rid of or destroy any property, including animals, except in the usual course of business or for necessities of life. In addition, the person must notify the other of any new or big expenses and explain them to the court. *(The person in ② cannot contact the person in ① if the court has made a "Personal Conduct"order.)*

Peaceful written contact through a lawyer or a process server or other person for service of legal papers related to a court case is allowed and does not violate this order.

This is a Court Order.

Revised January 1, 2012   **Restraining Order After Hearing (CLETS—OAH)**   DV-130, Page 3 of 6
(Order of Protection)   →
(Domestic Violence Prevention)

4A(e) Restraining Order After Hearing (DV-130)

Case Number:

(17) ☐ **Spousal Support**

Spousal support is ordered on the attached Form FL-343, *Spousal, Partner, or Family Support Order Attachment* or *(specify other form):* _____

(18) ☐ **Lawyer's Fees and Costs**

The person in **(2)** must pay the following lawyer's fees and costs:

Pay to: _____ For: _____ Amount: $_____ Due date: _____

Pay to: _____ For: _____ Amount: $_____ Due date: _____

(19) ☐ **Payments for Costs and Services**

The person in **(2)** must pay the following:

Pay to: _____ For: _____ Amount: $_____ Due date: _____

Pay to: _____ For: _____ Amount: $_____ Due date: _____

Pay to: _____ For: _____ Amount: $_____ Due date: _____

☐ *Check here if more payments ordered. Attach a sheet of paper and write, "DV-130, Payments for Costs and Services" as a title.*

(20) ☐ **Batterer Intervention Program**

The person in **(2)** must go to and pay for a 52-week batterer intervention program and show written proof of completion to the court. This program must be approved by the probation department.

(21) ☐ **Other Orders**

Other orders *(specify):* _____
_____

(22) **No Fee to Serve (Notify) Restrained Person**

If the sheriff or marshal serves this order, he or she will do it for free.

(23) **Service**

a. ☐ The people in **(1)** and **(2)** were at the hearing or agreed in writing to this order. No other proof of service is needed.

b. ☐ The person in **(1)** was at the hearing. The person in **(2)** was not.

    (1) ☐ Proof of service of Form DV-109 and Form DV-110 (if issued) was presented to the court. The judge's orders in this form are the same as in Form DV-110 except for the end date. The person in **(2)** must be served. This order can be served by mail.

    (2) ☐ Proof of service of Form DV-109 and Form DV-110 (if issued) was presented to the court. The judge's orders in this form are different from the orders in Form DV-110, or Form DV-110 was not issued. Someone—not the people in **(1)** or **(3)**—must personally "serve" a copy of this order to the person in **(2)**.

(24) ☐ **Criminal Protective Order**

a. ☐ Form CR-160, *Criminal Protective Order—Domestic Violence*, is in effect.

    Case Number: _____ County: _____ Expiration Date: _____

    (If more orders, list them on extra sheet of paper and write, "DV-130, Other Criminal Protective Orders" as a title.)

b. ☐ No information has been provided to the judge about a criminal protective order.

This is a Court Order.

4A(e) Restraining Order After Hearing (DV-130)

Case Number:

(25) ☐ **Attached pages are orders.**
- Number of pages attached to this six-page form: _____
- All of the attached pages are part of this order.
- Attachments include *(check all that apply):*
  - ☐ DV-140 ☐ DV-145 ☐ DV-150 ☐ FL-342 ☐ FL-343
  - ☐ Other *(specify):* _____
  _____

Date: _____   _____
                                      Judge (or Judicial Officer)

Certificate of Compliance With VAWA

This restraining (protective) order meets all "full faith and credit" requirements of the Violence Against Women Act, 18 U.S.C. § 2265 (1994) (VAWA) upon notice of the restrained person. This court has jurisdiction over the parties and the subject matter; the restrained person has been or will be afforded notice and a timely opportunity to be heard as provided by the laws of this jurisdiction. **This order is valid and entitled to enforcement in each jurisdiction throughout the 50 states of the United States, the District of Columbia, all tribal lands, and all U.S. territories, commonwealths, and possessions and shall be enforced as if it were an order of that jurisdiction.**

Warnings and Notices to the Restrained Person in ❷

If you do not obey this order, you can be arrested and charged with a crime.
- If you do not obey this order, you can go to jail or prison and/or pay a fine.
- It is a felony to take or hide a child in violation of this order.
- If you travel to another state or to tribal lands or make the protected person do so, with the intention of disobeying this order, you can be charged with a federal crime.

You cannot have guns, firearms, and/or ammunition.

You cannot own, have, possess, buy or try to buy, receive or try to receive, or otherwise get guns, other firearms, and/or ammunition while the order is in effect. If you do, you can go to jail and pay a $1,000 fine. You must sell to a licensed gun dealer or turn in to a law enforcement agency any guns or other firearms that you have or control. The judge will ask you for proof that you did so. If you do not obey this order, you can be charged with a crime. Federal law says you cannot have guns or ammunition while the order is in effect.

Instructions for Law Enforcement

Start Date and End Date of Orders
The orders *start* on the earlier of the following dates:
- The hearing date in item (5)(a) on page 2 or
- The date next to the judge's signature on this page.

The orders *end* on the expiration date in item (4) on page 1. If no date is listed, they end three years from the hearing date.

This is a Court Order.

4A(e) Restraining Order After Hearing (DV-130)

Case Number:

Arrest Required If Order Is Violated

If an officer has probable cause to believe that the restrained person had notice of the order and has disobeyed the order, the officer must arrest the restrained person. (Penal Code, §§ 836(c)(1), 13701(b).) A violation of the order may be a violation of Penal Code section 166 or 273.6.

Notice/Proof of Service

Law enforcement must first determine if the restrained person had notice of the orders. If notice cannot be verified, the restrained person must be advised of the terms of the orders, If the restrained person then fails to obey the orders, the officer must enforce them. (Family Code, § 6383.)

Consider the restrained person "served" (noticed) if:

- The officer sees a copy of the *Proof of Service* or confirms that the *Proof of Service* is on file; *or*
- The restrained person was at the restraining order hearing or was informed of the order by an officer. (Fam. Code, § 6383; Pen. Code, § 836(c)(2).) An officer can obtain information about the contents of the order in the Domestic Violence Restraining Orders System (DVROS). (Fam. Code, § 6381(b)(c).)

If the Protected Person Contacts the Restrained Person

Even if the protected person invites or consents to contact with the restrained person, the orders remain in effect and must be enforced. The protected person cannot be arrested for inviting or consenting to contact with the restrained person. The orders can be changed only by another court order. (Pen. Code, §13710(b).)

Child Custody and Visitation

- The custody and visitation orders are on Form DV-140, items ③ and ④. They are sometimes also written on additional pages or referenced in DV-140 or other orders that are not part of the restraining order.
- **Forms DV-100 and DV-105 are not orders. Do not enforce them.**

Enforcing the Restraining Order in California

Any law enforcement officer in California who receives, sees, or verifies the orders on a paper copy, the California Law Enforcement Telecommunications System (CLETS), or in an NCIC Protection Order File must enforce the orders.

Conflicting Orders

A protective order issued in a criminal case on Form CR-160 takes precedence in enforcement over any conflicting civil court order. (Pen. Code, § 136.2(e)(2).) Any nonconflicting terms of the civil restraining order remain in full force. An emergency protective order (Form EPO-001) that is in effect between the same parties and is more restrictive than other restraining orders takes precedence over all other restraining orders. (Pen. Code, § 136.2.)

(Clerk will fill out this part.)

—**Clerk's Certificate**—

Clerk's Certificate
[seal]

I certify that this *Restraining Order After Hearing (Order of Protection)* is a true and correct copy of the original on file in the court.

Date: _____ Clerk, by _____ , Deputy

This is a Court Order.

For your protection and privacy, please press the Clear This Form button after you have printed the form.   **Save This Form**   **Print This Form**   **Clear This Form**

4B   Emergency Court Order (FL-305)

FL-305

PETITIONER/PLAINTIFF: RESPONDENT/DEFENDANT: OTHER PARENT/PARTY:	CASE NUMBER:

TEMPORARY EMERGENCY COURT ORDERS
Attachment to *Request for Order* (FL-300)

The court makes the following orders, which are effective immediately and until the hearing:

1. ☐ PROPERTY RESTRAINT
   a. ☐   Petitioner ☐   Respondent ☐   Claimant   is restrained from transferring, encumbering, hypothecating, concealing, or in any way disposing of any property, real or personal, whether community, quasi-community, or separate, except in the usual course of business or for the necessities of life.
      ☐ The other party is to be notified of any proposed extraordinary expenditures, and an accounting of such is to be made to the court.
   b. ☐   Both parties are restrained and enjoined from cashing, borrowing against, canceling, transferring, disposing of, or changing the beneficiaries of any insurance or other coverage, including life, health, automobile, and disability, held for the benefit of the parties or their minor child or children.
   c. ☐   Neither party may incur any debts or liabilities for which the other may be held responsible, other than in the ordinary course of business or for the necessities of life.

2. ☐ PROPERTY CONTROL
   a. ☐   Petitioner ☐   Respondent   is given the exclusive temporary use, possession, and control of the following property that the parties own or are buying *(specify):*

   b. ☐   Petitioner ☐   Respondent   is ordered to make the following payments on liens and encumbrances coming due while the order is in effect:

Debt	Amount of payment	Pay to

3. ☐ MINOR CHILDREN
   a. ☐   Petitioner ☐   Respondent   will have the temporary physical custody, care, and control of the minor children of the parties ☐   subject to the other party's rights of visitation as follows:

   b. ☐   Petitioner ☐   Respondent   must not remove the minor child or children of the parties
      (1) ☐   from the state of California.
      (2) ☐   from the following counties *(specify):*
      (3) ☐   other *(specify):*
   c. ☐   Child abduction prevention orders are attached (see form FL-341(B)).
   d. (1) Jurisdiction: This court has jurisdiction to make child custody orders in this case under the Uniform Child Custody Jurisdiction and Enforcement Act (part 3 of the California Family Code, commencing with section 3400).
      (2) Notice and opportunity to be heard: The responding party was given notice and an opportunity to be heard as provided by the laws of the State of California.
      (3) Country of habitual residence: The country of habitual residence of the child or children is
         ☐ the United States of America ☐   other *(specify):*
      (4) **Penalties for violating this order: If you violate this order, you may be subject to civil or criminal penalties or both.**

4. ☐ OTHER ORDERS *(specify):*
      ☐ Additional orders are listed on Attachment 4.

Date: _____   _____
                                                    JUDGE OF THE SUPERIOR COURT

5. **The date of the court hearing is** *(insert date when known):*

CLERK'S CERTIFICATE

[SEAL]   I certify that the foregoing is a true and correct copy of the original on file in my office.

Date: _____   Clerk, by _____ , Deputy

Page 1 of 1

Form Adopted for Mandatory Use
Judicial Council of California
FL-305 [Rev. July 1, 2012]

TEMPORARY EMERGENCY COURT ORDERS

Family Code, §§ 2045, 6224, 6226, 6302,
6320–6326, 6380–6383
www.courts.ca.gov

Save This Form   Print This Form   Clear This Form

4C Ex Parte Declaration Sample

Appendix 4C

1 _____, SBN
   LAW OFFICES OF _____
2 _____
   _____
3
   TELEPHONE: (___) ___-_____
4 FACSIMILE: (___) ___-_____

5

6

7   **IN THE SUPERIOR COURT OF THE STATE OF CALIFORNIA**

8   **IN AND FOR THE COUNTY OF _____**

9

10 IN RE THE MATTER OF: NO. _____

11 Petitioner: _____   **EX PARTE DECLARATION**

12 Vs.

13 Respondent: _____

14 _____/

15
          I, _____, declare as follows:
16
          On, July _____, 20__ at _____ a.m/p.m.., I notified
17
    _____, that an Ex Parte Hearing had been set for _____,
18
    20___at _____ a.m./p.m. in Department _ of the _____ County Superior Court.
19
    _____ indicated that he/she would attend said hearing.
20
          I declare under penalty of perjury under the laws of the State of California that the
21
    foregoing is true and correct.
22

23
    Dated:_____   _____
24   _____
25

26

27

28

Declaration of Ex Parte Notice

4D Holiday Visitation—Example

VISITATION SCHEDULE (Minimum Contacts)

Every other weekend from Friday, 6:00 p.m. to Sunday, 6:00 p.m.

Midweek dinner with non-custodial parent; with overnight visit by agreement of the parties.

Summer Vacation: 2 weeks uninterrupted visitation with each parent

Occasion	Every Year	Odd Years	Even Years
Martin Luther King Day (if applicable)		Mother	Father
President's Day		Father	Mother
Spring Break		Mother	Father
Mother's Day	Mother		
Memorial Day		Father	Mother
Father's Day	Father		
4th of July		Mother	Father
Labor Day		Father	Mother
Veteran's Day (if applicable)		Mother	Father
Thanksgiving		Father	Mother
First Half Winter Break*		Mother	Father
Second Half - Winter Break*		Father	Mother

*may depend upon the way the school schedule and
the way Christmas and New Year's dates fall within
the break

4E Declaration (attachment to Request for Hearing)— Example

1 In re Marriage of Yonder, Case No: _____
   Declaration of O. Vera Yonder, Petitioner, in support of Request for Order
2

3 I declare as follows:

4 1. Child Custody

5 I request that the court order joint legal custody of our two minor children: Charles, age 10 and

6 Missy, age 7. I am attaching a copy of the Family Court Services report dated _____, 20__,

7 where the mediator recommend that I have primary custody of the children.

8   2. Visitation

9 I request that the court order that visitation will be as set forth in the Family Court Services

10 Report, as referenced above.

11 3. Child Support

12 I request that the court order Respondent to pay guideline child support. I have attached an

13 XSpouse print-out which indicates the timeshare of 26%, based on the visitation schedule in the

14 FCS Report, as well as on our current earnings. My Income & Expense Declaration has been

15 provided to the court, which indicates that I make $2,550 per month. Based on our previous joint

16 tax returns and personal knowledge, I believe the Respondent makes $6,500 per month and

17 support should be set using those earnings amounts.

18 I am also requesting that the court order that each parent should pay one-half of all work-related

19 child care. The current amount of child care is $600 per month.

20 I also request that Respondent continue to maintain the children on his health care plan, as I do

21 not currently have health care available for the children through my employment.

22 4. Spousal Support

23 I request that Respondent be ordered to pay Spousal Support as set forth on the Dissomaster/X-

24 Spouse printout I have attached. The support requested in this calculation is based on our

25 standard of living, our expenses and our respective incomes as set forth in the Income & Expense

26 Declarations I have filed and served herein. I believe that Respondent should pay this temporary

27 support until we have had an opportunity to discuss or reach an agreement regarding the division

28 of community property.

4E Declaration (attachment to Request for Hearing) — Example

1 | 5. Attorney Fees

2 | I am requesting that Respondent be ordered to pay my reasonable attorney fees and costs. I am

3 | unable to pay my attorney fees as I have only my net income from which I have to make the

4 | mortgage payment, pay for the utilities, and provide food for my children. I have been paying

5 | the entire sum of $600 per month to the child care provider since Respondent and I separated

6 | four months ago. I have had to borrow money from my parents to put gas in my car to that I

7 | could go to work.

8 | 6. Property

9 | I request that the Court order Respondent to make payments on the credit cards until such time as

10 | we either I am receiving child support and spousal support, or we have reached a settlement in

11 | this matter. I am unable to provide for my children and make payments on the credit cards with

12 | my current earnings. If the Court orders Respondent to pay support, I would then be able to pay

13 | one-half of the community bills.

14 | I declare under penalty of perjury that the foregoing is true and correct.

15 |

16 | Dated: _____   s/_____

17 | *[signed]*

18 |

19 |

20 |

21 |

22 |

23 |

24 |

25 |

26 |

27 |

28 |

5A Form Interrogatories (FL-145)

FL-145

To keep other people from seeing what you entered on your form, please press the Clear This Form button at the end of the form when finished.

ATTORNEY OR PARTY WITHOUT ATTORNEY *(Name, State Bar number, and address):*   TELEPHONE NO.:

ATTORNEY FOR *(Name):*

SUPERIOR COURT OF CALIFORNIA, COUNTY OF

SHORT TITLE:

FORM INTERROGATORIES–FAMILY LAW	CASE NUMBER:
Asking Party:	
Answering Party:	
Set No.:	

Sec. 1. Instructions to Both Parties

The interrogatories on page 2 of this form are intended to provide for the exchange of relevant information without unreasonable expense to the answering party. They do not change existing law relating to interrogatories, nor do they affect the answering party's right to assert any privilege or make any objection. **Privileges must be asserted.**

Sec. 2. Definitions

Words in **boldface** in these interrogatories are defined as follows:

(a) **Person** includes a natural person; a partnership; any kind of business, legal, or public entity; and its agents or employees.

(b) **Document** means all written, recorded,or graphic materials, however stored, produced, or reproduced.

(c) **Asset** or **property** includes any interest in real estate or personal property. It includes any interest in a pension, profit-sharing, or retirement plan.

(d) **Debt** means any obligation, including debts paid since the date of separation.

(e) **Support** means any benefit or economic contribution to the living expenses of another person, including gifts.

(f) If asked to **identify a person,** give the person's name, last known residence and business addresses, telephone numbers, and company affiliation at the date of the transaction referred to.

(g) If asked to **identify a document,** attach a copy of the document unless you explain why not. If you do not attach the copy, describe the document, including its date and nature, and give the name, address, telephone number, and occupation of the person who has the document.

Sec. 3. Instructions to the Asking Party

Check the box next to each interrogatory you want the answering party to answer.

Sec. 4. Instructions to the Answering Party

You must answer these interrogatories under oath within 30 days, in accordance with Code of Civil Procedure section 2030.260.

You must furnish all information you have or can reasonably find out, including all information (not privileged) from your attorneys or under your control. If you don't know, say so.

If an interrogatory is answered by referring to a document, the document must be attached as an exhibit to the response and referred to in the response. If the document has more than one page, refer to the page and section where the answer can be found.

If a document to be attached to the response may also be attached to the *Schedule of Assets and Debts* (form FL-142), the document should be attached only to the response, and the form should refer to the response.

If an interrogatory cannot be answered completely, answer as much as you can, state the reason you cannot answer the rest, and state any information you have about the unanswered portion.

Sec. 5. Oath

Your answers to these interrogatories must be under oath, dated, and signed. Use the following statement **at the end of your answers:**

> *I declare under penalty of perjury under the laws of the State of California that the foregoing answers are true and correct.*

▶

_____   _____
(DATE)   (SIGNATURE)

Form Approved for Optional Use
Judicial Council of California
FL-145 [Rev. January 1, 2006]

FORM INTERROGATORIES–FAMILY LAW

Code of Civil Procedure,
§§ 2030.010–2030.410, 2033.710
www.courtinfo.ca.gov

5A Form Interrogatories (FL-145)

1. **Personal history**. State your full name, current residence address and work address, social security number, any other names you have used, and the dates between which you used each name.

2. **Agreements.** Are there any agreements between you and your spouse or domestic partner, made before or during your marriage or domestic partnership or after your separation, that affect the disposition of **assets, debts,** or **support** in this proceeding? If your answer is yes, for each agreement state the date made and whether it was written or oral, and attach a copy of the agreement or describe its contents.

3. **Legal actions.** Are you a party or do you anticipate being a party to any legal or administrative proceeding other than this action? If your answer is yes, state your role and the name, jurisdiction, case number, and a brief description of each proceeding.

4. **Persons sharing residence.** State the name, age, and relationship to you of each **person** at your present address.

5. **Support provided others.** State the name, age, address, and relationship to you of each **person** for whom you have provided **support** during the past 12 months and the amount provided per month for each.

6. **Support received for others.** State the name, age, address, and relationship to you of each **person** for whom you have received **support** during the past 12 months and the amount received per month for each.

7. **Current income.** List all income you received during the past 12 months, its source, the basis for its computation, and the total amount received from each. Attach your last three paycheck stubs.

8. **Other income.** During the past three years, have you received cash or other property from any source not identified in item 7? If so, list the source, the date, and the nature and value of the property.

9. **Tax returns.** Attach copies of all tax returns and tax schedules filed by or for you in any jurisdiction for the past three calendar years.

10. **Schedule of assets and debts.** Complete the *Schedule of Assets and Debts* (form FL-142) served with these interrogatories.

11. **Separate property contentions.** State the facts that support your contention that an asset or debt is separate property.

12. **Property valuations.** During the past 12 months, have you received written offers to purchase or had written appraisals of any of the assets listed on your completed *Schedule of Assets and Debts?* If your answer is yes, **identify the document.**

13. **Property held by others.** Is there any **property** held by any third party in which you have any interest or over which you have any control? If your answer is yes, indicate whether the property is shown on the *Schedule of Assets and Debts* completed by you. If it is not, describe and identify each such asset, state its present value and the basis for your valuation, and **identify the person** holding the asset.

14. **Retirement and other benefits.** Do you have an interest in any disability, retirement, profit-sharing, or deferred compensation plan? If your answer is yes, **identify** each plan and provide the name, address, and telephone number of the administrator and custodian of records.

15. **Claims of reimbursement.** Do you claim the legal right to be reimbursed for any expenditures of your separate or community property? If your answer is yes, state all supporting facts.

16. **Credits.** Have you claimed reimbursement credits for payments of community debts since the date of separation? If your answer is yes, **identify** the source of payment, the creditor, the date paid, and the amount paid. State whether you have added to the debt since the separation.

17. **Insurance.** **Identify** each health, life, automobile, and disability insurance policy or plan that you now own or that covers you, your children, or your assets. State the policy type, policy number, and name of the company. **Identify** the agent and give the address.

18. **Health.** Is there any physical or emotional condition that limits your ability to work? If your answer is yes, state each fact on which you base your answer.

19. **Children's needs.** Do you contend that any of your children have any special needs? If so, identify the child with the need, the reason for the need, its cost, and its expected duration.

20. **Attorney fees.** State the total amount of attorney fees and costs incurred by you in this proceeding, the amount paid, and the source of the money paid. Describe the billing arrangements.

21. **Gifts.** List any gifts you have made without the consent of your spouse or domestic partner in the past 24 months, their values, and the recipients.

FORM INTERROGATORIES—FAMILY LAW

For your protection and privacy, please press the Clear This Form button after you have printed the form.

Save This Form | Print This Form | Clear This Form

5B   Request for Orders Regarding Noncompliance with Disclosure Requirements

	FL-316
PETITIONER:	CASE NUMBER:
RESPONDENT:	

REQUEST FOR ORDERS REGARDING NONCOMPLIANCE WITH DISCLOSURE REQUIREMENTS

Attachment to *Request for Order* (form FL-300)

1. ☐ Petitioner ☐ Respondent   has complied with mandatory disclosure requirements (you must attach a copy of your filed *Declaration Regarding Service of Declaration of Disclosure and Income and Expense Declaration* (form FL-141)), and requests an order that

   ☐ petitioner ☐ respondent

   a. ☐ provide a
      (1) ☐ preliminary declaration of disclosure under Family Code section 2104 as directed by court order.
      (2) ☐ final declaration of disclosure under Family Code section 2105 as directed by court order.

   b. ☐ provide a further response to his or her ☐ preliminary ☐ final declaration of disclosure under Family Code section 2107(b)(1).

   c. ☐ has failed to comply with disclosure requirements and is prevented from presenting evidence on the issues that should have been covered in the declaration of disclosure under Family Code section 2107(b)(2).

   d. ☐ be granted for good cause his or her request for voluntary waiver of receipt of ☐ preliminary ☐ final declaration of disclosure under Family Code section 2107(b)(3).

   e. ☐ for the reasons described below, be ordered to pay money sanctions for failure to comply with disclosure requirements. The amount of the money sanctions should be in an amount sufficient to deter him or her from repeating the conduct or comparable conduct, including reasonable attorney fees, costs incurred, or both, unless the court finds that the noncomplying party acted with substantial justification or that other circumstances make the imposition of the sanction unjust. (Family Code, § 2107(c).)

   f. ☐ be granted his or her request to set aside the judgment under Family Code section 2107(d).

   g. ☐ be ordered to comply with other, or alternative, relief, requested *(specify):*

2. ☐ FACTS IN SUPPORT of relief requested are *(specify):*
   ☐ Contained in the attached declaration. (You may use *Attached Declaration* (form MC-031) for this purpose).

I declare under penalty of perjury under the laws of the State of California that the foregoing is true and correct.

Date:

▶

_____   _____
(TYPE OR PRINT NAME)   (SIGNATURE OF APPLICANT)   **Page 1 of 1**

| Form Approved for Optional Use Judicial Council of California FL-316 [Rev. July 1, 2012] | **REQUEST FOR ORDERS REGARDING NONCOMPLIANCE WITH DISCLOSURE REQUIREMENTS** | Family Code, § 2107 www.courts.ca.gov |

Save This Form   Print This Form   Clear This Form

6A   Stipulation Examples

```
 1 | _____, SBN
   | LAW OFFICES OF _____
 2 | _____
   | _____
 3 |
   | Telephone: (___) ___-_____
 4 | Facsimile:  (___) ____-_____
   |
 5 | Attorney for:
   |
 6 |
   |
 7 |
   |                SUPERIOR COURT OF CALIFORNIA
 8 |
   |                   COUNTY OF _____
 9 |
   |
10 | Marriage of                    )    Case No:
   |                                )
11 | Petitioner: _____  )    STIPULATION AND ORDER
   |                                )    FOR _____
12 |                                )
   |                                )
13 | Respondent: _____  )
   | _____)
14 |
15 |        _____, Petitioner and _____ Respondent hereby stipulate and
   |
16 | agree that _____
   |
17 |
   |
18 |
   |
19 | Date: _____           _____
   |                                     Petitioner
20 |
   |
21 | Date:_____            _____
   |                                     Respondent
22 |
   |
23 | [Attorney signature as appropriate]
   |
24 |
25 |
26 |
27 |
28 |
   | _____ Page 1 _____
   | Marriage of _____; [document]
```

6A   Stipulation Examples

1

2   **ORDER**

3   Good cause appearing it is ordered that [or other language as appropriate]

4   _____

5   _____

6

7   Date: _____   _____
                                                JUDGE OF THE SUPERIOR COURT

8

9

10

11

12

13

14

15

16

17

18

19

20

21

22

23

24

25

26

27

28

Marriage of _____; [document]

6A Stipulation Examples

1 **Stipulation and Order for Continuance**:

2 _____ Petitioner and _____Respondent, hereby stipulate

3 that the hearing/trial set for _____ on [type of matter] shall be continued

4 to _____ [new date] at _____ [time] in Department

5 _____.

6 [If applicable] All temporary restraining orders granted by the Court on _____   will remain

7 in full force and effect until the new hearing date.]

8 [Order: The hearing/trial set for _____ on Petitioner/Respondent's _____ is

9 continued to _____ and time _____ in Department _____.] [Also include

10 temporary restraining order language as above if applicable.]

11 **Application for Continuance and Order**

12   I declare as follows:

13   1. I am the attorney for _____ Petitioner/Respondent in this action.

14   2. It is necessary that the hearing on Petitioner/Respondent's _____[matter]

15 filed on _____ [date and time} be continued to _____ [date &

16 time] in Department _____.

17   3. [Specify the reason for the application; ie., counsel just retained and inability to

18 prepare, taking of depositions, need for completion of mediation, etc.]

19   4. [If applicable] All temporary restraining orders granted by the Court on _____ [date]

20 shall remain in full force and effect until the new hearing date.

21   5. [If applicable] Manner of notice to be given.

22   I declare under penalty of perjury under the laws of the State of California that the

23 foregoing is true and correct.

24 Date: _____   _____

25   [Attorney's name]
                                                    Attorney for: _____

26

27

28

Page 3

Marriage of _____; [document]

6A Stipulation Examples

ORDER

Good cause appearing. It is ordered that the hearing on _____ Petitioner/

Respondent's _____ [action] filed on _____ shall be continued to

_____ in Department _____.

[If applicable: All temporary restraining orders granted by this Court on

_____ shall remain in full force and effect until the new hearing date.]

Date: _____   _____
                                                          JUDGE OF THE SUPERIOR COURT

Adoption of Mediation Report

_____ Petitioner and _____Respondent, hereby stipulate

and agree that the mediation report dated _____ and prepared by

_____ [name of mediator] be adopted [in its entirety or as amended as follows].

Said mediation is attached hereto as Exhibit "A" and incorporated in this document.

The parties further agree to comply with the mediation report until such time as the

parties agree in writing to any changes in custody and visitation of the minor children, until the

children have reached majority, or until further order of the court.

Date: _____   _____
                                                          Petitioner

Date:_____   _____
                                                          Respondent

[Attorney signature and/or notary as appropriate]

Page 4

Marriage of _____; [document]

6A Stipulation Examples

1

2   **ORDER**

3   Good cause appearing it is ordered that [or other language as appropriate]

4   _____

5   _____

6

7   Date: _____   _____
                                                  JUDGE OF THE SUPERIOR COURT
8

9

10

11

12

13

14

15

16

17

18

19

20

21

22

23

24

25

26

27

28
      _____Page 5_____
      Marriage of _____; [document]

6A Stipulation Examples

```
1   _____, SBN
    LAW OFFICES OF _____
2   _____

3   Telephone:
    Facsimile:
4

5   Attorney for:

6

7
                    SUPERIOR COURT OF CALIFORNIA
8
                         COUNTY OF _____
9

10
    Marriage of                    )      Case No:
11                                  )
    Petitioner: _____   )      STIPULATION AND ORDER
12                                  )      AFTER HEARING
                                    )      Date:
13                                  )      Time:
    Respondent: _____     )      Dept:
14  _____)

15
        This matter came on regularly for hearing on _____ at _____ in
16
    Department _____, before the Honorable _____.
17
        The parties stipulate and agree as follows:
18
    [Insert all matters/to which the parties agreed in court, based on the Minute Order]
19

20
    Date: _____          _____
21                                      Petitioner
22
    Date:_____           _____
23                                      Respondent
24
    Date: _____          _____
25                                      [Attorney's name]
                                        Attorney for:_____
26

27

28
                              Page 6
    _____
    Marriage of _____; [document]
```

6A   Stipulation Examples

1   Date:_____

2   _____
                                          [Attorney's name]
                                          Attorney for: _____

3

4   **ORDER**

5   Good cause appearing it is ordered that [or other language as appropriate]

6   _____

7   _____

8   Date: _____

9   _____
                                          JUDGE OF THE SUPERIOR COURT

10

11

12

13

14

15

16

17

18

19

20

21

22

23

24

25

26

27

28

                                          Page 7

Marriage of _____; [document]

6B *In re Marriage of Sullivan*

In re Marriage of Sullivan (1984) 37 CA3d 762

Janet and Mark Sullivan were married in 1967. Mark entered medical school immediately after the marriage and attended from 1968 -1971. He completed his residency in 1978 and received his license to practice medicine.

Janet worked full-time, and supported Mark during the entire time he was in medical school.

Shortly after Mark received his medical license the parties separated.

Janet requested that the Court place a "value" on Mark's medical license and that she receive her community portion of the equity in the license.

During the pendency of this matter, the California legislature enacted Civil Code Section 4800.3 (currently Family Code §2641), which created a right to reimbursement for "community contributions" made to the education or training that "substantially enhances the earning capacity" of the spouse. The Court will accept just about **any** education expenses, which were paid by the *working* spouse. Ordinary living expenses will not be considered, as those would have been necessary regardless of whether the person was obtaining an education or working.

The Court is given a great deal of discretion in determining if the education or training has "substantially enhanced" the student spouse's earning capacity, and the right and amount of reimbursement. The law clearly does not allow for the right to claim an interest in enhanced earnings, however.

The Legislature directed that the Court must also determine whether the community has **already** benefitted from the education and training. The Court must take into consideration the passage of time between when the education completed and/or the license received and the time that the parties separated. If the parties are married for a number of years after the professional status was attained, then the Court will usually determine that the community has already benefitted.

Family Code §2641 states as follows:

(a) "Community contributions to education or training" as used in this section means payments made with community or quasi-community property for education or training or for the repayment of a loan incurred for education or training, whether the payments were made while the parties were resident in this state or resident outside this state.

(b) Subject to the limitations provided in this section, upon dissolution of marriage or legal separation of the parties: (1) The community shall be reimbursed for community contributions to education or training of a party that substantially enhances the earning capacity of the party. The amount reimbursed shall be with interest at the legal rate, accruing from the end of the calendar year in which the contributions were made. (2) A loan incurred during marriage

6B *In re Marriage of Sullivan*

for the education or training of a party shall not be included among the liabilities of the community for the purpose of division pursuant to this division but shall be assigned for payment by the party.

(c) The reimbursement and assignment required by this section shall be reduced or modified to the extent circumstances render such a disposition unjust, including, but not limited to, any of the following: (1) The community has substantially benefited from the education, training, or loan incurred for the education or training of the party. There is a rebuttable presumption, affecting the burden of proof, that the community has not substantially benefited from community contributions to the education or training made less than 10 years before the commencement of the proceeding, and that the community has substantially benefited from community contributions to the education or training made more than 10 years before the commencement of the proceeding. (2) The education or training received by the party is offset by the education or training received by the other party for which community contributions have been made. (3) The education or training enables the party receiving the education or training to engage in gainful employment that substantially reduces the need of the party for support that would otherwise be required.

(d) Reimbursement for community contributions and assignment of loans pursuant to this section is the exclusive remedy of the community or a party for the education or training and any resulting enhancement of the earning capacity of a party. However, nothing in this subdivision limits consideration of the effect of the education, training, or enhancement, or the amount reimbursed pursuant to this section, on the circumstances of the parties for the purpose of an order for support pursuant to Section 4320.

(e) This section is subject to an express written agreement of the parties to the contrary.

6C   Spousal Support—Examples

Spousal Support Orders - Examples

Modifiable Amount for Indefinite Period

Petitioner shall pay to Respondent spousal support in the sum of $_____ per month, payable on the first day of each and every month commencing _____, 20___ until either party's death, Respondent's remarriage, modification or termination by further order of the court, whichever occurs first.

The Petitioner hereby waives spousal support from Respondent. The court has no jurisdiction to award spousal support to the Petitioner now or in the future.

Petitioner understands that it is public policy and the goal of the State of California that he/she shall attempt to be self-supporting within a reasonable amount of time, pursuant to Family Code Section 4320.

Modifiable Amount for Definite Period

Petitioner shall pay Respondent spousal support in the sum of $___ per month, payable on the first day of each and every month, commencing _____, 20___ until either party's death, respondent's remarriage or _____, 20___ [specific date], or further order of the court, whichever occurs first. Spousal support may be modified as to amount but not duration. If not terminated earlier, spousal support will terminate absolutely on _____, 20___ [same specific date as above] and the court's jurisdiction over spousal support shall terminate on said date.

The Petitioner hereby waives spousal support from Respondent. The court has no jurisdiction to award spousal support to the Petitioner now or in the future.

Petitioner understands that it is public policy and the goal of the State of California that he/she shall attempt to be self-supporting within a reasonable amount of time, pursuant to Family Code Section 4320.

Modifiable Amount for Definite Period of Time with Reservation of Jurisdiction

Petitioner shall pay Respondent spousal support in the sum of $___ per month, payable on the first day of each and every month, commencing _____, 20___ until either party's death, respondent's remarriage or _____, 20___ [specific date], modification or termination by order of the court, whichever occurs first. If _____, 20___ [same specific date as above] occurs first, then effective on that date spousal support will be reduced to zero, with the Court reserving jurisdiction, continuing until either party's death, respondent's remarriage, or further Court order.

6C Spousal Support—Examples

The Petitioner hereby waives spousal support from Respondent. The court has no jurisdiction to award spousal support to the Petitioner now or in the future.

Petitioner understands that it is public policy and the goal of the State of California that he/she shall attempt to be self-supporting within a reasonable amount of time, pursuant to Family Code Section 4320.

Modifiable Amount for Definite Period of Time; Burden of Proof Required to Avoid Termination

RICHMOND ORDER

Petitioner shall pay to Respondent spousal support the sum of $_____ per month, payable on the first day of each and every month, commencing _____, 20___, and continuing until either party's death, Respondent's remarriage, modification or termination or further Court order, or _____, 20__, whichever occurs first. If not terminated earlier, spousal support will terminate absolutely on _____, 20__, unless extended by Court order, on a showing by Respondent of good cause, on a motion filed on or before _____, 20____ [same date as above termination date].

Definite Decreasing Amounts

Petitioner shall pay to Respondent spousal support the sum of $____ per month, payable on the first day of each and every month, commencing _____, 20___, unless terminated earlier. Spousal Support shall be modified, unless terminated earlier, as follows:

$_____ per month for the period from _____, 20__ through _____, 20__;

$_____ per month for the period from _____, 20__ through _____, 20__;

$_____ per month for the period from _____, 20__ through _____, 20__;

Spousal support will be payable until either party's death, Respondent's remarriage, modification or termination by further Court order, or _____ [final date above], whichever occurs first. If not terminated earlier, spousal support shall terminate absolutely on _____, 20__ [final date above] unless extended by Court order, on a showing by Respondent of good cause, on a motion filed on or before _____, 20__ [final date above].

Petitioner understands that it is public policy and the goal of the State of California that he/she shall attempt to be self-supporting within a reasonable amount of time, pursuant to Family Code Section 4320.

6C Spousal Support—Examples

No Support; Reservation of Jurisdiction

Neither party shall pay spousal support to the other. The Court reserves jurisdiction, however, until either party's death, Respondent's remarriage, or modification or termination by further order of the Court, whichever occurs first, to order such support payable by Petitioner to Respondent on a proper showing of change of circumstances.

The parties understand that it is public policy and the goal of the State of California that he/she shall attempt to be self-supporting within a reasonable amount of time, pursuant to Family Code Section 4320.

No Support; Reservation Terminated.

Neither party shall pay spousal support to the other. Each party acknowledges that they understand their respective rights to future spousal support and are fully aware of the duties and forever discharge the other from any right, duty or obligation to support in the future, save and except solely as herein provided. In waiving any rights to future spousal support one from the other, each party has carefully considered not only the ability of the other party to pay, but his or her own individual ability to work and the risks and hazards of their future health and well-being. Regardless of all factors as herein set forth each party hereby waives any and all rights, claims, or demands on the other for future support and maintenance which he or she may now or hereafter have in the future.

Jurisdiction over spousal support is hereby terminated. No Court shall have jurisdiction to order spousal support payable to either party to the other at any time, regardless of any circumstances that may arise.

7A(1)   Disclosure Letter

Dear (Family Law Client)

Pursuant to Family Code §2104 you are required to completely disclose the identity, location, and value of **all your assets and obligations**, regardless of whether you claim a particular asset to be separate or community property. Additionally, if you have had an opportunity to make any investments since the date of separation that relates to the marriage, you must also disclose that information. If you operate or manage business, you must keep your spouse informed of the progress of that business. If you are aware of any material facts about the value of a particular asset, you must disclose same (for example if you have contacted a real estate agent about the value of your family residence).

Enclosed is a Declaration of Disclosure form which you must complete to the best of your ability and return to our office within _____ (__) days of this letter. There are five (5) numbered boxes on this form which must be checked, if applicable. They are as follows:

1. Section 1 requires that you complete the form entitled Schedule of Assets and Debts. This form is required for **all** clients. This form requires that you attach copies of written information relating to your assets. If you do not have copies, you will need to obtain them from your bank, insurance company, retirement fund, creditor or other entity. In completing this form remember that it is **your responsibility** to provide us with a true and accurate value of the community assets and obligations. If you do not know the value of a particular asset, then we may need to hire an expert to value that asset. The fee for such serves must be paid in advance. Please remember that you are valuing each asst as to what it is worth to you **today** in its present condition. We do not have Blue Books available in our office to assist you in valuing automobiles. You can obtain this information from the library or check on the Internet. With regard to valuing your household furniture, furnishings and appliances, we are enclosing a separate sheet for your convenience in itemizing and valuing these items. If you have other than a 100% interest in an asset or obligation, you must note that in the "Date Acquired" column. It is extremely important that you indicate each asset or debt which you feel is one party's **separate property or separate obligation**.

2. Section 2 requires that you complete an Income & Expense Declaration form. This form is required by all parties. The law states that "all material facts regarding the earnings, accumulations and expenses of each party" be disclosed.

7A(1)   Disclosure Letter

3. and 4. Sections 3 and 4 require that if you have any information (material facts) about your community assets and/or obligations of which your spouse is unaware, you must state these facts on a separate sheet of paper and return them to this along with the above referenced documents.

5. Section 5 requires that if you are aware of any investment opportunity that presents itself after the date of separation, and which results from any activity, involvement or investment of either spouse from the date of marriage to the date of separation, then you must provide that information. Please provide this information on a separate sheet of paper and return same to this office in sufficient time to advise your spouse so that he or she can make an informed decision as to whether to participate in the investment opportunity.

It is **very important** that you understand the concept of **Separate Property**. As required in the Schedule of Assets and Debts for, if you feel that a particular asset or debt is **separate**, then you must check the appropriate space in the first column of the form. If you have any question as to the concept of separate property, please discuss it with our office. For your information, separate property is generally:

(1) Property or debts owned prior to marriage. That is, an asset owned by a party prior to marriage that still exists when the parties separate (or an assets now in existence that can be traced to an asset owned prior to marriage. Also, any debt incurred prior to marriage that is still unpaid at the date of separation is generally that party's separate debt.

(2) Gifts. Property acquired during marriage by way of gift is generally the separate property of the party who receives the gift.

(3) Inheritance. If someone dies and leaves a party money or property, then the money or property so received is that party's sole and separate property, including any traceable assets purchased with that money.

(4) Personal Injury damages. Although sometimes considered to be community property, personal injury damages can be awarded 100% to the injured spouse depending upon the circumstances. If you have received a settlement during marriage as a result of a claim or lawsuit, please let me know.

(5) Property acquired **after** separation, or debts incurred after separation. If a party has purchased property after separation with money or earnings of that party acquired after separation, then that property can be deemed to be the party's sole and separate property. Likewise, a debt incurred after separation is generally that party's sole and separate debt.

(6) Title. In some cases, title to property may be held in one spouse's name only. Please

7A(1)   Disclosure Letter

let me know if you own property held solely in your name, as in certain instances, that property could be considered your sole and separate property. This category can also include U.S. Savings bonds held solely in one party's name.

We are required by the court to serve your spouse with the <u>Declaration of Disclosure</u> forms **regardless** of whether you and your spouse are in agreement as to how to divide your property within sixty (60) days of the date the Petition was filed. The court will **NOT** approve any marital settlement agreement or stipulated judgment until both the preliminary and the final Declaration of Disclosure are served on the other party.

Specifically, California Family Code Section 1100(e) provides in relevant part:

> "Each spouse shall act with respect to the other spouse in the management and control of the community assets and liabilities in accordance with the general rules governing fiduciary relationships with control the actions of persons having relationships of personal confidence as specified in Section 721, until such time as the assets and liabilities have been divided by the parties or by a court. This duty includes the obligation to make full disclosure to the other spouse of all material facts and information regarding the existence, characterization, and valuation of all assets in which community is or may be liable, and to provide equal access to all information, records, and books that pertain to the value and character of those assets and debts, upon request."

Once the preliminary <u>Declaration of Disclosure</u> is served on your spouse, the law requires that "each party has a continuing duty to **update and augment** that disclosure to the extent that there have been any material changes so that at the time the parties enter into an agreement for the resolution of any issues, each party will have a fall and complete knowledge of the relevant, underlying facts as is reasonably possible under the circumstances of the case." Thus, if any facts or conditions change **after** a <u>Disclosure</u> is served on your spouse that materially change your income or expenses, you have a continuing duty to notify us in writing, and an amended <u>Declaration of Disclosure</u> will have to be filed.

I realize that obtaining and furnishing us with the requested information will be a tedious, time-consuming task. However, by furnishing this information, sometimes it will not be necessary to incur the additional expense of formal discovery. We **cannot** proceed with, or complete your case, nor will a Judgment get approved by the court and entered, until these Disclosures are completed and served. If you refuse to complete the Disclosure, the court may order you to pay attorney fees, costs and possibly sanctions to your spouse for failure to disclose this information.

Yours very truly,

[Attorney]

7A(2) Notice of Fiduciary Responsibility

1 [Attorney Information]

2

3

4

5 Attorney for _____

6

7   IN THE SUPERIOR COURT OF THE STATE OF CALIFORNIA

8

9   COUNTY OF SACRAMENTO

10

11 In Re Marriage of: CASE NO:

12

13   , Petitioner   NOTICE OF FIDUCIARY DUTY OF
                                            SPOUSES TOWARD EACH OTHER
14 v.   RESPECTING THE MANAGEMENT
                                            AND CONTROL OF COMMUNITY
15   PROPERTY, DISCLOSURE AND
              , Respondent   INCOME & EXPENSE DECLARATIONS
16 _____/

17   TO: PETITIONER/RESPONDENT

18   NOTICE IS HEREBY GIVEN that Petitioner/Respondent, _____, shall

19 hold the Petitioner/Respondent _____, to that standard of care during the

20 marriage and after the date of separation until final division of the community property of the

21 parties as is set forth in California law, including, without limitation, California Family Code §§

22 721, 1100 and 2100, et. seq.

23   YOU ARE HEREBY PROVIDE NOTICE that Family Code § 721 states in relevant part:

24   "(b) Except as provided in Sections 143, 144, 146 and 16040, and 16047 of the Probate
         Code, in transactions between themselves, husband and wife are subject to the general
25   rules governing fiduciary relationship which control the action of persons occupying
         confidential relations with each other. This confidential relationship imposes a duty of
26   highest good faith and fair dealing on each spouse, and neither shall take any unfair
         advantage of the other. This confidential relationship is a fiduciary relationship subject
27   to the same rights and duties of nonmarital business partners, as provided in Sections
         16403, 16404, and 16503 of the Corporations Code, including, but not limited to the
28   following:

                                          1

7A(2) Notice of Fiduciary Responsibility

1
2
(1) Providing each spouse access at all times to any books kept regarding a transaction for the purposes of inspection and copying.

3
4
(2) Rendering upon request, true and full information of all things affecting any transaction which concerns the community property. Nothing in this section is intended to impose a duty for either spouse to keep detailed books and records of community property transactions.

5
6
(3) Accounting to the spouse, and holding as a trustee, any benefit or profit derived from any transaction by one spouse without the consent of the other spouse which concerns the community property."

7
YOU ARE HEREBY PROVIDED NOTICE that Family Code §1100 provides in

8
relevant part:

9
10
11
"(b) A spouse may not make a gift of community personal property, or dispose of community personal property for less than fair and reasonable value, without the written consent of the other spouse. This subdivision does not apply to gifts mutually given by both spouses to third parties and to gifts given by one spouse to the other spouse.

12
13
14
15
16
(e) Each spouse shall act with respect to the other spouse in the management and control of the community assets and liabilities in accordance with the general rules governing fiduciary relationship which control the actions of persons having relationships of personal confidence as specified in Section 721, until such time as the assets and liabilities have been divided by the parties or by a court. This duty includes the obligation to make full disclosure to the other spouse of all material facts and information regarding the existence, characterization, and valuation of all assets in which the community has or may have an interest and debts for which the community is or may be liable, and to provide equal access to all information, records, and books that pertain to the value and character of those assets and debts, upon request."

17
YOU ARE GIVEN FURTHER NOTICE that the laws of the State of California place

18
upon you an express obligation to disclose all assets and obligations, including without

19
limitation, all material facts and information regarding the existence, characterization, valuation,

20
and all things affecting any transaction which concerns the property of the parties which is, or

21
may be community property.

22
FURTHERMORE, you have the fiduciary duty to reveal all such documents and

23
information even if not specifically asked for. This duty remains in full force and effect until the

24
ultimate disposition of the property by the court.

25
YOUR FIDUCIARY DUTY is defined in California Family Code §2102, which defines

26
fiduciary duties as follow:

27
28
"(a) From the date of separation to the date of distribution of the community or quasi-community asset or liability in question, each party is subject to the standards provided in

2

7A(2)   Notice of Fiduciary Responsibility

Section 721, as to all activities that affect the assets and liabilities of the other party, including, but not limited to, the following activities:

(1) The accurate and complete disclosure of all assets and liabilities in which the party has or may have an interest or obligation and all current earnings, accumulations, and expenses, including an immediate, full and accurate update or augmentation to the extent there have been any material changes.

(2) The accurate and complete written disclosure of any investment opportunity, business opportunity, or other income-producing opportunity that presents itself after the date of separation, but that results from any investment, significant business activity outside the ordinary course of business, or other income-producing opportunity of either spouse from the date of marriage to the date of separation, inclusive. The written disclosure shall be made in sufficient time for the other spouse to make an informed decision as to whether he or she desired to participate in the investment opportunity, business, or other potential income-producing opportunity, and of the court to resolve any dispute regarding the right of the other spouse to participate in the opportunity. In the event of nondisclosure of any investment opportunity, the division of any gain resulting from that opportunity is governed by the standard provided in Section 2556.

(3) The operation or management of a business or an interest in a business in which the community may have an interest."

YOU ARE SUBJECT to the fiduciary standard set forth above "until the asset or liability

has actually been distributed pursuant to a valid, enforceable, and binding agreement. A

fiduciary duty no longer exists once a particular asset or liability has been distributed.

(California Family Code §2102(b).)

AT VARIOUS times during these proceedings, you will be obligated to complete an

Income and Expense Declaration. In preparing the Income and Expense Declaration, and as

events occur after the preparation of the Income and Expense Declaration, you must be informed

that California Family Code §2102(c) provides the following:

"(c) From the date of separation to the date of a valid, enforceable, and binding resolution of all issues relating to child or spouse support and professional fees, each party is subject to the standards provided in Section 721 as t o all issues relating to support and fees, including immediate, full, and accurate disclosure of all material facts and information regarding the income or expenses of the party."

YOUR OBLIGATIONS PURSUANT TO CALIFORNIA LAW are set forth above, and

are more particularly set forth in the attached copy of the California Family Code §§ 2100

through 2133.

YOU ARE HEREBY FURTHER NOTIFIED that, if you violate your fiduciary duty with

respect to the Petitioner/Respondent _____, there are significant economic damages

3

7A(2) Notice of Fiduciary Responsibility

1 which may be imposed against you, including without limitation, those set forth in Family Code

2 § 1101, which states in relevant part:

3 "(g) Remedies for breach of fiduciary duty by one spouse, including those set out in
Sections 721 and 1100, shall include, but not be limited to, an award to the other spouse

4 of 50 percent, or an amount equal to 50 percent, of any asset undisclosed or transferred in
breach of the fiduciary duty, plus attorney's fees and court costs. The value of the asset

5 shall be determined to be its highest value at the date of the breach of fiduciary duty, the
date of the sale or disposition of the asset, or the date of the award by the court.

6

7 (h) Remedies for breach of fiduciary duty by one spouse, including those set out in
Section 721 and 1100, when the breach falls within the ambit of Section 3294 of the Civil

8 Code shall include, but not be limited to, an award to the other spouse of 100 percent, or
an amount equal to 100 percent, of any asset undisclosed or transferred in breach of the

9 fiduciary duty."

10

11 Dated: _____

12 _____
[Attorney name]
Attorney for:

13

14

15

16

17

18

19

20

21

22

23

24

25

26

27

28

4

7B   Property Division Spreadsheet Examples

PROPERTY DISTRIBUTION SPREADSHEET (PROPOSAL)

Asset	Fair Market Value	Debt	Net Value	Husband	Wife
House	300,000	200,000	100,000	-0-	100,000
Vehicle 1	20,000	15,000	5,000	5,000	-0-
Vehicle 2	30,000	25,000	10,000	-0-	10,000
Retirement H	120,000	-0-	120,000	120,000	-0-
Retirement W	20,000	-0-	20,000	-0-	20,000
Furniture	5,000	-0-	5,000	2,500	2,500
xyz stocks	1,000	-0-	1,000	500	500
Total	496,000	246,000	261,000	128,000	133,000

Wife owes Husband an equalizing payment of $2,500 (one-half of $261,00 = 130,500 less 128,000 = 2,500)

7B Property Division Spreadsheet Examples

PROPERTY DISTRIBUTION SPREADSHEET (PROPOSAL)

Asset	Fair Market Value	Debt	Net Value	Husband	Wife
House	300,000	200,000	100,000	-0-	100,000
Vehicle 1	20,000	15,000	5,000	5,000	-0-
Vehicle 2	30,000	25,000	10,000	-0-	10,000
Retirement H	120,000	-0-	120,000	120,000	-0-
Retirement W	20,000	-0-	20,000	-0-	20,000
Furniture	5,000	-0-	5,000	2,500	2,500
xyz stocks	1,000	-0-	1,000	500	500
Citicard	-1,000	-1,000	-1,000	-0-	-1,000
Capital One	-1,000	-1,000	-1,000	-0-	-1,000
Target	- 500	- 500	- 500	-0-	500
Total	496,000	243,500	256,500	128,000	128,500

Husband owes Wife equalizing payment of $250.00 or they call it even, by mutual agreement

7B   Property Division Spreadsheet Examples

PROPERTY DISTRIBUTION SPREADSHEET (PROPOSAL)

Asset	Fair Market Value	Debt	Net Value	Husband	Wife
House	300,000	200,000	100,000	50,000	50,000
Vehicle 1	20,000	15,000	5,000	5,000	-0-
Vehicle 2	30,000	25,000	10,000	-0-	10,000
Retirement H	120,000	-0-	120,000	60,000	60,000
Retirement W	20,000	-0-	20,000	10,000	10,000
Furniture	5,000	-0-	5,000	2,500	2,500
xyz stocks	1,000	-0-	1,000	500	500
Total	496,000	246,000	261,000	130,500	130,500

(Note: there is no credit card debt included in this equation - possible Bankruptcy scenario; Alternatively you could pay the debts out of the proceeds of the sale of the house, which would eliminate the debts, however they should still be listed to show what happened to them.)

7B   Property Division Spreadsheet Examples

PROPERTY DISTRIBUTION SPREADSHEET (PROPOSAL)

Asset	Fair Market Value	Debt	Net Value	Husband	Wife
House	300,000	200,000	100,000	50,000	50,000
Vehicle 1	20,000	15,000	5,000	5,000	-0-
Vehicle 2	30,000	25,000	10,000	-0-	10,000
Retirement H	120,000	-0-	120,000	60,000	60,000
Retirement W	20,000	-0-	20,000	10,000	10,000
Furniture	5,000	-0-	5,000	2,500	2,500
xyz stocks	1,000	-0-	1,000	500	500
Target	-500	500	-500	-500	-0-
Citicard	-1,000	- 1,000	-1,000	-500	-0-
Capital One	-1,000	- 1,000	-1,000	-0-	1,000
Total	496,000	256,000	259,000	129,500	129,500

8A   Waiver of Rights Under Servicemembers Civil Relief Act

FL-130(A)

PETITIONER/PLAINTIFF:	CASE NUMBER:
RESPONDENT/DEFENDANT:	
OTHER PARENT:	

**DECLARATION AND CONDITIONAL WAIVER OF RIGHTS
UNDER THE SERVICEMEMBERS CIVIL RELIEF ACT OF 2003**
Attachment to *Appearance, Stipulations, and Waivers* (form FL-130)

Notice to Servicemember

The Servicemembers Civil Relief Act of 2003 (50 U.S.C. App. §§ 501–596), formerly known as the Soldiers' and Sailors' Civil Relief Act of 1940, is a federal law that provides protections for military members when they enter active duty. You may obtain a copy of the act from the public law library or from the website of the United States Department of Justice at *www.justice.gov.*

By signing this conditional waiver and attaching it to *Appearance, Stipulations, and Waivers* (form FL-130), I declare that I am entitled to the benefits of the Servicemembers Civil Relief Act, title 50 United States Code Appendix, sections 501–596 (SCRA), and:

1. To permit the court to decide this cause as an uncontested matter and enter a judgment that incorporates the terms of the written agreement made between the petitioner and me (a copy of which is attached to this form), I make a knowing, intelligent, and voluntary conditional waiver of the right to seek to set aside a default judgment entered against me in this matter, as provided by section 521 of the SCRA.

2. This waiver is conditioned as follows:

   a. The waiver applies only to a default judgment that incorporates the terms and conditions of the written agreement between the petitioner and me that is titled *(specify):*

      (1) ☐ Stipulation for Judgment

      (2) ☐ Marital Settlement Agreement

      (3) ☐ Other *(specify):*

   b. The court must enter a judgment in this case that incorporates only the terms and conditions of the above written agreement without any change; and

   c. Should the court enter a judgment that changes the above written agreement in any way, then I do not waive any of my rights under the SCRA, including my right to seek to set aside the judgment at any time.

3. This conditional waiver was executed during or after a period of military service.

I declare under penalty of perjury under the laws of the State of California that the foregoing is true and correct.

Date:

_____	_____
(TYPE OR PRINT NAME)	(SIGNATURE OF RESPONDENT)

Attention: Clerk of the Court
By law, a servicemember must not be charged a fee to file *Appearance, Stipulations, and Waivers* (form FL-130).

Page 1 of 1

Form Approved for Optional Use
Judicial Council of California
FL-130(A) [New January 1, 2011]
**DECLARATION AND CONDITIONAL WAIVER OF RIGHTS
UNDER THE SERVICEMEMBERS CIVIL RELIEF ACT OF 2003**
50 U.S.C. Appen. § 501 et seq.
Government Code, § 70673
www.courts.ca.gov

Save This Form | Print This Form | Clear This Form

8B   Default Judgment—Example

1 | _____, SBN
LAW OFFICES OF _____

2 | _____

3 | _____

   Telephone: (___) _____
4 | FAX: (___) _____

5 | Attorney For Petitioner: _____

6 |

7 | **IN THE SUPERIOR COURT OF THE STATE OF CALIFORNIA**

8 | **IN THE COUNTY OF _____**

9 |

10 |

   _____   CASE NO: _____
11 |
             Petitioner,   **DEFAULT JUDGMENT**
12 |
   and
13 |

   _____
14 | Respondent.

15 | _____/

16 |

   1.   **STATISTICAL INFORMATION**
17 |

     Petitioner declares that the following facts are true and correct:
18 |

     A. The parties married on _____, and ever since that time have been and now are
19 |

   Husband and Wife.
20 |

     B. There are three (3) minor child of this marriage.
21 |

              _____, born _____;
22 |

              _____, born _____; and,
23 |

              _____, born _____.
24 |

     C. The parties separated on _____, which is ___ (_) years and ____ (_)
25 |

   months from the date of marriage.
26 |

     D. A Petition for Dissolution was filed by Wife/Husband on _____, in the
27 |

   Superior Court of California, County of _____.
28 |

                                      1
   _____
   In re Marriage of _____; Default Judgment

8B   Default Judgment — Example

1   2. **<u>CHILD CUSTODY</u>**

2   A.   Petitioner acknowledges, agrees and accepts that this Superior Court of California,

3   County of _____, is the only court with jurisdiction over the custody of the minor children

4   referenced herein.

5   If either should party violate the custody and visitations orders as set forth below, that the

6   person may be subject to civil and/or criminal penalties pursuant to California Family Code Section

7   3048.

8   B. The parties will have joint legal custody. Mother shall have sole physical custody of the

9   minor children. Father shall have reasonable visitation with the minor children.

10   Joint legal custody under this paragraph means both parties have equal rights and

11   responsibilities toward the minor children. Specifically, decisions relating to the non-emergency

12   major medical care, dental, optometry, psychological, day care and educational needs of the child

13   shall require the mutual consent of both parties.

14   Each party shall provide the other with their current telephone number and address,

15   notifying the other within five (5) days of any changes of address or telephone number.

16   Pursuant to Section 4600.5(L) of the California Civil Code, both parties shall have access to

17   records and information pertaining to the minor child, including, but not limited to, medical, dental

18   and school records. This information shall not be denied to a party.

19   Each party shall be empowered to obtain emergency medical care for the children without

20   the consent of the other party. Each party shall notify the other party as soon as reasonably possible

21   of any serious illness requiring medical attention, or any emergency involving the children.

22   Each party shall exert every effort to maintain free access and unhampered contact between

23   the children and the other party, and to foster a feeling of affection between the children and the

24   other party. Neither party shall do anything which would estrange the children from the other,

25   which would injure the opinion of the child as to the other party or would impair the natural

26   development of the children's love and respect for the other party.

27   C.   The parties shall make good faith efforts to reach mutual agreements in the above

28   areas. In case a mutual agreement is not reached in any of the above areas, the parties shall seek

2

In re Marriage of _____; Default Judgment

8B   Default Judgment—Example

1   professional assistance from a licensed family counselor, private mediator or petition the court for

2   appointment of a mediator to resolve their differences. If an agreement is not reached after

3   attempted mediation, either party may come before the court for a resolution of the disputed issue(s).

4   The terms and conditions of the custody arrangement may be supplemented or revised as the

5   needs of the child changes. Such changes shall be in writing and signed by both parties. In the

6   event controversy arises, the existing Order of the Court shall remain in effect and the parties may

7   seek mediation prior to filing a motion with the Court for another hearing by filing a Petition for

8   Mediation.

9   3. **CHILD SUPPORT**

10   A. Father shall pay the sum of $_____ per month on the first day of each and every month

11 commencing _____, ____. Said support shall be payable by Wage Assignment. . The

12 needs of the children are adequately met by this Judgment. A _____ (printout) is attached and

13 incorporated as Exhibit "A."

14   Each party shall pay one-half of all work-related child care expenses.

15   1) The parties have been fully informed of their rights pursuant to Part 2, Child

16   Support, of the California Family Code §3900 et. seq.

17   2) The order is made without coercion or duress;

18   3) The order is in the best interests of the children involved;

19   4) The needs of the children will be adequately met by the order; and

20   5) The right to support has not been assigned to the County pursuant to Section 11477

21 of the Welfare & Institutions Code and no public assistance application is pending.

22   B. The Court shall reserve jurisdiction on the issue of child support until further order of the

23 Court, or until the children marry, die, are emancipated, reach the age of nineteen (19), or reach the

24 age of eighteen (18) and is not full-time students residing with a parent, whichever occurs first.

25   C. Support of the minor children is subject to an order of a Court of competent jurisdiction

26 at any time during the child's minority, and that this paragraph or any later child support order is

27 subject to modification.

28

3

In re Marriage of _____; Default Judgment

8B   Default Judgment—Example

4.   **MEDICAL AND DENTAL INSURANCE**

Father shall ensure that a policy of health and dental insurance for the minor children is in place as long as it is available at a reasonable cost through his employer.

5.   **MEDICAL AND DENTAL COSTS**

Any health care needs and costs not covered by such insurance, including but not limited to, deductibles, dental, orthodontic or opthamalagic, shall shared equally.

6.   **PROVISIONS RELATING TO SPOUSAL SUPPORT**

a. **Reservation of Jurisdiction**: Neither party shall pay spousal support to the other. The court shall retain jurisdiction as to spousal support for Petitioner, for a period of _____ (_) years from the entry of Judgment.

b. **Circumstances of Parties**: Each party is gainfully employed and expects to continue in this employment. Neither party has any known major medical condition which would render the continuation of gainful employment unlikely. There has been no award of pendente lite spousal support.

c. Petitioner understands that it is the public policy and the goal of the State of California that he/she shall attempt to be self-supporting within a reasonable amount of time, pursuant to Family Code Section 4320.

7.   **DIVISION OF COMMUNITY PROPERTY AND CO-OWNED PROPERTY**

A. **Wife** shall take the following assets as her separate property:

*   _____ (vehicle);

* Furniture, furnishings and appliance which are currently in her possession in the apartment located at _____;

All other personal property and jewelry which are in her possession.

B. **Husband** shall take the following assets as his separate property:

*   _____ (vehicle);

*   Any and all retirement benefits to which Respondent/Husband is entitled;

*   All personal property, jewelry, furniture, furnishings and appliances which are in his

---

4

In re Marriage of _____; Default Judgment

8B Default Judgment—Example

1 possession.

2

3 8. **COMMUNITY PROPERTY DEBT**

4   Future incurred personal debts shall be the responsibility of the purchasing party. Neither

5 party shall incur debt in each other's name. Each party shall assume and pay own personal debts.

6 All common credit card accounts and bank accounts will be closed.

7   **Wife** shall assume and is responsible for the following community debts:

8   None

9   B. **Husband** shall assume and is responsible for the following community debts:

10 * Sally Mae (Student) Loan; and,

11 * Debt of approximately $_____ due to _____.

12 9.. **OTHER PROVISIONS**

13   The parties are bound by the following additional terms and provisions:

14   A. RIGHT TO CONVEY OR WILL PROPERTY

15   Each party shall have an immediate right to sell, grant, transfer, and to dispose of by Will, his

16 or her respective interest in and to any property belonging to him or her from and after the date

17 hereof, and said right shall extend to all of the aforesaid future acquisitions of the property, earnings,

18 and income as well as to all property set over to either of the parties herein.

19   B. GOVERNING LAW

20   This Judgment is entered in the State of California and shall be construed and

21 interpreted under and in accordance with the law of the State of California applicable to Judgment

22 made to be wholly performed in the State of California.

23   C. RECONCILIATION

24   Any reconciliation between the parties shall not cancel, terminate or modify the force

25 or effect of any provision of this Judgment dealing with the assets or obligations of either party,

26 unless the parties agree to the contrary in writing.

27   D. CAPTIONS AND INTERPRETATIONS

28   The captions of this Judgment are employed solely for convenience and are not to be

5

In re Marriage of _____; Default Judgment

8B   Default Judgment—Example

1   used as an aid in interpretation. No provision in this Judgment is to be interpreted for or against

2   either party because that party or his or her legal representative drafted the provision.

3   E. NUMBER AND GENDER

4   Whenever the singular number is used in this Judgment, when required by the

5   context, the same shall include the plural, and the masculine, feminine and a neuter gender shall

6   each include the other; and the word "person" shall include corporation, firm, partnership, joint

7   venture, trust or estate.

8   F. ENFORCEMENT OF JUDGMENT - FEES AND COSTS

9   Should it be necessary for either party to bring an action in this or any other court for

10   the enforcement of any of the provisions of this Judgment, the prevailing party shall be entitled to an

11   award from the other party of their reasonable attorneys' fees and costs incurred in the action.

12   G. DOCUMENTS AND COOPERATION

13   1) Each party shall, on the request of the other, execute and deliver any instrument,

14   furnish any information and perform any other acts reasonably necessary to carry out the provision

15   of this Judgment without undue delay or expense. A party who fails to comply with this subsection

16   shall reimburse the other party for all costs and expenses, including attorney fees and court costs,

17   that as a result of their failure become reasonably necessary to carry out this Judgment. Upon a

18   party's failure to execute a document reasonably required to carry out the provision of this Judgment,

19   the court may appoint the County Clerk, or the County Clerk's deputy, upon ex parte application and

20   without formal notice, as an Elisor to sign those documents on behalf of the party who failed to do

21   so voluntarily. This section shall not constitute a waiver of any privilege afforded by law.

22   10.   **RETENTION OF JURISDICTION**

23   The _____ Superior Court shall retain, in addition to the jurisdiction

24   specifically mentioned elsewhere in this Judgment, the jurisdiction to:

25   A. Supervise the payment of any obligation to be paid by the terms of this Judgment;

26   B. Supervise the division and confirmation of assets by the terms of this Judgment;

27   C. Supervise the execution of any documents required or reasonably necessary to

28   carry out the terms of this Judgment;

6

In re Marriage of _____; Default Judgment

8B   Default Judgment—Example

1   / / / / / / /

2   / / / / / / /

3

4   D. Supervise the marital status of the parties; and

5   E. Supervise the overall enforcement of this Judgment

6

7   Dated:_____   _____

8   JUDGE OF THE SUPERIOR COURT

9

10

11

12

13

14

15

16

17

18

19

20

21

22

23

24

25

26

27

28

7

In re Marriage of _____; Default Judgment

8C Statement of Issues/Pre-trial Brief—Example

1 _____ SBN
   LAW OFFICES OF _____

2 _____
   _____

3 Telephone: (___) ___-_____

4 Attorney for Petitioner: _____

5

                    SUPERIOR COURT OF CALIFORNIA

6   COUNTY OF _____

7

8 In Re the Marriage of: CASE NO: _____

9 PETITIONER: _____   **PETITIONER'S STATEMENT**
                                    OF ISSUES, CONTENTIONS,
10   And   **AND PROPOSED DISPOSITION**
                                    Settlement Conference: _____
11 RESPONDENT: _____   Trial Date: _____
                                    Time: _____ a.m.
12 _____/ Department: ____, ____

13
          In accordance with the Local Rules of _____ County Superior Court, Petitioner,

14
   _____, submits the following Statement of Issues, Contentions and Proposed

15
   Disposition of this case:

16
                                     I

17
                     BACKGROUND INFORMATION

18
          Petitioner, _____, hereinafter referred to as "Husband," and Respondent,

19
   _____, hereinafter referred to as "Wife," were married on _____, ____. The

20
   parties separated on _____, ____. The duration of the marriage was ten (__) years and

21
   eight (_) months. There are no minor children of this marriage.

22
          Husband filed for Dissolution of Marriage on _____ , _____ in

23
   _____ County, Superior Court Case No: _____.

24
          An Order to Show Cause was filed by Wife on _____, ____ and the hearing on

25
   this matter was held on _____, ____ in Department ___ before the Honorable, _____

26
   _____.

27

28

                                     1

8C Statement of Issues/Pre-trial Brief—Example

II

ISSUES

A. CHILD CUSTODY

B. CHILD SUPPORT

C. SPOUSAL SUPPORT

D. DIVISION OF COMMUNITY PROPERTY

E. DIVISION OF COMMUNITY DEBTS

F. ATTORNEY FEES

III

CONTENTIONS AND PROPOSED DISPOSITION

A. <u>CHILD CUSTODY</u>

The parties have attended mediation. A copy of the agreement reached at mediation is attached as Exhibit "A" and incorporated hereto. Petitioner requests that the court adopt the mediation agreement.

B. <u>CHILD SUPPORT</u>

Husband and Wife have been unable to reach an agreement regarding child support. Petitioner requests that the Court order guideline child support. A _____ (child support calculation) is attached and incorporated hereto as Exhibit "B." Petitioner has provided Respondent with a copy of his current Income & Expense Declarations. Said documents have been filed with the Court as required prior to trial.

The _____ (support calculation) indicates guideline child support as _____. This amount is based on Petitioner's net income and the time share based on the parenting agreement, as referenced above. Said time share is 52% for Respondent (Mother) and 48% for Petitioner (Father).

/ / / / /

/ / / / /

/ / / / /

2

8C Statement of Issues/Pre-trial Brief—Example

1 C. <u>SPOUSAL SUPPORT</u>

2 Husband was ordered to pay Wife the sum of $_____ per month commencing

3 _____. Husband paid all ordered spousal support and there are no arrears.

4 Husband requests that the court order spousal support to be terminated at trial. Wife is

5 now gainfully employed and has adequate means of support.

6 D. <u>DIVISION OF COMMUNITY PROPERTY</u>:

7 Husband has responded to each of Wife's settlement offers, with fair and equitable

8 settlement offers, which are attached and incorporated herein. Wife has rejected these settlement

9 offers and has failed to negotiate in good faith to reach an agreement.

10 A copy of a spreadsheet showing a fair and equitable settlement of all property is

11 attached and incorporated as Exhibit "C."

12 Petitioner has complied with all disclosure requirements. An updated Schedule of

13 Assets and Debts has been served and filed with the court prior to trial as required.

14 E. <u>DIVISION OF COMMUNITY DEBTS</u>:

15 Husband agrees that each party should pay the balance on their respective credit cards as

16 set forth in his proposed settlement agreement.

17 Husband has been paying the obligation on the ____ since the date of separation, as

18 evidenced in the statement attached as Exhibit "D," and requests that he be credited for the

19 amount he has paid on this community property debt, using separate property. Said

20 reimbursement is included in the property spreadsheet which is attached as Exhibit "C."

21 F. <u>ATTORNEY FEES</u>:

22 Husband has previously paid Wife's attorney fees in the sum of $1,000.00, as ordered on

23 _____, ____. Husband contends Wife has failed to negotiate in good faith to each a

24 settlement without further litigation. Husband therefore proposes that Wife be ordered to pay

25 any and all attorney's fees which she has incurred in this matter since the that time.

26

27 _____
   Attorney for Petitioner

28

3

8C Statement of Issues/Pre-trial Brief—Example

1 _____, SBN

2 LAW OFFICES OF _____

   _____

3 _____

   Telephone: (___) ___-____

4 Attorney for Petitioner: _____

5

6   SUPERIOR COURT OF CALIFORNIA

7   COUNTY OF _____

8 In Re the Marriage of: CASE NO: _____

9 PETITIONER: _____   **PROOF OF SERVICE BY**
                                        FACSIMILE AND REGULAR
10   And   **MAIL**

11 RESPONDENT: _____

12 _____/

13 _____, declares:

14   I am over the age of 18 and not a party to this action. My business address is

15 _____, Suite ___, _____, California, _____.

16   On _____ I sent by facsimile at _____, California, and I

17 prepared for deposit in the U.S. mail at Citrus Heights, California, in a sealed envelope with

18 postage prepaid, a copy of the attached: PETITIONER'S STATEMENT OF ISSUES,

19 CONTENTIONS AND PROPOSED DISPOSITION addressed as follows:

20 _____

   ATTORNEY AT LAW

21 _____

   _____

22

23   I declare under penalty of perjury that the foregoing is true and correct and that this

24 declaration was executed on _____ at _____, California.

25   _____

26   _____

27

28

                              4

8D(a) Request for Separate Trial (Bifurcation)

FL-315

PETITIONER:	CASE NUMBER:
RESPONDENT:	

☐ **REQUEST FOR SEPARATE TRIAL**   OR   ☐ **RESPONSE TO REQUEST FOR SEPARATE TRIAL**

Attachment to ☐ *Request for Order*   ☐ *Responsive Declaration to Request for Order*
(form FL-300)   (form FL-320)

1. I am the ☐ petitioner ☐ respondent and ☐ request ☐ oppose the request   that the court sever
    (bifurcate) and grant an early and separate trial on the following issue or issues:

    a. ☐ Permanent custody and visitation of the children of the marriage or domestic partnership

    b. ☐ Date of separation of the parties

    c. ☐ Alternate valuation date for property

    d. ☐ Validity of agreement entered into before or during the marriage or domestic partnership

    e. ☐ Dissolution of the status of the marriage or domestic partnership

    (1) I will serve with this application or response my preliminary *Declaration of Disclosure* (form FL-140) and completed
         Schedule of Assets and *Debts* (form FL-142) *and Income and Expense Declaration* (FL-150) unless they have been
         previously served or the parties have stipulated in writing to defer service.

    (2) All pension or retirement plans in which the community has an interest are listed below or on attachment 1e(2):

    (3) All pension or retirement plans listed in 1e(2) have been joined as a party to this proceeding, unless joinder is
         precluded or made unnecessary as a matter of law. *(See* Retirement Plan Joinder—Information Sheet (form
         FL-318-INFO) *to determine if a joinder is required.)*

    (4) I understand that the court may make the orders specified or requested on pages 2 and 3 if the motion is granted to
         bifurcate the status of the marriage and the marriage is ended.

    (5) ☐ I request that the court make the orders indicated on pages 2 and 3 and any attachments.

    *NOTE: A request for an early termination of your marital or partnership status may have a significant impact on your
    rights or responsibilities in your case. If you do not understand this form, you should speak with an attorney.*

    f. ☐ Other *(specify):*

2. a. ☐ I request that the court conduct this separate trial on the hearing date.

    b. ☐ I will, at the hearing, ask the court to set a date for this separate trial.

3. The reasons in support of this request are *(specify):*
    ☐ Memorandum attached.   ☐ Supporting declarations attached.

Page 1 of 3

Form Adopted for Mandatory Use Judicial Council of California FL-315 [Rev. July 1, 2012]	**REQUEST OR RESPONSE TO REQUEST FOR SEPARATE TRIAL** **(Family Law)**	Family Code, § 2337 *www.courts.ca.gov*

8D(a) Request for Separate Trial (Bifurcation)

FL-315

PETITIONER:	CASE NUMBER:
RESPONDENT:	

4. Conditions relating to bifurcation of the status of the marriage or partnership:

   a. I understand that the court must enter an order to preserve the claims of each spouse or domestic partner in all retirement plan benefits upon entry of judgment granting a dissolution of the status of the marriage or domestic partnership.

   b. I request that the court order the following as a condition of granting the bifurcation and ending the marriage upon an early and separate trial:

     (1) ☐ **Division of property**

       The ☐ petitioner ☐ respondent and his or her estate must indemnify and hold me harmless from any taxes, reassessments, interest, and penalties that I have to pay in connection with the division of the community estate that I would not have had to pay if we were still married or in a domestic partnership at the time the division was made.

     (2) ☐ **Health insurance**

       Until a judgment has been entered and filed on the remaining issues, the ☐ petitioner ☐ respondent must maintain all existing health and medical insurance coverage for me and any minor children as named dependents as long as he or she is eligible to do so. If at any time during this period, he or she is not eligible to maintain that coverage, he or she must, at his or her sole expense, provide and maintain health and medical insurance coverage that is comparable to the existing health and medical insurance coverage to the extent it is available.

       To the extent that coverage is not available, the ☐ petitioner ☐ respondent must be responsible for paying, and demonstrate to the court's satisfaction the ability to pay, for health and medical care for me and the minor children to the extent that care would have been covered by the existing insurance coverage but for the dissolution of marital status or domestic partnership, and must otherwise indemnify and hold me harmless from any adverse consequences resulting from the loss or reduction of the existing coverage.

     (3) ☐ **Probate homestead**

       Until a judgment has been entered and filed on all remaining issues, the ☐ petitioner ☐ respondent must indemnify and hold me harmless from any adverse consequences if the bifurcation results in a termination of my right to a probate homestead in the residence in which I am residing at the time the severance is granted.

     (4) ☐ **Probate family allowance**

       Until a judgment has been entered and filed on all remaining issues, the ☐ petitioner ☐ respondent must indemnify and hold me harmless from any adverse consequences if the bifurcation results in the loss of my right to a probate family allowance as the surviving spouse or surviving domestic partner.

     (5) ☐ **Retirement benefits**

       Until a judgment has been entered and filed on all remaining issues, the ☐ petitioner ☐ respondent must indemnify and hold me harmless from any adverse consequences if the bifurcation results in the loss of my rights with respect to any retirement, survivor, or deferred compensation benefits under any plan, fund, or arrangement, or to any elections or options associated those benefits, to the extent that I would have been entitled to those benefits or elections as the spouse or surviving spouse or the domestic partner or surviving domestic partner.

     (6) ☐ **Social security benefits**

       The ☐ petitioner ☐ respondent must indemnify and hold me harmless from any adverse consequences if the bifurcation results in the loss of rights to social security benefits or elections to the extent that I would have been entitled to those benefits or elections as the surviving spouse or surviving domestic partner.

REQUEST OR RESPONSE TO REQUEST FOR SEPARATE TRIAL
(Family Law)

8D(a) Request for Separate Trial (Bifurcation)

FL-315

PETITIONER:	CASE NUMBER:
RESPONDENT:	

(7) ☐ **Beneficiary designation—nonprobate transfer**

The ☐ petitioner ☐ respondent   must maintain the beneficiary designation specified for each Nonprobate Transfer Asset (Probate Code section 5000) identified on the attached list in the percentage indicated. *(See Attachment 7 (not a form), which lists each asset and proposed percentage.)* This designation must stay in effect until judgment has been entered with respect to the community ownership of that asset and until my interest in it has been distributed to me.

(8) ☐ **Individual Retirement Accounts**

To preserve the ability of the nonowner to defer the distribution of an Individual Retirement Account (IRA) or annuity upon the death of the owner, the court should make the attached orders assigning and transferring the community interest of ☐ petitioner ☐ respondent   in each listed IRA to that party. *(See Attachment 8 (not a form), which lists names of IRAs, account numbers, and amount to be awarded.)*

(9) ☐ **Enforcement of community property rights**

Because it will be difficult to enforce either of our community property rights if one of us dies before the division and distribution or compliance with any court-ordered payment of any community property interest, the court should make the attached order to provide enforcement security for ☐ petitioner ☐ respondent. *(See attachment 9 (not a form), which specifies the security interest to be ordered as provided by Family Code section 2337(c)(9).)*

(10) ☐ **Other conditions that are just and equitable**

The court makes the following additional orders:

5. Number of pages attached after this page: _____

I declare under penalty of perjury under the laws of the State of California that the foregoing is true and correct.

Date:

▶

_____   _____
(TYPE OR PRINT NAME)   (SIGNATURE OF DECLARANT)

| FL-315 [Rev. July 1, 2012] | **REQUEST OR RESPONSE TO REQUEST FOR SEPARATE TRIAL**
(Family Law) | Page 3 of 3 |

Save This Form   Print This Form   Clear This Form

8D(b) Request for Separate Trial (Bifurcation)

FL-347

PETITIONER:	CASE NUMBER:
RESPONDENT:	

BIFURCATION OF STATUS OF MARRIAGE OR DOMESTIC PARTNERSHIP
ATTACHMENT TO ☐ **JUDGMENT (FL-180)** ☐ **FINDINGS AND ORDER AFTER HEARING (FL-340)**

The court grants the request of ☐ petitioner ☐ respondent to bifurcate and grant a separate trial on the issue of the dissolution of the status of the marriage or domestic partnership apart from other issues.

Date marital or domestic partnership status ends *(specify):*

THE COURT FINDS

1. A preliminary declaration of disclosure with a completed schedule of assets and debts and income and expense declaration has been served on the nonmoving party, or the parties have stipulated in writing to defer service of the preliminary declaration of disclosure until a later time.

2. Each retirement or pension plan of the parties has been joined as a party to the proceeding for dissolution unless joinder is precluded or made unnecessary by applicable law.

THE COURT ORDERS

3. a. To preserve the claims of each party in all retirement plan benefits on entry of judgment granting a dissolution of the status of the marriage or domestic partnership, the court makes one of the following orders for each retirement plan in which either party is a participant:

   (1) A final domestic relations order or qualified domestic relations order under Family Code section 2610 disposing of each party's interest in retirement plan benefits, including survivor and death benefits.

   (2) An interim order preserving the nonemployee party's right to retirement plan benefits, including survivor and death benefits, pending entry of judgment on all remaining issues.

   (3) A provisional order on *Pension Benefits—Attachment to Judgment* (form FL-348) incorporated as an attachment to the judgment of dissolution of the status of marriage or domestic partnership (*Judgment (Family Law)*(form FL-180)). This order provisionally awards to each party a one-half interest in all retirement benefits attributable to employment during the marriage or domestic partnership.

   b. Name of plan:

	Type of order attached		
	3a(1)	3a(2)	3a(3)
	☐	☐	☐
	☐	☐	☐
	☐	☐	☐

   ☐ See attachment 3b for additional plans.

   c. The moving party must promptly serve on the retirement or pension plan administrator a copy of any order entered under items a and b above and a copy of the judgment granting dissolution of the status of the marriage or domestic partnership (form FL-180).

4. Jurisdiction is reserved for later determination of all other pending issues in this case.

5. The court makes the following additional orders as conditions for granting the severance on the issue of dissolution of the status of marriage or domestic partnership. In the case of the moving party's death, the order continues to be binding on that moving party's estate and will be enforceable against any asset, including the proceeds thereof, to the same extent that these obligations would have been enforceable before the person's death.

   a. ☐ **Division of property**

   The ☐ petitioner ☐ respondent must indemnify and hold the other party harmless from any ☐ taxes, ☐ reassessments, ☐ interest, and ☐ penalties payable by the other party in connection with the division of the community estate that would not have been payable if the parties were still married or domestic partners at the time the division was made.

Page 1 of 3

Form Adopted for Mandatory Use
Judicial Council of California
FL-347 [Rev. July 1, 2012]

**BIFURCATION OF STATUS OF MARRIAGE
OR DOMESTIC PARTNERSHIP—ATTACHMENT
(Family Law)**

Family Code, §§ 2337, 2610;
Probate Code, §§ 160 et seq., 5000 et seq.
www.courts.ca.gov

8D(b) Request for Separate Trial (Bifurcation)

FL-347

PETITIONER:	CASE NUMBER:
RESPONDENT:	

5. b. ☐ **Health insurance**

Until a judgment has been entered and filed on all remaining issues, the ☐ petitioner ☐ respondent must maintain all existing health and medical insurance coverage for the other party, and that party must also maintain any minor children as named dependents, as long as that party is eligible to do so. If at any time during this period the ☐ petitioner ☐ respondent is not eligible to maintain that coverage, that party must, at his or her sole expense, provide and maintain health and medical insurance coverage that is comparable to the existing health and medical insurance coverage to the extent it is available.

If that coverage is not available, the ☐ petitioner ☐ respondent is responsible for paying the health and medical care for the other party and the minor children to the extent that care would have been covered by the existing insurance coverage but for the dissolution of marital status or domestic partnership, and will otherwise indemnify and hold the other party harmless from any adverse consequences resulting from the loss or reduction of the existing coverage. "Health and medical insurance coverage" includes any coverage under any group or individual health or other medical plan, fund, policy, or program.

c. ☐ **Probate homestead**

Until a judgment has been entered and filed on all remaining issues, the ☐ petitioner ☐ respondent must indemnify and hold the other party harmless from any adverse consequences to the other party if the bifurcation results in a termination of the other party's right to a probate homestead in the residence in which the other party resides at the time the severance is granted.

d. ☐ **Probate family allowance**

Until a judgment has been entered and filed on all remaining issues, the ☐ petitioner ☐ respondent must indemnify and hold the other party harmless from any adverse consequences to the other party if the bifurcation results in the loss of the rights of the other party to a probate family allowance as the surviving spouse or surviving domestic partner.

e. ☐ **Retirement benefits**

Except for any retirement plan, fund, or arrangement identified in any order issued and attached as set out in paragraph 3, until a judgment has been entered on all remaining issues, the ☐ petitioner ☐ respondent must indemnify and hold the other party harmless from any adverse consequences to the other party if the bifurcation results in the loss of the other party's rights with respect to any retirement, survivor, or deferred compensation benefits under any plan, fund, or arrangement, or to any elections or options associated with them, to the extent that the other party would have been entitled to those benefits or elections as the spouse or surviving spouse or the domestic partner or surviving domestic partner of the moving party.

f. ☐ **Social security benefits**

The moving party must indemnify and hold the other party harmless from any adverse consequences if the bifurcation results in the loss of rights to social security benefits or elections to the extent the other party would have been entitled to those benefits or elections as the surviving spouse or surviving domestic partner of the moving party.

g. ☐ **Beneficiary designation— Nonprobate transfer**

Attachment 5(g), Order Re: Beneficiary Designation for Nonprobate Transfer Assets, will remain in effect for each covered asset until the division of any community interest therein has been completed.

h. ☐ **Individual Retirement Account**

Attachment 5(h), Order Re: Division of IRA Under Internal Revenue Code Section 408(d)(6), has been issued to preserve the ability of ☐ petitioner ☐ respondent to defer distribution of his or her community interest on the death of the IRA owner.

8D(b)   Request for Separate Trial (Bifurcation)

FL-347

PETITIONER:	CASE NUMBER:
RESPONDENT:	

5. i. ☐ **Enforcement of community property rights**

   Good cause exists to make additional orders as set out in Family Code section 2337(c)(9). See Attachment 5(i).

   j. ☐ **Other conditions that are just and equitable**

   Other:

6. Number of attachments: _____

> **WARNING:** *Judgment (Family Law)* (form FL-180) (status only) must be completed in addition to this form for the status of the marriage or domestic partnership to be ended.

For your protection and privacy, please press the Clear This Form button after you have printed the form.

Save This Form   **Print This Form**   **Clear This Form**

9A Marital Settlement Agreement—Example

1

2

3 _____

4 _____
   _____

5 TELEPHONE: (916) _____

6 Attorney for Petitioner/Respondent, _____

7

8

9   IN THE SUPERIOR COURT OF THE STATE OF CALIFORNIA

10   IN AND FOR THE COUNTY OF SACRAMENTO

11

12 IN RE THE MARRIAGE OF   NO. _____

13 Petitioner: _____   MARRIAGE SETTLEMENT
                                       AGREEMENT
14   Vs.

15 Respondent: _____

16 _____/

17   1. **STATISTICAL INFORMATION**

18   A. _____, hereinafter referred as "Husband", and

19 _____, hereinafter referred as "Wife", were married on _____,

20 and from that time forward have been Husband and Wife.

21

22   B. Differences have arisen between the parties and have continued to the present time, as

23 a result of which the marriage of the parties has broken down irretrievably, and the parties desire

24 to live apart. Therefore, the parties were separated on _____ _, ____, which is _____

25 (__) years and _____ (__) months from the date of marriage.

26

27   C. The parties have two (2) minor children of this marriage:

28   _____, born on _____, and

9A Marital Settlement Agreement—Example

_____ , born on _____ .

D. A Petition for Dissolution of Marriage was filed by Wife on

_____ , in the Superior Court of Sacramento County, State of California,

Case Number _____ . Pursuant to stipulation and agreement by the parties, the court makes

the following findings and orders:

2. **PURPOSES OF AGREEMENT**

The purposes of this Agreement are to:

      A.   Settle all property interests and rights that each party may have with

respect to the other.

      B.   Settle the obligations of each party for the support of the other.

      C.   Relinquish any and all past, present, or future claims that each may have

against the property or estate of the other party and his or her executors, administrators,

representatives, successors, and assigns, except as otherwise provided herein.

3. **CHILD CUSTODY**

      A. The parties herein acknowledge, agree and accept that this Superior Court of

California, County of Sacramento, is the only court with jurisdiction over the custody of the

minor children referenced herein. The parties further agree and acknowledge that should either

party violate the custody and visitations orders as set forth below, that they may be subject to

civil and/or criminal penalties pursuant to California Family Code Section 3048.

2

Marriage of ____ ; Marital Settlement Agreement

9A Marital Settlement Agreement—Example

1

2   B. Both parents shall share joint legal custody. Mother shall have primary

3   physical custody of the minor children and Father shall have reasonable parenting time, as more

4   specifically set forth in paragraph 4 below..

5
   OR Both parents shall share joint legal and physical custody of the minor children. Each
6
7   party shall assure that the children shall have frequent and continuing contact with each parent.

8   C. Joint legal custody under this paragraph means both parties have equal rights

9   and responsibilities toward the minor children. Specifically, decisions relating to the non-

10 emergency major medical care, dental, optometry, psychological, day care and educational needs

11
    of the child shall require the mutual consent of both parties.
12

13   D. The parties shall make good faith efforts to reach mutual agreements in the

14 above areas. In case a mutual agreement is not reached in any of the above areas, the parties

15 shall seek professional assistance from a licensed family counselor, private mediator or petition

16
    the court for appointment of a mediator to resolve their differences. If an agreement is not
17
18 reached after attempted mediation, either party may come before the court for a resolution of the

19 disputed issue(s).

20   E. Any additional parenting time mutually agreed upon by both parties shall be

21 allowed and encouraged.

22
        F. The terms and conditions of this custody arrangement may be supplemented or
23
24 revised as the needs of the child changes. Such changes shall be in writing and signed by both

25 parties. In the event controversy arises, the existing Order of the Court shall remain in effect and

26 the parties may seek mediation prior to filing a motion with the Court for another hearing by

27

28   3

    Marriage of ____; Marital Settlement Agreement

9A　Marital Settlement Agreement—Example

filing a Petition for Mediation.

　　　　G.　Each party shall provide the other with their current telephone number and address, notifying the other within five (5) days of any changes of address or telephone number.

　　　　H.　Pursuant to Section 4600.5(L) of the California Civil Code, both parties shall have access to records and information pertaining to the minor child, including, but not limited to, medical, dental and school records. This information shall not be denied to a party.

　　　　I.　Each party shall be empowered to obtain emergency medical care for the children without the consent of the other party. Each party shall notify the other party as soon as reasonably possible of any serious illness requiring medical attention, or any emergency involving the children.

　　　　J.　Each party shall exert every effort to maintain free access and unhampered contact between the children and the other party, and to foster a feeling of affection between the children and the other party. Neither party shall do anything which would estrange the children from the other, which would injure the opinion of the child as to the other party or would impair the natural development of the children's love and respect for the other party.

4.　PHYSICAL CUSTODY OR PARENTING TIME

Father shall have parenting time as follows:

　　　　The parties agree to adopt the Family Court Services Report dated

_____, which is attached as Exhibit ___ and incorporated herein.

4

Marriage of _____; Marital Settlement Agreement

9A Marital Settlement Agreement—Example

OR

    A.   Father shall have parenting time with the minor children every Wednesday and every Thursday, in addition to every other weekend from Friday night to Sunday night.

    B.   Mother shall have the children at all other times.

    C.   All other parenting time shall be my mutual agreement of the parties.

**A holiday schedule may be included at this point, if the parties wish to specify said schedule, or that portion of the Family Court Services report might be adopted.

5. CHILD SUPPORT

A. Each party agrees that Father shall pay to mother as and for the support of the minor children the sum of $_____.00 per month, payable beginning on _____, payable by the first day of each and every month. Said support is based on a gross monthly income of the Petitioner in the sum of $1,500.00 and a gross monthly income of the Respondent in the amount of $6,000.00. The Court shall reserve jurisdiction on the issue of child support until further order of court, or until the child marries, dies, is emancipated, reaches the age of nineteen (19) or reaches eighteen (18) and is a not full-time student residing with a parent, whichever occurs first.

B. Father further agrees to pay one-half of the children's daycare expenses to the school, as additional child support, each and every month, commencing _____ . Said one-half of the daycare is currently $_____.

C. The parties acknowledge that they are fully informed of their rights under the guidelines and specifically pursuant to California FAMILY CODE, Section 4065 et seq., and that

5

Marriage of ____; Marital Settlement Agreement

9A   Marital Settlement Agreement—Example

the child support order herein being agreed to without coercion or duress. The parties declare

that this agreement, which is less than the guideline support, is in the best interests of the minor

child and his needs will be adequately met by the terms of this agreement. The parties also

declare that the right to receive child support has not been assigned to any county pursuant to

Section 11477 of the California Welfare and Institutions Code and that no public assistance

application is pending.   D. The parties acknowledge that support of the minor child

is subject to order of a court of competent jurisdiction at any time during the child's minority,

and that this paragraph or any later child support order is subject to modification.

        6. **DEPENDENCY EXEMPTION   OPTIONAL**

        Both parties agree that each parent shall be entitled to claim the dependency exemption

for one child under Sections 151 and 152 of the Internal Revenue Code on their respective tax

returns.

        7. **MEDICAL AND DENTAL INSURANCE**

        Husband shall continue to provide a policy of health and dental insurance for the minor

child for as long as such is available through his employment at a reasonable cost.

        8. **MEDICAL AND DENTAL COSTS**

        Any health needs and expenses not covered by such insurance, including, but not limited

to, deductibles, dental or orthodontic, shall be shared equally by both parties.

        9. **SPOUSAL SUPPORT**

        The court shall hereby terminate its jurisdiction over spousal support. Each of the parties

acknowledges that they understand their respective rights to future spousal support and are fully

                                                    6

Marriage of ____; Marital Settlement Agreement

9A Marital Settlement Agreement—Example

1
2 aware of the duties and forever discharge the other from any right, duty or obligation to support

3 in the future, save and except solely as herein provided. In waiving any rights to future spousal

4 support one from the other, each party has carefully considered not only the ability of the other

5 party to pay, but his or her own individual ability to work and the risks and hazards of their

6
7 future health and well-being. Regardless of all factors as herein set forth each party hereby

8 waives any and all rights, claims, or demands on the other for future support and maintenance

9 which he or she may now or hereafter have in the future.

10 **OR**

11
12   A. The Respondent shall pay to the Petitioner spousal support in the sum of

13 $_____ per month commencing _____, and is payable by wage

14 assignment.

15   B. Spousal support shall terminate upon Wife's remarriage, either party's death,

16
17 or further order of the court, whichever occurs first, except with regard to any payments in

18 arrears. Any payments in arrears at the time of Husband's death shall constitute a charge against

19 his estate.   C. All sums payable under this paragraph 9 for the support of Wife are

20 intended to qualify as alimony in compliance with the Internal Revenue Code and shall be

21 deducted from Husband's income and included in Wife's income for all federal and state income

22
23 tax purposes.

24   D.   Wife acknowledges that it is the goal of this state that each party shall

25 make reasonable good faith efforts to become self-supporting as provided for in Family Code

26 Section 4320. The failure to make reasonable good faith efforts, may be one of the factors

27

28
                                              7

Marriage of ____; Marital Settlement Agreement

9A   Marital Settlement Agreement—Example

considered by the court as a basis for modifying or terminating support.

E.   Husband hereby waives any and all rights to receive any manner of spousal support from Wife.

10. **COMMUNITY PROPERTY**

All community assets, including all household items and personal properties, have been equally and equitably divided and each party now possesses all that property to which he or she shall be entitled.

Except as specifically set forth hereinabove, each party is awarded those items of personal property presently in their possession.

A. The parties agree that Husband shall be entitled to the following community property:

**List those items of property which will be awarded to Husband such as family residence, automobile, furniture and furnishings, 1/2 of his community interest in his retirement, etc. If the parties agree to sell the home, 1/2 of the proceeds of the sale of the home. If you chose to have the husband keep the home, he will have to make an community property equalization payment to wife, set forth how that will work here and under a separate paragraph titled equalization.

1.

2.

3.

4.

8

Marriage of ____; Marital Settlement Agreement

9A   Marital Settlement Agreement — Example

B. The parties agree that Wife shall be entitled to the following community property:

**List those items of property which will be awarded to Wife such as family residence, automobile, furniture and furnishings, 1/2 of husband's community interest in his retirement, etc., and 1/2 of proceeds of home if it is sold. If Wife retains home, set forth who will pay the mortgage, whether there is a deferred sale, etc.

1.

2.

3.

4.

ASSIGNMENT OF ENCUMBRANCES: Except as otherwise provided for herein, all property assigned pursuant to this agreement is assigned subject to all existing encumbrances and liens thereon. The assignee agrees to indemnify and hold the other party free and harmless from and of any claim or liability that the other party may suffer or may be required to pay on account of such encumbrances or liens. All insurance on the property being assigned hereunder is assigned to the party receiving such property. All insurance premiums from the date hereof shall be paid by the party to whom the insurance is assigned.

11. **COMMUNITY PROPERTY DEBTS**

A. Except as otherwise provided for herein, the parties shall assume and pay and to hold and save the other harmless as to, and to indemnify the other against any liability for payment of, any and all present, existing, or unpaid community indebtedness heretofore incurred

9A   Marital Settlement Agreement—Example

or contracted by either of them. Neither of the parties has incurred nor shall incur any debts or obligations or liabilities against or upon the credit of the other and shall hold the other harmless from and to indemnify the other against all such debts, obligations, or liabilities.

B. Husband shall assume, pay and hold Wife harmless and to indemnify her against any liability for payment of the following debts:

1.

2.

3.

4.

C. Wife shall assume, pay and hold Husband harmless and to indemnify him against any liability for payment of the following debts:

1.

2.

3.

4.

D. The parties shall close any joint credit accounts.

E. Neither of the parties shall hereafter incur any indebtedness chargeable against the other, or his or her estate, from and after the date hereof, nor contract any debt or obligation in the name of the other, and each of us shall indemnify and hold harmless the other from and against any such indebtedness incurred or created by such indemnifying party. Each of the parties warrants to the other that he or she has not incurred any unpaid liability or obligation on

10

Marriage of _____; Marital Settlement Agreement

9A Marital Settlement Agreement—Example

which the other is or may be liable (except as expressly provided in this agreement), and each of them shall indemnify and hold harmless the other from and against any such liability or obligation. The parties shall each forthwith surrender and cancel all credit cards and charge accounts presently outstanding upon which the other is or would or may become liable, unless specifically provided otherwise herein.

F. Further, if any claim, action, or proceeding shall hereafter be brought seeking to hold Wife liable on account of any debt, liability, or obligation which Husband is obligated to pay under this agreement, Husband shall at his sole expense defend Wife against any such claim or demand, or threat thereof, whether or not well founded, and hold Wife harmless therefrom, together with reasonable attorneys' fees and costs in connection with any defense there against.

G. Further, if any claim, action, or proceeding shall hereafter be brought seeking to hold Husband liable on account of any debt, liability, or obligation which Wife is obligated to pay under this agreement, Wife shall at her sole expense defend Husband against any such claim or demand, or threat thereof, whether or not well founded, and hold Husband harmless therefrom, together with reasonable attorneys' fees and costs in connection with any defense there against.

12. **PENSION PLANS**

The parties acknowledge that they are fully informed as to their community property rights as to the other's retirement plans and survivor benefits. For consideration received, each party hereby relinquishes and waives any and all rights, benefits, shares and interest in the other's retirement plans, benefits and/or, survivor benefits that have accrued during the marriage and

11

Marriage of ____; Marital Settlement Agreement

9A Marital Settlement Agreement — Example

hereby confirm that all existing benefits of such plans are the sole personal property of the participating member.

OR

Husband and Wife agree that there is a community interest in the retirement benefits of Husband. The parties agree that Husband's employment by the State of California commenced on _____ and that Husband and Wife separated on _____.

The community interest of each spouse in the retirement benefits of Husband shall be awarded to each respective spouse and shall be equal to one-half of the total community interest in the retirement benefits as determined in this paragraph. The total community interest in the retirement benefits shall be equal to the product obtained by multiplying the amount of each benefit payment by a fraction, the numerator of which is the number of months of Husband's employment by the State of California during the marriage prior to the separation date of the parties, and denominator of which is the total number of months of Husband's employment by the State of California. Any remaining interest shall be the sole and separate property of Husband.

Husband and Wife further agree that the court in their dissolution proceeding shall reserve jurisdiction to make any others necessary to carry out the provisions of his Agreement regarding the Plan and the division of benefits under the Plan.

13. **SEPARATE PROPERTY**

A. The property listed below is the separate property of Husband:

12

Marriage of _____; Marital Settlement Agreement

9A Marital Settlement Agreement—Example

1. The respective Social Security and disability accounts of Husband; however nothing in this order shall be construed as affecting either Husband's or Wife's derivative Social Security benefits that they may have in the other's Social Security and/or disability accounts;

2. Furniture, furnishings, appliances and all other assets acquired prior to the date of marriage and after the date of separation as well as during marriage by way of gift, bequest, devise, or inheritance.

3. Retirement benefits, if any, acquired prior to the date of marriage, and after the date of separation.

4.

B. The property listed below is the separate property of Wife:

1. The respective Social Security and disability accounts of Wife; however nothing in this order shall be construed as affecting either Husband's or Wife's derivative Social Security benefits that they may have in the other's Social Security and/or disability accounts;

2. Furniture, furnishings, appliances and all other assets acquired prior to the date of marriage and after the date of separation as well as during marriage by way of gift, bequest, devise, or inheritance.

3. Retirement benefits, acquired prior to the date of marriage, and after the date of separation.

4.

13

Marriage of ____; Marital Settlement Agreement

9A Marital Settlement Agreement — Example

14. **NECESSARY DOCUMENTS**

Each party hereto shall execute and deliver, at any time and from time to time, upon request of the other, good and sufficient instruments necessary or proper to vest the title and property in the respective parties hereto, in accordance with the terms hereof, and any and all documents which may be necessary or proper to carry out the purpose of this Judgment or to establish a record of the sole and separate ownership of said parties in the manner herein ordered. If either party for any reason shall fail or refuse to execute any such documents, then this Judgment shall, from and after the effective date, constitute a full and present transfer, assignment, and conveyance of all rights and property herein provided as being transferred, assigned, or conveyed, and a full and effective release, waiver, and relinquishment of all rights herein provided as being released, waived, or relinquished. Notwithstanding the foregoing, to the extent that a privilege against disclosing any or all of a separately filed tax return is provided for by law, nothing in this Judgment shall be construed as a waiver of said privilege.

15. **ATTORNEY'S FEES**

The parties agree that they shall each pay one-half (1/2) of the attorney's fees incurred by Wife, in the amount of_____, in this matter to _____, for a total of_____ each. Respondent shall commence payment of said attorney fees to _____ on _____, with additional payments of _____ each on _____ and _____.

OR

The parties agree that they will each pay their own attorney's fees in this matter.

14

Marriage of ____; Marital Settlement Agreement

9A Marital Settlement Agreement—Example

16. **NOTICE REGARDING DEATH BENEFITS**

Notice: Please review your Will, insurance policies, retirement benefit plans, and other matters that you may want to change in view of the dissolution of your marriage. Ending your marriage may automatically change a disposition made by your Will to your former spouse. California Civil Code Section 4352.

17. **GENERAL PROVISIONS**

A. Each party acknowledges that this Agreement constitutes a substantially equal division of the community property, but to the extent that it may be unequal, each party waives their right to an equal division. Both parties acknowledge that they have agreed to the values of all property and debts divided herein and that Attorney _____ has not been directed to make any independent investigation of values of property. Nevertheless, the parties hereto are satisfied that the division of property constitutes an equal division.

B. If any community assets are discovered at a later date, either party may petition the court for one-half of said assets.

C. Both parties understand that although an obligation based on a contract is or may be assigned to one party as part of the division of the community property pursuant to Civil Code Section 4800.6, in the event that the party to whom the obligation was assigned defaults on the contract, the creditor may have a cause of action against the other party.

D. Each party expressly waives all rights to the estate of the other party.

E. Both parties waive any and all claims they may have for any credits pursuant to the property division of property set forth herein, including but not limited to credits claimed

15

Marriage of ____; Marital Settlement Agreement

9A   Marital Settlement Agreement—Example

under

In Re the Marriage of Epstein and In Re the Marriage of Watts.

F.   Each party intends that this order be a Qualified Domestic Relations Order (QDRO) pursuant to the Retirement Equity Act of 1984, and its provisions administered in conformity with the Act.

G.   BOTH PARTIES DO HEREBY EXPRESSLY WAIVE THE FOLLOWING:

1.   MAKING ANY MOTIONS BEFORE THE ENTRY OF JUDGEMENT;

2.   NOTICE OF TIME, DATE AND PLACE OF TRIAL;

3.   THE SIXTY (60) DAY APPEAL PERIOD WHEREIN APPEAL FROM ENTRY OF JUDGMENT MAY BE FILED; AND

4.   FINDINGS OF FACT AND CONCLUSIONS OF LAW.

H.   If the Parties reconcile, this Agreement shall continue in full force until modified, altered, or terminated in writing and signed by each Party.

I.   The captions of various paragraphs in this Agreement are for convenience only, and none of them is intended to be any part of the text of this Agreement, nor intended to be referred to as construing any of the provision of this Agreement.

J.   This Agreement shall inure to the benefit of and be binding on the Parties and their respective heirs, executors, administrators, successors, assigns and legal representatives.

K.   If any portion of this Agreement is held illegal, unenforceable, void or voidable by any Court of competent jurisdiction, each of the remaining terms shall continue in

16

Marriage of ____; Marital Settlement Agreement

9A Marital Settlement Agreement—Example

force as a separate contract.

L.   This Agreement shall be subject to and interpreted under the laws of the State of California.

M.   Both parties acknowledge that each of them has read this Agreement, understands and is satisfied with its provisions and its legal effect, and understands that it will be legally binding when executed by both of us.

18. The parties agree that the execution of this Agreement shall be, and is intended to be, a full, complete, and final adjustment of all of our property rights existing as of the date of this agreement, except as otherwise expressly provided for herein, and supersedes any prior agreement between us, written or oral. Each agrees there has been no promise, agreement or undertaking by either of them to the other as a matter of inducement to enter into this Agreement.   The parties have read and understand all the terms and conditions included in this Agreement and agree to be bound by said terms and conditions.

DATED:_____   _____
                                                            _____,
                                                            Petitioner

DATED:_____   _____
                                                            _____,
                                                            Respondent

DATED:_____   _____
                                                            _____,
                                                            Attorney for Petitioner

Marriage of ____; Marital Settlement Agreement

9A Marital Settlement Agreement — Example

STATE OF CALIFORNIA   )
)
COUNTY OF SACRAMENTO   )

On _____ before me, _____ personally appeared, _____ personally known to me (or proved to me on the basis of satisfactory evidence) to be the person(s) whose name(s) is/are subscribed to the within instrument and acknowledged to me that he/she/they executed the same in his/her/their authorized capacity(ies), and that by his/her/their signature(s) on the instrument the person(s), or the entity(ies) upon behalf of which the person(s) acted, executed the instrument.

WITNESS my hand and official seal. _____

[seal]

Dated: _____   _____
                         JUDGE OF THE SUPERIOR COURT

18

Marriage of _____ ; Marital Settlement Agreement

10A(a) Order to Show Cause and Affidavit for Contempt (FL-410)

FL-410

ATTORNEY OR PARTY WITHOUT ATTORNEY *(Name, state bar number, and address)*:

> To keep other people from seeing what you entered on your form, please press the Clear This Form button at the end of the form when finished.

TELEPHONE NO.:   FAX NO.:

ATTORNEY FOR *(Name)*:

SUPERIOR COURT OF CALIFORNIA, COUNTY OF

STREET ADDRESS:

MAILING ADDRESS:

CITY AND ZIP CODE:

BRANCH NAME:

PETITIONER/PLAINTIFF:

RESPONDENT/DEFENDANT:

OTHER PARENT:

ORDER TO SHOW CAUSE AND AFFIDAVIT FOR CONTEMPT	CASE NUMBER:

NOTICE!	¡AVISO!
A contempt proceeding is criminal in nature. If the court finds you in contempt, the possible penalties include jail sentence, community service, and fine.	Un proceso judicial por desacato es de índole criminal. Si la corte le declara a usted en desacato, las sanciones posibles incluyen penas de prisión y de servicio a la comunidad, y multas.
You are entitled to the services of an attorney, who should be consulted promptly in order to assist you. If you cannot afford an attorney, the court may appoint an attorney to represent you.	Usted tiene derecho a los servicios de un abogado, a quien debe consultar sin demora para obtener ayuda. Si no puede pagar a un abogado, la corte podrá nombrar a un abogado para que le represente.

1. TO CITEE *(name of person you allege has violated the orders):*

2. YOU ARE ORDERED TO APPEAR IN THIS COURT AS FOLLOWS, TO GIVE ANY LEGAL REASON WHY THIS COURT SHOULD NOT FIND YOU GUILTY OF CONTEMPT, PUNISH YOU FOR WILLFULLY DISOBEYING ITS ORDERS AS SET FORTH IN THE AFFIDAVIT BELOW AND ANY ATTACHED *AFFIDAVIT OF FACTS CONSTITUTING CONTEMPT*; AND REQUIRE YOU TO PAY, FOR THE BENEFIT OF THE MOVING PARTY, THE ATTORNEY FEES AND COSTS OF THIS PROCEEDING.

a. Date: Time: Dept.:   Rm.:

b. Address of court: ☐ same as noted above ☐ other *(specify):*

Date:

_____
JUDICIAL OFFICER

AFFIDAVIT SUPPORTING ORDER TO SHOW CAUSE FOR CONTEMPT

3. ☐ An *Affidavit of Facts Constituting Contempt* (form FL-411 or FL-412) is attached.

4. Citee has willfully disobeyed certain orders of this court as set forth in this affidavit and any attached affidavits.

5. a. Citee had knowledge of the order in that
      (1) ☐ citee was present in court at the time the order was made.
      (2) ☐ citee was served with a copy of the order.
      (3) ☐ citee signed a stipulation upon which the order was based.
      (4) ☐ other *(specify):*

      ☐ Continued on Attachment 5a(4).
    b. Citee was able to comply with each order when it was disobeyed.

6. Based on the instances of disobedience described in this affidavit
    a. ☐ I have not previously filed a request with the court that the citee be held in contempt.
    b. ☐ I have previously filed a request with the court that the citee be held in contempt *(specify date filed and results):*

☐ Continued on Attachment 6b.   Page 1 of 4

Form Adopted for Mandatory Use
Judicial Council of California
FL-410 [Rev. January 1, 2003]

ORDER TO SHOW CAUSE AND AFFIDAVIT FOR CONTEMPT

Family Code, § 292;
Code of Civil Procedure, §§ 1211.5, 2015.5
www.courtinfo.ca.gov

10A(a) Order to Show Cause and Affidavit for Contempt (FL-410)

PETITIONER/PLAINTIFF:	CASE NUMBER:
RESPONDENT/DEFENDANT:	
OTHER PARENT:	

7. ☐ Citee has previously been found in contempt of a court order *(specify case, court, date):*

    ☐ Continued on Attachment 7.

8. ☐ Each order disobeyed and each instance of disobedience is described as follows:

    a. ☐ Orders for child support, spousal support, family support, attorney fees, and court or other litigation costs (see attached *Affidavit of Facts Constituting Contempt* (form FL-411))

    b. ☐ Domestic violence restraining orders and child custody and visitation orders (see attached *Affidavit of Facts Constituting Contempt* (form FL-412))

    c. ☐ Injunctive or other order *(specify which order was violated, how the order was violated, and when the order was violated):*

    ☐ Continued on Attachment 8c.

    d. ☐ Other material facts, including facts indicating that the violation of the orders was without justification or excuse *(specify):*

    ☐ Continued on Attachment 8d.

    e. ☐ I am requesting that attorney fees and costs be awarded to me for the costs of pursuing this contempt action. (A copy of my *Income and Expense Declaration* (form FL-150) is attached.)

WARNING: IF YOU PURSUE THIS CONTEMPT ACTION, IT MAY AFFECT THE ABILITY OF THE DISTRICT ATTORNEY TO PROSECUTE THE CITEE CRIMINALLY FOR THE SAME VIOLATIONS.

I declare under penalty of perjury under the laws of the State of California that the foregoing is true and correct.

Date:

▶

_____   _____
(TYPE OR PRINT NAME)   (SIGNATURE)

FL-410 [Rev. January 1, 2003]   Page 2 of 4

ORDER TO SHOW CAUSE AND AFFIDAVIT FOR CONTEMPT

For your protection and privacy, please press the Clear This Form button after you have printed the form.

| Print This Form | | Clear This Form |

10A(a)　Order to Show Cause and Affidavit for Contempt (FL-410)

INFORMATION SHEET FOR ORDER TO SHOW CAUSE
AND AFFIDAVIT OF FACTS CONSTITUTING CONTEMPT

(Do NOT deliver this Information Sheet to the court clerk.)

Please follow these instructions to complete the *Order to Show Cause and Affidavit for Contempt* (form FL-410) if you do not have an attorney to represent you. Your attorney, if you have one, should complete this form, as well as the *Affidavit of Facts Constituting Contempt* (form FL-411 or form FL-412). You may wish to consult an attorney for assistance. Contempt actions are very difficult to prove. An attorney may be appointed for the citee.

INSTRUCTIONS FOR COMPLETING THE ORDER TO SHOW CAUSE AND AFFIDAVIT OF FACTS CONSTITUTING CONTEMPT (TYPE OR PRINT FORM IN INK):

If the top section of the form has already been filled out, skip down to number 1 below. If the top section of the form is blank, you must provide this information.

<u>Front page, first box, top of form, left side</u>: Print your name, address, telephone number, and fax number, if any, in this box. If you have a restraining order and wish to keep your address confidential, you may use any address where you can receive mail. **You can be legally served court papers at this address.**

<u>Front page, second box, left side</u>: Print the name of the county where the court is located and insert the address and any branch name of the court building where you are seeking to obtain a contempt order. You may get this information from the court clerk. This should be the same court in which the original order was issued.

<u>Front page, third box, left side</u>: Print the names of the Petitioner, Respondent, and Other Parent (if any) in this box. Use the same names as appear on the most recent court order disobeyed.

<u>Front page, first box, top of form, right side</u>: Leave this box blank for the court's use.

<u>Front page, second box, right side</u>: Print the court case number in this box. This number is also shown on the most recent court order disobeyed.

<u>Item 1</u>: Insert the name of the party who disobeyed the order ("the citee").

<u>Item 2</u>: The court clerk will provide the hearing date and location.

<u>Item 3</u>: Either check the box in item 3 and attach an *Affidavit of Facts Constituting Contempt* (form FL-411 for financial orders or form FL-412 for domestic violence, or custody and visitation orders), or leave the box in item 3 blank but check and complete item 8.

<u>Item 5</u>: Check the box that describes how the citee knew about the order that has been disobeyed.

<u>Item 6</u>: a. Check this box if you have not previously applied for a contempt order.

　　　　 b. Check this box if you have previously applied for a contempt order and briefly explain when you requested the order and results of your request. If you need more space, check the box that says "continued on Attachment 6b" and attach a separate sheet to this order to show cause.

<u>Item 7</u>: Check this box if the citee has previously been found in contempt by a court of law. Briefly explain when the citee was found in contempt and for what. If there is not enough space to write all the facts, check the box that says "continued on Attachment 7" and attach a separate sheet to this order to show cause.

<u>Item 8</u>: a. Check this box if the citee has disobeyed orders for child support, custody, visitation, spousal support, family support, attorney fees, and court or litigation costs. Refer to item 1a on *Affidavit of Facts Constituting Contempt* (form FL-411).

　　　　 b. Check this box if the citee has disobeyed domestic violence orders or child custody and visitation orders. Refer to *Affidavit of Facts Constituting Contempt* (form FL-412).

ORDER TO SHOW CAUSE AND AFFIDAVIT FOR CONTEMPT

10A(a) Order to Show Cause and Affidavit for Contempt (FL-410)

Information Sheet *(continued)*

<u>Item 8</u>: c. If you are completing this item, use facts personally known to you or known to the best of your knowledge. State the facts in detail. if there is not enough space to write all the facts, check the box that says "continued on Attachment 8c" and attach a separate sheet to this order to show cause, including facts indicating that the violation of the orders was without justification or excuse.

d. Use this item to write other facts that are important to this order. If you are completing this item, insert facts personally known to you, or known to the best of your knowledge. State facts in detail. If there is not enough space to write all the facts, check the box that says "Continued on Attachment 8d" and attach a separate sheet to the order to show cause.

e. If you request attorney fees and/or costs for pursuing this contempt action, check this box. Attach a copy of your *Income and Expense Declaration* (form FL-150).

Type or print and sign your name at the bottom of page 2.

If you checked the boxes in item 3 and item 8a or 8b, complete the appropriate *Affidavit of Facts Constituting Contempt* (form FL-411), following the instructions for the affidavit above.

Make at least three copies of the *Order to Show Cause and Affidavit for Contempt* (form FL-410) and any supporting *Affidavit of Facts Constituting Contempt* (form FL-411 or FL-412) and the *Income and Expense Declaration* (form FL-150) for the court clerk, the citee, and yourself. If the district attorney or local child support agency is involved in your case, you must provide a copy to the district attorney or local child support agency.

Take the completed form(s) to the court clerk's office. The clerk will provide hearing date and location in item 2, obtain the judicial officer's signature, file the originals, and return the copies to you.

Have someone who is at least 18 years of age, who is not a party, serve the order and any attached papers on the disobedient party. For example, a process server or someone you know may serve the papers. **You may not serve the papers yourself. Service must be personal; service by mail is insufficient.** The papers must be served at least 21 calendar days before the court hearing. The person serving papers must complete a *Proof of Personal Service* (form FL-330) and give the original to you. Keep a copy for yourself and file the original *Proof of Personal Service* (form FL-330) with the court.

If you need assistance with these forms, contact an attorney or the Family Law Facilitator in your county.

FL-410 [Rev. January 1, 2003]   Page 4 of 4

ORDER TO SHOW CAUSE AND AFFIDAVIT FOR CONTEMPT

For your protection and privacy, please press the Clear This Form button after you have printed the form.   Save This Form   Print This Form   Clear This Form

10A(b) Declaration in Support of Contempt—Example

Declaration in Support of Motion for Contempt

I, Sandie Shores, am the obligee in this matter. I declare under penalty of perjury that the following is true:

On, June 10, 2004, Rocky Shores was ordered to pay child support for his minor children as follows:

"Respondent to pay $1,000 to Petitioner, as and for child support of his two minor children, commencing on June 1, 2004. Said support to be paid on the first day of each and every month, by wage assignment, until the age of majority."

On June 15, 2004 a Order/Notice to Withhold was served on Respondent's employer. A copy of the Order and the Proof of Service are attached for the Court's reference. Approximately 12 days after the notice was received by Respondent's employer, and just prior to any support being withheld on June 30, 2004, Respondent called his employer and stated that he quit. I am attaching a copy of the Declaration that was prepared by ZZZZ Company, stating that Rocky Shores stated that he was "never going to pay one red cent to my ex-wife" and that "I am quitting so she doesn't get anything."

Since that time, I have attempted to ascertain where Respondent is working. I know that he is working because he is living by himself and therefore must have some means of support. On approximately September 5, 2004, I learned that Respondent was working for YYYY Company and served the Order/Notice to Withhold on them. I received one partial amount of support on September 15, 2004 and then did not receive any additional checks. I contacted YYYY company and they told me that on September 16, 2004, Respondent quit.

I have contacted Respondent and asked him to please pay support as it is affecting his children. He simply shouts at me and says I am never going to "get one red cent" from him. He said he would go to another state and "work under the table" if I continue to hound him for money.

10A(b) Declaration in Support of Contempt—Example

I believe that Respondent is now working for ABC Group, at that is what his Mother told me when she dropped off our son's birthday present last week. I contacted them, but they do not return my calls. I have also served a copy of the Order/Notice to Withhold on January 3, 2005, but they have not sent me any support checks.

Respondent does not appear to be indigent when I have seen him for the exchange of the children's visitation. The children inform me that he takes them to movies, to dinner and on other outings. Mutual friends have told me that he is working, but they won't tell me where.

I served Respondent with an Order to Show Cause to establish arrears that I had filed. He did not appear at the hearing on February 10, 2005. The Judge established the arrears, and I served an amended Order/Notice to Withhold. To date I have not received any support and I have no means of collecting.

I believe that Respondent is willfully hiding his income. He has the ability to work and I believe that he is working. He has the ability to pay child support, but refuses to do so. I therefore believe that he should be cited for contempt. I understand that if he is cited for contempt, that he may be put in jail. However, I believe that this is the only way that Respondent will understand that he has an obligation to support his children and that he must do so.

I have attached a copy of the arrearages owed by Respondent as of the date of the last hearing, the on-going support and the amount owed to date, plus interest at the legal rate.

Dated: _____, ____   _____
                                              Sandie Shores, Petitioner

10B(a)   Registration of Out-of-State Custody Order (FL-580)

FL-580

ATTORNEY OR PARTY WITHOUT ATTORNEY *(Name, State Bar number, and address):*	To keep other people from seeing what you entered on your form, please press the Clear This Form button at the end of the form when finished.

TELEPHONE NO.:   FAX NO. *(Optional):*

E-MAIL ADDRESS *(Optional):*

ATTORNEY FOR *(Name):*

SUPERIOR COURT OF CALIFORNIA, COUNTY OF

STREET ADDRESS:

MAILING ADDRESS:

CITY AND ZIP CODE:

BRANCH NAME:

PETITIONER:

RESPONDENT:

REGISTRATION OF OUT-OF-STATE CUSTODY ORDER	CASE NUMBER:

1. The minor children covered by the out-of-state custody order are *(name each):*

Child's name   Date of birth   Age   Sex

2. a. Petitioner has been awarded ☐ custody ☐ visitation of those minor children.

   b. Petitioner is the ☐ mother ☐ father ☐ other *(specify):*   of those minor children.

   c. Petitioner's address is:*

3. a. Respondent has been awarded ☐ custody ☐ visitation of those minor children.

   b. Respondent is the ☐ mother ☐ father ☐ other *(specify):*   of those minor children.

   c. Respondent's address is:*

4. ☐ a. Another person *(specify name):*   has been awarded
       ☐ custody ☐ visitation of those minor children.
   b. That person is the ☐ mother ☐ father ☐ other *(specify):*   of those minor children.
   c. That person's address is:*

   * If there are issues of domestic violence or child abuse, you may give a mailing address instead.

5. A completed *Declaration Under Uniform Child Custody Jurisdiction and Enforcement Act (UCCJEA)* (form FL-105) is attached to this registration.

6. I request that the attached out-of-state custody order be registered in this court.
   a. The court, county, and state where order was made are *(specify):*
   b. The date when the most recent order for child custody/visitation was made in that case *(specify):*
   c. Two copies, including one certified copy of that out-of-state order, are attached to this registration and made a part of it.
   d. To the best of my knowledge and belief, this order has not been modified.

Date:

I declare under penalty of perjury under the laws of the State of California that the foregoing is true and correct.

▶

_____   _____
(TYPE OR PRINT NAME)   (SIGNATURE)

Page 1 of 2

Form Approved for Optional Use Judicial Council of California FL-580 [Rev. January 1, 2006]	**REGISTRATION OF OUT-OF-STATE CUSTODY ORDER**	Family Code, §§ 3429, 3445 www.courtinfo.ca.gov

10B(a) Registration of Out-of-State Custody Order (FL-580)

PETITIONER:	CASE NUMBER:
RESPONDENT:	

NOTICE OF REGISTRATION OF OUT-OF-STATE CUSTODY ORDER

1. To:
    a. Petitioner at address on 2(c) on page 1

    b. Respondent at address on 3(c) on page 1

    c. ☐ Other person who has been awarded custody or visitation in this custody order at address on 4(c) on page 1

2. The attached out-of-state custody order can be enforced as of the date of registration in the same manner as an order issued by a California court.

3. If you want to contest the validity of this registered out-of-state custody order, you must request a hearing date that is within 20 days of the date that this notice was mailed to you (see clerk's date of mailing below). A request for a hearing must be in writing and filed in this case.

4. If you do not request this hearing, the out-of-state order will be confirmed in California and you will not be able to challenge its validity in the future.

5. At the hearing, the court will confirm the out-of-state order unless you can prove one of the following:
    a. The issuing court did not have jurisdiction under chapter 2 of the California Family Code (commencing with section 3421).
    b. The child custody determination sought to be registered has been vacated, stayed, or modified by a court having jurisdiction to do so under chapter 2 of the California Family Code (commencing with section 3421).
    c. You were entitled to notice of the original order, but did not receive that notice in accordance with the standards of California Family Code section 3408 in the proceedings before the court that issued the order for which registration is sought.

CLERK'S CERTIFICATE OF MAILING

I certify that I am not a party to this case and that a copy of this *Registration of Out-of-State Custody Order* and all attachments was sent to each person named in item 1 above by first-class mail. The copies were enclosed in envelopes with postage fully prepaid. The envelopes were addressed to the persons named in item 1 at the addresses listed above, sealed, and deposited with the United States Postal Service.

At *(place):* _____

On *(date):* _____

Date: _____   Clerk by: _____, Deputy

For your protection and privacy, please press the Clear This Form button after you have printed the form.	Save This Form	Print This Form	Clear This Form

10B(b) Request for Hearing Regarding Registration of Out-of-State Custody Decree (FL-585)

FL-585

ATTORNEY OR PARTY WITHOUT ATTORNEY *(Name, state bar number, and address):*	
TELEPHONE NO.: FAX NO.:	To keep other people from seeing what you entered on your form, please press the Clear This Form button at the end of the form when finished.
ATTORNEY FOR *(Name):*	

SUPERIOR COURT OF CALIFORNIA, COUNTY OF
STREET ADDRESS:
MAILING ADDRESS:
CITY AND ZIP CODE:
BRANCH NAME:

PETITIONER:

RESPONDENT:

REQUEST FOR HEARING REGARDING REGISTRATION OF OUT-OF-STATE CUSTODY DECREE	CASE NUMBER:

NOTICE OF HEARING

1. A hearing on this application will be held as follows:

   a. Date: Time: Dept: Div.:   Room:

   b. The address of the court is ☐ same as noted above ☐ other *(specify):*

2. I request that service of the registration of custody be vacated (canceled) because:
   a. ☐ The court or tribunal that issued the order did not have personal jurisdiction over me.
   b. ☐ The custody order has been vacated, stayed, or modified by a later order made by a court having jurisdiction to do so. *(Please attach a copy of the later order.)*
   c. ☐ I was entitled to notice of the original order, but did not receive that notice in the proceedings before the court that issued the order.
   d. ☐ Other *(specify):*

I declare under penalty of perjury under the laws of the State of California that the foregoing is true and correct.

Date:

▶

_____   _____
(TYPE OR PRINT NAME)   (SIGNATURE OF DECLARANT)

Page 1 of 2

Form Approved for Optional Use
Judicial Council of California
FL-585 [New January 1, 2003]

**REQUEST FOR HEARING REGARDING
REGISTRATION OF OUT-OF-STATE CUSTODY DECREE**

Family Code, § 3445
www.courtinfo.ca.gov

10B(b) Request for Hearing Regarding Registration of Out-of-State Custody Decree (FL-585)

PETITIONER:	CASE NUMBER:
RESPONDENT:	

CLERK'S CERTIFICATE OF MAILING

I certify that I am not a party to this cause and that a true copy of the *Request for Hearing Regarding Registration of Out-of-State Custody Decree* was mailed first class, postage fully prepaid, in a sealed envelope addressed as shown below, and that the notice was mailed

at *(place)*:   , California,

on *(date)*:

Date: Clerk, by _____ , Deputy

REQUEST FOR HEARING REGARDING REGISTRATION OF OUT-OF-STATE CUSTODY DECREE

For your protection and privacy, please press the Clear This Form button after you have printed the form.

Save This Form   Print This Form   Clear This Form

10B(c) Notice of Registration of Out-of-State Support Order (FL-570)

FL-570

SUPERIOR COURT OF CALIFORNIA, COUNTY OF STREET ADDRESS: MAILING ADDRESS: CITY AND ZIP CODE: BRANCH NAME: PETITIONER/PLAINTIFF: RESPONDENT/DEFENDANT:	To keep other people from seeing what you entered on your form, please press the Clear This Form button at the end of the form when finished.
NOTICE OF REGISTRATION OF OUT-OF-STATE SUPPORT ORDER ☐ **Support Order** ☐ **Income Withholding Order**	CASE NUMBER:

1. To *(name):*

2. You are notified that an ☐ Out-of-State Support Order ☐ Out-of-State Order for Income Withholding has been registered with this court. A copy of the order and the Registration Statement are attached.

3. The amount of arrears is specified in item 1 on the attached Registration Statement.

4. The registered order is enforceable in the same manner as a support order made by a California court as of the date the Registration Statement is filed.

5. If you want to contest the validity or enforcement of the registered order, you must request a hearing within 25 days of the date that this notice was mailed to you *(see below for clerk's date of mailing)*. You can request a hearing by completing and filing a *Request for Hearing Regarding Registration of Support Order* (form FL-575).

6. If you fail to contest the validity or enforcement of the attached order within 25 days of the date this notice was mailed, the order will be confirmed by the court and you will not be able to contest any portion of the order including the amount of arrears as specified in item 1 of the Registration Statement.

CLERK'S CERTIFICATE OF MAILING

1. I certify that I am not a party to this cause and that a copy of the registration statement with a copy of the out-of-state order were sent to the person named in item 1 by first-class mail. The copies were enclosed in an envelope with postage fully prepaid. The envelope was addressed to the person named in item 1 only at the address in the registration statement, sealed, and deposited with the United States Postal Service
   at *(place):*
   on *(date):*

2. Copy sent to local child support agency on *(date):*

Date: _____   Clerk, by _____ , Deputy

Page 1 of 1

Form Approved for Optional Use
Judicial Council of California
FL-570 [Rev. January 1, 2003]

NOTICE OF REGISTRATION OF OUT-OF-STATE SUPPORT ORDER

Family Code, §§ 4952, 4954
www.courtinfo.ca.gov

For your protection and privacy, please press the Clear This Form button after you have printed the form.

Save This Form   **Print This Form**   **Clear This Form**

10B(d) Request for Hearing Regarding Registration of Out-of-State Support Order (FL-575)

FL-575

ATTORNEY OR PARTY WITHOUT ATTORNEY *(Name, state bar number, and address):*	FOR COURT USE ONLY

TELEPHONE NO.:   FAX NO.:

ATTORNEY FOR *(Name):*

SUPERIOR COURT OF CALIFORNIA, COUNTY OF

STREET ADDRESS:

MAILING ADDRESS:

CITY AND ZIP CODE:

BRANCH NAME:

PETITIONER/PLAINTIFF:

RESPONDENT/DEFENDANT:

OTHER PARENT:

REQUEST FOR HEARING REGARDING REGISTRATION OF SUPPORT ORDER ☐ California Support Order ☐ Out-of-State Support Order	CASE NUMBER:

NOTICE OF HEARING

1. A hearing on this application will be held as follows *(see instructions on how to get a hearing date):*

   a. Date: Time: Dept: Div: Room:

   b. The address of the court: ☐ same as noted above ☐ other *(specify):*

2. I request that service of the registration of support be vacated (canceled) because:

   a. ☐ I am not the Obligor named in the Registration Statement.

   b. ☐ The court or tribunal that issued the order did not have personal jurisdiction over me.

   c. ☐ The support order was obtained by fraud.

   d. ☐ The support order has been vacated, suspended, or modified by a later order. *(Please attach a copy of the later order.)*

   e. ☐ The order has been stayed pending appeal.

   f. ☐ The amount of arrears in section 1 of the Registration Statement is incorrect. The correct amount of arrears is *(specify amount):* $ ☐ Supporting documents attached.

   g. ☐ Some or all of the arrears are not enforceable.

   h. ☐ Other *(specify):*

I declare under penalty of perjury under the laws of the State of California that the foregoing is true and correct.

Date:

▶

_____   _____
(TYPE OR PRINT NAME)   (SIGNATURE OF DECLARANT)

Page 1 of 4

Form Adopted for Mandatory Use Judicial Council of California FL-575 [Rev. July 1, 2007]	**REQUEST FOR HEARING REGARDING REGISTRATION OF SUPPORT ORDER**	Family Code §§ 4955, 4956, 5603 www.courtinfo.ca.gov

10B(d) Request for Hearing Regarding Registration of Out-of-State Support Order (FL-575)

FL-575

PETITIONER/PLAINTIFF:	CASE NUMBER:
RESPONDENT/DEFENDANT:	
OTHER PARENT:	

CLERK'S CERTIFICATE OF MAILING

I certify that I am not a party to this cause and that a true copy of the *Request for Hearing Regarding Registration of Support Order* was mailed first class, postage fully prepaid, in a sealed envelope addressed as shown below, and that the notice was mailed

at *(place):* _____ , California,

on *(date):*

Date: _____   Clerk, by _____ , Deputy

**REQUEST FOR HEARING REGARDING
REGISTRATION OF SUPPORT ORDER**

10C Request for Production of an Income and Expense Declaration after Judgment (FL-396)

FL-396

ATTORNEY OR PARTY WITHOUT ATTORNEY *(Name and Address)*:	TELEPHONE NO.:

ATTORNEY FOR *(Name)*:

SUPERIOR COURT OF CALIFORNIA, COUNTY OF
STREET ADDRESS:
MAILING ADDRESS:
CITY AND ZIP CODE:
BRANCH NAME:

PETITIONER/PLAINTIFF:

RESPONDENT/DEFENDANT:

REQUEST FOR PRODUCTION OF AN INCOME AND EXPENSE DECLARATION AFTER JUDGMENT	CASE NUMBER:

> To keep other people from seeing what you entered on your form, please press the Clear This Form button at the end of the form when finished.

(NOTE: This request must be served on the petitioner or respondent and not on an attorney who was or is representing that party.)

To *(name):*

1. a. As permitted by Family Code section 3664(a), declarant requires that you complete and return the attached *Income and Expense Declaration* (form FL-150) within 30 days after the date this request is served on you. Family Code section 3665(a) requires you to attach copies of your most recent state and federal income tax returns (whether individual or joint) to the completed *Income and Expense Declaration* (form FL-150).

   b. The completed *Income and Expense Declaration* (form FL-150) should be mailed to the following person at the following address *(specify):*

2. You may consult an attorney about completion of the *Income and Expense Declaration* (form FL-150) or you may proceed without an attorney. The information provided will be used to determine whether to ask for a modification of child, spousal, or family support at this time.

3. If you wish to do so, you may serve a request for a completed *Income and Expense Declaration* (form FL-150) on me. Each of us may use this procedure once a year after judgment even though no legal matter is pending.

Date:

▶

_____
(TYPE OR PRINT NAME)

_____
(SIGNATURE OF DECLARANT)

> WARNING: If a court later finds that the information provided in response to this request is incomplete or inaccurate or missing the prior year's tax returns, or that you did not submit the information in good faith, the court may order you to pay all costs necessary for me to get complete and accurate information. In addition you could be found to be in contempt and receive other penalties.

Page 1 of 2

Form Adopted for Mandatory Use
Judicial Council of California
FL-396 [Rev. January 1, 2003]

**REQUEST FOR PRODUCTION OF AN INCOME
AND EXPENSE DECLARATION AFTER JUDGMENT**

Family Code, §§ 3664,
3665, 3668
www.courtinfo.ca.gov

10C Request for Production of an Income and Expense Declaration after Judgment (FL-396)

PETITIONER/PLAINTIFF:	CASE NUMBER:
RESPONDENT/DEFENDANT:	

PROOF OF SERVICE BY MAIL
REQUEST FOR PRODUCTION OF AN INCOME AND EXPENSE DECLARATION AFTER JUDGMENT

1. I am at least 18 years old and **not a party to this cause.** I am a resident of or employed in the county where the mailing took place, and my residence or business address is *(specify):*

2. I served a copy of the following documents:
   a. a completed *Request for Production of an Income and Expense Declaration After Judgment,* and
   b. a **blank** *Income and Expense Declaration* (a four-page form) (form FL-150).

3. I served a copy of the foregoing documents by mailing them in a sealed envelope with postage fully prepaid, certified mail, return receipt requested, as follows:
   a. ☐ I deposited the envelope with the United States Postal Service.
   b. ☐ I placed the envelope for collection and processing for mailing following this business's ordinary practice with which I am readily familiar. On the same day correspondence is placed for collection and mailing, it is deposited in the ordinary course of business with the United States Postal Service.

4. Manner of service
   a. Date of mailing:
   b. Place mailed from:
   c. Addressed as follows:
         Name:

         Street:

      City, state, and zip code:

   I declare under penalty of perjury under the laws of the State of California that the foregoing is true and correct.

Date:

_____   ▶   _____
            (TYPE OR PRINT NAME)   (SIGNATURE OF DECLARANT)

FL-396 [Rev. January 1, 2003]   **REQUEST FOR PRODUCTION OF AN INCOME
AND EXPENSE DECLARATION AFTER JUDGMENT**

For your protection and privacy, please press the Clear This Form button after you have printed the form. | Save This Form | Print This Form | Clear This Form |

11A Citation to Natural Parent—Example

1 | _____, SBN
  | LAW OFFICE OF _____
2 | _____
  | _____
3 |
  | TELEPHONE: (____) ____-_____
4 |
5 | Attorney for Petitioner, _____
6 |
7 | IN THE SUPERIOR COURT OF CALIFORNIA
8 | IN AND FOR THE COUNTY OF _____
9 |
  | In the Matter of the Adoption of   CASE NO: _____
10|
  | _____, Petitioner   **CITATION TO PARENT**
11| **ON PETITION TO**
  | Adopting Parent.   **TERMINATE PARENTAL**
12| _____/   **RIGHTS** (FC§7662)
13| THE PEOPLE OF THE STATE OF CALIFORNIA
14| TO: _____ [natural parent]
15| YOU ARE HEREBY CITED to appear at ____ a/p.m. on _____, 20___ in Department ___
16| of the above entitled court, located at _____ _____, California. At that time
17| and place, you must show cause why the Petition of _____ to adopt your minor child,
18| _____, should not be granted without your consent in the above entitled proceeding,
19| on the ground that you have abandoned _____. The above-referenced petition alleges
20| that for a period of one year after _____, you willfully failed to communicate with, and to
21| pay for the care, support and education of the above children although you were able to do so. A
22| copy of the petition is attached.
23|
24| YOU ARE FURTHER ADVISED that if you appear at the above hearing and wish to have legal
25| counsel but are unable to afford counsel, the court will appoint counsel on your behalf.
26|
27| Dated:_____   _____
28| Clerk of the Superior Court

1

11B Petition for Stepparent Adoption—Example

1 _____ SBN
   LAW OFFICES OF _____

2 _____

3 _____

   TELEPHONE: (___) ___-____

4 Attorney for Petitioner, _____

5

6

7
                IN THE SUPERIOR COURT OF THE STATE OF CALIFORNIA

8   IN AND FOR THE COUNTY OF _____

9

10 IN THE MATTER OF THE ADOPTION   )   CASE NO:

11   )
    _____, Petitioner,   )   PETITION FOR ADOPTION
12   )
                  Adopting Parent.   )   (Stepparent)
13 _____)

14 Petitioner alleges:

15   1. The names of the child who is the subject of this petition was registered at birth as

16 follows: _____, a fe/male, born on _____, _____.

17   2. Petitioner is an adult who desires to adopt the children. Petitioner is the husband of

18 _____, who is the natural mother of the children and who has physical

19 custody of the child. Petitioner and his spouse and the children reside in _____ County,

20 California.

21   3. The mother of the child, _____, was married to the Petitioner on

22 _____, at _____, California. She is prepared to consent to the child's adoption

23 by the petitioner, retaining all of her rights of custody and control.

24   4. The child's natural mother, _____, and the child's natural father,

25 _____, were married on _____. The marriage was terminated on

26 _____ by a Judgment of Dissolution entered in the _____ County

27

28 In Re Adoption of _____; Petition for Step-parent Adoption   Page 1 of 2

11B   Petition for Stepparent Adoption—Example

1 Superior Court in proceeding _____, a copy of which is attached hereto as Exhibit A.

2   A Petition for Termination of Parental Rights has been filed herein.

3   5. The welfare of the child will be served and the minor's best interests promoted by this

4 adoption. The Petitioner is willing and able to care for and educate the child and to adopt the

5 child and treat him/her in all respects as if they were Petitioner's lawful child.

6   6. The minor is not the subject of a petition for the appointment of a guardian.

7   WHEREFORE, Petitioner prays that the court grant this petition and decree that the

8 children mentioned herein has been duly and legally adopted by the Petitioner; and that

9 Petitioner and children shall thereafter sustain toward each other the legal relation of parent and

10 children, with all rights and duties of that relation, and that the children shall be known as

11 follows: _____.

12
    DATED:_____   _____ ____
13   _____, Petitioner

14

15

16

17

18

19

20

21

22

23

24

25

26

27

28 In Re Adoption of _____; Petition for Step-parent Adoption   Page 2 of 2

11C Petition to Terminate Parental Rights

1
2
3

Phone: _____

4

5 Attorney for Petitioner(s), _____

6

7   IN THE SUPERIOR COURT OF CALIFORNIA

8   IN AND FOR THE COUNTY OF _____

9

In the Matter of the Adoption of   CASE NO:

10

                _____   **PETITION TO TERMINATE**
11   **PARENTAL RIGHTS**
        Adopting Parent.   Family Code §7662
12 _____/

13   Petitioners respectfully request:

14   1.   Petitioner, _____, has sole physical custody of

15 _____, a fe/male, born _____. The Father/Mother of the subject minor

16 children consents to the adoption of the children by his/her wife/husband, _____.

17   2. Petitioners have filed in the above-entitled proceeding a Petition for Adoption of the

18 Minor children.

19   3. The child's natural Father/Mother, _____, and the Mother/Father

20 of the child, _____ were married on _____. The marriage was terminated

21 by Judgment of Dissolution which was entered on _____ by _____

22 Court, Case No: _____. _____ will consent   to Petitioner,

23 _____'s adoption of the minor child, retaining all of his/her parental rights of custody and

24 control over the minor child. [OR: The minor does not have a presumed father under Section

25 7004(a) of the Civil Code, does not have a father to whom the minor is a legitimate child under prior

26 law of California, and does not have a father to whom the minor is a legitimate child under the law

27 of another jurisdiction.

28

Petition to Terminate Parental Rights   1

11C Petition to Terminate Parental Rights

1 No declaration of paternity has been executed under Section 7571 of the Family Code. **If you use**

2 **this option #3 do not use #4 below.**]

3   4. The child's natural Mother/Father,_____ for a period in excess of

4 one year, has willfully failed to communicate with and to pay the care, support and education of the

5 child although he/she was able to do so. Consent of the natural Mother/Father, _____,

6 the adoption of said minor child by_____, is not therefore necessary. <u>Adoption of Van Anda</u>

7 (1976) 62 Cal.App.3d 189, 193. <u>Family Code§8304(b)</u>.

8   5. Petitioner, _____, is willing and able to care for and educate the child, to adopt

9 the child, and to treat him/her in all respects as if he/she were his/her natural child.

10   6. The child is proper subject for adoption. It is in the best interest of the minor child that

11 the parental rights of _____, be terminated so that the adoption may be granted because

12 has accepted no responsibility to the child for over one (1) year. In contract, Petitioner stands willing

13 and able to provide a suitable home for the child and has done so for the past _____ (_)

14 months. The welfare of the child will be served and their best interest promoted by this adoption.

15   7. The minor are not subject to a petition for appointment of a guardian.

16

17 WHEREFORE, Petitioner prays judgment as follows:

18   1. For an order declaring the minor child, _____, is free from the custody and

19 control of _____, birth parent and terminating all of his rights and

20 responsibilities with regarding to the minor child, _____ [OR child does not

21 have a presumed father and therefore is free for adoption]

22   2. For an order allowing, _____ to Petition for adoption under Family

23 Code §7662.

24 Dated:_____   By:_____

25   _____, Petitioner

26 Dated:_____   By:_____

27   _____, Petitioner

28

Petition to Terminate Parental Rights   2

11C Petition to Terminate Parental Rights

Dated:_____   By: _____
                                    _____
                                    Attorney for Petitioners

Petition to Terminate Parental Rights   3

11C Petition to Terminate Parental Rights

1

2 **VERIFICATION**

3   I, _____, am the Petitioner in this proceeding. I have read the

4 foregoing petition and know the contents thereof. The same is true of my own knowledge, except

5 as to those matters that are therein alleged on information and belief, and so to those matters, I

6 believe to be true.

7   I declare under penalty of perjury under the laws of the State of California that the foregoing

8 is true and correct.

9 Dated:_____   _____
                                                _____

10

11

12 **VERIFICATION**

13   I, _____, am the Petitioner in this proceeding. I have read the foregoing

14 petition and know the contents thereof. The same is true of my own knowledge, except as to those

15 matters that are therein alleged on information and belief, and so to those matters, I believe to be

16 true.

17   I declare under penalty of perjury under the laws of the State of California that the foregoing

18 is true and correct.

19 Dated:_____   _____
                                                _____

20

21

22

23

24

25

26

27

28

Petition to Terminate Parental Rights   4

11D Order Declaring Minor Free from Custody and Control—Example

1 _____

2 _____

3 Telephone: _____
   Facsimile: _____

4

5 Attorney for Petitioner, _____

6

7   **IN THE SUPERIOR COURT OF CALIFORNIA**

8   **IN AND FOR THE COUNTY OF _____**

9

10 In re the Matter of Adoption of   CASE NO: _____

11   _____   **ORDER DECLARING MINOR**
                                         FREE FROM PARENTAL
12   **CUSTODY AND CONTROL**
    Adopting Parent.

13 _____/

14   The Petition of _____ for the order of this court declaring

15 _____, a minor, free from the parental control of _____ came on

16 regularly for hearing on _____ , ____, at ____ a.m./p.m. in Department _____.

17 Having examined the Petitioner, the minor child and other witnesses, and other evidence both

18 oral and documentary having been introduced, and good cause appearing, this court finds:

19   1. All of the allegations in the petition are true insofar as they pertain to the defaulting

20 Respondent and that each ground has been proven by clear and convincing evidence.

21   2. Notice of the hearing on petition was given as prescribed by law.

22   3. The written investigation and report of the

23 _____Department was received into evidence, including a

24 recommendation to declare the minor child free from the custody and control of _____.

25

26

27

28 Order Declaring Minor Free from Parental Custody & Control   Page 1

11D Order Declaring Minor Free from Custody and Control — Example

1   It is hereby ordered that the petition is granted and the minor child is free from the

2 custody and control of _____ .

3 Dated: _____

                  _____

4   JUDGE OF THE SUPERIOR COURT

5

6

7

8

9

10

11

12

13

14

15

16

17

18

19

20

21

22

23

24

25

26

27

28 Order Declaring Minor Free from Parental Custody & Control   Page 2

11E(a) Consent of Natural Parent to Adoption by Petitioner

1 _____ SBN

2 _____

3 _____

4 (__) __-____

5 Attorney for Petitioner, _____

6

7   IN THE SUPERIOR COURT OF CALIFORNIA

8   IN AND FOR THE COUNTY OF _____

9 In the Matter of the Adoption of   CASE NO: _____

10   **CONSENT OF NATURAL PARENT**
11   _____,   **TO ADOPTION BY PETITIONER**

        Adopting Parent.
12 _____/

13   I, _____, being the natural Father/Mother of _____, born

14 _____, ____ in _____, California, who is the subject of the adoption proceedings

15

16 herein, do hereby give my consent to the adoption of said child. I fully understand, by signing this

    consent, that my consent may not be withdrawn except with court approval, and that upon the
17
    signing of the Order of Adoption by the Court, I shall forever give up all of my rights of custody,
18
    services and earnings of said child, and that the child cannot be reclaimed by me.
19

20

21 Dated:_____   _____
22   _____, [Natural Parent]

23

24

25

26

27

28

    In re Adoption of _____   1

11E(b) Consent to Adoption by Parent in California (Stepparent)

1 _____SBN
LAW OFFICES OF _____

2 _____

3 _____

TELEPHONE: (___) ___-____

4 Attorneys for Petitioner, _____

5

6   IN THE SUPERIOR COURT OF THE STATE OF CALIFORNIA

7   IN AND FOR THE COUNTY OF _____

8

9 In the Matter of the Adoption   )   CASE NO: _____

10   )
_____, Petitioner   )

11   )   **CONSENT TO THE ADOPTION**
     Adopting Parent.   )   **BY PARENT IN CALIFORNIA**

12 _____)   (STEPPARENT)

13   I, the undersigned petitioner, having petitioned this court for the approval of the

14 adoption of _____, do hereby agree with the State of California that the

15 children shall be adopted and treated in all respects as my own lawful children.

16 DATED:_____   _____

17   _____

SIGNED IN THE PRESENCE OF

18

19 JUDGE OF THE SUPERIOR COURT   Dated: _____

20

21

22

23

24

25

26

27

28 In re Adoption of _____; Case No: _____; Consent of Adopting Parent

11F   Petition for Adoption (Adult)

```
1    _____, SBN _____

2    _____
     _____
3    Telephone:    _____
     Facsimile:    _____
4

5

6

7              IN THE SUPERIOR COURT OF THE STATE OF CALIFORNIA

8                   IN AND FOR THE COUNTY OF _____

9

10   In re the Matter of the Adoption of        CASE NO:

11   _____,                PETITION FOR ADOPTION
                                                        (ADULT)
12   an adult person.

13   _____/

14   _____ [Adoptive parent] and _____ [child],

15   petitioners, allege:

16         1. The Petitioner, _____, is __ years of age, having been born on

17   _____, ____ in the city of _____, State of _____, and now resides in

18   _____ County, California; and that Petitioner, _____, is __ years

19   of age, having been born on _____, ____, in the city of _____, State of California, and now

20   resides in _____ County, California.

21         2. That on or about _____, 200_, Petitioners herein did enter into and

22   execute an agreement in writing wherein and whereby Petitioner, _____ agreed to

23   adopt _____, the latter agreed to be adopted by the former, and the parties

24   agreed to assume towards each other the legal relation of parent and child and to have all of the

25   rights and be subject to all of the duties and responsibilities of that relationship; that an exact

26   copy of said agreement of adoption is attached hereto, marked Exhibit "A" and by this reference

27   made a part thereof as though set out in full herein.

28         3. The Petitioner, _____, is the stepfather/mother of Petitioner, _____
```

11F   Petition for Adoption (Adult)

1   _____.

2   4. That the spouse of Petitioner, _____, herein has, in writing, consented

3   to such adoption; that an exact copy of the consent of spouse/natural parent is attached hereto,

4   marked as Exhibit "B" and by this reference made a part hereof as though set out in full herein.

5   The natural parent and mother of Petitioner, _____, consents to the adoption

6   of his/her adult child by his/her spouse without relinquishing any of his/her rights, duties or

7   responsibilities.

8   5. That Petitioner, _____, desires to adopt said

9   _____ and give said _____ the name of _____

10   _____, and _____, desires to be so adopted and given such name.

11   6. Petitioner, _____ has known Petitioner, _____

12   since _____, when his/her father/mother married said Petitioner and has since resided

13   in Petitioner's home.

14   7. No petition for adoption was completed during the minority of Petitioner.

15   8. This adoption is in the best interests of petitioners and the public because it will

16   establish between then the legal rights and obligations of parent and child, including the rights

17   relating to inheritance and duties of support.

18   9. Petitioner, _____' father/mother lives at _____,

19   _____, _____ County, California

20   WHEREFORE, the Petitioners pray the court to permit all persons concerned in this

21   matter to attend and be heard and that the court examine all persons thus appearing before it as

22   required by law and, if satisfied that the best interest of the parties and the public interest will be

23   promoted by the adoption proposed, grant said petition, approve said agreement of adoption, and

24   make an order that said adult persons, _____, has been duly adopted by

25   Petitioner, _____, and that said _____, shall hereafter bear

26   the name of _____.

27

28

11F Petition for Adoption (Adult)

1 DATED:_____   _____
2   _____

3 DATED:_____   _____
4   _____

5 DATED:_____   _____
              [Attorney]

6

7

8

9

10

11

12

13

14

15

16

17

18

19

20

21

22

23

24

25

26

27

28

11G(a) Adoption Agreement (Adult)

1	_____ SBN
2	_____
	_____
3	Telephone: _____
	Facsimile: _____
4	
5	
6	
7	IN THE SUPERIOR COURT OF THE STATE OF CALIFORNIA
8	IN AND FOR THE COUNTY OF _____
9	
10	In re the Matter of the Adoption of CASE NO:
11	_____ AGREEMENT OF ADOPTION
	(ADULT)
12	an adult person.
13	_____/
14	This Agreement is entered into by and between _____ [Adoptive Parent] and
15	_____ [Child].
16	W-I-T-N-E-S-S-E-T-H:
17	
18	WHEREAS, _____, age ___, who lives at
19	_____, _____, California, _____, desires to adopt
20	_____, age __, who lives at _____, _____,
21	California, and
22	WHEREAS, _____, wishes to be adopted by _____;
23	and
24	WHEREAS, the parties desire to assume toward each other the legal relation of parent
25	and child and to have all of the rights and be subject to all of the duties and responsibilities of
26	that relationship;
27	
28	

11G(a) Adoption Agreement (Adult)

1   NOW, THEREFORE, in consideration of the premises, the parties agree as follows:

2   1. That _____ will adopt _____, and that

3 _____ will be adopted by _____.

4   2. That the parties will assume toward each other the legal relation of parent and child,

5 and agree to be subject to all the rights, duties and responsibilities of that relationship;

6   3. That they will file a petition in the Superior Court of California, County of

7 _____, praying for approval of this Agreement of Adoption and decree that

8 _____ is the child of _____ and that s/he bear the name of

9 _____.

10   In WITNESS WHEREOF, we have hereunto set our hands this ___ day of

11 _____ 200_, _____, California.

12

13 DATED:_____   _____

14   _____

15 DATED:_____   _____

16   _____

17

18

19

20

21

22

23

24

25

26

27

28

11G(b) Consent to the Adoption (Adult)

1 _____, SBN
   LAW OFFICES OF _____

2 _____

3 _____

4 (__) ___-___

5 Attorney for Petitioner(s), _____

6

7   IN THE SUPERIOR COURT OF THE STATE OF CALIFORNIA

8   IN AND FOR THE COUNTY OF _____

9

10 In the Matter of the Adoption   )   CASE NO: _____

)

11 _____, Petitioner   )

12   Adopting Parent.   )   **CONSENT TO THE ADOPTION**
)   **(ADULT)**

13 _____)

14   I, the undersigned, being the _____ [relationship, e.g. wife/husband] r

15 of _____, do hereby give my full and free consent to the adoption of

16 _____ by _____, the Petitioner(s). I respectfully ask that

17 the petition be granted.

18

19 DATED:_____   _____

20   _____

21 SIGNED IN THE PRESENCE OF

22

23

24 _____

25 JUDGE OF THE SUPERIOR COURT   DATED: _____

26

27

28 In re Adoption of _____; Case No: _____; Consent of _____

11H   Decree of Adoption (Adult)

1   _____, SBN _____

2   _____
     _____
3   Telephone: _____
     Facsimile: _____
4

5

6

7   IN THE SUPERIOR COURT OF THE STATE OF CALIFORNIA

8   IN AND FOR THE COUNTY OF _____

9

10   In re the Matter of the Adoption of   CASE NO: _____

11   _____   DECREE OF ADOPTION
                                                (ADULT)
12   an adult person.

13   _____/

14   The Petition of _____ for the adoption of the adult child,

15   _____, named in the Petition herein, came on regularly for hearing on

16   _____, 200_ at ____ a.m/pm in Department ____ of the _____ County

17   Superior Court. _____, Attorney appeared as attorney for Petitioner,

18   _____, _____, and _____ also appeared.

19   Each person appearing was examined separately by the Court, from which examination it

20   is found that Petitioner, _____, the person being adopted herein, is

21   younger than Petitioner, _____, the adopting person; that Petitioner, _____

22   _____, is a resident of the County of _____, California; that _____, the

23   natural mother of _____, consents to said adoption; that Petitioner _____

24   _____ and _____ have entered into an agreement in writing whereby,

25   Petitioner, _____ has agreed to adopt _____, the latter

26   agreed to be adopted by the former, and the said parties agreed to assume toward each other the

27   legal relation of parent and child and have all the rights and be subject to all the duties and

28   responsibilities of that relationship; and the court, after hearing the evidence, being satisfied, and

     In Re Adoption of _____; Decree   Page 1

11H   Decree of Adoption (Adult)

1   finding that said adoption will be for the best interests of the parties and in the public interest and

2   that there is no reason why the petition herein should not be granted.

3   IT IS HEREBY ORDERED, ADJUDGED, AND DECREED that the petition herein be

4   and hereby is granted, and that said agreement of adoption is hereby approved, and that

5   Petitioner _____ is hereby adopted by the Petitioner,

6   _____, and that _____ shall hereafter be regarded and

7   treated in all respects as the child of _____ and shall hereafter bear the name of

8   _____

9

10

11   DATED: _____   _____
                                                       Judge of the Superior Court
12

13

14

15

16

17

18

19

20

21

22

23

24

25

26

27

28

In Re Adoption of _____; Decree   Page 2

11I Cohabitation Agreement—Example

Cohabitation Agreement

I

Intent

_____ and _____ declare that they are not married to each other, although they are living together. By this agreement they intend to protect and define their individual rights as to future services rendered, accumulated earnings and property and any other matters set forth in this agreement.

The parties expressly agree that the consent of either party to cohabit sexually is not a consideration, either in whole or part, for the making of this agreement. The purpose of this agreement is to expressly agree that any and all agree that the property of each party shall be the separate property of that party who earns or acquires said property. Said property will not be considered community property or joint property. The non-earning or non-acquiring party will not have any interest in same.

II

Representations to the Public/No Common Law Marriage

It is expressly agreed that neither party will represent to the public, in any manner, that they are husband and wife. Should any representation to the contrary be made, it will be for social convenience only and will not imply that sexual services are a consideration for either party.

The parties understand that California does not recognize common law marriage. The parties agree that although they are cohabiting, and there may be an appearance they are married, they do not intend to assert a "common law marriage." This agreement is **not** an agreement to marry, nor are the parties to be considered married for the proposes of California family law.

III

Property, Earnings and Accumulations

It is expressly agree that all property, including but not limited to the earnings and income resulting from personal services, skill, effort, and work of either party to this agreement will be the separate property of the respective party. Neither party shall have any interest in any property acquired by either of them either prior to their cohabitation, or after cohabitation which is received by gift, inheritance or purchase.

11I Cohabitation Agreement — Example

IV

Services Rendered

It is expressly agreed that any domestic work or services, including but not limited to homemaking, cooking, cleaning and entertaining, that either party may contribute to the other or to their common residence will be voluntary and without compensation. Such work is done without expectation of monetary compensation or reward.

V

Debts and Obligations

It is expressly agreed that all debts and obligations acquired by either party which is for the benefit of that party will be debt or obligation of that party only. If one party is forced to pay a debt or obligation which belongs to or benefits the other party, the obligated party agrees to reimburse, indemnify and hold harmless the party who paid the debt or obligation.

The debts and obligations which are for the benefit of both parties, such as rent, telephone, utilities, and insurance will be paid in such sums and in proportion by each party as is mutually agreed.

VI

Primary "Ownership" of Premises

It is expressly agreed that any property rented for the mutual benefit of the parties will "belong" to the person who first rented the property. If the parties separate, the second party will leave the premises taking only their personal property he or she owned prior to moving into the property.

If the parties jointly rent the premises, it is agreed that they will have a third party flip a coin (or some other mechanism for determining by chance) to determine which party will stay and which will leave.

VII

Rent or Mortgage Payments

It is expressly agreed that the parties will split the rent or mortgage payments in whatever proportion they choose. If one party contributes to the mortgage payment of a property being purchased, which is in the name of the other party, that contribution is considered rent. Said rent will be non-refundable and will not create any ownership interest in the property.

11I Cohabitation Agreement—Example

VIII

Separate Accounts

It is expressly agreed that in order to conform with the intentions of the parties, each party will maintain separate bank accounts, credit accounts, automobile ownership, deeds, insurance and other types of accounts. Each party will file their own tax return. Each party will make purchases of personal property, including but not limited to, furniture, appliances, art, electronic equipment in order to avoid confusion as to the ownership of said purchases. Each party will keep their own records evidencing the purchase and ownership of their property.

IX

Duration of Agreement

It is expressly agreed that this agreement will remain in effect from the date the parties commence cohabiting until either party leaves or removes him or herself from the common residence with the intention not to return, or until a new agreement is executed between the parties. The parties agree that if they marry, this agreement becomes null and void.

X
Attorney Fees & Costs

It is expressly agreed that they will act in good faith to follow the provisions of this agreement. If either party should breach the agreement, or fail to act in good faith, such party will pay to the other any attorney fees and costs as are reasonable in order to enforce the provisions of this agreement.

XI

Waiver of Support

It is expressly agreed that each party waives any rights to "spousal" support from the other in the event their relationship is terminated.

Dated: _____   _____

Dated: _____   _____

[Notary acknowledgment]

11J Pre-Nuptial Agreement — Example

Pre-Nuptial Agreement (Sample Clauses)

This agreement is made this _____ day of _____ between _____ and _____.

Whereas the parties contemplate marriage on or about _____, _____ ;

Whereas the parties acknowledge that each of them own or expect to own certain property;

Whereas the parties have made a full and complete disclosure of all their assets and liabilities and have attached a copy of said schedules to this agreement;

Whereas each party has consulted individual their an attorney of law and said attorney has executed an acknowledgment of having reviewed and discussed this agreement with the respective party;

The parties agree to the following terms:

1. Wife's Property.

A. _____ [wife] shall have full right and authority to use, enjoy, manage, control, mortgage, convey and dispose of all of her present and future property and estate, including the right to dispose of said property by will or trust.

B. _____ [husband] releases to _____ [wife], her heirs, legal representatives, and assigns every right, claim and estate, whether actual or contingent, which he may have by reason of his marriage to _____ [wife].

C. If any child of this marriage survives _____ [wife], and is a minor upon her death, _____ [husband] releases every right, claim and estate he may have to any inheritance. Such property is subject to any bequest or devise made by _____ [wife].

D. _____ [husband] agrees that he will execute, acknowledge and deliver, any additional instruments that may reasonably be necessary to effectuate the terms and conditions of this agreement.

2. Husband's Property.

A. _____ [husband] shall have full right and authority to use, enjoy, manage, control, mortgage, convey and dispose of all of her present and future property and estate, including the right to dispose of said property by will or trust.
B. _____ [wife] releases to _____ [husband], his heirs, legal

11J Pre-Nuptial Agreement—Example

representatives, and assigns every right, claim and estate, whether actual or contingent, which she may have by reason of his marriage to _____ [wife].

      C. If any child of this marriage survives _____ [husband], and is a minor upon his death, _____ [wife] releases every right, claim and estate she may have to any inheritance. Such property is subject to any bequest or devise made by _____ [husband].

      D. _____ [wife] agrees that he will execute, acknowledge and deliver, any additional instruments that may reasonably be necessary to effectuate the terms and conditions of this agreement.

3. Control of Separate Property.

      A. During their marriage, each party will have full right to own, control and dispose of his or her own separation property the same is if the marriage did not exit. Each party will have the full right to dispose of and sell any and all real or personal property now or owned by each of them without the other party joining. Either party to this agreement will convey the same title to said transfer which would convey the property as though the marriage did not exist.

This agreement limits the right of either party to participate in the estate of the other, whether the marriage has been terminated by death or legal proceedings, except to the extent that each party has executed a Will and/or Trust as to the distribution of their separate and community property.

4. Community Property

      A. The parties agree that they may acquire community property after the date of their marriage. Any such property shall be held as joint tenants and shall be distributed as set forth in the probate code if either party should die intestate. If the parties have a Will and/or Trust at their death, said documents should be created for the benefit of the parties' community benefit and for any children that the parties may have between them.

The parties further agree that should the marriage dissolved, this agreement will be controlling in the dividing of any community property.

5. Transmutation of Separate Property to Community Property.

      A. The parties agree that if at any time, they wish to transfer any separate property to community property they will execute a transmutation agreement memorializing the transfer of said property.

11J Pre-Nuptial Agreement—Example

6. General Provisions.

    A. The parties agree that each shall retain an original of this document.

    B. This agreement cannot be revoked, except by written agreement of both parties.

I declare under penalty of perjury that I have made a full and final disclosure of all of my assets and liabilities and that I have consulted with an attorney of my choice and he or she has advised me of my legal rights relative to this agreement.

Dated: _____   _____
                                                        Husband

Dated:_____   _____
                                                        Wife

Dated:_____   _____
                                                     Attorney for Husband

Dated: _____   _____
                                                     Attorney for Wife

Appendix 11G

11J Pre-Nuptial Agreement — Example

Exhibit "A"

Schedule of Husband's Assets and Liabilities

Exhibit "B"

Schedule of Wife's Assets and Liabilities

Exhibit "C"

Schedule of Community Assets and Liabilities (may be added and modified as acquired)

11K *In re Marriage of Bonds*

In re Marriage of Bonds (2000) 24 Cal. 4th 1, 5 P.3d 815

Case History: Barry Bonds married Susann (Sun) Bonds while playing for the Pittsburgh Pirates. He was earning $106,000 per year. Just prior to their marriage, Barry and Sun signed a premarital agreement, which was prepared by Barry's attorney. The agreement stated that Sun waived any interest in his earnings during the marriage.

At the time of their divorce, he was playing for the San Francisco Giants and earning several million dollars per year.

Sun Bonds contended that she did not have independent counsel and that the agreement was not signed voluntarily. She also stated that she did not understand the agreement and what she was waiving, and that she was under duress to sign he agreement.

The trial court found that Sun did enter the agreement voluntarily and that she understood the terms of the agreement. She appealed to the Court of Appeal. They reversed the decision and directed a re-trial on the issue of voluntariness. Barry Bonds appealed the decision to the California Supreme Court.

Chief Justice George wrote the opinion for the Supreme Court.

Sun and Barry met in Montreal in the summer of 1987 and maintained a relationship during ensuring months through telephone contacts. In October 1987, at Barry's invitation, Sun visited him for 10 days at his home in Phoenix, Arizona. In November 1987, Sun moved to Phoenix to take up residence with Barry and, one week later, the two became engaged to be married. In January 1988, they decided to marry before the commencement of professional baseball's spring training. On February 5, 19088, in Phoenix, the parties entered into a written premarital agreement in which each party waive any interest in the earnings and acquisitions of the other party during marriage....That same day, they flew to Las Vegas, and were married the following day.

Each of the parties then was 23 years of age. Barry, who had attended college for three years and who had begun his career in professional baseball in 1985, had a contract to play for the Pittsburgh Pirates. His annual salary at the time of the marriage ceremony was approximately $106,000. Sun had emigrated to Canada from Sweden in 1985, had worked as a waitress and bartender, and had undertaken some training as a cosmetologist, having expressed an interest in embarking upon a career as a makeup artist for celebrity clients. Although her native language was Swedish, she had used both French and English in her employment, education, and personal relationships when she lived in Canada. She was unemployed at the time she entered into the prenuptial agreement.

[Barry sought a dissolution of marriage in May of 1994. Sun was awarded custody of their two minor children and child support.] in the amount of $10,000 per month per child. Spousal

11K *In re Marriage of Bonds*

support was awarded in the amount of $10,000 per month, to terminate December 20, 1998. On the first issue - the validity of the premarital agreement - is before the court.

Barry testified that he was aware of teammates and other persons who had undergone bitter marital dissolution proceedings involving the division of property, and recalled that from the beginning of his relationship with Sun he told her that he believed his earnings and acquisitions during marriage should be his own. He informed her he would not marry without a premarital agreement, and she had no objection. He also recalled that from the beginning of the relationship, Sun agreed that their earnings and acquisitions should be separate, saying "what's mine is mine, what's yours is yours." Indeed, she informed him that this was the practice with respect to marital property in Sweden. She stated that she planned to pursue a career and wished to be financially independent. Sun knew that Barry did not anticipate that she would shoulder her living expenses, while she was not employed. She was not, in fact, employed during the marriage. Barry testified that he and Sun had no difficulty communicating.

Although Barry testified that he had previous experience working with lawyers in the course of baseball contract negotiations and the purchase of real property, his testimony at trial did not demonstrate an understanding of the legal fine points of the agreement.

Sun's testimony at trial differed from Barry's in material respects. She testified that her English language skills in 1987 and 1988 were limited. Out of pride, she did not disclose to Barry that she often did not understand him. She testified that she and Barry never discussed money or property during the relationship that preceded their marriage. She agreed that she had expressed interest in a career as a cosmetologist and had said she wished to be financially independent. She had very few assets when she took up residence with Barry, and he paid for all their needs. Their wedding arrangements were very informal, with no written invitations or caterer, and only Barry's parents and a couple of friends, including Barry's godfather Willie Mays, were invited to attend. No marriage license or venue had been arranged in advance of their arrival in Las Vegas.

Several persons testified as to the circumstances surrounding the signing of the premarital agreement. Sun testified that on the evening before the premarital agreement was signed, Barry first informed her that they needed to go the following day to the offices of his lawyers, Leonard Brown and his associate Sabinus Megwa. She was uncertain, however, whether Barry made any reference to a premarital agreement. She testified that only at the parking lot of the law office where the agreement was to be entered into did she learn, from Barry's financial advisor, Mel Wilcox, that Barry would not marry her unless she signed a premarital agreement. She was not upset. She was surprised, however, because Barry never had said that signing the agreement was a precondition to marriage. She did not question Barry or anyone else at this point. She was under the impression that Barry wished to retain separate ownership of property he owned before the marriage, and that this was the sole object of the premarital agreement. She was unaware the agreement would affect her future and was not concerned about the matter, because she was nervous and excited about getting married and trusted Barry. Wilcox's statement had little effect on her, because she had no question, but that she and Barry were to be married the following day.

11K *In re Marriage of Bonds*

Sun recalled having to hurry to arrive at the lawyer's office in time both to accomplish their business there and make the scheduled departure of the airplane to Las Vegas so that she and Barry could marry the next day. Sun recalled that once they arrived at the lawyer's office on February 5, 1988, she, her friend Margareta Forsberg, Barry, and Barry's financial advisor Mel Wilcox were present in a conference room. She did not recall asking questions or her friend asking questions, nor did she recall that any changes were made to the agreement. She declared that her English language skills were limited at the time and she did not understand the agreement, but she did not ask questions of anyone other than Margareta Forsberg or ask for more time, because she did not want to miss her flight and she was focused on the forthcoming marriage ceremony. She did not believe that Barry understood the agreement either. Forsberg was unable to assist her. Sun did not recall the lawyers telling her that she should retain her own lawyer, that they were representing Barry and not her, that the applicable community property law provided that a spouse has an interest in the earnings and in acquisitions of the other spouse during marriage, or that she would be waiving this right if she signed the agreement. The lawyers may have mentioned the possibility of her being represented by her own lawyer, but she did not believe she needed one. She did not inform anyone at the meeting that she was concerned about the agreement; the meeting and discussion were not cut short, and no one forced her to sign the agreement.

Forsberg, a native of Sweden and 51 years of age at the time the agreement was signed, confirmed that she as present when attorneys Brown and Megwa explained the agreement, that Wilcox also was present that no changes to the agreement were made at Sun's or Forsberg's request, and that she had been unable to answer Sun's questions or explain to Sun the terminology used in the agreement. She confirmed that Sun's English was limited, that the lawyers had explained the agreement, and that Sun never stated that she did not understand it, or that she was not signing of her own free will. Sun never said that Barry threatened her or forced her to sign, that she wanted to consult independent counsel concerning the agreement, ro that she felt pressured. Forsberg understood that Brown and Megwa were Barry's attorney's, not Sun's. She testified that when the attorneys explained the agreement, she did not recall any discussion of Sun's community property rights.

Barry and other witnesses offered a different picture of the circumstances leading to the signing of the premarital agreement, an account found by the trial court to be more credible in material aspects, as reflected in its statement of decision. Barry and his attorney Brown recalled that approximately two weeks before the parties signed the formal agreement, they discussed with Sun the drafting of an agreement to keep earnings and acquisitions separate. Brown testified that he told Sun at this meeting that he represented Barry and that it might be in her best interest to obtain independent counsel.

Barry, Brown, and Megwa testified that Wilcox was not present at the February 5, 1988, meeting, which lasted between one and two hours, and that at the meeting the attorneys informed Sun of her right to independent counsel. All three recalled that Sun stated she did not want her own counsel, and Megwa recalled explaining that he and Brown did not represent her.

11K *In re Marriage of Bonds*

Additionally, all three recalled that the attorneys read the agreement to her paragraph by paragraph and explained it as they went through it, also informing her of a spouse's basic community property rights in earnings and acquisitions and that Sun would be waiving these rights. Megwa recalled it was clearly explained that Barry's income and acquisitions during the marriage would remain Barry's separate property, and he recalled that Sun stated that such arrangements were the practice in Sweden. Furthermore, Barry and the two attorneys each confirmed that Sun and Forsberg asked questions during the meeting and were left alone on several occasions to discuss its terms, that Sun did not exhibit any confusion, and that Sun indicated she understood the agreement. They also testified that changes were made to the agreement at Sun's behest. Brown and Megwa experienced no difficulty in communicating with Sun, found her confident and happy, and had no indication that she was nervous or confused, intimidated, or pressured. No threat was uttered that unless she signed the agreement, the wedding would be cancelled, nor did they hear her express any reservations about signing the agreement. Additionally, legal secretary Illa Washington recalled that Wilcox waited in another room while the agreement was discussed, that Sun asked questions and that changes were made to the agreement at her behest, that Sun was informed she could secure independent counsel, that Sun said she understood the contract and did not want to consult another attorney, and that she appeared to understand the discussions and to feel comfortable and confident.....

[The trial court concluded that Barry had demonstrated by clear and convincing evidence that the agreement and its execution were free from the taint of fraud, coercions, or undue influence and that Sun entered the agreement with full knowledge of the property involved and her rights therein. The court of appeal reversed and directed a retrial on the issue of voluntariness. The court stressed that Sun lacked independent counsel and had not waived counsel effectively. It asserted that attorneys Brown and Megwa failed to explain that Sun's interests conflicted with Barry's, failed to urge her to retain separate counsel, and may have led Sun to believe they actually represented her interests as they explained the agreement paragraph by paragraph. The court of appeal concluded that the trial court erred in failing to give proper weight to the circumstance that Sun was not represented by independent counsel. It also pointed to Sun's limited English-language skills and lack of "legal or business sophistication" and stated that she "received no explanation of the legal consequences to her ensuing from signing the contract" and "was told there would be 'no marriage' if she did not immediately sign the agreement." It also referred to typographical errors and omissions in the agreement, the imminence of the wedding and the inconvenience and embarrassment of canceling it, Sun's asserted lack of understanding that she was waiving her statutory right to a community property interest in Barry's earnings, and the absence of an attorney acting as an advocate on her behalf.]

Pursuant to Family Code section 1615 [based on the Uniform Premarital Agreement Act], a premarital agreement will be enforced unless the party resisting enforcement of the agreement can demonstrate either (1) that he or she did not enter into the contract voluntarily, or (2) that the contract was unconscionable when entered into and that he or she did not have the actual or constructive knowledge of the assets and obligations of the other party and did not voluntarily waive knowledge of such assets and obligations. In the present case, the trial court found no lack of knowledge regarding the nature of the parties' assets, a necessary predicate to consider the

11K *In re Marriage of Bonds*

issue of unconscionability, and the Court of Appeal accepted the trial court's determination on this point. We do not reconsider this factual determination, and thus the question of unconscionability is not before us.....[T]he only issue we face concerns the trial court's determination that Sun entered into the agreement voluntarily.

[Family Code §1615 does not define] the term "voluntarily."......*Black's Law Dictionary* defines "voluntarily" as "Done by design...Intentionally and without coercion." (Black's Law Dict. (6th ed 1990) p. 1575.) The same source defines "voluntary" as "Proceeding from the free and unrestrained will of the person. Produced in or by an act of choice. Resulting from free choice, without compulsion or solicitation. The word, especially in statutes, often implies knowledge of essential facts." (Ibid.) The *Oxford English Dictionary* defines "voluntary" as "[o]f one's own free will or accord; without compulsion, constraint, or undue influence by others; freely, willingly." (19 *Oxford English Dict.* (2d ed. 1989) p. 753.)

[A number of factors are relevant to the issue of voluntariness. A court should examine whether the evidence indicates coercion or lack of knowledge and consider] the impact upon the parties of such factors as the coercion that may arise from the proximity of the execution of the agreement to the wedding, or from surprise in the presentation of the agreement; the presence or absence of independent counsel; inequality of bargaining power in some cases indicated by the relative age and sophistication of the parties; whether there was full disclosure of assets; and the parties' understanding of the rights being waived under the agreement or at least their awareness of the intent of the agreement......[T]he parties' general understanding of the effect of the agreement constitutes a factor for the court to consider in determining whether the parties entered into the agreement voluntarily........

In *In re Marriage of Dawley*, 17 Cal.3d 342, 131 Cal. Rptr. 3, 551 P.2d 323, we rejected the wife's claim that a premarital agreement waiving community property rights had been obtained through undue influence, pointing out that in the particular case the pressure to marry created by an unplanned pregnancy fell equally on both parties, that both parties were educated and employed, and that the party challenging the agreement did not rely upon the other party's advise, but consulted her own attorney. [See also] *La Liberty v La Liberty*, (1932) 127 Cal. App. 669, 16 P.2d. 681 (rejecting lack of independent counsel as a basis for rescission, given the parties' apparent understanding fo the meaning of the premarital agreement.)......

We have considered the range of factors that may be relevant to establish the involuntariness of a premarital agreement in order to consider whether the Court of Appeal erred in according such great weight to one factor- the presence or absence of independent counsel for each party.....

[Nothing in our statute] makes the absence of assistance of independent legal counsel a condition for the unenforceability of a premarital agreement....[The presence of independent counsel or a reasonable opportunity to consult counsel is] merely one factor among several that a court should consider in examining a challenge to the voluntariness of a premarital agreement.

11K *In re Marriage of Bonds*

[W]e conclude that the trial court's determination that Sun voluntarily entered into the premarital agreement in the present case is supported by substantial evidence....

The Court of Appeal held the trial court erred in finding the parties' agreement to be voluntary. The appellate court stressed the absence of counsel for Sun, and ....pointed to Sun's limited English language skills and lack of "legal or business sophistication," stated that she "received no explanation of the legal consequences to her ensuing from signing the contract," and "was told there would be 'no marriage' if she did not immediately sign the agreement." It also referred to typographical errors and omissions in the agreement, the imminence of the wedding and the inconvenience and embarrassment of cancelling it, and Sun's asserted lack of understanding that she was waiving her statutory right to a community property interest in Barry's earnings.

The trial court, however, determined that Sun entered into the premarital contract voluntarily, without being subject to fraud, coercion, or undue influence, and with full understanding of the terms and effect of the agreement.......It determined that [Barry] had demonstrated by clear and convincing evidence that the agreement had been entered into voluntarily.

The trial court made specific findings of fact regarding the factors we had identified as relevant to the determination of voluntariness. The findings are supported by substantial evidence and should have been accepted by the Court of Appeal.....

The trial court determined that there had been no coercion. It declared that Sun had not been subjected to any threats, that she had not been forced to sign the agreement, and that she never expressed any reluctance to sign the agreement. It found that the temporal proximity of the wedding to the signing of the agreement was no coercive, because under the particular circumstances of the case, including the small number of guest and the informality of the wedding arrangements, little embarrassment would have followed from postponement of the wedding. It found that the presentation of the agreement did not come as a surprise to Sun, noting that she was aware of Barry's desire to "protect his present property and future earnings," and that she had been aware for at least a week before the parties signed the formal premarital agreement that one was planned.

These findings were supported by substantial evidence. Several witnesses, including Sun herself, stated that she was not threatened. The witnesses were unanimous in observing that Sun expressed no reluctance to sign the agreement, and they observed in addition that she appeared calm, happy, and confident as she participated in discussions of the agreement. Attorney Brown testified that Sun had indicated a desire at their first meeting to enter into the agreement, and that during the discussion preceding execution fo the document, she stated that she understood the agreement. As the trail court determined, although the wedding between Sun and Barry was planned for the day following the signing of the agreement, the wedding was impromptu–the parties had not secured a license or a place to be married, and the few family members and close friends who were invited could have changed their plans without difficulty (For example, guests

11K *In re Marriage of Bonds*

were not arriving from Sweden.) In view of these circumstances, the evidence supported the inference, drawn by the trial court, that the coercive force of the normal desire to avoid social embarrassment or humiliation was diminished and absent. Finally, Barry's testimony that the parties early in their relationship had discussed their desire to keep separate their property and earnings, in addition to the testimony of Barry and Brown that they had met with Sun at least once week before the document was signed to discuss the need for an agreement, and the evidence establishing that Sun understood and concurred in the agreement, constituted substantial evidence to support the trial court's conclusion that Sun was not subjected to the type of coercion that may arise from the surprise and confusion caused by a last-minute presentation of a new plan to keep earnings and property separate during marriage. In this connection, certain statements in the opinion rendered by the Court of Appeal....that Sun was subjected to aggressive threats from financial advisor Mel Wilcox[;] that the temporal proximity of the wedding was coercive under the circumstances of this case; and that defects in the text of the agreement indicate it was prepared in a rush, came as a surpi9se when presented, and was impossible to understand–are inconsistent with factual determinations made by the trial court that we have determined ware supported by substantial evidence.

With respect to the presence of independent counsel, although Sun lacked legal counsel, the trial court determined that she had reasonable opportunity to obtain counsel. The trial court stated: "Respondent had sufficient awareness and understanding of her right t, and need for, independent counsel. Respondent also had an adequate and reasonable opportunity to obtain independent counsel prior to execution of the Agreement. Respondent was advised at a meeting with Attorney Brown at least one week prior to execution of the Agreement that she had the right to have an attorney represent her and that Attorneys Brown and Megwa represented Petitioner, not Respondent. On at least two occasions during the February 5, 1988, meeting, Respondent was told that she could have separate counsel if she chose. Respondent declined. Respondent was capable of understanding this admonition."

These factual findings are supported by substantial evidence. Brown testified that at the meeting that preceded the February 5, 1988, meeting at which the premarital agreement was executed, both Sun and Barry indicated they wished to enter into a premarital agreement, and that Brown informed Sun that he represented Barry and that therefore it might be in her best interest to have her own attorney. She declined. Brown testified that at th February 5, 1988, session he explained the basics of community property law, telling Sun that she would be disavowing the protection of community property law by agreeing that income and acquisitions during marriage would be separate property . He informed her of h er right to separate counsel, and told both parties that the agreement did not have to be signed that day. He again informed Sun that he represented Barry. He testified that Sun stated that it was not necessary for her to have counsel, and that she said she understood how the contract affected her interest under the community property law. Attorney Megwa also testified that the attorneys discussed basic community property law with Sun and told her that she did not have to sign the agreement. He testified that the subject of h er obtaining her own counsel came up at least three times during the February 5, 1988, meeting, and that she stated explicitly that she did not wish to submit the agreement to separate counsel for review. Megwa testified that he had cautioned Sun that she should not sign

11K *In re Marriage of Bonds*

the agreement (which she had reviewed herself and which then had been explained to her clause by clause) unless it reflected her intentions, and that she said she understood the agreement.

The Court of Appeal.....rejected the conclusion of the trial court that Sun understood why she should consult separate counsel. This determination by the appellate court contradicts the specific finding of the trial court's finding is supported by the language of the agreement itself, including the indication in paragraph 10 that the earnings and accumulations of each spouse "during marriage' would be separate property, and additional language stating that "[w]e desire by this instrument to agree as to the treatment of separate and community property *after* the marriage...." [italics added for emphasis].   The trial court's finding also was supported by evidence establishing that the attorneys explained to Sun the rights she would have under community property law In addition, Barry testified that ever since the issue first came up at the beginning of the relationship, Sun had agreed that the parties' earnings and acquisitions should be separate. Further, the attorneys testified that during the February 5, 1988, meeting, Sun stated her intent to keep marital property separate. These circumstances establish that Sun did not forgo separate legal advise out of ignorance. Instead she declined to invoke her interests under the community property law because she agreed, for her own reasons, that Barry's and her earnings and acquisitions after marriage should be separate property.

The Court of Appeal....surmised that Sun did not have a reasonable opportunity to consult counsel because of a copy of the agreement was not provided in advance of the February 5, 1988, meeting, and because Sun had insufficient funds to retain counsel and was not informed that Barry would pay for independent counsel's services. Again, this determination is contradicted by the conclusion of the trial court that Sun had "an adequate and reasonable opportunity to ob tain independent counsel prior to execution of the Agreement." The trial court's determination was supported by evidence that Sun had been told about the agreement and her potential need for counsel at least a week before the document was executed and that she was told at the February 5, 19088, meeting that she could consult separate counsel and was not required to sign the contract that day. Additionally, there was evidence supporting the inference that she declined counsel because she understood and agreed with the terms of the agreement, and not because she had insufficient funds to employ counsel.

With respect to the question of inequality of bargaining power, the trial court determined that Sun was intelligent and, evidently not crediting her claim that limited English made her unable to understand the import of the agreement or the explanations offered by Barry's counsel, found that she was capable of understanding the agreement and the explanations proffered by Barry's attorneys. There is ample evidence to support the trial court's determination regarding Sun's English-language skills, in view of the circumstances that for two years prior to marriage she had undertaken employment and education in a trade that required such skills, and before meeting Barry had maintained close personal relationships with persons speaking only English before meeting Barry. In addition, Barry and his witnesses all testified that Sun appeared to have no language problems at the time she signed the agreement. Brown and Megwa testified that Sun indicated at the February 5, 1988, meeting that she understood the agreement, and indeed the contract contains a paragraph indicated that the parties attest that they "fully understand [ ]" the

11K *In re Marriage of Bonds*

terms of the agreement. The trial court's findings with respect to the notice and opportunity Sun received to obtain independent counsel at least one week before the agreement was executed, as well as evidence indicating Sun long h ad known and agreed that the marriage would entail separation of earnings and acquisitions, tend to undercut any inference that coercion arose from unequal bargaining power, including Barry's somewhat great sophistication and the involvement of two attorneys and a financial advisor on Barry's behalf. In addition, although these persons represented Barry, there is substantial evidence that they did not pressure Sun or even urge her to sign the agreement. Further, although Barry had three years of college studies as well as some experience in negotiating contracts, while Sun had only recently passed her high school equivalency exam (in English) and had little commercial experience, there is evidence that Barry did not understand the legal fine points of the agreement any more than Sun did. In addition, the basis purport of the agreement–that the parties would hold their earnings and accumulations during the marriage as separate property, thereby giving up the protection of marital property law – was a relatively simple concept that did not require great legal sophistication to comprehend and that was, as the trail court found, understood by Sun. Finally, we observe that the evidence supports the inference that Sun was intrepid rather than a person whose will is easily overborne. She emigrated from her homeland at a young age, found employment and friends in a new country using two languages other than her native tongue, and in two years moved to yet another country, expressing the desire to take up a career and declaring to Barry that she "didn't want his money." These circumstances support the inference that an inequality in bargaining power – arising primarily from the absence of independent counsel who could have advised Sun not to sign the agreement or urged Barry to abandon the idea of keeping his earnings separate - was not coercive.

With respect to full disclosure of the property involved, the trial court found that Sun was aware of what separate property was held by Barry prior to the marriage, and as the Court of Appeal noted, she failed to identify any property of which she later became aware that was not on the list of property referred to by the parties when they executed the contract. The trial court also determined that Sun was aware of what was at stake – of what normally would be community property, namely earnings and acquisitions of the parties during marriage. Substantial evidence supports this conclusion, including Sun's states to Barry before marriage, the terms used in the contract, and Brown and Megwa's testimony that they painstakingly explained this matter to Sun.

With respect to the question of knowledge, as already explained it is evident that the trial court was impressed with the extent of Sun's awareness. The trial court did not credit her claim that before the premarital agreement was presented to her, the parties never had discussed keeping their earnings and acquisitions separate during marriage. Nor did the trial court credit her claim that the subject and content of the agreement came as a surprise to her, or that she did not understand that absent the agreement, she would be entitled to share in Barry's earnings and acquisitions during marriage. The finding that she was sufficiently aware of her statutory rights and how the agreement "adversely affected these rights" is supported by the testimony of Barry, Brown, and Megwa that the attorneys explained these matters before Sun signed the agreement. In addition, as noted, Barry testified that he and Sun agreed long before their marriage that their

11K *In re Marriage of Bonds*

earnings and acquisitions would remain separate...

The factors we have identified in assessing the voluntariness of the agreement entered into between Barry and Sun was not rigidly separate considerations; rather the presence of one factor may influence the weight to be given evidence considered primarily under another factor. In this respect, the trail court's finding that Sun had advance knowledge of the meaning and intent of the agreement and what was at state for her is influential, as we have seen, in considering some of the other factors.

In considering evidence that Sun responded to Barry's suggestion that she secure independent counsel with the observation that she did not need counsel because she had nothing, the Court of Appeal....drew the inference least in support of the judgment – namely, that this statement indicated Sun did not understand that she did have property interests at state in the form of the community property rights that would accrue to her under applicable statutes, in the absence of a premarital agreement. We believe that this was error on the part of the appellate court, because substantial evidence supported the trial court's determination to the contrary. It is clear from the testimony of Brown and Megwa that, even if Sun did not peruse the entire document herself, they read it to her paragraph by paragraph, thoroughly explaining the matter to her. Barry's testimony further established that he and Sun had agreed from the beginning of their relationship that each would forgo any interest in the other's earnings and acquisitions during marriage.

Family Code section 1615 places on the party seeking to avoid a premarital agreement the burden of demonstrating that the agreement was involuntary. The trial court determined that Sun did not carry her burden, and we believe that its factual findings in support of this conclusion are supported by substantial evidence.

The judgment of the Court of Appeal is reversed.....

Glossary

Ability to pay

A person's actual earnings at that specific time, which will be used to determine his or her ability to pay an order of the court.

Abstract of judgment

A notice of a court's order which is recorded in the County where the judgment debtor is likely to have property or resides. The order acknowledging the debt will become a lien on any and all property in the county(ies) where the abstract is filed.

Agnos Act

A legislative act which established state-wide, mandatory, two-tier system of child support guidelines, which was intended to reduce the gap between welfare payments and child support payments. Child support was to be no less than the mandatory minimum amount paid by the supporting parent under welfare guidelines. The legislature also established discretionary orders for support that was above the minimum guideline.

Alternate Valuation Date

Assets to be divided in a dissolution of marriage are generally valued as of the date of trial. The Court may allow the date of separation to be used in certain circumstances.

Annulment

See nullity.

Apportionment

The manner in which a separate property interest in a community property asset is determined.

Automatic Temporary Restraining Orders

The restraining orders which are part of the family law Summons.

Bankruptcy

A procedure for relief of a debtor, through the federal court system, whereby the debtor is allowed an alternative economic means of re-paying or eliminating their debts.

Bifurcation

The separation or "splitting out" of issues within a dissolution of marriage. The court retains jurisdiction of the marital status, while resolving other issues such as custody, support and property.

Citation

An order to appear.

Citee

A person who is alleged to have violated the court's orders and is thereby ordered to appear in court (via a citation) to defend the charges. This term is used most often in contempt proceedings.

Cohabitation

Two or more people living together as roommates.

Cohabitation Agreement

A written agreement between persons living together, either as roommates or where the parties are not married. The contract would incorporate financial and related matters while they are living together.

Collaborative Practice

A law practice which utilizes experts and mediation as a means to resolving family law issues. Usually agreed to by the parties prior to commencing a "litigation" process.

Commingling

The act of combining or mixing separate and community assets to the extent that it is no longer clear what the source of the assets was.

Common law

The law that came from England and which has been handed down over the years, usually through case law.

Community

The marital estate.

Community property

All real and/or personal property, which was acquired during marriage while domiciled in California.

Confidential Marriage

A marriage performed before a county clerk. The clerk may only provide third parties with confirmation that the parties are married. The clerk will not verify the date or location of the marriage.

Contempt

The procedure, usually through an Order to Show cause, whereby a party alleges that court orders have been violated. The alleging party usually requests that the person who did not obey the Court's order be held accountable. The court may "punish" the non-complying party by ordering them to compensate the "injured" party, as well as to obey the Court's previous orders.

Contract

A promise to perform an act or provide services. Requires consideration. A contract can be oral or written.

Custody

The manner in which the parents of minor children will have responsibility and exercise control over their children subsequent to a dissolution or legal separation.

Defense of Marriage Act

Defense of Marriage Action (DOMA) is a federal statute that allows a state to deny recognition to marriage between same sex partners that were validly entered in a sister state. Restricts the definition of marriage to heterosexual couples.

Deferred Compensation

Earnings or compensation paid for the benefit of an employee. The compensation is paid at a later date, rather than while the person is employed. (See also retirement benefits.)

Deferred Sale of Home Order

An Order wherein the Court has authorized the deferment of the sale of the family home until the minor(s) have reached majority, or until some other specified condition. Usually ordered as a means of additional child support. Often referred to as a *Duke Order*.

Defined benefit plan

A type of deferred compensation or retirement plan. The employee contributes a portion of their earnings in proportion to the amount that they will receive upon retirement.

Defined contribution plan

A retirement or deferred compensation plan to which the employee contributes each month. The amount of retirement which will be received by the employee upon retirement is not known, as the amount is based on the investment return.

Discovery

The various procedures which my be used by the parties to obtain as much information as possible about the other party's "case" or position. Types of discovery are: interrogatories, depositions, requests for production of documents, and requests for admissions.

Dissolution

The process of terminating a marriage.

Domestic Violence Prevention Act

The statutory definitions and guidelines which were enacted to "prevent the recurrence of acts of violence and sexual abuse and to provide for a separation of the persons involved in the domestic violence for a period sufficient to seek a resolution of the causes of the violence."

Domicile

A person's *permanent* place of residence. Evidenced by voter's registration and the payment of income tax.

Due process

Jurisdictional and constitutional safeguards which accord all litigants the right to their property. All persons involved in the litigation process must be given an opportunity to participate in the legal proceedings which affect their rights.

Duke Order

See Deferred Sale of Home Order.

Earning capacity

A person's earning capacity is usually evidenced by their education, skill and experience. Also known as their earning potential.

Emancipation

The process of a minor being declared an adult and therefore independent of parental control.

Epstein reimbursement credits

The process for determining the reimbursement to a spouse for using separate property to make post-separation payments on community property assets and debts.

Equity

Equity is the value of property after deducting any debt or liens on the property. Often referred to as fair market value.

Ex Parte

The manner of noticing an opposing party when there is not adequate time to give proper notice as prescribed by law.

Federal Parental Kidnapping Act

Federal law which regulates situations wherein a parent may kidnap their own children.

Fiduciary duty

Married persons have a duty of trust and confidence to each other.

Freeman Order

Considered a minimum, standard visitation order, which is approximately a 20% time share to the non-custodial parent.

Full disclosure

Family law requires a high level of disclosure of all assets and debts. The law requires that no aspect of marital property may be left undisclosed.

Full faith and credit

Federal term which requires all states to recognize the judgments and orders made in other states. It is considered a constitutional right.

***Gavron* warning**

The landmark case which recognized that all cases where an order is made for spousal support or where jurisdiction is retained over the issue of child support should contain a notification to the supported party that it is the public policy of the state that the party become self-supporting.

Gift

The transfer of an item of value from one person to another, which is made gratuitously and without receiving anything in return (without consideration).

Goodwill

The concept of repeat patronage of a business which results in an expectation of future earnings.

Gross income

Earnings received before any deductions are made.

Imputed income

Income or earnings which may be assigned to an individual based on their previous earnings or an expectation of earnings resulting from their education, skill and/or training.

Independent Adoption

Adoptions that are typically arranged outside of the scope of the supervision of an agency, usually by an attorney.

Inheritance

A gift received by one person as the result of another person's death.

Irreconcilable differences

The basis for a "no fault" dissolution, wherein the Petitioner has stated the marriage cannot be salvages and that they are not asking for a "wrong" to be determined by the court. Used most commonly in conjunction with the term "irremedial breakdown."

Irremedial breakdown

The statutory term used for a "no fault" dissolution in California. Considered the "grounds" for a dissolution and infers that there is no change that the parties cannot reconcile. Usually used in conjunction with the term "irreconcilable differences."

Joinder

A "third party" may be joined into family law proceedings, so that the court can exercise it's jurisdiction over said third party. Most comply used for pension plans and grand-parent visitation.

Joint Legal Custody

The parents will share equally in the rights and responsibilities relating to their minor children. Specifically, they will share in the decisions as to the health, education and welfare of their children.

Joint Physical Custody

Often referred to as "shared parenting." This type of custody infers that the children will spend nearly equal time with each parent or at least with have significant periods of time with each parent.

Judgment creditor

The person to whom money is owned by a judgment debtor.

Judgment debtor

The person owing money and who is required to pay the judgment creditor.

Judicial council forms

Court forms that have been created and pre-printed for use in filing with the court. The forms may be approved for use in civil matters and other types of cases. Family law forms, in most cases, have been adopted as mandatory and must be used for dissolutions, legal separations and annulments, as well as paternity, child custody and support cases, domestic violence and most adoptions.

Jurisdiction

The court's power to hear a matter.

Jurisdictional stepdown

Term used with respect to spousal support orders. The court's jurisdiction is reduced or held at a certain level.

Laches

The concept of a party "sitting" on their rights. When a party knows his or her rights, but chooses to take no action to preserve or protect their rights, he or she may affect the rights of the other party or cause them to be adversely affected.

Legal custody

The right of a parent to exercise control, power and responsibility over their minor child. Those rights and responsibilities include the health, safety and welfare, which include medical treatment, education and religion.

Legal separation

The process of severing and resolving the custody, support and property issues of a married couple, while maintaining their marital status.

Lengthy marriage

Typically considered a marriage of at least ten years duration.

Lis Pen Dens

A document used to "cloud the title" of a piece of real property. It is recorded with the county recorder where the property is located and notifies anyone researching the title of such property that it is subject to pending litigation.

Marital or Property Settlement Agreement

A written contract between a married couple disposing of their marital property and resolving the issues of custody and support. Usually made without Court intervention, except as to temporary orders.

Mediation

In the family law context it is the process of determining the best interests of the children with respect to custody and visitation. Voluntary mediation may also be used to assist the parties in coming to an agreement as to the division of marital property and any other issues they wish to mediate.

Memorandum of Points & Authorities

The document which usually accompanies a Motion and which sets for the legal argument(s) of the case. The Points & Authorities usually follow a specific format and will contain the "point(s)" being made by the attorney, the case law that supports that point, and the request (or conclusion) that is being requested of the court.

Minimum contacts

California states that the "minimum contact" is sufficient for the court to have personal jurisdiction or power over that person. "Mere presence" may be all that is required.

Minor child

A child who is under the age of eighteen, or who is under the age of nineteen and who is a full-time student residing with a parent is defined as a minor in California.

Moore/Marsden

Case law precedents (rules) which are used to determine the apportionment of separate property and community property interests in real estate.

Net Income

The amount of money that remains after federal and state taxes, state disability (if applicable), medicare, and social security have been deducted from gross income. Often referred to as "take home pay." In California, other deductions such as mandatory retirement, health insurance and union dues may be deducted from the gross earnings, at the discretion of the court.

No fault

See irreconcilable differences and irremedial breakdown.

Noticed Motion

Written request by a party, to the court, usually requesting a determination of a question of law. The Motion (form) can be signed by an attorney rather than a Judge, as it is not a notice to appear. A motion does not require an appearance by the opposing party. Usually accompanied by Points & Authorities, which reference case law supporting the finding of law. Witnesses cannot be called.

Nullity

A petition to the court to determine that a marriage is invalid.

Nunc Pro Tunc

Literally meaning to go back. A method or procedure for "back dating" a dissolution of marriage or the marital status of the parties.

Order to Show Cause

Written request by a party, to the court requesting a determination by the Court based on facts. The OSC (form) must be signed by a Judge, as it is an order to appear. The opposing party is ordered to appear and witnesses can be called.

Paternity

The conclusive presumption that a husband of a cohabitating wife, is the father of any child born during that marriage. Alternatively, paternity has more recently become the guideline for establishing the identity of a "natural" father where there is no marriage between the parents.

Pendente Lite

Latin for "pending litigation." Most often used to notice a party or third party that actions may or may not be taken while the matter is pending. Also refers to temporary orders.

Pereira/Van Camp rules

Case laws (methods) used to apportion separate and community property interests in marital assets.

Permanent spousal support

Spousal support that is ordered either my agreement of the parties subsequent to a trial, for the purpose of maintaining the supported spouse's standard of living acquired during marriage. Often referred to as "long term" spousal support.

Personal jurisdiction

The jurisdiction or power the court has over a person involved in litigation.

Personal property

Considered tangible property or items, which is not real property.

Petition

The initial document filed in family law matters. Comparable to the Complaint in civil matters.

Petitioner

The person filing the initial family law documents. Comparable to the Plaintiff.

Physical custody

The parent with whom a minor child primarily resides has physical custody.

Postnuptial agreement

A contract entered into by parties after they have married, which identifies the separate property of each party, as well as any property that is to be considered community property. Such agreements may also address spousal support issues.

Prenuptial agreement

A contract entered into by parties to a prospective marriage, which identifies the separate property of each party, which they owned prior to their marriage. Such agreements may also address spousal support issues.

Presumption

A matter of fact or law that is deemed established.

Property

Items of tangible value which may be owned.

Putative spouse

A party to a void or voidable marriage, who is entitled to marital assets, although they are not considered a "spouse." A putative spouse may enjoy the same benefits and protections afforded a spouse, even though they were attained as the results of the "bad acts" of their spouse. Property acquired during a putative marriage is considered quasi-marital property.

Qualified Domestic Relations Order (QDRO)

Federal rules and regulations which establish guidelines for orders governing the division of federal pension plans.

Quasi-community property

Property acquired by married persons which is located in another state.

Quasi-criminal

Used most frequently in the family law context with contempt proceeding, which are not solely criminal in nature. The person being cited for contempt, however, may have imposed upon them criminal penalties and punishments, such as jail.

Quasi-marital property

Property acquired as a the result of an invalid marriage. (See putative spouse.)

Real property

Land and real estate. Includes any structures affixed to the property.

Rebuttable presumption

Presumption which may be overcome by disproving the presumed fact.

Relocation

Pertains to issues, in the family law context, of moving the minor children to another location.

Reservation of jurisdiction

The superior court may agree to maintain jurisdiction over a particular issue in family law matters. Examples: child support, *Duke orders*, spousal support. The Court will always retain jurisdiction over the minor children regardless of the parents' circumstances and the orders made.

Residence

The place a person lives, such as a vacation home or while they are working on a temporary work assignment. A person may have more than one residence, but can only have one domicile, although they may be the same.

Residency requirement

California requires that a person filing (Petitioner) for a dissolution in this state must have been domiciled in the state for six months and in the county of filing (venue) for at least three months.

Respondent

The person required to respond. Defendant in civil cases.

Response

The pleading used to respond in family law matters. Comparable to the Answer.

Retirement benefits

Compensation that is earned by an employee, but which is paid to the employee at a later date, usually upon retirement. Some retirement benefits may be transferred to another type of retirement account if the employee terminates employment.

Richmond order

Case which established spousal support which is paid for a specific period of time or until a specific occurrence. Support will eventually reach zero. The burden of proving support needs to continue past that specific date is on the supported party.

Sanctions

An award for payment of attorney fees when an attorney has failed to comply, sometimes on behalf of his or her client, to a court order.

Separate property

All property owned prior to marriage, during marriage by gift, bequest or inheritance, or after the date of separation. Also includes any rents, issues, or profits from said property.

Service of process

The process of notifying a party of the pending litigation and the type of action against them.

Sister state judgment

The Sister State Money Judgment Act (SSMJA) is the procedure for applying for the entry of a judgment made in one state in another state. SSMJA judgments are made for non-support Judgments. Support Judgments also require an application, however that application is made under the Uniform Interstate Family Support Act (UIFSA).

Sole Legal Custody

One parent has the sole discretion as to the health, education, and welfare of the child(ren).

Sole Physical Custody

One parent has primary responsibility for the day-to-day care and supervision of the child(ren), while the other parent has visitation.

Special appearance

An appearance made to challenge the validity of the court's jurisdiction over him or her.

Spousal support

Support (alimony) paid by one spouse to another either temporarily and/or permanently which is meant to maintain the status quo of the standard of living while the parties were married.

Statute of limitations

The time period in which a matter must come under the court's jurisdiction, after which time a person's legal rights must be protected.

Statutory law

Laws that have been created by legislature or statute, as opposed to case law.

Stay of service

The court may order that service of an assignment order be stayed provided that there is a finding of good cause or if an alternative arrangement exists for payment.

Stepparent adoption

The proceeding wherein a stepparent petitions the court, requesting that they be considered the natural parent of the stepchild. The child's relationship with their natural parent is terminated and the stepparent assumes all rights and obligations of that of the natural parent.

Stipulated Judgment

An Agreement or Judgment (contract) executed by the parties after a settlement conference and/or trial.

Subject matter jurisdiction

The court's power to exercise control over a specific legal subject matter.

Substantive stepdown

An award of permanent spousal support, wherein the support will be reduced by specific amounts at specific intervals, or upon the occurrence of a specific event, until support ultimately reaches zero. The Court retains jurisdiction over the issue of spousal support until the support reaches zero or is terminated for other reasons.

Summary dissolution

A process for easily terminating a marriage when the parties have a short-term marriage, do not have children, and do not own any real property or valuable tangible property. The process is meant to be completed without needing an attorney and has very strict statutory guidelines.

Summons

The document issued by the clerk in the county where the action is filed, which serves to officially notify the Respondent of the legal proceedings.

Superior court

The court having subject matter jurisdiction over all family law matters.

Temporary restraining orders

An order of brief duration which prohibits a party or parties from certain actions, until a hearing or further order of the court.

Temporary spousal support

Spousal support (alimony) paid temporarily during the pendency (pendente lite) of the dissolution process.

Title documents

Documents which establish evidence of ownership to property.

Tracing

The process of proving a rebuttable presumption that property acquired during marriage is community property if the source of the funds can be traced to separate property assets of one party.

Transmutation

An agreement between spouses which changes the status (vesting) of an asset from separate to community or community to separate.

Uniform Child Custody Jurisdiction Enforcement Act

An Act adopted by all 50 states, designed to provide a uniform means of a state's jurisdiction over all issues pertaining to minor children.

Uniform Interstate Family Support Act

The Uniform Interest Family Support Act (UIFSA) was established to standardized support Judgments throughout the 50 states. An application for enforcement of a support order may be made in California, even though the Judgment or Order was made in another state, provided the child now resides in California.

Venue

In the family law context, the county where the matter will be filed. That county where the Petitioner has resided for at least three months in order to file a dissolution of marriage.

Vesting

The amount of "actual" ownership that an individual has in property. For real property it is the manner in which a person holds "title." For other types of property, particularly retirement or deferred compensation plans, vesting refers to the length of employment, which may affect the benefit the employee will receive upon retirement or termination of employment.

Visitation

The period of time a non-custodial parent may spend their time minor child(ren). Visitation infers that one parent is the primary custodian, or has primary physical custody of more than 51%, and that the other parent "visits" with the child(ren).

Void marriage

A marriage that is invalid at its inception, and which has no force and effect.

Voidable marriage

A marriage that was valid at its inception, but is being voided based on statutory proof that the marriage should be set aside.

Wage Assignment

A document issued by a court clerk, which is based on a Judgment, and which orders the employer to withhold, either a specific amount or percentage, from the judgment debtor's (employee's) wages. The employer then pays the withheld funds to the judgment creditor in order to satisfy the Judgment on which the wage assignment is based.

Watts reimbursement credits

Case law which establishes the right to reimbursement a spouse may assert when they have been denied the use of a community property asset, post-separation, when the rental value exceeds its original cost. (See Epstein reimbursement credits.)

Writ of Execution

A document issued by a court clerk, which is based on a Judgment, and which orders a *levying officer*, usually the sheriff, to take possession of the assets of the judgment debtor in order to satisfy the Judgment. Such assets can be property or cash. (Similar to a Writ of Possession.) The judgment creditor will then be sent or notified that the sheriff is in possession of the property.

Writ of Possession

A document issued by a court clerk, which is based on a Judgment, and which orders a *levying officer*, usually the sheriff, to take possession of property of the judgment debtor. The Writ may also require that the assets or property be sold in order to satisfy the Judgment. The property or the proceeds of the sale of the property will then be sent to the judgment creditor.

Bibliography

2013 Practice Under the Family Code (Dissolution, Legal Separation, Nullity), Continuing Education of the Bar, Contributing Editors: M. Dee Samuels, Esq. and Judge Frederick A. Manabach.

California Family Law for Paralegals, Fourth Edition, Marshall W. Waller, Aspen Law & Business Publishing.

Family Law, Sixth Edition, William P. Statsky, West-Thomson Learning.

Family Law Hypotheticals (Law School Edition), The Rutter Group, 1995.

Introduction to Family Law, N.R. Gallow, Thomson Delmar Learning, West Legal Studies, 2012.

Case Index

Index